Regulation of Lawyers:
Statutes and Standards

1993 Edition

Regulation of Lawyers: Statutes and Standards

1993 Edition

Stephen Gillers
Professor of Law
New York University

Roy D. Simon, Jr.
Professor of Law
Hofstra University

Little, Brown and Company
Boston Toronto London

Library of Congress Catalog Card No. 92-85088

ISBN No. 0-316-31435-8

MV-NY

Published simultaneously in Canada
by Little, Brown & Company (Canada) Limited

Printed in the United States of America

Summary of Contents

Acknowledgments

Roy Simon is grateful to his secretaries, Monica Groth and Roslyn Weiss, and to his research assistants, Chris Perzan, Class of 1992, and Chris Boehning, Class of 1994, at Washington University School of Law, who performed careful and indispensable research. He also thanks his wife, Karen, and his children, Daniel, Nicole, Joshua, and Rebecca, for their support.

Stephen Gillers thanks his secretary, Shirley Gray, for her help on this volume. As always, he is indebted to his wife, Barbara, and his children, Heather and Gillian.

Finally, the authors deeply appreciate the exceptional work done by Richard Audet and Julie Nahil, manuscript editors at Little, Brown and Company, and by the others at Little, Brown who helped to produce this book.

The authors thank the following copyright holders for their permission to reprint the materials in this book:

The American Bar Association, for permission to reprint the ABA Model Rules of Professional Conduct, the Model Code of Professional Conduct, and numerous other items, all of which are separately acknowledged where the materials appear.

The American Arbitration Association, for permission to reprint its Code of Ethics for Arbitrators in Commercial Disputes.

The American Law Institute, for permission to reprint excerpts from tentative drafts of the Restatement (Third) of the Law Governing Lawyers.

The American Trial Lawyer's Association, for permission to reprint its 1988 Code of Conduct and its 1986 Victim's Bill of Rights.

The Federal Bar Association, for permission to reprint excerpts from the Model Rules of Professional Conduct for Federal Lawyers.

The American Academy of Matrimonial Lawyers, for permission to reprint excerpts from the Bounds of Advocacy.

The Roscoe Pound Foundation (formerly the Roscoe Pound-American Trial Lawyers Foundation), for permission to reprint excerpts from the 1982 Revised Draft of the American Lawyer's Code of Conduct.

TRIAL magazine, for permission to reprint excerpts from the Preface to the American Lawyer's Code of Conduct. (The Preface originally appeared in TRIAL magazine.)

The Society of Professionals in Dispute Resolution (SPIDR), for permission to reprint its Ethical Standards of Professional Conduct.

The Association of American Law Schools, for permission to reprint its Statement of Good Practices by Law Professors in the Discharge of Their Ethical and Professional Responsibilities.

Introduction to the Regulation of Lawyers

This book contains rules regulating the behavior of lawyers and judges. These rules come from many sources: statutes, administrative regulations, rules of evidence and procedure, and, most prominently, ethical codes. These rules continue to grow and change. The 1993 edition of this book has hundreds of changes, some of them substantial, from the 1992 edition.

The most important ethical codes for lawyers are those promulgated by the American Bar Association. The ABA's first effort at codifying ethical rules was the adoption of the Canons of Professional Ethics in 1908. These (as amended) remained in effect — though with diminishing influence — for 62 years.

Effective in 1970, the ABA replaced the Canons with the Model Code of Professional Responsibility. Within a few years, every state had adopted the new Code in some form. States varied somewhat in their adoptions, changing a word here or a sentence there, but most of the variations were modest. The only variation that was truly different appeared in California, which rejected or substantially revised many of the Model Code's Disciplinary Rules and deleted all of the Ethical Considerations.

In 1977, the President of the American Bar Association appointed a new commission to prepare a new set of rules. That commission soon became known as the Kutak Commission, after Robert J. Kutak, an energetic and visionary lawyer from Omaha, Nebraska, who chaired the commission until his death in early 1983. After much debate and several drafts, the ABA House of Delegates approved the Model Rules of Professional Conduct on August 2, 1983.

It is often instructive to compare the Model Rules as adopted with parallel provisions in the Kutak Commission's drafts. Many of these parallel provisions are contained in the Legislative History sections following each Model Rule. It is also often instructive to compare the Model Rules as adopted with state variations governing the same conduct. The states have been giving careful attention

to the Model Rules. As of fall 1992, more than 35 states and the District of Columbia have adopted all or significant portions of the Model Rules.

Several states, including New York, Oregon, Vermont, and Massachusetts,
have rejected the Model Rules. New York, however, has amended its Code to
include provisions of the Model Rules. California also has chosen not to adopt
the Rules, but has amended its Rules of Professional Conduct to incorporate
Model Rules provisions. This book contains both the amended California Rules
and the amended New York Code of Professional Responsibility. It also contains important statutory material from both California and New York and the
New York court rules for sanctioning lawyers.

Many states that have adopted the Model Rules have deviated from its
"model" text in significant ways. Sometimes a state will opt for language derived from a draft of the Model Rules. Sometimes a state will choose to retain
language contained in the Model Code of Professional Responsibility. Some jurisdictions, like Virginia, have adopted some provisions of the Model Rules but
have retained the Code's format. We have identified interesting state variations
on particular Model Rules in a section called "Selected State Variations" following each Model Rule. While we have presented variations from dozens of
American jurisdictions, we have concentrated on these: Arizona, District of Columbia, Florida, Georgia, Illinois, Michigan, Missouri, New Jersey, North Carolina, Pennsylvania, Texas, and Virginia.

Several areas of variation deserve special attention. These areas are confidentiality, corporate representation, and lawyer advertising and solicitation. Model
Rules 1.6, 3.3, and 4.1 prominently address the issue of confidentiality. Rule
1.13 addresses the responsibilities of a lawyer whose client is an organization.
Rules 7.1, 7.2, and 7.3 are concerned with various methods for marketing legal
services.

Other areas in which we see significant variation among jurisdictions or between drafts of the Model Rules and the final document include conflicts of interest (Rules 1.7, 1.8, 1.9, 1.10, and 1.11); fairness to opposing parties and
counsel (Rule 3.4); relationships between lawyers and nonlawyers (Rule 5.4);
and pro bono service (Rule 6.1).

Two dominant concerns underlie the provisions containing these variations.
The first concern is the proper scope of the lawyer's loyalty to current and former clients, including the scope of the lawyer's duty to protect client confidences. Competing demands on this loyalty come from the justice system, third
persons, other clients, and the lawyer's personal or financial interests.

The second concern is competition, from within and from outside the profession, in marketing and profiting from legal services. One question is whether
nonlawyers should be permitted to invest in or share profits from organizations
that sell legal services for a profit. This question brings up competition between
lawyers and persons outside the legal profession. Another question is what limits
should be placed on the ways in which lawyers compete with other lawyers.
This question addresses issues of lawyer advertising and solicitation. Recently, a
tangential issue has emerged: Should lawyers be permitted to own "ancillary"

non-law businesses (such as title insurance companies, investment advisors, and real estate developers) that serve both clients and non-clients? By a slim vote, the ABA said "no" when it adopted Rule 5.7 in 1991. But only a year later, again by a slim margin, the ABA reversed course and said "yes," repealing Rule 5.7.

The areas we have identified are, we believe, those where controversy was most prominent and variation among jurisdictions most frequent and pronounced. But other provisions of the Model Rules were also seriously debated and are also the subject of variation among the states. As we show in the Legislative History section for each Model Rule, the Kutak Commission's early drafts usually differed markedly from the Rules as finally adopted. And as we show in the Selected State Variations sections for each Model Rule, the states have often adopted divergent provisions. The legislative history and the selected state variations for each Rule, together with our extensive California and New York materials, should thus dispel any misconception that the ABA Model Rules are "the rules." The Model Rules are influential, but they continue to generate considerable disagreement.

To make it easier to roam within the Model Rules, each Rule is followed by a list of cross-references identifying every other Rule or Comment that mentions the annotated Rule. These cross-references should help readers appreciate each Rule's implications throughout the Rules as a whole.

The Model Rules are only one source of authority and guidance within the legal profession. As our Related Materials show, lawyers may be subject to many obligations and restrictions beyond those imposed by the Model Rules. In addition, the Model Rules give little or no guidance in many areas of practice. We have therefore included other sources of authority such as federal statutes and regulations, rules of evidence and procedure, the tentative Restatement of the Law Governing Lawyers (still in progress), and recently emerging creeds of courtesy and professionalism. We have also reprinted all or significant parts of several specialized codes, such as the ABA Standards for Criminal Justice, the ABA Standards of Practice for Lawyer Mediators in Family Disputes, the Bounds of Advocacy of the American Academy of Matrimonial Lawyers (whose Reporter was Professor Robert Aronson of the University of Washington Law School), the Code of Conduct for Lawyers in the European Community, a statement of good practices for law professors from the Association of American Law Schools, the Ethical Standards of Professional Conduct of the Society of Professionals in Dispute Resolution, and the Federal Bar Association's Model Rules of Professional Conduct for Federal Lawyers.

Finally, judges are subject to special regulations beyond those that govern practicing lawyers. Some of these are in statutory law, such as §455 of Title 28 of the United States Code. Others are in codes of judicial ethics. The most prominent ethics code is the ABA's Code of Judicial Conduct, first promulgated in 1972 and adopted by 47 states and the District of Columbia. In 1990 the ABA revised the Code of Judicial Conduct. Although the revised document has not yet seen significant adoption, we reprint it, rather than its predecessor, because it addresses issues the earlier Code ignored. Part III of the Report of the ABA Standing Committee recommending the new Code highlights principal changes from the predecessor. We reprint this part of the Report so readers can readily identify the significant revisions.

In sum, this book presents a wide range of statutes, rules, regulations, and model codes that govern lawyers and judges. We have aimed to make these materials accessible and understandable, and to give readers an appreciation for the rich and variegated landscape of the regulation of lawyers.

Stephen Gillers
Roy D. Simon, Jr.

September 1992

Regulation of Lawyers: Statutes and Standards

1993 Edition

Model Codes and Standards

ABA Model Rules of
Professional Conduct*
As amended through August 1992

Editors' Introduction. In 1977, only eight years after adopting the Model Code of Professional Responsibility, the ABA appointed a Commission on the Evaluation of Professional Standards to recommend revisions to the Code. The Commission was chaired by attorney Robert Kutak and is commonly referred to as the Kutak Commission.

It soon became clear to the Kutak Commission that the Code needed to be substantially rewritten and reorganized. Between 1979 and 1982, the Kutak Commission circulated four major drafts of its proposed Model Rules of Professional Conduct: the 1979 Unofficial Pre-Circulation Draft; the 1980 Discussion Draft; the 1981 Draft; and the 1982 Draft. After making some significant revisions, the ABA House of Delegates formally adopted the Model Rules on August 2, 1983. Since 1983, about three dozen states have adopted some form of the Model Rules. However, there are significant variations among the states, especially regarding such key issues as conflicts, confidentiality, and advertising.

We have used a seven-part format to present each Rule:

(1) the black letter Model Rule itself;

(2) the official ABA Comment (with the paragraphs numbered, in brackets, for convenience);

(3) the Model Code Comparison, written by the ABA to compare each Rule to the Model Code of Professional Responsibility;

(4) Cross-references in the Rules, compiled especially for this book to show each place in the Rules and Comments where a particular Rule is mentioned;

(5) Legislative History, which we compiled to show interesting excerpts from earlier drafts and amendments to the Rules since their adoption;

(6) Selected State Variations, which we compiled to show some of the ways in which states have diverged from the ABA Model Rule; and

ABA Model Rules of Professional Conduct

(7) Related Materials, which we compiled to show such things as historical antecedents in the old ABA Canons of Professional Ethics, counterparts in the American Lawyer's Code of Conduct, the Restatement of the Law Governing Lawyers (in progress), and the Bounds of Advocacy of the American Academy of Matrimonial Lawyers, and brief descriptions or quotations from other items that shed light on a particular Rule.

An overview of the Rules, including the legislative history of the Rules, the major differences between the Rules and the Model Code, and the trends in state variations on the Rules, is contained in our introductory essay at pages ix-xii.

Contents

Preamble: A Lawyer's Responsibilities
Scope
Terminology

ABA Model Rules of Professional Conduct

PREAMBLE: A LAWYER'S RESPONSIBILITIES

[1] A lawyer is a representative of clients, an officer of the legal system and a public citizen having special responsibility for the quality of justice.

[2] As a representative of clients, a lawyer performs various functions. As advisor, a lawyer provides a client with an informed understanding of the client's legal rights and obligations and explains their practical implications. As advocate, a lawyer zealously asserts the client's position under the rules of the adversary system. As negotiator, a lawyer seeks a result advantageous to the client but consistent with requirements of honest dealing with others. As intermediary between clients, a lawyer seeks to reconcile their divergent interests as an advisor and, to a limited extent, as a spokesman for each client. A lawyer acts as evaluator by examining a client's legal affairs and reporting about them to the client or to others.

[3] In all professional functions a lawyer should be competent, prompt and diligent. A lawyer should maintain communication with a client concerning the representation. A lawyer should keep in confidence information relating to representation of a client except so far as disclosure is required or permitted by the Rules of Professional Conduct or other law.

[4] A lawyer's conduct should conform to the requirements of the law, both in professional service to clients and in the lawyer's business and personal affairs. A lawyer should use the law's procedures only for legitimate purposes and not to harass or intimidate others. A lawyer should demonstrate respect for the legal system and for those who serve it, including judges, other lawyers and public officials. While it is a lawyer's duty, when necessary, to challenge the rectitude of official action, it is also a lawyer's duty to uphold legal process.

[5] As a public citizen, a lawyer should seek improvement of the law, the administration of justice and the quality of service rendered by the legal profession. As a member of a learned profession, a lawyer should cultivate knowledge of the law beyond its use for clients, employ that knowledge in reform of the law and work to strengthen legal education. A lawyer should be mindful of deficiencies in the administration of justice and of the fact that the poor, and sometimes persons who are not poor, cannot afford adequate legal assistance, and should therefore devote professional time and civic influence in their behalf. A lawyer should aid the legal profession in pursuing these objectives and should help the bar regulate itself in the public interest.

[6] Many of a lawyer's professional responsibilities are prescribed in the Rules of Professional Conduct, as well as substantive and procedural law. However, a lawyer is also guided by personal conscience and the approbation of professional peers. A lawyer should strive to attain the highest level of skill, to improve the law and the legal profession and to exemplify the legal profession's ideals of public service.

[7] A lawyer's responsibilities as a representative of clients, an officer of the legal system and a public citizen are usually harmonious. Thus, when an opposing party is well represented, a lawyer can be a zealous advocate on behalf of a client and at the same time assume that justice is being done. So also, a lawyer can be sure that preserving client confidences ordinarily serves the public interest because people are more likely to seek legal advice, and thereby heed their legal obligations, when they know their communications will be private.

[8] In the nature of law practice, however, conflicting responsibilities are encountered. Virtually all difficult ethical problems arise from conflict between a lawyer's responsibilities to clients, to the legal system and to the lawyer's own interest in remaining an upright person while earning a satisfactory living. The Rules of Professional Conduct prescribe terms for resolving such conflicts. Within the framework of these Rules many difficult issues of professional discretion can arise. Such issues must be resolved through the exercise of sensitive professional and moral judgment guided by the basic principles underlying the Rules.

[9] The legal profession is largely self-governing. Although other professions also have been granted powers of self-government, the legal profession is unique in this respect because of the close relationship between the profession and the processes of government and law enforcement. This connection is manifested in the fact that ultimate authority over the legal profession is vested largely in the courts.

[10] To the extent that lawyers meet the obligations of their professional calling, the occasion for government regulation is obviated. Self-regulation also helps maintain the legal profession's independence from government domination. An independent legal profession is an important force in preserving government under law, for abuse of legal authority is more readily challenged by a profession whose members are not dependent on government for the right to practice.

[11] The legal profession's relative autonomy carries with it special responsibilities of self-government. The profession has a responsibility to assure that its regulations are conceived in the public interest and not in furtherance of parochial or self-interested concerns of the bar. Every lawyer is responsible for observance of the Rules of Professional Conduct. A lawyer should also aid in securing their observance by other lawyers. Neglect of these responsibilities compromises the independence of the profession and the public interest which it serves.

[12] Lawyers play a vital role in the preservation of society. The fulfillment of this role requires an understanding by lawyers of their relationship to our legal

system. The Rules of Professional Conduct, when properly applied, serve to define that relationship.

SCOPE

[1] The Rules of Professional Conduct are rules of reason. They should be interpreted with reference to the purposes of legal representation and of the law itself. Some of the Rules are imperatives, cast in the terms "shall" or "shall not." These define proper conduct for purposes of professional discipline. Others, generally cast in the term "may," are permissive and define areas under the Rules in which the lawyer has professional discretion. No disciplinary action should be taken when the lawyer chooses not to act or acts within the bounds of such discretion. Other Rules define the nature of relationships between the lawyer and others. The Rules are thus partly obligatory and disciplinary and partly constitutive and descriptive in that they define a lawyer's professional role. Many of the Comments use the term "should." Comments do not add obligations to the Rules but provide guidance for practicing in compliance with the Rules.

[2] The Rules presuppose a larger legal context shaping the lawyer's role. That context includes court rules and statutes relating to matters of licensure, laws defining specific obligations of lawyers and substantive and procedural law in general. Compliance with the Rules, as with all law in an open society, depends primarily upon understanding and voluntary compliance, secondarily upon reinforcement by peer and public opinion and finally, when necessary, upon enforcement through disciplinary proceedings. The Rules do not, however, exhaust the moral and ethical considerations that should inform a lawyer, for no worthwhile human activity can be completely defined by legal rules. The Rules simply provide a framework for the ethical practice of law.

[3] Furthermore, for purposes of determining the lawyer's authority and responsibility, principles of substantive law external to these Rules determine whether a client-lawyer relationship exists. Most of the duties flowing from the client-lawyer relationship attach only after the client has requested the lawyer to render legal services and the lawyer has agreed to do so. But there are some duties, such as that of confidentiality under Rule 1.6, that may attach when the lawyer agrees to consider whether a client-lawyer relationship shall be established. Whether a client-lawyer relationship exists for any specific purpose can depend on the circumstances and may be a question of fact.

[4] Under various legal provisions, including constitutional, statutory and common law, the responsibilities of government lawyers may include authority concerning legal matters that ordinarily reposes in the client in private client-lawyer relationships. For example, a lawyer for a government agency may have

8

authority on behalf of the government to decide upon settlement or whether to appeal from an adverse judgment. Such authority in various respects is generally vested in the attorney general and the state's attorney in state government, and their federal counterparts, and the same may be true of other government law officers. Also, lawyers under the supervision of these officers may be authorized to represent several government agencies in intragovernmental legal controversies in circumstances where a private lawyer could not represent multiple private clients. They also may have authority to represent the "public interest" in circumstances where a private lawyer would not be authorized to do so. These Rules do not abrogate any such authority.

[5] Failure to comply with an obligation or prohibition imposed by a Rule is a basis for invoking the disciplinary process. The Rules presuppose that disciplinary assessment of a lawyer's conduct will be made on the basis of the facts and circumstances as they existed at the time of the conduct in question and in recognition of the fact that a lawyer often has to act upon uncertain or incomplete evidence of the situation. Moreover, the Rules presuppose that whether or not discipline should be imposed for a violation, and the severity of a sanction, depend on all the circumstances, such as the willfulness and seriousness of the violation, extenuating factors and whether there have been previous violations.

[6] Violation of a Rule should not give rise to a cause of action nor should it create any presumption that a legal duty has been breached. The Rules are designed to provide guidance to lawyers and to provide a structure for regulating conduct through disciplinary agencies. They are not designed to be a basis for civil liability. Furthermore, the purpose of the Rules can be subverted when they are invoked by opposing parties as procedural weapons. The fact that a Rule is a just basis for a lawyer's self-assessment, or for sanctioning a lawyer under the administration of a disciplinary authority, does not imply that an antagonist in a collateral proceeding or transaction has standing to seek enforcement of the Rule. Accordingly, nothing in the Rules should be deemed to augment any substantive legal duty of lawyers or the extra-disciplinary consequences of violating such a duty.

[7] Moreover, these Rules are not intended to govern or affect judicial application of either the attorney-client or work product privilege. Those privileges were developed to promote compliance with law and fairness in litigation. In reliance on the attorney-client privilege, clients are entitled to expect that communications within the scope of the privilege will be protected against compelled disclosure. The attorney-client privilege is that of the client and not of the lawyer. The fact that in exceptional situations the lawyer under the Rules has a limited discretion to disclose a client confidence does not vitiate the proposition that, as a general matter, the client has a reasonable expectation that information relating to the client will not be voluntarily disclosed and that disclosure of such information may be judicially compelled only in accordance with recognized exceptions to the attorney-client and work product privileges.

[8] The lawyer's exercise of discretion not to disclose information under Rule 1.6 should not be subject to reexamination. Permitting such reexamination would be incompatible with the general policy of promoting compliance with law through assurances that communications will be protected against disclosure.

[9] The Comment accompanying each Rule explains and illustrates the meaning and purpose of the Rule. The Preamble and this note on Scope provide general orientation. The Comments are intended as guides to interpretation, but the text of each Rule is authoritative. Research notes were prepared to compare counterparts in the ABA Model Code of Professional Responsibility (adopted 1969, as amended) and to provide selected references to other authorities. The notes have not been adopted, do not constitute part of the Model Rules, and are not intended to affect the application or interpretation of the Rules and Comments.

Cross-References in Rules

Rule 1.3, Comment 7: "[I]n a matter involving the conduct of government officials, a government lawyer may have authority to question such conduct more extensively than that of a lawyer for a private organization in similar circumstances. This Rule does not limit that authority. See note on **Scope**."

Rule 1.6, Comment 5: "A lawyer may not disclose such confidential information except as authorized or required by the Rules of Professional Conduct or other law. See also **Scope**."

Rule 1.7, Comment 2: "As to whether a client-lawyer relationship exists or, having once been established, is continuing, see Comment to Rule 1.3 and **Scope**."

Rule 1.7, Comment 15: "Where the conflict is such as clearly to call in question the fair or efficient administration of justice, opposing counsel may properly raise the question. Such an objection should be viewed with caution, however, for it can be misused as a technique of harassment. See **Scope**."

Legislative History

1980 Discussion Draft contained the following Preface:

The decade past has witnessed an extraordinary concern with professional responsibility. Barely ten years ago, the American Bar Association adopted its Model Code of Professional Responsibility, the product of a committee chaired by Edward L. Wright. . . . [I]n every sphere one finds searching inquiry into the meaning of professionally responsible conduct.

That inquiry has led to reconsideration of the Model Code, the creation of the Commission on Evaluation of Professional Standards, and, finally, the development of this document — the Discussion Draft of the Model Rules of Profession•l Conduct.

In reconsidering the concepts of professional standards, the Commission soon realized that more than a series of amendments or a general restatement of the Model Code of Professional Responsibility was in order. The Commission determined that a comprehensive reformulation was required. We have built on the Code's foundation, but we make no apology for having pushed beyond it. . . .

Selected State Variations

District of Columbia: Scope Note provides:

In appropriate cases, violation of a Rule may be evidence admissible in connection with a claim that a substantive duty has been violated, but in other cases evidence of such violations may not be admissible on the issue of the liability of the lawyer to others. Such issues are to be resolved by the tribunal having jurisdiction with respect to the substantive claims. Furthermore, nothing in these Rules, the Comments associated with them, or this Scope section is intended to alter existing requirements that the testimony of expert witnesses or other modes of proof must be employed in determining the scope of a lawyer's duty to others. Finally, nothing in the Rules or associated Comments or this Scope section is intended to confer rights on an adversary of a lawyer to enforce the Rules in a proceeding other than a disciplinary proceeding. A tribunal presented with claims that the conduct of a lawyer appearing before that tribunal requires, for example, disqualification of the lawyer and/or the lawyer's firm may take such action as seems appropriate in the circumstances, which may or may not involve disqualification.

Related Materials

ABA Canons: The Preamble to the Canons* provided as follows:

In America, where the stability of Courts and of all departments of government rests upon the approval of the people, it is peculiarly essential that the system for establishing and dispensing Justice be developed to a high point of efficiency and so maintained that the public shall have absolute confidence in the integrity and impartiality of its administration. The future of the Republic, to a great extent, depends upon our maintenance of Justice pure and unsullied. It cannot be so maintained unless the conduct and the motives of the members of our profession are such as to merit the approval of all just men.

No code or set of rules can be framed, which will particularize all the duties of the lawyer in the varying phases of litigation or in all the relations of professional life. The following canons of ethics are adopted by the American Bar Association as a general guide, yet the enumeration of particular duties should not be construed as a denial of the existence of others equally imperative, though not specifically mentioned.

Editors' Note. In 1982, the Roscoe Pound-American Trial Lawyer's Foundation circulated a revised draft of a proposed code of legal ethics entitled the American Lawyer's Code of Conduct (ALCC). The ALCC was intended as an alternative to the ABA's Model Rules of Professional Conduct, drafts of which were then being circulated for public comment by the Kutak Commission. The ALCC differs from the ABA Model Rules on many issues, especially confidentiality. The overall tone of the differences is reflected in the Preface and Preamble to the ALCC, which harshly criticized the Kutak Commission's 1982 Draft of the ABA Model Rules.

Preface to American Lawyer's Code of Conduct*

We continue to disagree with the Kutak Commission in our basic approach to legal eth-ics. We believe that a code of lawyers' conduct is important legislation for the entire commu-nity, because it affects every person's ability to exercise basic rights. We believe that the basic purpose of such a code should be to enable lawyers to help people — to leave the individual lawyer free to help the individual client.

The Kutak Commission sees lawyers as ombudsmen, who serve the system as much as they serve clients. This is a collectivist, bureaucratic concept. It is the sort of thinking you get from a commission made up of lawyers who work for institutional clients, in institutional firms, and who have lost sight of the lawyer's basic function. Lawyers are not licensed to write prospectuses for giant corporations, or to haggle with federal agencies over regulations and operating rights. We are licensed to represent people in court, which often means people in trouble with the law, and with the government. We are the citizens' champions against official tyranny.

We cannot continue to have a democratic system, as we know it, without a legal profes-sion whose members are free to perform that function. The Kutak Rules contain some useful changes in regulating peripheral aspects of law practice, but they embody a core conviction about the lawyer's role that is fundamentally at odds with the American constitutional system. . . .

Preamble to American Lawyer's Code of Conduct

. . . The individual rights most relevant to lawyers' duties relate to what we call one's "day in court" — the rights to due process of law, counsel, and trial by jury. Also relevant are rights relating to self-incrimination, confrontation, bail, search and seizure, and cruel and unusual punishment. The right to litigate is also an essential aspect of freedom of speech and of the right to petition for redress of grievances.

As a result of the enormous volume and complexity of our law, ordinary citizens need the assistance of lawyers simply to comprehend and cope with the rules governing their actions. The lawyer therefore serves the most basic individual right, that of personal autonomy: the right to make those decisions that most affect one's own life and values. Without professional assistance, the individual citizen is often unaware of the range of choices available, and of the means to pursue particular choices.

The assistance of counsel is thus essential to justice under law, and to equal protection of the laws. Leaving each person to his or her own resources, without the aid of counsel in com-prehending and coping with the complexities of the legal system, would produce gross dis-parities in justice under law. . . .

The legal system that gives context and meaning to basic American rights is the ad-versary system. It is the adversary system which assures each of us a "champion against a hostile world," and which thereby helps to preserve and enhance our dignity as individuals.

Recognizing that the American attorney functions in an adversary system, and that such a system expresses fundamental American values, helps us to appreciate the emptiness of some cliches of lawyers' ethics. It is said, for example, that the lawyer is an "officer of the court," or an "officer of the legal system." Out of context, such phrases are at best meaning-less, and at worst misleading. In the context of the adversary system, it is clear that the law-yer for a private party is and should be an officer of a court only in the sense of serving a court

*The American Lawyer's Code of Conduct is copyright © 1982 by the Roscoe Pound Founda-tion; the excerpts here and elsewhere in this chapter are reprinted with its permission. The Preface to the ALCC, which first appeared in the July 1982 issue of TRIAL magazine, is copyright © 1982 by TRIAL magazine and is reprinted with the permission of the Association of Trial Lawyers of America.

as a zealous, partisan advocate of one side of the case before it, and in the sense of having been licensed by a court to play that very role.

TERMINOLOGY

[1] "Belief" or "Believes" denotes that the person involved actually supposed the fact in question to be true. A person's belief may be inferred from circumstances.

[2] "Consult" or "Consultation" denotes communication of information reasonably sufficient to permit the client to appreciate the significance of the matter in question.

[3] "Firm" or "Law Firm" denotes a lawyer or lawyers in a private firm, lawyers employed in the legal department of a corporation or other organization and lawyers employed in a legal services organization. See Comment, Rule 1.9.

[4] "Fraud" or "Fraudulent" denotes conduct having a purpose to deceive and not merely negligent misrepresentation or failure to apprise another of relevant information.

[5] "Knowingly," "Known," or "Knows" denotes actual knowledge of the fact in question. A person's knowledge may be inferred from circumstances.

[6] "Partner" denotes a member of a partnership and a shareholder in a law firm organized as a professional corporation.

[7] "Reasonable" or "Reasonably" when used in relation to conduct by a lawyer denotes the conduct of a reasonably prudent and competent lawyer.

[8] "Reasonable belief" or "Reasonably believes" when used in reference to a lawyer denotes that a lawyer of reasonable prudence and competence would ascertain the matter in question.

[9] "Reasonably should know" when used in reference to a lawyer denotes that a lawyer of reasonable prudence and competence would ascertain the matter in question.

[10] "Substantial" when used in reference to degree or extent denotes a material matter of clear and weighty importance.

Selected State Variations

District of Columbia Terminology provides:

[2] "Consent" denotes a client's uncoerced assent to a proposed course of action, following consultation with the lawyer regarding the matter in question.

[7] "Law clerk" denotes a person, typically a recent law school graduate, who acts, typically for a limited period, as confidential assistant to a judge or judges of a court; to an administrative law judge or a similar administrative hearing officer; or to the head of a governmental agency or to a member of a governmental commission, either of which has authority to adjudicate or to promulgate rules or regulations of general application. . . .

[12] "Tribunal" denotes a court, regulatory agency, commission, and any other body or individual authorized by law to render decisions of a judicial or quasi-judicial nature, based on information presented before it, regardless of the degree of formality or informality of the proceedings.

Illinois retains the Model Code definitions of "confidence" and "secret" and adds the following terminology:

"Contingent fee agreement" denotes an agreement for the provision of legal services by a lawyer under which the amount of the lawyer's compensation is contingent in whole or in part upon the successful completion of the subject matter of the agreement, regardless of whether the fee is established by formula or is a fixed amount.

"Disclose" or "disclosure" denotes communication of information reasonably sufficient to permit the client to appreciate the significance of the matter in question.

"Person" denotes natural persons, partnerships, business corporations, not-for-profit corporations, public and quasi-public corporations, municipal corporations, State and Federal governmental bodies and agencies, or any other type of lawfully existing entity.

New York: See end of New York Code for definition of "fraud."

Texas adds or modifies the following definitions:

"Adjudicatory Official" denotes a person who serves on a Tribunal.

"Adjudicatory Proceeding" denotes the consideration of a matter by a Tribunal.

"Competent" or "Competence" denotes possession or the ability to timely acquire the legal knowledge, skill, and training reasonably necessary for the representation of the client.

"Consult" or "Consultation" denotes communication of information and advice reasonably sufficient to permit the client to appreciate the significance of the matter in question.

"Firm" or "Law firm" denotes a lawyer or lawyers in a private firm; or a lawyer or lawyers employed in the legal department of a corporation, legal services organization, or other organization, or in a unit of government.

"Fitness" denotes those qualities of physical, mental and psychological health that enable a person to discharge a lawyer's responsibilities to clients in conformity with the Texas Rules of Professional Conduct. Normally a lack of fitness is indicated most clearly by a persistent inability to discharge, or unreliability in carrying out, significant obligations.

"Should know" when used in reference to a lawyer denotes that a reasonable lawyer under the same or similar circumstances would know the matter in question.

"Substantial" when used in reference to degree or extent denotes a matter of meaningful significance or involvement.

"Tribunal" denotes any governmental body or official or any other person engaged in a process of resolving a particular dispute or controversy. "Tribunal" includes such institutions as courts and administrative agencies when engaging in adjudicatory or licensing activities as defined by applicable law or rules of practice or procedure, as well as judges, magistrates, special masters, referees, arbitrators, mediators, hearing officers and comparable persons empowered to resolve or to recommend a resolution of a particular matter; but it does not include jurors, prospective jurors, legislative bodies or their committees, members or staffs, nor does it include other governmental bodies when acting in a legislative or rule-making capacity.

Related Materials

American Lawyer's Code of Conduct uses the following terminology:

A lawyer *knows* certain facts, or acts *knowingly* or with *knowledge* of facts, when a person with that lawyer's professional training and experience would be reasonably certain of those facts in view of all the circumstances of which the lawyer is aware. A duty to investigate or inquire is not implied by the use of these words, but may be explicitly required under particular rules. Even in the absence of a duty to investigate, however, a studied rejection of reasonable inferences is inadequate to avoid ethical responsibility.

Reasonable belief, reasonably believes or *reasonable understanding* is the standard used to denote a lawyer's mental state when the lawyer may be required or permitted to act on the basis of incomplete knowledge of relevant facts, as when the lawyer is predicting future events, or is compelled to act on the basis of assumptions or inferences because all the relevant facts cannot be ascertained. The lawyer must understand or suppose the fact or circumstance to be so, and the circumstances must make that understanding or supposition a reasonable one.

Model Rules of Professional Conduct for Federal Lawyers* add the following definitions:

"Federal Agency" means: (1) An Executive agency, including an Executive department, military department, Government corporation, Government controlled corporation, and an independent establishment; (2) The Congress, committees of Congress, members of Congress who employ lawyers, and Congressional agencies; (3) The courts of the United States and agencies of the Judiciary; (4) The Governments of the territories and possessions of the United States; or (5) The Government of the District of Columbia.

"Federal lawyer" means a Government lawyer or a Non-Government lawyer, as hereinafter defined.

"Government lawyer" means a Government employee who holds a position as an attorney with a Federal Agency or serves as a judge advocate in one of the Armed Forces, but only while performing official duties. The term includes a lawyer in private practice who has contracted with or been specially retained by a Federal Agency to represent the Agency or another person while engaged in the performance of the contractual obligation.

"Non-Government lawyer" means an individual who is a member of the bar of a Federal court or the highest court of a State or Territory, who represents persons before a Federal Agency. When a Government lawyer is engaged in the private practice of law or pro bono representation not related to the Government lawyer's official duties, the lawyer is considered a Non-Government lawyer.

"Supervisory lawyer" means a Federal lawyer within an office or organization with authority over or responsibility for the direction, coordination, evaluation, or assignment of responsibilities and work of subordinate lawyers, contract legal representation, nonlawyer assistants (e.g., paralegals), and clerical personnel.

ARTICLE 1. CLIENT-LAWYER RELATIONSHIP

Editors' Note. The 1980 Discussion Draft included the following introduction to Article 1:

A client usually seeks legal assistance to deal with unfamiliar circumstances and relationships. The client's position is ordinarily one of need and frequently one of adversity; the client's problem may involve significant personal and property interests, individual freedom

*This and all other excerpts from the Model Rules of Professional Conduct for Federal Lawyers, copyright © 1990 Federal Bar Association, 1815 H Street, NW, Washington, D.C. 20006-3697, have been directly quoted here with the permission of the Federal Bar Association.

15

and responsibility, or even life itself. To obtain effective advice and assistance in such matters, the client must place trust in the lawyer. To provide such advice and assistance the lawyer must be skillful, diligent, and trustworthy. At the same time, the lawyer must be faithful to the requirements of law and the Rules of Professional Conduct and respectful of the interests of third persons.

These responsibilities commence when a lawyer is asked to assist a client. They continue in all the functions that a lawyer may perform on behalf of a client. . . .

Rule 1.1 Competence

A lawyer shall provide competent representation to a client. Competent representation requires the legal knowledge, skill, thoroughness and preparation reasonably necessary for the representation.

COMMENT

Legal Knowledge and Skill

[1] In determining whether a lawyer employs the requisite knowledge and skill in a particular matter, relevant factors include the relative complexity and specialized nature of the matter, the lawyer's general experience, the lawyer's training and experience in the field in question, the preparation and study the lawyer is able to give the matter and whether it is feasible to refer the matter to, or associate or consult with, a lawyer of established competence in the field in question. In many instances, the required proficiency is that of a general practitioner. Expertise in a particular field of law may be required in some circumstances.

[2] A lawyer need not necessarily have special training or prior experience to handle legal problems of a type with which the lawyer is unfamiliar. A newly admitted lawyer can be as competent as a practitioner with long experience. Some important legal skills, such as the analysis of precedent, the evaluation of evidence and legal drafting, are required in all legal problems. Perhaps the most fundamental legal skill consists of determining what kind of legal problems a situation may involve, a skill that necessarily transcends any particular specialized knowledge. A lawyer can provide adequate representation in a wholly novel field through necessary study. Competent representation can also be provided through the association of a lawyer of established competence in the field in question.

[3] In an emergency a lawyer may give advice or assistance in a matter in which the lawyer does not have the skill ordinarily required where referral to or consultation or association with another lawyer would be impractical. Even in an emergency, however, assistance should be limited to that reasonably necessary in the circumstances, for ill considered action under emergency conditions can jeopardize the client's interest.

[4] A lawyer may accept representation where the requisite level of competence can be achieved by reasonable preparation. This applies as well to a lawyer who is appointed as counsel for an unrepresented person. See also Rule 6.2.

Thoroughness and Preparation

[5] Competent handling of a particular matter includes inquiry into and analysis of the factual and legal elements of the problem, and use of methods and procedures meeting the standards of competent practitioners. It also includes adequate preparation. The required attention and preparation are determined in part by what is at stake; major litigation and complex transactions ordinarily require more elaborate treatment than matters of lesser consequence.

Maintaining Competence

[6] To maintain the requisite knowledge and skill, a lawyer should engage in continuing study and education. If a system of peer review has been established, the lawyer should consider making use of it in appropriate circumstances.

Model Code Comparison

DR 6-101(A)(1) provided that a lawyer shall not handle a matter "which he knows or should know that he is not competent to handle, without associating himself with a lawyer who is competent to handle it"; DR 6-101(A)(2) requires "preparation adequate in the circumstances." Rule 1.1 more fully particularizes the elements of competence. Whereas DR 6-101(A)(3) prohibited the "neglect of a legal matter," Rule 1.1 does not contain such a prohibition. Instead, Rule 1.1 affirmatively requires the lawyer to be competent.

Cross-References in Rules

Rule 1.2, Comment 5: "[T]he client may not be asked to agree to representation so limited in scope as to violate **Rule 1.1**."

Rule 1.7, Comment 6: "[A] lawyer's need for income should not lead the lawyer to undertake matters that cannot be handled competently and at a reasonable fee" (citing **Rule 1.1**).

Rule 1.17, Comment 11 provides that a lawyer selling a law practice has an "obligation to exercise competence in identifying a purchaser qualified to assume the practice and the purchaser's obligation to undertake the representation competently (see **Rule 1.1**)."

Rule 6.2, Comment 2: A lawyer has good cause to decline appointment by a court to represent a person "if the lawyer could not handle the matter competently, see **Rule 1.1.** . . ."

Legislative History

1979 Unofficial Pre-Circulation Draft:

. . . (b) A lawyer acts incompetently in a particular matter, if:

(i) He or she fails to use the knowledge, skill, preparation, and judgment that a reasonably competent lawyer would use in the circumstances; and

(ii) The result of the lawyer's act or failure to act is substantial expense, delay, harm, or risk of harm to a client or other person for whose benefit the advice or assistance is provided.

1980 Discussion Draft: "A lawyer shall undertake representation only in matters in which the lawyer can act with adequate competence. . . ."

1981 Draft defined competence to include "efficiency."

1982 Draft was adopted.

Selected State Variations

California: See Rule 3-110 (Failing to Act Competently).

District of Columbia: Rule 1.1(b) adds that a lawyer "shall serve a client with skill and care commensurate with that generally afforded to clients by other lawyers in similar matters."

Illinois adds the following subparagraphs to Rule 1.1:

(b) A lawyer shall not represent a client in a legal matter in which the lawyer knows or reasonably should know that the lawyer is not competent to provide representation, without the association of another lawyer who is competent to provide such representation.

(c) After accepting employment on behalf of a client, a lawyer shall not thereafter delegate to another lawyer not in the lawyer's firm the responsibility for performing or completing that employment, without the client's consent.

Michigan retains the language of the Code in its Rule 1.1.

New Hampshire substitutes for Rule 1.1:

(a) A lawyer shall provide competent representation to a client.

(b) Legal competence requires at a minimum:

(1) specific knowledge about the fields of law in which the lawyer practices;

(2) performance of the techniques of practice with skill;

(3) identification of areas beyond the lawyer's competence and bringing those areas to the client's attention;

(4) proper preparation; and

(5) attention to details and schedules necessary to assure that the matter undertaken is completed with no avoidable harm to the client's interest.

(c) In the performance of client service, a lawyer shall at a minimum:

(1) gather sufficient facts regarding the client's problem from the client, and from other relevant sources;

(2) formulate the material issues raised, determine applicable law and identify alternative legal responses;

(3) develop a strategy, in collaboration with the client, for solving the legal problems of the client; and

(4) undertake actions on the client's behalf in a timely and effective manner including, where appropriate, associating with another lawyer who possesses the skill and knowledge required to assure competent representation.

New Jersey: A lawyer shall not:

(a) Handle or neglect a matter entrusted to the lawyer in such manner that the lawyer's conduct constitutes gross negligence.

(b) Exhibit a pattern of negligence or neglect in the lawyer's handling of legal matters generally.

New York: Same or substantially the same as the ABA Model Code — see Model Code Comparison above.

North Carolina retains the language of DR 6-101(A)(1)-(2) and adds the second sentence of Rule 1.1.

Texas: Rule 1.01 provides:

(a) A lawyer shall not accept or continue employment in a legal matter which the lawyer knows or should know is beyond the lawyer's competence, unless:

(1) another lawyer who is competent to handle the matter is, with the prior informed consent of the client, associated in the matter; or

(2) the advice or assistance of the lawyer is reasonably required in an emergency and the lawyer limits the advice and assistance to that which is reasonably necessary in the circumstances.

(b) In representing a client, a lawyer shall not:

(1) neglect a legal matter entrusted to the lawyer; or

(2) frequently fail to carry out completely the obligations that the lawyer owes to a client or clients.

(c) As used in this Rule, "neglect" signifies inattentiveness involving a conscious disregard for the responsibilities owed to a client or clients.

Virginia: DR 6-101(A) provides that a lawyer may undertake representation "only in matters in which: (1) The lawyer can act with competence and demonstrate the specific legal knowledge, skill, efficiency, and thoroughness in preparation employed in acceptable legal practice by lawyers undertaking similar matters; or (2) The lawyer has associated another lawyer who is competent in those matters."

Related Materials

ABA Model Rule for Minimum Continuing Legal Education (MCLE): In 1988, to give states guidance on implementing MCLE programs, the ABA adopted a Model Rule for MCLE. It is reprinted in the ABA/BNA Lawyers' Manual on Professional Conduct.

*ABA Standards for Imposing Lawyer Discipline:**

---

*This and all subsequent Standards for Imposing Lawyer Discipline are copyright © 1986 by the American Bar Association. All rights reserved. Reprinted with permission of the American Bar Association.

4.51. Disbarment is generally appropriate when a lawyer's course of conduct demonstrates that the lawyer does not understand the most fundamental legal doctrines or procedures, and the lawyer's conduct causes injury or potential injury to a client.

4.52. Suspension is generally appropriate when a lawyer engages in an area of practice in which the lawyer knows he or she is not competent, and causes injury or potential injury to a client.

American Academy of Matrimonial Lawyers: The "Bounds of Advocacy" drafted by the American Academy of Matrimonial Lawyers contains the following provisions and commentary:

1.3. An attorney should not advise a client about a matter concerning which the attorney is not sufficiently competent.

Comment to Rule 1.3

No attorney has complete command of every field of the law or every issue that may be encountered in a family law matter. Clients, however, often ask matrimonial lawyers to provide psychological or investment counseling or to provide advice on issues of real estate and corporate law. A matrimonial lawyer should recommend that such a client consult more knowledgeable lawyers or other professionals when in the best interest of the client.

American Lawyer's Code of Conduct: Rules 4.1 through 4.4 and 4.6 provide:

4.1. At a minimum, a lawyer shall serve a client with skill and care commensurate with that generally afforded to clients by other lawyers in similar matters.

4.2. A lawyer who has held himself or herself out to a client as having special skill and competence relative to a matter in which the client has retained the lawyer shall serve the client with that skill and care generally afforded to clients by lawyers of such skill and competence.

4.3. A lawyer shall take such legal action as is necessary and reasonably available to protect and advance a client's interests in the matter entrusted to the lawyer by the client.

4.4. A lawyer shall seek out all facts and legal authorities that are reasonably available and relevant to a client's interests in the matter entrusted to the lawyer by the client. In so doing, the lawyer shall give due regard not only to established rules of law, but also to developing legal concepts that might affect the client's interests.

4.6. A lawyer shall seek out reasonably available resources that are necessary to protect and advance a client's interests, such as experts in specialized areas of the law or experts in non-legal disciplines.

State MCLE Programs: About 35 states have adopted minimum continuing legal education (MCLE) programs to help raise the general level of lawyer competence.

Restatement of the Law Governing Lawyers: The American Law Institute has tentatively approved the following provision:

§28. Lawyer's Duties to Client in General

To the extent consistent with the lawyer's legal duties and subject to the other provisions of this Restatement, a lawyer must:

(1) In matters covered by the representation, act in a manner reasonably calculated to advance a client's lawful objectives, as defined by the client after disclosure and consultation;

(2) Act in the matter with reasonable competence and diligence;

(3) Safeguard the client's confidences and property, avoid impermissible conflicting interests, deal honestly with the client, and not employ adversely to the client powers arising from the client-lawyer relationship; and

(4) Fulfil any valid contractual obligation to the client.

Rule 1.2 Scope of Representation

(a) A lawyer shall abide by a client's decisions concerning the objectives of representation, subject to paragraphs (c), (d) and (e), and shall consult with the client as to the means by which they are to be pursued. A lawyer shall abide by a client's decision whether to accept an offer of settlement of a matter. In a criminal case, the lawyer shall abide by the client's decision, after consultation with the lawyer, as to a plea to be entered, whether to waive jury trial and whether the client will testify.

(b) A lawyer's representation of a client, including representation by appointment, does not constitute an endorsement of the client's political, economic, social or moral views or activities.

(c) A lawyer may limit the objectives of the representation if the client consents after consultation.

(d) A lawyer shall not counsel a client to engage, or assist a client, in conduct that the lawyer knows is criminal or fraudulent, but a lawyer may discuss the legal consequences of any proposed course of conduct with a client and may counsel or assist a client to make a good faith effort to determine the validity, scope, meaning or application of the law.

(e) When a lawyer knows that a client expects assistance not permitted by the rules of professional conduct or other law, the lawyer shall consult with the client regarding the relevant limitations on the lawyer's conduct.

COMMENT

Scope of Representation

[1] Both lawyer and client have authority and responsibility in the objectives and means of representation. The client has ultimate authority to determine the purposes to be served by legal representation, within the limits imposed by law and the lawyer's professional obligations. Within those limits, a client also has a right to consult with the lawyer about the means to be used in pursuing those objectives. At the same time, a lawyer is not required to pursue objectives or employ means simply because a client may wish that the lawyer do so. A clear distinction between objectives and means sometimes cannot be drawn, and in many cases the client-lawyer relationship partakes of a joint undertaking. In questions of means, the lawyer should assume responsibility for technical and legal tactical issues, but should defer to the client regarding such questions as

the expense to be incurred and concern for third persons who might be adversely affected. Law defining the lawyer's scope of authority in litigation varies among jurisdictions.

[2] In a case in which the client appears to be suffering mental disability, the lawyer's duty to abide by the client's decisions is to be guided by reference to Rule 1.14.

Independence from Client's Views or Activities

[3] Legal representation should not be denied to people who are unable to afford legal services, or whose cause is controversial or the subject of popular disapproval. By the same token, representing a client does not constitute approval of the client's views or activities.

Services Limited in Objectives or Means

[4] The objectives or scope of services provided by a lawyer may be limited by agreement with the client or by the terms under which the lawyer's services are made available to the client. For example, a retainer may be for a specifically defined purpose. Representation provided through a legal aid agency may be subject to limitations on the types of cases the agency handles. When a lawyer has been retained by an insurer to represent an insured, the representation may be limited to matters related to the insurance coverage. The terms upon which representation is undertaken may exclude specific objectives or means. Such limitations may exclude objectives or means that the lawyer regards as repugnant or imprudent.

[5] An agreement concerning the scope of representation must accord with the Rules of Professional Conduct and other law. Thus, the client may not be asked to agree to representation so limited in scope as to violate Rule 1.1, or to surrender the right to terminate the lawyer's services or the right to settle litigation that the lawyer might wish to continue.

Criminal, Fraudulent and Prohibited Transactions

[6] A lawyer is required to give an honest opinion about the actual consequences that appear likely to result from a client's conduct. The fact that a client uses advice in a course of action that is criminal or fraudulent does not, of itself, make a lawyer a party to the course of action. However, a lawyer may not knowingly assist a client in criminal or fraudulent conduct. There is a critical distinction between presenting an analysis of legal aspects of questionable conduct and recommending the means by which a crime or fraud might be committed with impunity.

[7] When the client's course of action has already begun and is continuing, the lawyer's responsibility is especially delicate. The lawyer is not permitted to reveal the client's wrongdoing, except where permitted by Rule 1.6. However, the lawyer is required to avoid furthering the purpose, for example, by suggesting how it might be concealed. A lawyer may not continue assisting a client in conduct that the lawyer originally supposes is legally proper but then discovers is criminal or fraudulent. Withdrawal from the representation, therefore, may be required.

[8] Where the client is a fiduciary, the lawyer may be charged with special obligations in dealings with a beneficiary.

[9] Paragraph (d) applies whether or not the defrauded party is a party to the transaction. Hence, a lawyer should not participate in a sham transaction; for example, a transaction to effectuate criminal or fraudulent escape of tax liability. Paragraph (d) does not preclude undertaking a criminal defense incident to a general retainer for legal services to a lawful enterprise. The last clause of paragraph (d) recognizes that determining the validity or interpretation of a statute or regulation may require a course of action involving disobedience of the statute or regulation or of the interpretation placed upon it by governmental authorities.

Model Code Comparison

Paragraph (a) has no counterpart in the Disciplinary Rules of the Model Code. EC 7-7 stated: "In certain areas of legal representation not affecting the merits of the cause or substantially prejudicing the rights of a client, a lawyer is entitled to make decisions on his own. But otherwise the authority to make decisions is exclusively that of the client. . . ." EC 7-8 stated that "[I]n the final analysis, however, the . . . decision whether to forego legally available objectives or methods because of nonlegal factors is ultimately for the client. . . . In the event that the client in a nonadjudicatory matter insists upon a course of conduct that is contrary to the judgment and advice of the lawyer but not prohibited by Disciplinary Rules, the lawyer may withdraw from the employment." DR 7-101(A)(1) provided that a lawyer "shall not intentionally . . . fail to seek the lawful objectives of his client through reasonably available means permitted by law. . . . A lawyer does not violate this Disciplinary Rule, however, by . . . avoiding offensive tactics. . . ."

Paragraph (b) has no counterpart in the Model Code.

With regard to paragraph (c), DR 7-101(B)(1) provided that a lawyer may, "where permissible, exercise his professional judgment to waive or fail to assert a right or position of his client."

With regard to paragraph (d), DR 7-102(A)(7) provided that a lawyer shall not "counsel or assist his client in conduct that the lawyer knows to be illegal or fraudulent." DR 7-102(A)(6) provided that a lawyer shall not "participate in the creation or preservation of evidence when he knows or it is obvious that the evidence is false." DR 7-106 provided that a lawyer shall not "advise his client to disregard a standing rule of a tribunal or a ruling of a tribunal . . . but he may take appropriate steps in good faith to test the validity of such rule or ruling." EC 7-5 stated that a lawyer "should never encourage or aid his client to commit criminal acts or counsel his client on how to violate the law and avoid punishment therefor."

With regard to Rule 1.2(e), DR 2-110(C)(1)(c) provided that a lawyer may withdraw from representation if a client "insists" that the lawyer engage in "conduct that is illegal or that is prohibited under the Disciplinary Rules." DR 9-101(C) provided that "a lawyer shall not state or imply that he is able to influence improperly . . . any tribunal, legislative body or public official."

Cross-References in Rules

Rule 1.3, Comment 1: "A lawyer has professional discretion in determining the means by which a matter should be pursued. See **Rule 1.2.**"

Rule 1.4, Comment 1: "A lawyer who receives from opposing counsel an offer of settlement in a civil controversy or a proffered plea bargain in a criminal case should promptly inform the client of its substance unless prior discussions with the client have left it clear that the proposal will be unacceptable. See **Rule 1.2(a).**"

Rule 1.6, Comment 10: "[T]he lawyer may not counsel or assist a client in conduct that is criminal or fraudulent. See **Rule 1.2(d).** Similarly, a lawyer has a duty under Rule 3.3(a)(4) not to use false evidence. This duty is essentially a special instance of the duty prescribed in **Rule 1.2(d)** to avoid assisting a client in criminal or fraudulent conduct."

Rule 1.6, Comment 11: "[T]he lawyer may have been innocently involved in past conduct by the client that was criminal or fraudulent. In such a situation the lawyer has not violated **Rule 1.2(d),** because to 'counsel or assist' criminal or fraudulent conduct requires knowing that the conduct is of that character."

Rule 1.13, Comment 6: "If the lawyer's services are being used by an organization to further a crime or fraud by the organization, **Rule 1.2(d)** can be applicable."

Rule 1.14, Comment 4: "If the lawyer represents the guardian as distinct from the ward, and is aware that the guardian is acting adversely to the ward's interest, the lawyer may have an obligation to prevent or rectify the guardian's misconduct. See **Rule 1.2(d).**"

Rule 3.3, Comment 2: "The obligation prescribed in **Rule 1.2(d)** not to counsel a client to commit or assist the client in committing a fraud applies in litigation. Regarding compliance with **Rule 1.2(d),** see the Comment to that Rule."

Rule 3.3, Comment 6: The alternative to disclosing a client's deception to the court or to the other party is that the lawyer "cooperate in deceiving the court, thereby subverting the truth-finding process which the adversary system is designed to implement. See **Rule 1.2(d).**"

Rule 3.3, Comment 10: "[A]n advocate has an obligation, not only in professional ethics but under the law as well, to avoid implication in the commission of perjury or other falsification of evidence. See **Rule 1.2(d).**"

Rule 6.4, Comment: "Lawyers involved in organizations seeking law reform generally do not have a client-lawyer relationship with the organization. . . . See also **Rule 1.2(b).**"

Rule 8.4, Comment 2: "The provisions of **Rule 1.2(d)** concerning a good faith challenge to the validity, scope, meaning or application of the law apply to challenges of legal regulation of the practice of law."

Legislative History

1980 Discussion Draft (then called Rule 1.3):

(a) A lawyer shall accept a client's decisions concerning the objectives of the representation and the means by which they are to be pursued except as stated in paragraphs (b) and (c).

(b) A lawyer shall not pursue a course of action on behalf of a client in violation of law or the rules of professional conduct.

(c) The lawyer may decline to pursue a lawful course of action . . . and, if the client insists upon such course of action, the lawyer may withdraw from representation subject to the provisions of Rule 1.16.

The 1980 Draft also contained the following separate rules (then called Rules 2.3 and 2.4):

Advice Concerning Wrongful Conduct

(a) A lawyer shall not give advice which the lawyer can reasonably foresee will:

(1) Be used by the client to further an illegal course of conduct except as part of a good faith effort to determine the validity, scope, meaning, or application of the law; or

(2) Aid the client in contriving false testimony or making a legally wrongful misrepresentation.

(b) A lawyer may decline to give advice that might assist the client in any conduct that would violate the law or . . . that the lawyer considers repugnant.

Duty to Offer Advice

A lawyer who knows that a client contemplates a course of action which has a substantial likelihood of serious legal consequences shall warn the client of the legal implications of the conduct, unless a client has expressly or by implication asked not to receive such advice.

The 1980 Draft also contained the following rule (then called Rule 4.1) similar to the adopted version of Rule 1.2(a):

Disclosures to a Client

A lawyer conducting negotiations for a client shall:

(a) inform the client of facts relevant to the matter and of communications from another party that may significantly affect resolution of the matter;

(b) in connection with an offer, take reasonable steps to assure that the judgment of the client rather than that of the lawyer determines whether the offer will be accepted.

1981 Draft of Rule 1.2(d) prohibited a lawyer from counseling or assisting a client "in the preparation of a written instrument containing terms the lawyer knows or reasonably should know are legally prohibited. . . ."

1982 Draft of Rule 1.2 was the same as adopted, except that Rule 1.2(d) also prohibited a lawyer from counseling or assisting "in the preparation of a written instrument containing terms the lawyer knows are expressly prohibited by law. . . ."

Selected State Variations

California: See Rule 3-210 (Advising the Violation of Law) and B & P Code §6068(c).

District of Columbia: Rule 1.2(d) provides:

> A government lawyer's authority and control over decisions concerning the representation may, by statute or regulation, be expanded beyond the limits imposed by paragraphs (a) and (c).

Florida adds the words "or reasonably should know" in Rule 1.2(d) and (e). In addition, Florida's Statement of Client's Rights, which must be provided to every contingent fee client (see Florida Rule 1.5(D)), provides that "[y]ou, the client, have the right to make the final decision regarding settlement of a case. . . ."

Georgia forbids a lawyer to "institute, cause to be instituted or settle a legal proceeding or claim without obtaining proper authorization from his client." DR 7-102(A)(9).

Illinois includes language from DR 7-102(A)-(B) as paragraphs (f)-(h), and adds the following new paragraph (based on DR 7-105) as Rule 1.2(e): "A lawyer shall not present, participate in presenting, or threaten to present criminal charges or professional disciplinary actions to obtain an advantage in a civil matter."

Louisiana adds to Rule 1.2(a): "Both lawyer and client have authority and responsibility in the objectives and means of representation. The client has ultimate authority to determine the purposes to be served by legal representation within the limits imposed by law and the lawyer's professional obligations."

Maryland adds "when appropriate" before the words "shall consult" in Rule 1.2(a).

Michigan deletes Rule 1.2(b) and adds the following sentence to Rule 1.2(a): "In representing a client, a lawyer may, where permissible, exercise professional judgment to waive or fail to assert a right or position of the client."

Minnesota deletes Rule 1.2(b) entirely.

New Jersey: In Rule 1.2(d), New Jersey forbids a lawyer to assist a client "in the preparation of a written instrument containing terms the lawyer knows are expressly prohibited by the law."

New York: Same or substantially the same as the ABA Model Code — see Model Code Comparison above — except see New York Materials for New York's version of DR 7-102(B)(1). See also EC 2-27, EC 4-7, and DR 4-101(C)(5) of the New York Code.

North Carolina retains the language of DR 7-101 and adds the language of Rule 1.2 except for Rule 1.2(b) and the first sentence of Rule 1.2(a).

Virginia: Substantially the same as the Model Code.

Related Materials

ABA Canons: Canons 16, 24, and 32 provided:

16. Restraining Clients from Improprieties

A lawyer should use his best efforts to restrain and to prevent his clients from doing those things which the lawyer himself ought not to do, particularly with reference to their conduct towards Courts, judicial officers, jurors, witnesses and suitors. If a client persists in such wrongdoing the lawyer should terminate their relation.

24. Right of Lawyer to Control the Incidents of the Trial

As to incidental matters pending the trial, not affecting the merits of the cause, or working substantial prejudice to the rights of the client, such as forcing the opposite lawyer to trial when he is under affliction or bereavement; forcing the trial on a particular day to the injury of the opposite lawyer when no harm will result from a trial at a different time; agreeing to an extension of time for signing a bill of exceptions, cross interrogatories and the like, the lawyer must be allowed to judge. In such matters no client has a right to demand that his counsel shall be illiberal, or that he do anything therein repugnant to his own sense of honor and propriety.

32. The Lawyer's Duty in Its Last Analysis

No client, corporate or individual, however powerful, nor any cause, civil or political, however important, is entitled to receive nor should any lawyer render any service or advice involving disloyalty to the law whose ministers we are, or disrespect of the judicial office, which we are bound to uphold, or corruption of any person or persons exercising a public office or private trust, or deception or betrayal of the public. When rendering any such improper service or advice, the lawyer invites and merits stern and just condemnation. Correspondingly, he advances the honor of his profession and the best interests of his client when he renders service or gives advice tending to impress upon the client and his undertaking exact compliance with the strictest principles of moral law. He must also observe and advise his client to observe the statute law, though until a statute shall have been construed and interpreted by competent adjudication, he is free and is entitled to advise as to its validity and as to what he conscientiously believes to be its just meaning and extent. But above all a lawyer will find his highest honor in a deserved reputation for fidelity to private trust and to public duty, as an honest man and as a patriotic and loyal citizen.

American Academy of Matrimonial Lawyers: The "Bounds of Advocacy" drafted by the American Academy of Matrimonial Lawyers contains the following provisions and commentary:

2.13. An attorney should never encourage a client to hide or dissipate assets.

Comment to Rule 2.13

It is improper for an attorney to "counsel a client to engage, or assist a client, in conduct that the lawyer knows is criminal or fraudulent, but a lawyer may discuss the legal consequences of any proposed course of conduct with a client. . . ." Whether the client proposes opening up an out-of-state bank account or having a family member hold sums of cash for the purpose of concealment, the advice to the client must be the same: "Don't do it." Hiding assets is a fraud upon the client's spouse and likely to result in a fraud upon the court. However, advice to protect, rather than hide, assets is appropriate. The client must also be advised not to conceal data about his property, fail to furnish relevant documents, insist on placing unrealistic values on properties in, or omit assets from, sworn financial statements.

On the other hand, "[t]here is a critical distinction between presenting an analysis of legal aspects of questionable conduct and recommending the means by which a crime or fraud might be committed with impunity." It may sometimes be difficult to determine whether a client's questions concerning legal aspects of predivorce planning are asked to facilitate an improper purpose. Although the attorney should initially give the client the benefit of any doubt, later discovery of improper conduct mandates that the attorney cease such assistance and may require withdrawal from representation.

2.27. An attorney should refuse to assist in vindictive conduct toward a spouse or third person and should not do anything to increase the emotional level of the dispute.

Comment to Rule 2.27

Although the client has the right to determine the "objectives of representation," after consulting with the client the attorney may limit the objectives and the means by which the objectives are to be pursued. The matrimonial lawyer should make every effort to lower the emotional level of the interaction between the parties and their counsel. Some dissension and bad feelings can be avoided by a frank discussion with the client at the outset of how the attorney handles cases, including what the attorney will and will not do regarding vindictive conduct or actions likely to adversely affect the children's interests. Although not essential, a letter to the client confirming the understanding, before specific issues or requests arise, is advisable. To the extent that the client is unwilling to accept any limitations on objectives or means, the attorney should decline the representation.

If such a discussion did not occur, or the client despite a prior understanding asks the attorney to engage in conduct the attorney believes to be imprudent or repugnant, the attorney should attempt to convince the client to work toward family harmony or the interests of the children. Conduct in the interests of the children or family will almost always be in the client's long term best interests.

American Lawyer's Code of Conduct: Rules 3.3 and 3.4 provide:

3.3. A lawyer shall not advise a client about the law when the lawyer knows that the client is requesting the advice for an unlawful purpose likely to cause death or serious physical injury to another person.

3.4. A lawyer shall not knowingly encourage a client to engage in illegal conduct, except in a good faith effort to test the validity or scope of the law.

Restatement of the Law Governing Lawyers: The American Law Institute has tentatively approved the following provision:

§30. Limited Representation and Waiver of Client or Lawyer Duties

(1) Subject to other requirements stated in this Restatement, a lawyer and an adequately informed client may agree to limit the scope or objectives of the representation.

(2) Subject to other requirements stated in this Restatement, a client may agree to waive a duty that a lawyer would otherwise owe to the client if:

(a) The client gives informed consent, having adequate information about the risks and advantages of waiving the duty; and

(b) The terms of the waiver are reasonable in the circumstances.

(3) A lawyer may agree to waive a client's duty to pay or other duty that a client would otherwise owe to the lawyer.

§31. Lawyer's Duty to Inform and Consult with Client

(1) A lawyer must keep a client reasonably informed about the status of a matter and must consult with a client to a reasonable extent concerning decisions to be made by the lawyer under §§32-34.

(2) A lawyer must promptly comply with a client's reasonable requests for information.

(3) A lawyer must notify a client of decisions to be made by a client under §§32-34, such as whether to accept a settlement offer, and must explain a matter to the extent reasonably necessary to permit the client to make informed decisions regarding the representation.

§32. Allocating Authority to Decide Between Client and Lawyer

As between client and lawyer:

(1) A client and lawyer may agree which of them will make specified decisions. Such an agreement is valid if consistent with the requirements stated in §§29A, 30, 33, 34, and other provisions of this Restatement. It may be superseded by another valid agreement.

(2) A client may instruct a lawyer during the representation. Such an instruction binds the lawyer if consistent with requirements stated in §§33, 34, and other provisions of this Restatement and any valid existing agreement between client and lawyer.

(3) To the extent that the authority to decide is not allocated to the client by §33, other provisions of this Restatement, or a valid agreement or instruction, a lawyer may take any lawful measure reasonably calculated to advance a client's objectives as defined by the client in a matter in which the lawyer represents the client, consulting with the client as required by §31.

(4) A client may ratify an act of a lawyer that was unauthorized under §33 or other parts of this Section.

§33. Authority Reserved to Client

As between client and lawyer, decisions such as the following are allocated to the client within the meaning of §32(3) and may not be irrevocably delegated to the lawyer: whether and on what terms to settle a claim; how to plead in a criminal prosecution; whether to choose to waive jury trial in a criminal prosecution; whether to testify in a criminal prosecution; and whether to appeal in a civil proceeding or criminal prosecution. A client may from time to time authorize a lawyer to make those decisions for the client, except to the extent that other law (such as criminal procedure rules governing pleas, jury trial waiver, and defendant testimony) requires the client's personal participation or approval.

§34. Authority Reserved to Lawyer

As between client and lawyer, a lawyer retains the authority, which may not be overridden by an agreement or an instruction from the client:

(1) To refuse to perform, counsel or assist future or ongoing acts that the lawyer reasonably believes to be unlawful;

(2) To make decisions that law or an order of a tribunal requires the lawyer to make; and

(3) To decide what should be done on behalf of the client when law or an order of a tribunal requires an immediate decision without time to consult the client.

§37. Presumption that Appearing Lawyer Represents Client

A lawyer who files an appearance before a tribunal on behalf of a person is presumed to represent that person as a client. The presumption may be rebutted by persuading the tribunal of the lawyer's lack of authority.

§38. A Lawyer's Actual Authority

A lawyer's act is considered to be that of a client in proceedings before a tribunal or in dealings with third persons when:

(1) The client has authorized the act;

(2) As stated in §32 the client has conferred authority on the lawyer to decide to perform the act;

(3) Authority to perform the act is reserved to the lawyer as stated in §34; or

(4) The client ratifies the act.

§39. A Lawyer's Apparent Authority

A lawyer's act is considered to be that of a client in proceedings before a tribunal or in dealings with a third person when:

(1) The tribunal or third person believes that the lawyer is authorized to do the act; and

(2) (a) The act reasonably appears calculated to advance the client's objectives in a matter in which the lawyer represents the client and authority over the act is not reserved to the client as stated in §33; or

(b) The decision is so reserved but the client's conduct known to the tribunal or third person reasonably indicates that the lawyer is authorized to do the act.

§40. Attributing Lawyer's Knowledge and Statements to Client

(1) What a lawyer knows, during and relating to the representation of a client, is attributed to the client for the purpose of determining the client's rights and liabilities in matters in which the lawyer represents the client, unless the law governing those rights and liabilities requires proof of the client's personal knowledge or intentions.

(2) Unless applicable law otherwise provides, a third person may give notification to a client, in a matter in which the client is represented by a lawyer, by giving notification to the client's lawyer, unless the third person knows of circumstances reasonably indicating that the client has abrogated the lawyer's authority to receive notification.

(3) A lawyer's unprivileged statement is admissible in evidence against a client as an admission of the client if:

(a) The client authorized the lawyer to make a statement concerning the subject; or

(b) The statement concerns a matter within the scope of the representation and was made by the lawyer during it.

§41. When a Client May Show Lawyer's Conduct to Disclaim Client's Responsibility

(1) When a client's knowing violation of law or malice is in issue, a tribunal may consider otherwise admissible evidence of a lawyer's advice to the client.

(2) When deciding whether to sanction a person or release a person from a criminal or civil ruling, default, or judgment, a tribunal may consider otherwise admissible evidence that the person should not in fairness be bound by a lawyer's representation of the person because the lawyer represented the person inadequately or contrary to the client's instructions or was otherwise to blame.

§42. Lawyer's Liability for Acts on Behalf of Client

(1) For acts performed while representing a client, a lawyer is subject to professional discipline as stated in Chapter 1, to tort liability as stated in Chapter 4, and to criminal prosecution.

(2) A lawyer is liable to third persons on contracts the lawyer entered into on behalf of a client, unless the lawyer or third person disclaimed such liability, if:

(a) The client's existence or identity was not disclosed to the third person; or

(b) The contract is with a third person who provides goods or services used by lawyers and who normally deals with lawyers rather than clients.

(3) A lawyer is liable to a third person for damages for loss caused by the lawyer's acting without authority from a client under §38 if:

(a) The lawyer tortiously misrepresents to the third person that the lawyer has authority to make a contract, conveyance, or representation on behalf of the client and the third person reasonably relies on the misrepresentation; or

(b) The lawyer purports to make a contract, conveyance, or representation on behalf of the client, unless the lawyer manifests that the lawyer does not warrant that the lawyer is authorized to act or the other party knows that the lawyer is not authorized to act.

§132. Exception for Client Crimes and Frauds

The attorney-client privilege does not apply to a communication occurring when a client consults a lawyer for the purpose of obtaining assistance in engaging in conduct or aiding a third person in engaging in conduct if the client, at the time of the communication, knows or reasonably should know that the conduct is a crime or fraud.

Substantive Criminal Law: In many jurisdictions, a lawyer's violation of Rule 1.2(d) would also violate criminal laws prohibiting anyone from aiding or abetting the commission of a crime.

Rule 1.3 Diligence

A lawyer shall act with reasonable diligence and promptness in representing a client.

COMMENT

[1] A lawyer should pursue a matter on behalf of a client despite opposition, obstruction or personal inconvenience to the lawyer, and may take whatever lawful and ethical measures are required to vindicate a client's cause or endeavor. A lawyer should act with commitment and dedication to the interests of the client and with zeal in advocacy upon the client's behalf. However, a lawyer is not bound to press for every advantage that might be realized for a client. A lawyer has professional discretion in determining the means by which a matter should be pursued. See Rule 1.2. A lawyer's workload should be controlled so that each matter can be handled adequately.

[2] Perhaps no professional shortcoming is more widely resented than procrastination. A client's interests often can be adversely affected by the passage of time or the change of conditions; in extreme instances, as when a lawyer overlooks a statute of limitations, the client's legal position may be destroyed. Even when the client's interests are not affected in substance, however, unreasonable delay can cause a client needless anxiety and undermine confidence in the lawyer's trustworthiness.

[3] Unless the relationship is terminated as provided in Rule 1.16, a lawyer should carry through to conclusion all matters undertaken for a client. If a lawyer's employment is limited to a specific matter, the relationship terminates when the matter has been resolved. If a lawyer has served a client over a substantial period in a variety of matters, the client sometimes may assume that the lawyer will continue to serve on a continuing basis unless the lawyer gives notice of withdrawal. Doubt about whether a client-lawyer relationship still exists should be clarified by the lawyer, preferably in writing, so that the client will not mistakenly suppose the lawyer is looking after the client's affairs when the lawyer has ceased to do so. For example, if a lawyer has handled a judicial or administrative proceeding that produced a result adverse to the client but has not been specifically instructed concerning pursuit of an appeal, the lawyer should advise the client of the possibility of appeal before relinquishing responsibility for the matter.

Model Code Comparison

DR 6-101(A)(3) required that a lawyer not "[n]eglect a legal matter entrusted to him." EC 6-4 stated that a lawyer should "give appropriate attention to his legal work." Canon 7 stated that "a lawyer should represent a client zealously within the bounds of the law." DR 7-101(A)(1) provided that a lawyer "shall not intentionally . . . fail to seek the lawful objectives of his client through reasonably available means permitted by law and the Disciplinary Rules. . . ." DR 7-101(A)(3) provided that a lawyer "shall not intentionally . . . [p]rejudice or damage his client during the course of the relationship. . . ."

Cross-References in Rules

Rule 1.7, Comment 1: "As to whether a client-lawyer relationship exists or, having once been established, is continuing, see Comment to **Rule 1.3** and Scope."

Rule 3.2 does not refer to Rule 1.3 but does require a lawyer to make reasonable efforts to "expedite" litigation.

Legislative History

1980 Discussion Draft:

A lawyer shall attend promptly to matters undertaken for a client and give them adequate attention until completed or until the lawyer has properly withdrawn from representing the client.

1981 and 1982 Drafts were the same as adopted.

Selected State Variations

California: See Rule 3-110(B) (Failing to Act Competently).
District of Columbia: Rule 1.3 provides:

(a) A lawyer shall represent a client zealously and diligently within the bounds of the law.
(b) A lawyer shall not intentionally:
(1) fail to seek the lawful objectives of a client through reasonably available means permitted by law and the disciplinary rules; or
(2) prejudice or damage a client during the course of the professional relationship.
(c) A lawyer shall act with reasonable promptness in representing a client.

New Hampshire adds Rule 1.3(b), which provides:

Performance by a lawyer is prompt and diligent when:
(1) it is carried out in the manner and within the time parameters established by the agreement between the client and the lawyer; however, the lawyer may not rely upon the terms of an agreement to excuse performance which is not prompt and diligent in light of changes in circumstances, known to the lawyer, which require adjustments to the agreed upon schedule of performance.
(2) in all other matters of representation, it is carried out with no avoidable harm to the client's interest nor to the lawyer-client relationship.

New York: Same or substantially the same as the ABA Model Code — see Model Code Comparison above.
Texas omits Rule 1.3.
Virginia: DR 6-101(B) provides that a lawyer "shall attend promptly to matters undertaken for a client until completed or until the lawyer has properly and completely withdrawn from representing the client."

Related Materials

ABA Canons: Canon 21 provided:

21. Punctuality and Expedition

It is the duty of the lawyer not only to his client, but also to the Courts and to the public to be punctual in attendance, and to be concise and direct in the trial and disposition of causes.

ABA Standards for Imposing Lawyer Discipline:

4.41. Disbarment is generally appropriate when:
(a) a lawyer abandons the practice and causes serious or potentially serious injury to a client; or
(b) a lawyer knowingly fails to perform services for a client and causes serious or potentially serious injury to a client; or
(c) a lawyer engages in a pattern of neglect with respect to client matters and causes serious or potentially serious injury to a client.
4.42. Suspension is generally appropriate when:

(a) a lawyer knowingly fails to perform services for a client and causes injury or potential injury to a client; or

(b) a lawyer engages in a pattern of neglect and causes injury or potential injury to a client.

American Lawyer's Code of Conduct: Rule 3.1 provides:

A lawyer shall use all legal means that are consistent with the retainer agreement, and reasonably available, to advance a client's interests as the client perceives them.

Rule 1.4 Communication

(a) A lawyer shall keep a client reasonably informed about the status of a matter and promptly comply with reasonable requests for information.

(b) A lawyer shall explain a matter to the extent reasonably necessary to permit the client to make informed decisions regarding the representation.

COMMENT

[1] The client should have sufficient information to participate intelligently in decisions concerning the objectives of the representation and the means by which they are to be pursued, to the extent the client is willing and able to do so. For example, a lawyer negotiating on behalf of a client should provide the client with facts relevant to the matter, inform the client of communications from another party and take other reasonable steps that permit the client to make a decision regarding a serious offer from another party. A lawyer who receives from opposing counsel an offer of settlement in a civil controversy or a proffered plea bargain in a criminal case should promptly inform the client of its substance unless prior discussions with the client have left it clear that the proposal will be unacceptable. See Rule 1.2(a). Even when a client delegates authority to the lawyer, the client should be kept advised of the status of the matter.

[2] Adequacy of communication depends in part on the kind of advice or assistance involved. For example, in negotiations where there is time to explain a proposal, the lawyer should review all important provisions with the client before proceeding to an agreement. In litigation a lawyer should explain the general strategy and prospects of success and ordinarily should consult the client on tactics that might injure or coerce others. On the other hand, a lawyer ordinarily cannot be expected to describe trial or negotiation strategy in detail. The guiding principle is that the lawyer should fulfill reasonable client expectations for information consistent with the duty to act in the client's best interests, and the client's overall requirements as to the character of representation.

[3] Ordinarily, the information to be provided is that appropriate for a client who is a comprehending and responsible adult. However, fully informing the client according to this standard may be impracticable, for example, where the

client is a child or suffers from mental disability. See Rule 1.14. When the client is an organization or group, it is often impossible or inappropriate to inform everyone of its members about its legal affairs; ordinarily, the lawyer should address communications to the appropriate officials of the organization. See Rule 1.13. Where many routine matters are involved, a system of limited or occasional reporting may be arranged with the client. Practical exigency may also require a lawyer to act for a client without prior consultation.

Withholding Information

[4] In some circumstances, a lawyer may be justified in delaying transmission of information when the client would be likely to react imprudently to an immediate communication. Thus, a lawyer might withhold a psychiatric diagnosis of a client when the examining psychiatrist indicates that disclosure would harm the client. A lawyer may not withhold information to serve the lawyer's own interest or convenience. Rules or court orders governing litigation may provide that information supplied to a lawyer may not be disclosed to the client. Rule 3.4(c) directs compliance with such rules or orders.

Model Code Comparison

Rule 1.4 has no direct counterpart in the Disciplinary Rules of the Model Code. DR 6-101(A)(3) provided that a lawyer shall not "[n]eglect a legal matter entrusted to him." DR 9-102(B)(1) provided that a lawyer shall "[p]romptly notify a client of the receipt of his funds, securities, or other properties." EC 7-8 stated that a lawyer "should exert his best efforts to insure that decisions of his client are made only after the client has been informed of relevant considerations." EC 9-2 stated that a "lawyer should fully and promptly inform his client of material developments in the matters being handled for the client."

Cross-References in Rules

Rule 2.1, Comment 5: "[W]hen a lawyer knows that a client proposes a course of action that is likely to result in substantial adverse legal consequences to the client, duty to the client under **Rule 1.4** may require that the lawyer act if the client's course of action is related to the representation."

Rule 2.2, Comment 6: "In a common representation, the lawyer is still required both to keep each client adequately informed and to maintain confidentiality of information relating to the representation. See **Rules 1.4** and 1.6."

Rule 2.2, Comment 9: Paragraph (b) of Rule 2.2, requiring consultation with clients while acting as an intermediary, "is an application of the principle expressed in **Rule 1.4.**"

Legislative History

1979 Unofficial Pre-Circulation Draft (then Rule 1.3):

> (a) A lawyer shall keep a client informed about a matter in which the lawyer's services are being rendered. Informing the client includes:
> (1) Periodically advising the client of the status and progress of the matter;
> (2) Explaining the legal and practical aspects of the matter and foreseeable effects of alternative courses of action; and . . .
> (c) A lawyer may withhold information to which a client is otherwise entitled only when doing so is necessary to protect the client's interest or some superior interest.

1980 Discussion Draft prohibited a lawyer from withholding information to which a client was entitled "except when doing so is clearly necessary to protect the client's interest or to comply with the requirements of law or the rules of professional conduct."

1981 Draft provided:

> (b) A lawyer shall explain the legal and practical aspects of a matter and alternative courses of action to the extent reasonably necessary to permit the client to make informed decisions regarding the representation.

1982 Draft was adopted.

Selected State Variations

California: Rule 3-500 (Communication), Rule 3-510 (Communication of Settlement Offer), and B & P Code §6068(m) (regarding communication generally).

District of Columbia adds Rule 1.4(c), which provides:

> A lawyer who receives an offer of settlement in a civil case or a proffered plea bargain in a criminal case shall inform the client promptly of the substance of the communication.

Florida: Florida's Statement of Client's Rights, which must be provided to every contingent fee client (see Florida Rule 1.5(D)), provides:

> 10. . . . Your lawyer must notify you of all offers of settlement before and after the trial. Offers during the trial must be immediately communicated and you should consult with your lawyer regarding whether to accept a settlement. However, you must make the final decision to accept or reject a settlement.

Louisiana adds to Rule 1.4(b): "The lawyer shall give the client sufficient information to participate intelligently in decisions concerning the object of the representation and the means by which they are to be pursued, to the extent the client is willing and able to do so."

Michigan adds to Rule 1.4(a): "A lawyer shall notify the client promptly of all settlement offers, mediation evaluations, and proposed plea bargains."

New York: Same or substantially the same as the ABA Model Code — see Model Code Comparison above.

Virginia: DR 6-101(D) adds that a lawyer "shall inform his client . . . of communications from another party that may significantly affect settlement or resolution of a matter."

Related Materials

ABA Canons: Canon 8 provided:

Advising upon the Merits of a Client's Cause

A lawyer should endeavor to obtain full knowledge of his client's cause before advising thereon, and he is bound to give a candid opinion of the merits and probable result of pending or contemplated litigation. The miscarriages to which justice is subject, by reason of surprises and disappointments in evidence and witnesses, and through mistakes of juries and errors of Courts, even though only occasional, admonish lawyers to beware of bold and confident assurances to clients, especially where the employment may depend upon such assurance. Whenever the controversy will admit of fair adjustment, the client should be advised to avoid or to end the litigation.

ABA Standards for Imposing Lawyer Discipline:

4.61. Disbarment is generally appropriate when a lawyer knowingly deceives a client with the intent to benefit the lawyer or another, and causes serious injury or potentially serious injury to a client.

4.62. Suspension is generally appropriate when a lawyer knowingly deceives a client, and causes injury or potential injury to the client.

American Academy of Matrimonial Lawyers: The "Bounds of Advocacy" drafted by the American Academy of Matrimonial Lawyers contains the following provision and commentary:

2.6 An attorney should keep the client informed of developments in the representation and promptly respond to letters and telephone calls.

Comment to Rule 2.6

The duty of keeping the client reasonably informed and promptly complying with reasonable requests for information, includes the attorney or a staff member responding to telephone calls, normally by the end of the next business day. The client should be informed at the outset, however, that communications with the attorney are chargeable. In addition, the attorney should routinely: send the client a copy of all pleadings and correspondence, except in unusual circumstances; provide the client with frequent statements of costs and fees (see Standards 2.1-2.5); provide notice before incurring any major costs; provide notice of any calendar changes, scheduled court appearances, and discovery proceedings; communicate all settlement offers, no matter how trivial or facetious; advise of major changes in the law affecting the proceedings; and provide periodic status reports on progress in the case and major changes in case strategy.

Frequent communication with the client on important matters (1) empowers the client, (2) satisfies the client's need for information about the progress of the case, (3) helps to build a positive attorney-client relationship, and (4) helps the client understand the amount and nature of the work the attorney is performing, thereby reducing concern that nothing is happening and that the attorney is not earning her fees. While the attorney should understand that a pending divorce is usually the single most important matter in the life of the client, the client should understand that a successful lawyer has many clients, all of whom believe their case to be the most important.

American Lawyer's Code of Conduct: Rules 4.5 and 5.2 provide:

4.5. A lawyer shall keep a client currently apprised of all significant developments in the matter entrusted to the lawyer by the client, unless the client has instructed the lawyer to do otherwise.

5.2. As soon as practicable after being retained, a lawyer shall make clear to a client, in writing, the material terms of the retainer agreement, including the scope of what the lawyer is undertaking to do for the client, the limits of that undertaking, and the fee and any other obligations the client is assuming.

Rule 1.5 Fees

(a) A lawyer's fee shall be reasonable. The factors to be considered in determining the reasonableness of a fee include the following:

(1) the time and labor required, the novelty and difficulty of the questions involved, and the skill requisite to perform the legal service properly;

(2) the likelihood, if apparent to the client, that the acceptance of the particular employment will preclude other employment by the lawyer;

(3) the fee customarily charged in the locality for similar legal services;

(4) the amount involved and the results obtained;

(5) the time limitations imposed by the client or by the circumstances;

(6) the nature and length of the professional relationship with the client;

(7) the experience, reputation, and ability of the lawyer or lawyers performing the services; and

(8) whether the fee is fixed or contingent.

(b) When the lawyer has not regularly represented the client, the basis or rate of the fee shall be communicated to the client, preferably in writing, before or within a reasonable time after commencing the representation.

(c) A fee may be contingent on the outcome of the matter for which the service is rendered, except in a matter in which a contingent fee is prohibited by paragraph (d) or other law. A contingent fee agreement shall be in writing and shall state the method by which the fee is to be determined, including the percentage or percentages that shall accrue to the lawyer in the event of settlement, trial or appeal, litigation and other expenses to be deducted from the recovery, and whether such expenses are to be deducted before or after the contingent fee is calculated. Upon conclusion of a contingent fee matter, the lawyer shall provide the client with a written statement stating the outcome of the matter and, if there is a recovery, showing the remittance to the client and the method of its determination.

(d) A lawyer shall not enter into an arrangement for, charge, or collect:

(1) any fee in a domestic relations matter, the payment or amount of which is contingent upon the securing of a divorce or upon the amount of alimony or support, or property settlement in lieu thereof; or

(2) a contingent fee for representing a defendant in a criminal case.

(e) A division of fee between lawyers who are not in the same firm may be made only if:

(1) the division is in proportion to the services performed by each lawyer or, by written agreement with the client, each lawyer assumes joint responsibility for the representation;

(2) the client is advised of and does not object to the participation of all the lawyers involved; and

(3) the total fee is reasonable.

COMMENT

Basis or Rate of Fee

[1] When the lawyer has regularly represented a client, they ordinarily will have evolved an understanding concerning the basis or rate of the fee. In a new client-lawyer relationship, however, an understanding as to the fee should be promptly established. It is not necessary to recite all the factors that underlie the basis of the fee, but only those that are directly involved in its computation. It is sufficient, for example, to state that the basic rate is an hourly charge or a fixed amount or an estimated amount, or to identify the factors that may be taken into account in finally fixing the fee. When developments occur during the representation that render an earlier estimate substantially inaccurate, a revised estimate should be provided to the client. A written statement concerning the fee reduces the possibility of misunderstanding. Furnishing the client with a simple memorandum or a copy of the lawyer's customary fee schedule is sufficient if the basis or rate of the fee is set forth.

Terms of Payment

[2] A lawyer may require advance payment of a fee, but is obliged to return any unearned portion. See Rule 1.16(d). A lawyer may accept property in payment for services, such as an ownership interest in an enterprise, providing this does not involve acquisition of a proprietary interest in the cause of action or subject matter of the litigation contrary to Rule 1.8(j). However, a fee paid in property instead of money may be subject to special scrutiny because it involves questions concerning both the value of the services and the lawyer's special knowledge of the value of the property.

[3] An agreement may not be made whose terms might induce the lawyer improperly to curtail services for the client or perform them in a way contrary to the client's interest. For example, a lawyer should not enter into an agreement whereby services are to be provided only up to a stated amount when it is foreseeable that more extensive services probably will be required, unless the situation is adequately explained to the client. Otherwise, the client might have to bargain for further assistance in the midst of a proceeding or transaction. However, it is proper to define the extent of services in light of the client's ability to pay. A law-

yer should not exploit a fee arrangement based primarily on hourly charges by using wasteful procedures. When there is doubt whether a contingent fee is consistent with the client's best interest, the lawyer should offer the client alternative bases for the fee and explain their implications. Applicable law may impose limitations on contingent fees, such as a ceiling on the percentage.

Division of Fee

[4] A division of fee is a single billing to a client covering the fee of two or more lawyers who are not in the same firm. A division of fee facilitates association of more than one lawyer in a matter in which neither alone could serve the client as well, and most often is used when the fee is contingent and the division is between a referring lawyer and a trial specialist. Paragraph (e) permits the lawyers to divide a fee on either the basis of the proportion of services they render or by agreement between the participating lawyers if all assume responsibility for the representation as a whole and the client is advised and does not object. It does not require disclosure to the client of the share that each lawyer is to receive. Joint responsibility for the representation entails the obligations stated in Rule 5.1 for purposes of the matter involved.

Disputes over Fees

[5] If a procedure has been established for resolution of fee disputes, such as an arbitration or mediation procedure established by the bar, the lawyer should conscientiously consider submitting to it. Law may prescribe a procedure for determining a lawyer's fee, for example, in representation of an executor or administrator, a class or a person entitled to a reasonable fee as part of the measure of damages. The lawyer entitled to such a fee and a lawyer representing another party concerned with the fee should comply with the prescribed procedure.

Model Code Comparison

DR 2-106(A) provided that a lawyer "shall not enter into an agreement for, charge, or collect an illegal or clearly excessive fee." DR 2-106(B) provided that a fee is "clearly excessive when, after a review of the facts, a lawyer of ordinary prudence would be left with a definite and firm conviction that the fee is in excess of a reasonable fee." The factors of a reasonable fee in Rule 1.5(a) are substantially identical to those listed in DR 2-106(B). EC 2-17 states that a lawyer "should not charge more than a reasonable fee. . . ."

There was no counterpart to Rule 1.5(b) in the Disciplinary Rules of the Model Code. EC 2-19 stated that it is "usually beneficial to reduce to writing the understanding of the parties regarding the fee, particularly when it is contingent."

There was no counterpart to paragraph (c) in the Disciplinary Rules of the Model Code. EC 2-20 provided that "[c]ontingent fee arrangements in civil cases have long been commonly accepted in the United States," but that "a lawyer generally should decline to accept employment on a contingent fee basis by one who is able to pay a reasonable fixed fee. . . ."

With regard to paragraph (d), DR 2-106(C) prohibited "a contingent fee in a criminal case." EC 2-20 provided that "contingent fee arrangements in domestic relation cases are rarely justified."

With regard to paragraph (e), DR 2-107(A) permitted division of fees only if: "(1) The client consents to employment of the other lawyer after a full disclosure that a division of fees will be made. (2) The division is in proportion to the services performed and responsibility assumed by each. (3) The total fee does not exceed clearly reasonable compensation. . . ." Paragraph (e) permits division with regard to the services rendered by each lawyer if they assume joint responsibility for the representation.

Cross-References in Rules

Rule 1.7, Comment 5: "[A] lawyer's need for income should not lead the lawyer to undertake matters that cannot be handled competently and at a reasonable fee. See **Rules** 1.1 and **1.5.**"

Rule 1.8, Comment 3 states that Rule 1.8(d) (prohibiting a lawyer from acquiring media rights to a client's story until the representation is over) "does not prohibit a lawyer from agreeing that the lawyer's fee shall consist of a share in ownership in the property, if the arrangement conforms to **Rule 1.5**" and Rule 1.8(j).

Rule 1.8, Comment 6: Rule 1.8(j) "states the traditional general rule that lawyers are prohibited from acquiring a proprietary interest in litigation. This general rule . . . is subject to . . . the exception for reasonable contingent fees set forth in **Rule 1.5.** . . ."

Legislative History

1979 Unofficial Pre-Circulation Draft (then Rule 1.4):

(b) A fee agreement shall . . .

(2) State with reasonable definiteness, expressly or by implication, the nature and extent of the services to be provided; and . . .

(c) A fee agreement shall be expressed or confirmed in writing before the lawyer has rendered substantial services in the matter, except:

(1) Where an agreement as to the fee is implied by the fact that the lawyer's services are of the same general kind as previously rendered to and paid for by the client;

(2) For services rendered in an emergency where a written agreement or confirmation is impracticable. . . .

1980 Discussion Draft (then Rule 1.6):

(b) The basis or rate of a lawyer's fee shall be put in writing before the lawyer has rendered substantial services in the matter, except when:

(1) An agreement as to the fee is implied by the fact that the lawyer's services are of the same general kind as previously rendered to and paid for by the client; or

(2) The services are rendered in an emergency where a writing is impracticable.

(c) The form of a fee and the terms of a fee agreement shall involve no inducement for the lawyer to perform the services in a manner inconsistent with the best interests of the client. . . .

(e) A division of fee between lawyers who are not in the same firm may be made only if:

(1) The division is in proportion to the services performed by each lawyer, or both lawyers expressly assume responsibility as if they were partners;

(2) The terms of the division are disclosed to the client. . . .

1981 Draft of Rule 1.5(b) continued to require that the "basis or rate of a lawyer's fee shall be communicated to the client in writing before the lawyer renders substantial services in a matter. . . ."

1982 Draft was substantially the same as adopted.

Selected State Variations

California: See Rule 4-200 (Fees for Legal Services), B & P Code §§6147-6149 (governing contingency fee contracts and other fee arrangements), and B & P Code §§6200-6206 (establishing system and procedures for arbitrating fee disputes).

Connecticut deletes Rule 1.5(e)(1).

District of Columbia: Rule 1.5(b) requires all fee agreements to be communicated in writing if the lawyer has not regularly represented the client. Comment 7 to Rule 1.5 states: "Contingent fees in domestic relations cases, while rarely justified, are not prohibited by Rule 1.5." Comments 10, 11, and 12 to Rule 1.5(e) provide:

[10] Paragraph (e) permits the lawyers to divide a fee on either the basis of the proportion of services they render or by agreement between the participating lawyers if all assume responsibility for the representation as a whole. . . . Permitting a division on the basis of joint responsibility . . . is intended to encourage lawyers to affiliate other counsel, who are better equipped by reason of experience or specialized background to serve the client's needs, rather than to retain sole responsibility for the representation in order to avoid losing the right to a fee.

[11] The concept of joint responsibility is not, however, merely a technicality or incantation. The lawyer who refers the client to another lawyer, or affiliates another lawyer in the representation, remains fully responsible to the client, and is accountable to the client for deficiencies in the discharge of the representation by the lawyer who has been brought into the representation. If a lawyer wishes to avoid such responsibility for the potential deficiencies of another lawyer, the matter must be referred to the other lawyer without retaining a right to participate in fees beyond those fees justified by services actually rendered.

[12] The concept of joint responsibility does not require the referring lawyer to perform any minimum portion of the total legal services rendered. The referring lawyer may agree that the lawyer to whom the referral is made will perform substantially all of the services to be rendered in connection with the representation, without review by the referring lawyer. Thus, the referring lawyer is not required to review pleadings or other documents, attend hearings or depositions, or otherwise participate in a significant and continuing manner. The referring lawyer does not, however, escape the implications of joint responsibility, see Comment [11], by avoiding direct participation.

Florida has adopted an elaborate rule with these main features:

Rule 1.5(B) provides that a fee "is clearly excessive when, after a review of the facts, a lawyer of ordinary prudence would be left with a definite and firm conviction that the fee is in excess of a reasonable fee."

Rule 1.5(D)(4)(a)(1) says that a contingent fee contract must contain the following provision (among others):

> This contract may be cancelled by written notification to the attorney at any time within three (3) business days of the date the contract was signed, and if cancelled the client shall not be obligated to pay any fees to the attorney(s) for the work performed during that time.

Rule 1.5(D)(4)(b)(1) provides:

> Without prior court approval as specified below any contingent fee which exceeds the following standards shall be presumed, unless rebutted, to be clearly excessive:
>   (a) 25% of any recovery regardless of amount, prior to filing of suit;
>   (b) $33\frac{1}{3}$% of any recovery up to $1 million through the time of filing of an answer or the demand for appointment of arbitrators;
>   (c) 40% of any recovery up to $1 million through the trial of the case;
>   (d) 30% of any recovery between $1 and $2 million;
>   (e) 20% of any recovery in excess of $2 million;
>   (f) If a defendant admits liability at the time of filing an answer and requests a trial only on damages:
>   (i) $33\frac{1}{3}$% of any recovery up to $1 million from that defendant through trial;
>   (ii) 20% of any recovery from that defendant between $1 and $2 million;
>   (iii) 15% of any recovery from that defendant in excess of $2 million;
>   (g) 5% of any recovery if an appeal is necessary. Such 5% may be in addition to the fee limitations stated above.

Rule 1.5(D)(4)(c) provides that before a lawyer enters into a contingent fee contract, the lawyer "shall provide the client with a statement of the client's rights. . . ." The Statement of Client's Rights contains ten paragraphs and is set forth in full at the end of Florida's Rule 1.5.

With respect to Model Rule 1.5(e), Florida's statement of Client's Rights says:

> 5. If your lawyer intends to refer your case to another lawyer or counsel with other lawyers, your lawyer should tell you about that at the beginning. If your lawyer takes the case and later decides to refer it to another lawyer or to associate with other lawyers, you should sign a new contract which includes the new lawyers. You, the client, also have the right to consult with each lawyer working on your case and each lawyer is legally responsible to represent your interests and is legally responsible for the acts of the other lawyers involved in the case.

In addition, Florida's new advertising rules (adopted in December 1990) require that advertisements describing legal fees of any kind must disclose whether the client will be liable for costs or expenses in the absence of recovery, and whether a contingent fee will be computed before or after expenses are deducted.

To prevent lawyers from advertising for cases that they have no intention of handling but intend only to refer to another lawyer in exchange for a share of the fee, Florida's new advertising rules state that an advertisement "shall be presumed to be misleading if the lawyer reasonably believes that a lawyer or law firm not associated with the originally retained lawyer or law firm will be associated or act as primary counsel in representing the client. In determining whether the statement is misleading in this respect, the history of prior conduct by the lawyer in similar matters may be considered."

Florida also amended its solicitation rule (Rule 4-7.4) to prohibit "a fee for professional employment obtained in violation of" the solicitation rule, and Florida simultaneously amended Model Rule 1.5(a) to prohibit a fee "generated by employment that was obtained through advertising or solicitation not in compliance" with Florida's advertising and solicitation rules.

Finally, in December 1990 the Florida Supreme Court gave itself the power to order any lawyer found guilty of violating the fee rules "to forfeit the fee or any part thereof," either by returning the excessive part of any fee to the client or by forfeiting all or part of an otherwise improper fee to the Florida Bar Clients' Security Fund. See Florida Rule 3-5.1(i).

Georgia's version of Rule 1.5 continues to permit fee-splitting only under the circumstances identified in the Code. DR 2-107. Georgia's Rules do not forbid contingent fees in domestic relations matters.

Illinois provides that "the prohibition set forth in Rule 1.5(d)(1) shall not extend to representation in matters subsequent to final judgments in such cases."

Illinois adds a new subparagraph providing:

> (e) Notwithstanding Rule 1.5(c), a contingent fee agreement regarding the collection of commercial accounts or of insurance company subrogation claims may be made in accordance with the customs and practice in the locality for such legal services.

Illinois also adds the following new subparagraphs:

> (g) A division of fees [between lawyers not in the same firm] shall be made in proportion to the services performed and responsibility assumed by each lawyer, except where the primary service performed by one lawyer is the referral of the client to another lawyer and
> > (1) the receiving lawyer discloses that the referring lawyer has received or will receive economic benefit from the referral and the extent and basis of such economic benefit; and
> > (2) the referring lawyer agrees to assume the same legal responsibility for the performance of the services in question as would a partner of the receiving lawyer.
> (h) The total fee of the lawyers shall be reasonable.
> (i) For purposes of Rule 1.5 "economic benefit" shall include:
> > (1) the amount of participation in the fee received with regard to the particular matter;
> > (2) any other form of remuneration passing to the referring lawyer from the receiving lawyer, whether or not with regard to the particular matter; and
> > (3) an established practice of referrals to and from or from and to the receiving lawyer and the referring lawyer.
> (j) Notwithstanding Rule 1.5(f), a payment may be made to a lawyer formerly in the firm, pursuant to a separation or retirement agreement.

Kansas: Rule 1.5(c) adds that a court's determination that a fee is not reasonable "shall not be presumptive evidence of a violation that requires discipline of the attorney." Rule 1.5(e) adds:

> Upon application by the client, all fee contracts shall be subject to review and approval by the appropriate court having jurisdiction of the matter and the court shall have the authority to determine whether the contract is reasonable. If the court finds the contract is not reasonable, it shall set and allow a reasonable fee.

Maryland adds that a fee cannot be contingent upon a client's "securing custody of a child."

Michigan retains the Code articulation in lieu of Rule 1.5(a). In Rule 1.5(d), Michigan forbids contingent fees in "a domestic relations matter" without qualification.

Michigan and *Pennsylvania* do not require a writing in Rule 1.5(e), and do not distinguish fee-sharing arrangements based on services provided from those based on assumption of responsibility.

Minnesota adds to Rule 1.5(e)(2) that the client must be "advised of the share that each lawyer is to receive."

New Jersey requires a fee agreement to be in writing if the lawyer has not regularly represented the client. In addition, New Jersey has adopted various court rules that tightly control contingent fees, especially in tort cases. Supreme Court Rule 1:21-7, for example, provides as follows:

> (c) In any matter where a client's claim for damages is based upon the alleged tortious conduct of another, including products liability claims, and the client is not a subrogee, an attorney shall not contract for, charge, or collect a contingent fee in excess of the following limits:
>
> (1) 33 1/3% on the first $250,000 recovered;
>
> (2) 25% on the next $250,000 recovered;
>
> (3) 20% on the next $500,000 recovered; and
>
> (4) on all amounts recovered in excess of the above by application for reasonable fee in accordance with the provisions of paragraph (f) hereof; and
>
> (5) where the amount recovered is for the benefit of a client who was an infant or incompetent when the contingent fee arrangement was made, the foregoing limits shall apply, except that the fee on any amount recovered by settlement without trial shall not exceed 25%.
>
> . . . (f) If at the conclusion of a matter an attorney considers the fee permitted by paragraph (c) to be inadequate, an application on written notice to the client may be made to the Assignment Judge for the hearing and determining of a reasonable fee in light of all the circumstances. A copy of any such application and of all papers filed in support of or in opposition thereto, together with a copy of the court order fixing the fee shall be filed with the Administrative Office of the Courts. This rule shall not preclude the exercise of a client's existing right to a court review of the reasonableness of an attorney's fee.
>
> . . . (h) Calculation of Fee in Structured Settlements. . . . For purposes of paragraph (c), the basis for calculation of a contingent fee shall be the value of the structured settlement as herein defined. Value shall consist of any cash payment made upon consummation of the settlement plus the actual cost . . . of the deferred payment aspects thereof. . . . [T]he party making the settlement shall disclose to the party receiving the settlement its actual cost and, if it does not purchase the deferred payment aspect of the settlement, the factors and assumptions used by it in assigning actual cost.

New Jersey also controls fees in matrimonial cases. Supreme Court Rule 1:21-7A provides: "All agreements for legal services by an attorney or attorneys in connection with family actions shall be in writing signed by the attorney and client."

New York: Same or substantially the same as the ABA Model Code — see Model Code Comparison above — except that New York permits lawyers to divide fees if the division is "in proportion to the services performed by each lawyer or, by a writing given to the client, each lawyer assumes joint responsibility for the representation." See EC 2-22 and DR 2-106(C), DR 2-106(D), and DR 2-107(A)(2) of the New York Code.

North Carolina: Rule 2.6 combines the language of DR 2-106 with the language of Rule 1.5(e).

Ohio's version of Rule 1.5(e) adopts its language but also provides for mediation or arbitration in the event of a dispute over the fees between the participating lawyers. DR 2-107(B).

Pennsylvania Rule 1.5(b) requires a written fee agreement if a lawyer has not regularly represented a client.

Texas Rule 1.04(a) forbids "illegal" or "unconscionable" fees and lists the same considerations as in Rule 1.5. The Texas Rules do not forbid contingent fees in family law matters but the Comment says they are "rarely justified." Texas Rule 1.04(f) provides that a division "or agreement for division" of a fee between lawyers who are not in the same firm shall not be made unless the division is "(i) in proportion to the professional services performed by each lawyer; (ii) made with a forwarding lawyer; or (iii) made, by written agreement with the client, with a lawyer who assumes joint responsibility for the representation. . . ."

Virginia: DR 2-105 requires that a lawyer's fees must be reasonable "and adequately explained to the client," and that the basis or rate of the fee "shall be furnished on request of the lawyer's client." DR 2-105(D) allows a division of fees between lawyers not in the same firm only if the client "consents to the employment of additional counsel," the attorneys "expressly" assume responsibility to the client, and the "terms of the division are disclosed to the client. . . ."

Washington adds that a fee may not be contingent on securing an "annulment."

Wyoming Rule 1.5(e)(1) provides that a division of fees between lawyers must be in proportion to the services performed by each lawyer *"and"* by written agreement with the client, each lawyer assumes joint responsibility. Wyoming also prohibits a lawyer from receiving a fee solely for making a referral to another lawyer.

Related Materials

ABA Canons: Canons 12, 13, 14, and 42 provided:

12. Fixing the Amount of the Fee

In fixing fees, lawyers should avoid charges which overestimate their advice and services, as well as those which undervalue them. A client's ability to pay cannot justify a charge in excess of the value of the service, though his poverty may require a less charge, or even none at all. The reasonable requests of brother lawyers, and of their widows and orphans without ample means, should receive special and kindly consideration.

In determining the amount of the fee, it is proper to consider: (1) the time and labor required, the novelty and difficulty of the questions involved and the skill requisite properly to conduct the cause; (2) whether the acceptance of employment in the particular case will preclude the lawyer's appearance for others in cases likely to arise out of the transaction, and in which there is a reasonable expectation that otherwise he would be employed, or will involve the loss of other employment while employed in the particular case or antagonisms with other clients; (3) the customary charges of the Bar for similar services; (4) the amount involved in the controversy and the benefits resulting to the client from the services; (5) the contingency or the certainty of the compensation; and (6) the character of the employment, whether casual or for an established and constant client. No one of these considerations in itself is controlling. They are mere guides in ascertaining the real value of the service.

In determining the customary charges of the Bar for similar services, it is proper for a lawyer to consider a schedule of minimum fees adopted by a Bar Association, but no lawyer should permit himself to be controlled thereby or to follow it as his sole guide in determining the amount of his fee.

In fixing fees it should never be forgotten that the profession is a branch of the administration of justice and not a mere money-getting trade.

13. Contingent Fees

A contract for a contingent fee, where sanctioned by law, should be reasonable under all the circumstances of the case, including the risk and uncertainty of the compensation, but should always be subject to the supervision of a court, as to its reasonableness.

14. Suing a Client for a Fee

Controversies with clients concerning compensation are to be avoided by the lawyer so far as shall be compatible with his self-respect and with his right to receive reasonable recompense for his services; and lawsuits with clients should be resorted to only to prevent injustice, imposition or fraud.

42. Expenses of Litigation

A lawyer may not properly agree with a client that the lawyer shall pay or bear the expenses of litigation; he may in good faith advance expenses as a matter of convenience, but subject to reimbursement.

American Academy of Matrimonial Lawyers: The "Bounds of Advocacy" drafted by the American Academy of Matrimonial Lawyers contains the following provisions and commentary:

Fees

Many divorce clients have never before hired an attorney and are vulnerable because of fear and insecurity. Matrimonial lawyers and their clients may not have the long-standing relationship out of which business lawyers and their clients often evolve an understanding about fees.

It is not unusual for one party to a divorce to lack sufficient funds to pay an attorney. This lack of resources, various strictures against contingent fee contracts, the unwillingness of some courts to redress the economic imbalance between the parties with fee awards, and the tendency of overwrought clients to misunderstand the fee agreement or to blame their attorneys for undesirable results can make collection of fees extremely difficult.

These factors help to explain why the records of fee dispute committees indicate that the number of disputes arising from family law cases is several times greater than those from any other category. Thus, financial arrangements with clients should be clearly explained, agreed upon, and documented.

2.1 Fee agreements should be reduced to writing.

Comment to Rule 2.1

At the outset the matrimonial lawyer must tell the client the basis on which fees will be charged and when and how the attorney expects to be paid. Fee agreements should be presented to the client in a manner that allows the client an opportunity to reflect upon the terms, consult another attorney before signing, and obtain answers to any questions in order to fully understand the agreement prior to entering into it.

2.2 An attorney should provide periodic statements of accrued fees and costs.

Comment to Rule 2.2

This information can be part of the necessary communications concerning the case addressed in **Standard 2.6 and Comment.** The statement should be sufficiently detailed to apprise the client of the time and charges incurred. In addition, the matrimonial lawyer should comply with fee regulations in his jurisdiction which may be more detailed or restrictive in requiring information about fees and costs.

2.3 All transactions in which an attorney obtains security for fees should be properly documented.

Comment to Rule 2.3

All security agreements should be arms-length transactions. When taking mortgages on real property from a client, the client should be independently represented. If an attorney takes personal property as security, it must be appraised, photographed and identified by a qualified appraiser in order to establish concretely its precise identity and value. The attorney must then secure it in a safe place (usually a safe deposit box) where there is no danger that it can be removed, substituted, or lost.

American Lawyer's Code of Conduct: Rule 5.4, regarding division of fees among lawyers, provides:

Lawyers who are not openly associated in the same firm shall not share a fee unless: (a) the division reflects the proportion of work performed by each attorney and the normal billing rate of each; or (b) the client has been informed pursuant to Rule 5.2 of the fact of fee-sharing and the effect on the total fee, and the client consents.

Comment to Rule 5.4

Rule 5.4, governing the division of fees by lawyers not openly associated in the same firm, is less restrictive than any other provision or proposal known to the Commission. . . .

It must be emphasized that the purpose of allowing fee splitting is to encourage lawyers to refer clients to competent specialists. The proposed Rules of Professional Conduct would continue the existing practice of penalizing such referrals outside one's own firm; even the Massachusetts and California rules prohibit a division that increases the amount of the fee (but only when the two lawyers are not members of the same firm). Such rules exalt the form of association over the substance of client consent and providing better service for the client, particularly in the context of recent increases in the number and size of multi-office firms. It prohibits some lawyers from doing something that other lawyers may do with impunity, and that many lawyers in fact do. It is more realistic to regulate a common practice than to prohibit it on a discriminatory basis, especially when the practice may actually improve the quality of service made available to clients.

See also Rule 5.6(d) (permitting contingency fee agreements). The ALCC Comment to Rule 5.6(d) provides:

Rule 5.6(d) permits fees to be contingent in whole or in part on the outcome of any case. Such fees have long been recognized as proper when the client is a plaintiff in civil litigation. The principal reason is that, as a practical matter, most people would not be in a position to seek vindication of their legal rights, however meritorious, if litigating those rights could result in substantial financial loss as well as loss in time and the other burdens of litigation. Since there is little if any incentive to lawyers to take frivolous cases on contingent fees, such cases are screened out through a contingent fee system more effectively than they might be in a system based exclusively upon retainers. Moreover, any concern that contingent fees will induce unethical conduct on the part of lawyers seems fanciful. A lawyer unscrupulous enough to fabricate a case to earn a contingent fee will undoubtedly not hesitate to do so to earn a retainer or to establish a reputation for winning cases. . . .

There is even more reason for allowing contingent fees for the accused in criminal cases, because the accused who goes to prison, thereby losing any opportunity to earn a living, is far less able to pay a fee than is the accused who is acquitted. Also, lawyers would accept such arrangements only when the defense appeared sufficiently strong to warrant it, and the unscrupulous lawyer would be no more likely to fabricate a defense to earn a contingent fee than to earn a retainer. . . .

Restatement of the Law Governing Lawyers: The American Law Institute has tentatively approved the following provisions:

§29A. Client-Lawyer Contracts

(1) A contract between a lawyer and client concerning the basis or rate of the lawyer's compensation or other matters involving the client-lawyer relationship may be enforced by either party if the contract meets other applicable requirements, except that:

(a) If the contract is made after the lawyer has been retained and when obtaining a different lawyer would significantly inconvenience the client but before the lawyer has finished providing services, the client may avoid it unless the lawyer shows that the contract and the circumstances of its formation were fair and reasonable to the client; and

(b) If the contract is made after the lawyer has finished providing services, the client may avoid it if the client was not informed of facts needed to evaluate the appropriateness of the lawyer's compensation or other benefits conferred on the lawyer by the contract.

(2) A tribunal should construe a contract between client and lawyer as a reasonable person in the circumstances of the client would have construed it.

§46. Lawful and Reasonable Fees

A lawyer may not charge a fee that is greater than is reasonable in the circumstances or that is unlawful.

§47. Contingent-Fee Arrangements

A lawyer may agree with a client for a fee the size or payment of which is contingent on success in a matter, unless the agreement violates another provision of this Restatement or the size or payment of the fee is:

(1) Contingent on success in prosecuting or defending a criminal proceeding; or

(2) Contingent on securing a divorce or a decree awarding or modifying custody of a child, except where that arrangement is reasonably necessary for the client to secure adequate representation.

§49. Forfeiture of a Lawyer's Fee

A lawyer engaging in clear serious violation of duty to a client may forfeit some or all of the lawyer's compensation for the matter. In determining whether and to what extent forfeiture is appropriate, relevant considerations include the extent of the violation, its wilfulness, any threatened or actual harm to the client, and the adequacy of other remedies.

§50. *Client-Lawyer Fee Contracts*

(1) Before or within a reasonable time after beginning to represent a client in a matter, a lawyer must communicate to the client, in writing when applicable rules so provide, the basis or rate of the fee, unless the communication is unnecessary for the client because the lawyer has previously represented that client on the same basis or rate. . . .

(3) Unless the contract construed in the circumstances indicates otherwise:

(a) The lawyer cannot charge an amount in addition to the stated basis or rate for the lawyer's office and overhead expenses;

(b) Payments that the law requires an opposing party or that party's lawyer to pay as attorney fee awards or sanctions are credited to the client, not the client's lawyer, absent a contrary statute or court order;

(c) When the lawyer requests and receives a fee payment that is not for services already rendered, that payment is to be credited against whatever fee the lawyer may be entitled to collect; and

(d) When the lawyer has contracted for a percentage contingent fee, the lawyer is entitled to receive the specified percentage of the client's damages recovery only when the client receives payment.

§51. *A Lawyer's Fee When There Is No Contract*

Unless a lawyer and client have made a valid agreement providing for another measure of compensation, a client owes a lawyer who has performed legal services for the client the fair value of the lawyer's services.

§53. *Abusive Fee Collection Methods*

In seeking claimed compensation from a client or former client, a lawyer may not employ collection methods forbidden by law, use confidential information (as defined in Chapter Five) in excess of what §117 permits, or harass the client.

(Restatement §117 is reprinted in the Related Materials following Model Rule 1.6.)

§54. *Remedies and Burden of Persuasion*

(1) A fee dispute between a lawyer and a client may be adjudicated in any appropriate proceeding, including a suit by the lawyer to recover an unpaid fee, a suit for a refund by a client, an arbitration to which both parties consent unless applicable law renders the lawyer's consent unnecessary, or in the court's discretion a proceeding ancillary to a pending suit in which the lawyer performed the services in question.

(2) In any such proceeding the lawyer has the burden of persuading the trier of fact, when relevant, of the existence and terms of any fee agreement, the making of any disclosures to the client required to render an agreement enforceable, and the extent and value of the lawyer's services.

Rule 1.6   Confidentiality of Information

(a) A lawyer shall not reveal information relating to representation of a client unless the client consents after consultation, except for disclosures that are

impliedly authorized in order to carry out the representation, and except as stated in paragraph (b).

(b) A lawyer may reveal such information to the extent the lawyer reasonably believes necessary:

(1) to prevent the client from committing a criminal act that the lawyer believes is likely to result in imminent death or substantial bodily harm; or

(2) to establish a claim or defense on behalf of the lawyer in a controversy between the lawyer and the client, to establish a defense to a criminal charge or civil claim against the lawyer based upon conduct in which the client was involved, or to respond to allegations in any proceeding concerning the lawyer's representation of the client.

COMMENT

[1] The lawyer is part of a judicial system charged with upholding the law. One of the lawyer's functions is to advise clients so that they avoid any violation of the law in the proper exercise of their rights.

[2] The observance of the ethical obligation of a lawyer to hold inviolate confidential information of the client not only facilitates the full development of facts essential to proper representation of the client but also encourages people to seek early legal assistance.

[3] Almost without exception, clients come to lawyers in order to determine what their rights are and what is, in the maze of laws and regulations, deemed to be legal and correct. The common law recognizes that the client's confidences must be protected from disclosure. Based upon experience, lawyers know that almost all clients follow the advice given, and the law is upheld.

[4] A fundamental principle in the client-lawyer relationship is that the lawyer maintain confidentiality of information relating to the representation. The client is thereby encouraged to communicate fully and frankly with the lawyer even as to embarrassing or legally damaging subject matter.

[5] The principle of confidentiality is given effect in two related bodies of law, the attorney-client privilege (which includes the work product doctrine) in the law of evidence and the rule of confidentiality established in professional ethics. The attorney-client privilege applies in judicial and other proceedings in which a lawyer may be called as a witness or otherwise required to produce evidence concerning a client. The rule of client-lawyer confidentiality applies in situations other than those where evidence is sought from the lawyer through compulsion of law. The confidentiality rule applies not merely to matters communicated in confidence by the client but also to all information relating to the representation, whatever its source. A lawyer may not disclose such information except as authorized or required by the Rules of Professional Conduct or other law. See also Scope.

[handwritten margin note: embraces > client ⊏ [more than]]

[handwritten: communications]

[6] The requirement of maintaining confidentiality of information relating to representation applies to government lawyers who may disagree with the policy goals that their representation is designed to advance.

Authorized Disclosure

[7] A lawyer is impliedly authorized to make disclosures about a client when appropriate in carrying out the representation, except to the extent that the client's instructions or special circumstances limit that authority. In litigation, for example, a lawyer may disclose information by admitting a fact that cannot properly be disputed, or in negotiation by making a disclosure that facilitates a satisfactory conclusion.

[8] Lawyers in a firm may, in the course of the firm's practice, disclose to each other information relating to a client of the firm, unless the client has instructed that particular information be confined to specified lawyers.

Disclosure Adverse to Client

[9] The confidentiality rule is subject to limited exceptions. In becoming privy to information about a client, a lawyer may foresee that the client intends serious harm to another person. However, to the extent a lawyer is required or permitted to disclose a client's purposes, the client will be inhibited from revealing facts which would enable the lawyer to counsel against a wrongful course of action. The public is better protected if full and open communication by the client is encouraged than if it is inhibited.

[10] Several situations must be distinguished. First, the lawyer may not counsel or assist a client in conduct that is criminal or fraudulent. See Rule 1.2(d). Similarly, a lawyer has a duty under Rule 3.3(a)(4) not to use false evidence. This duty is essentially a special instance of the duty prescribed in Rule 1.2(d) to avoid assisting a client in criminal or fraudulent conduct.

[11] Second, the lawyer may have been innocently involved in past conduct by the client that was criminal or fraudulent. In such a situation the lawyer has not violated Rule 1.2(d), because to "counsel or assist" criminal or fraudulent conduct requires knowing that the conduct is of that character.

[12] Third, the lawyer may learn that a client intends prospective conduct that is criminal and likely to result in imminent death or substantial bodily harm. As stated in paragraph (b)(1), the lawyer has professional discretion to reveal information in order to prevent such consequences. The lawyer may make a disclosure in order to prevent homicide or serious bodily injury which the lawyer reasonably believes is intended by a client. It is very difficult for a lawyer to "know" when such a heinous purpose will actually be carried out, for the client may have a change of mind.

[13] The lawyer's exercise of discretion requires consideration of such factors as the nature of the lawyer's relationship with the client and with those who might be injured by the client, the lawyer's own involvement in the transaction and factors that may extenuate the conduct in question. Where practical, the lawyer should seek to persuade the client to take suitable action. In any case, a disclosure adverse to the client's interest should be no greater than the lawyer reasonably believes necessary to the purpose. A lawyer's decision not to take preventive action permitted by paragraph (b)(1) does not violate this Rule.

Withdrawal

> **Editors' Note.** Paragraphs 14 and 15 of the Comment to Rule 1.6 — which permit a "noisy withdrawal" — were added to the Kutak Commission's draft of the Comment after the ABA House of Delegates rejected the Kutak Commission's 1982 proposal to allow disclosure of information necessary to "rectify the consequences of a client's criminal or fraudulent act in the furtherance of which the lawyer's services had been used."

[14] If the lawyer's services will be used by the client in materially furthering a course of criminal or fraudulent conduct, the lawyer must withdraw, as stated in Rule 1.16(a)(1).

[15] After withdrawal the lawyer is required to refrain from making disclosure of the clients' confidences, except as otherwise provided in Rule 1.6. Neither this rule nor Rule 1.8(b) nor Rule 1.16(d) prevents the lawyer from giving notice of the fact of withdrawal, and the lawyer may also withdraw or disaffirm any opinion, document, affirmation, or the like.

[16] Where the client is an organization, the lawyer may be in doubt whether contemplated conduct will actually be carried out by the organization. Where necessary to guide conduct in connection with this Rule, the lawyer may make inquiry within the organization as indicated in Rule 1.13(b).

Dispute Concerning Lawyer's Conduct

[17] Where a legal claim or disciplinary charge alleges complicity of the lawyer in a client's conduct or other misconduct of the lawyer involving representation of the client, the lawyer may respond to the extent the lawyer reasonably believes necessary to establish a defense. The same is true with respect to a claim involving the conduct or representation of a former client. The lawyer's right to respond arises when an assertion of such complicity has

been made. Paragraph (b)(2) does not require the lawyer to await the commencement of an action or proceeding that charges such complicity, so that the defense may be established by responding directly to a third party who has made such an assertion. The right to defend, of course, applies where a proceeding has been commenced. Where practicable and not prejudicial to the lawyer's ability to establish the defense, the lawyer should advise the client of the third party's assertion and request that the client respond appropriately. In any event, disclosure should be no greater than the lawyer reasonably believes is necessary to vindicate innocence, the disclosure should be made in a manner which limits access to the information to the tribunal or other persons having a need to know it, and appropriate protective orders or other arrangements should be sought by the lawyer to the fullest extent practicable.

[18] If the lawyer is charged with wrongdoing in which the client's conduct is implicated, the rule of confidentiality should not prevent the lawyer from defending against the charge. Such a charge can arise in a civil, criminal or professional disciplinary proceeding, and can be based on a wrong allegedly committed by the lawyer against the client, or on a wrong alleged by a third person; for example, a person claiming to have been defrauded by the lawyer and client acting together. A lawyer entitled to a fee is permitted by paragraph (b)(2) to prove the services rendered in an action to collect it. This aspect of the rule expresses the principle that the beneficiary of a fiduciary relationship may not exploit it to the detriment of the fiduciary. As stated above, the lawyer must make every effort practicable to avoid unnecessary disclosure of information relating to a representation, to limit disclosure to those having the need to know it, and to obtain protective orders or make other arrangements minimizing the risk of disclosure.

Disclosures Otherwise Required or Authorized

[19] The attorney-client privilege is differently defined in various jurisdictions. If a lawyer is called as a witness to give testimony concerning a client, absent waiver by the client, Rule 1.6(a) requires the lawyer to invoke the privilege when it is applicable. The lawyer must comply with the final orders of a court or other tribunal of competent jurisdiction requiring the lawyer to give information about the client.

[20] The Rules of Professional Conduct in various circumstances permit or require a lawyer to disclose information relating to the representation. See Rules 2.2, 2.3, 3.3 and 4.1. In addition to these provisions, a lawyer may be obligated or permitted by other provisions of law to give information about a client. Whether another provision of law supersedes Rule 1.6 is a matter of interpretation beyond the scope of these Rules, but a presumption should exist against such a supersession.

Former Client

[21] The duty of confidentiality continues after the client-lawyer relationship has terminated.

Model Code Comparison

Rule 1.6 eliminates the two-pronged duty under the Model Code in favor of a single standard protecting all information about a client "relating to the representation." Under DR 4-101, the requirement applied only to information governed by the attorney-client privilege and to information "gained in" the professional relationship that "the client has requested be held inviolate or the disclosure of which would be embarrassing or would be likely to be detrimental to the client." EC 4-4 added that the duty differed from the evidentiary privilege in that it existed "without regard to the nature or source of the information or the fact that others share the knowledge." Rule 1.6 imposes confidentiality on information relating to the representation even if it is acquired before or after the relationship existed. It does not require the client to indicate information that is to be confidential, or permit the lawyer to speculate whether particular information might be embarrassing or detrimental.

Paragraph (a) permits a lawyer to disclose information where impliedly authorized to do so in order to carry out the representation. Under DR 4-101(B) and (C), a lawyer could not reveal "confidences" unless the client first consented after disclosure.

Paragraph (b) redefines the exceptions to the requirement of confidentiality. Regarding paragraph (b)(1), DR 4-101(C)(3) provided that a lawyer "may reveal . . . [t]he intention of his client to commit a crime and the information necessary to prevent the crime." This option existed regardless of the seriousness of the proposed crime.

With regard to paragraph (b)(2), DR 4-101(C)(4) provided that a lawyer may reveal "[c]onfidences or secrets necessary to establish or collect his fee or to defend himself or his employers or associates against an accusation of wrongful conduct." Paragraph (b)(2) enlarges the exception to include disclosure of information relating to claims by the lawyer other than for the lawyer's fee — for example, recovery of property from the client.

Cross-References in Rules

Scope ¶3: "Most of the duties flowing from the client-lawyer relationship attach only after the client has requested the lawyer to render legal services and the lawyer has agreed to do so. But there are some duties, such as that of confidentiality under **Rule 1.6**, that may attach when the lawyer agrees to consider whether a client-lawyer relationship shall be established."

Scope ¶7: "The fact that in exceptional situations the lawyer under the Rules has a limited discretion to disclose a client confidence does not vitiate the proposition that, as a general matter, the client has a reasonable expectation that information relating to the client will not be voluntarily disclosed and that disclosure of such information may be judicially compelled only in accordance with recognized exceptions to the attorney-client and work product privileges."

Scope ¶8: "The lawyer's exercise of discretion not to disclose information under **Rule 1.6** should not be subject to reexamination."

Rule 1.2, Comment 7: "The lawyer is not permitted to reveal the client's wrongdoing, except where permitted by **Rule 1.6**."

Rule 1.8, Comment 4: When a third party pays fees, the arrangement must "conform to the requirements of **Rule 1.6** concerning confidentiality. . . ."

Rule 1.9(b): "A lawyer shall not knowingly represent a person in the same or a substantially related matter in which a firm with which the lawyer formerly was associated had previously represented a client whose interests are materially adverse to that person and about whom the lawyer had acquired information protected by **Rules 1.6** and 1.9(c) that is material to the matter. . . ."

Rule 1.9(c): "A lawyer who has formerly represented a client in a matter or whose present or former firm has formerly represented a client . . . shall not thereafter: . . . (1) use information . . . to the disadvantage of the former client except as **Rule 1.6** or Rule 3.3 would permit or require . . . ; or (2) reveal information relating to the representation except as **Rule 1.6** or Rule 3.3 would permit or require with respect to a client."

Rule 1.9, Comment 9: "Paragraph (b) operates to disqualify the lawyer only when the lawyer involved has actual knowledge of information protected by **Rules 1.6** and 1.9(c)."

Rule 1.9, Comment 10: "Independent of the question of disqualification of a firm, a lawyer changing a professional association has a continuing duty to preserve confidentiality of information about a client formerly represented. See **Rules 1.6** and 1.9."

Rule 1.10(b)(2) restricts representation when "any lawyer remaining in the firm has information protected by **Rules 1.6** and 1.9(c) that is material to the matter."

Rule 1.10, Comment 4: When a lawyer moves from government to a private practice, or vice versa, the lawyer "is bound by the Rules generally, including **Rule 1.6**. . . ."

Rule 1.10, Comment 5: "The government is entitled to protection of its client confidences, and therefore to the protections provided in **Rule 1.6**. . . ."

Rule 1.10, Comment 7: When a lawyer who represents or formerly represented a client leaves a firm, the firm may not represent a person with interests adverse to that client where the matter is the same or substantially related and "any other lawyer currently in the firm has material information protected by **Rules 1.6** and 1.9(c)."

Rule 1.13, Comment 3: "When one of the constituents of an organizational client communicates with the organization's lawyer in that person's organizational capacity, the communication is protected by **Rule 1.6**. Thus, by way of example, if an organizational client requests its lawyer to investigate allegations of wrongdoing, interviews made in the course of that investigation between the lawyer and the client's employees or other constituents are covered by **Rule 1.6**. This does not mean, however, that constituents of an organizational client are the clients of the lawyer. The lawyer may not disclose to such constituents information relating to the representation except for disclosures explicitly or impliedly authorized by the organizational client in order to carry out the representation or as otherwise permitted by **Rule 1.6**."

Rule 1.13, Comment 6: "[T]his Rule does not limit or expand the lawyer's responsibility under **Rules 1.6**, 1.8, and 1.16, 3.3 or 4.1."

Rule 1.17, Comment 6 provides: "Negotiations between seller and prospective purchaser prior to disclosure of information relating to a specific representation of an identifiable client no more violate the confidentiality provisions of **Model Rule 1.6** than do preliminary discussions concerning the possible association of another lawyer or mergers between firms, with respect to which client consent is not required. Providing the purchaser access to client-specific information relating to the representation and to the file, however, requires client consent."

Rule 1.17, Comment 11 provides that a lawyer selling a law practice has an "obligation to protect information relating to the representation (see **Rules 1.6** and 1.9).*"*

Rule 2.2, Comment 6: "In a common representation, the lawyer is still required both to keep each client adequately informed and to maintain confidentiality of information relating to the representation. See **Rules** 1.4 and **1.6**."

Rule 2.3(b): "Except as disclosure is required in connection with a report of an evaluation, information relating to the evaluation is otherwise protected by **Rule 1.6**."

Rule 3.3(b): "The duties stated in paragraph (a) continue to the conclusion of the proceeding, and apply even if compliance requires disclosure of information otherwise protected by **Rule 1.6**."

Rule 4.1(b): "In the course of representing a client a lawyer shall not knowingly . . . fail to disclose a material fact to a third person when disclosure is necessary to avoid assisting a criminal or fraudulent act by a client, unless disclosure is prohibited by **Rule 1.6**."

Rule 4.1, Comment 3: "Paragraph (b) recognizes that substantive law may require a lawyer to disclose certain information to avoid being deemed to have assisted the client's crime or fraud. The requirement of disclosure created by this paragraph is, however, subject to the obligations created by **Rule 1.6**."

Rule 8.1(b): "[T]his rule does not require disclosure of information otherwise protected by **Rule 1.6**."

Rule 8.3(c): "This rule does not require disclosure of information otherwise protected by **Rule 1.6**."

Rule 8.3, Comment 2: "A report about misconduct is not required where it would involve violation of **Rule 1.6**."

Legislative History

1979 Unofficial Pre-Circulation Draft:

(a) In giving testimony or providing evidence concerning a client's affairs, a lawyer shall not disclose matter concerning the client except as permitted under the applicable law of evidentiary privilege. In other circumstances, a lawyer shall not disclose information about a client acquired in serving the client in a professional capacity except as stated in paragraphs (b), (c) and (d).

(b) A lawyer shall disclose information about a client when directed to do so by the client and may do so when disclosure is necessary in the representation.

(c) A lawyer shall disclose information about a client

(1) to the extent necessary to prevent the client from committing an act that would seriously endanger the life or safety of a person, result in wrongful detention or incarceration of a person or wrongful destruction of substantial property, or corrupt judicial or governmental procedure;

(2) when disclosure by the lawyer is required by law or the rules of professional conduct.

(d) A lawyer may disclose information about a client

(1) to the extent necessary to prevent or rectify the consequences of a deliberately wrongful act by the client in which the lawyer's services are or were involved, except

when the lawyer has been employed after the commission of such an act to represent the client concerning the act or its consequences. . . .

1980 Discussion Draft:

(b) A lawyer shall disclose information about a client to the extent it appears necessary to prevent the client from committing an act that would result in death or serious bodily harm to another person, and to the extent required by law or the rules of professional conduct.

(c) A lawyer may disclose information about a client only:

(1) For the purposes of serving the client's interest, unless it is information the client has specifically requested not to be disclosed;

(2) To the extent it appears necessary to prevent or rectify the consequences of a deliberately wrongful act by the client, except when the lawyer has been employed after the commission of such an act to represent the client concerning the act or its consequences. . . .

1981 Draft:

(b) A lawyer may reveal such information to the extent the lawyer believes necessary:

(1) to serve the client's interests, unless it is information the client has specifically requested not to be disclosed;

(2) to prevent the client from committing a criminal or fraudulent act that the lawyer believes is likely to result in death or substantial bodily harm, or substantial injury to the financial interest or property of another;

(3) to rectify the consequences of a client's criminal or fraudulent act in the commission of which the lawyer's services had been used. . . .

1982 Draft:

(b) A lawyer may reveal such information to the extent the lawyer reasonably believes necessary:

(1) to prevent the client form committing a criminal or fraudulent act that the lawyer reasonably believes is likely to result in death or substantial bodily harm, or in substantial injury to the financial interests or property of another;

(2) to rectify the consequences of a client's criminal or fraudulent act in the furtherance of which the lawyer's services had been used. . . .

1991 Proposal: At the ABA's August 1991 Annual Meeting, the Standing Committee on Ethics and Professional Responsibility proposed an amendment to Rule 1.6(b) that would have permitted a lawyer to reveal information that the lawyer reasonably believed necessary to "rectify the consequences of a client's criminal or fraudulent act in the commission of which the lawyer's services had been used." The House of Delegates defeated this proposal by a vote of 251 to 158. The rejected amendment was virtually identical to the Kutak Commission draft that was rejected by the ABA in 1982. By rejecting the 1991 proposal to amend the text of Rule 1.6, the House of Delegates also rejected the following amendments to various paragraphs of the Comment to Rule 1.6:

To the extent a lawyer is prohibited from making disclosure, the interests of the potential victim are sacrificed in favor of preserving the client's confidences even though the client's purpose is wrongful.

Generally speaking, information relating to the representation must be kept confidential. . . . However, where the client is or has been engaged in criminal or fraudulent conduct or the integrity of the lawyer's own conduct is involved, the principle of confidentiality may have to yield, depending on the lawyer's knowledge about and relationship to the conduct in question, and the seriousness of the conduct.

Even if the [lawyer's] involvement was innocent . . . the fact remains that the lawyer's professional services were made the instrument of the client's crime or fraud. The lawyer, therefore, has a legitimate interest in being able to rectify the consequences of such conduct, and has the professional right, although not a professional duty, to rectify the situation. Exercising that right may require revealing information relating to the representation.

Selected State Variations

Arizona, Arkansas, Idaho, Indiana, Kansas, Michigan, Minnesota, Mississippi, North Carolina, Washington, and *Wyoming* permit a lawyer to reveal "the intention of a client to commit a crime" (or use words to that effect).

Arizona, Connecticut, Illinois, Nevada, North Dakota, and *Texas* mandate disclosure of information to prevent the client from committing serious violent crimes.

Arkansas places the language in paragraph 15 of the Comment in the text of the Rule as paragraph (c).

California: B & P Code §6068(e) provides that it is the duty of an attorney "[t]o maintain inviolate the confidence, and at every peril to himself or herself to preserve the secrets, of his or her client." (California's Rules of Professional Conduct do not expressly cover confidentiality.)

Connecticut, Maryland, New Hampshire, New Mexico, North Dakota, and *Pennsylvania* permit a lawyer to reveal information necessary to prevent the client from committing a criminal act "likely to result in substantial injury to the financial interest or property of another" (or words to that effect). Maryland permits the same when the act is only fraudulent.

Connecticut, Pennsylvania, Maryland, Michigan, New Jersey, and *Wisconsin* permit lawyers to reveal confidential information "to rectify the consequences of a client's criminal or fraudulent act in the furtherance of which the lawyer's services were used" (or words to that effect).

District of Columbia: Rule 1.6 provides:

(a) Except when permitted under paragraph (c) or (d), a lawyer shall not knowingly:
(1) reveal a confidence or secret of the lawyer's client;
(2) use a confidence or secret of the lawyer's client to the disadvantage of the client;
(3) use a confidence or secret of the lawyer's client for the advantage of the lawyer or of a third person. . . .
(c) A lawyer may reveal client confidences and secrets, to the extent reasonably necessary:
(1) to prevent a criminal act that the lawyer reasonably believes is likely to result in death or substantial bodily harm absent disclosure of the client's secrets or confidences by the lawyer; or
(2) to prevent the bribery or intimidation of witnesses, jurors, court officials, or other persons who are involved in proceedings before a tribunal if the lawyer reasonably believes that such acts are likely to result absent disclosure of the client's confidences or secrets by the lawyer.
(d) A lawyer may use or reveal client confidences or secrets: . . .
(2) (A) when permitted by these rules or required by law or court order; and
(B) if a government lawyer, when permitted or authorized by law;
(3) to the extent reasonably necessary to establish a defense to a criminal charge, disciplinary charge, or civil claim, formally instituted against the lawyer, based upon con-

duct in which the client was involved, or to the extent reasonably necessary to respond to specific allegations by the client concerning the lawyer's representation of the client;

(4) when the lawyer has reasonable grounds for believing that a client has impliedly authorized disclosure of a confidence or secret in order to carry out the representation; or

(5) to the minimum extent necessary in an action instituted by the lawyer to establish or collect the lawyer's fee.

(e) A lawyer shall exercise reasonable care to prevent the lawyer's employees, associates and others whose services are utilized by the lawyer from disclosing or using confidences or secrets of a client, except that a lawyer may reveal the information required to be disclosed by paragraph (c) and the information permitted to be disclosed by paragraph (d) through such persons.

(f) The lawyer's obligation to preserve the client's confidences and secrets continues after termination of the lawyer's employment.

(g) The obligation of a lawyer under paragraph (a) also applies to confidences and secrets learned prior to becoming a lawyer in the course of providing assistance to another lawyer.

(h) A lawyer who serves as a member of the D.C. Bar Lawyer Counseling Committee, or as a trained intervenor for that Committee, shall be deemed to have a lawyer-client relationship with respect to any lawyer-counselee being counseled under programs conducted by or on behalf of the Committee. Information obtained from another lawyer being counselled under the auspices of the Committee, or in the course of and associated with such counseling, shall be treated as a confidence or secret within the terms of paragraph (b). Such information may be disclosed only to the extent permitted by this rule.

(i) The client of the government lawyer is the agency that employs the lawyer unless expressly provided to the contrary by appropriate law, regulation, or order.

Comment to Rule 1.6

[29] There are circumstances in which a person who ultimately becomes a lawyer provides assistance to a lawyer while serving in a non-lawyer capacity. The typical situation is that of the law clerk or summer associate in a law firm or government agency. Paragraph (g) addresses the confidentiality obligations of such a person after becoming a member of the Bar; the same confidentiality obligations are imposed as would apply if the person had been a member of the Bar at the time confidences or secrets were received.

Florida provides that a lawyer "shall reveal" information the lawyer believes "necessary (1) to prevent a client from committing a crime or (2) to prevent death or substantial bodily harm to another." In addition, Florida Rule 1.6(c) permits a lawyer to reveal information necessary "(1) To serve the client's interest unless it is information the client specifically requires not to be disclosed . . . or (5) To comply with the Rules of Professional Conduct." Florida also adds Rule 1.6(d): "When required by a tribunal to reveal such information, a lawyer may first exhaust all appellate remedies."

Georgia retains the language of DR 4-101.

Illinois: Rule 1.6 provides:

(a) Except when required under Rule 1.6(b) or permitted under Rule 1.6(c), a lawyer shall not, during or after termination of the professional relationship with the client, use or reveal a confidence or secret of the client unless the client consents after disclosure.

(b) A lawyer shall reveal information about a client to the extent it appears necessary to prevent the client from committing an act that would result in death or serious bodily harm.

(c) A lawyer may use or reveal:

(1) confidences or secrets when permitted under these Rules or required by law or court order;

(2) the intention of a client to commit a crime in circumstances other than those enumerated in Rule 1.6(b); or

(3) confidences or secrets necessary to establish or collect the lawyer's fee or to defend the lawyer or the lawyer's employees or associates against an accusation of wrongful conduct.

Illinois also adds:

(d) The relationship of trained intervenor and a lawyer or a judge who seeks or receives assistance through the Lawyer's Assistance Program, Inc., shall be the same as that of lawyer and client for purposes of the application of Rule 8.3 and Rule 1.6.

(e) Any information received by a lawyer in a formal proceeding before a trained intervenor, or panel of intervenors, of the Lawyer's Assistance Program, Inc., shall be deemed to have been received from a client for purposes of the application of Rules 1.6 and 8.3.

New Jersey, in addition to above, requires a lawyer to reveal confidential information "to prevent a client from committing a criminal, illegal or fraudulent act . . . likely to result in death or substantial bodily harm or substantial injury to the financial interest or property of another." New Jersey also requires a lawyer to reveal confidences to prevent a client from committing "a criminal, illegal or fraudulent act that the lawyer reasonably believes is likely to perpetrate a fraud upon a tribunal."

New York: Same or substantially the same as the ABA Model Code — see Model Code Comparison above — except see New York Materials for New York's version of DR 7-102(B)(1) and New York's versions of EC 4-7 and DR 4-101(C)(5).

Texas, in addition to above, Rule 1.02(d) and (e) provides:

(d) When a lawyer has confidential information clearly establishing that a client is likely to commit a criminal or fraudulent act that is likely to result in substantial injury to the financial interests or property of another, the lawyer shall promptly make reasonable efforts under the circumstances to dissuade the client from committing the crime or fraud.

(e) When a lawyer has confidential information clearly establishing that the lawyer's client has committed a criminal or fraudulent act in the commission of which the lawyer's services have been used, the lawyer shall make reasonable efforts under the circumstances to persuade the client to take corrective action.

Texas Rule 1.05 distinguishes between "privileged information" and "unprivileged client information." The former is information protected by the attorney-client privilege. The latter "means all information relating to a client or furnished by the client, other than privileged information, acquired by the lawyer in the course of or by reason of the representation of the client." Both categories of information comprise a third category called "confidential information." A lawyer "may reveal confidential information" in eight instances, including when "the lawyer has reason to believe it is necessary to do so in order to prevent the client from committing a criminal or fraudulent act," and to "the extent revelation reasonably appears necessary to rectify the consequences of a client's criminal or fraudulent act in the commission of which the lawyer's services had been used." Rule 1.05(c)(7) and (8).

Virginia: DR 4-101(D)(1) provides that a lawyer "shall" reveal:

(1) The intention of his client, as stated by the client, to commit a crime and the information necessary to prevent the crime, but before revealing such information, the attorney shall, where feasible, advise his client of the possible legal consequences of his action, urge the

client not to commit the crime, and advise the client that the attorney must reveal the client's criminal intention unless thereupon abandoned, and, if the crime involves perjury by the client, that the attorney shall seek to withdraw as counsel.

Virginia DR 4-101(D)(2) retains the language of DR 7-102(B)(1) relating to a client's fraud on a tribunal, but adds that information "is clearly established when the client acknowledges to the attorney that he has perpetrated a fraud upon a tribunal."

Related Materials

ABA Canons: Canon 37 provided:

37. Confidences of a Client

It is the duty of a lawyer to preserve his client's confidences. This duty outlasts the lawyer's employment, and extends as well to his employees; and neither of them should accept employment which involves or may involve the disclosure or use of these confidences, either for the private advantage of the lawyer or his employees or to the disadvantage of the client, without his knowledge and consent, and even though there are other available sources of such information. A lawyer should not continue employment when he discovers that this obligation prevents the performance of his full duty to his former or to his new client.

If a lawyer is accused by his client, he is not precluded from disclosing the truth in respect to this accusation. The announced intention of a client to commit a crime is not included within the confidences which he is bound to respect. He may properly make such disclosures as may be necessary to prevent the act or protect those against whom it is threatened.

ABA Standards for Imposing Lawyer Discipline:

4.21. Disbarment is generally appropriate when a lawyer, with the intent to benefit the lawyer or another, knowingly reveals information relating to representation of a client not otherwise lawfully permitted to be disclosed, and this disclosure causes injury or potential injury to a client.

4.22. Suspension is generally appropriate when a lawyer knowingly reveals information relating to the representation of a client not otherwise lawfully permitted to be disclosed, and this disclosure causes injury or potential injury to a client.

4.23. Reprimand is generally appropriate when a lawyer negligently reveals information relating to representation of a client not otherwise lawfully permitted to be disclosed and this disclosure causes injury or potential injury to a client.

4.24. Admonition is generally appropriate when a lawyer negligently reveals information relating to representation of a client not otherwise lawfully permitted to be disclosed and this disclosure causes little or no actual or potential injury to a client.

American Academy of Matrimonial Lawyers: The "Bounds of Advocacy" drafted by the American Academy of Matrimonial Lawyers contains the following provisions and commentary:

2.10 An Attorney should not permit a client's relatives, friends, lovers, employers, or other third persons to interfere with the representation, affect the attorney's independent professional judgment, or make decisions affecting the representation, except with the client's express consent.

Comment to Rule 2.10

Third persons often try to play a part in matrimonial cases. Frequently, the client has requested that one or more of these persons be present at conferences and consulted about major decisions. The potential conflicts are exacerbated when the third person is paying expenses or the attorney's fee. Neither payment of litigation expenses nor sincere concern about the welfare of the client make those third persons clients. To the extent specifically authorized by the client, the lawyer may discuss choices with third parties, provided all concerned are aware that such discussions may waive any attorney-client privilege. While it is important for persons going through a divorce to receive advice and support from those they trust, the client, with the advice of the attorney, should make the decisions with which the client must ultimately live.

Both the client and the person paying for the representation must be informed at the outset that nothing related by the client in confidence will be disclosed without the client's consent. The duty to protect confidential information also requires that the attorney raise the issue of the effect on confidentiality of the parents, friends, lovers, children or employers' being present. Usually, the presence of a third person not necessary to the rendition of legal services waives the attorney-client privilege. For this and other reasons, an attorney should discourage family members and other third persons from participating in client conferences. In addition to the potential loss of confidentiality, a more accurate account of the client's desires and best interests can usually be obtained when third persons are not present.

2.26 An attorney should disclose evidence of a substantial risk of physical or sexual abuse of a child by the attorney's client.

Comment to Rule 2.26

While engaged in efforts on the client's behalf, the matrimonial lawyer may become convinced that the client has abused one of the children. Or the client, who seems a good parent, has a live-in lover who has abused one of the children. Under traditional analysis in most jurisdictions, the attorney should refuse to assist the client. The attorney may withdraw if the client will not be adversely affected and the court grants any required permission.

It may also be appropriate to seek the appointment of a guardian ad litem or attorney for the children. The entire thrust of the family law system is intended to make the child's well-being the highest priority. The vindictiveness of a parent, the ineffective legal representation of the spouse, or the failure of the court to perceive sua sponte the need to protect the child's interests do not justify an attorney's failure to act. However, even the appointment of a guardian or lawyer for the child is insufficient if the matrimonial lawyer is aware of physical abuse or similarly extreme parental deficiency. Nor would withdrawal (even if permitted) solve the problem if the attorney is convinced that the child will suffer adverse treatment by the client.

In the most extreme cases, the attorney may reveal information reasonably believed necessary "to prevent the client from committing a criminal act that the lawyer believes is likely to result in imminent death or substantial bodily harm." Many states permit the attorney to reveal the intention of the client to commit any crime and the information necessary to prevent it. The rules do not appear to address, however, revelation of conduct that may be severely detrimental to the well-being of the child, but not criminal.

Notwithstanding the importance of the attorney-client privilege, the obligation of the matrimonial lawyer to consider the welfare of children, coupled with the client's lack of any legitimate interest in preventing his attorney from revealing information to protect the children from likely physical abuse, requires disclosure of a substantial risk of abuse and the information necessary to prevent it. If the client insists on seeking custody or unsupervised visitation, even without the attorney's assistance, the attorney should report specific knowledge of child abuse to the authorities for the protection of the child.

American Lawyer's Code of Conduct: The terminology section states:

A *client's confidence*, protected by this Code, includes any information obtained by the client's lawyer in the course of and by reason of the lawyer-client relationship.

Rules 1.1 through 1.6 provide:

1.1. Beginning with the initial interview with a prospective client, a lawyer shall strive to establish and maintain a relationship of trust and confidence with the client. The lawyer shall impress upon the client that the lawyer cannot adequately serve the client without knowing everything that might be relevant to the client's problem, and that the client should not withhold information that the client might think is embarrassing or harmful to the client's interests. The lawyer shall explain to the client the lawyer's obligation of confidentiality.

1.2. Without the client's knowing and voluntary consent, a lawyer shall not directly or indirectly reveal a confidence of a client or former client, or use it in any way detrimental to the interests of the client, except as provided in Rules 1.3 to 1.6, and Rule 6.5. (Rules 1.3 to 1.6 permit divulgence under compulsion of law; to avoid proceeding before a corrupted judge or juror; to defend the lawyer or the lawyer's associates from charges of misconduct; and to prevent imminent danger to human life. Rule 6.5 permits withdrawal in noncriminal cases when the client has induced the lawyer to act through material misrepresentation, even though withdrawal might indirectly divulge a confidence.)

1.3. A lawyer may reveal a client's confidence to the extent required to do so by law, rule of court, or court order, but only after good faith efforts to test the validity of the law, rule, or order have been exhausted.

1.4. A lawyer may reveal a client's confidence when the lawyer knows that a judge or juror in a pending proceeding in which the lawyer is involved has been bribed or subjected to extortion. In such a case, the lawyer shall use all reasonable means to protect the client, consistent with preventing the case from going forward with a corrupted judge or juror.

1.5. A lawyer may reveal a client's confidence to the extent necessary to defend the lawyer or the lawyer's associate or employee against charges of criminal, civil, or professional misconduct asserted by the client, or against formally instituted charges of such conduct in which the client is implicated.

[1.6. A lawyer may reveal a client's confidence when and to the extent that the lawyer reasonably believes that divulgence is necessary to prevent imminent danger to human life. The lawyer shall use all reasonable means to protect the client's interests that are consistent with preventing loss of life.]

Commission's Note: Rule 1.6 was not approved by the Commission [on Professional Responsibility of the Roscoe Pound Foundation], but was supported by so many members that it is included in this Revised Draft as a Supplemental Rule.

Comment to Rules 1.1-1.6

These Rules reject the previously recognized exception permitting lawyers to violate confidentiality to collect an unpaid fee. The reason for the exception — the lawyer's financial interest — is not sufficiently weighty to justify impairing confidentiality. On the other hand, a limited exception is permitted, when a lawyer or the lawyer's associate is formally charged with criminal or unprofessional conduct. . . .

This Code rejects permitting violation of confidentiality in all cases of "future (or continuing) crimes." First, the category of "crimes" is too broad; it lumps offenses that are openly done and relatively harmless, with those that are clandestine and involve life and death. At the same time, the requirement of a crime may be too narrow; if saving a life, for example, is sufficiently important to justify an exception to confidentiality, then the exception should not turn on technicalities. . . .

Attorney-Client Privilege: Wigmore's treatise on the law of evidence defines the attorney-client privilege as follows:

> (1) Where legal advice of any kind is sought (2) from a professional legal advisor in his capacity as such, (3) the communications relating to that purpose, (4) made in confidence (5) by the client, (6) are at his [the client's] instance permanently protected (7) from disclosure by himself or the legal advisor, (8) except the protection be waived.

Federal Rules of Civil Procedure: In September 1992, the Judicial Conference of the United States proposed an amendment to Fed. R. Civ. P. 26(a)(1) that would require parties to produce lists of witnesses and documents soon after litigation commenced, even if the opposing party did not serve a formal discovery request. This "automatic discovery" provision would require parties to identify people "likely to have discoverable information relevant to disputed facts alleged with particularity in the pleadings" and would impose a parallel duty to identify or produce relevant documents. (Pursuant to the Civil Justice Reform Act of 1990, a few federal district courts have already implemented similar mandatory disclosure rules on an experimental basis.) If the proposal to amend Rule 26(a)(1) is not blocked or altered by the Supreme Court or Congress, it will take effect on December 1, 1993.

Model Rules of Professional Conduct for Federal Lawyers: Rule 1.6(b) provides: "A federal lawyer shall reveal such information to the extent the Federal lawyer reasonably believes necessary to prevent the client from committing a criminal act that the Federal lawyer believes is likely to result in imminent death or substantial bodily harm, or imminent and significant impairment of national security or defense." The Comment also cautions that government lawyers have confidentiality obligations under many federal statutes and regulations, so "in addition to determining the extent to which Rule 1.6 applies to a given situation, it is always advisable for Government lawyers to review the applicable Federal law . . . and to consult with their supervisors."

Restatement of the Law Governing Lawyers: The American Law Institute has tentatively approved the following provisions:

§26. Formation of a Client-Lawyer Relationship

A relationship of client and lawyer arises when:
(1) A person manifests to a lawyer the person's intent that the lawyer provide legal services for the person; and
(2)(a) The lawyer manifests to the person consent to do so, or (b) fails to manifest lack of consent to do so, when the lawyer knows or reasonably should know that the person reasonably relies on the lawyer to provide the services, or (c) a tribunal with power to do so appoints the lawyer to provide the services.

§27. A Lawyer's Duties to a Prospective Client

When a person discusses with a lawyer the possibility of their forming a client-lawyer relationship and even if no such relationship arises, the lawyer must:
(1) Protect the person's confidential information as stated in Chapter 5 and the person's property as stated in §§56-58 and avoid conflicts of interest as stated in §213; and
(2) Use reasonable care to the extent the lawyer advises or provides other legal services for the person.

§111. Lawyer's Duty to Safeguard Confidential Client Information

Except as provided in §§113-117B, during and following the time that a lawyer represents a client or consults with a prospective client:

(1) The lawyer shall not use or disclose confidential client information within the meaning of §112 about a client if there is a reasonable likelihood that doing so will adversely affect a material interest of the client or if the client has directed that the lawyer not use or disclose it; and

(2) The lawyer shall take steps reasonable under the circumstances to protect confidential client information within the meaning of §112 against use or disclosure by others that may adversely affect a material interest of the client.

§112. Definition of "Confidential Client Information"

Confidential client information consists of information about a client or a client's matter contained in oral communications, documents, or other forms of communications, other than information that is generally known, if the lawyer or the lawyer's agent learns or comes into possession of the information:

(1) During the course of representing a client or consulting with a prospective client, regardless of the relationship of the information to the matter involved in the representation or consultation; or

(2) At a time before a representation begins or after it ends, the information concerns a specific client (other than a prospective client whom the lawyer never represents as a client), and the information is entrusted to the lawyer under circumstances reasonably indicating that the lawyer is to employ and safeguard the information in behalf of the client whom the information concerns.

§113. Using or Disclosing Information to Advance Client Interests or for Purposes of Law Practice

Unless the client has directed otherwise, a lawyer may use or disclose confidential client information:

(1) When the lawyer reasonably believes it will advance the interests of the client in the representation, for example:

(a) By providing it in confidence to colleagues of the lawyer such as employees, other agents, contractors, and other persons who aid the lawyer in representing the client;

(b) By presenting evidence or argument in proceedings; or

(c) By disclosing confidential client information to other persons; or

(2) When the lawyer reasonably believes it is appropriate and not inconsistent with the client's interests to provide such information in confidence to colleagues of the lawyer such as employees, other agents, contractors, and other persons aiding the lawyer in facilitating the business affairs and law practice of the lawyer's firm and for purposes of professional development.

§114. Using or Disclosing Information with Client Consent

A lawyer may use or disclose confidential client information:

(1) With respect to the relationship between client and lawyer, when the client consents after the client is adequately informed concerning the use or disclosure; or

(2) With respect to the interests of third persons, when the lawyer acts with actual or apparent authority.

§115. Using or Disclosing Information When Required by Law

A lawyer may use or disclose confidential client information when required by law, for example when ordered to do so by a tribunal, if the lawyer takes reasonably appropriate steps to assert that the information is privileged or otherwise protected against disclosure.

§116. Using or Disclosing Information in Lawyer's Self-Defense

A lawyer may use or disclose confidential client information to the extent that the lawyer reasonably believes necessary in order to defend the lawyer against a charge by any person that the lawyer or a person for whose conduct the lawyer is responsible acted wrongfully during the course of representing the client whose information the lawyer uses or discloses.

§117. Using or Disclosing Information in Compensation Dispute

A lawyer may use or disclose confidential client information to the extent that the lawyer reasonably believes necessary in order to permit the lawyer to resolve a dispute with the client concerning compensation or reimbursement that the lawyer reasonably claims is due to the lawyer.

(Sections 118 through 135 of the tentative Restatement concern the attorney-client privilege, and are reprinted below in the chapter on the attorney-client privilege.)

Rule 1.7 Conflict of Interest: General Rule

(a) A lawyer shall not represent a client if the representation of that client will be directly adverse to another client, unless:

(1) the lawyer reasonably believes the representation will not adversely affect the relationship with the other client; and

(2) each client consents after consultation.

(b) A lawyer shall not represent a client if the representation of that client may be materially limited by the lawyer's responsibilities to another client or to a third person, or by the lawyer's own interests, unless:

(1) the lawyer reasonably believes the representation will not be adversely affected; and

(2) the client consents after consultation. When representation of multiple clients in a single matter is undertaken, the consultation shall include explanation of the implications of the common representation and the advantages and risks involved.

COMMENT

Loyalty to a Client

[1] Loyalty is an essential element in the lawyer's relationship to a client. An impermissible conflict of interest may exist before representation is undertaken,

in which event the representation should be declined. The lawyer should adopt reasonable procedures, appropriate for the size and type of firm and practice, to determine in both litigation and non-litigation matters the parties and issues involved and to determine whether there are actual or potential conflicts of interest.

> **Editors' Note.** The last sentence of paragraph 1 of the Comment was added by the ABA House of Delegates in 1987.

[2] If such a conflict arises after representation has been undertaken, the lawyer should withdraw from the representation. See Rule 1.16. Where more than one client is involved and the lawyer withdraws because a conflict arises after representation, whether the lawyer may continue to represent any of the clients is determined by Rule 1.9. See also Rule 2.2(c). As to whether a client-lawyer relationship exists or, having once been established, is continuing, see Comment to Rule 1.3 and Scope.

[3] As a general proposition, loyalty to a client prohibits undertaking representation directly adverse to that client without that client's consent. Paragraph (a) expresses that general rule. Thus, a lawyer ordinarily may not act as advocate against a person the lawyer represents in some other matter, even if it is wholly unrelated. On the other hand, simultaneous representation in unrelated matters of clients whose interests are only generally adverse, such as competing economic enterprises, does not require consent of the respective clients. Paragraph (a) applies only when the representation of one client would be directly adverse to the other.

[4] Loyalty to a client is also impaired when a lawyer cannot consider, recommend or carry out an appropriate course of action for the client because of the lawyer's other responsibilities or interests. The conflict in effect forecloses alternatives that would otherwise be available to the client. Paragraph (b) addresses such situations. A possible conflict does not itself preclude the representation. The critical questions are the likelihood that a conflict will eventuate and, if it does, whether it will materially interfere with the lawyer's independent professional judgment in considering alternatives or foreclose courses of action that reasonably should be pursued on behalf of the client. Consideration should be given to whether the client wishes to accommodate the other interest involved.

Consultation and Consent

[5] A client may consent to representation notwithstanding a conflict. However, as indicated in paragraph (a)(1) with respect to representation directly adverse to a client, and paragraph (b)(1) with respect to material limitations on representation of a client, when a disinterested lawyer would conclude that the client should not agree to the representation under the circumstances, the lawyer involved cannot properly ask for such agreement or provide representation

on the basis of the client's consent. When more than one client is involved, the question of conflict must be resolved as to each client. Moreover, there may be circumstances where it is impossible to make the disclosure necessary to obtain consent. For example, when the lawyer represents different clients in related matters and one of the clients refuses to consent to the disclosure necessary to permit the other client to make an informed decision, the lawyer cannot properly ask the latter to consent.

Lawyer's Interests

[6] The lawyer's own interests should not be permitted to have adverse effect on representation of a client. For example, a lawyer's need for income should not lead the lawyer to undertake matters that cannot be handled competently and at a reasonable fee. See Rules 1.1 and 1.5. If the probity of a lawyer's own conduct in a transaction is in serious question, it may be difficult or impossible for the lawyer to give a client detached advice. A lawyer may not allow related business interests to affect representation, for example, by referring clients to an enterprise in which the lawyer has an undisclosed interest.

Conflicts in Litigation

[7] Paragraph (a) prohibits representation of opposing parties in litigation. Simultaneous representation of parties whose interests in litigation may conflict, such as co-plaintiffs or co-defendants, is governed by paragraph (b). An impermissible conflict may exist by reason of substantial discrepancy in the parties' testimony, incompatibility in positions in relation to an opposing party or the fact that there are substantially different possibilities of settlement of the claims or liabilities in question. Such conflicts can arise in criminal cases as well as civil. The potential for conflict of interest in representing multiple defendants in a criminal case is so grave that ordinarily a lawyer should decline to represent more than one co-defendant. On the other hand, common representation of persons having similar interests is proper if the risk of adverse effect is minimal and the requirements of paragraph (b) are met. Compare Rule 2.2 involving intermediation between clients.

[8] Ordinarily, a lawyer may not act as advocate against a client the lawyer represents in some other matter, even if the other matter is wholly unrelated. However, there are circumstances in which a lawyer may act as advocate against a client. For example, a lawyer representing an enterprise with diverse operations may accept employment as an advocate against the enterprise in an unrelated matter if doing so will not adversely affect the lawyer's relationship with the enterprise or conduct of the suit and if both clients consent upon consultation. By the same token, government lawyers in some circumstances may represent government employees in proceedings in which a government agency is

the opposing party. The propriety of concurrent representation can depend on the nature of the litigation. For example, a suit charging fraud entails conflict to a degree not involved in a suit for a declaratory judgment concerning statutory interpretation.

[9] A lawyer may represent parties having antagonistic positions on a legal question that has arisen in different cases, unless representation of either client would be adversely affected. Thus, it is ordinarily not improper to assert such positions in cases pending in different trial courts, but it may be improper to do so in cases pending at the same time in an appellate court.

Interest of Person Paying for a Lawyer's Service

[10] A lawyer may be paid from a source other than the client, if the client is informed of that fact and consents and the arrangement does not compromise the lawyer's duty of loyalty to the client. See Rule 1.8(f). For example, when an insurer and its insured have conflicting interests in a matter arising from a liability insurance agreement, and the insurer is required to provide special counsel for the insured, the arrangement should assure the special counsel's professional independence. So also, when a corporation and its directors or employees are involved in a controversy in which they have conflicting interests, the corporation may provide funds for separate legal representation of the directors or employees, if the clients consent after consultation and the arrangement ensures the lawyer's professional independence.

Other Conflict Situations

[11] Conflicts of interest in contexts other than litigation sometimes may be difficult to assess. Relevant factors in determining whether there is potential for adverse effect include the duration and intimacy of the lawyer's relationship with the client or clients involved, the functions being performed by the lawyer, the likelihood that actual conflict will arise and the likely prejudice to the client from the conflict if it does arise. The question is often one of proximity and degree.

[12] For example, a lawyer may not represent multiple parties to a negotiation whose interests are fundamentally antagonistic to each other, but common representation is permissible where the clients are generally aligned in interest even though there is some difference of interest among them.

[13] Conflict questions may also arise in estate planning and estate administration. A lawyer may be called upon to prepare wills for several family members, such as husband and wife, and, depending upon circumstances, a conflict of interest may arise. In estate administration the identity of the client may be unclear under the law of a particular jurisdiction. Under one view, the client is the fiduciary; under another view the client is the estate or trust, including its

beneficiaries. The lawyer should make clear the relationship to the parties involved.

[14] A lawyer for a corporation or other organization who is also a member of its board of directors should determine whether the responsibilities of the two roles may conflict. The lawyer may be called on to advise the corporation in matters involving actions of the directors. Consideration should be given to the frequency with which such situations may arise, the potential intensity of the conflict, the effect of the lawyer's resignation from the board and the possibility of the corporation's obtaining legal advice from another lawyer in such situations. If there is material risk that the dual role will compromise the lawyer's independence of professional judgment, the lawyer should not serve as a director.

Conflict Charged by an Opposing Party

[15] Resolving questions of conflict of interest is primarily the responsibility of the lawyer undertaking the representation. In litigation, a court may raise the question when there is reason to infer that the lawyer has neglected the responsibility. In a criminal case, inquiry by the court is generally required when a lawyer represents multiple defendants. Where the conflict is such as clearly to call in question the fair or efficient administration of justice, opposing counsel may properly raise the question. Such an objection should be viewed with caution, however, for it can be misused as a technique of harassment. See Scope.

Model Code Comparison

DR 5-101(A) provided that "[e]xcept with the consent of his client after full disclosure, a lawyer shall not accept employment if the exercise of his professional judgment on behalf of the client will be or reasonably may be affected by his own financial, business, property, or personal interests." DR 5-105(A) provided that a lawyer "shall decline proffered employment if the exercise of his independent professional judgment in behalf of a client will be or is likely to be adversely affected by the acceptance of the proffered employment, or if it would be likely to involve him in representing differing interests, except to the extent permitted under DR 5-105(C)." DR 5-105(C) provided that "a lawyer may represent multiple clients if it is obvious that he can adequately represent the interest of each and if each consents to the representation after full disclosure of the possible effect of such representation on the exercise of his independent professional judgment on behalf of each." DR 5-107(B) provided that a lawyer "shall not permit a person who recommends, employs, or pays him to render legal services for another to direct or regulate his professional judgment in rendering such services."

Rule 1.7 clarifies DR 5-105(A) by requiring that, when the lawyer's other interests are involved, not only must the client consent after consultation but also that, independent of such consent, the representation reasonably appears not to be adversely affected by the lawyer's other interests. This requirement appears to be the intended meaning of the provision in DR 5-105(C) that "it is obvious that he can adequately represent" the client, and was implicit in EC 5-2, which stated that a lawyer "should not accept proffered employment if his personal interests or desires will, or there is a reasonable probability that they will, affect adversely the advice to be given or services to be rendered the prospective client."

Cross-References in Rules

Rule 1.8, Comment 4: When a lawyer allows a third party to pay a client's fee, the arrangement must "conform to the requirements of . . . **Rule 1.7** concerning conflict of interest."

Rule 1.8, Comment 5: "Related lawyers in the same firm are governed by **Rules 1.7,** 1.9, and 1.10."

Rule 1.9, Comment 1: "The principles in **Rule 1.7** determine whether the interest of the present and former client are adverse."

Rule 1.9, Comment 14: "With regard to an opposing party's raising a question of conflict of interest, see Comment to **Rule 1.7."**

Rule 1.10(a): "While lawyers are associated in a firm, none of them shall knowingly represent a client when any one of them practicing alone would be prohibited from doing so by **Rules 1.7,** 1.8(c), 1.9 or 2.2."

Rule 1.10(c): "A disqualification prescribed by this rule may be waived by the affected client under the conditions stated in **Rule 1.7."**

Rule 1.10, Comment 4: A lawyer changing from government to private practice, or vice versa, "is bound by the Rules generally, including **Rules** 1.6, **1.7,** and 1.9."

Rule 1.10, Comment 7: Despite Rule 1.10(b), a law firm "may not represent a person with interests adverse to those of a present client of the firm, which would violate **Rule 1.7."**

Rule 1.11, Comment 2: "A lawyer representing a government agency, whether employed or specially retained by the government, is subject to the Rules of Professional Conduct, including the prohibition against representing adverse interests stated in **Rule 1.7. . . ."**

Rule 1.11, Comment 8: "Paragraphs (a) and (c) do not prohibit a lawyer from jointly representing a private party and a government agency when doing so is permitted by **Rule 1.7** and is not otherwise prohibited by law."

Rule 1.13(e): "A lawyer representing an organization may also represent any of its directors, officers, employees, members, shareholders or other constituents, subject to the provisions of **Rule 1.7.** If the organization's consent to the dual representation is required by **Rule 1.7,** the consent shall be given by an appropriate official of the organization other than the individual who is to be represented, or by the shareholders."

Rule 1.13, Comment 12: If a claim involves "serious charges of wrongdoing by those in control of the organization, a conflict may arise between the lawyer's duty to the organization and the lawyer's relationship with the board. In those circumstances, **Rule 1.7** governs who should represent the directors and the organization."

Rule 1.17, Comment 5 provides that if the purchaser of a law practice "is unable to undertake all client matters because of a conflict of interest in a specific matter respecting which the purchaser is not permitted by **Rule 1.7** or another rule to represent the client, the requirement of Rule 1.17 that there be a single purchaser is nevertheless satisfied."

Rule 1.17, Comment 11 provides that a lawyer selling a law practice has an "obligation to avoid disqualifying conflicts, and to secure client consent after consultation for those conflicts which can be agreed to (see **Rule 1.7**)".

Rule 2.2: There is no formal reference to **Rule 1.7,** but note the close parallel between **Rule 1.7(b)(2)** and Rule 2.2(a)(1).

Rule 3.7(b): "A lawyer may act as advocate in a trial in which another lawyer in the lawyer's firm is likely to be called as a witness unless precluded from doing so by **Rule 1.7** or Rule 1.9."

Rule 3.7, Comment 5: "Whether the combination of roles involves an improper conflict of interest with respect to the client is determined by **Rule 1.7** or 1.9. . . . Determining whether or not such a conflict exists is primarily the responsibility of the lawyer involved. See Comment to **Rule 1.7.**"

Rule 5.2, Comment 2: "[I]f a question arises whether the interests of two clients conflict under **Rule 1.7,** the supervisor's reasonable resolution of the question should protect the subordinate professionally if the resolution is subsequently challenged."

Rule 5.7, Comment 9 (deleted): "[T]he existence of an ownership interest by lawyers in other entities (especially clients) may implicate conflict of interest concerns (see Model Rules of Professional Conduct 1.7 and 1.8) and may require disclosure by the lawyers pursuant to these rules."

Rule 6.4, Comment: In determining the nature and scope of law reform activities, "a lawyer should be mindful of obligations to clients under other Rules, particularly **Rule 1.7.**"

Rule 6.3(a): A lawyer "shall not knowingly participate in a decision or action" of a legal services organization "if participating in the decision or action would be incompatible with the lawyer's obligation to a client under **Rule 1.7.**"

Legislative History

1980 Discussion Draft (then Rule 1.8) provided as follows:

> In circumstances in which a lawyer has interests, commitments, or responsibilities that may adversely affect the representation of a client, a lawyer shall not represent the client unless:
>
> (a) the Services contemplated in the representation can otherwise be performed in accordance with the rules of professional conduct; and
>
> (b) the client consents after adequate disclosure of the circumstances.

1981 Draft:

> (a) A lawyer shall not represent a client if the lawyer's ability to consider, recommend or carry out a course of action on behalf of the client will be adversely affected by the lawyer's responsibilities to another client or to a third person, or by the lawyer's own interests.
>
> (b) When a lawyer's own interests or other responsibilities might adversely affect the representation of a client, the lawyer shall not represent the client unless:
>
> (1) the lawyer reasonably believes the other responsibilities or interests involved will not adversely affect the best interest of the client; and . . .

1982 Draft was adopted.

1987 Amendment: The ABA House of Delegates added the last sentence of Comment 1 to Rule 1.7, and placed other parts of Comment 1 into a separate paragraph, which is now Comment 2.

Selected State Variations

California: See Rule 3-310 (Avoiding the Representation of Adverse Interests).
District of Columbia: Rule 1.7 provides:

(a) A lawyer shall not represent a client with respect to a position to be taken in a matter if that position is adverse to a position taken or to be taken in the same matter by another client represented with respect to that position by the same lawyer.

(b) Except as permitted by paragraph (c) below, a lawyer shall not represent a client with respect to a matter if:

(1) A position to be taken by that client in that matter is adverse to a position taken or to be taken by another client in the same matter;

(2) Such representation will be or is likely to be adversely affected by representation of another client;

(3) Representation of another client will be or is likely to be adversely affected by such representation; or

(4) The lawyer's professional judgment on behalf of the client will be or reasonably may be adversely affected by the lawyer's responsibilities to or interests in a third party or the lawyer's own financial, business, property or personal interests.

Comment to Rule 1.7

[3] The concept of a "matter" is typically apparent in on-the-record adversary proceedings or other proceedings in which a written record of the position of parties exists. In other situations, it may not be clear to a lawyer whether the representation of one client is adverse to the interests of another client. For example, a lawyer may represent a client only with respect to one or a few of the client's areas of interest. Other lawyers, or non-lawyers (such as lobbyists), or employees of the client (such as government relations personnel) may be representing that client on many issues whose scope and content are unknown to the lawyer. A lawyer may not undertake a representation known to be adverse to the interests of another client, whether that representation is in a court proceeding, an on-the-record administrative hearing, a notice-and-comment rulemaking, or in an effort to influence policy or achieve a legislative result. However, clients often have many representatives acting for them, including multiple law firms, nonlawyer lobbyists, and client employees. A lawyer retained for a limited purpose may not be aware of the full range of a client's other interests or positions on issues. A lawyer is not required to inquire of a client concerning the full range of that client's interests in issues, unless it is clear to the lawyer or to any affiliated lawyer that there is a potential for concrete adversity between the interests of clients of the lawyer or firm. Unless a lawyer is aware that representing one client involves seeking a result to which another client is opposed, Rule 1.7 is not violated by a representation which eventuates in the lawyer unwittingly taking a position for one client adverse to the interests of another client. . . .

[18] In the government lawyer context, Rule 1.7(b) is not intended to apply to conflicts between agencies or components of government (federal, state or local) where the resolution of such conflicts has been entrusted by law, order or regulation to a specific individual or entity.

Florida: Rule 1.7(a)(1) applies when "the representation will not adversely affect the lawyer's responsibilities to and relationship with the other client."

Georgia retains the Code formulation on concurrent conflicts of interest. DR 5-105.

New Jersey Rule 1.7(a)(2) provides that "a public entity cannot consent to any such representation." New Jersey also adds Rule 1.7(c):

(c) This rule shall not alter the effect of case law or ethics opinions to the effect that:

(1) in certain cases or categories of cases involving conflicts or apparent conflicts, consent to continued representation is immaterial, and

(2) in certain cases or situations creating an appearance of impropriety rather than an actual conflict, multiple representation is not permissible, that is, in those situations in which an ordinary knowledgeable citizen acquainted with the facts would conclude that the multiple representation poses substantial risk of disservice to either the public interest or the interest of one of the clients.

New York: Same or substantially the same as the ABA Model Code — see Model Code Comparison above.

North Carolina: Rule 5.1(A) adds that a lawyer shall not represent a client if the representation "is likely to be" directly adverse to another client.

Texas: Rule 1.06 provides:

(a) A lawyer shall not represent opposing parties to the same litigation.

(b) In other situations and except to the extent permitted by paragraph (c), a lawyer shall not represent a person if the representation of that person:

(1) involves a substantially related matter in which that person's interests are materially and directly adverse to the interests of another client of the lawyer or the lawyer's firm; or

(2) reasonably appears to be or become adversely limited by the lawyer's or law firm's responsibilities to another client or to a third person or by the lawyer's or law firm's own interests.

(c) A lawyer may represent a client in the circumstances described in (b) if:

(1) the lawyer reasonably believes the representation of each client will not be materially affected; and

(2) each affected or potentially affected client consents to such representation after full disclosure of the existence, nature, implications, and possible adverse consequences of the common representation and the advantages involved, if any.

(d) A lawyer who has represented multiple parties in a matter shall not thereafter represent any of such parties in a dispute among the parties arising out of the matter, unless prior consent is obtained from all such parties to the dispute.

(e) If a lawyer has accepted representation in violation of this Rule, or if multiple representation properly accepted becomes improper under this Rule, the lawyer shall promptly withdraw from one or more representations to the extent necessary for any remaining representation not to be in violation of these Rules.

(f) If a lawyer would be prohibited by this Rule from engaging in particular conduct, no other lawyer while a member or associated with that lawyer's firm may engage in that conduct.

Virginia: Substantially the same as the Model Code.

Wisconsin requires that consent under Rule 1.7(a) and (b) be in writing after consultation.

Related Materials

ABA Canons: Canon 6 provided:

6. Adverse Influences and Conflicting Interests

It is the duty of a lawyer at the time of retainer to disclose to the client all the circumstances of his relations to the parties, and any interest in or connection with the controversy, which might influence the client in the selection of counsel.

It is unprofessional to represent conflicting interests, except by express consent of all concerned given after a full disclosure of the facts. Within the meaning of this canon, a lawyer represents conflicting interests when, in behalf of one client, it is his duty to contend for that which duty to another client requires him to oppose.

The obligation to represent the client with undivided fidelity and not to divulge his secrets or confidences forbids also the subsequent acceptance of retainers or employment from others in matters adversely affecting any interest of the client with respect to which confidence has been reposed.

ABA Standards for Imposing Lawyer Discipline:

4.3. Failure to Avoid Conflicts of Interest

4.31. Disbarment is generally appropriate when a lawyer, without the informed consent of client(s):

(a) engages in representation of a client knowing that the lawyer's interests are adverse to the client's with the intent to benefit the lawyer or another, and causes serious or potentially serious injury to the client; or

(b) simultaneously represents clients that the lawyer knows have adverse interests with the intent to benefit the lawyer or another, and causes serious or potentially serious injury to a client; or

(c) represents a client in a matter substantially related to a matter in which the interests of a present or former client are materially adverse, and knowingly uses information relating to the representation of a client with the intent to benefit the lawyer or another, and causes serious or potentially serious injury to a client.

4.32. Suspension is generally appropriate when a lawyer knows of a conflict of interest and does not fully disclose to a client the possible effect of that conflict, and causes injury or potential injury to a client.

4.33. Reprimand is generally appropriate when a lawyer is negligent in determining whether the representation of a client may be materially affected by the lawyer's own interests, or whether the representation will adversely affect another client, and causes injury or potential injury to a client.

4.34. Admonition is generally appropriate when a lawyer engages in an isolated instance of negligence in determining whether the representation of a client may be materially affected by the lawyer's own interests, or whether the representation will adversely affect another client, and causes little or no actual or potential injury to a client.

American Academy of Matrimonial Lawyers: The "Bounds of Advocacy" drafted by the American Academy of Matrimonial Lawyers contains the following provisions and commentary:

Conflict of Interest

Conflict of interest dilutes a lawyer's loyalty to the client. A lawyer's loyalty may be diluted by a number of personal interests (financial security, prestige, and self-esteem) and interests of third persons (family, friends, business associates, employer, legal profession, and society as a whole). Under the RPC, a conflict exists if the representation of a client "may be materially limited by the lawyer's responsibilities to another client or to a third person, or by the lawyer's own interests." The key to preventing unintentional violations of the conflict of interest rules lies in anticipating the probability or possibility that a conflict situation will develop.

The influences that might dilute a matrimonial lawyer's loyalty to a client are unlimited. The interests of the children, relatives, friends, lovers, employers and the opposing party, along with a perceived obligation to the court and the interest of society, may be compelling in a given case. In family law matters, where "winning" and "losing" in the traditional sense often lose their meaning, determination of the appropriate ethical conduct can be extremely difficult.

2.16 An attorney should never have a sexual relationship with a client or opposing counsel during the time of the representation.

Comment to Rule 2.16

Persons in need of a matrimonial lawyer are often in a highly vulnerable emotional state. Some degree of social contact (particularly if a social relationship existed prior to the events that occasioned the representation) may be desirable, but a more intimate relationship may endanger both the client's welfare and the lawyer's objectivity.

Attorneys are expected to maintain personal relationships with other attorneys, but must be sensitive to the threat to independent judgment and the appearance of impropriety when an intimate relationship exists with opposing counsel or others involved in the proceedings.

2.22 An attorney should not simultaneously represent both a client and a person with whom the client is sexually involved.

Comment to Rule 2.22

A matrimonial lawyer is often asked to represent a client and the client's lover. Joint representation may make it difficult to advise the client of the need to recover from the emotional trauma of divorce, the desirability of a prenuptial agreement, or the dangers of early remarriage. The testimony of either might be adverse to the other at deposition or trial. In addition, the client may desire to waive support payments because she believes she is going to marry her lover. The inherent conflicts in attempting to represent both the client and her lover render such representation improper. Even when the client's new partner is not represented by the attorney, but wishes to participate in consultations and other aspects of the representation, the attorney must be alert to the danger of the client's undermining her own best interests in an effort to accommodate her new partner.

Children

One of the most troubling issues in family law is determining a lawyer's obligations to children. The lawyer must represent the client zealously, but not at the expense of children. The parents' fiduciary obligations for the well-being of a child provide a basis for the attorney's consideration of the child's best interests consistent with traditional adversary and client loyalty principles. It is accepted doctrine that the attorney for a trustee or other fiduciary has an ethical obligation to the beneficiaries to whom the fiduciary's obligations run. To the extent that statutory or decisional law imposes a duty on the parent to act in the child's best interests, the attorney for the parent might be considered to have an obligation to the child that would, in some instances, justify subordinating the express wishes of the parent. For example, "If the lawyer represents the guardian as distinct from the ward, and is aware that the guardian is acting adversely to the ward's interest, the lawyer may have an obligation to prevent or rectify the guardian's misconduct." For this analysis to be of benefit to practitioners, however, a clearer mandate must be adopted as part of the ethical code or its official interpretations.

2.23 In representing a parent, an attorney should consider the welfare of children.

Comment to Rule 2.23

Although the substantive law in most jurisdictions concerning custody, abuse, and termination of parental rights is premised upon the "best interests of the child," the ethical codes provide little (or contradictory) guidance for an attorney whose client's expressed wishes or interests are in direct conflict with the well-being of children. This provision stresses the welfare of a client's children.

3.5 An attorney should discourage the client from interfering in the spouse's effort to obtain effective representation.

Comment to Rule 3.5

Clients who file or anticipate the filing of a divorce proceeding occasionally telephone or interview numerous attorneys as a means of denying their spouse access to effective representation. The attorney should discourage such practices and should not assist the client, for example, by responding to the client's request for a list of matrimonial lawyers if improper motives are suspected. When the client has already contacted other lawyers for the purpose of disqualifying them, the client's attorney should attempt to persuade the client to waive any conflicts so created.

Professional Cooperation and the Administration of Justice

Many jurisdictions have elaborated upon the general principles in this section by adopting codes of professional courtesy. In jurisdictions where such codes have been adopted, matrimonial lawyers should adhere to them scrupulously.

American Lawyer's Code of Conduct: Rules 2.1, 2.4, and 8.8 provide:

2.1. In a matter entrusted to a lawyer by a client, the lawyer shall give undivided fidelity to the client's interests as perceived by the client, unaffected by any interest of the lawyer or of any other person, or by the lawyer's perception of the public interest.

2.4. A lawyer may serve one or more clients, despite a divided loyalty, if each client who is or may be adversely affected by the divided loyalty is fully informed of the actual or potential adverse effects, and voluntarily consents.

8.8. A lawyer shall not commence having sexual relations with a client during the lawyer-client relationship.

Comment to Rule 8.8

. . . Rule 8.8 forbids a lawyer to commence having sexual relations with a client during the lawyer-client relationship. This rule . . . recognizes the dependency of a client upon a lawyer, the high degree of trust that a client is entitled to place in a lawyer, and the potential for unfair advantage in such a relationship. Other professionals, such as psychiatrists, have begun to face up to analogous problems.

Restatement of the Law Governing Lawyers: The American Law Institute has tentatively approved the following provisions:

§201. Basic Prohibition of Conflict of Interest

Unless all affected clients consent to the representation under the limitations and conditions provided in §202, a lawyer may not represent a client if the representation would constitute a conflict of interest. A conflict of interest exists if there is a substantial risk that the lawyer's representation of the client would be materially and adversely affected by the lawyer's own interests or by the lawyer's duties to another current client, to a former client, or to a third person.

§202. *Client Consent to a Conflict of Interest*

(1) A lawyer may represent a client notwithstanding a conflict of interest prohibited by §201 if each affected client gives informed consent to the lawyer's representation. Informed consent requires that the client have adequate information about the risks and advantages of such representation to that client.

(2) Notwithstanding each affected client's consent, a lawyer may not represent a client if:

(a) The lawyer represents an opposing party in the same litigation;

(b) One or more of the clients is legally incapable of giving consent; or

(c) Special circumstances render it unlikely that the lawyer will be able to provide adequate representation to one or more of the clients.

(Restatement §§203–204 concern imputed conflicts of interest and are reprinted in the Related Materials following Model Rule 1.9 below; §205 has not yet been written but the section number has been "reserved.")

§206. *Lawyer's Personal Interest Affecting Representation of a Client*

Unless the affected client consents to the representation under the conditions and limitations provided in §202, a lawyer may not undertake or continue to represent a client if a substantial risk exists that a financial or other personal interest of the lawyer will materially and adversely affect the lawyer's representation of the client.

(Restatement §§207-208 concern lawyer-client business transactions and gifts, and are reprinted below in the Related Materials following Model Rule 1.8.)

§209. *Representing Parties with Conflicting Interests in Civil Litigation*

Unless all affected clients consent to the representation under the limitations and conditions provided in §202, a lawyer in civil litigation may not:

(1) Represent more than one client in a matter if there is a substantial risk that the lawyer's representation of one of the clients would materially and adversely affect the lawyer's representation of another client in the matter; or

(2) Represent one client in asserting or defending a claim against another client currently represented by the lawyer, even if the matters are not related.

§210. *Conflicts of Interest in Criminal Litigation*

Unless all affected clients consent to the representation under the limitations and conditions provided in §202, a lawyer in a criminal case may not represent:

(1) Two or more defendants or potential defendants in the same matter; or

(2) A single defendant, if the representation would involve a conflict of interest as stated in §201.

§211. *Simultaneous Representation in Non-Litigated Matters*

Unless all affected clients consent to the representation under the limitations and conditions provided in §202, a lawyer may not represent two or more clients in any matters not involving litigation if there is a substantial risk that the lawyer's representation of one or more of the clients would be materially and adversely affected by the lawyer's duties to one or more of the other clients.

§216. Lawyer with a Fiduciary or Other Legal Obligation to Another

Unless the affected client consents to the representation under the limitations and conditions provided in §202, a lawyer may not represent a client in any matter with respect to which the lawyer has a fiduciary or other legal obligation to another person if there is a substantial risk that the obligation would materially and adversely affect the lawyer's representation of the client.

With respect to "the implications of the common representation" under Rule 1.7(b), the ALI has tentatively approved the following provisions:

§125. The Limited Privilege for Co-Clients

If two or more persons are jointly represented by the same lawyer in a matter, the communications of each co-client with the lawyer or other privileged person that otherwise qualify as privileged under §§118-122:

(1) Are privileged as against a third person, and any co-client may assert the privilege; but

(2) Unless the co-clients have explicitly agreed otherwise, are not privileged as between the co-clients in subsequent litigation between them.

§126. Pooled-Information Arrangements

If two or more clients represented by separate lawyers share a common interest in a matter, the communications of each separately represented client that otherwise qualify as privileged under §§118-122:

(1) Are privileged as against a third person, and any such client may assert the privilege, if the communication is made in confidence between such a client, the client's communicating agents, the client's lawyer, or the lawyer's representing agent, and another commonly interested client or such a client's communicating agent, lawyer, or representing agent; but

(2) Unless the affected clients in the pooled-information arrangement have explicitly agreed otherwise, a communication within subsection (1) is not privileged as between such clients in subsequent litigation between two or more of the clients when it is offered against the client who originally made the communication, or on whose behalf it was made, by a client who learned of the communication in the circumstances described in subsection (1).

(Restatement §§118-122 are reprinted below in the chapter on the attorney-client privilege.)

Rule 1.8 Conflict of Interest: Prohibited Transactions

(a) A lawyer shall not enter into a <u>business transaction with a client</u> or knowingly acquire an ownership, possessory, security or other pecuniary interest adverse to a client unless:

(1) the transaction and terms on which the lawyer acquires the interest are fair and reasonable to the client and are fully disclosed and transmitted in writing to the client in a manner which can be reasonably understood by the client;

(2) the client is given a reasonable opportunity to seek the advice of independent counsel in the transaction; and

(3) the client consents in writing thereto.

(b) A lawyer shall not use information relating to representation of a client to the disadvantage of the client unless the client consents after consultation, except as permitted or required by Rule 1.6 or Rule 3.3.

(c) A lawyer shall not prepare an instrument giving the lawyer or a person related to the lawyer as parent, child, sibling, or spouse any substantial gift from a client, including a testamentary gift, except where the client is related to the donee.

(d) Prior to the conclusion of representation of a client, a lawyer shall not make or negotiate an agreement giving the lawyer literary or media rights to a portrayal or account based in substantial part on information relating to the representation.

(e) A lawyer shall not provide financial assistance to a client in connection with pending or contemplated litigation, except that:

(1) a lawyer may advance court costs and expenses of litigation, the repayment of which may be contingent on the outcome of the matter; and

(2) a lawyer representing an indigent client may pay court costs and expenses of litigation on behalf of the client.

(f) A lawyer shall not accept compensation for representing a client from one other than the client unless:

(1) the client consents after consultation;

(2) there is no interference with the lawyer's independence of professional judgment or with the client-lawyer relationship; and

(3) information relating to representation of a client is protected as required by Rule 1.6.

(g) A lawyer who represents two or more clients shall not participate in making an aggregate settlement of the claims of or against the clients, or in a criminal case an aggregated agreement as to guilty or nolo contendere pleas, unless each client consents after consultation, including disclosure of the existence and nature of all the claims or pleas involved and of the participation of each person in the settlement.

(h) A lawyer shall not make an agreement prospectively limiting the lawyer's liability to a client for malpractice unless permitted by law and the client is independently represented in making the agreement, or settle a claim for such liability with an unrepresented client or former client without first advising that person in writing that independent representation is appropriate in connection therewith.

(i) A lawyer related to another lawyer as parent, child, sibling or spouse shall not represent a client in a representation directly adverse to a person who the lawyer knows is represented by the other lawyer except upon the consent by the client after consultation regarding the relationship.

(j) A lawyer shall not acquire a <u>proprietary interest in the cause of action</u> or subject matter of litigation the lawyer is conducting for a client, except that the lawyer may:

(1) acquire a lien granted by law to secure the lawyer's fee or expenses; and

(2) contract with a client for a reasonable contingent fee in a civil case.

COMMENT

Transactions Between Client and Lawyer

[1] As a general principle, all transactions between client and lawyer should be fair and reasonable to the client. In such transactions a review by independent counsel on behalf of the client is often advisable. Furthermore, a lawyer may not exploit information relating to the representation to the client's disadvantage. For example, a lawyer who has learned that the client is investing in specific real estate may not, without the client's consent, seek to acquire nearby property where doing so would adversely affect the client's plan for investment. Paragraph (a) does not, however, apply to standard commercial transactions between the lawyer and the client for products or services that the client generally markets to others, for example, banking or brokerage services, medical services, products manufactured or distributed by the client, and utilities services. In such transactions, the lawyer has no advantage in dealing with the client, and the restrictions in paragraph (a) are unnecessary and impracticable.

[2] A lawyer may accept a gift from a client, if the transaction meets general standards of fairness. For example, a simple gift such as a present given at a holiday or as a token of appreciation is permitted. If effectuation of a substantial gift requires preparing a legal instrument such as a will or conveyance, however, the client should have the detached advice that another lawyer can provide. Paragraph (c) recognizes an exception where the client is a relative of the donee or the gift is not substantial.

Literary Rights

[3] An agreement by which a lawyer acquires literary or media rights concerning the conduct of the representation creates a conflict between the interests of the client and the personal interests of the lawyer. Measures suitable in the representation of the client may detract from the publication value of an ac-

count of the representation. Paragraph (d) does not prohibit a lawyer representing a client in a transaction concerning literary property from agreeing that the lawyer's fee shall consist of a share in ownership in the property, if the arrangement conforms to Rule 1.5 and paragraph (j).

Person Paying for Lawyer's Services

[4] Rule 1.8(f) requires disclosure of the fact that the lawyer's services are being paid for by a third party. Such an arrangement must also conform to the requirements of Rule 1.6 concerning confidentiality and Rule 1.7 concerning conflict of interest. Where the client is a class, consent may be obtained on behalf of the class by court-supervised procedure.

Family Relationships Between Lawyers

[5] Rule 1.8(i) applies to related lawyers who are in different firms. Related lawyers in the same firm are governed by Rules 1.7, 1.9, and 1.10. The disqualification stated in Rule 1.8(i) is personal and is not imputed to members of firms with whom the lawyers are associated.

Acquisition of Interest in Litigation

[6] Paragraph (j) states the traditional general rule that lawyers are prohibited from acquiring a proprietary interest in litigation. This general rule, which has its basis in common law champerty and maintenance, is subject to specific exceptions developed in decisional law and continued in these Rules, such as the exception for reasonable contingent fees set forth in Rule 1.5 and the exception for certain advances of the costs of litigation set forth in paragraph (e).

[7] This Rule is not intended to apply to customary qualification and limitations in legal opinions and memoranda.

Model Code Comparison

With regard to paragraph (a), DR 5-104(A) provided that a lawyer "shall not enter into a business transaction with a client if they have differing interests therein and if the client expects the lawyer to exercise his professional judgment therein for the protection of the client, unless the client has consented after full disclosure." EC 5-3 stated that a lawyer "should not seek to persuade his client to permit him to invest in an undertaking of his client nor make improper use of his professional relationship to influence his client to invest in an enterprise in which the lawyer is interested."

With regard to paragraph (b), DR 4-101(B)(3) provided that a lawyer should not use "a confidence or secret of his client for the advantage of himself, or of a third person, unless the client consents after full disclosure."

There was no counterpart to paragraph (c) in the Disciplinary Rules of the Model Code. EC 5-5 stated that a lawyer "should not suggest to his client that a gift be made to himself or for his benefit. If a lawyer accepts a gift from his client, he is peculiarly susceptible to the charge that he unduly influenced or overreached the client. If a client voluntarily offers to make a gift to his lawyer, the lawyer may accept the gift, but before doing so, he should urge that the client secure disinterested advice from an independent, competent person who is cognizant of all the circumstances. Other than in exceptional circumstances, a lawyer should insist that an instrument in which his client desires to name him beneficially be prepared by another lawyer selected by the client."

Paragraph (d) is substantially similar to DR 5-104(B), but refers to "literary or media" rights, a more generally inclusive term than "publication" rights.

Paragraph (e)(1) is similar to DR 5-103(B), but eliminates the requirement that "the client remains ultimately liable for such expenses."

Paragraph (e)(2) has no counterpart in the Model Code.

Paragraph (f) is substantially identical to DR 5-107(A)(1).

Paragraph (g) is substantially identical to DR 5-106.

The first clause of paragraph (h) is similar to DR 6-102(A). There was no counterpart in the Model Code to the second clause of paragraph (h).

Paragraph (i) has no counterpart in the Model Code.

Paragraph (j) is substantially identical to DR 5-103(A).

Cross-References in Rules

Rule 1.5, Comment 2: "A lawyer may accept property in payment for services . . . this does not involve acquisition of a proprietary interest in the cause of action or subject matter of the litigation contrary to **Rule 1.8(j).**"

Rule 1.6, Comment 15: "Neither this Rule nor **Rule 1.8(b)** . . . prevents the lawyer from giving notice of the fact of withdrawal, and the lawyer may also withdraw or disaffirm any opinion, document, affirmation, or the like."

Rule 1.7, Comment 10: "A lawyer may be paid from a source other than the client, if the client is informed of that fact and consents and the arrangement does not compromise the lawyer's duty of loyalty to the client. See **Rule 1.8(f).**"

Rule 1.10(a): "While lawyers are associated in a firm, none of them shall knowingly represent a client when any one of them practicing alone would be prohibited from doing so by **Rules** 1.7, **1.8(c),** 1.9 or 2.2."

Rule 1.13, Comment 6: Rule 1.13 "does not limit or expand the lawyer's responsibility under" **Rule 1.8.**

Rule 5.7, Comment 9 (deleted): "[T]he existence of an ownership interest by lawyers in other entities (especially clients) may implicate conflict of interest concerns (see Model Rules of Professional Conduct 1.7 and **1.8**) and may require disclosure by the lawyers pursuant to these rules."

Rule 5.7, Comment 15 (deleted): "[B]efore providing ancillary services to a client, a law firm must comply with appropriate disclosure requirements (as mandated in Model Rule of Professional Conduct 1.8 . . . .)."

Legislative History

1979 Unofficial Pre-Circulation Draft:

(e) A lawyer shall not provide financial assistance to a client in connection with pending or contemplated litigation, except that a lawyer may advance expenses, including:

Alternative (1): Court costs, expenses of investigation, medical and other experts, and obtaining and presenting evidence.

Alternative (2): Court costs, expenses of litigation, and living expenses.

1980 Discussion Draft (then called Rule 1.9):

(f) A lawyer may serve as general counsel to a corporation or other organization of which the lawyer is a director only if:

(1) There is adequate disclosure to and consent by all persons having an investment interest in the organization; or

(2) When doing so would not involve serious risk of conflict between the lawyer's responsibilities as general counsel and those as director.

1981 and 1982 Drafts were substantially the same as adopted, except that Rule 1.8(f) contained no restrictions other than the client's consent "after consultation."

Selected State Variations

California: See Rule 3-300 (Avoiding Adverse Interests — compare to Model Rule 1.8(a)); Rule 3-310(E) (compare to Model Rule 1.8(f)); Rule 3-310(C) (compare to Model Rule 1.8(g)); Rule 3-320 (Relationship with Other Party's Lawyer — compare to Model Rule 1.8(i)); Rule 3-400 (Limiting Liability to Client — compare to Model Rule 1.8(h)); and Rule 4-210 (Payment of Personal or Business Expenses Incurred by or for a Client — compare to Model Rule 1.8(e)).

Connecticut and **Michigan:** Rule 1.8(e)(1) requires nonindigent clients to remain ultimately responsible for advanced costs and expenses.

District of Columbia: Rule 1.8 provides:

(d) While representing a client in connection with contemplated or pending litigation or administrative proceedings, a lawyer shall not advance or guarantee financial assistance to the client, except that a lawyer may pay or otherwise provide:

(1) the expenses of litigation or administrative proceedings, including court costs, expenses of investigation, expenses of medical examination, costs of obtaining and presenting evidence; and

(2) other financial assistance which is reasonably necessary to permit the client to institute or maintain the litigation or administrative proceeding. . . .

(i) A lawyer shall not impose a lien upon any part of a client's files, except upon the lawyer's own work product, and then only to the extent that the work product has not been paid for. This work product exception shall not apply when the client has become unable to pay, or when withholding the lawyer's work product would present a significant risk to the client of irreparable harm.

Comment to Rule 1.8

[5] Historically, under the Code of Professional Responsibility, lawyers could only advance the costs of litigation. The client remained ultimately responsible, and was re-

quired to pay such costs even if the client lost the case. That rule was modified by this Court in 1980 in an amendment to DR 5-103(B) which eliminated the requirement that the client remain ultimately liable for costs of litigation, even if the litigation was unsuccessful. The provisions of Rule 1.8(d) embrace the result of the 1980 modification, but go further by providing that a lawyer may also pay certain expenses of a client which are not litigation expenses. Thus, under Rule 1.8(d), a lawyer may pay medical or living expenses of a client to the extent necessary to permit the client to continue the litigation. The payment of these additional expenses is limited to those strictly necessary to sustain the client during the litigation, such as medical expenses and minimum living expenses. The purpose of permitting such payments is to avoid situations in which a client is compelled by exigent financial circumstances to settle a claim on unfavorable terms in order to receive the immediate proceeds of settlement. This provision does not permit lawyers to "bid" for clients by offering financial payments beyond those minimum payments necessary to sustain the client until the litigation is completed. Regardless of the types of payments involved, assuming such payments are proper under Rule 1.8(d), client reimbursement of the lawyer is not required. . . .

[8] Rule 1.16(d) requires a lawyer to surrender papers and property to which the client is entitled when representation of the client terminates. Paragraph (i) of this Rule states a narrow exception to Rule 1.16(d); a lawyer may retain the lawyer's own work product if the client has not paid for the work. However, if the client has paid for the work product, the client is entitled to receive it, even if the client has not previously seen or received a copy of the work product. Furthermore, the lawyer may not retain work product for which the client has not paid, if the client has become unable to pay or if withholding the work product might irreparably harm the client's interest.

[9] Under Rule 1.16(d), for example, a lawyer would be required to return all papers received from a client, such as birth certificates, wills, tax returns, or "green cards." Rule 1.8(i) does not permit retention of such papers to secure payment of any fee due. Only the lawyer's own work product — results of factual investigations, legal research and analysis, and similar materials generated by the lawyer's own effort — could be retained. (The term "work product" as used in paragraph (i) is not limited to materials falling within the "work product doctrine," but includes any material generated by the lawyer whether or not in connection with pending or anticipated litigation.) And a lawyer could not withhold all work product merely because a portion of the lawyer's fees had not been paid.

[10] There are situations in which withholding work product would not be permissible because of irreparable harm to the client. The possibility of involuntary incarceration or criminal conviction constitutes one category of irreparable harm. The realistic possibility that a client might irretrievably lose a significant right or become subject to a significant liability because of the withholding of work product constitutes another category of irreparable harm. On the other hand, the mere fact that the client might have to pay another lawyer to replicate the work product does not, standing alone, constitute irreparable harm. These examples are merely indicative of the meaning of the term "irreparable harm," and are not exhaustive.

Georgia allows lawyers to advance litigation and related costs but the client must remain "ultimately liable" for them. Financial assistance cannot be guaranteed or advanced. DR 5-103(C).

Illinois: The Illinois version of Rule 1.8(a) provides:

(a) Unless the client has consented after disclosure, a lawyer shall not enter into a business transaction with the client if:

(1) the lawyer knows or reasonably should know that the lawyer and the client have or may have conflicting interests therein; or

(2) the client expects the lawyer to exercise the lawyer's professional judgment therein for the protection of the client.

Illinois omits Rule 1.8(b), and modifies Rule 1.8(c) as follows:

(b) Unless all aspects of the matter giving rise to the employment have been concluded, a lawyer shall not enter into any arrangement or understanding with a client or a prospective client by which the lawyer acquires an interest in publication, media, or other literary rights with respect to the subject matter of employment or proposed employment.

Illinois modifies Rule 1.8(e) as follows:

(d) While representing a client in connection with contemplated or pending litigation, a lawyer shall not advance or guarantee financial assistance to the client, except that a lawyer may advance or guarantee the expenses of litigation, including, but not limited to, court costs, expenses of investigation, expenses of medical examination, and costs of obtaining and presenting evidence if:
    (1) the client remains ultimately liable for such expenses; or
    (2) the repayment is contingent on the outcome of the matter; or
    (3) the client is indigent.

Illinois modifies Rule 1.8(h) as follows:

(g) A lawyer shall not settle a claim against the lawyer made by an unrepresented client or former client without first advising that person in writing that independent representation is appropriate in connection therewith.

Illinois adds the following new subparagraph:

(h) A lawyer shall not enter into an agreement with a client or former client limiting or purporting to limit the right of the client or former client to file or pursue any complaint before the Attorney Registration and Disciplinary Commission.

Louisiana adds the following prior to Rule 1.8(a): "As a general principle, all transactions between client and lawyer should be fair and reasonable to the client. Furthermore, a lawyer may not exploit his representation of a client or information relating to the representation to the client's disadvantage."

Minnesota Rule 1.8(e)(3) allows a lawyer to guarantee a loan necessary for a client to withstand litigation delay.

New Jersey Rule 1.8(a)(2) adds that the client must be "advised of the desirability of seeking independent counsel." New Jersey permits agreements prospectively limiting malpractice only when the client rejects the lawyer's advice and the lawyer continues to represent the client. The balance of Rule 1.8(h) is the same. New Jersey also adds a Rule 1.8(k) making the provisions of Rule 1.7(c) applicable to Rule 1.8. See Selected State Variations under Rule 1.7.

New York: Same or substantially the same as the ABA Model Code — see Model Code Comparison above. See DR 5-103(B)(2), DR 6-102(A), and DR 9-101(D) of the New York Code for the Model Rules' influence.

North Carolina: Rules 5.3 through 5.9 parallel the language of Rule 1.8, except that North Carolina substitutes the wording of DR 5-103 and DR 5-104 for Rules 1.8(a), (b), (d), and (e). Rule 5.4(A) adds that a lawyer "shall not enter into a business transaction with a client under any circumstances unless it is fair to the client." Rule 5.4(C) adds:

During or after a representation, a lawyer shall not enter into a business transaction with a client for which a fee or commission will be charged in lieu of, or in addition to, a legal fee, if

the business transaction is related to the subject matter of the legal representation, any financial proceeds from the representation, or any information, confidential or otherwise, acquired by the lawyer during the course of the representation.

In addition, North Carolina Rule 5.9 expressly states that disqualifications based on a
spouse or relative "shall not be construed to disqualify other lawyers in the affected lawyer's firm."

Pennsylvania Rule 1.8(a) requires the lawyer to advise the client to seek independent
advice.

Texas Rule 1.08(c) and (d) provides:

(c) Prior to the conclusion of all aspects of the matter giving rise to the lawyer's employment, a lawyer shall not make or negotiate an agreement with a client, prospective client, or
former client giving the lawyer literary or media rights to a portrayal or account based in
substantial part on information relating to the representation.

(d) A lawyer shall not provide financial assistance to a client in connection with pending
or contemplated litigation or administrative proceedings, except that:

(1) a lawyer may advance or guarantee court costs, expenses of litigation or administrative proceedings, and reasonably necessary medical and living expenses, the repayment of which may be contingent on the outcome of the matter; and

(2) a lawyer representing an indigent client may pay court costs and expenses of litigation on behalf of the client.

Virginia: Substantially the same as the Model Code.
Washington deletes Rule 1.8(e)(2).

Related Materials

ABA Canons: Canons 10, 11, and 38 provided:

10. Acquiring Interest in Litigation

The lawyer should not purchase any interest in the subject matter of the litigation which
he is conducting.

11. Dealing with Trust Property

The lawyer should refrain from any action whereby for his personal benefit or gain he
abuses or takes advantage of the confidence reposed in him by his client.

38. Compensation, Commissions and Rebates

A lawyer should accept no compensation, commissions, rebates or other advantages from
others without the knowledge and consent of his client after full disclosure.

ABA Tort and Insurance Practice Section (TIPS): In April 1991, TIPS approved
Guidelines for the Selection and Performance of Retained Counsel. The Guidelines are
reprinted in the Fall 1991 issue of The Brief. The following provisions relate to Rule
1.8(f):

c. Relationships Involving Three Parties—Attorney, Insured,
   and Insurer—Must Be Balanced with Legal and Contractual
   Obligations

Counsel is charged with a high degree of care and fidelity to the client. When counsel is retained by an insurer to represent an insured, counsel's duty is owed to both clients to the extent that the interests of each party are aligned. When the interests of the insurer and the insured conflict, counsel's primary duty is to the insured.

When counsel is retained by an insurer to represent an insured and a conflict exists between insured and insurer, counsel for the insured may not provide counsel to the insurer. All potential conflicts between insurer and insured must be identified and disclosed in detail to the insured by the insurer.

If the insurer agrees to retain counsel to defend an insured (a) under a reservation of rights to deny coverage or (b) while contending that some of the allegations asserted against the insured are not covered by the insurance policy, counsel's primary duty is to the insured. In such a case, counsel should defend the action so as to avoid prejudice to, or impairment of, the rights of the insured.

Where there are matters within the policy coverage and matters potentially outside the policy coverage, the insurer should advise the insured of the excess exposure and inform the insured of the right to retain personal counsel.

American Lawyer's Code of Conduct: Rules 5.6, 8.7, and 8.8 provide:

5.6. A lawyer shall not give money or anything of substantial value to any person in order to induce that person to become or to remain a client, or to induce that person to retain or to continue the lawyer as counsel on behalf of someone else. However, a lawyer may (a) advance money to a client on any terms that are fair; (b) give money to a client as an act of charity; (c) give money to a client to enable the client to withstand delays in litigation that would otherwise induce the client to settle a case because of financial hardship, rather than on the merits of the client's claim; or (d) charge a fee that is contingent in whole or in part on the outcome of the case.

8.7. A lawyer shall not enter into a commercial transaction or other business relationship with a person who is or was recently a client, unless that person is represented by independent counsel. This Rule does not affect the specific transactions covered by Chapter V of this Code, relating to retainer agreements and financial arrangements with clients.

8.8. A lawyer shall not commence having sexual relations with a client during the lawyer-client relationship.

Restatement of the Law Governing Lawyers: The American Law Institute has tentatively approved the following provisions:

§48. Forbidden Client-Lawyer Financial Arrangements

(1) A lawyer may not acquire a proprietary interest in the cause of action or subject matter of litigation that the lawyer is conducting for a client, except that the lawyer may:

(a) Acquire a lien as provided by §55 to secure the lawyer's fee or expenses; and

(b) Contract with a client for a contingent fee in a civil case except when prohibited as stated in §47.

(2) A lawyer may not make or guarantee a loan to a client in connection with pending or contemplated litigation that the lawyer is conducting for the client, except that the lawyer may:

(a) Advance or guarantee a loan covering court costs and expenses of litigation, the repayment of which to the lawyer may be contingent on the outcome of the matter; and

(b) Make or guaranty a loan on fair terms, the repayment of which to the lawyer may be contingent on the outcome of the matter, if the loan is needed to enable the client to withstand delay in litigation that otherwise might unjustly induce the client to settle or dismiss a case because of financial hardship rather than on the merits.

(3) A lawyer may not, before the lawyer ceases to represent a client, make an agreement giving the lawyer literary or media rights to a portrayal or account based in substantial part on information relating to the representation.

(Restatement §47 is reprinted above in the Related Materials following Model Rule 1.5.)

§55. Lawyer Liens

(1) Except as provided in Subsection (2), a lawyer does not acquire a lien entitling the lawyer to retain the client's property (including documents) in the lawyer's possession in order to secure payment of the lawyer's fee. A lawyer may decline to deliver to a client or former client an original or copy of any document prepared by the lawyer when the client or former client has not paid all fees or disbursements then due for the lawyer's work in preparing the document and nondelivery would not reasonably harm the client or former client.

(2) A client and lawyer may agree that the lawyer shall have a security interest in property of the client in the lawyer's possession or recovered for the client through the lawyer's efforts as follows:

(a) The lawyer may contract in writing with a client for a lien on the proceeds of a representation to secure payment for the lawyer's services and disbursements in that matter;

(b) The lien becomes binding on a third party when an action has been commenced and when the lawyer has given notice of the lien to that party;

(c) The lawyer may seek to withhold under the lien only the amount of fees claimed reasonably and in good faith for the lawyer's services already performed in the representation, and the lawyer may not unreasonably impede the speedy and inexpensive resolution of any dispute concerning those fees or the lien; and

(d) On request of the client or lawyer, the tribunal where the action is pending may in its discretion adjudicate any fee or other dispute concerning the lien, provide for custody of the sum, release all or part of the sum to the client or lawyer, and grant such other relief as justice may require.

(3) With respect to property neither in the lawyer's possession nor recovered by the client through the lawyer's efforts, the lawyer may obtain a security interest on property of a client only as provided by other law and consistent with §§29A and 207. Acquisition of such a security interest is a business or financial transaction with a client within the meaning of §207.

(Restatement §29A appears under Rule 1.5; §207 is reprinted below.)

§207. Business Transactions Between Lawyer and Client

A lawyer may not be involved in a business or financial transaction with a client, except a standard commercial transaction in which the lawyer does not render legal services, unless:

(1) The client knows the terms of the transaction and the risks presented by the lawyer's involvement in it;

(2) The terms and circumstances of the transaction are fair and reasonable to the client;

(3) The client consents to the lawyer's role in the transaction under the limitations and conditions provided in §202 after being encouraged and given a reasonable opportunity to seek competent, independent advice concerning the transaction; and

(4) When required by law, disclosure of the terms of the transaction and the expression of consent by the client are in writing.

(Restatement §202 is reprinted above in the Related Materials following Model Rule 1.7.)

§208. *Client Gifts to Lawyers*

A lawyer may not solicit and accept a gift from a client, including a testamentary gift, or prepare any instrument effecting any gift from a client, unless:

(1) The benefit to the lawyer is insubstantial in amount;

(2) The lawyer is a relative of the client and a natural object of the client's generosity; or

(3) The client has been encouraged and given a reasonable opportunity to seek competent, independent advice before making the gift.

§215. *Fee Payment by a Third Person*

(1) A lawyer may not represent a client under circumstances in which someone other than the client will compensate the lawyer for the representation, unless the client consents under the limitations and conditions provided in §202, with knowledge of the circumstances and conditions of the payment.

(2) A lawyer's professional judgment on behalf of a client may be materially influenced by the source or any conditions of the compensation only if the influence is reasonable in scope and character and the client expressly consents to the possible influence before the lawyer undertakes the representation.

Rule 1.9 Conflict of Interest: Former Client

Editors' Note. At its February 1989 Mid-Year Meeting, the ABA House of Delegates amended Rule 1.9 and the Comment to Rule 1.9. The amendments moved the text of former Rule 1.10(b) to Rule 1.9(b), and renumbered former Rule 1.9(b) as new Rule 1.9(c).

(a) A lawyer who has formerly represented a client in a matter shall not thereafter represent another person in the same or a substantially related matter in which that person's interests are materially adverse to the interests of the former client unless the former client consents after consultation.

(b) A lawyer shall not knowingly represent a person in the same or a substantially related matter in which a firm with which the lawyer formerly was associated had previously represented a client,

(1) whose interests are materially adverse to that person; and

(2) about whom the lawyer had acquired information protected by Rules 1.6 and 1.9(c) that is material to the matter;
unless the former client consents after consultation.

(c) A lawyer who has formerly represented a client in a matter or whose present or former firm has formerly represented a client in a matter shall not thereafter:

(1) use information relating to the representation to the disadvantage of the former client except as Rule 1.6 or Rule 3.3 would permit or require with respect to a client, or when the information has become generally known; or

(2) reveal information relating to the representation except as Rule 1.6 or Rule 3.3 would permit or require with respect to a client.

COMMENT

[1] After termination of a client-lawyer relationship, a lawyer may not represent another client except in conformity with this Rule. The principles in Rule 1.7 determine whether the interests of the present and former client are adverse. Thus, a lawyer could not properly seek to rescind on behalf of a new client a contract drafted on behalf of the former client. So also a lawyer who has prosecuted an accused person could not properly represent the accused in a subsequent civil action against the government concerning the same transaction.

[2] The scope of a "matter" for purposes of this Rule may depend on the facts of a particular situation or transaction. The lawyer's involvement in a matter can also be a question of degree. When a lawyer has been directly involved in a specific transaction, subsequent representation of other clients with materially adverse interests clearly is prohibited. On the other hand, a lawyer who recurrently handled a type of problem for a former client is not precluded from later representing another client in a wholly distinct problem of that type even though the subsequent representation involves a position adverse to the prior client. Similar considerations can apply to the reassignment of military lawyers between defense and prosecution functions within the same military jurisdiction. The underlying question is whether the lawyer was so involved in the matter that the subsequent representation can be justly regarded as a changing of sides in the matter in question.

> **Editors' Note.** Paragraphs 3 through 9 and 11 of the Comment to Rule 1.9 originally appeared as Comments 7 through 15 to Rule 1.10. In 1989, the ABA moved the substance of these comments, with minor modifications, to Rule 1.9.

Lawyers Moving Between Firms [*ABA Note:* Substance moved here from Comment to Rule 1.10.]

[3] When lawyers have been associated in a firm but then end their association, the question of whether a lawyer should undertake representation is more complicated. There are several competing considerations. First, the client previously represented by the former firm must be reasonably assured that the principle of loyalty to the client is not compromised. Second, the rule should not be so broadly cast as to

preclude other persons from having reasonable choice of legal counsel. Third, the rule should not unreasonably hamper lawyers from forming new associations and taking on new clients after having left a previous association. In this connection, it should be recognized that today many lawyers practice in firms, many to some degree limit their practice to one field or another, and many move from one association to another several times in their careers. If the concept of imputed disqualification were applied with unqualified rigor, the result would be radical curtailment of the opportunity of lawyers to move from one practice setting to another and of the opportunity of clients to change counsel.

[4] Reconciliation of these competing principles in the past has been attempted under two rubrics. One approach has been to seek per se rules of disqualification. For example, it has been held that a partner in a law firm is conclusively presumed to have access to all confidences concerning all clients of the firm. Under this analysis, if a lawyer has been a partner in one law firm and then becomes a partner in another law firm, there may be a presumption that all confidences known by a partner in the first firm are known to all partners in the second firm. This presumption might properly be applied in some circumstances, for example, where the client has been represented on many matters by numerous lawyers in the firm. This presumption may, however, be unrealistic in other circumstances, for example, where the client has been represented in a single matter of short duration by only one or two lawyers in a larger firm such that broad dissemination of client confidences within the firm is unlikely. Furthermore, such a rigid rule exaggerates the difference between a partner and an associate in modern law firms.

[5] The other rubric formerly used for dealing with disqualification is the appearance of impropriety proscribed in Canon 9 of the ABA Model Code of Professional Responsibility. This rubric has a twofold problem. First, the appearance of impropriety can be taken to include any new client-lawyer relationship that might make a former client feel anxious. If that meaning were adopted, disqualification would become little more than a question of subjective judgment by the former client. Second, since "impropriety" is undefined, the term "appearance of impropriety" is question-begging. It therefore has to be recognized that the problem of disqualification cannot be properly resolved either by simple analogy to a lawyer practicing alone or by the very general concept of appearance of impropriety.

[6] A rule based on a functional analysis is more appropriate for determining the question of disqualification. Two functions are involved: preserving confidentiality and avoiding positions adverse to a client.

Confidentiality [*ABA Note:* Substance moved here from Comment to Rule 1.10.]

[7] Preserving confidentiality is a question of access to information. Access to information, in turn, is essentially a question of fact in particular circumstances,

aided by inferences, deductions or working presumptions that reasonably may be made about the way in which lawyers work together. A lawyer may have general access to files of all clients of a law firm and may regularly participate in discussions of their affairs; it should be inferred that such a lawyer in fact is privy to all information about all the firm's clients. In contrast, another lawyer may have access to the files of only a limited number of clients and participate in discussion of the affairs of no other clients; in the absence of information to the contrary, it should be inferred that such a lawyer in fact is privy to information about the clients actually served but not those of other clients.

[8] Application of paragraph (b) depends on a situation's particular facts. In any such inquiry, the burden of proof should rest upon the firm whose disqualification is sought.

[9] Paragraph (b) operates to disqualify the lawyer only when the lawyer involved has actual knowledge of information protected by Rules 1.6 and 1.9(c). Thus, if a lawyer while with one firm acquired no knowledge of information relating to a particular client of the firm, neither the lawyer individually nor the second firm is disqualified from representing another client in the same or a related matter even though the interests of the two clients conflict. See Rule 1.10(b) for the restrictions on a firm once a lawyer has terminated association with the firm.

[10] Independent of the question of disqualification of a firm, a lawyer changing professional association has a continuing duty to preserve confidentiality of information about a client formerly represented. See Rules 1.6 and 1.9.

Adverse Positions [*ABA Note:* Substance of first paragraph moved here from Comment to Rule 1.10.]

[11] The second aspect of loyalty to client is the lawyer's obligation to decline subsequent representations involving positions adverse to a former client arising in substantially related matters. This obligation requires abstention from adverse representation by the individual lawyer involved, but does not properly entail abstention of other lawyers through imputed disqualification. Hence, this aspect of the problem is governed by Rule 1.9(a). Thus, if a lawyer left one firm for another, the new affiliation would not preclude the firms involved from continuing to represent clients with adverse interests in the same or related matters, so long as the conditions of paragraphs (b) and (c) concerning confidentiality have been met.

[12] Information acquired by the lawyer in the course of representing a client may not subsequently be revealed by the lawyer or used by the lawyer to the disadvantage of the client. However, the fact that a lawyer has once served a client does not preclude the lawyer from using generally known information about that client when later representing another client.

[13] Disqualification from subsequent representation is for the protection of clients and can be waived by them. A waiver is effective only if there is disclosure of the circumstances, including the lawyer's intended role in behalf of the new client.

[14] With regard to an opposing party's raising a question of conflict of interest, see Comment to Rule 1.7. With regard to disqualification of a firm with which a lawyer is or was formerly associated, see Rule 1.10.

Model Code Comparison

Editors' Note. The following Model Code Comparison has been revised by the editors to reflect the ABA's 1989 amendments to Rules 1.9 and 1.10.

There was no counterpart to paragraphs (a) and (c) in the Disciplinary Rules of the Model Code. The problem addressed in paragraph (a) was sometimes dealt with under the rubric of Canon 9 of the Model Code, which provided: "A lawyer should avoid even the appearance of impropriety." EC 4-6 stated that the "obligation of a lawyer to preserve the confidences and secrets of his client continues after the termination of his employment."

The provision in paragraph (a) for waiver by the former client is similar to DR 5-105(C).

The exception in the last sentence of paragraph (c) permits a lawyer to use information relating to a former client that is in the "public domain," a use that was also not prohibited by the Model Code, which protected only "confidences and secrets." Since the scope of paragraph (a) is much broader than "confidences and secrets," it is necessary to define when a lawyer may make use of information about a client after the client-lawyer relationship has terminated.

Cross-References in Rules

Terminology: "'Firm' or 'Law firm' denotes a lawyer or lawyers in a private firm, lawyers employed in the legal department of a corporation or other organization and lawyers employed in a legal services organization. See Comment, **Rule 1.9.**"

Rule 1.7, Comment 2: "Where more than one client is involved and the lawyer withdraws because a conflict arises after representation, whether the lawyer may continue to represent any of the clients is determined by **Rule 1.9.**"

Rule 1.8, Comment 5: "Related lawyers in the same firm are governed by **Rules** 1.7, **1.9,** and 1.10."

Rule 1.10(a): "While lawyers are associated in a firm, none of them shall knowingly represent a client when any one of them practicing alone would be prohibited from doing so by **Rules** 1.7, 1.8(c), **1.9** or 2.2."

Rule 1.10(b)(2): When a lawyer leaves a firm, the firm may represent interests adverse to the departed lawyer's former clients unless "any lawyer remaining in the firm has information protected by **Rules** 1.6 and **1.9(c)** that is material to the matter."

Rule 1.10, Comment 4: A lawyer who moves from government to private practice, or vice versa, "is bound by the Rules generally, including **Rules** 1.6, 1.7, and **1.9.**"

Rule 1.10, Comment 5: "The government is entitled to protection of its client confidences, and therefore to the protections provided in **Rules** 1.6, **1.9(a) and (c),** and 1.11. However, if the more extensive disqualification in Rule **1.9(b)** were applied to former government lawyers, the potential effect on the government would be unduly burdensome. . . . The government's recruitment of lawyers would be seriously impaired if **Rule 1.9(b)** were applied to the government."

Rule 1.10, Comment 6: "When a lawyer moves from one firm to another, the situation is governed by **Rules 1.9(b)** and 1.10(b)."

Rule 1.10, Comment 7: When a lawyer who represents or formerly represented a client leaves a firm, the firm may not represent a person with interests adverse to that client where the matter is the same or substantially related and "any other lawyer currently in the firm has material information protected by **Rules** 1.6 and **1.9(c).**"

Rule 1.11, Comment 1: Rule 1.11 "is a counterpart of **Rule 1.9(b),** which applies to lawyers moving from one firm to another."

Rule 1.11, Comment 2: "A lawyer representing a government agency . . . is subject to . . . the protections afforded former clients in **Rule 1.9.**"

Rule 1.17, Comment 11 provides that a lawyer selling a law practice has an "obligation to protect information relating to the representation (see **Rules** 1.6 and 1.9)."

Rule 2.2, Comment 10: In a common representation, each client "has the right to . . . the protection of **Rule 1.9** concerning obligations to a former client."

Rule 3.7(b): "A lawyer may act as advocate in a trial in which another lawyer in the lawyer's firm is likely to be called as a witness unless precluded from doing so by Rule 1.7 or **Rule 1.9.**"

Rule 3.7, Comment 5: "Whether the combination of roles involves an improper conflict of interest with respect to the client is determined by **Rule** 1.7 or **1.9.**"

Legislative History

1980 Discussion Draft: Rule 1.9(c) (then Rule 1.10(a)(2)) provided that a lawyer who has represented a client in a matter shall not thereafter "make use of information acquired in service to the client in a manner disadvantageous to the client . . . unless the information has become generally known *or accessible.*"

1981 Draft was substantially the same as adopted.

1982 Draft was adopted.

1989 Amendments: At its February 1989 Mid-Year Meeting, the ABA House of Delegates moved former Rule 1.10(b) to its current position as Rule 1.9(b), amended and renumbered former Rule 1.9(b) as current Rule 1.9(c), and made some minor amendments to the balance of Rule 1.9. The Comments to Rules 1.9 and 1.10 were changed to correspond to these amendments. The Committee Report to the House of Delegates gave the following explanation for amending Rule 1.9(c).

> The addition of explanatory language to . . . paragraph (c), is intended to eliminate another oversight in the drafting of Rule 1.9. The added language makes clear that a lawyer's duty of confidentiality with respect to former clients applies to clients who were personally represented by the lawyer and to clients who, although not personally represented by the lawyer, were represented by the lawyer's firm. In addition, a prohibition on the "revelation"

of confidential information is added to Rule 1.9. As originally drafted, Rule 1.9 prohibited only the "use" of such information to the disadvantage of the former client. . . . The Comments to Rules 1.9 and 1.10 are amended in conformity with the amendments to the black letter Rules.

Selected State Variations

California: See Rule 3.310(D) (regarding employment adverse to former clients), and B & P Code §6068(e) (regarding client confidences).

District of Columbia: Rule 1.10(b) applies only when the lawyer in question has "in fact" acquired protected information, and the rule adds the following clause relating to law students:

> The disqualification of the firm does not apply if the lawyer participated in a previous representation or acquired information under the circumstances covered by Rule 1.6(g).

District of Columbia Rule 1.6(g) provides:

> The [confidentiality] obligation of a lawyer under paragraph 1.6(a) also applies to confidences and secrets learned prior to becoming a lawyer in the course of providing assistance to another lawyer.

Illinois Rule 1.10(b) provides:

> (b) When a lawyer becomes associated with a firm, the firm may not represent a person in a matter that the firm knows or reasonably should know is the same or substantially related to a matter in which the newly associated lawyer, or a firm with which that lawyer was associated, had previously represented a client whose interests are materially adverse to that person unless:
>   (1) the newly associated lawyer has no information protected by Rule 1.6 or Rule 1.9 that is material to the matter; or
>   (2) the newly associated lawyer is screened from any participation in the matter. . . .
> (e) For purposes of Rule 1.10, Rule 1.11, and Rule 1.12, a lawyer in a firm will be deemed to have been screened from any participation in a matter if:
>   (1) the lawyer has been isolated from confidences, secrets, and material knowledge concerning the matter;
>   (2) the lawyer has been isolated from all contact with the client or any agent, officer, or employee of the client and any witness for or against the client;
>   (3) the lawyer and the firm have been precluded from discussing the matter with each other; and
>   (4) the firm has taken affirmative steps to accomplish the foregoing.

Michigan and *Pennsylvania* also permit screening of transient lawyers who would otherwise disqualify a firm.

New Jersey adds the following language in Rule 1.10(d): "When lawyers terminate an association in a firm, none of them, nor any other lawyer with whom any of them subsequently becomes associated shall knowingly represent a client when doing so involves a material risk of violating Rule 1.6 or 1.9." Rule 1.9(a) requires "a full disclosure of the circumstances" to the former client as a condition of consent. Rule 1.9(c) applies New Jersey's Rule 1.7(c) to Rule 1.9. See Rule 1.7, Selected State Variations.

New York: Amendments to the New York version of the Code substantially adopt the provisions of Rule 1.9(a) and (c). See New York Code DR 5-105(D) and DR 5-108.

Oregon permits screening but requires "the personally disqualified lawyer" and his or her firm to serve affidavits at the outset and, on request, the conclusion of the matter attesting to the screen and its observance. DR 5-105(F).

Texas Rule 1.09 provides:

(a) Without prior consent, a lawyer who personally has formerly represented a client in a matter shall not thereafter represent another person in a matter adverse to the former client:

(1) in which such other person questions the validity of the lawyer's services or work product for the former client;

(2) if the representation in reasonable probability will involve a violation of Rule 1.05; or

(3) if it is the same or a substantially related matter.

Virginia retains the language of DR 5-105.

Related Materials

ABA Canons: Canon 37 provided:

37. Confidences of a Client

It is the duty of a lawyer to preserve his client's confidences. This duty outlasts the lawyer's employment. . . .

ABA Standards for Imposing Lawyer Discipline: See Standard 4.3 in the Related Materials following Model Rule 1.7.

American Lawyer's Code of Conduct: Rule 8.3 provides:

When a lawyer has represented a client, or when, because of the lawyer's association with a law firm, a client of that firm could reasonably believe that the lawyer has had access to the client's confidences, the lawyer shall not thereafter accept employment by any other party whose interests are in any way adverse to the client's and could be materially affected by the lawyer's presumed knowledge of the client's confidences.

Restatement of the Law Governing Lawyers: The American Law Institute has tentatively approved the following provision:

§213. Representation Contrary to the Interest of a Former Client

Unless both the affected present and former clients consent to the representation under the limitations and conditions provided in §202, a lawyer who has represented a client in a matter may not thereafter represent another client with interests materially adverse to interests of the former client in the same or a substantially related matter. A current matter is substantially related to an earlier matter if:

(1) The current matter involves the work the lawyer performed for the former client; or

(2) There is a substantial risk that representation of the present client will involve the use of confidential information of the former client in violation of §111.

(Restatement §111 is reprinted above in the Related Materials following Model Rule 1.6; §202 follows Model Rule 1.7.)

Rule 1.10 Imputed Disqualification: General Rule

Editors' Note. At its February 1989 Mid-Year Meeting, the ABA House of Delegates amended Rule 1.10 and the Comment to Rule 1.10. The essence of the amendments was to move the text of former Rule 1.10(b) to Rule 1.9(b), change Rule 1.9(b) to 1.9(c), and renumber former Rules 1.10(c) and (d) as new Rules 1.10(b) and (c).

(a) While lawyers are associated in a firm, none of them shall knowingly represent a client when any one of them practicing alone would be prohibited from doing so by Rules 1.7, 1.8(c), 1.9 or 2.2.

(b) When a lawyer has terminated an association with a firm, the firm is not prohibited from thereafter representing a person with interests materially adverse to those of a client represented by the formerly associated lawyer, and not currently represented by the firm, unless:

(1) the matter is the same or substantially related to that in which the formerly associated lawyer represented the client; and

(2) any lawyer remaining in the firm has information protected by Rules 1.6 and 1.9(c) that is material to the matter.

(c) A disqualification prescribed by this rule may be waived by the affected client under the conditions stated in Rule 1.7.

COMMENT

Definition of "Firm"

[1] For purposes of the Rules of Professional Conduct, the term "firm" includes lawyers in a private firm, and lawyers employed in the legal department of a corporation or other organization, or in a legal services organization. Whether two or more lawyers constitute a firm within this definition can depend on the specific facts. For example, two practitioners who share office space and occasionally consult or assist each other ordinarily would not be regarded as constituting a firm. However, if they present themselves to the public in a way suggesting that they are a firm or conduct themselves as a firm, they should be regarded as a firm for purposes of the Rules. The terms of any formal agreement between associated lawyers are relevant in determining whether they are a firm, as is the fact that they have mutual access to confidential information concerning the clients they serve. Furthermore, it is relevant in doubtful cases to consider the underlying purpose of the rule that is involved. A group of lawyers could be regarded as a firm for purposes of the rule that the same lawyer should not represent opposing parties in litigation, while it might not be so regarded for purposes of the rule that information acquired by one lawyer is attributed to another.

[2] With respect to the law department of an organization, there is ordinarily no question that the members of the department constitute a firm within the meaning of the Rules of Professional Conduct. However, there can be uncertainty as to the identity of the client. For example, it may not be clear whether the law department of a corporation represents a subsidiary or an affiliated corporation, as well as the corporation by which the members of the department are directly employed. A similar question can arise concerning an unincorporated association and its local affiliates.

[3] Similar questions can also arise with respect to lawyers in legal aid. Lawyers employed in the same unit of a legal service organization constitute a firm, but not necessarily those employed in separate units. As in the case of independent practitioners, whether the lawyers should be treated as associated with each other can depend on the particular rule that is involved, and on the specific facts of the situation.

[4] Where a lawyer has joined a private firm after having represented the government, the situation is governed by Rule 1.11(a) and (b); where a lawyer represents the government after having served private clients, the situation is governed by Rule 1.11(c)(1). The individual lawyer involved is bound by the Rules generally, including Rules 1.6, 1.7, and 1.9.

[5] Different provisions are thus made for movement of a lawyer from one private firm to another and for movement of a lawyer between a private firm and the government. The government is entitled to protection of its client confidences, and therefore to the protections provided in Rules 1.6, 1.9(a) and (c), and 1.11. However, if the more extensive disqualification in Rule 1.9(b) were applied to former government lawyers, the potential effect on the government would be unduly burdensome. The government deals with all private citizens and organizations, and thus has a much wider circle of adverse legal interests than does any private law firm. In these circumstances, the government's recruitment of lawyers would be seriously impaired if Rule 1.9(b) were applied to the government. On balance, therefore, the government is better served in the long run by the protections stated in Rule 1.11.

Principles of Imputed Disqualification

[6] The rule of imputed disqualification stated in paragraph (a) gives effect to the principle of loyalty to the client as it applies to lawyers who practice in a law firm. Such situations can be considered from the premise that a firm of lawyers is essentially one lawyer for purposes of the rules governing loyalty to the client, or from the premise that each lawyer is vicariously bound by the obligation of loyalty owed by each lawyer with whom the lawyer is associated. Paragraph (a) operates only among the lawyers currently associated in a firm. When a lawyer moves from one firm to another, the situation is governed by Rules 1.9(b) and 1.10(b).

Editors' Note. The following paragraph (paragraph 7) was added by the ABA House of Delegates in 1989.

[7] Rule 1.10(b) operates to permit a law firm, under certain circumstances, to represent a person with interests directly adverse to those of a client represented by a lawyer who formerly was associated with the firm. The Rule applies regardless of when the formerly associated lawyer represented the client. However, the law firm may not represent a person with interests adverse to those of a present client of the firm, which would violate Rule 1.7. Moreover, the firm may not represent the person where the matter is the same or substantially related to that in which the formerly associated lawyer represented the client and any other lawyer currently in the firm has material information protected by Rules 1.6 and 1.9(c).

Editors' Note. At its February 1989 Mid-Year Meeting, the ABA moved the substance of the remaining paragraphs of the original Comment to Rule 1.10 (then paragraphs 7 through 15) to the Comment to Rule 1.9.

Model Code Comparison

DR 5-105(D) provided that "[i]f a lawyer is required to decline or to withdraw from employment under a Disciplinary Rule, no partner, or associate, or any other lawyer affiliated with him or his firm, may accept or continue such employment."

Cross-References in Rules

Rule 1.8, Comment 5: "Related lawyers in the same firm are governed by **Rules** 1.7, 1.9, and **1.10.**"

Rule 1.9, Comment 9: "See **Rule 1.10(b)** for the restrictions on a firm once a lawyer has terminated association with the firm."

Rule 1.9, Comment 14: "With regard to disqualification of a firm with which a lawyer is or was formerly associated, see **Rule 1.10.**"

Rule 3.7, Comment 4: "The principle of imputed disqualification in **Rule 1.10** has no application to" the problem addressed in Rule 3.7(a)(3).

Rule 3.7, Comment: "If a lawyer who is a member of a firm may not act as both advocate and witness by reason of conflict of interest, **Rule 1.10** disqualifies the firm also."

Legislative History

1980 Discussion Draft had no comparable provision on imputed disqualification.
1981 Draft:

(b) When lawyers terminate an association in a firm, none of them, nor any other lawyer with whom any of them subsequently become associated, shall undertake or continue representation that involves a material risk of revealing information relating to representation of a client in violation of Rule 1.6, or of making use of information to the disadvantage of a former client in violation of Rule 1.9.

1982 Draft:

(b) When lawyers terminate an association in a firm, none of them, nor any other lawyer with whom any of them subsequently becomes associated, shall knowingly represent a client when doing so involves a material risk of violating Rule 1.6 or Rule 1.9.

1989 Amendments: At its 1989 Mid-Year Meeting, the House of Delegates amended Rule 1.10 by moving former Rule 1.10(b) to its current position as Rule 1.9(b), by moving former Rule 1.10(c) to current Rule 1.10(b), by adding a phrase to new Rule 1.10(b), and by moving former Rule 1.10(d) to its current position as Rule 1.10(c). An excerpt from the Committee Report explaining the changes is reprinted in the Legislative History following Rule 1.9. The Committee's explanation regarding the amendment to former Rule 1.10(c) states:

Paragraph (c) (now paragraph (b)) of Rule 1.10 was never intended to permit the representation of a client whose interests are directly adverse to the interests of a present client of a firm. Such representation would violate Rule 1.7. In order to make it clear that when a lawyer leaves a law firm, this paragraph does not override the proscription in Rule 1.7, the limiting words "and not currently represented by the firm" are proposed to be added to Rule 1.10(b).

Selected State Variations

California: See Rule 3-310(A) and 3-310(D) (Avoiding the Representation of Adverse Interests).

Illinois extends the prohibition of Rule 1.10(a) to any lawyer who "knows or reasonably should know" that another lawyer in the firm is disqualified. Illinois also adds a new provision, Rule 1.10(e), to define "screened." This new provision is quoted in the Selected State Variations following Rule 1.9.

New Jersey adds the following Rule 1.10(e):

A disqualification prescribed by this rule may be waived by the affected client under the conditions stated in Rule 1.7 except where prohibited by law or regulation, such as the prohibition against a public entity waiving an attorney conflict of interest.

New York: For New York's imputed disqualification rule, see DR 5-105(D).

North Carolina: Rule 5.11(A) imputes disqualification to all lawyers in a firm when any one of them practicing alone would be disqualified "by the Rules of Professional Conduct, unless otherwise specifically provided herein." Rule 5.11(C) parallels Model Rule 1.10(b) but omits the phrase, "and not currently represented by the firm."

Texas Rule 1.09 provides:

(b) Except to the extent authorized by Rule 1.10 [concerning government lawyers], when lawyers are or have become members of or associated with a firm, none of them shall knowingly represent a client if any one of them practicing alone would be prohibited from doing so by paragraph (a).

(c) When the association of a lawyer with a firm has terminated, the lawyers who were then associated with that lawyer shall not knowingly represent a client if the lawyer whose association with that firm has terminated would be prohibited from doing so by paragraph (a)(1) or if the representation in reasonable probability will involve a violation of Rule 1.05.

Virginia: Substantially the same as the Model Code.

Related Materials

Model Rules of Professional Conduct for Federal Lawyers: Rule 1.10(a) provides that "Government lawyers working in the same Federal Agency are not automatically disqualified from representing a client because any of them practicing alone would be prohibited from doing so by Rules 1.7, 1.8(c), 1.9 or 2.2." The Comment states:

> The circumstances of Government service may require representation of opposing sides by Government lawyers working in the same Federal Agency. Such representation is permissible so long as conflicts of interest are avoided and independent judgment, zealous representation, and protection of client confidences are not compromised. Thus, the principle of imputed disqualification is not automatically controlling for Government lawyers. The knowledge, action, and conflicts of interest of one Government lawyer are not to be imputed to another simply because they operate from the same office. . . .

Restatement of the Law Governing Lawyers: The American Law Institute has tentatively approved the following provisions:

§203. Imputation of Conflicts of Interest to Affiliated Lawyers

Unless all affected clients consent to the representation under the limitations and conditions provided in §202 or unless imputation hereunder is removed as provided in §204, the restrictions upon a lawyer imposed by §§207-214 also restrict other lawyers who:
    (1) Are associated with that lawyer in rendering legal services to others through a law partnership, professional corporation, sole proprietorship, or similar association;
    (2) Are employed with that lawyer by an organization to render legal services either to that organization or to others to advance the interests of the organizaiton; or
    (3) Share office space under circumstances that fail to assure that confidential client information will not be available to other lawyers in the shared office.

§204. Removing Imputation

The restrictions upon an affiliated lawyer specified in §203 do not restrict that lawyer when:
    (1) The affiliation between the lawyer and the personally-prohibited lawyer that created the imputed prohibition has been terminated and no confidential information of the client, material to the matter, has been communicated to the lawyer or any other lawyer who remains affiliated with the lawyer;
    (2) The restriction is of representation adverse to a former client as provided in §213 and there is no reasonable prospect that confidential information of the former client will be used with material adverse effect on the former client because:
        (a) The confidential client information communicated to the personally-prohibited lawyer is not likely to be significant in the later case;
        (b) Adequate screening measures are in effect to eliminate involvement by the personally-prohibited lawyer in the representation; and

(c) Timely and adequate notice of the screening has been provided to all affected clients; or

(3) The restriction is of a representation prohibited as provided in §214 and:

(a) Adequate screening measures are in effect to eliminate involvement by the personally-prohibited lawyer in the representation; and

(b) Timely and adequate notice of the screening has been provided to the appropriate government agency.

(Restatement §202 is reprinted in the Related Materials following Rule 1.7; §§207-214 are reprinted following Rules 1.8, 1.9, 1.11, and 1.13; the phrase "confidential client information" is defined in Restatement §111, reprinted following Rule 1.6.)

Rule 1.11 Successive Government and Private Employment

(a) Except as law may otherwise expressly permit, a lawyer shall not represent a private client in connection with a matter in which the lawyer participated personally and substantially as a public officer or employee, unless the appropriate government agency consents after consultation. No lawyer in a firm with which that lawyer is associated may knowingly undertake or continue representation in such a matter unless:

(1) the disqualified lawyer is screened from any participation in the matter and is apportioned no part of the fee therefrom; and

(2) written notice is promptly given to the appropriate government agency to enable it to ascertain compliance with the provisions of this rule.

(b) Except as law may otherwise expressly permit, a lawyer having information that the lawyer knows is confidential government information about a person acquired when the lawyer was a public officer or employee, may not represent a private client whose interests are adverse to that person in a matter in which the information could be used to the material disadvantage of that person. A firm with which that lawyer is associated may undertake or continue representation in the matter only if the disqualified lawyer is screened from any participation in the matter and is apportioned no part of the fee therefrom.

(c) Except as law may otherwise expressly permit, a lawyer serving as a public officer or employee shall not:

(1) participate in a matter in which the lawyer participated personally and substantially while in private practice or nongovernmental employment, unless under applicable law no one is, or by lawful delegation may be, authorized to act in the lawyer's stead in the matter; or

(2) negotiate for private employment with any person who is involved as a party or as attorney for a party in a matter in which the lawyer is participating personally and substantially, except that a lawyer serving as a law clerk to a judge, other adjudicative officer or arbitrator may negotiate for private employment as permitted by Rule 1.12(b) and subject to the conditions stated in Rule 1.12(b).

(d) As used in this rule, the term "matter" includes:

(1) any judicial or other proceeding, application, request for a ruling or other determination, contract, claim, controversy, investigation, charge, accusation, arrest or other particular matter involving a specific party or parties; and

(2) any other matter covered by the conflict of interest rules of the appropriate government agency.

(e) As used in this rule, the term "confidential government information" means information which has been obtained under governmental authority and which, at the time this rule is applied, the government is prohibited by law from disclosing to the public or has a legal privilege not to disclose, and which is not otherwise available to the public.

COMMENT

[1] This Rule prevents a lawyer from exploiting public office for the advantage of a private client. It is a counterpart of Rule 1.9(b), which applies to lawyers moving from one firm to another.

[2] A lawyer representing a government agency, whether employed or specially retained by the government, is subject to the Rules of Professional Conduct, including the prohibition against representing adverse interests stated in Rule 1.7 and the protections afforded former clients in Rule 1.9. In addition, such a lawyer is subject to Rule 1.11 and to statutes and government regulations regarding conflict of interest. Such statutes and regulations may circumscribe the extent to which the government agency may give consent under this Rule.

[3] Where the successive clients are a public agency and a private client, the risk exists that power or discretion vested in public authority might be used for the special benefit of a private client. A lawyer should not be in a position where benefit to a private client might affect performance of the lawyer's professional functions on behalf of public authority. Also, unfair advantage could accrue to the private client by reason of access to confidential government information about the client's adversary obtainable only through the lawyer's government service. However, the rules governing lawyers presently or formerly employed by a government agency should not be so restrictive as to inhibit transfer of employment to and from the government. The government has a legitimate need to attract qualified lawyers as well as to maintain high ethical standards. The provisions for screening and waiver are necessary to prevent the disqualification rule from imposing too severe a deterrent against entering public service.

[4] When the client is an agency of one government, that agency should be treated as a private client for purposes of this Rule if the lawyer thereafter represents an agency of another government, as when a lawyer represents a city and subsequently is employed by a federal agency.

[5] Paragraphs (a)(1) and (b)(1) do not prohibit a lawyer from receiving a salary or partnership share established by prior independent agreement. They

prohibit directly relating the attorney's compensation to the fee in the matter in which the lawyer is disqualified.

[6] Paragraph (a)(2) does not require that a lawyer give notice to the government agency at a time when premature disclosure would injure the client; a requirement for premature disclosure might preclude engagement of the lawyer. Such notice is, however, required to be given as soon as practicable in order that the government agency or affected person will have a reasonable opportunity to ascertain that the lawyer is complying with Rule 1.11 and to take appropriate action if they believe the lawyer is not complying.

[7] Paragraph (b) operates only when the lawyer in question has knowledge of the information, which means actual knowledge; it does not operate with respect to information that merely could be imputed to the lawyer.

[8] Paragraphs (a) and (c) do not prohibit a lawyer from jointly representing a private party and a government agency when doing so is permitted by Rule 1.7 and is not otherwise prohibited by law.

[9] Paragraph (c) does not disqualify other lawyers in the agency with which the lawyer in question has become associated.

Model Code Comparison

Paragraph (a) is similar to DR 9-101(B), except that the latter used the terms "in which he had substantial responsibility while he was a public employee."

Paragraphs (b), (c), (d), and (e) have no counterparts in the Model Code.

Cross-References in Rules

Rule 1.10, Comment 4: "Where a lawyer has joined a private firm after having represented the government, the situation is governed by **Rule 1.11(a) and (b)**; where a lawyer represents the government after having served private clients, the situation is governed by **Rule 1.11(c)(1)**."

Rule 1.10, Comment 5: "The government is entitled to protection of its client confidences, and therefore to the protections provided in **Rules** 1.6, 1.9(a) and (c), and **1.11**. However, if the more extensive disqualification in Rule 1.9(b) were applied to former government lawyers, the potential effect on the government would be unduly burdensome. . . . [O]n balance, therefore, the government is better served in the long run by the protections stated in Rule **1.11**."

Rule 1.12, Comment 1: "This Rule generally parallels Rule **1.11**. . . . Compare the Comment to Rule **1.11**."

Legislative History

1980 Discussion Draft:

... (e) If a lawyer is required by this rule to decline representation on account of personal and substantial participation in a matter, except where the participation was as a judicial law clerk, no lawyer in a firm with the disqualified lawyer may accept such employment. ...

1981 and 1982 Drafts were substantially the same as adopted.

Selected State Variations

California has no direct counterpart.
District of Columbia: Rule 1.11 provides:

(a) A lawyer shall not accept other employment in connection with a matter which is the same as, or substantially related to, a matter in which the lawyer participated personally and substantially as a public officer or employee. Such participation includes acting on the merits of a matter in a judicial or other adjudicative capacity.

(b) If a lawyer is required to decline or to withdraw from employment under Paragraph (a) on account of personal and substantial participation in a matter, no partner or associate of that lawyer, or lawyer with an of counsel relationship to that lawyer, may accept or continue such employment except as provided in Paragraphs (c) and (d) below. The disqualification of such other lawyers does not apply if the sole form of participation was as a judicial law clerk.

(c) The prohibition stated in Paragraph (b) shall not apply if the personally disqualified lawyer is screened from any form of participation in the matter or representation as the case may be, and from sharing in any fees resulting therefrom, and if the requirements of Paragraphs (d) and (e) are satisfied.

(d) Except as provided in Paragraph (e), when any of counsel, lawyer, partner or associate of a lawyer personally disqualified under Paragraph (a) accepts employment in connection with a matter giving rise to the personal disqualification, the following notifications shall be required:

(1) The personally disqualified lawyer shall submit to the public department or agency by which the lawyer was formerly employed and serve on each other party to any pertinent proceeding a signed document attesting that during the period of disqualification the personally disqualified lawyer will not participate in any manner in the matter or the representation, will not discuss the matter or the representation with any partner, associate, or of counsel lawyer, and will not share in any fees for the matter or the representation.

(2) At least one affiliated lawyer shall submit to the same department or agency and serve on the same parties a signed document attesting that all affiliated lawyers are aware of the requirement that the personally disqualified lawyer be screened from participating in or discussing the matter or the representation and describing the procedures being taken to screen the personally disqualified lawyer.

(e) If a client requests in writing that the fact and subject matter of a representation subject to Paragraph (d) not be disclosed by submitting the signed statements referred to in Paragraph (d), such statements shall be prepared concurrently with undertaking the representation and filed with bar counsel under seal. If at any time thereafter the fact and subject matter of the representation are disclosed to the public or become a part of the public record, the signed statements previously prepared shall be promptly submitted as required by Paragraph (d).

(f) Signed documents filed pursuant to Paragraph (d) shall be available to the public, except to the extent that a lawyer submitting a signed document demonstrates to the satisfaction of the public department or agency upon which such documents are served that public disclosure is inconsistent with Rule 1.6 or provisions of law.

(g) As used in this Rule, a "matter" is any judicial or other proceeding, application, request for a ruling or other determination, contract, claim, controversy, investigation, charge, accusation, arrest or other particular matter involving a specific party or parties.

(h) A lawyer who participates in a program of temporary service to the Office of Corporation Counsel of the kind described in Rule 1.10(e) shall be treated as having served as a public officer or employee for purposes of paragraph (a), and the provisions of paragraphs (b)-(e) shall apply to the lawyer and to lawyers affiliated with the lawyer.

Subparagraph (h) is new and "is being adopted on a trial basis," effective February 1, 1992, to January 31, 1994. The adoption of Rule 1.11(h) was accompanied by new comments 19-23 to Rule 1.10 and new comments 12-13 to Rule 1.11 of the D.C. Rules. Comment 19 to Rule 1.10 explains:

> The [D.C.] Office of Corporation Counsel may experience periods of peak need for legal services which cannot be met by normal hiring programs, or may experience problems in dealing with a large backlog of matters requiring legal services. In such circumstances, the public interest is served by permitting private firms to provide the services of lawyers affiliated with such private firms on a temporary basis to assist the Office of Corporation Counsel. Such arrangements do not fit within the classical pattern of situations involving the general imputation rule of [Rule 1.10(a)]. Provided that safeguards are in place which preclude the improper disclosure of client confidences or secrets, and the improper use of one client's confidences or secrets on behalf of another client, the public interest benefits of such arrangements justify an exception to the general imputation rule. . . .

Illinois: Rule 1.11(a) covers any lawyer who knows "or reasonably should know" of the former government lawyer's prior participation. Rules 1.11(a)(1) and 1.11(b) condition the exceptions on apportioning the disqualified lawyer "no specific share" of the fee.

New Hampshire adds a Rule 1.11A dealing with the responsibilities of "a lawyer actively engaged in the practice of law, who is a member of [a] governmental body."

New Jersey Rules 1.11(a) and 1.11(b) provide:

> (a) Except as law may otherwise expressly permit, a lawyer shall not represent a private client in connection with a matter (i) in which the lawyer participated personally and substantially as a public officer or employee, (ii) about which the lawyer acquired knowledge of confidential information as a public officer or employee, or (iii) for which the lawyer had substantial responsibility as a public officer or employee.
>
> (b) An appearance of impropriety may arise from a lawyer representing a private client in connection with a matter that relates to the lawyer's former employment as public officer or employee even if the lawyer did not personally and substantially participate in it, have actual knowledge of it, or substantial responsibility for it. In such an event, the lawyer may not represent a private client, but a firm with which that lawyer is associated may undertake or continue representation if: (1) the disqualified lawyer is screened from any participation in the matter and is apportioned no part of the fee therefrom, and (2) written notice is promptly given to the appropriate government agency to enable it to ascertain compliance with the provisions of this rule.

New York: DR 9-101(B) of the New York Code substantially adopts language from Rule 1.11(a), (b), and (c), with modifications.

North Carolina: Rule 9.1 does not allow a law firm to escape from imputed disqualification by using screens, but does permit other lawyers in a firm to undertake a representation with "the consent of the public agency involved" in circumstances covered by Model Rule 1.11(a), or "with the consent of the person about whom the [confidential government] information was obtained" in circumstances covered by Model Rule 1.11(b).

Texas Rule 1.10(f) specifically excludes "regulation-making" and "rule-making" from the definition of "matter".

Virginia: Substantially the same as the Model Code.

Related Materials

American Lawyer's Code of Conduct: Rules 9.14 through 9.21 provide:

9.14. A lawyer shall not accept private employment relating to any matter in which the lawyer participated personally and substantially while in public service.

9.15. When a lawer is disqualified from representing a client under Rule 9.14, no partner or associate of the lawyer, and no one with an of counsel relationship to the lawyer, shall represent the client.

9.16. A lawyer in public service shall not participate in any matter in which the lawyer participated personally and substantially in private practice.

9.17. While a lawyer in public service is participating personally and substantially in a matter in which a private attorney's client has a material interest, neither lawyer shall comment to the other about the government lawyer's private employment possibilities.

Supplementary Provisions [to the American Lawyer's Code of Conduct]*

9.18. For one year after leaving public service, a lawyer shall not counsel or otherwise represent a client who was previously involved in any matter in which the lawyer participated personally and substantially within one year prior to leaving public service.

9.19. For one year after leaving public service, a lawyer shall not become a partner or associate of, or have an of counsel relationship with, any law firm that represented an interested party in any matter in which the lawyer participated personally and substantially within one year prior to leaving public service.

9.20. For one year after entering public service, a lawyer shall not participate in any matter in which an interested party was the lawyer's client within one year before the lawyer entered public service, or in which an interested party is represented by a lawyer who was the partner or associate of, or had an of counsel relationship to, the lawyer within one year before the lawyer entered public service, unless (a) the lawyer was appointed to office by the chief executive officer of the jurisdiction, with approval of a legislative body, or (b) the lawyer's participation is approved by a superior who was appointed by the chief executive officer with approval of a legislative body, or (c) the lawyer was elected to office.

9.21. When a lawyer is disqualified from representing a client under Rules 9.18 or 9.19, no partner or associate of the lawyer, and no one of counsel to the lawyer, shall represent the client.

Comment to Rules 9.14-9.21

. . . The principal argument in favor of permitting a screening-waiver device is that the government would find it impossible to hire competent lawyers if the screening-waiver exception is rejected, because lawyers would fear becoming unemployable. But if concern over the denial of waivers would indeed result in the unemployability of former government lawyers, that problem would prevail as long as there were any significant risk that waivers would be denied in particular cases. That is, unless the waiver device

---

*These provisions have not been approved by the Commission, principally because of concern about their effect in smaller communities served by very few lawyers. [Footnote in original. — EDS.]

were a sham, and waivers were to be granted as a matter of course whenever requested, the asserted risks of hiring former government employees would still discourage law firms from employing them, and would thus discourage lawyers from entering government service.

In fact, however, no instance has ever been given of a government employee who would be rendered unemployable by the rejection of a waiver-screening exception. Unquestionably, a particular lawyer might have to forgo employment with a particular law firm, or even with three or four firms, but that is hardly the sweeping effect that has been projected by opponents of the ethical rule.

It should be emphasized, however, that these rules are not motivated by disapproval of the so-called revolving door between government service and private practice, but by the serious likelihood of professional impropriety inherent in the lawyer's switching from one side to the other.

In addition to dealing with the problem of the lawyer who switches sides in the same matter, these rules seek also to discourage the situation in which a lawyer is representing the government's interests and, at the same time, may be contemplating leaving government service and going to work for a party or a law firm whose interests the government lawyer is able to affect. Because it is easy for understandings of future employment to be reached without any realistic opportunity to discover or to prove that to have been the case, the Supplementary Provisions establish time bars to employment of former government lawyers by some parties and firms in some circumstances.

"Confidential government information": Model Rule 1.11(e) defines "confidential government information" to include information the government is "prohibited by law from disclosing" or "has a legal privilege not to disclose, " *and* (having satisfied one of those two criteria) that also is "not otherwise available to the public." As to prohibitions, various federal statutes prohibit disclosure — see, e.g., the Privacy Act, 5 U.S.C. §552a, and the Trade Secrets Act, 18 U.S.C. §1905. As to privileges, the government has successfully claimed various privileges under Federal Rule of Evidence 501, including the executive privilege, the deliberate privilege, the national security privilege, and the attorney-client privilege. As to availability to the public, the Freedom of Information Act (FOIA), 5 U.S.C. §552, makes a broad range of government information available to the public on demand.

"Revolving door" provisions: Rule 1.11(d)(2) refers to "the conflict of interest rules of the appropriate government agency." All former lawyers for the federal government are covered by the "revolving door" provision in 18 U.S.C. §207 (reprinted in this volume at pages 563-565), which prohibits former government lawyers from opposing the government, either directly or in matters in which the government has "a direct and substantial interest," for two years after leaving government, if the lawyer was involved in the matter while in federal government service. See 5 C.F.R. §2637 for the general implementation of 18 U.S.C. §207. In addition, several agencies of the federal government have their own "revolving door" provisions. See e.g., 45 C.F.R. §680 (National Science Foundation), 32 C.F.R. §1690 (Selective Service System), 22 C.F.R. §18 (Foreign Service). Many states have enacted parallel provisions.

Restatement of the Law Governing Lawyers: The American Law Institute has tentatively approved the following provision:

§214. Former Government Lawyer or Officer

A lawyer may not act on behalf of a client with respect to a matter in which the lawyer was personally and substantially involved while acting as a government lawyer or officer unless both the government and the client consent to the representation under the limitations and conditions provided in §202.

(Restatement §202 is reprinted above in the Related Materials following Model Rule 1.7.)

Rule 1.12 Former Judge or Arbitrator

(a) Except as stated in paragraph (d), a lawyer shall not represent anyone in connection with a matter in which the lawyer participated personally and substantially as a judge or other adjudicative officer, arbitrator or law clerk to such a person, unless all parties to the proceeding consent after consultation.

(b) A lawyer shall not negotiate for employment with any person who is involved as a party or as attorney for a party in a matter in which the lawyer is participating personally and substantially as a judge or other adjudicative officer, or arbitrator. A lawyer serving as a law clerk to a judge, other adjudicative officer or arbitrator may negotiate for employment with a party or attorney involved in a matter in which the clerk is participating personally and substantially, but only after the lawyer has notified the judge, other adjudicative officer or arbitrator.

(c) If a lawyer is disqualified by paragraph (a), no lawyer in a firm with which that lawyer is associated may knowingly undertake or continue representation in the matter unless:

(1) the disqualified lawyer is screened from any participation in the matter and is apportioned no part of the fee therefrom; and

(2) written notice is promptly given to the appropriate tribunal to enable it to ascertain compliance with the provisions of this rule.

(d) An arbitrator selected as a partisan of a party in a multi-member arbitration panel is not prohibited from subsequently representing that party.

COMMENT

This Rule generally parallels Rule 1.11. The term "personally and substantially" signifies that a judge who was a member of a multimember court, and thereafter left judicial office to practice law, is not prohibited from representing a client in a matter pending in the court, but in which the former judge did not participate. So also the fact that a former judge exercised administrative responsibility in a court does not prevent the former judge from acting as a lawyer in a matter where the judge had previously exercised remote or incidental administrative responsibility that did not affect the merits. Compare the Comment to Rule 1.11. The term "adjudicative officer" includes such officials as judges pro tempore, referees, special masters, hearing officers and other parajudicial officers, and also lawyers who serve as part-time judges. Compliance Canons A (2), B (2) and C of the Model Code of Judicial Conduct provide that a part-time judge, judge pro tempore or retired judge recalled to active service, may not "act as a lawyer in any proceeding in which he served as a judge or in any other proceeding related thereto." Although phrased differently from this Rule, those rules correspond in meaning.

Model Code Comparison

Paragraph (a) is substantially similar to DR 9-101(A), which provided that a lawyer "shall not accept private employment in a matter upon the merits of which he has acted in a judicial capacity." Paragraph (a) differs, however, in that it is broader in scope and states more specifically the persons to whom it applies. There was no counterpart in the Model Code to paragraphs (b), (c), or (d).

With regard to arbitrators, EC 5-20 stated that "a lawyer [who] has undertaken to act as an impartial arbitrator or mediator, . . . should not thereafter represent in the dispute any of the parties involved." DR 9-101(A) did not permit a waiver of the disqualification applied to former judges by consent of the parties. However, DR 5-105(C) was similar in effect and could be construed to permit waiver.

Cross-References in Rules

None.

Legislative History

1980 Discussion Draft (then Rules 1.11(d), 1.11(e), and 1.11(f)):

> (d) A lawyer who has served as a judge in an adjudicatory proceeding shall not thereafter represent anyone in connection with the subject matter of the proceeding.
> (e) If a lawyer is required by this rule to decline representation on account of personal and substantial participation in a matter, except where the participation was as a judicial law clerk, no lawyer in a firm with the disqualified lawyer may accept such employment.
> (f) . . . The disqualification stated in paragraph (d) may be waived by the consent of all parties to the adjudication.

1981 and 1982 Drafts: Substantially the same as adopted.

Selected State Variations

California has no direct counterpart to Rule 1.12.

District of Columbia: Rule 1.12(a) omits reference to judges and deletes subparagraphs 1.12(b) and (c).

Illinois: Rule 1.12(c) covers any lawyer who "knows or reasonably should know" of the former judge's or arbitrator's disqualification. Rule 1.12(c)(1) requires that the disqualified lawyer receive "no specific share" of the fee.

New Jersey deletes Rule 1.12(c).

New York: Same or substantially the same as the ABA Model Code — see Model Code Comparison above — except see New York Materials for New York's version of DR 5-105(D).
Virginia: Substantially the same as the Model Code.

Related Materials

ABA Canons: Canon 36 provided:

36. Retirement from Judicial Position of Public Employment

> A lawyer should not accept employment as an advocate in any matter upon the merits of which he has previously acted in a judicial capacity.
>
> A lawyer, having once held public office or having been in the public employ, should not after his retirement accept employment in connection with any matter which he has investigated or passed upon while in such office or employ.

Restatement of the Law Governing Lawyers: The American Law Institute has tentatively approved §204 explaining general methods of removing imputation. Section 204 is reprinted in the Related Materials following Model Rule 1.10.

Code of Conduct for Law Clerks: In a student piece entitled Ethics for Judicial Clerks, 4 Geo. L.J. 771, 786-790 (1991), the author proposes a Code of Conduct for Law Clerks. Proposed Canon 3(D) of this Code, which relates to Model Rule 1.12(b), provides:

> A law clerk should inform the appointing judge of any circumstance or activity of the law clerk that might serve as a basis for disqualification of the judge, e.g., a prospective employment relation with a law firm, association of the law clerk's spouse with a law firm or litigant, etc.

Rule 1.13 Organization as Client

(a) A lawyer employed or retained by an organization represents the organization acting through its duly authorized constituents.

(b) If a lawyer for an organization knows that an officer, employee or other person associated with the organization is engaged in action, intends to act or refuses to act in a matter related to the representation that is a violation of a legal obligation to the organization, or a violation of law which reasonably might be imputed to the organization, and is likely to result in substantial injury to the organization, the lawyer shall proceed as is reasonably necessary in the best interest of the organization. In determining how to proceed, the lawyer shall give due consideration to the seriousness of the violation and its consequences, the scope and nature of the lawyer's representation, the responsibility in the organization and the apparent motivation of the person involved, the policies of the organization concerning such matters and any other relevant considerations. Any measures taken shall be designed to minimize disruption of the organization and the risk of revealing information relating to the representation to persons outside the organization. Such measures may include among others:

(1) asking reconsideration of the matter;

(2) advising that a separate legal opinion on the matter be sought for presentation to appropriate authority in the organization; and

(3) referring the matter to higher authority in the organization, including, if warranted by the seriousness of the matter, referral to the highest authority that can act in behalf of the organization as determined by applicable law.

(c) If despite the lawyer's efforts in accordance with paragraph (b), the highest authority that can act on behalf of the organization insists upon action, or a refusal to act, that is clearly a violation of law and is likely to result in substantial injury to the organization, the lawyer may resign in accordance with Rule 1.16.

(d) In dealing with an organization's directors, officers, employees, members, shareholders or other constituents, a lawyer shall explain the identity of the client when it is apparent that the organization's interests are adverse to those of the constituents with whom the lawyer is dealing.

(e) A lawyer representing an organization may also represent any of its directors, officers, employees, members, shareholders or other constituents, subject to the provisions of Rule 1.7. If the organization's consent to the dual representation is required by Rule 1.7, the consent shall be given by an appropriate official of the organization other than the individual who is to be represented, or by the shareholders.

COMMENT

The Entity as the Client

[1] An organizational client is a legal entity, but it cannot act except through its officers, directors, employees, shareholders and other constituents.

[2] Officers, directors, employees and shareholders are the constituents of the corporate organizational client. The duties defined in this Comment apply equally to unincorporated associations. "Other constituents" as used in this Comment means the positions equivalent to officers, directors, employees and shareholders held by persons acting for organizational clients that are not corporations.

[3] When one of the constituents of an organizational client communicates with the organization's lawyer in that person's organizational capacity, the communication is protected by Rule 1.6. Thus, by way of example, if an organizational client requests its lawyer to investigate allegations of wrongdoing, interviews made in the course of that investigation between the lawyer and the client's employees or other constituents are covered by Rule 1.6. This does not mean, however, that constituents of an organizational client are the clients of the lawyer. The lawyer may not disclose to such constituents information relat-

ing to the representation except for disclosures explicitly or impliedly authorized by the organizational client in order to carry out the representation or as otherwise permitted by Rule 1.6.

[4] When constituents of the organization make decisions for it, the decisions ordinarily must be accepted by the lawyer even if their utility or prudence is doubtful. Decisions concerning policy and operations, including ones entailing serious risk, are not as such in the lawyer's province. However, different considerations arise when the lawyer knows that the organization may be substantially injured by action of constituent that is in violation of law. In such a circumstance, it may be reasonably necessary for the lawyer to ask the constituent to reconsider the matter. If that fails, or if the matter is of sufficient seriousness and importance to the organization, it may be reasonably necessary for the lawyer to take steps to have the matter reviewed by a higher authority in the organization. Clear justification should exist for seeking review over the head of the constituent normally responsible for it. The stated policy of the organization may define circumstances and prescribe channels for such review, and a lawyer should encourage the formulation of such a policy. Even in the absence of organization policy, however, the lawyer may have an obligation to refer a matter to higher authority, depending on the seriousness of the matter and whether the constituent in question has apparent motives to act at variance with the organization's interest. Review by the chief executive officer or by the board of directors may be required when the matter is of importance commensurate with their authority. At some point it may be useful or essential to obtain an independent legal opinion.

[5] In an extreme case, it may be reasonably necessary for the lawyer to refer the matter to the organization's highest authority. Ordinarily, that is the board of directors or similar governing body. However, applicable law may prescribe that under certain conditions highest authority reposes elsewhere; for example, in the independent directors of a corporation.

Relation to Other Rules

[6] The authority and responsibility provided in paragraph (b) are concurrent with the authority and responsibility provided in other Rules. In particular, this Rule does not limit or expand the lawyer's responsibility under Rules 1.6, 1.8, and 1.16, 3.3, or 4.1. If the lawyer's services are being used by an organization to further a crime or fraud by the organization, Rule 1.2(d) can be applicable.

Government Agency

[7] The duty defined in this Rule applies to governmental organizations. However, when the client is a governmental organization, a different balance

may be appropriate between maintaining confidentiality and assuring that the wrongful official act is prevented or rectified, for public business is involved. In addition, duties of lawyers employed by the government or lawyers in military service may be defined by statutes and regulation. Therefore, defining precisely the identity of the client and prescribing the resulting obligations of such lawyers may be more difficult in the government context. Although in some circumstances the client may be a specific agency, it is generally the government as a whole. For example, if the action or failure to act involves the head of a bureau, either the department of which the bureau is a part or the government as a whole may be the client for purpose of this Rule. Moreover, in a matter involving the conduct of government officials, a government lawyer may have authority to question such conduct more extensively than that of a lawyer for a private organization in similar circumstances. This Rule does not limit that authority. See note on Scope.

Clarifying the Lawyer's Role

[8] There are times when the organization's interest may be or become adverse to those of one or more of its constituents. In such circumstances the lawyer should advise any constituent, whose interest he finds adverse to that of the organization of the conflict or potential conflict of interest, that the lawyer cannot represent such constituent, and that such person may wish to obtain independent representation. Care must be taken to assure that the individual understands that, when there is such adversity of interest, the lawyer for the organization cannot provide legal representation for that constituent individual, and that discussions between the lawyer for the organization and the individual may not be privileged.

[9] Whether such a warning should be given by the lawyer for the organization to any constituent individual may turn on the facts of each case.

Dual Representation

[10] Paragraph (e) recognizes that a lawyer for an organization may also represent a principal officer or major shareholder.

Derivative Actions

[11] Under generally prevailing law, the shareholders or members of a corporation may bring suit to compel the directors to perform their legal obligations in the supervision of the organization. Members of unincorporated associations have essentially the same right. Such an action may be brought

nominally by the organization, but usually is, in fact, a legal controversy over management of the organization.

[12] The question can arise whether counsel for the organization may defend such an action. The proposition that the organization is the lawyer's client does not alone resolve the issue. Most derivative actions are a normal incident of an organization's affairs, to be defended by the organization's lawyer like any other suit. However, if the claim involves serious charges of wrongdoing by those in control of the organization, a conflict may arise between the lawyer's duty to the organization and the lawyer's relationship with the board. In those circumstances, Rule 1.7 governs who should represent the directors and the organization.

Model Code Comparison

There was no counterpart to this Rule in the Disciplinary Rules of the Model Code. EC 5-18 stated that a "lawyer employed or retained by a corporation or similar entity owes his allegiance to the entity and not to a stockholder, director, officer, employee, representative, or other person connected with the entity. In advising the entity, a lawyer should keep paramount its interests and his professional judgment should not be influenced by the personal desires of any person or organization. Occasionally, a lawyer for an entity is requested by a stockholder, director, officer, employee, representative, or other person connected with the entity to represent him in an individual capacity; in such case the lawyer may serve the individual only if the lawyer is convinced that differing interests are not present." EC 5-24 stated that although a lawyer "may be employed by a business corporation with non-lawyers serving as directors or officers, and they necessarily have the right to make decisions of business policy, a lawyer must decline to accept direction of his professional judgment from any layman." DR 5-107(B) provided that a lawyer "shall not permit a person who . . . employs . . . him to render legal services for another to direct or regulate his professional judgment in rendering such legal services."

Cross-References in Rules

Rule 1.4, Comment 3: "When the client is an organization or group, it is often impossible or inappropriate to inform every one of its members about its legal affairs; ordinarily, the lawyer should address communications to the appropriate officials of the organization. See **Rule 1.13**."

Rule 1.6, Comment 16: "The requirement of maintaining confidentiality of information relating to representation applies to government lawyers who may disagree with the policy goals that their representation is designed to advance."

Legislative History

1980 Discussion Draft:

An Organization as the Client

(a) A lawyer employed or retained by an organization represents the organization as distinct from its directors, officers, employees, members, shareholders, or other constituents.

(b) If a lawyer for an organization knows that an officer, employee, or other person associated with the organization is engaged in or intends action, or a refusal to act, that is a violation of law and is likely to result in significant harm to the organization, the lawyer shall use reasonable efforts to prevent the harm. In determining the appropriate measures, the lawyer shall give due consideration to the seriousness of the legal violation and its consequences, the scope and nature of the lawyer's representation, the responsibility in the organization of the person involved, and the policies of the organization concerning such matters. The measures taken shall be designed to minimize disruption and the risk of disclosing confidences. Such measures may include:

(1) Asking reconsideration of the matter;

(2) Seeking a separate legal opinion on the matter for presentation to appropriate authority in the organization;

(3) Referring the matter to higher authority in the organization, including, if necessary, referral to the highest authority that can act in behalf of the organization as determined by applicable law.

(c) If, despite the lawyer's efforts in accordance with paragraph (b), the highest authority that can act on behalf of the organization insists upon action, or a refusal to act, that is clearly a violation of law and is likely to result in substantial injury to the organization, the lawyer may take further remedial action, including disclosure of client confidences to the extent necessary, if the lawyer reasonably believes such action to be in the best interest of the organization.

(d) A lawyer representing an organization may also represent any of its directors, officers, members, or shareholders subject to the provisions of Rule 1.8. A lawyer undertaking such dual representation shall disclose that fact to an appropriate official of the organization other than the person so represented.

(e) When a shareholder or member of an organization brings a derivative action, the lawyer for the organization may act as its advocate only as permitted by Rule 1.8.

(f) In dealing with an organization's officials and employees, a lawyer shall explain the identity of the client when necessary to avoid embarrassment or unfairness to them.

1981 Draft: Rule 1.13(a) was the same as 1980 Draft. In Rule 1.13(b), a lawyer discovering conduct likely to result in "material" injury (rather than "significant" injury) to the corporation was to "proceed as is reasonably necessary in the best interest of the organization." Rule 1.13(c), describing remedial action, provided:

Such action may include revealing information relating to the representation of the organization only if the lawyer reasonably believes that:

(1) the highest authority in the organization has acted to further the personal or financial interests of members of that authority which are in conflict with the interests of the organization; and

(2) revealing the information is necessary in the best interest of the organization.

1982 Draft: Substantially the same as 1981 Draft.

Selected State Variations

California: See Rule 3-600 (Organization as Client).
District of Columbia deletes subparagraphs 1.13(b) and (c).

Maryland, Michigan, New Hampshire, and *New Jersey* permit revelation outside the corporation under the same or substantially the same circumstances described in the ABA's 1981 Draft of Rule 1.13. Michigan and New Jersey also retain the language of Rule 1.13(a) as it appeared in the Kutak Commission's 1980 draft.

Minnesota deletes "and is likely to result in substantial injury to the organization" from Rule 1.13(b). In Rule 1.13(c), Minnesota provides: "If despite the lawyer's efforts in accordance with paragraph (b), a violation of law appears likely, the lawyer may resign in accordance with Rule 1.16 and if the violation is criminal or fraudulent, may reveal it in accordance with Rules of Professional Conduct."

New York: Amendments to the New York Code adopt substantial portions of Rule 1.13 in EC 5-18 and DR 5-109(A).

North Carolina: Rule 5.10 substitutes the following short paragraph for all of Model Rule 1.13:

> A lawyer who represents a corporation or other organization represents and owes his allegiance to the entity and shall not permit his professional judgment to be compromised in favor of any other entity or individual.

Texas Rule 1.12(a) says that a lawyer retained or employed by an organization "represents the entity." Texas Rule 1.12(d) relieves the lawyer of responsibilities to the entity when the lawyer properly withdraws from the representation.

Virginia omits Rule 1.13.

Washington omits Rule 1.13.

Related Materials

American Lawyer's Code of Conduct: Rule 2.5 provides:

> A lawyer representing a corporation shall, as early as possible in the lawyer-client relationship, inform the board of directors of potential conflicts that might develop among the interests of the board, corporate officers, and shareholders. The lawyer shall receive from the board instructions in advance as to how to resolve such conflicts, and shall take reasonable steps to ensure that officers with whom the lawyer deals, and the shareholders, are made aware of how the lawyer has been instructed to resolve conflicts of interest.

Model Rules of Professional Conduct for Federal Lawyers: Rule 1.13 differs significantly. It provides:

> (a) Except when representing another client pursuant to paragraphs (e), (f) and (g), a *Government lawyer represents the Federal Agency that employs the Government lawyer.* Government lawyers are often formally employed by a Federal Agency but assigned to an organizational element within the Federal Agency. Unless otherwise specifically provided, the Federal Agency, not the organizational element, is ordinarily considered the client. The Federal Agency acts through its authorized officials. These officials include the heads of organizational elements within the Federal Agency. When a Government lawyer is assigned to an organizational element and designated to provide legal services and advice to the head of that organization, the client-lawyer relationship exists between the Government lawyer and the Federal Agency, as represented by the head of the organization. *The head of the organization may only invoke the attorney-client privilege or the rule of confidentiality for the benefit of the Federal*

Agency. In so invoking either the attorney-client privilege or attorney-client confidentiality on behalf of the Federal Agency, the head of the organization is subject to being overruled by higher agency authority.

(b) . . . [The measures a Government lawyer may take] may include, among others: . . .

(3) Advising the person that the lawyer is ethically obligated to preserve the interests of the Federal agency and, as a result, must consider discussing the matter with supervisory lawyers within the Government lawyer's office or at a higher level within the Federal Agency.

(c) If, despite the Government lawyer's efforts in accordance with paragraph (b), the highest authority that can act concerning the matter insists upon action, or refusal to act, that is clearly a violation of law, the Government lawyer *shall terminate representation* with respect to the matter in question. *In no event may the Government lawyer participate or assist in the illegal activity.* . . .

(e) A Government lawyer shall not form a client-lawyer relationship or represent a client other than the Federal Agency unless specifically authorized or authorized by competent authority. . . .

(g) A Government lawyer who has been duly assigned or authorized to represent an individual who is subject to disciplinary action or administrative proceedings, or to provide civil legal assistance to an individual, has, for those purposes, a lawyer-client relationship with that individual. [Emphasis added.]

The Comment to these Rules states:

Except when a Government lawyer is assigned to represent the interest of another client, the Federal Agency that employs the Government lawyer is the client. This principle is critical to the application of these Rules, since the identity of the client affects significant confidentiality and conflict issues.

. . . Although arguments have been made that the Government lawyer's ultimate obligation is to serve the public interest or the "government as a whole," for practical purposes, these may be unworkable ethical guidelines, particularly with regard to client control and confidentiality.

A Federal Agency may, of course, establish different client-lawyer obligations by Executive or court order, regulation, or statute. See e.g., 5 U.S.C. 2302.

Nevertheless, the conclusion that the Government lawyer's client is the lawyer's employing agency does not answer every ethical question. There are special considerations that affect the ethical responsibilities of the Government lawyer. For example, the Government lawyer has a responsibility to question the conduct of agency officials more extensively than a lawyer for a private organization would in similar circumstances. Government lawyers, in many situations, are asked to represent diverse client interests. For example, Government lawyers in the Executive branch also represent other branches of Government in a number of different situations. Here it becomes especially clear that the Government attorney's responsibilities are affected by the attorney's more general obligations to the United States, as for example, when it is necessary to refuse to defend an unconstitutional statute or regulation or to resist the encroachment by one branch on another's sphere of power. The client-lawyer obligations of Government lawyers in other branches of Government raise still different considerations. For example, lawyers engaged by the Senate or the House of Representatives, by Congressional committees, or on the staffs of individual members of Congress may develop client-lawyer relationships with those bodies, committees or individuals. Yet these relationships must themselves be viewed in the context of the Government lawyer's broader obligations to the Congress as a whole and ultimately to the United States.

Restatement of the Law Governing Lawyers: The American Law Institute has tentatively approved the following provisions:

§123. Scope of the Privilege for Organizations

Where a client is a corporation, unincorporated association, partnership, sole proprietorship, or other for-profit or not-for-profit organization, the attorney-client privilege extends to a communication if:

(1) The communication otherwise qualifies as privileged under §§118-122;

(2) The communication is between a person communicating pursuant to an agency relationship with the organization and a privileged person within the meaning of §120;

(3) The communication concerns a legal matter of interest to the organization; and

(4) The communication is shared only with:

(a) Privileged persons as defined in §§120 and 123(2); and

(b) Other agents of the organization who reasonably need to know of the communication in order to act for the organization.

(Restatement §§118-123 are reprinted in the chapter on attorney-client privilege.)

§134. Exception for Organizational Fiduciaries

In a proceeding involving a dispute between an organizational client and shareholders, members, or other constituents of the organization toward whom the controlling directors or officers of the organization bear fiduciary responsibilities, the attorney-client privilege of the organization does not apply to a communication if:

(1) Directors or officers of the organization are charged with breach of their obligations toward the shareholders, members, or other beneficial owners or toward the organization itself;

(2) The communication occurred prior to the suit and relates directly to those charges; and

(3) The tribunal concludes that the need of the requesting party to discover or introduce the communication is sufficiently compelling and the threat to confidentiality sufficiently confined to justify setting the privilege aside.

§212. Conflicts of Interest in Representing an Organization

(1) A lawyer employed or retained to represent an organization represents the interests of the organization as defined by its responsible agents acting pursuant to the organization's decision-making procedures.

(2) Unless all affected clients consent to the representation under the limitations and conditions provided in §202, a lawyer employed or retained to represent an organization may not represent in the same matter one or more of the directors, officers, employees, shareholders, owners, members, or other individuals or organizations associated with the organization if a substantial risk exists that the interests of the organization in the matter will be materially adverse to those of the associated individual or organization.

(Restatement §202 is reprinted above in the Related Materials following Model Rule 1.7.)

Rule 1.14 Client Under a Disability

(a) When a client's ability to make adequately considered decisions in connection with the representation is impaired, whether because of minority, mental disability or for some other reason, the lawyer shall, as far as rea-

sonably possible, maintain a normal client-lawyer relationship with the client.

(b) A lawyer may seek the appointment of a guardian or take other protective action with respect to a client, only when the lawyer reasonably believes that the client cannot adequately act in the client's own interest.

COMMENT

[1] The normal client-lawyer relationship is based on the assumption that the client, when properly advised and assisted, is capable of making decisions about important matters. When the client is a minor or suffers from a mental disorder or disability, however, maintaining the ordinary client-lawyer relationship may not be possible in all respects. In particular, an incapacitated person may have no power to make legally binding decisions. Nevertheless, a client lacking legal competence often has the ability to understand, deliberate upon, and reach conclusions about matters affecting the client's own well-being. Furthermore, to an increasing extent the law recognizes intermediate degrees of competence. For example, children as young as five or six years of age, and certainly those of ten or twelve, are regarded as having opinions that are entitled to weight in legal proceedings concerning their custody. So also, it is recognized that some persons of advanced age can be quite capable of handling routine financial matters while needing special legal protection concerning major transactions.

[2] The fact that a client suffers a disability does not diminish the lawyer's obligation to treat the client with attention and respect. If the person has no guardian or legal representative, the lawyer often must act as de facto guardian. Even if the person does have a legal representative, the lawyer should as far as possible accord the represented person the status of client, particularly in maintaining communication.

[3] If a legal representative has already been appointed for the client, the lawyer should ordinarily look to the representative for decisions on behalf of the client. If a legal representative has not been appointed, the lawyer should see to such an appointment where it would serve the client's best interests. Thus, if a disabled client has substantial property that should be sold for the client's benefit, effective completion of the transaction ordinarily requires appointment of a legal representative. In many circumstances, however, appointment of a legal representative may be expensive or traumatic for the client. Evaluation of these considerations is a matter of professional judgment on the lawyer's part.

[4] If the lawyer represents the guardian as distinct from the ward, and is aware that the guardian is acting adversely to the ward's interest, the lawyer may have an obligation to prevent or rectify the guardian's misconduct. See Rule 1.2(d).

Disclosure of the Client's Condition

[5] Rules of procedure in litigation generally provide that minors or persons suffering mental disability shall be represented by a guardian or next friend if they do not have a general guardian. However, disclosure of the client's disability can adversely affect the client's interests. For example, raising the question of disability could, in some circumstances, lead to proceedings for involuntary commitment. The lawyer's position in such cases is an unavoidably difficult one. The lawyer may seek guidance from an appropriate diagnostician.

Model Code Comparison

There was no counterpart to this Rule in the Disciplinary Rules of the Model Code. EC 7-11 stated that the "responsibilities of a lawyer may vary according to the intelligence, experience, mental condition or age of a client. . . . Examples include the representation of an illiterate or an incompetent." EC 7-12 stated that "[a]ny mental or physical condition of a client that renders him incapable of making a considered judgment on his own behalf casts additional responsibilities upon his lawyer. Where an incompetent is acting through a guardian or other legal representative, a lawyer must look to such representative for those decisions which are normally the prerogative of the client to make. If a client under disability has no legal representative, his lawyer may be compelled in court proceedings to make decisions on behalf of the client. If the client is capable of understanding the matter in question or of contributing to the advancement of his interests, regardless of whether he is legally disqualified from performing certain acts, the lawyer should obtain from him all possible aid. If the disability of a client and the lack of a legal representative compel the lawyer to make decisions for his client, the lawyer should consider all circumstances then prevailing and act with care to safeguard and advance the interests of his client. But obviously a lawyer cannot perform any act or make any decision which the law requires his client to perform or make, either acting for himself if competent, or by a duly constituted representative if legally incompetent."

Cross-References in Rules

Rule 1.2, Comment 2: "In a case in which the client appears to be suffering mental disability, the lawyer's duty to abide by the client's decisions is to be guided by reference to **Rule 1.14**."

Rule 1.4, Comment 3: "Ordinarily, the information to be provided is that appropriate for a client who is a comprehending and responsible adult. However, fully informing the client according to this standard may be impracticable, for example, where the client is a child or suffers from mental disability. See **Rule 1.14**."

Rule 1.16, Comment 6: "If the client is mentally incompetent, the client may lack the legal capacity to discharge the lawyer, and in any event the discharge may be seriously adverse to the client's interests. The lawyer should make special effort to help the client consider the consequences and, in an extreme case, may initiate proceedings for a conservatorship or similar protection of the client. See **Rule 1.14**."

Legislative History

1980 Discussion Draft:

. . . (b) A lawyer shall secure the appointment of a guardian or other legal representative, or seek a protective order with respect to a client, when doing so is necessary in the client's best interests.

1981 Draft: Rule 1.14(a) was the same as the version finally adopted. Rule 1.14(b) required a lawyer to seek appointment of a guardian or a protective order "only when the lawyer reasonably believes that the client cannot adequately communicate or exercise judgment in the client-lawyer relationship."

1982 Draft was adopted.

Selected State Variations

California has no counterpart to Rule 1.14.

New York: Same or substantially the same as the ABA Model Code — see Model Code Comparison above.

North Carolina omits Rule 1.14.

Texas Rule 1.02(g) provides:

A lawyer shall take reasonable action to secure the appointment of a guardian or other legal representative for, or seek other protective orders with respect to, a client whenever the lawyer reasonably believes that the client lacks legal competence and that such action should be taken to protect the client.

Virginia omits Rule 1.14.

Related Materials

ABA Criminal Justice Mental Health Standards: In 1983, the ABA Standing Committee for Association Standards on Criminal Justice published a First Tentative Draft of Criminal Justice Mental Health Standards. Approved by the ABA in 1984, they contain many useful guidelines for representing mentally ill or mentally retarded clients.

American Academy of Matrimonial Lawyers: The "Bounds of Advocacy" drafted by the American Academy of Matrimonial Lawyers contains the following provision and commentary:

1.2 An attorney should be sensitive to common emotional and psychological problems. When an attorney believes that such problems are interfering with effective representation or with the client's ability to function, he should suggest that the client seek the help of a mental health professional.

Comment to Rule 1.2

Clients often come to matrimonial lawyers with "emotional baggage" that hinders their ability to make well-considered decisions about their case or interact in a constructive manner with other family members, opposing counsel, or their own attorney. Recognizing and helping the client deal with emotional problems may be essential to an effective attorney-client relationship. Competent representation may require that the attorney recommend that the client consult a mental health professional. See Standards 2.9, 2.10, 2.11 and fn. 22.

Restatement of the Law Governing Lawyers: The American Law Institute has tentatively approved the following provision:

§35. *Client Under a Disability*

(1) When a client's ability to make adequately considered decisions in connection with the representation is impaired, whether because of minority, old age, physical illness, or mental disability or for some other reason, the lawyer must, as far as reasonably possible, maintain a normal client-lawyer relationship with the client and act in the best interests of the client as stated in Subsection (2).

(2) A lawyer representing a person whom the lawyer reasonably believes to be a client described in Subsection (1) and for whom no guardian or other representative is available to act must, with respect to a question within the scope of the representation, pursue the lawyer's reasonable view of the client's objectives or interests as the client would define them if able to exercise rational judgment on the question, even if the client expresses no wishes or gives contrary instructions.

(3) If a client described in Subsection (1) has a guardian or other person legally entitled to act for the client, the client's lawyer must treat the guardian or other person as the person entitled to act with respect to the client's interests in the matter, unless:

    (a) The lawyer represents the client in a matter against the interests of such person; or

    (b) The person instructs the lawyer to act in a manner that the lawyer knows will violate the person's legal duties toward the client.

(4) A lawyer representing a person whom the lawyer reasonably believes to be a client described in Subsection (1) may seek the appointment of a guardian or take other protective action with respect to a decision on a question within the scope of the representation when doing so is practical and will advance the client's objectives or interests, determined as stated in Subsection (2).

§202. *Client Consent to a Conflict of Interest*

. . . (2) Notwithstanding each affected client's consent, a lawyer may not represent a client if:

    . . . (b) One or more of the clients is legally incapable of giving consent. . . .

Rule 1.15 Safekeeping Property

(a) A lawyer shall hold property of clients or third persons that is in a lawyer's possession in connection with a representation separate from the lawyer's own property. Funds shall be kept in a separate account maintained in the state where the lawyer's office is situated, or elsewhere with the consent of

the client or third person. Other property shall be identified as such and appropriately safeguarded. Complete records of such account funds and other property shall be kept by the lawyer and shall be preserved for a period of [five years] after termination of the representation.

(b) Upon receiving funds or other property in which a client or third person has an interest, a lawyer shall promptly notify the client or third person. Except as stated in this rule or otherwise permitted by law or by agreement with the client, a lawyer shall promptly deliver to the client or third person any funds or other property that the client or third person is entitled to receive and, upon request by the client or third person, shall promptly render a full accounting regarding such property.

(c) When in the course of representation a lawyer is in possession of property in which both the lawyer and another person claim interests, the property shall be kept separate by the lawyer until there is an accounting and severance of their interests. If a dispute arises concerning their respective interests, the portion in dispute shall be kept separate by the lawyer until the dispute is resolved.

COMMENT

[1] A lawyer should hold property of others with the care required of a professional fiduciary. Securities should be kept in a safe deposit box, except when some other form of safekeeping is warranted by special circumstances. All property which is the property of clients or third persons should be kept separate from the lawyer's business and personal property and, if monies, in one or more trust accounts. Separate trust accounts may be warranted when administering estate monies or acting in similar fiduciary capacities.

[2] Lawyers often receive funds from third parties from which the lawyer's fee will be paid. If there is risk that the client may divert the funds without paying the fee, the lawyer is not required to remit the portion from which the fee is to be paid. However, a lawyer may not hold funds to coerce a client into accepting the lawyer's contention. The disputed portion of the funds should be kept in trust and the lawyer should suggest means for prompt resolution of the dispute, such as arbitration. The undisputed portion of the funds shall be promptly distributed.

[3] Third parties, such as a client's creditors, may have just claims against funds or other property in a lawyer's custody. A lawyer may have a duty under applicable law to protect such third-party claims against wrongful interference by the client, and accordingly may refuse to surrender the property to the client. However, a lawyer should not unilaterally assume to arbitrate a dispute between the client and the third party.

[4] The obligations of a lawyer under this Rule are independent of those arising from activity other than rendering legal services. For example, a lawyer who serves as an escrow agent is governed by the applicable law relating

to fiduciaries even though the lawyer does not render legal services in the transaction.

[5] A "client's security fund" provides a means through the collective efforts of the bar to reimburse persons who have lost money or property as a result of dishonest conduct of a lawyer. Where such a fund has been established, a lawyer should participate.

Model Code Comparison

With regard to paragraph (a), DR 9-102(A) provided that "funds of clients" are to be kept in an identifiable bank account in the state in which the lawyer's office is situated. DR 9-102(B)(2) provided that a lawyer shall "identify and label securities and properties of a client . . . and place them in . . . safekeeping. . . ." DR 9-102(B)(3) required that a lawyer "[m]aintain complete records of all funds, securities, and other properties of a client. . . ." Paragraph (a) extends these requirements to property of a third person that is in the lawyer's possession in connection with the representation.

Paragraph (b) is substantially similar to DR 9-102(B)(1), (3), and (4).

Paragraph (c) is similar to DR 9-102(A)(2), except that the requirement regarding disputes applies to property concerning which an interest is claimed by a third person as well as by a client.

Cross-References in Rules

None.

Legislative History

1980 Discussion Draft (then Rule 1.12) provided in (a) that funds "shall be kept in a *trust* account." Subparagraph (d) provided:

> (d) When a lawyer and another person both have interests in property, the property shall be treated by the lawyer as trust property until an accounting and severance of their interests. If a dispute arises concerning their respective interests, the portion in dispute shall be treated as trust property until the dispute is resolved.

1981 and 1982 Drafts were substantially the same as adopted.

Selected State Variations

California: See Rule 4-100 (Preserving Identity of Funds and Property of a Client) and accompanying standards.

Delaware adds a long list of requirements.

District of Columbia adds subparagraphs (d) and (e), which provide:

(d) Advances of legal fees and costs become the property of the lawyer upon receipt. Any unearned amount of prepaid fees must be returned to the client at the termination of the lawyer's services in accordance with Rule 1.16(d).

(e) Nothing in this rule shall prohibit a lawyer or law firm from placing clients' funds which are nominal in amount or to be held for a short period of time in one or more interest-bearing accounts for the benefit of the charitable purposes of a court-approved "Interest on Lawyers Trust Account (IOLTA)" program.

The District of Columbia has also added a lengthy new Rule 1.17 entitled "Trust Account Overdraft Notification." The rule requires lawyers to maintain trust funds only in financial institutions approved by the D.C. Bar, and requires such approved financial institutions to notify the D.C. Bar Counsel of every overdraft or "dishonored instrument" relating to the trust account, and every instrument that was honored even though it was presented against insufficient funds in the trust account. At the same time, the District of Columbia adopted new definitions of "Law Firm" and "Financial Institution" to define terms used in Rule 1.17.

Hawaii has adopted the following "Addendum" to ensure that attorneys comply with Hawaii's version of Rule 1.15:

Maintenance of Books and Records

To establish compliance with the applicable provisions of the Code of Professional Responsibility relating to funds and property held in a fiduciary capacity, every attorney engaged in the private practice of law, or the partnership or professional corporation of which the attorney is a member, associate or employee, should maintain the books and records described below. Equivalent books and records demonstrating the same information in an easily accessible manner and in substantially the same detail would be acceptable. Books and records may be prepared manually, by machine or by computer.

The following books and records should be maintained for funds and property received and disbursed in a fiduciary capacity for clients or others:

1. A cash receipts journal listing the sources of the receipt and the date of the receipt. Receipts should be deposited intact and the duplicate deposit slip should be sufficiently detailed to identify each item.
2. A disbursements journal listing the date of the disbursement and payee. All disbursements should be made by check.
3. A subsidiary ledger containing a separate page for each person or company for whom monies have been received in trust showing the date of receipt and the amount, the date of the disbursement and the amount, and any unexpended balance.
4. Bank statements, cancelled checks and duplicate deposit slips.
5. A record showing all property, specifically identified, other than cash, held in trust, provided that routine files and documents which are not expected to be held indefinitely need not be so recorded.

Illinois provides:

(d) All nominal or short-terms funds of clients paid to a lawyer or law firm, including advances for costs and expenses, shall be deposited in one or more pooled interest-bearing trust accounts established with a bank or savings and loan association, with the Lawyers Trust Fund of Illinois designated as income beneficiary. . . .

The Illinois rule then sets forth detailed guidelines for maintaining these mandatory IOLTA accounts.

Michigan provides for IOLTA accounts in Rule 1.15(d).

Missouri: Rule 1.15(d) through (g) and Appendix 1 to Supreme Court Rule 4 provide for the Missouri Lawyer Trust Account Foundation, an IOLTA program.

New York: See New York version of DR 9-102.

North Carolina: Rules 10.1 and 10.2 set forth detailed rules for preserving, keeping records of, and accounting for client property, and Rule 10.3 establishes an IOLTA program.

Virginia generally keeps the language of DR 9-102, but has included an IOLTA program in DR 9-102 and has added extensive rules in DR 9-103 to govern record-keeping for client funds and property.

Related Materials

ABA Canons: Canon 11 provided:

11. Dealing with Trust Property

Money of the client or collected for the client or other trust property coming into the possession of the lawyer should be reported and accounted for promptly, and should not under any circumstances be commingled with his own or be used by him.

ABA Standards for Imposing Lawyer Discipline:

4.11. Disbarment is generally appropriate when a lawyer knowingly converts client property and causes injury or potential injury to a client.

4.12. Suspension is generally appropriate when a lawyer knows or should know that he is dealing improperly with client property and causes injury or potential injury to a client.

4.13. Reprimand is generally appropriate when a lawyer is negligent in dealing with client property and causes injury or potential injury to a client.

4.14. Admonition is generally appropriate when a lawyer is negligent in dealing with client property and causes little or no actual or potential injury to a client.

Client Protection Funds: In keeping with Comment 5 of Rule 1.15, many states have established client protection funds (sometimes called client security funds) for the purpose of reimbursing clients who have lost money or property as a result of dishonest conduct by lawyers. For example, chapter 7 of Florida's Supreme Court Rules authorizes establishment of a Clients' Security Fund "to provide monetary relief to persons who suffer reimbursable losses as a result of misappropriation, embezzlement, or other wrongful taking or conversion" by a Florida lawyer. In several states, these client protection funds have paid out so many claims that they have run out of money. The ABA adopted Model Rules for Lawyers' Funds for Client Protection at its 1989 Annual Meeting. These Model Rules replaced similar rules first adopted in 1981, then called Model Rules for Clients' Security Funds.

Model Rules of Professional Conduct for Federal Lawyers add a new subparagraph (d) that provides: "When property of a client or third party is admitted into evidence or otherwise included in the record of a proceeding, the Federal lawyer should take reasonable action to ensure its prompt return."

Restatement of the Law Governing Lawyers: The American Law Institute has tentatively approved the following provisions:

§56. Safeguarding and Segregating Property

(1) A lawyer must take reasonable steps to safeguard funds and other property in the lawyer's possession belonging to a client or third person to whom the lawyer owes fiduciary duties or in which a client or such a third person claims an interest. In particular, the lawyer must hold such property separate from the lawyer's property, keep records of it, deposit funds in a separate account, identify tangible objects, and comply with related requirements imposed by regulatory authorities.

(2) Upon receiving funds or other property in which a client or a third person to whom the lawyer owes fiduciary duties owns or claims an interest, a lawyer shall promptly notify the client or third person. The lawyer shall promptly render a full accounting regarding such property upon request by the client or third person.

§57. Surrendering Possession of Property

(1) Except as provided in Subsection (2), a lawyer must promptly deliver, to the client or third person so entitled, funds or other property in the lawyer's possession belonging to a client or third person to whom the lawyer owes fiduciary duties.

(2) A lawyer may retain possession of funds or other property of a client or third person to whom the lawyer owes fiduciary duties if:

(a) The client or third person consents;

(b) The lawyer's client is entitled to the property, the lawyer appropriately possesses the property for purposes of the representation, and the client has not asked for delivery of the property;

(c) The lawyer has a valid lien on the property (see §55);

(d) There are substantial grounds for a dispute existing as to the person entitled to the property; or

(e) Delivering the property to the client or third person would violate a court order or other legal obligation of the lawyer.

(Restatement §55 is reprinted in the Related Materials following Model Rule 1.8.)

Rule 1.16 Declining or Terminating Representation

(a) Except as stated in paragraph (c), a lawyer shall not represent a client or, where representation has commenced, shall withdraw from the representation of a client if:

(1) the representation will result in violation of the rules of professional conduct or other law;

(2) the lawyer's physical or mental condition materially impairs the lawyer's ability to represent the client; or

(3) the lawyer is discharged.

(b) Except as stated in paragraph (c), a lawyer may withdraw from representing a client if withdrawal can be accomplished without material adverse effect on the interests of the client, or if:

(1) the client persists in a course of action involving the lawyer's services that the lawyer reasonably believes is criminal or fraudulent;

(2) the client has used the lawyer's services to perpetrate a crime or fraud;

(3) a client insists upon pursuing an objective that the lawyer considers repugnant or imprudent;

(4) the client fails substantially to fulfill an obligation to the lawyer regarding the lawyer's services and has been given reasonable warning that the lawyer will withdraw unless the obligation is fulfilled;

(5) the representation will result in an unreasonable financial burden on the lawyer or has been rendered unreasonably difficult by the client; or

(6) other good cause for withdrawal exists.

(c) When ordered to do so by a tribunal, a lawyer shall continue representation notwithstanding good cause for terminating the representation.

(d) Upon termination of representation, a lawyer shall take steps to the extent reasonably practicable to protect a client's interests, such as giving reasonable notice to the client, allowing time for employment of other counsel, surrendering papers and property to which the client is entitled and refunding any advance payment of fee that has not been earned. The lawyer may retain papers relating to the client to the extent permitted by other law.

COMMENT

[1] A lawyer should not accept representation in a matter unless it can be performed competently, promptly, without improper conflict of interest and to completion.

Mandatory Withdrawal

[2] A lawyer ordinarily must decline or withdraw from representation if the client demands that the lawyer engage in conduct that is illegal or violates the Rules of Professional Conduct or other law. The lawyer is not obliged to decline or withdraw simply because the client suggests such a course of conduct; a client may make such a suggestion in the hope that a lawyer will not be constrained by a professional obligation.

[3] When a lawyer has been appointed to represent a client, withdrawal ordinarily requires approval of the appointing authority. See also Rule 6.2. Difficulty may be encountered if withdrawal is based on the client's demand that the lawyer engage in unprofessional conduct. The court may wish an explanation for the withdrawal, while the lawyer may be bound to keep confidential the facts that would constitute such an explanation. The lawyer's statement that

professional considerations require termination of the representation ordinarily should be accepted as sufficient.

Discharge

[4] A client has a right to discharge a lawyer at any time, with or without cause, subject to liability for payment for the lawyer's services. Where future dispute about the withdrawal may be anticipated, it may be advisable to prepare a written statement reciting the circumstances.

[5] Whether a client can discharge appointed counsel may depend on applicable law. A client seeking to do so should be given a full explanation of the consequences. These consequences may include a decision by the appointing authority that appointment of successor counsel is unjustified, thus requiring the client to represent himself.

[6] If the client is mentally incompetent, the client may lack the legal capacity to discharge the lawyer, and in any event the discharge may be seriously adverse to the client's interests. The lawyer should make special effort to help the client consider the consequences and, in an extreme case, may initiate proceedings for a conservatorship or similar protection of the client. See Rule 1.14.

Optional Withdrawal

[7] A lawyer may withdraw from the representation in some circumstances. The lawyer has the option to withdraw if it can be accomplished without material adverse effect on the client's interests. Withdrawal is also justified if the client persists in a course of action that the lawyer reasonably believes is criminal or fraudulent, for a lawyer is not required to be associated with such conduct even if the lawyer does not further it. Withdrawal is also permitted if the lawyer's services were misused in the past even if that would materially prejudice the client. The lawyer also may withdraw where the client insists on a repugnant or imprudent objective.

[8] A lawyer may withdraw if the client refuses to abide by the terms of an agreement relating to the representation, such as an agreement concerning fees or court costs or an agreement limiting the objectives of the representation.

Assisting the Client upon Withdrawal

[9] Even if the lawyer has been unfairly discharged by the client, a lawyer must take all reasonable steps to mitigate the consequences to the client. The lawyer may retain papers as security for a fee only to the extent permitted by law.

[10] Whether or not a lawyer for an organization may under certain unusual circumstances have a legal obligation to the organization after withdrawing or being discharged by the organization's highest authority is beyond the scope of these Rules.

Model Code Comparison

With regard to paragraph (a), DR 2-109(A) provided that a lawyer "shall not accept employment . . . if he knows or it is obvious that [the prospective client] wishes to . . . [b]ring a legal action . . . or otherwise have steps taken for him, merely for the purpose of harassing or maliciously injuring any person. . . ." Nor may a lawyer accept employment if the lawyer is aware that the prospective client wishes to "[p]resent a claim or defense . . . that is not warranted under existing law, unless it can be supported by good faith argument for an extension, modification, or reversal of existing law." DR 2-110(B) provided that a lawyer "shall withdraw from employment . . . if":

(1) He knows or it is obvious that his client is bringing the legal action . . . or is otherwise having steps taken for him, merely for the purpose of harassing or maliciously injuring any person.

(2) He knows or it is obvious that his continued employment will result in violation of a Disciplinary Rule.

(3) His mental or physical condition renders it unreasonably difficult for him to carry out the employment effectively.

(4) He is discharged by his client.

With regard to paragraph (b), DR 2-110(C) permitted withdrawal regardless of the effect on the client if:

(1) His client: (a) Insists upon presenting a claim or defense that is not warranted under existing law and cannot be supported by good faith argument for an extension, modification, or reversal of existing law; (b) Personally seeks to pursue an illegal course of conduct; (c) Insists that the lawyer pursue a course of conduct that is illegal or that is prohibited under the Disciplinary Rules; (d) By other conduct renders it unreasonably difficult for the lawyer to carry out his employment effectively; (e) Insists, in a matter not pending before a tribunal, that the lawyer engage in conduct that is contrary to the judgment and advice of the lawyer but not prohibited under the Disciplinary Rules; (f) Deliberately disregards an agreement or obligation to the lawyer as to expenses and fees.

(2) His continued employment is likely to result in a violation of a Disciplinary Rule.

(3) His inability to work with co-counsel indicates that the best interest of the client likely will be served by withdrawal.

(4) His mental or physical condition renders it difficult for him to carry out the employment effectively.

(5) His client knowingly and freely assents to termination of his employment.

(6) He believes in good faith, in a proceeding pending before a tribunal, that the tribunal will find the existence of other good cause for withdrawal.

With regard to paragraph (c), DR 2-110(A)(1) provided: "If permission for withdrawal from employment is required by the rules of a tribunal, the lawyer shall not withdraw . . . without its permission."

The provisions of paragraph (d) are substantially identical to DR 2-110(A)(2) and (3).

Cross-References in Rules

Rule 1.3, Comment 3: "Unless the relationship is terminated as provided in **Rule 1.16**, a lawyer should carry through to conclusion all matters undertaken for a client."

Rule 1.5, Comment 2: "A lawyer may require advance payment of a fee, but is obliged to return any unearned portion. See **Rule 1.16(d)**."

Rule 1.6, Comment 14: "If the lawyer's services will be used by the client in materially furthering a course of criminal or fraudulent conduct, the lawyer must withdraw, as stated in **Rule 1.16(a)(1)**."

Rule 1.6, Comment 15: "After withdrawal the lawyer is required to refrain from making disclosure of the clients' confidences, except as otherwise provided in Rule 1.6. Neither this Rule nor Rule 1.8(b) nor **Rule 1.16(d)** prevents the lawyer from giving notice of the fact of withdrawal, and the lawyer may also withdraw or disaffirm any opinion, document, affirmation, or the like."

Rule 1.7, Comment 2: "If . . . a conflict arises after representation has been undertaken, the lawyer should withdraw from the representation. See **Rule 1.16**."

Rule 1.13(c) provides that a lawyer "may resign in accordance with **Rule 1.16**."

Rule 1.13, Comment 6: "[T]his Rule does not limit or expand the lawyer's responsibility under" **Rule 1.16**.

Rule 1.17, Comment 12 provides: "If approval of the substitution of the purchasing attorney for the selling attorney is required by the rules of any tribunal in which a matter is pending, such approval must be obtained before the matter can be included in the sale (see **Rule 1.16**)."

Rule 2.2, Comment 10: "Common representation does not diminish the rights of each client in the client-lawyer relationship. Each has the right to loyal and diligent representation, the right to discharge the lawyer as stated in **Rule 1.16**, and the protections of Rule 1.9. . . ."

Legislative History

1980 Discussion Draft: Rule 1.16(b) provided:

(b) Except as stated in paragraph (c), a lawyer may withdraw from representing a client if:

(1) Withdrawal can be effected without material prejudice to the client;

(2) The client persists in a course of conduct that is illegal or unjust; or

(3) The client fails to fulfill an obligation to the lawyer regarding the lawyer's services.

1981 and 1982 Drafts were substantially the same as adopted.

Selected State Variations

California: See Rule 3-700 (Termination of Employment).

District of Columbia: A lawyer may withdraw if "obdurate or vexatious conduct on the part of the client has rendered the representation unreasonably difficult."

Georgia retains the substance of the Code provision on withdrawal.

Illinois provides:

(a) A lawyer representing a client before a tribunal shall withdraw from employment (with permission of the tribunal if such permission is required), and a lawyer representing a client in other matters shall withdraw from employment, if:

(1) the lawyer knows or reasonably should know that the client is bringing the legal action, conducting the defense, or asserting a position in the litigation, or is otherwise having steps taken, merely for the purpose of harassing or maliciously injuring any person;

(2) the lawyer knows or reasonably should know that such continued employment will result in violation of these rules;

(3) the lawyer's mental or physical condition renders it unreasonably difficult for the lawyer to carry out the employment effectively; or

(4) the lawyer is discharged by the client.

(b) Except as required in Rule 1.16(a), a lawyer shall not request permission to withdraw in matters pending before a tribunal, and shall not withdraw in other matters, unless such request or such withdrawal is because

(1) the client:

(A) insists upon presenting a claim or defense that is not warranted under existing law and cannot be supported by a reasonable argument for an extension, modification, or reversal of existing law;

(B) seeks to pursue an illegal course of conduct;

(C) insists that the lawyer pursue a course of conduct that is illegal or that is prohibited by these Rules;

(D) by other conduct renders it unreasonably difficult for the lawyer to carry out the employment effectively;

(E) insists, in a matter not pending before a tribunal, that the lawyer engage in conduct that is contrary to the judgment and advice of the lawyer although not prohibited by these Rules; or

(F) substantially fails to fulfill an agreement or obligation to the lawyer as to expenses or fees;

(2) the lawyer's inability to work with co-counsel indicates that the best interests of the client likely will be served by withdrawal;

(3) the client consents to termination of the lawyer's employment after disclosure; or

(4) the lawyer reasonably believes that a tribunal will, in a proceeding pending before the tribunal, find the existence of other good cause for withdrawal.

Illinois subparagraphs (c), (d), and (e) to Rule 1.16 are substantially the same as DR 2-110(A)(1)-(3).

Massachusetts: DR 2-110(A)(4) gives former clients significant rights to papers within former counsel's possession. It provides:

An attorney must make available to a former client, within a reasonable time following the client's request for his or her file, the following:

(a) All papers, documents, and other materials the client supplied to the attorney. The attorney may at his or her own expense retain copies of any such materials.

(b) All pleadings and other papers filed with or by the court or served by or upon any party. The client may be required to pay any copying charge consistent with the attorney's actual cost for these materials, unless the client has already paid for such materials.

(c) All investigatory or discovery documents for which the client has paid the attorney's out-of-pocket costs, including but not limited to medical records, photographs, tapes, disks, investigative reports, expert reports, depositions, and demonstrative evidence. The attorney may at his or her own expense retain copies of any such materials.

(d) If the attorney and the client have not entered into a contingent fee agreement, the client is entitled only to that portion of the attorney's work product (as defined in paragraph (f) below) for which the client has paid.

(e) If the attorney and the client have entered into a contingent fee agreement, the attorney must provide copies of the attorney's work product (as defined in paragraph (f) below). The client may be required to pay any copying charge consistent with the attorney's actual cost for the copying of these materials.

(f) For purposes of this Disciplinary Rule, work product shall consist of documents and tangible things prepared in the course of the representation of the client by the attorney or at the attorney's direction by his or her employee, agent, or consultant, and not described in paragraphs (b) or (c) above. Examples of work product include without limitation legal research, records of witness interviews, reports of negotiations, and correspondence.

(g) Notwithstanding anything in this Disciplinary Rule to the contrary, an attorney may not refuse, on grounds of nonpayment, to make available materials in the client's file when retention would prejudice the client unfairly.

New York: Same or substantially the same as the ABA Model Code — see Model Code Comparison above.

North Carolina: Substantially the same as the Model Code.

Virginia: DR 2-107 retains the language of DR 2-109 on declining employment. DR 2-108(A)(1) mandates withdrawal if continuing the representation will result in "a course of conduct by the lawyer that is illegal or inconsistent" with the Rules. DR 2-108(B)(2) permits withdrawal if the client persists in a course of conduct that is "illegal or unjust" (as opposed to "criminal or fraudulent"), and DR 2-108(B)(3) permits withdrawal if the client fails to fulfill an obligation to the lawyer "and such failure continues after reasonable notice to the client" (in place of "reasonable warning that the lawyer will withdraw"). Virginia has no equivalent to Rule 1.16(b)(2), (3), and (6).

Related Materials

ABA Canons: Canons 7 and 44 provided:

7. Professional Colleagues and Conflicts of Opinion

A client's proffer of assistance of additional counsel should not be regarded as evidence of want of confidence, but the matter should be left to the determination of the client. A lawyer should decline association as colleague if it is objectionable to the original counsel, but if the lawyer first retained is relieved, another may come into the case.

When lawyers jointly associated in a cause cannot agree as to any matter vital to the interest of the client, the conflict of opinion should be frankly stated to him for his final determination. His decision should be accepted unless the nature of the difference makes it impracticable for the lawyer whose judgment has been overruled to cooperate effectively. In this event it is his duty to ask the client to relieve him.

Efforts, direct or indirect, in any way to encroach upon the professional employment of another lawyer, are unworthy of those who should be brethren at the Bar; but, nevertheless, it is the right of any lawyer, without fear or favor, to give proper advice to those seeking relief against unfaithful or neglectful counsel, generally after communication with the lawyer of whom the complaint is made.

44. Withdrawal from Employment as Attorney or Counsel

The right of an attorney or counsel to withdraw from employment, once assumed, arises only from good cause. Even the desire or consent of the client is not always sufficient. The lawyer should not throw up the unfinished task to the detriment of his client except for reasons of honor or self-respect. If the client insists upon an unjust or immoral course in the conduct of his case, or if he persists over the attorney's remonstrance in presenting frivolous defenses, or if he deliberately disregards an agreement or obligation as to fees or expenses, the lawyer may be warranted in withdrawing on due notice to the client, allowing him time to employ another lawyer. So also when a lawyer discovers that his client has no case and the client is determined to continue it; or even if the lawyer finds himself incapable of conducting the case effectively. Sundry other instances may arise in which withdrawal is to be justified. Upon withdrawing from a case after a retainer has been paid, the attorney should refund such part of the retainer as has not been clearly earned.

American Lawyer's Code of Conduct: Rules 5.5 and 6.2 through 6.6 provide:

5.5. A lawyer shall not impose a lien upon any part of a client's files, except upon the lawyer's own work product, and then only to the extent that the work product has not been paid for. This work-product exception shall be inapplicable when the client is in fact unable to pay, or when withholding the lawyer's work product would present a significant risk to the client of imprisonment, deportation, destruction of essential evidence, loss of custody of a child, or similar irreparable harm.

6.2. A lawyer may withdraw from representing a client at any time and for any reason if (a) withdrawal will cause no significant harm to the client's interests, (b) the client is fully informed of the consequences of withdrawal and voluntarily assents to it, or (c) withdrawal is pursuant to the terms of the retainer agreement. . . .

6.3. A lawyer may withdraw from representing a client if the lawyer reasonably believes that continued employment in the case would be likely to have a seriously adverse effect upon the lawyer's health.

6.4. Unless the lawyer knows that withdrawal would result in significant and irreparable harm to the client, a lawyer may withdraw from representing a client if (a) the client commits a clear and substantial violation of a written agreement regarding fees or expenses, or (b) the lawyer encounters continuing, unavoidable and substantial difficulties in working with co-counsel or with the client.

6.5. In any matter other than criminal litigation, a lawyer may withdraw from representing a client if the lawyer comes to know that the client has knowingly induced the lawyer to take the case or to take action on behalf of the client on the basis of material misrepresentations about the facts of the case, and if withdrawal can be accomplished without a direct violation of confidentiality.

6.6. A lawyer shall decline or withdraw from representing a client when the lawyer knows that such action is necessary to avoid commission by the lawyer of a disciplinary violation, unless such action would result in a violation of Rule 1.2, proscribing direct or indirect divulgence of a client's confidences.

Comment to Rule 6.6

. . . A lawyer is forbidden to knowingly present false evidence. Therefore, withdrawal from representation would be required by Rule 6.6 when the client intends to present false evidence, and when withdrawal would not result in violating a confidence. When the lawyer reasonably believes that refusal to present false evidence could result in violating a confidence, however, Rules 1.2, 3.7, and 6.6 require the lawyer to continue in the case.

Model Rules of Professional Conduct for Federal Lawyers: Rule 1.16(c) provides: "When properly ordered to do so by a tribunal or other competent authority, a Federal lawyer shall continue representation notwithstanding good cause for terminating the representation."

Restatement of the Law Governing Lawyers: The American Law Institute has tentatively approved the following provisions:

§29. *Client's Duties to Lawyer*

Subject to the other provisions of this Restatement, a client must, in matters covered by the representation:

(1) Compensate a lawyer for services and expenses as stated in Chapter 3;

(2) Indemnify the lawyer for liabilities to which the client has exposed the lawyer without the lawyer's fault; and

(3) Fulfil any valid contractual obligation to the lawyer.

§43. *Termination of Lawyer's Authority*

(1) Subject to Subsection (2), a lawyer's actual authority to represent a client ends when:

(a) The client discharges the lawyer;

(b) The client dies;

(c) The lawyer withdraws;

(d) The lawyer dies or becomes physically or mentally incapable of providing representation or is disbarred or suspended from practicing law; or

(e) The representation ends as provided by agreement or because the lawyer has completed the contemplated services.

(2) Notwithstanding Subsection (1), a lawyer must comply with applicable law requiring notice or permission of a tribunal when terminating a representation and with any order of a tribunal (in accord with §[————] [Chapter 9]) requiring the representation to continue.

(3) A lawyer's apparent authority to represent a client ends when the third person knows or has reason to know of facts from which it can be reasonably inferred that the lawyer lacks actual authority including knowledge of any event described in Subsection (1).

§44. *Discharge by Client and Withdrawal by Lawyer*

(1) A client may discharge a lawyer at any time.

(2) Except as stated in Subsection (4), a lawyer shall not represent a client or, where representation has commenced, shall withdraw from the representation of a client if:

(a) The representation will result in the lawyer's violating rules of professional conduct or other law;

(b) The lawyer's physical or mental condition materially impairs the lawyer's ability to represent the client; or

(c) The client discharges the lawyer.

(3) Except as stated in Subsection (4), a lawyer may withdraw from representing a client if withdrawal can be accomplished without material adverse effect on the interests of the client, or if:

(a) The lawyer is required to withdraw under Subsection (2);

(b) The client consents;

(c) The client persists in a course of action involving the lawyer's services that the lawyer reasonably believes is criminal or fraudulent;

(d) The client has used the lawyer's services to perpetrate a crime or fraud;

(e) The client insists on taking action that the lawyer considers repugnant or imprudent;

(f) The client fails substantially to fulfill an obligation to the lawyer regarding the lawyer's services and the lawyer has given the client reasonable warning that the lawyer will withdraw unless the client fulfills the obligation;

(g) The representation has been rendered unreasonably difficult by the client or by the irreparable breakdown of the client-lawyer relationship; or

(h) Other good cause for withdrawal exists.

(4) When ordered to do so by a tribunal, a lawyer shall continue representation notwithstanding cause for terminating the representation.

§45. A Lawyer's Duties to a Former Client

(1) Upon termination of a representation, a lawyer shall take reasonable steps to protect a client's interests, such as giving notice to the client of the termination, allowing time for employment of other counsel, surrendering papers and property to which the client is entitled, and refunding any advance payment of fee the lawyer has not earned.

(2) A lawyer shall:

(a) Follow requirements stated in other provisions of this Restatement concerning former clients such as those dealing with client confidences (Chapter 5), conflicts of interest (Chapter 9), client property and documents (§§56-58), and fee collection (§53);

(b) Take no action on behalf of a former client without new authorization and give reasonable notice to those who might otherwise be misled that the lawyer lacks authority to act for the client;

(c) Take reasonable steps to convey to the former client any material communication the lawyer receives relating to the matter involved in the representation; and

(d) Take no unfair advantage of a former client by abusing knowledge or trust acquired by means of the representation.

§52. Fees on Termination

When the client-lawyer relationship ends before the lawyer has completed the services due for a matter:

(1) A lawyer who has been discharged without forfeiting the lawyer's fee under §49 and after substantially performing the services due, or any severable part of them, may recover the compensation provided by any otherwise enforceable agreement, less the value of the services covered by that contractual compensation that the lawyer did not provide because of the discharge; and

(2) When a lawyer's compensation is not forfeited under §49 and the lawyer is not entitled to recover under Subsection (1), the lawyer may recover the lesser of the fair value of the lawyer's services as determined under §51 and the compensation provided by any otherwise enforceable agreement between lawyer and client for the services performed.

(Sections 49 and 51 are reprinted in the Related Materials following Model Rule 1.5.)

§58. Documents Relating to a Representation

(1) A lawyer must take reasonable steps to safeguard documents in the lawyer's possession relating to the representation of a client or former client.

(2) On request, a lawyer must allow a client or former client to inspect and copy any document possessed by the lawyer relating to the representation, unless substantial grounds exist not to do so.

(3) Unless the client or former client consents to nondelivery or substantial grounds exist for refusing to make delivery, a lawyer must deliver to the client or former client, at an appropriate time and in any event promptly after the representation ends, such originals and copies of other documents possessed by the lawyer relating to the representation as a client or former client reasonably needs.

(4) Notwithstanding Subsections (2) and (3), a lawyer may decline to deliver to a client or former client an original or copy of any document under circumstances permitted by §55(1).

(Section 55 is reprinted in the Related Materials following Model Rule 1.8.)

Editors' Note.　Rule 1.17 was added by the ABA at its February 1990 Mid-Year Meeting.

Rule 1.17　Sale of Law Practice

A lawyer or a law firm may sell or purchase a law practice, including good will, if the following conditions are satisfied:

(a) The seller ceases to engage in the private practice of law [in the geographic area] [in the jurisdiction] (a jurisdiction may elect either version) in which the practice has been conducted;

(b) The practice is sold as an entirety to another lawyer or law firm;

(c) Actual written notice is given to each of the seller's clients regarding:

(1) the proposed sale;

(2) the terms of any proposed change in the fee arrangement authorized by paragraph (d);

(3) the client's right to retain other counsel or to take possession of the file; and

(4) the fact that the client's consent to the sale will be presumed if the client does not take any action or does not otherwise object within ninety (90) days of receipt of the notice.

If the client cannot be given notice, the representation of that client may be transferred to the purchaser only upon entry of an order so authorizing by a court having jurisdiction. The seller may disclose to the court *in camera* information relating to the representation only to the extent necessary to obtain an order authorizing the transfer of a file.

(d) The fees charged clients shall not be increased by reason of the sale. The purchaser may, however, refuse to undertake the representation unless the client consents to pay the purchaser fees at a rate not exceeding the fees charged by the purchaser for rendering substantially similar services prior to the initiation of the purchase negotiations.

COMMENT

[1] The practice of law is a profession, not merely a business. Clients are not commodities that can be purchased and sold at will. Pursuant to this Rule, when a lawyer or an entire firm ceases to practice and another lawyer or firm takes over the representation, the selling lawyer or firm may obtain compensation for the reasonable value of the practice as may withdrawing partners of law firms. See Rules 5.4 and 5.6.

Termination of Practice by the Seller

[2] The requirement that all of the private practice be sold is satisfied if the seller in good faith makes the entire practice available for sale to the purchaser. The fact that a number of the seller's clients decide not to be represented by the purchaser but take their matters elsewhere, therefore, does not result in a violation. Neither does a return to private practice as a result of an unanticipated change in circumstances result in a violation. For example, a lawyer who has sold the practice to accept an appointment to judicial office does not violate the requirement that the sale be attendant to cessation of practice if the lawyer later resumes private practice upon being defeated in a contested or a retention election for the office.

[3] The requirement that the seller cease to engage in the private practice of law does not prohibit employment as a lawyer on the staff of a public agency or a legal services entity which provides legal services to the poor, or as in-house counsel to a business.

[4] The Rule permits a sale attendant upon retirement from the private practice of law within the jurisdiction. Its provisions, therefore, accommodate the lawyer who sells the practice upon the occasion of moving to another state. Some states are so large that a move from one locale therein to another is tantamount to leaving the jurisdiction in which the lawyer has engaged in the practice of law. To also accommodate lawyers so situated, states may permit the sale of the practice when the lawyer leaves the geographic area rather than the jurisdiction. The alternative desired should be indicated by selecting one of the two provided for in Rule 1.17(a).

Single Purchaser

[5] The Rule requires a single purchaser. The prohibition against piecemeal sale of a practice protects those clients whose matters are less lucrative and who might find it difficult to secure other counsel if a sale could be limited to substantial fee-generating matters. The purchaser is required to undertake all client matters in the practice, subject to client consent. If, however, the purchaser is unable to undertake all client matters because of a conflict of interest in a spe-

cific matter respecting which the purchaser is not permitted by Rule 1.7 or another rule to represent the client, the requirement that there be a single purchaser is nevertheless satisfied.

Client Confidences, Consent and Notice

[6] Negotiations between seller and prospective purchaser prior to disclosure of information relating to a specific representation of an identifiable client no more violate the confidentiality provisions of Model Rule 1.6 than do preliminary discussions concerning the possible association of another lawyer or mergers between firms, with respect to which client consent is not required. Providing the purchaser access to client-specific information relating to the representation and to the file, however, requires client consent. The Rule provides that before such information can be disclosed by the seller to the purchaser the client must be given actual written notice of the contemplated sale, including the identity of the purchaser and any proposed change in the terms of future representation, and must be told that the decision to consent or make other arrangements must be made within 90 days. If nothing is heard from the client within that time, consent to the sale is presumed.

[7] A lawyer or law firm ceasing to practice cannot be required to remain in practice because some clients cannot be given actual notice of the proposed purchase. Since these clients cannot themselves consent to the purchase or direct any other disposition of their files, the Rule requires an order from a court having jurisdiction authorizing their transfer or other disposition. The Court can be expected to determine whether reasonable efforts to locate the client have been exhausted, and whether the absent client's legitimate interests will be served by authorizing the transfer of the file so that the purchaser may continue the representation. Preservation of client confidences requires that the petition for a court order be considered *in camera*. (A procedure by which such an order can be obtained needs to be established in jurisdictions in which it presently does not exist.)

[8] All the elements of client autonomy, including the client's absolute right to discharge a lawyer and transfer the representation to another, survive the sale of the practice.

Fee Arrangements Between Client and Purchaser

[9] The sale may not be financed by increases in fees charged the clients of the practice. Existing agreements between the seller and the client as to fees and the scope of the work must be honored by the purchaser, unless the client consents after consultation. The purchaser may, however, advise the client that the

purchaser will not undertake the representation unless the client consents to pay the higher fees the purchaser usually charges. To prevent client financing of the sale, the higher fee the purchaser may charge must not exceed the fees charged by the purchaser for substantially similar service rendered prior to the initiation of the purchase negotiations.

[10] The purchaser may not intentionally fragment the practice which is the subject of the sale by charging significantly different fees in substantially similar matters. Doing so would make it possible for the purchaser to avoid the obligation to take over the entire practice by charging arbitrarily higher fees for less lucrative matters, thereby increasing the likelihood that those clients would not consent to the new representation.

Other Applicable Ethical Standards

[11] Lawyers participating in the sale of a law practice are subject to the ethical standards applicable to involving another lawyer in the representation of a client. These include, for example, the seller's obligation to exercise competence in identifying a purchaser qualified to assume the practice and the purchaser's obligation to undertake the representation competently (see Rule 1.1); the obligation to avoid disqualifying conflicts, and to secure client consent after consultation for those conflicts which can be agreed to (see Rule 1.7); and the obligation to protect information relating to the representation (see Rules 1.6 and 1.9).

[12] If approval of the substitution of the purchasing attorney for the selling attorney is required by the rules of any tribunal in which a matter is pending, such approval must be obtained before the matter can be included in the sale (see Rule 1.16).

Applicability of the Rule

[13] This Rule applies to the sale of a law practice by representatives of a deceased, disabled or disappeared lawyer. Thus, the seller may be represented by a non-lawyer representative not subject to these Rules. Since, however, no lawyer may participate in a sale of a law practice which does not conform to the requirements of this Rule, the representatives of the seller as well as the purchasing lawyer can be expected to see to it that they are met.

[14] Admission to or retirement from a law partnership or professional association, retirement plans and similar arrangements, and a sale of tangible assets of a law practice, do not constitute a sale or purchase governed by this Rule.

[15] This Rule does not apply to the transfers of legal representation between lawyers when such transfers are unrelated to the sale of a practice.

Model Code Comparison

EC 4-6 provided that "a lawyer should not attempt to sell a law practice as a going business because, among other reasons, to do so would involve the disclosure of confidences and secrets."

Cross-References in Rules

Rule 5.4(a)(2) provides that "a lawyer who purchases the practice of a deceased, disabled, or disappeared lawyer may, pursuant to the provisions of **Rule 1.17**, pay to the estate or other representative of that lawyer the agreed-upon purchase price."

Rule 5.6, Comment 3: "This Rule does not apply to prohibit restrictions that may be included in the terms of the sale of a law practice pursuant to **Rule 1.17**."

Rule 7.2(c)(3) permits a lawyer to "pay for a law practice in accordance with **Rule 1.17**."

Rule 7.2, Comment 6: "A lawyer is allowed to pay for advertising permitted by this Rule and for the purchase of a law practice in accordance with the provisions of **Rule 1.17**, but otherwise is not permitted to pay another person for channeling professional work."

Legislative History

Rule 1.17 was adopted by the ABA House of Delegates at the ABA's February 1990 Mid-Year Meeting. It is an entirely new Rule and was not proposed in any form in Kutak Commission drafts. The proposal to add Rule 1.17 to the Model Rules was initiated by the State Bar of California, based on California Rule 2-300, and was joined by the ABA Section of General Practice and the ABA Section of Law Practice Management. The Committee Report submitted to the House of Delegates in support of adding Rule 1.17 explained the Rule as follows:

Impetus for Formulation of the Rule

Protection of Clients

[California] Rule of Professional Conduct 2-300 and proposed Model Rule 1.17 are consumer protection measures designed to address the disparity between the treatment of the clients of sole practitioners and the clients of law firms when the attorney handling the client matter leaves the practice, by ensuring that the client matters handled by sole practitioners are attended to when the sole practitioner leaves the practice.

If the attorney leaving the practice is or was part of a law firm, in most cases, the firm continues to handle the matter. In the majority of situations, the transition for the client is very smooth. However, if the attorney was in sole practice, the transition is not so smooth because there is no law firm standing ready to continue to handle the client matter. The clients of sole practitioners who leave the practice of law are relatively unprotected because there are no regulations in place to protect them during the transition.

Sole Practitioners in Unfair Financial Position

In addition to the issues of the client protection, sole practitioners are in an unfair financial position concerning the "good will" of their law practice. The "good will" of a business is "the expectation of continued public patronage." . . . Attorneys, like other business persons, may sell the physical assets of their law practice, such as equipment, the library or the furniture. However, case authority and ethics opinions held that the sale of "good will" of a law practice is unethical and against public policy. . . .

Treatment of "good will" in other contexts presents a mixed picture. For example, attorneys who are members of firms with two or more members may ethically enter into retirement agreements which may require lump sum payments that implicitly include sums for the attorney's share of the firm's "good will."

The estate of a deceased attorney may receive payments from the attorney who completes the unfinished client matters of the deceased attorney. However, in the absence of a rule like that which is being proposed, the payments are limited to the "proportion of the total compensation which fairly represents the services rendered by the deceased member" and thus do not permit an allowance for "good will."

Pursuant to agreements entered into between an attorney not in sole practice and the attorney's firm, partner or associate, the estate of the attorney may receive payments over a reasonable period of time after the attorney's death. Note that there is no requirement that the payments be related to any services the attorney performed. Thus, it appears that the payments to the estate can include the value of "good will."

In marital dissolution proceedings, the "good will" of the attorney-spouse's share in his or her law practice may be valued for the purpose of determining the community or other divisible assets.

This inconsistent treatment of "good will" resulted in a series of awkward results: the estate of a sole practitioner could not receive payment for the "good will" of the law practice, while the estate of an attorney who was a member of a law firm could; upon retirement, an attorney who was a member of a law firm could receive compensation including "good will," while the compensation received by a sole practitioner could not include "good will"; the "good will" of a sole practice may be considered an asset of the marital community for purposes of a dissolution, but could not be sold.

The Committee Report also cited two prominent cases holding that sole practitioners could not sell good will: O'Hara v. Ahlgren, Blumenfeld and Kempster, 537 N.E.2d 730 (Ill. 1989), and Geffen v. Moss, 53 Cal. App. 3d 215, 226 (1975).

Selected State Variations

California: See Rule 2-300.

Illinois: The Illinois Supreme Court rejected Rule 1.17 even though it was recommended by the Illinois State Bar Association.

Michigan has adopted Rule 1.17 in nearly identical form. It adds Rule 1.17(e), which permits the "sale of the good will of a law practice . . . conditioned upon the seller ceasing to engage in the private practice of law for a reasonable period of time within the geographical area in which the practice has been conducted."

New York: No comparable provision.

ARTICLE 2. COUNSELOR

Editors' Note. The *1980 Discussion Draft* contained the following Introduction to the section entitled "Attorney as Advisor":

The lawyer's professional function historically originated as attorney and advocate, that is, appearing on behalf of a party to litigation. Giving legal advice evolved from giving advice about how to proceed in litigation. Today, serving as adviser is the lawyer's predominant role.

As adviser, a lawyer informs clients about their legal rights and obligations and their practical implications. Giving advice is ordinarily an incident of other functions a lawyer performs on behalf of a client, such as advocacy or negotiation, but in many matters giving advice may be the lawyer's sole function. Legal advice may be given orally or in writing. It may be reflected in documents effectuating courses of action by the client, such as wills, articles of organization of an enterprise, by-laws, contracts, formal opinions, and draft legislation or government regulations. In giving advice, a lawyer should consider not only the literal terms of the law but also its purposes and changing course. A lawyer should also take into account equitable and ethical considerations and problems of cost and feasibility.

Rule 2.1 Advisor

In representing a client, a lawyer shall exercise independent professional judgment and render candid advice. In rendering advice, a lawyer may refer not only to law but to other considerations such as moral, economic, social and political factors, that may be relevant to the client's situation.

COMMENT

Scope of Advice

[1] A client is entitled to straightforward advice expressing the lawyer's honest assessment. Legal advice often involves unpleasant facts and alternatives that a client may be disinclined to confront. In presenting advice, a lawyer endeavors to sustain the client's morale and may put advice in as acceptable a form as honesty permits. However, a lawyer should not be deterred from giving candid advice by the prospect that the advice will be unpalatable to the client.

[2] Advice couched in narrowly legal terms may be of little value to a client, especially where practical considerations, such as cost or effects on other people, are predominant. Purely technical legal advice, therefore, can sometimes be inadequate. It is proper for a lawyer to refer to relevant moral and ethical considerations in giving advice. Although a lawyer is not a moral advisor as such, moral and ethical considerations impinge upon most legal questions and may decisively influence how the law will be applied.

[3] A client may expressly or impliedly ask the lawyer for purely technical advice. When such a request is made by a client experienced in legal matters, the lawyer may accept it at face value. When such a request is made by a client inex-

perienced in legal matters, however, the lawyer's responsibility as advisor may include indicating that more may be involved than strictly legal considerations.

[4] Matters that go beyond strictly legal questions may also be in the domain of another profession. Family matters can involve problems within the professional competence of psychiatry, clinical psychology or social work; business matters can involve problems within the competence of the accounting profession or of financial specialists. Where consultation with a professional in another field is itself something a competent lawyer would recommend, the lawyer should make such a recommendation. At the same time, a lawyer's advice at its best often consists of recommending a course of action in the face of conflicting recommendations of experts.

Offering Advice

[5] In general, a lawyer is not expected to give advice until asked by the client. However, when a lawyer knows that a client proposes a course of action that is likely to result in substantial adverse legal consequences to the client, duty to the client under Rule 1.4 may require that the lawyer act if the client's course of action is related to the representation. A lawyer ordinarily has no duty to initiate investigation of a client's affairs or to give advice that the client has indicated is unwanted, but a lawyer may initiate advice to a client when doing so appears to be in the client's interest.

Model Code Comparison

There was no direct counterpart to this Rule in the Disciplinary Rules of the Model Code. DR 5-107(B) provided that a lawyer "shall not permit a person who recommends, employs, or pays him to render legal services for another to direct or regulate his professional judgment in rendering such legal services." EC 7-8 stated that "[a]dvice of a lawyer to his client need not be confined to purely legal considerations. . . . In assisting his client to reach a proper decision, it is often desirable for a lawyer to point out those factors which may lead to a decision that is morally just as well as legally permissible. . . . In the final analysis, however, . . . the decision whether to forego legally available objectives or methods because of nonlegal factors is ultimately for the client. . . ."

Cross-References in Rules

None.

Legislative History

1980 Discussion Draft:

2.1 Independence and Candor

In advising a client a lawyer shall exercise independent and candid professional judgment, uncontrolled by the interests or wishes of a third person, or by the lawyer's own interests or wishes.

In addition, Rule 2.2 (now incorporated into Rule 2.1) provided:

Scope of Advice

In rendering advice a lawyer may refer to all relevant considerations unless in the circumstances it is evident that the client desires advice confined to strictly legal considerations.

1981 and 1982 Drafts were the same as adopted.

Selected State Variations

California has no direct counterpart to Rule 2.1.
New York: Same or substantially the same as the ABA Model Code — see Model Code Comparison above.
North Carolina omits Rule 2.1.
Texas Rule 2.01 deletes the second sentence of Rule 2.1.
Virginia omits Rule 2.1.

Related Materials

American Academy of Matrimonial Lawyers: The "Bounds of Advocacy" drafted by the American Academy of Matrimonial Lawyers contains the following provisions and commentary:

2.12 An attorney should advise the client of the emotional and economic impact of divorce and the possibility or advisability of reconciliation.

Comment to Rule 2.12

The duty of vigorous advocacy in no way prohibits the matrimonial lawyer from counseling the client to be cautious in embarking on divorce. The divorce process exacts a heavy economic and emotional toll. An attorney should ask if reconciliation might be possible, or at least whether the client is receptive to counseling. If the client exhibits uncertainty or ambivalence, the lawyer should assist in obtaining a counselor. In no event should an attorney urge a client to file suit, unless necessary to protect the client's interests.

It is generally assumed that a lawyer's role in family matters is to act not only as an advocate, but to some extent as a counselor or advisor. And the RPC specifically permit the lawyer to address moral, economic, social and political factors, which may be relevant to the client's situation. Further, "[w]here consultation with a professional in another field is itself something a competent lawyer would recommend, the lawyer should make such a recommendation." Although few attorneys are qualified to do personal counseling, a thorough discussion of the probable emotional and monetary repercussions of divorce is permissible.

If the client has begun counseling in hopes of reconciliation, the matrimonial lawyer should attempt to mitigate litigation-related activities that might prejudice marital harmony. It is important, however, for the attorney to be mindful that clients may make damaging admissions during joint marriage counseling. One spouse may use a "breathing spell" afforded by counseling to deplete the marital estate. The lawyer should advise the client of these risks and take precautions to protect the client in the interim.

Predivorce Planning

A client is entitled to know what laws govern divorce and the consequence of those laws on a dissolution of his marriage. A matrimonial lawyer should advise a client about the repercussions of any matrimonial litigation, including factors that are likely to be considered in economic and custody determinations. However, predivorce planning carries the potential for fraud.

2.14 An attorney should advise the client of the potential effect of the client's conduct on a custody dispute.

Comment to Rule 2.14

Predivorce conduct of the parents may significantly affect custody decisions. The client is entitled to advice where there is a custody issue. Conduct conforming to such advice often will benefit both the children and the client's spouse, independent of any custody dispute. Suggesting that the client spend more time with the child and consult from time-to-time with the child's doctor, teacher, and babysitter is appropriate. It is also proper to describe the potentially harmful legal consequences of an adulterous relationship, substance abuse, or other inappropriate behavior.

The lawyer must consider whether the custody claim will be made in good faith. If not, the lawyer must advise the client of the harmful consequences of a meritless custody claim to the client, the child, and the client's spouse. If the client still demands advice to build a spurious custody case or to use a custody claim as a bargaining chip or as a means of inflicting revenge (see Standard 2.25 and Comment), the lawyer should withdraw.

Rule 2.2 Intermediary

(a) A lawyer may act as intermediary between clients if:

(1) the lawyer consults with each client concerning the implications of the common representation, including the advantages and risks involved, and the effect on the attorney-client privileges, and obtains each client's consent to the common representation;

(2) the lawyer reasonably believes that the matter can be resolved on terms compatible with the clients' best interests, that each client will be able to make adequately informed decisions in the matter and that there is little risk of material prejudice to the interests of any of the clients if the contemplated resolution is unsuccessful; and

(3) the lawyer reasonably believes that the common representation can be undertaken impartially and without improper effect on other responsibilities the lawyer has to any of the clients.

(b) While acting as intermediary, the lawyer shall consult with each client concerning the decisions to be made and the considerations relevant in making them, so that each client can make adequately informed decisions.

(c) A lawyer shall withdraw as intermediary if any of the clients so requests, or if any of the conditions stated in paragraph (a) is no longer satisfied. Upon withdrawal, the lawyer shall not continue to represent any of the clients in the matter that was the subject of the intermediation.

COMMENT

[1] A lawyer acts as intermediary under this Rule when the lawyer represents two or more parties with potentially conflicting interests. A key factor in defining the relationship is whether the parties share responsibility for the lawyer's fee, but the common representation may be inferred from other circumstances. Because confusion can arise as to the lawyer's role where each party is not separately represented, it is important that the lawyer make clear the relationship.

[2] The Rule does not apply to a lawyer acting as arbitrator or mediator between or among parties who are not clients of the lawyer, even where the lawyer has been appointed with the concurrence of the parties. In performing such a role the lawyer may be subject to applicable codes of ethics, such as the Code of Ethics for Arbitration in Commercial Disputes prepared by a joint Committee of the American Bar Association and the American Arbitration Association.

[3] A lawyer acts as intermediary in seeking to establish or adjust a relationship between clients on an amicable and mutually advantageous basis; for example, in helping to organize a business in which two or more clients are entrepreneurs, working out the financial reorganization of an enterprise in which two or more clients have an interest, arranging a property distribution in settlement of an estate or mediating a dispute between clients. The lawyer seeks to resolve potentially conflicting interests by developing the parties' mutual interests. The alternative can be that each party may have to obtain separate representation, with the possibility in some situations of incurring additional cost, complication or even litigation. Given these and other relevant factors, all the clients may prefer that the lawyer act as intermediary.

[4] In considering whether to act as intermediary between clients, a lawyer should be mindful that if the intermediation fails the result can be additional cost, embarrassment and recrimination. In some situations the risk of failure is so great that intermediation is plainly impossible. For example, a lawyer cannot undertake common representation of clients between whom contentious litigation is imminent or who contemplate contentious negotiations. More generally, if the relationship between the parties has already assumed definite antagonism, the possibility that the clients' interests can be adjusted by intermediation ordinarily is not very good.

[5] The appropriateness of intermediation can depend on its form. Forms of intermediation range from informal arbitration, where each client's case is presented by the respective client and the lawyer decides the outcome, to mediation, to common representation where the clients' interests are substantially though not entirely compatible. One form may be appropriate in circumstances

150

where another would not. Other relevant factors are whether the lawyer subsequently will represent both parties on a continuing basis and whether the situation involves creating a relationship between the parties or terminating one.

Confidentiality and Privilege

[6] A particularly important factor in determining the appropriateness of intermediation is the effect on client-lawyer confidentiality and the attorney-client privilege. In a common representation, the lawyer is still required both to keep each client adequately informed and to maintain confidentiality of information relating to the representation. See Rules 1.4 and 1.6. Complying with both requirements while acting as intermediary requires a delicate balance. If the balance cannot be maintained, the common representation is improper. With regard to the attorney-client privilege, the prevailing rule is that as between commonly represented clients the privilege does not attach. Hence, it must be assumed that if litigation eventuates between the clients, the privilege will not protect any such communications, and the clients should be so advised.

[7] Since the lawyer is required to be impartial between commonly represented clients, intermediation is improper when that impartiality cannot be maintained. For example, a lawyer who has represented one of the clients for a long period and in a variety of matters might have difficulty being impartial between that client and one to whom the lawyer has only recently been introduced.

Consultation

[8] In acting as intermediary between clients, the lawyer is required to consult with the clients on the implications of doing so, and proceed only upon consent based on such a consultation. The consultation should make clear that the lawyer's role is not that of partisanship normally expected in other circumstances.

[9] Paragraph (b) is an application of the principle expressed in Rule 1.4. Where the lawyer is intermediary, the clients ordinarily must assume greater responsibility for decisions than when each client is independently represented.

Withdrawal

[10] Common representation does not diminish the rights of each client in the client-lawyer relationship. Each has the right to loyal and diligent representation, the right to discharge the lawyer as stated in Rule 1.16, and the protection of Rule 1.9 concerning obligations to a former client.

Model Code Comparison

There was no direct counterpart to this Rule in the Disciplinary Rules of the Model Code. EC 5-20 stated that a "lawyer is often asked to serve as an impartial arbitrator or mediator in matters which involve present or former clients. He may serve in either capacity if he first discloses such present or former relationships." DR 5-105(B) provided that a lawyer "shall not continue multiple employment if the exercise of his independent judgment in behalf of a client will be or is likely to be adversely affected by his representation of another client, or if it would be likely to involve him in representation of differing interests, except to the extent permitted under DR 5-105(C)." DR 5-105(C) provided that "a lawyer may represent multiple clients if it is obvious that he can adequately represent the interests of each and if each consents to the representation after full disclosure of the possible effect of such representation on the exercise of his independent professional judgment on behalf of each."

Cross-References in Rules

Rule 1.6, Comment 20: "The Rules of Professional Conduct in various circumstances permit or require a lawyer to disclose information relating to the representation. See **Rules 2.2**, 2.3, 3.3 and 4.1."

Rule 1.7, Comment 2: "Where more than one client is involved and the lawyer withdraws because a conflict arises after representation, whether the lawyer may continue to represent any of the clients is determined by Rule 1.9. See also **Rule 2.2(c)**."

Rule 1.7, Comment 7: "[C]ommon representation of persons having similar interests is proper if the risk of adverse effect is minimal and the requirements of paragraph (b) are met. Compare **Rule 2.2** involving intermediation between clients."

Rule 1.10(a): "While lawyers are associated in a firm, none of them shall knowingly represent a client when any one of them practicing alone would be prohibited from doing so by **Rules** 1.7, 1.8(c), 1.9 or **2.2**."

Legislative History

1980 Discussion Draft (then Rules 5.1 and 5.2) began with the following Introduction:

Intermediary Between Clients

A lawyer acts as intermediary in seeking to establish or adjust a relationship between clients on an amicable and mutually advantageous basis. A lawyer acts as intermediary, for example, in drafting the documents organizing a business in which two or more clients are entrepreneurs but have differing financial or personal interests in the enterprise. A lawyer acts as intermediary in working out a plan of financial reorganization for an enterprise on behalf of two or more clients who have differing financial interests in the enterprise, or in arranging the distribution of specific property in settlement of an estate among distributees. Under some circumstances, a lawyer may act as intermediary between spouses in arranging the terms of an uncontested separation or divorce settlement. A lawyer may act as intermediary in mediating a dispute between clients.

In all such situations, the lawyer seeks to resolve potentially conflicting interests by developing the parties' mutual interests. The alternative often is that each party may have to obtain separate representation, with the possibility in some situations of incurring added burdens of cost, complication, and even litigation. In some nonlitigation situations, the stakes involved may be so modest that separate representation of the parties is financially impractical. Given these factors, all the clients may prefer that the lawyer act as intermediary. If they do, and if the lawyer's independent professional judgment indicates that acting as intermediary will further the clients' mutual interest, a lawyer may undertake that function.

This Rule does not deal with a lawyer acting as mediator or arbitrator between parties with whom the lawyer does not have a client-lawyer relationship, nor does it govern a situation where a lawyer represents a party in negotiation with a party who is unrepresented. A lawyer acts as intermediary under this Rule when the lawyer represents both parties. A key factor in defining the relationship is whether the parties share responsibility for paying the lawyer's fee, but the existence of a joint or common representation can be inferred from other circumstances. Because confusion can arise as to the lawyer's role and responsibility where each party is not separately represented, it is important that the lawyer make clear whom he represents in such situations.

Rules 5.1 and 5.2 of the 1980 Discussion Draft provided:

Conditions for Acting as an Intermediary

(a) A lawyer may act as an intermediary between clients if:
   (1) the possibility of adjusting the clients' interests is strong; and
   (2) each client will be able to make adequately informed decisions in the matter, and there is little likelihood that any of the clients will be significantly prejudiced if the contemplated adjustment of interests is unsuccessful; and
   (3) the lawyer can act impartially and without improper effect on other services the lawyer is performing for any of the clients; and
   (4) the lawyer fully explains to each client the implications of the common representation, including the advantages and risks involved, and obtains each client's consent to the common representation.

(b) Before serving as intermediary a lawyer shall explain fully to each client the decisions to be made and the considerations relevant to making them, so that each client can make adequately informed decisions.

Withdrawal as an Intermediary

A lawyer shall withdraw as intermediary if any of the clients so requests, if the conditions stated in Rule 5.1 cannot be met, or if it becomes apparent that a mutually advantageous adjustment of interests cannot be made. Upon withdrawal, the lawyer may continue to represent any of the clients only to the extent compatible with the lawyer's responsibilities to the other client or clients.

1981 Draft: Rule 2.2(c) required a lawyer to withdraw if the conditions in (a) could not be met "or if in the light of subsequent events the lawyer reasonably should know that a mutually advantageous resolution cannot be achieved."

1982 Draft: Rule 2.2(a)(1) was substantially the same as adopted except that it did not require the lawyer to explain "the effect on the attorney-client privileges." Rule 2.2(c)'s second sentence provided: "Upon withdrawal, the lawyer shall not continue to represent any of the clients unless doing so is clearly compatible with the lawyer's responsibilities to the other client or clients." The remainder of Rule 2.2 was substantially the same as adopted.

Selected State Variations

California: See Rule 3-310(B) (generally governing concurrent conflicts — California has no direct counterpart to Rule 2.2).

District of Columbia: Rule 2.2(b) provides:

> A lawyer should, except in unusual circumstances that may make it infeasible, provide both clients with an explanation in writing of the risks involved in the common representation and of the circumstances that may cause separate representation later to be necessary or desirable. The consent of the clients shall also be in writing.

Illinois omits Rule 2.2.

New Jersey makes Rule 2.2 "subject to the provisions of Rule 1.7."

New York: Same or substantially the same as the ABA Model Code — see Model Code Comparison above.

North Carolina omits Rule 2.2.

Texas Rule 2.02 deletes paragraph (b).

Virginia omits Rule 2.2.

Related Materials

Editors' Note.   Comment 2 to Rule 2.2 notes that the Rule "does not apply to a lawyer acting as arbitrator or mediator." However, a number of codes and standards are available to give guidance to lawyers acting as artibrators or mediators. Here are a few examples:

ABA Standards of Practice for Lawyer Mediators in Family Disputes: In 1984, the ABA House of Delegates formally adopted Standards for Lawyer Mediators in Family Disputes. They are reprinted in this volume at pages 506-510.

American Academy of Matrimonial Lawyers: The "Bounds of Advocacy" drafted by the American Academy of Matrimonial Lawyers contains the following provisions and commentary:

> 1.4 An attorney should be knowledgeable about alternative ways to resolve matrimonial disputes.

Comment to Rule 1.4

> Matrimonial law is not simply a matter of winning or losing. At its best, matrimonial law should result in disputes being resolved fairly for all parties, including children. An alternative to courtroom confrontation may achieve a fair outcome. Parties are more likely to abide by their own promises than by an outcome imposed by a court. In some cases, alternative dispute resolution mechanisms may not be appropriate or workable due to the nature of the dispute or the animosity of the parties. Under certain circumstances, litigation may be the best course, but a negotiated resolution is desirable in most family law disputes.
> Alternative dispute resolution mechanisms may establish a positive tone for continuing

post-divorce relations by avoiding the animosity and pain of court battles. Parents who litigate their custody disputes are more likely to believe the process had a detrimental effect on relations with the divorcing spouse than parents whose custody disputes are mediated. When resolution requires complex trade-offs, the parties may be better able than the court to forge a resolution that addresses their individual values and needs. Alternatives to litigation are often less expensive; however, the client should be informed that such mechanisms may not necessarily reduce the cost because the matrimonial lawyer may need to prepare the case as thoroughly as for trial. Thus, it is essential that matrimonial lawyers have sufficient knowledge about alternative dispute resolution to enable them to understand its advantages and disadvantages. The attorney may then be able to determine when it is appropriate to recommend alternative methods to the client.

1.5 An attorney should act as a mediator or arbitrator only if competent to do so.

Comment to Rule 1.5

No one should engage in the mediation or arbitration of marital disputes without adequate education and training. There are many ways to acquire the necessary knowledge and skill, including continuing legal education, formal training programs, informal training by peers, law school training programs and experience.

A matrimonial lawyer is in the best position to understand the likely outcome of the adjudication of a legal dispute and is best able to ensure the validity of any agreement or other legal document resulting from a mediated agreement. Mediation and arbitration are skills that, like trial advocacy, require study and training.

2.15 An attorney should encourage the settlement of marital disputes through negotiation, mediation, or arbitration.

Comment to Rule 2.15

The litigation process is expensive and emotionally draining. In matrimonial matters, the highly charged atmosphere makes a speedy, cooperative resolution of disputes highly desirable. In many cases, the parties will have continuing contact with each other and need to cooperate for years to come. There is evidence that parties to a matrimonial dispute are more willing to abide by an agreement voluntarily entered into than by a court-ordered resolution following litigation. And, there is increasing evidence of the destructive effect on the children of protracted, adversarial proceedings between the spouses. It is therefore in the family's interest to seek to settle disputes cooperatively.

2.20 An attorney should not represent both husband and wife even if they do not wish to obtain independent representation.

Comment to Rule 2.20

The temptation to represent potentially conflicting interests is particularly difficult to resist in family disputes. Often the attorney is the "family lawyer" and previously represented husband, wife, family corporations, and even the children. Serving as an intermediary between husband and wife is not prohibited by the RPC. However, it is impossible for the attorney to provide impartial advice to both parties, and even a seemingly amicable separation or divorce may result in bitter litigation over financial matters or custody. A matrimonial lawyer should not attempt to represent both husband and wife even with the consent of both.

The attorney may be asked to represent family members in a nonlitigation setting. If separation or divorce is foreseeable or if one of the parents desires defense in a battered child action, the lawyer may see her role as counselor or negotiator for all concerned. This temptation should be resisted. However, this Standard does not apply in adoption proceedings or other matters where the spouses' positions are not adverse.

Association of Family Conciliation Courts Model Standards of Practice for Family and Divorce Mediation: In 1984, the Association of Family and Conciliation Courts promulgated standards "intended to assist public and private, voluntary and mandatory mediation" (Preamble). They can be found in the December 1984 Dispute Resolution Forum published by the National Institute for Dispute Resolution.

Code of Ethics for Arbitrators in Commercial Disputes: A Joint Committee of the ABA and the American Arbitration Association (AAA) has prepared a code of ethics for commercial arbitrators. It is mentioned in Comment 2 to Rule 2.2, and is reprinted in this volume at page 150.

Model Rules of Professional Conduct for Federal Lawyers: Federal lawyers are permitted to act as intermediaries only between two individuals. After withdrawal as an intermediary, a federal lawyer may continue to represent some of the clients in the same matter if each client consents.

Restatement of the Law Governing Lawyers: The American Law Institute has tentatively approved the following provision:

§211. Simultaneous Representation in Non-Litigated Matters

Unless all affected clients consent to the representation under the limitations and conditions provided in §202, a lawyer may not represent two or more clients in any matters not involving litigation if there is a substantial risk that the lawyer's representation of one or more of the clients would be materially and adversely affected by the lawyer's duties to one or more of the other clients.

(Restatement §202 is reprinted above in the Related Materials following Model Rule 1.7.)

Rule 2.3 Evaluation for Use by Third Persons

(a) A lawyer may undertake an evaluation of a matter affecting a client for the use of someone other than the client if:

(1) the lawyer reasonably believes that making the evaluation is compatible with other aspects of the lawyer's relationship with the client; and

(2) the client consents after consultation.

(b) Except as disclosure is required in connection with a report of an evaluation, information relating to the evaluation is otherwise protected by Rule 1.6.

COMMENT

Definition

[1] An evaluation may be performed at the client's direction but for the primary purpose of establishing information for the benefit of third parties; for ex-

ample, an opinion concerning the title of property rendered at the behest of a vendor for the information of a prospective purchaser, or at the behest of a borrower for the information of a prospective lender. In some situations, the evaluation may be required by a government agency; for example, an opinion concerning the legality of the securities registered for sale under the securities laws. In other instances, the evaluation may be required by a third person, such as a purchaser of a business.

[2] Lawyers for the government may be called upon to give a formal opinion on the legality of contemplated government agency action. In making such an evaluation, the government lawyer acts at the behest of the government as the client but for the purpose of establishing the limits of the agency's authorized activity. Such an opinion is to be distinguished from confidential legal advice given agency officials. The critical question is whether the opinion is to be made public.

[3] A legal evaluation should be distinguished from an investigation of a person with whom the lawyer does not have a client-lawyer relationship. For example, a lawyer retained by a purchaser to analyze a vendor's title to property does not have a client-lawyer relationship with the vendor. So also, an investigation into a person's affairs by a government lawyer, or by special counsel employed by the government, is not an evaluation as that term is used in this Rule. The question is whether the lawyer is retained by the person whose affairs are being examined. When the lawyer is retained by that person, the general rules concerning loyalty to client and preservation of confidences apply, which is not the case if the lawyer is retained by someone else. For this reason, it is essential to identify the person by whom the lawyer is retained. This should be made clear not only to the person under examination, but also to others to whom the results are to be made available.

Duty to Third Person

[4] When the evaluation is intended for the information or use of a third person, a legal duty to that person may or may not arise. That legal question is beyond the scope of this Rule. However, since such an evaluation involves a departure from the normal client-lawyer relationship, careful analysis of the situation is required. The lawyer must be satisfied as a matter of professional judgment that making the evaluation is compatible with other functions undertaken in behalf of the client. For example, if the lawyer is acting as advocate in defending the client against charges of fraud, it would normally be incompatible with that responsibility for the lawyer to perform an evaluation for others concerning the same or a related transaction. Assuming no such impediment is apparent, however, the lawyer should advise the client of the implications of the evaluation, particularly the lawyer's responsibilities to third persons and the duty to disseminate the findings.

Access to and Disclosure of Information

[5] The quality of an evaluation depends on the freedom and extent of the investigation upon which it is based. Ordinarily a lawyer should have whatever latitude of investigation seems necessary as a matter of professional judgment. Under some circumstances, however, the terms of the evaluation may be limited. For example, certain issues or sources may be categorically excluded, or the scope of search may be limited by time constraints or the noncooperation of persons having relevant information. Any such limitations which are material to the evaluation should be described in the report. If after a lawyer has commenced an evaluation, the client refuses to comply with the terms upon which it was understood the evaluation was to have been made, the lawyer's obligations are determined by law, having reference to the terms of the client's agreement and the surrounding circumstances.

Financial Auditors' Requests for Information

[6] When a question concerning the legal situation of a client arises at the instance of the client's financial auditor and the question is referred to the lawyer, the lawyer's response may be made in accordance with procedures recognized in the legal profession. Such a procedure is set forth in the American Bar Association Statement of Policy Regarding Lawyers' Responses to Auditors' Requests for Information, adopted in 1975.

Model Code Comparison

There was no counterpart to this Rule in the Model Code.

Cross-References in Rules

Rule 1.6, Comment 20: "The Rules of Professional Conduct in various circumstances permit or require a lawyer to disclose information relating to the representation. See **Rules** 2.2, **2.3**, 3.3 and 4.1."

Legislative History

1980 Discussion Draft (then Rules 6.1 through 6.3):

Confidential Evaluation (Rule 6.1)

A lawyer undertakes a confidential evaluation of a matter affecting a client when a report of the evaluation is to be given to the client alone and to be disclosed to others only at the direction of the client.

Independent Evaluation (Rule 6.2)

(a) A lawyer undertakes an independent evaluation of a matter affecting a client when a report of the evaluation is to be given to someone other than the client. A lawyer may make an independent evaluation if:

(1) Making the evaluation is compatible with other aspects of the lawyer's relationship with the client; and

(2) The terms upon which the evaluation is made are clearly described, particularly the lawyer's access to information and the persons to whom the report of the evaluation is to be made; and

(3) The client agrees that the lawyer may, within the terms upon which the evaluation is made, disclose information about the client, including matter otherwise confidential or privileged, that the lawyer determines ought to be disclosed in making a fair and accurate evaluation; and

(4) After adequate disclosure of the terms upon which the evaluation is to be made and their implications for the client, the client requests the lawyer to make the evaluation.

(b) In reporting the evaluation, the lawyer shall indicate any limitations on the scope of the inquiry that are reasonably necessary to a proper interpretation of the report.

(c) If, after a lawyer has commenced an independent evaluation, the client refuses to comply with the terms upon which it is to be made, the lawyer shall give to the person for whom the evaluation is intended the fullest report that can be made in the circumstances.

(d) Except as disclosure is required in connection with a report of the evaluation, information relating to an independent evaluation is confidential under Rule 1.7.

Financial Auditors' Requests for Information (Rule 6.3)

When a question concerning the legal situation of a client arises at the instance of the client's financial auditor and the question is referred to the lawyer, the lawyer's response shall be made in accordance with procedures recognized in the legal profession unless some other procedure is established after consent by the client upon adequate disclosure.

1981 Draft: Rule 2.3(a)(2) provided:

the terms upon which the evaluation is to be made are stated in writing, particularly the terms relating to the lawyer's access to information, the contemplated disclosure of otherwise confidential information and the persons to whom report of the evaluation is to be made . . .

Rule 2.3(b) provided: "In reporting the evaluation, the lawyer shall indicate any material limitations that were imposed on the scope of the inquiry or on the disclosure of information."

1982 Draft: Rule 2.3(a)(2) required that "the conditions of the evaluation [be] described to the client in writing, including contemplated disclosure of information otherwise protected by Rule 1.6. . . ."

Selected State Variations

California has no direct counterpart to Rule 2.3.

New Jersey adds a requirement that "the conditions of the evaluation are described to the client in writing, including contemplated disclosure of information otherwise protected by Rule 1.6."

New York: No comparable provision.

North Carolina and *Virginia* omit Rule 2.3.

ARTICLE 3. ADVOCATE

Editors' Note. The *1980 Discussion Draft* contained the following Introduction to this article:

As advocate, a lawyer presents evidence and argument before a tribunal in behalf of a client. The advocate's duty in the adversary system is to present the client's case as persuasively as possible, leaving presentation of the opposing case to the other party. An advocate may not present a claim or defense lacking serious merit for the purpose of delay, although an advocate for the defendant in a criminal case may insist on proof of the offense charged. An advocate does not vouch for the justness of a client's cause but only its legal merit.

Rule 3.1 Meritorious Claims and Contentions

A lawyer shall not bring or defend a proceeding, or assert or controvert an issue therein, unless there is a basis for doing so that is not frivolous, which includes a good faith argument for an extension, modification or reversal of existing law. A lawyer for the defendant in a criminal proceeding, or the respondent in a proceeding that could result in incarceration, may nevertheless so defend the proceeding as to require that every element of the case be established.

COMMENT

[1] The advocate has a duty to use legal procedure for the fullest benefit of the client's cause, but also a duty not to abuse legal procedure. The law, both procedural and substantive, establishes the limits within which an advocate may proceed. However, the law is not always clear and never is static. Accordingly, in determining the proper scope of advocacy, account must be taken of the law's ambiguities and potential for change.

[2] The filing of an action or defense or similar action taken for a client is not frivolous merely because the facts have not first been fully substantiated or because the lawyer expects to develop vital evidence only by discovery. Such action is not frivolous even though the lawyer believes that the client's posi-

tion ultimately will not prevail. The action is frivolous, however, if the client desires to have the action taken primarily for the purpose of harassing or maliciously injuring a person or if the lawyer is unable either to make a good faith argument on the merits of the action taken or to support the action taken by a good faith argument for an extension, modification or reversal of existing law.

Model Code Comparison

DR 7-102(A)(1) provided that a lawyer may not "[f]ile a suit, assert a position, conduct a defense, delay a trial, or take other action on behalf of his client when he knows or when it is obvious that such action would serve merely to harass or maliciously injure another." Rule 3.1 is to the same general effect as DR 7-102(A)(1), with three qualifications. First, the test of improper conduct is changed from "merely to harass or maliciously injure another" to the requirement that there be a basis for the litigation measure involved that is "not frivolous." This includes the concept stated in DR 7-102(A)(2) that a lawyer may advance a claim or defense unwarranted by existing law if "it can be supported by good faith argument for an extension, modification, or reversal of existing law." Second, the test in Rule 3.1 is an objective test, whereas DR 7-102(A)(1) applied only if the lawyer "knows or when it is obvious" that the litigation is frivolous. Third, Rule 3.1 has an exception that in a criminal case, or a case in which incarceration of the client may result (for example, certain juvenile proceedings), the lawyer may put the prosecution to its proof even if there is no nonfrivolous basis for defense.

Cross-References in Rules

Rule 3.3, Comment 2: "An advocate is responsible for pleadings and other documents prepared for litigation, but is usually not required to have personal knowledge of matters asserted therein, for litigation documents ordinarily present assertions by the client, or by someone on the client's behalf, and not assertions by the lawyer. Compare **Rule 3.1**."

Legislative History

1980 Discussion Draft provided:

 (a) A lawyer shall not:
  (1) file a complaint, motion, or pleading other than one that puts the prosecution to its proof in a criminal case, unless according to the lawyer's belief there is good ground to support it;

1982 and 1982 Drafts were substantially the same as adopted.

Selected State Variations

California: See Rule 3-200 (Prohibited Objectives of Employment) and B & P Code §6068(c).

District of Columbia: Rule 3.1 provides in part:

> ... A lawyer for the defendant in a criminal proceeding, or for the respondent in a proceeding that could result in involuntary institutionalization, shall, if the client elects to go to trial or to a contested fact-finding hearing, nevertheless so defend the proceeding as to require that the government carry its burden of proof.

New Jersey adds "the lawyer knows or reasonably believes" after "unless" in the first sentence.

New York: Same or substantially the same as the ABA Model Code — see Model Code Comparison above. See also New York Sanctioning Provisions in the New York Materials.

North Carolina: Rule 7.2 retains the language of the Model Code, but adds the phrase "controvert an issue" and adds the second sentence of Model Rule 3.1 (relating to criminal proceedings).

Texas's version of Rule 3.01 ends after "frivolous."

Virginia: Substantially the same as the Model Code.

Related Materials

ABA Canons: Canons 5, 15, 30, and 31 provided:

5. The Defense or Prosecution of Those Accused of Crime

It is the right of the lawyer to undertake the defense of a person accused of crime, regardless of his personal opinion as to the guilt of the accused; otherwise innocent persons, victims only of suspicious circumstances, might be denied proper defense. Having undertaken such defense, the lawyer is bound, by all fair and honorable means, to present every defense that the law of the land permits, to the end that no person may be deprived of life or liberty, but by due process of law.

15. How Far a Lawyer May Go in Supporting a Client's Cause

Nothing operates more certainly to create or to foster popular prejudice against lawyers as a class, and to deprive the profession of that full measure of public esteem and confidence which belongs to the proper discharge of its duties than does the false claim, often set up by the unscrupulous in defense of questionable transactions, that it is the duty of the lawyer to do whatever may enable him to succeed in winning his client's cause.

It is improper for a lawyer to assert in argument his personal belief in his client's innocence or in the justice of his cause.

30. Justifiable and Unjustifiable Litigations

The lawyer must decline to conduct a civil cause or to make a defense when convinced that it is intended merely to harass or to injure the opposite party or to work oppression or wrong. But otherwise it is his right, and, having accepted retainer, it becomes his duty to insist upon the judgment of the Court as to the legal merits of his client's claim. His appearance in Court should be deemed equivalent to an assertion on his honor that in his opinion his client's case is one proper for judicial determination.

31. Responsibility for Litigation

The responsibility for advising as to questionable transactions, for bringing questionable suits, for urging questionable defenses, is the lawyer's responsibility. He cannot escape it by urging as an excuse that he is only following his client's instructions.

American Academy of Matrimonial Lawyers: The "Bounds of Advocacy" drafted by the American Academy of Matrimonial Lawyers contains the following provision and commentary:

2.25 An attorney should not contest child custody or visitation for either financial leverage or vindictiveness.

Comment to Rule 2.25

Clients in contested dissolutions sometimes ask attorneys to contest custody even though they concede that the other spouse is the better parent. It is improper for the matrimonial lawyer to assist the client in such conduct. Proper consideration of the welfare of the children requires that they not be used as pawns in the adversary process. If despite the attorney's advice the client persists, the attorney should seek to withdraw.

Federal Rules of Civil Procedure: Rule 11, which closely tracks the language of Model Rule 3.1, has been an active weapon in fighting frivolous and unwarranted lawsuits. An attorney who violates Rule 11 is subject to "an appropriate sanction," which may include the opposing party's reasonable attorney fees caused by the violation. However, Rule 11 has also caused much controversy. We reprint the full text of the Rule and a proposed amendment at pages 606-608. The Rule provides in pertinent part as follows:

Every pleading, motion, and other paper of a party represented by an attorney shall be signed by at least one attorney of record in the attorney's individual name. . . . The signature of an attorney or party constitutes a certificate by the signer that the signer has read the pleading, motion, or other paper; that to the best of the signer's knowledge, information, and belief formed after reasonable inquiry it is well grounded in fact and is warranted by existing law or a good faith argument for the extension, modification, or reversal of existing law, and that it is not interposed for any improper purpose, such as to harass or to cause unnecessary delay or needless increase in the cost of litigation. . . .

In addition, Fed. R. Civ. P. 16, which governs pretrial conferences, provides that the participants at any pretrial conference "may consider and take action with respect to . . . the elimination of frivolous claims or defenses."

Federal Rules of Appellate Procedure: Rule 38 provides that "[i]f a court of appeals shall determine that an appeal is frivolous, it may award just damages and single or double costs to the appellee."

Rule 3.2 Expediting Litigation

A lawyer shall make reasonable efforts to expedite litigation consistent with the interests of the client.

COMMENT

Dilatory practices bring the administration of justice into disrepute. Delay should not be indulged merely for the convenience of the advocates, or for the purpose of frustrating an opposing party's attempt to obtain rightful redress or repose. It is not a justification that similar conduct is often tolerated by the bench and bar. The question is whether a competent lawyer acting in good faith would regard the course of action as having some substantial purpose other than delay. Realizing financial or other benefit from otherwise improper delay in litigation is not a legitimate interest of the client.

Model Code Comparison

DR 7-101(A)(1) stated that a lawyer does not violate the duty to represent a client zealously "by being punctual in fulfilling all professional commitments." DR 7-102(A)(1) provided that a lawyer "shall not . . . file a suit, assert a position, conduct a defense [or] delay a trial . . . when he knows or when it is obvious that such action would serve merely to harass or maliciously injure another."

Cross-References in Rules

None.

Legislative History

1980 Discussion Draft (then Rule 3.3(a)) provided:

A lawyer shall make every effort consistent with the legitimate interests of the client to expedite litigation. Realizing financial or other benefit from otherwise improper delay in litigation is not a legitimate interest of the client. A lawyer shall not engage in any procedure or tactic having no substantial purpose other than delay or increasing the cost of litigation to another party.

1981 Draft: "A lawyer shall make reasonable effort consistent with the *legitimate* interests of the client to expedite litigation."
1982 Draft was adopted.

Selected State Variations

California: See B & P Code §6128(b). (California's Rules of Professional Conduct have no comparable provision.)

District of Columbia: Rule 3.2(a) adds the following language based on DR 7-102(A)(1): "a lawyer shall not delay a proceeding when the lawyer knows or when it is obvious that such action would serve solely to harass or maliciously injure another."

New Jersey adds "and shall treat with courtesy and consideration all persons involved in the legal process" at the end of Rule 3.2.

New York: Same or substantially the same as the ABA Model Code — see Model Code Comparison above.

North Carolina: Rules 7.1 and 7.2 are substantially the same as the Model Code.

Texas Rule 3.02 provides:

> In the course of litigation, a lawyer shall not take a position that unreasonably increases the costs or other burdens of the case or that unreasonably delays resolution of the matter.

Virginia: Substantially the same as the Model Code.

Related Materials

Federal Rules of Civil Procedure: Fed. R. Civ. P. 1 provides that the Federal Rules of Civil Procedure "shall be construed to secure the just, *speedy*, and inexpensive determination of every action [emphasis added]." Fed. R. Civ. P. 11, the broadest and most frequently invoked sanctions rule, requires attorneys to sign every pleading, motion, or other paper to certify that (among other things) the paper is "not interposed for any improper purpose, such as to harass or to *cause unnecessary delay* or needless increase in the cost of the litigation . . . [emphasis added]." Fed. R. Civ. P. 26(g), part of the general rule governing discovery, requires the identical certification pertaining to discovery requests, responses, and objections. Fed. R. Civ. P. 56(g), part of the rule on summary judgment, provides sanctions whenever the court finds "that any of the affidavits presented pursuant to this rule are presented in bad faith *or solely for the purpose of delay* [emphasis added]."

Federal Rules of Appellate Procedure: Rule 38, entitled "Damages for Delay," provides as follows: "If a court of appeals shall determine that an appeal is frivolous, it may award just damages and single or double costs to the appellee."

Federal Rules of Evidence: Rule 102 of the Federal Rules of Evidence provides that the Rules shall be construed to secure "elimination of unjustifiable expense and delay. . . ."

Model Rules of Professional Conduct for Federal Lawyers: Rule 3.2 provides: "A Federal lawyer shall make reasonable efforts to expedite litigation and other proceedings consistent with the interests of the client *and the lawyer's responsibilities to the tribunal to avoid unwarranted delay* [emphasis added]."

28 U.S.C. §1927: A major federal statutory provision available to penalize litigants who engage in abusive delay and other improper litigation tactics is 28 U.S.C. §1927, which provides as follows:

Counsel's Liability for Excessive Costs

Any attorney . . . who so multiplies the proceedings in any case unreasonably and vexatiously may be required by the court to satisfy personally the excess costs, expenses, and attorneys' fees reasonably incurred because of such conduct.

Rule 3.3 Candor Toward the Tribunal

(a) A lawyer shall not knowingly:

(1) make a false statement of material fact or law to a tribunal;

(2) fail to disclose a material fact to a tribunal when disclosure is necessary to avoid assisting a criminal or fraudulent act by the client;

(3) fail to disclose to the tribunal legal authority in the controlling jurisdiction known to the lawyer to be directly adverse to the position of the client and not disclosed by opposing counsel; or

(4) offer evidence that the lawyer knows to be false. If a lawyer has offered material evidence and comes to know of its falsity, the lawyer shall take reasonable remedial measures.

(b) The duties stated in paragraph (a) continue to the conclusion of the proceeding, and apply even if compliance requires disclosure of information otherwise protected by Rule 1.6.   5 o – 5 1 .

(c) A lawyer may refuse to offer evidence that the lawyer reasonably believes is false.

(d) In an ex parte proceeding, a lawyer shall inform the tribunal of all material facts known to the lawyer which will enable the tribunal to make an informed decision, whether or not the facts are adverse.

COMMENT

[1] The advocate's task is to present the client's case with persuasive force. Performance of that duty while maintaining confidences of the client is qualified by the advocate's duty of candor to the tribunal. However, an advocate does not vouch for the evidence submitted in a cause; the tribunal is responsible for assessing its probative value.

Representations by a Lawyer

[2] An advocate is responsible for pleadings and other documents prepared for litigation, but is usually not required to have personal knowledge of matters asserted therein, for litigation documents ordinarily present assertions by the client, or by someone on the client's behalf, and not assertions by the lawyer. Compare Rule 3.1. However, an assertion purporting to be on the lawyer's own knowledge, as in an affidavit by the lawyer or in a statement in open court, may

properly be made only when the lawyer knows the assertion is true or believes it to be true on the basis of a reasonably diligent inquiry. There are circumstances where failure to make a disclosure is the equivalent of an affirmative misrepresentation. The obligation prescribed in Rule 1.2(d) not to counsel a client to commit or assist the client in committing a fraud applies in litigation. Regarding compliance with Rule 1.2(d), see the Comment to that Rule. See also the Comment to Rule 8.4(b).

Misleading Legal Argument

[3] Legal argument based on a knowingly false representation of law constitutes dishonesty toward the tribunal. A lawyer is not required to make a disinterested exposition of the law, but must recognize the existence of pertinent legal authorities. Furthermore, as stated in paragraph (a)(3), an advocate has a duty to disclose directly adverse authority in the controlling jurisdiction which has not been disclosed by the opposing party. The underlying concept is that the legal argument is a discussion seeking to determine the legal premises properly applicable to the case.

False Evidence

[4] When evidence that a lawyer knows to be false is provided by a person who is not the client, the lawyer must refuse to offer it regardless of the client's wishes.

[5] When false evidence is offered by the client, however, a conflict may arise between the lawyer's duty to keep the client's revelations confidential and the duty of candor to the court. Upon ascertaining that material evidence is false, the lawyer should seek to persuade the client that the evidence should not be offered or, if it has been offered, that its false character should immediately be disclosed. If the persuasion is ineffective, the lawyer must take reasonable remedial measures.

[6] Except in the defense of a criminal accused, the rule generally recognized is that, if necessary to rectify the situation, an advocate must disclose the existence of the client's deception to the court or to the other party. Such a disclosure can result in grave consequences to the client, including not only a sense of betrayal but also loss of the case and perhaps a prosecution for perjury. But the alternative is that the lawyer cooperate in deceiving the court, thereby subverting the truth-finding process which the adversary system is designed to implement. See Rule 1.2(d). Furthermore, unless it is clearly understood that the lawyer will act upon the duty to disclose the existence of false evidence, the client can simply reject the lawyer's advice to reveal the false evidence and insist that the lawyer keep silent. Thus the client could in effect coerce the lawyer into being a party to fraud on the court.

Perjury by a Criminal Defendant

[7] Whether an advocate for a criminally accused has the same duty of disclosure has been intensely debated. While it is agreed that the lawyer should seek to persuade the client to refrain from perjurious testimony, there has been dispute concerning the lawyer's duty when that persuasion fails. If the confrontation with the client occurs before trial, the lawyer ordinarily can withdraw. Withdrawal before trial may not be possible, however, either because trial is imminent, or because the confrontation with the client does not take place until the trial itself, or because no other counsel is available.

[8] The most difficult situation, therefore, arises in a criminal case where the accused insists on testifying when the lawyer knows that the testimony is perjurious. The lawyer's effort to rectify the situation can increase the likelihood of the client's being convicted as well as opening the possibility of a prosecution for perjury. On the other hand, if the lawyer does not exercise control over the proof, the lawyer participates, although in a merely passive way, in deception of the court.

[9] Three resolutions of this dilemma have been proposed. One is to permit the accused to testify by a narrative without guidance through the lawyer's questioning. This compromises both contending principles; it exempts the lawyer from the duty to disclose false evidence but subjects the client to an implicit disclosure of information imparted to counsel. Another suggested resolution, of relatively recent origin, is that the advocate be entirely excused from the duty to reveal perjury if the perjury is that of the client. This is a coherent solution but makes the advocate a knowing instrument of perjury.

[10] The other resolution of the dilemma is that the lawyer must reveal the client's perjury if necessary to rectify the situation. A criminal accused has a right to the assistance of an advocate, a right to testify and a right of confidential communication with counsel. However, an accused should not have a right to assistance of counsel in committing perjury. Furthermore, an advocate has an obligation, not only in professional ethics but under the law as well, to avoid implication in the commission of perjury or other falsification of evidence. See Rule 1.2(d).

Remedial Measures

[11] If perjured testimony or false evidence has been offered, the advocate's proper course ordinarily is to remonstrate with the client confidentially. If that fails, the advocate should seek to withdraw if that will remedy the situation. If withdrawal will not remedy the situation or is impossible, the advocate should make disclosure to the court. It is for the court then to determine what should be done — making a statement about the matter to the trier of fact, ordering a mistrial or perhaps nothing. If the false testimony was that of the client, the client may controvert the lawyer's version of their communication when the lawyer

discloses the situation to the court. If there is an issue whether the client has committed perjury, the lawyer cannot represent the client in resolution of the issue, and a mistrial may be unavoidable. An unscrupulous client might in this way attempt to produce a series of mistrials and thus escape prosecution. However, a second such encounter could be construed as a deliberate abuse of the right to counsel and as such a waiver of the right to further representation.

Constitutional Requirements

[12] The general rule — that an advocate must disclose the existence of perjury with respect to a material fact, even that of a client — applies to defense counsel in criminal cases, as well as in other instances. However, the definition of the lawyer's ethical duty in such a situation may be qualified by constitutional provisions for due process and the right to counsel in criminal cases. In some jurisdictions these provisions have been construed to require that counsel present an accused as a witness if the accused wishes to testify, even if counsel knows the testimony will be false. The obligation of the advocate under these Rules is subordinate to such a constitutional requirement.

Duration of Obligation

[13] A practical time limit on the obligation to rectify the presentation of false evidence has to be established. The conclusion of the proceeding is a reasonably definite point for the termination of the obligation.

Refusing to Offer Proof Believed to Be False

[14] Generally speaking, a lawyer has authority to refuse to offer testimony or other proof that the lawyer believes is untrustworthy. Offering such proof may reflect adversely on the lawyer's ability to discriminate in the quality of evidence and thus impair the lawyer's effectiveness as an advocate. In criminal cases, however, a lawyer may, in some jurisdictions, be denied this authority by constitutional requirements governing the right to counsel.

Ex Parte Proceedings

[15] Ordinarily, an advocate has the limited responsibility of presenting one side of the matters that a tribunal should consider in reaching a decision; the conflicting position is expected to be presented by the opposing party. However, in an ex parte proceeding, such as an application for a temporary restraining order, there is no balance of presentation by opposing advocates. The object of

an ex parte proceeding is nevertheless to yield a substantially just result. The judge has an affirmative responsibility to accord the absent party just consideration. The lawyer for the represented party has the correlative duty to make disclosures of material facts known to the lawyer and that the lawyer reasonably believes are necessary to an informed decision.

Model Code Comparison

Paragraph (a)(1) is substantially identical to DR 7-102(A)(5), which provided that a lawyer shall not "knowingly make a false statement of law or fact."

Paragraph (a)(2) is implicit in DR 7-102(A)(3), which provided that "a lawyer shall not . . . knowingly fail to disclose that which he is required by law to reveal."

Paragraph (a)(3) is substantially identical to DR 7-106(B)(1).

With regard to paragraph (a)(4), the first sentence of this subparagraph is similar to DR 7-102(A)(4), which provided that a lawyer shall not "knowingly use" perjured testimony or false evidence. The second sentence of paragraph (a)(4) resolves an ambiguity in the Model Code concerning the action required of a lawyer who discovers that the lawyer has offered perjured testimony or false evidence. DR 7-102(A)(4), quoted above, did not expressly deal with this situation, but the prohibition against "use" of false evidence can be construed to preclude carrying through with a case based on such evidence when that fact has become known during the trial. DR 7-102(B)(1), also noted in connection with Rule 1.6, provided that a lawyer "who receives information clearly establishing that . . . [h]is client has . . . perpetrated a fraud upon . . . a tribunal shall [if the client does not rectify the situation] . . . reveal the fraud to the . . . tribunal. . . ." Since use of perjured testimony or false evidence is usually regarded as "fraud" upon the court, DR 7-102(B)(1) apparently required disclosure by the lawyer in such circumstances. However, some states have amended DR 7-102(B)(1) in conformity with an ABA-recommended amendment to provide that the duty of disclosure does not apply when the "information is protected as a privileged communication." This qualification may be empty, for the rule of attorney-client privilege has been construed to exclude communications that further a crime, including the crime of perjury. On this interpretation of DR 7-102(B)(1), the lawyer has a duty to disclose the perjury.

Paragraph (c) confers discretion on the lawyer to refuse to offer evidence that the lawyer "reasonably believes" is false. This gives the lawyer more latitude than DR 7-102(A)(4), which prohibited the lawyer from offering evidence the lawyer "knows" is false.

There was no counterpart in the Model Code to paragraph (d).

Cross-References in Rules

Rule 1.6, Comment 10: "[A] lawyer has a duty under **Rule 3.3(a)(4)** not to use false evidence."

Rule 1.6, Comment 20: "The Rules of Professional Conduct in various circumstances permit or require a lawyer to disclose information relating to the representation. See **Rules** 2.2, 2.3, **3.3** and 4.1."

Rule 1.13, Comment 6: "[T]his Rule does not limit or expand the lawyer's responsibility under **Rules** 1.6, 1.8, and 1.16, **3.3** or 4.1."

Rule 3.8, Comment 1: "See also **Rule 3.3(d)**, governing ex parte proceedings, among which grand jury proceedings are included."

Rule 3.9: "A lawyer representing a client before a legislative or administrative tribunal in a nonadjudicative proceeding shall disclose that the appearance is in a representative capacity and shall conform to the provisions of **Rules 3.3(a)** through **(c)**, 3.4(a) through (c), and 3.5."

Legislative History

1980 Discussion Draft (then Rule 3.1) provided:

(a) A lawyer shall not: . . .

(2) make a knowing misrepresentation of fact;

(3) except as provided in paragraph (f), offer evidence that the lawyer is convinced beyond a reasonable doubt is false, or offer without suitable explanation evidence that the lawyer knows is substantially misleading; or

(4) make a representation about existing legal authority that the lawyer knows to be inaccurate or so incomplete as to be substantially misleading.

(b) Except as provided in paragraph (f), if a lawyer discovers that evidence or testimony presented by the lawyer is false, the lawyer shall disclose that fact and take suitable measures to rectify the consequences, even if doing so requires disclosure of a confidence of the client or disclosure that the client is implicated in the falsification.

(c) If a lawyer discovers that the tribunal has not been apprised of legal authority known to the lawyer that would probably have a substantial effect on the determination of a material issue, the lawyer shall advise the tribunal of that authority.

(d) Except as provided in paragraph (f), a lawyer shall disclose a fact known to the lawyer, even if the fact is adverse, when disclosure:

(1) is required by law or the Rules of Professional Conduct; or

(2) is necessary to correct a manifest misapprehension resulting from a previous representation the lawyer has made to the tribunal.

(e) Except as provided in paragraph (f), a lawyer may apprise another party of evidence favorable to that party and may refuse to offer evidence that the lawyer believes with substantial reason to be false.

(f) A lawyer for a defendant in a criminal case:

(1) is not required to apprise the prosecutor or the tribunal of evidence adverse to the accused, except as law may otherwise provide;

(2) may not disclose facts as required by paragraph (d) if doing so is prohibited by applicable law;

(3) shall offer evidence regardless of belief as to whether it is false if the client so demands and applicable law requires that the lawyer comply with such a demand.

(g) A prosecutor has the further duty of disclosure stated in Rule 3.10.

1981 Draft was substantially the same as adopted except for the following parts of subparagraph (a):

(a) A lawyer shall not knowingly:

(1) make a false statement of fact or law to a tribunal, or fail to disclose a fact in circumstances where the failure to make the disclosure is the equivalent of the lawyer's making a material misrepresentation;

(2) fail to make a disclosure of fact necessary to prevent a fraud on the tribunal. . . .

1982 Draft was adopted.

Selected State Variations

California: See Rule 5-200 (Trial Conduct), and B & P Code §6068(d) (regarding false statements to a judge) and §6128(a) (regarding intention to deceive a court).

District of Columbia: Rule 3.3 provides:

> (b) When the witness who intends to give evidence that the lawyer knows to be false is the lawyer's client and is the accused in a criminal case, the lawyer shall first make a good faith effort to dissuade the client from presenting the false evidence; if the lawyer is unable to dissuade the client, the lawyer shall seek leave of the tribunal to withdraw. If the lawyer is unable to dissuade the client or to withdraw without seriously harming the client, the lawyer may put the client on the stand to testify in a narrative fashion, but the lawyer shall not examine the client in such manner as to elicit testimony which the lawyer knows to be false, and shall not argue the probative value of the client's testimony in closing argument.
>
> (c) The duties stated in paragraph (a) continue to the conclusion of the proceeding.
>
> (d) A lawyer who receives information clearly establishing that a fraud has been perpetrated upon the tribunal shall promptly reveal the fraud to the tribunal unless compliance with this duty would require disclosure of information otherwise protected by Rule 1.6, in which case the lawyer shall promptly call upon the client to rectify the fraud.

In 1992, the District of Columbia deleted former paragraphs 9-11 of the Comment to Rule 3.3 and substituted the following new language:

> [9] Generally speaking, a lawyer may not offer testimony or other proof, through a non-client, that the lawyer knows to be false. Furthermore, a lawyer may not offer evidence of a client if the evidence is known by the lawyer to be false, except to the extent permitted by paragraph (b) where the client is a defendant in a criminal case.

Florida: In 1990, the Florida Supreme Court amended Rule 3.3 to provide that a lawyer shall not

> (a)(4) Permit any witness, including a criminal defendant, to offer testimony or other evidence that the lawyer knows to be false. A lawyer may not offer testimony which he knows to be false in the form of a narrative unless so ordered by the tribunal.

The next sentence of Florida's Rule 3.3(a)(4) is the same as the second sentence of ABA Model Rule 3.3(a)(4). Florida also provides in Rule 3.3(b) that the "duties stated in paragraph (a) continue beyond the conclusion of the proceeding. . . ."

Georgia's version of Rule 3.3(a) and (b) is the Code version as originally adopted without the 1974 amendment. See Model Code Comparison above.

Illinois Rule 3.3(a) provides:

> (a) In appearing in a professional capacity before a tribunal, a lawyer shall not:
>
> (1) make a statement of material fact or law to a tribunal which the lawyer knows or reasonably should know is false; . . .
>
> (5) participate in the creation or preservation of evidence when the lawyer knows or reasonably should know the evidence is false;
>
> (6) counsel or assist the client in conduct the lawyer knows to be illegal or fraudulent; . . .
>
> (8) fail to disclose the identities of the clients represented and of the persons who employed the lawyer unless such information is privileged or irrelevant;

(9) intentionally degrade a witness or other person by stating or alluding to personal facts concerning that person which are not relevant to the case; . . .

(12) fail to use reasonable efforts to restrain and to prevent clients from doing those things that the lawyer ought not to do;

(13) suppress any evidence that the lawyer or client has a legal obligation to reveal or produce;

(14) advise or cause a person to become unavailable as a witness by leaving the jurisdiction or making secret their whereabouts within the jurisdiction; or

(15) pay, offer to pay, or acquiesce in the payment of compensation to a witness contingent upon the content of the witness' testimony or the outcome of the case, but a lawyer may advance, guarantee, or acquiesce in the payment of expenses reasonably incurred in attending or testifying, and a reasonable fee for the professional services of an expert witness.

(b) The duties stated in paragraph (a) are continuing duties and apply even if compliance requires disclosure of information otherwise protected by Rule 1.6.

Illinois also adds to its Rule 1.2 the following subparagraphs, which substantially retain the language of DR 7-102(B) of the Code of Professional Responsibility as amended in 1974 (see Model Code Comparison to Rule 3.3 above):

(g) A lawyer who knows a client has, in the course of the representation, perpetrated a fraud upon a person or tribunal shall promptly call upon the client to rectify the same, and if the client refuses or is unable to do so, the lawyer shall reveal the fraud to the affected person or tribunal, except when the information is protected as a privileged communication.

(h) A lawyer who knows that a person other than the client has perpetrated a fraud upon a tribunal shall promptly reveal the fraud to the tribunal.

Maryland adds the following subparagraph (e): "notwithstanding paragraphs (a) through (d), a lawyer for an accused in a criminal case need not disclose that the accused intends to testify falsely or has testified falsely if the lawyer reasonably believes that the disclosure would jeopardize any constitutional right of the accused."

New Jersey adds the following subparagraph (a)(5): "fail to disclose to the tribunal a material fact with knowledge that the tribunal may tend to be misled by such failure." New Jersey adds the client's "illegal" acts to Rule 3.3(a)(2). New Jersey also requires a lawyer to reveal confidences to prevent a client from committing "a criminal, illegal or fraudulent act that the lawyer reasonably believes is likely to perpetrate a fraud upon a tribunal."

New York: Same or substantially the same as the ABA Model Code — see Model Code Comparison above — except see New York Materials for New York's versions of DR 7-102(B)(1), EC 4-7, and DR 4-101(C)(5).

North Carolina: Rule 7.2 is substantially the same as DR 7-102(B), but adds that "if the representation involves litigation, the lawyer shall (if applicable rules require) request the tribunal to permit him to withdraw, but without necessarily revealing his reason for wishing to withdraw." Rule 7.6(B) is equivalent to Model Rule 3.3(a)(3), but adds that a lawyer "shall disclose . . . [u]nless privileged or irrelevant, the identities of the clients he represents and the persons who employed him."

Texas Rule 3.03(b) and (c) provides:

(b) If a lawyer has offered material evidence and comes to know of its falsity, the lawyer shall make a good faith effort to persuade the client to authorize the lawyer to correct or withdraw the false evidence. If such efforts are unsuccessful, the lawyer shall take reasonable remedial measures, including disclosure of the true facts.

(c) The duties stated in paragraphs (a) and (b) continue until remedial legal measures are no longer reasonably possible.

Virginia: Substantially the same as the Model Code, except that DR 7-105 deletes the obligation to disclose adverse legal authority, and DR 7-105(C)(6) is identical to Model Rule 3.3(a)(4).

Washington's version of Rule 3.3(b) does *not* allow disclosure of information protected by Rule 1.6.

Related Materials

ABA Canons: Canons 22 and 41 provided:

22. Candor and Fairness

The conduct of the lawyer before the Court and with other lawyers should be characterized by candor and fairness.

It is not candid or fair for the lawyer knowingly to misquote the contents of a paper, the testimony of a witness, the language or the argument of opposing counsel, or the language of a decision or a textbook; or with knowledge of its invalidity, to cite as authority a decision that has been overruled, or a statute that has been repealed; or in argument to assert as a fact that which has not been proved, or in those jurisdictions where a side has the opening and closing arguments to mislead his opponent by concealing or withholding positions in his opening argument upon which his side then intends to rely.

It is unprofessional and dishonorable to deal other than candidly with the facts in taking the statements of witnesses, in drawing affidavits and other documents, and in the presentation of causes.

A lawyer should not offer evidence which he knows the Court should reject, in order to get the same before the jury by argument for its admissibility, nor should he address to the Judge arguments upon any point not properly calling for determination by him. Neither should he introduce into an argument, addressed to the court, remarks or statements intended to influence the jury or bystanders.

These and all kindred practices are unprofessional and unworthy of an officer of the law charged, as is the lawyer, with the duty of aiding in the administration of justice.

41. Discovery of Imposition and Deception

When a lawyer discovers that some fraud or deception has been practiced, which has unjustly imposed upon the court or a party, he should endeavor to rectify it; at first by advising his client, and if his client refuses to forego the advantage thus unjustly gained, he should promptly inform the injured person or his counsel, so that they may take appropriate steps.

ABA Standards for Criminal Justice: See Defense Function Standard 4-7.5. The original draft of The Defense Function contained the following version of Standard 4-7.7:

(a) If the defendant has admitted to defense counsel facts which establish guilt and counsel's independent investigation established that the admissions are true but the defendant insists on the right to trial, counsel must strongly discourage the defendant against taking the witness stand to testify perjuriously.

174

(b) If, in advance of trial, the defendant insists that he or she will take the stand to testify perjuriously, the lawyer may withdraw from the case, if that is feasible, seeking leave of the court if necessary, but the court should not be advised of the lawyer's reason for seeking to do so.

(c) If withdrawal from the case is not feasible or is not permitted by the court, or if the situation arises immediately preceding trial or during the trial and the defendant insists upon testifying perjuriously in his or her own behalf, it is unprofessional conduct for the lawyer to lend aid to the perjury or use the perjured testimony. Before the defendant takes the stand in these circumstances, the lawyer should make a record of the fact that the defendant is taking the stand against the advice of counsel in some appropriate manner without revealing the fact to the court. The lawyer may identify the witness as the defendant and may ask appropriate questions of the defendant when it is believed that the defendant's answers will not be perjurious. As to matters for which it is believed the defendant will offer perjurious testimony, the lawyer should seek to avoid direct examination of the defendant in the conventional manner; instead, the lawyer should ask the defendant if he or she wishes to make any additional statement concerning the case to the trier or triers of the facts. A lawyer may not later argue the defendant's known false version of facts to the jury as worthy of belief, and may not recite or rely upon the false testimony in his or her closing argument.

When Standard 4-7.7 was published, it was accompanied by the following official Editorial Note written by the ABA:

> This proposed standard was approved by the ABA Standing Committee on Association Standards for Criminal Justice but was withdrawn prior to submission of this chapter to the ABA House of Delegates. Instead, the question of what should be done in situations dealt with by the standard has been deferred until the ABA Special Commission on Evaluation of Professional Standards [the Kutak Commission] reports its final recommendations.

The final recommendation of the Kutak Commission is found in Rule 3.3 of the ABA Model Rules and in the accompanying Comments. Comment 9 to Rule 3.3 refers to the "narrative" suggested in Standard 4-7.7, but both Rule 3.3 and the accompanying Comment appear to reject the narrative proposal. ABA Opinion 353 (1987) does so explicitly. Nevertheless, some courts continue to approve it. See also Nix v. Whiteside, 475 U.S. 157 (1986).

ABA Standards for Imposing Lawyer Discipline:

6.11. Disbarment is generally appropriate when a lawyer, with the intent to deceive the court, makes a false statement, submits a false document, or improperly withholds material information, and causes serious or potentially serious injurt to a party, or causes a significant or potentially significant adverse effect on the legal proceeding.

6.12. Suspension is generally appropriate when a lawyer knows that false statements or documents are being submitted to the court or that material information is improperly being withheld, and takes no remedial action, and causes injury or potential injury to a party to the legal proceeding, or causes an adverse or potentially adverse effect on the legal proceeding.

6.13. Reprimand is generally appropriate when a lawyer is negligent either in determining whether statements or documents are false or in taking remedial action when material information is being withheld, and causes injury or potential injury to a party to the legal proceeding, or causes an adverse or potentially adverse effect on the legal proceeding.

6.14. Admonition is generally appropriate when a lawyer engages in an isolated instance of neglect in determining whether submitted statements or documents are false or in failing to disclose material information upon learning of its falsity, and causes little or no actual or potential injury to a party, or causes little or no adverse or potentially adverse effect on the legal proceeding.

6.31. Disbarment is generally appropriate when a lawyer:

. . . (b) makes an ex parte communication with a judge or juror with intent to affect the outcome of the proceeding, and causes serious or potentially serious injury to a party, or causes significant or potentially significant interference with the outcome of the legal proceeding. . . .

American Academy of Matrimonial Lawyers: The "Bounds of Advocacy" drafted by the American Academy of Matrimonial Lawyers contains the following provision and commentary:

3.11 An attorney should not seek an ex parte order without prior notice to opposing counsel except in exigent circumstances.

Comment to Rule 3.11

There are few things more damaging to a client's confidence in his lawyer, or to relationships between lawyers, than for a party to be served with an ex parte order about which his lawyer knows nothing. Even where there are exigent circumstances (substantial physical or financial risk to the client), or local rules permit ex parte proceedings, notice to, or the appearance of, opposing counsel usually will not prevent appropriate relief from issuing.

Federal Rules of Civil Procedure: Rule 26(e) requires parties to supplement discovery responses under certain circumstances, including when the party "obtains information upon the basis of which (A) the party knows that the response was incorrect when made, or (B) the party knows that the response though correct when made is no longer true and the circumstances are such that a failure to amend the response is in substance a knowing concealment."

Model Rules of Professional Conduct for Federal Lawyers add a new Rule 3.3(a)(5), which states that a federal lawyer shall not "[d]isobey an obligation or order imposed by a tribunal, unless done openly before the tribunal in a good faith assertion that no valid obligation or order should exist." (This rule is similar to Rule 3.4(c), but the Federal Lawyers version of that rule covers only obligations to opposing parties and counsel.)

Rule 3.4 Fairness to Opposing Party and Counsel

A lawyer shall not:

(a) unlawfully obstruct another party's access to evidence or unlawfully alter, destroy or conceal a document or other material having potential evidentiary value. A lawyer shall not counsel or assist another person to do any such act;

(b) falsify evidence, counsel or assist a witness to testify falsely, or offer an inducement to a witness that is prohibited by law;

(c) knowingly disobey an obligation under the rules of a tribunal except for an open refusal based on an assertion that no valid obligation exists;

(d) in pretrial procedure, make a frivolous discovery request or fail to make reasonably diligent effort to comply with a legally proper discovery request by an opposing party;

(e) in trial, allude to any matter that the lawyer does not reasonably believe is relevant or that will not be supported by admissible evidence, assert personal knowledge of facts in issue except when testifying as a witness, or state a personal opinion as to the justness of a cause, the credibility of a witness, the culpability of a civil litigant or the guilt or innocence of an accused; or

(f) request a person other than a client to refrain from voluntarily giving relevant information to another party unless:

(1) the person is a relative or an employee or other agent of a client; and

(2) the lawyer reasonably believes that the person's interests will not be adversely affected by refraining from giving such information.

COMMENT

[1] The procedure of the adversary system contemplates that the evidence in a case is to be marshalled competitively by the contending parties. Fair competition in the adversary system is secured by prohibitions against destruction or concealment of evidence, improperly influencing witnesses, obstructive tactics in discovery procedure, and the like.

[2] Documents and other items of evidence are often essential to establish a claim or defense. Subject to evidentiary privileges, the right of an opposing party, including the government, to obtain evidence through discovery or subpoena is an important procedural right. The exercise of that right can be frustrated if relevant material is altered, concealed or destroyed. Applicable law in many jurisdictions makes it an offense to destroy material for purpose of impairing its availability in a pending proceeding or one whose commencement can be foreseen. Falsifying evidence is also generally a criminal offense. Paragraph (a) applies to evidentiary material generally, including computerized information.

[3] With regard to paragraph (b), it is not improper to pay a witness's expenses or to compensate an expert witness on terms permitted by law. The common law rule in most jurisdictions is that it is improper to pay an occurrence witness any fee for testifying and that it is improper to pay an expert witness a contingent fee.

[4] Paragraph (f) permits a lawyer to advise employees of a client to refrain from giving information to another party, for the employees may identify their interests with those of the client. See also Rule 4.2.

Model Code Comparison

With regard to paragraph (a), DR 7-109(A) provided that a lawyer "shall not suppress any evidence that he or his client has a legal obligation to reveal." DR 7-109(B) provided that a lawyer "shall not advise or cause a person to secrete himself . . . for the purpose of making him unavailable as a witness. . . ." DR 7-106(C)(7) provided that a lawyer shall not "[i]ntentionally or habitually violate any established rule of procedure or of evidence."

With regard to paragraph (b), DR 7-102(A)(6) provided that a lawyer shall not participate "in the creation or preservation of evidence when he knows or it is obvious that the evidence is false." DR 7-109(C) provided that a lawyer "shall not pay, offer to pay, or acquiesce in the payment of compensation to a witness contingent upon the content of his testimony or the outcome of the case. But a lawyer may advance, guarantee or acquiesce in the payment of: (1) Expenses reasonably incurred by a witness in attending or testifying; (2) Reasonable compensation to a witness for his loss of time in attending or testifying; [or] (3) A reasonable fee for the professional services of an expert witness." EC 7-28 stated that witnesses "should always testify truthfully and should be free from any financial inducements that might tempt them to do otherwise."

Paragraph (c) is substantially similar to DR 7-106(A), which provided that "A lawyer shall not disregard . . . a standing rule of a tribunal or a ruling of a tribunal made in the course of a proceeding, but he may take appropriate steps in good faith to test the validity of such rule or ruling."

Paragraph (d) has no counterpart in the Model Code.

Paragraph (e) substantially incorporates DR 7-106(C)(1), (2), (3), and (4). DR 7-106(C)(2) proscribed asking a question "intended to degrade a witness or other person," a matter dealt with in Rule 4.4. DR 7-106(C)(5), providing that a lawyer shall not "fail to comply with known local customs of courtesy or practice," was too vague to be a rule of conduct enforceable as law.

With regard to paragraph (f), DR 7-104(A)(2) provided that a lawyer shall not "give advice to a person who is not represented . . . other than the advice to secure counsel, if the interests of such person are or have a reasonable possibility of being in conflict with the interests of his client."

Cross-References in Rules

Rule 1.4, Comment 4: "Rules or court orders governing litigation may provide that information supplied to a lawyer may not be disclosed to the client. **Rule 3.4(c)** directs compliance with such rules or orders."

Rule 3.6, Comment 3: "Special rules of confidentiality may validly govern proceedings in juvenile, domestic relations and mental disability proceedings, and perhaps other types of litigation. **Rule 3.4(c)** requires compliance with such Rules."

Rule 3.9: "A lawyer representing a client before a legislative or administrative tribunal in a nonadjudicative proceeding shall disclose that the appearance is in a representative capacity and shall conform to the provisions of **Rules** 3.3(a) through (c), **3.4(a) through (c)**, and 3.5."

Rule 4.2, Comment 2: "If an agent or employee of the organization is represented in the matter by his or her own counsel, the consent by that counsel to a communication will be sufficient for purposes of this Rule. Compare **Rule 3.4(f)**."

Legislative History

1980 Discussion Draft (then Rule 3.2):

(a) A lawyer shall be fair to other parties and their counsel, accord them their procedural rights, and fulfill obligations under the procedural law and established practices of the tribunal.

(b) A lawyer shall not:

(1) improperly obstruct another party's access to evidence, destroy, falsify or conceal evidence, or use illegal methods of obtaining evidence;

(2) disobey an obligation under procedural law, except for an open refusal based on a good faith belief that no valid obligation exists;

(3) refer in a proceeding to a matter that the lawyer has no reasonable basis to believe is relevant thereto, or does not reasonably expect will be supported by admissible evidence;

(4) make a knowing misrepresentation of fact or law to an opposing party or counsel;

(5) interview or otherwise communicate with a party who the lawyer knows is represented by other counsel concerning the subject matter of the representation, except with the consent of that party's counsel or as authorized by law.

In addition, the 1980 Discussion Draft contained the following separate Rules (then Rules 2.5 and 3.4):

2.5 Alteration or Destruction of Evidence

A lawyer shall not advise a client to alter or destroy a document or other material when the lawyer reasonably should know that the material is relevant to a pending proceeding or one that is clearly foreseeable.

3.4 Respect for the Interests of Others

(a) In preparing and presenting a cause, a lawyer shall respect the interests of third persons, including witnesses, jurors, and persons incidentally concerned with the proceeding.

(b) A lawyer shall not:

(1) use means of obtaining evidence that violate a third person's legal rights; or

(2) use a procedure having no substantial purpose other than to embarrass, delay, or burden a third person.

1981 Draft: Substantially the same as finally adopted, except subparagraph (a), which provided:

A lawyer shall not:

(a) unlawfully obstruct another party's access to evidence or alter, destroy or conceal a document or other material that the lawyer knows or reasonably should know is relevant to a pending proceeding or one that is reasonably foreseeable. A lawyer shall not counsel or assist another person to do any such act;

1982 Draft was adopted.

Selected State Variations

California: See Rule 5-200 (Trial Conduct), Rule 5-310 (Prohibited Contact with Witnesses), and B & P Code §§6068(d), 6103, and 6128(a).

Connecticut forbids a lawyer to "present, participate in presenting, or threaten to present criminal charges solely to obtain an advantage in a civil matter." Rule 3.4(g).

Delaware: Rule 3.4 provides that a lawyer shall not:

falsify evidence, counsel or assist a witness to testify falsely, or pay, offer to pay or acquiesce in the payment of compensation, or participate in offering any inducement to a witness contingent upon the content of his testimony or the outcome of the case. But a lawyer may advance, guarantee or acquiesce in the payment of:
>(i) expenses reasonably incurred by a witness in attending or testifying;
>(ii) reasonable compensation to a witness for his loss of time in attending or testifying;
>(iii) a reasonable fee for the professional services of an expert witness.

District of Columbia: Rule 3.4(a) provides that a lawyer shall not:

>Obstruct another party's access to evidence or alter, destroy or conceal evidence, or counsel or assist another person to do so, if the lawyer reasonably should know that the evidence is or may be the subject of discovery or subpoena in any pending or imminent proceeding. Unless prohibited by law, a lawyer may receive physical evidence of any kind from the client or from another person. If the evidence received by the lawyer belongs to anyone other than the client, the lawyer shall make a good faith effort to preserve it and to return it to the owner, subject to Rule 1.6.

Illinois provides, in Rule 3.3(a)(15), that a lawyer shall not "pay, offer to pay, or acquiesce in the payment of compensation to a witness contingent upon the content of the witness' testimony or the outcome of the case, but a lawyer may advance, guarantee, or acquiesce in the payment of expenses reasonably incurred in attending or testifying, and a reasonable fee for the professional services of an expert witness." In addition, Illinois omits Rules 3.4(c)-(d) and moves an amplified version of Rule 3.4(e) to Illinois Rule 3.3(a)(10).

New Jersey Rule 3.4(d) refers to "requests" and "efforts" in the plural so that a violation will depend on showing a "pattern of behavior."

New York: Same or substantially the same as the ABA Model Code — see Model Code Comparison above.

North Carolina: Rule 7.6 provides that a lawyer shall not disregard "or advise his client to disregard" a ruling or standing rule of a tribunal, or "[f]ail to comply with known local customs or courtesy or practice of the bar or of a particular tribunal" without giving timely notice to opposing counsel.

Pennsylvania Rule 3.4(b) retains the substance of DR 7-109(C). Pennsylvania adds at the end of Rule 3.4(d)(2) "and such conduct is not prohibited by Rule 4.2."

Texas Rule 3.04(b) retains the substance of DR 7-109(C). Rule 3.04(a), (c), and (d) provides:

>A lawyer shall not:
>(a) unlawfully obstruct another party's access to evidence; in anticipation of a dispute unlawfully alter, destroy or conceal a document or other material that a competent lawyer would believe has potential or actual evidentiary value; or counsel or assist another person to do any such act. . . .
>(c) except as stated in paragraph (d), in representing a client before a tribunal:
>>(1) habitually violate an established rule of procedure or of evidence;
>>(2) state or allude to any matter that the lawyer does not reasonably believe is relevant to such proceeding or that will not be supported by admissible evidence, or assert personal knowledge of facts in issue except when testifying as a witness;
>>(3) state a personal opinion as to the justness of a cause, the credibility of a witness, the culpability of a civil litigant or the guilt or innocence of an accused, except that a

lawyer may argue on his analysis of the evidence and other permissible considerations for any position or conclusion with respect to the matters stated herein;

(4) ask any question intended to degrade a witness or other person except where the lawyer reasonably believes that the question will lead to relevant and admissible evidence; or

(5) engage in conduct intended to disrupt the proceedings.

(d) knowingly disobey, or advise the client to disobey, an obligation under the standing rules of or a ruling by a tribunal except for an open refusal based either on an assertion that no valid obligation exists or on the client's willingness to accept any sanctions arising from such disobedience.

Virginia: Substantially the same as the Model Code.
Washington deletes subparagraph (f).

Related Materials

ABA Canons: Canons 3, 15, 25, and 39 provided:

3. Attempts to Exert Personal Influence on the Court

Marked attention and unusual hospitality on the part of a lawyer to a Judge, uncalled for by the personal relations of the parties, subject both the Judge and the lawyer to misconstructions of motive and should be avoided. A lawyer should not communicate or argue privately with the Judge as to the merits of a pending cause, and he deserves rebuke and denunciation for any device or attempt to gain from a Judge special personal consideration or favor. A self-respecting independence in the discharge of professional duty, without denial or diminution of the courtesy and respect due the Judge's station, is the only proper foundation for cordial personal and official relations between Bench and Bar.

15. How Far a Lawyer May Go in Supporting a Client's Cause

The lawyer owes "entire devotion to the interest of the client, warm zeal in the maintenance and defense of his rights and the exertion of his utmost learning and ability," to the end that nothing be taken or be withheld from him, save by the rules of law, legally applied. No fear of judicial disfavor or public unpopularity should restrain him from the full discharge of his duty. In the judicial forum the client is entitled to the benefit of any and every remedy and defense that is authorized by the law of the land, and he may expect his lawyer to assert every such remedy or defense. But it is steadfastly to be borne in mind that the great trust of the lawyer is to be performed within and not without the bounds of the law. The office of attorney does not permit, much less does it demand of him for any client, violation of law or any manner of fraud or chicane. He must obey his own conscience and not that of his client.

25. Taking Technical Advantage of Opposite Counsel; Agreements with Him

A lawyer should not ignore known customs or practice of the Bar or of a particular Court, even when the law permits, without giving timely notice to the opposing counsel. As far as possible, important agreements, affecting the rights of clients, should be reduced to writing; but it is dishonorable to avoid performance of an agreement fairly made because it is not reduced to writing, as required by rules of Court.

39. Witnesses

A lawyer may properly interview any witness or prospective witness for the opposing side in any civil or criminal action without the consent of opposing counsel or party. In doing so, however, he should scrupulously avoid any suggestion calculated to induce the witness to suppress or deviate from the truth, or in any degree to affect his free and untrammeled conduct when appearing at the trial or on the witness stand.

ABA Standards for Criminal Justice: See Prosecution Function Standards 3-5.2, 3-5.6; Defense Function Standards 4-1.2, 4-4.3, 4-4.5, 4-7.1.
ABA Standards for Imposing Lawyer Discipline:

6.2. Abuse of the Legal Process

6.21. Disbarment is generally appropriate when a lawyer knowingly violates a court order or rule with the intent to obtain a benefit for the lawyer or another, and causes serious injury or potentially serious injury to a party, or causes serious or potentially serious interference with a legal proceeding.

6.22. Suspension is appropriate when a lawyer knows that he is violating a court order or rule, and there is injury or potential injury to a client or a party, or interference or potential interference with a legal proceeding.

See also Standard 6.3 printed in the Related Materials following Model Rule 4.2.

American Academy of Matrimonial Lawyers: The "Bounds of Advocacy" drafted by the American Academy of Matrimonial Lawyers contains the following provision and commentary:

3.14 An attorney should promptly and completely comply with all reasonable discovery requests.

Comment to Rule 3.14

This may require convincing the client of the necessity of full compliance with such discovery requests as document production and answers to interrogatories and that concealing information is detrimental to the client's own case.

American Lawyer's Code of Conduct: In addition, Rule 3.10 provides:

A lawyer shall not give a witness money or anything of substantial value, or threaten a witness with harm, in order to induce the witness to testify or dissuade the witness from testifying. However, a lawyer may pay a fee to an expert witness; a lawyer may reimburse a witness' actual, reasonable financial losses and expenses of appearing; a lawyer may give a witness protection against physical harm; and a prosecutor may immunize a witness from prosecution in order to avoid an assertion of the constitutional privilege against self-incrimination.

Federal Rules of Civil Procedure: Various provisions of the rules of procedure penalize the kinds of behavior condemned in Rule 3.4. With respect to Rule 3.4(c), Fed. R. Civ. P. 41(b) provides: "For failure of the plaintiff to prosecute or to comply with these rules or any order of court, a defendant may move for dismissal of an action or of any claim against the defendant," and such a dismissal ordinarily operates as "an adjudication upon the merits." Fed. R. Civ. P. 45(f) provides: "Failure by any person without adequate excuse to obey a subpoena served upon that person may be deemed a contempt of the court from which the subpoena issued." With respect to Rule 3.4(d), Fed. R. Civ. P. 26(g) provides sanctions for improper or bad faith conduct in discovery, and Fed. R. Civ.

P. 37, which also governs discovery problems, gives courts power to compel a party to respond to discovery requests and, in the case of an unjustified failure to respond to discovery, a court "shall" sanction "the party or attorney advising such conduct or both of them. . . ."

Federal Rules of Appellate Procedure: Fed. R. App. P. 46(c) empowers a federal court of appeals, after notice and hearing, to "take any appropriate disciplinary action against any attorney who practices before it for conduct unbecoming a member of the bar or for failure to comply with these rules or any rule of the court."

Model Rules of Professional Conduct for Federal Lawyers clarify that Rule 3.4 applies to an obligation "to an opposing party and counsel." (The Rules for Federal Lawyers address obligations to a tribunal in a new Rule 3.3(a)(5), quoted after Rule 3.3.) The Comment to Rule 3.4 states:

> A federal lawyer who receives . . . an item of physical evidence implicating the client in criminal conduct shall disclose the location of or shall deliver that item to proper authorities when required by law or court order. Thus, if a Federal lawyer receives contraband, the Federal lawyer has no legal right to possess it and must always surrender it to lawful authorities. If a Federal lawyer receives stolen property, the Federal lawyer must surrender it to the owner or lawful authority to avoid violating the law. . . . When a client informs the Federal lawyer about the existence of material having potential evidentiary value adverse to the client or when the client presents, but does not relinquish possession of, such material to the Federal lawyer, the Federal lawyer should inform the client of the Federal lawyer's legal and ethical obligations regarding evidence. Frequently, the best course for the Federal lawyer is to refrain from either taking possession of such material or advising the client as to what course of action should be taken regarding it. . . . If a Federal lawyer discloses the location of or delivers an item of physical evidence to proper authorities, it should be done in the way best designed to protect the client's interest. The Federal lawyer should consider methods of return or disclosure that best protect (a) the client's identity; (b) the client's words concerning the item; (c) other confidential information; and (d) the client's privilege against self-incrimination. . . .
>
> With regard to paragraph (c), a "rule of a tribunal" includes Rule 6(e) of the Federal Rules of Criminal Procedure governing discussion of grand jury testimony.

Rule 3.5 Impartiality and Decorum of the Tribunal

A lawyer shall not:

(a) seek to influence a judge, juror, prospective juror or other official by means prohibited by law;

(b) communicate ex parte with such a person except as permitted by law; or

(c) engage in conduct intended to disrupt a tribunal.

COMMENT

[1] Many forms of improper influence upon a tribunal are proscribed by criminal law. Others are specified in the ABA Model Code of Judicial Conduct,

with which an advocate should be familiar. A lawyer is required to avoid contributing to a violation of such provisions.

[2] The advocate's function is to present evidence and argument so that the cause may be decided according to law. Refraining from abusive or obstreperous conduct is a corollary of the advocate's right to speak on behalf of litigants. A lawyer may stand firm against abuse by a judge but should avoid reciprocation; the judge's default is no justification for similar dereliction by an advocate. An advocate can present the cause, protect the record for subsequent review and preserve professional integrity by patient firmness no less effectively than by belligerence or theatrics.

Model Code Comparison

With regard to paragraphs (a) and (b), DR 7-108(A) provided that "[b]efore the trial of a case a lawyer . . . shall not communicate with . . . anyone he knows to be a member of the venire. . . ." DR 7-108(B) provided that during the trial of a case a lawyer "shall not communicate with . . . any member of the jury." DR 7-110(B) provided that a lawyer shall not "communicate . . . as to the merits of the cause with a judge or an official before whom the proceeding is pending, except . . . upon adequate notice to opposing counsel," or as "otherwise authorized by law."

With regard to paragraph (c), DR 7-106(C)(6) provided that a lawyer shall not engage in "undignified or discourteous conduct which is degrading to a tribunal."

Cross-References in Rules

Rule 3.9: "A lawyer representing a client before a legislative or administrative tribunal in a nonadjudicative proceeding shall disclose that the appearance is in a representative capacity and shall conform to the provisions of **Rules** 3.3(a) through (c), 3.4(a) through (c), and **3.5**."

Legislative History

1980 Discussion Draft (then called Rule 3.7) provided as follows:

(a) A lawyer shall assist a tribunal in maintaining impartiality and conducting the proceedings with decorum.
(b) A lawyer shall not:
(1) seek improperly to influence a judge, juror, or other decision-maker, or, except as permitted by law, communicate ex parte with such a person;
(2) seek improperly to influence a witness;
(3) be abusive or obstreperous;
(4) refuse to comply with an obligation of procedural law or an order of the tribunal, except for an open refusal based on a good faith belief that compliance is not legally required.

1981 Draft was substantially the same as adopted, except that subparagraph (a) used the phrase "other decision-maker" instead of "other official."
1982 Draft was adopted.

Selected State Variations

Arkansas: Subparagraph (b) provides that a lawyer shall not "communicate ex parte with such a person *on the merits of the cause* except as permitted by law."
California: See Rule 5-300 (Contact with Officials).
Delaware adds the following language to subparagraph (c): "or engage in undignified or discourteous conduct which is degrading to a tribunal."
Florida, Maryland, and *Minnesota* add language to Rule 3.5 drawing on DR 7-108. (See Model Code Comparison above.)
Illinois: Rule 3.5 provides:

(a) Before the trial of a case, a lawyer connected therewith shall not communicate with or cause another to communicate with anyone the lawyer knows to be a member of the venire from which the jury will be selected for the trial of the case.

(b) During the trial of a case:

(1) a lawyer connected therewith shall not communicate with or cause another to communicate with a juror; and

(2) a lawyer who is not connected therewith shall not communicate with or cause another to communicate with a juror concerning the case.

(c) Notwithstanding Rules 3.5(a) and (b), a lawyer may communicate with members of the venire or jury in the course of official proceedings.

(d) After discharge of the jury from further consideration of a case with which the lawyer was connected, the lawyer shall not ask questions of or make comments to a juror until the venire of which such juror is a member has been discharged, nor shall the lawyer thereafter ask question of or make comments to a member of the venire that are calculated merely to harass or embarrass the juror or to influence such juror's actions in future jury service.

(e) A lawyer shall not conduct or cause another to conduct, by financial support or otherwise, a vexatious or harassing investigation of members of the venire or jury.

(f) All restrictions imposed by Rule 3.5 also apply to communications with or investigations of the families of members of the venire or jury.

(g) A lawyer shall reveal promptly to the court the lawyer's knowledge of improper conduct by a member of the venire or jury or by another toward such a person or a member of such person's family.

(h) A lawyer shall not give or lend anything of value to a judge, official, or employee of a tribunal, except those gifts or loans which a judge or a member of the judge's family may receive under Rule 65(C)(4) of the Code of Judicial Conduct, and except that a lawyer may: make a gift, bequest, loan or campaign contribution to a judge that the judge is permitted to accept under the Code of Judicial Conduct, provided that no campaign contribution to a judge or candidate for judical office may be made other than by means of a check, draft, or other instrument payable to or to the order of an entity which the lawyer reasonably believes to be a political committee supporting such judge or candidate, provided further, however, that the provision of volunteer services by a lawyer to a political committee shall not be deemed to violate this Rule.

(i) [Combines language from DR 7-108 and DR 7-110.]

Kansas forbids a lawyer to "engage in undignified or discourteous conduct degrading to a tribunal." Rule 3.5(d).

Michigan's version of Rule 3.5(c) forbids a lawyer to "engage in undignified or discourteous conduct toward the tribunal."

New York: Same or substantially the same as the ABA Model Code — see Model Code Comparison above.

North Carolina: Rules 7.6, 7.8, and 7.10 are substantially the same as the Model Code.

Texas Rule 3.06 provides:

> (a) A lawyer shall not:
> (1) conduct or cause another, by financial support or otherwise, to conduct a vexatious or harassing investigation of a venireman or juror; or
> (2) seek to influence a venireman or juror concerning the merits of a pending matter by means prohibited by law or applicable rules of practice or procedure.
> (b) Prior to discharge of the jury from further consideration of a matter, a lawyer connected therewith shall not communicate with or cause another to communicate with anyone he knows to be a member of the venire from which the jury will be selected or any juror or alternate juror, except in the course of official proceedings.
> (c) During the trial of a case, a lawyer not connected therewith shall not communicate with or cause another to communicate with a juror or alternate juror concerning the matter.
> (d) After discharge of the jury from further consideration of a matter with which the lawyer was connected, the lawyer shall not ask questions of or make comments to a member of that jury that are calculated merely to harass or embarass the juror or to influence his actions in future jury service.
> (e) All restrictions imposed by this Rule upon a lawyer also apply to communications with or investigations of members of a family of a venireman or a juror.
> (f) A lawyer shall reveal promptly to the court improper conduct by a venireman or a juror, or by another toward a venireman or a juror or a member of his family, of which the lawyer has knowledge.
> (g) As used in this Rule, the terms "matter" and "pending" have the meanings specified in Rule 3.05(c).

Virginia: Substantially the same as the Model Code, but omits the prohibition in DR 7-106(C)(6) on "undignified or discourteous conduct," and bars intentional or habitual violations of the rules of procedure or evidence "where such conduct is disruptive of the proceedings."

Related Materials

ABA Canons: Canons 17 and 23 provided:

17. Ill-Feeling and Personalities Between Advocates

Clients, not lawyers, are the litigants. Whatever may be the ill-feeling existing between clients, it should not be allowed to influence counsel in their conduct and demeanor toward each other or toward suitors in the case. All personalities between counsel should be scrupulously avoided. In the trial of a cause it is indecent to allude to the personal history or the personal peculiarities and idiosyncrasies of counsel on the other side. Personal colloquies between counsel which cause delay and promote unseemly wrangling should also be carefully avoided.

23. Attitude Toward Jury

All attempts to curry favor with juries by fawning, flattery or pretended solicitude for their personal comfort are unprofessional. Suggestions of counsel, looking to the comfort or convenience of jurors, and propositions to dispense with argument, should be made to the Court out of the jury's hearing. A lawyer must never converse privately with jurors about the case; and both before and during the trial he should avoid communicating with them, even as to matters foreign to the cause.

ABA Model Code of Judicial Conduct, cited in Rule 3.5, Comment 1, is reprinted in full later in this volume at pages 435-508.

ABA Standards for Criminal Justice: See Prosecution Function Standard 3-2.8; Standards for Special Functions of the Trial Judge.

ABA Standards for Imposing Lawyer Discipline: See Standard 6.3 printed in the Related Materials following Model Rule 4.2.

Federal Rules of Civil Procedure: Rule 65(b), governing ex parte communications in proceedings to obtain temporary restraining orders, provides, in pertinent part, as follows:

Temporary Restraining Order; Notice; Hearing; Duration. A temporary restraining order may be granted without written or oral notice to the adverse party or that party's attorney only if (1) it clearly appears from specific facts shown by affidavit or by the verified complaint that immediate and irreparable injury, loss, or damage will result to the applicant before the adverse party or that party's attorney can be heard in opposition, and (2) the applicant's attorney certifies to the court in writing the efforts, if any, which have been made to give the notice and the reasons supporting the claim that notice should not be required. . . .

Model Rules of Professional Conduct for Federal Lawyers: Rule 3.5(a) prohibits a federal lawyer from seeking to influence "a tribunal, a member of a tribunal, a prospective member of a tribunal, or other official by means prohibited by law."

Editors' Note. In Gentile v. Nevada State Bar, 111 S. Ct. 2720 (1991), the Supreme Court construed the First Amendment rights of a criminal defense lawyer who held a press conference at which he made statements that allegedly violated Nevada's version of Rule 3.6.

Rule 3.6 Trial Publicity

(a) A lawyer shall not make an extrajudicial statement that a reasonable person would expect to be disseminated by means of public communication if the lawyer knows or reasonably should know that it will have a substantial likelihood of materially prejudicing an adjudicative proceeding.

(b) A statement referred to in paragraph (a) ordinarily is likely to have such an effect when it refers to a civil matter triable to a jury, a criminal matter, or any other proceeding that could result in incarceration, and the statement relates to:

(1) the character, credibility, reputation or criminal record of a party, suspect in a criminal investigation or witness, or the identity of a witness, or the expected testimony of a party or witness;

(2) in a criminal case or proceeding that could result in incarceration, the possibility of a plea of guilty to the offense or the existence or contents of any confession, admission, or statement given by a defendant or suspect or that person's refusal or failure to make a statement;

(3) the performance or results of any examination or test or the refusal or failure of a person to submit to an examination or test, or the identity or nature of physical evidence expected to be presented;

(4) any opinion as to the guilt or innocence of a defendant or suspect in a criminal case or proceeding that could result in incarceration;

(5) information the lawyer knows or reasonably should know is likely to be inadmissible as evidence in a trial and would if disclosed create a substantial risk of prejudicing an impartial trial; or

(6) the fact that a defendant has been charged with a crime, unless there is included therein a statement explaining that the charge is merely an accusation and that the defendant is presumed innocent until and unless proven guilty.

(c) Notwithstanding paragraph (a) and (b) (1-5), a lawyer involved in the investigation or litigation of a matter may state without elaboration:

(1) the general nature of the claim or defense;

(2) the information contained in a public record;

(3) that an investigation of the matter is in progress, including the general scope of the investigation, the offense or claim or defense involved and, except when prohibited by law, the identity of the persons involved;

(4) the scheduling or result of any step in litigation;

(5) a request for assistance in obtaining evidence and information necessary thereto;

(6) a warning of danger concerning the behavior of a person involved, when there is reason to believe that there exists the likelihood of substantial harm to an individual or to the public interest; and

(7) in a criminal case:

(i) the identity, residence, occupation and family status of the accused;

(ii) if the accused has not been apprehended, information necessary to aid in apprehension of that person;

(iii) the fact, time and place of arrest; and

(iv) the identity of investigating and arresting officers or agencies and the length of the investigation.

COMMENT

[1] It is difficult to strike a balance between protecting the right to a fair trial and safeguarding the right of free expression. Preserving the right to a

fair trial necessarily entails some curtailment of the information that may be disseminated about a party prior to trial, particularly where trial by jury is involved. If there were no such limits, the result would be the practical nullification of the protective effect of the rules of forensic decorum and the exclusionary rules of evidence. On the other hand, there are vital social interests served by the free dissemination of information about events having legal consequences and about legal proceedings themselves. The public has a right to know about threats to its safety and measures aimed at assuring its security. It also has a legitimate interest in the conduct of judicial proceedings, particularly in matters of general public concern. Furthermore, the subject matter of legal proceedings is often of direct significance in debate and deliberation over questions of public policy.

[2] No body of rules can simultaneously satisfy all interests of fair trial and all those of free expression. The formula in this Rule is based upon the ABA Model Code of Professional Responsibility and the ABA Standards Relating to Fair Trial and Free Press, as amended in 1978.

[3] Special rules of confidentiality may validly govern proceedings in juvenile, domestic relations and mental disability proceedings, and perhaps other types of litigation. Rule 3.4(c) requires compliance with such Rules.

Model Code Comparison

Rule 3.6 is similar to DR 7-107, except as follows: First, Rule 3.6 adopts the general criteria of "substantial likelihood of materially prejudicing an adjudicative proceeding" to describe impermissible conduct. Second, Rule 3.6 transforms the particulars in DR 7-107 into an illustrative compilation that gives fair notice of conduct ordinarily posing unacceptable dangers to the fair administration of justice. Finally, Rule 3.6 omits DR 7-107(C)(7), which provided that a lawyer may reveal "[a]t the time of seizure, a description of the physical evidence seized, other than a confession, admission or statement." Such revelations may be substantially prejudicial and are frequently the subject of pre-trial suppression motions, which, if successful, may be circumvented by prior disclosure to the press.

Cross-References in Rules

Rule 3.8(e) provides that the prosecutor in a criminal case shall "exercise reasonable care to prevent investigators . . . or other persons . . . from making an extrajudicial statement that the prosecutor would be prohibited from making under **Rule 3.6**."

Legislative History

1980 Discussion Draft (then Rule 3.8) provided as follows:

(a) To ensure a fair trial, a lawyer involved in the investigation of a criminal matter or in criminal or civil litigation shall not, except as provided in paragraph (b), make an extrajudicial statement:

(1) intended to induce the tribunal to determine the matter otherwise than in accordance with law; or

(2) when the matter under investigation or in litigation is a criminal case or a civil case triable to a jury and the statement relates to:

(i) the identity, character, credibility, reputation, or criminal record of a party, suspect in a criminal investigation, or witness, or the expected testimony of a party or witness;

(ii) in a criminal case, the possibility of a plea of guilty to the offense, or the existence or contents of any confession, admission, or statement given by the accused or the accused's refusal or failure to make a statement;

(iii) the performance or results of any examination or test or the refusal or failure of a person to submit to an examination or test, or the identity or nature of physical evidence expected to be presented.

(iv) any opinion as to the guilt or innocence of an accused or suspect in a criminal case or as to the merits of a criminal or civil case;

(v) information the lawyer knows or reasonably should know would be inadmissible as evidence in a trial;

(vi) any other matter that similarly creates a serious and imminent risk of prejudicing an impartial trial.

(b) A lawyer involved in the investigation or litigation of a matter may state without elaboration;

(1) information contained in a public record;

(2) that investigation of the matter is in progress, including the general scope of the investigation, the offense or claim or defense involved, and, except when prohibited by law, the identity of the persons involved;

(3) the scheduling or result of any step in evidence;

(4) a request for assistance in obtaining evidence;

(5) a warning of danger concerning the behavior of a person involved, when there is reason to believe that such danger exists; and

(6) in a criminal case:

(i) the name, age, residence, occupation, and family status of the accused;

(ii) if the accused has not been apprehended, information necessary to aid in apprehension of the accused;

(iii) the fact, time, and place of arrest, resistance, pursuit, and use of weapons;

(iv) the identity of investigating and arresting officers or agencies and the length of the investigation;

(v) at the same time of seizure, a description of the physical evidence seized, other than a confession, admission or statement; and

(vi) that the accused denies the charges.

(c) When evidence or information received in or relating to a proceeding is by law or order of a tribunal to be kept confidential, the lawyer shall not unlawfully disclose the evidence or information.

1981 Draft was the same as adopted, except (b)(7)(iii), which provided: "the fact, time, and place of arrest, *resistance, pursuit and use of weapons.*"

1982 Draft was adopted.

Selected State Variations

California: No comparable provision.

Delaware deletes Rule 3.6(b)(6).

District of Columbia: Rule 3.6 states only:

> A lawyer engaged in a case being tried to a judge or jury shall not make an extrajudicial statement that a reasonable person would expect to be disseminated by means of mass public communication if the lawyer knows or reasonably should know that the statement will create a serious and imminent threat to the impartiality of the judge or jury.

Illinois Rule 3.6(a) applies to statements that would "pose a serious and imminent threat to the fairness of an adjudicative proceeding." Rule 3.6(b)(1) refers to "the prior criminal record (including arrests, indictments or other charges of crime)." Illinois omits the requirement in ABA Model Rule 3.6(b)(5) that the inadmissible evidence "would if disclosed create a substantial risk of prejudicing an impartial trial." Illinois completely omits Rule 3.6(b)(6).

Michigan places Rule 3.6(b) and (c) in its Comment to Rule 3.6.

Minnesota deletes subparagraphs (b) and (c) of Rule 3.6 in their entirety.

Montana adds the following language to (b)(4): "or a substantial likelihood of materially prejudicing the outcome of a hearing or trial."

New Jersey substitutes "reasonable lawyer" for "reasonable person" in Rule 3.6(a).

New York: Amendments to the New York Code substantially adopt the text of Rule 3.6. See DR 7-107.

Virginia: DR 7-106(A) prohibits a lawyer "participating in or associated with the investigation or the prosecution or the defense of a criminal matter that may be tried by a jury" from making an extrajudicial statement that "constitutes a clear and present danger of interfering with the fairness of the trial by jury."

Related Materials

ABA Canons: Canon 20 provided:

20. Newspaper Discussion of Pending Litigation

> Newspaper publications by a lawyer as to pending or anticipated litigation may interfere with a fair trial in the Courts and otherwise prejudice the due administration of justice. Generally they are to be condemned. If the extreme circumstances of a particular case justify a statement to the public, it is unprofessional to make it anonymously. An *ex parte* reference to the facts should not go beyond quotation from the records and papers on file in the court; but even in extreme cases it is better to avoid any *ex parte* statement.

ABA Standards of Criminal Justice: See Prosecution Function Standard 3-1.4 (Public Statements). See also Standards Relating to Fair Trial and Free Press (cited in Rule 3.6, Comment 2), Standard 8-1.1.

American Academy of Matrimonial Lawyers: The "Bounds of Advocacy" drafted by the American Academy of Matrimonial Lawyers contains the following provision and commentary:

> 2.19 An attorney should not communicate with the news media about the representation except with the client's prior consent.

Comment to Rule 2.19

Statements to the media by an attorney representing a party in a matrimonial matter are potentially improper because they tend to prejudice an adjudicative proceeding. An attorney's interest in obtaining publicity should not be allowed to obstruct settlement, cause embarrassment, diminish the opportunity for reconciliation, or harm the family. Nor should an attorney attempt to gain an advantage for the client by providing information to the media to embarrass or humiliate the opposing party or counsel.

Code of Federal Regulations: See 28 C.F.R. §50.2 in the material on Federal Regulations.

Model Rules of Professional Conduct for Federal Lawyers: Rule 3.6(a) prohibits extrajudicial statements likely to prejudice an adjudicative proceeding "or an official review process thereof." Rule 3.6(b)(4) makes clear that Rule 3.6 applies to any proceeding that could result in incarceration "or other adverse action." The Rules for Federal Lawyers also add Rule 3.6(d), which provides: "The protection and release of information in matters pertaining to the Government shall be consistent with law."

Rule 3.7 Lawyer as Witness

(a) A lawyer shall not act as advocate at a trial in which the lawyer is likely to be a necessary witness except where:

(1) the testimony relates to an uncontested issue;

(2) the testimony relates to the nature and value of legal services rendered in the case; or

(3) disqualification of the lawyer would work substantial hardship on the client.

(b) A lawyer may act as advocate in a trial in which another lawyer in the lawyer's firm is likely to be called as a witness unless precluded from doing so by Rule 1.7 or Rule 1.9.

COMMENT

[1] Combining the roles of advocate and witness can prejudice the opposing party and can involve a conflict of interest between the lawyer and client.

[2] The opposing party has proper objection where the combination of roles may prejudice that party's rights in the litigation. A witness is required to testify on the basis of personal knowledge, while an advocate is expected to explain and comment on evidence given by others. It may not be clear whether a statement by an advocate-witness should be taken as proof or as an analysis of the proof.

[3] Paragraph (a)(1) recognizes that if the testimony will be uncontested, the ambiguities in the dual role are purely theoretical. Paragraph (a)(2) recognizes that where the testimony concerns the extent and value of legal services ren-

dered in the action in which the testimony is offered, permitting the lawyers to testify avoids the need for a second trial with new counsel to resolve that issue. Moreover, in such a situation the judge has first hand knowledge of the matter in issue; hence, there is less dependence on the adversary process to test the credibility of the testimony.

[4] Apart from these two exceptions, paragraph (a)(3) recognizes that a balancing is required between the interests of the client and those of the opposing party. Whether the opposing party is likely to suffer prejudice depends on the nature of the case, the importance and probable tenor of the lawyer's testimony, and the probability that the lawyer's testimony will conflict with that of other witnesses. Even if there is risk of such prejudice, in determining whether the lawyer should be disqualified due regard must be given to the effect of disqualification on the lawyer's client. It is relevant that one or both parties could reasonably foresee that the lawyer would probably be a witness. The principle of imputed disqualification stated in Rule 1.10 has no application to this aspect of the problem.

[5] Whether the combination of roles involves an improper conflict of interest with respect to the client is determined by Rule 1.7 or 1.9. For example, if there is likely to be substantial conflict between the testimony of the client and that of the lawyer or a member of the lawyer's firm, the representation is improper. The problem can arise whether the lawyer is called as a witness on behalf of the client or is called by the opposing party. Determining whether or not such a conflict exists is primarily the responsibility of the lawyer involved. See Comment to Rule 1.7. If a lawyer who is a member of a firm may not act as both advocate and witness by reason of conflict of interest, Rule 1.10 disqualifies the firm also.

Model Code Comparison

DR 5-102(A) prohibited a lawyer, or the lawyer's firm, from serving as advocate if the lawyer "learns or it is obvious that he or a lawyer in his firm ought to be called as a witness on behalf of his client." DR 5-102(B) provided that a lawyer, and the lawyer's firm, may continue representation if the "lawyer learns or it is obvious that he or a lawyer in his firm may be called as a witness other than on behalf of his client . . . until it is apparent that his testimony is or may be prejudicial to his client." DR 5-101(B) permitted a lawyer to testify while representing a client: "(1) If the testimony will relate solely to an uncontested matter; (2) If the testimony will relate solely to a matter of formality and there is no reason to believe that substantial evidence will be offered in opposition to the testimony; (3) If the testimony will relate solely to the nature and value of legal services rendered in the case by the lawyer or his firm to the client; (4) As to any matter if refusal would work a substantial hardship on the client because of the distinctive value of the lawyer or his firm as counsel in the particular case."

The exception stated in paragraph (a)(1) consolidates provisions of DR 5-101(B)(1) and (2). Testimony relating to a formality, referred to in DR 5-101(B)(2), in effect defines the phrase "uncontested issue" and is redundant.

Cross-References in Rules

None.

Legislative History

1980 Discussion Draft (then Rule 3.9) prohibited a lawyer from acting as an advocate, "except on the lawyer's own behalf, in litigation in which the lawyer's own conduct is a material issue or in which the lawyer is likely to be a witness," unless the lawyer satisfied exceptions that were substantially the same as finally adopted.

1981 Draft was substantially the same as adopted.

1982 Draft was adopted.

Selected State Variations

Arkansas totally deletes subparagraph (b).

California: See Rule 5-210 (Member as Witness).

District of Columbia adds the following clause to Rule 3.7(b):

The provisions of this Paragraph (b) do not apply if the lawyer who is appearing as an advocate is employed by, and appears on behalf of, a government agency.

Georgia's DR 5-102 provides:

When a lawyer is a witness for his client, except as to merely formal matters, such as the attestation or custody of an instrument and the like, he should leave the trial of the case to other counsel. Except when essential to the ends of justice, a lawyer should avoid testifying in court in behalf of his client.

Illinois Rule 3.7 distinguishes between a witness on behalf of a client and a witness not on behalf of a client. Illinois Rule 3.7(a) essentially tracks DR 5-101(B), and Illinois Rule 3.7(b) essentially tracks DR 5-102(B).

New Mexico deletes subparagraph (a)(3).

New York: The language of DR 5-101 and DR 5-102 is retained except that disqualification is not imputed within a firm.

North Carolina: Rule 5.2 is substantially the same as the Model Code.

Texas Rule 3.08(a) disqualifies a lawyer whose testimony will be "necessary to establish an essential fact on behalf of the lawyer's client." Rules 3.08(b) and (c) provide:

(b) A lawyer shall not continue as an advocate in a pending adjudicatory proceeding if the lawyer believes that the lawyer will be compelled to furnish testimony that will be substantially adverse to the lawyer's client, unless the client consents after full disclosure.

(c) Without the client's informed consent, a lawyer may not act as advocate in an adjudicatory proceeding in which another lawyer in the lawyer's firm is prohibited by paragraphs (a) or (b) from serving as advocate. If the lawyer to be called as a witness could not also serve as an advocate under this Rule, that lawyer shall not take an active role before the tribunal in the presentation of the matter.

Virginia: Substantially the same as the Model Code.

Washington's version of subparagraph (a)(3) is as follows: "the trial judge finds that disqualification of the lawyer would work a substantial hardship on the client and that the likelihood of the lawyer being a necessary witness was not reasonably foreseeable before trial." Washington also adds the following new subparagraph (a)(4): "the lawyer has been called by the opposing party and the court rules that the lawyer may continue to act as an advocate."

Related Materials

ABA Canons: Canon 19 provided:

19. Appearance of Lawyer as Witness for His Client

When a lawyer is a witness for his client, except as to merely formal matters, such as the attestation or custody of an instrument and the like, he should leave the trial of the case to other counsel. Except when essential to the ends of justice, a lawyer should avoid testifying in court in behalf of his client.

Model Rules of Professional Conduct for Federal Lawyers: Rule 3.7(a)(2) permits a lawyer to testify to "the nature, value, *and quality* of legal services rendered in the case."

Rule 3.8 Special Responsibilities of a Prosecutor

The prosecutor in a criminal case shall:

(a) refrain from prosecuting a charge that the prosecutor knows is not supported by probable cause;

(b) make reasonable efforts to assure that the accused has been advised of the right to, and the procedure for obtaining, counsel and has been given reasonable opportunity to obtain counsel;

(c) not seek to obtain from an unrepresented accused a waiver of important pretrial rights, such as the right to a preliminary hearing;

(d) make timely disclosure to the defense of all evidence or information known to the prosecutor that tends to negate the guilt of the accused or mitigates the offense, and, in connection with sentencing, disclose to the defense and to the tribunal all unprivileged mitigating information known to the prosecutor, except when the prosecutor is relieved of this responsibility by a protective order of the tribunal; and

(e) exercise reasonable care to prevent investigators, law enforcement personnel, employees or other persons assisting or associated with the prosecutor in a criminal case from making an extrajudicial statement that the prosecutor would be prohibited from making under Rule 3.6.

(f) not subpoena a lawyer in a grand jury or other criminal proceeding to present evidence about a past or present client unless:

(1) the prosecutor reasonably believes:

(i) the information sought is not protected from disclosure by any applicable privilege;

(ii) the evidence sought is essential to the successful completion of an ongoing investigation or prosecution;

(iii) there is no other feasible alternative to obtain the information; and

(2) the prosecutor obtains prior judicial approval after an opportunity for an adversarial proceeding.

Editors' Note. Subparagraph (f) was added by the ABA at its Mid-Year Meeting in February 1990.

COMMENT

[1] A prosecutor has the responsibility of a minister of justice and not simply that of an advocate. This responsibility carries with it specific obligations to see that the defendant is accorded procedural justice and that guilt is decided upon the basis of sufficient evidence. Precisely how far the prosecutor is required to go in this direction is a matter of debate and varies in different jurisdictions. Many jurisdictions have adopted the ABA Standards of Criminal Justice Relating to Prosecution Function, which in turn are the product of prolonged and careful deliberation by lawyers experienced in both criminal prosecution and defense. See also Rule 3.3(d), governing ex parte proceedings, among which grand jury proceedings are included. Applicable law may require other measures by the prosecutor and knowing disregard of those obligations or a systematic abuse of prosecutorial discretion could constitute a violation of Rule 8.4.

[2] Paragraph (c) does not apply to an accused representing himself with the approval of the tribunal. Nor does it forbid the lawful questioning of a suspect who has knowingly waived his rights to counsel and silence.

[3] The exception in paragraph (d) recognizes that a prosecutor may seek an appropriate protective order from the tribunal if disclosure of information to the defense could result in substantial harm to an individual or to the public interest.

Editors' Note. Comment paragraph 4, which follows, was added by the ABA when it added Rule 3.8(f) in 1990.

[4] Paragraph (f) is intended to limit the issuance of lawyer subpoenas in grand jury and other criminal proceedings to those situations in which there is a

genuine need to intrude into the client-lawyer relationship. The prosecutor is required to obtain court approval for the issuance of the subpoena after an opportunity for an adversarial hearing is afforded in order to assure an independent determination that the applicable standards are met.

Model Code Comparison

DR 7-103(A) provided that a "public prosecutor . . . shall not institute . . . criminal charges when he knows or it is obvious that the charges are not supported by probable cause." DR 7-103(B) provided that "[a] public prosecutor . . . shall make timely disclosure . . . of the existence of evidence, known to the prosecutor . . . that tends to negate the guilt of the accused, mitigate the degree of the offense, or reduce the punishment."

Paragraph (f) has no counterpart in the Model Code.

Cross-References in Rules

None.

Legislative History

1980 Discussion Draft (then Rule 3.10) provided as follows:

> The prosecutor in a criminal case shall:
> (a) refrain from prosecuting a charge that the prosecutor knows is not supported by probable cause;
> (b) advise the defendant of the right to counsel and provide assistance in obtaining counsel;
> (c) not induce an unrepresented defendant to surrender important procedural rights, such as the right to a preliminary hearing;
> (d) seek all evidence, whether or not favorable to the accused, and make timely disclosure to the defense of all evidence supporting innocence of mitigating the offense;
> (e) not discourage a person from giving relevant information to the defense;
> (f) in connection with sentencing, disclose to the defendant and to the court all unprivileged information known to the prosecution that is relevant thereto.

1980 Discussion Draft also contained a separate rule, with no counterpart in the Rules as adopted, that read as follows:

Special Responsibilities of Defense Counsel in a Criminal Case

> A lawyer for the accused in a criminal case, shall not:
> (a) agree to represent a person proposing to commit a crime, except as part of a good faith effort to determine the validity, scope, meaning, or application of the law;

(b) act in a case in which the lawyer's partner or other professional associate is or has been the prosecutor;

(c) accept payment of fees by one person for the defense of another except with the consent of the accused after adequate disclosure; or

(d) charge a contingent fee.

1981 Draft: Substantially the same as adopted, except subparagraph (d), which included an obligation to "make reasonable efforts to seek all evidence, whether or not favorable to the defendant," but which did not refer to protective orders. Also, 1981 Draft did not include subparagraph (e) of the rule as adopted.

1982 Draft: Same as adopted, except that subparagraph (e) was not yet in the Rule.

1990 Amendment: At its 1990 Mid-Year Meeting, the ABA House of Delegates added subparagraph (f) to Rule 3.8 and added paragraph 4 to the Comment. The reasons for adding Rule 3.8(f) were exhaustively explained in a Report and Recommendation by the ABA's Standing Committee on Ethics and Professional Responsibility that provided, in part, as follows:

> . . . In February 1986, the ABA House of Delegates approved a resolution requiring prior judicial approval of all subpoenas sought to be issued to attorneys for information relating to clients, and incorporation of several substantive standards to govern when such approval should be granted. This resolution was prompted by the ABA's concern over the increasing incidence of subpoenas directed to attorneys for information relating to clients, and by the effect these subpoenas might have on the adversary system and the attorney-client relationship — the trust placed by the clients in their attorneys and the confidentiality implicit in that relationship itself.
>
> However, the problem has not been corrected. In the seven months preceding the 1986 resolution, according to Department of Justice statistics, approximately 170 federal grand jury subpoenas were issued to attorneys for information about a client — an average of about one each working day (24 per month). In the thirteen months immediately after the 1986 resolution was approved, approximately 525 federal grand jury and trial subpoenas were issued to attorneys for information about a client — an average of almost two per working day (40 per month).
>
> In February 1988, the ABA House of Delegates adopted a new resolution which modified and strengthened the 1986 resolution. . . .
>
> Notwithstanding the laudable objectives of the ABA's February 1988 resolution, the problem of attorney subpoenas continues to "pose for resolution a critical problem in criminal law today." Statistics released by the Department of Justice indicate that during a single twenty month period from 1985 through 1987 almost 700 attorney subpoenas were being authorized by the Department (an annual rate of 420 per year). More recently, in a four month period from October 1988 through January 1989, attorney subpoenas for 179 attorneys were issued by the Department of Justice (an annual rate of nearly 540 per year). These numbers, of course, do not include attorney subpoenas issued by state prosecutors. . . .
>
> Proper operation of our adversary system of justice requires full recognition and protection of the relation of trust and confidence between a client and attorney. One, but only one, aspect of that relation is the privilege not to disclose confidential communications between the client and the attorney, the oldest privilege for confidential communications known to the common law. The United States Supreme Court has observed that "the purpose of the privilege is to encourage clients to make full disclosure to their attorneys." The full and frank communication encouraged by the privilege promotes "broader interests in the observance of law and the administration of justice. The privilege recognizes that sound legal advice or advocacy serves public ends and that such advice or advocacy depends on the lawyer's being fully informed by the client." Any rule regulating subpoenas to lawyers must, at a minimum, provide for full protection of the privilege.

A subpoena rule which does no more than recognize the attorney-client privilege, however, will ignore other important aspects of the relationship between a client and his attorney. In those jurisdictions which have adopted the Model Rules of Professional Conduct, Rule 1.6(a) prohibits an attorney from revealing any information relating to representation of a client. Similarly, DR 4-101 requires an attorney to keep a client's "confidences and secrets," the latter term being defined as "information gained in the professional relationship which the client has requested be held inviolate or the disclosure of which would be embarrassing or would be likely to be detrimental to the client."

Because information protected by the attorney-client privilege is not coterminous with information which an ethical attorney is supposed to hold confidential, there is much information in the hands of an attorney which remains exposed to the subpoena power, even if that power is limited by the privilege. For example, the prevailing judicial position is that, absent special circumstances, an attorney may be compelled by subpoena to reveal information about the identity of the client and the size and source of the fee — information frequently sought by government attorneys. Similarly, an attorney in possession of documents received from a client in the course of a case may be compelled by subpoena to produce those documents, assuming that the client personally could be compelled to produce the documents were they in the client's hands.

Since a subpoena may compel production of information which, though unprivileged, is certainly confidential under Rule 1.6 and DR 4-101, the mere issuance of the subpoena undermines the client's confidence and trust. . . .

[T]he trust and confidence which is the foundation of the attorney-client relationship do not rest solely on the expectation that only privileged communications between client and attorney will remain undisclosed. Clients seeking counsel in criminal proceedings do not draw fine distinctions or follow the nuances of the privilege and its expectations. Confronted by a powerful adversary and by a seemingly bewildering array of procedures, with their liberty at stake, clients rightfully expect that their lawyer will, within the constraints of the law and the profession's code of ethics, zealously argue their case at every turn. There could be few things more destructive of this expectation than the spectacle of their own attorney forced by their adversary to supply information detrimental to their interest.

In addition, a prosecutor's subpoena of a defense lawyer may have a significant inhibiting effect on the lawyer. . . . [O]f those members of the National Association of Criminal Defense Lawyers responding to the study by Professor Genego, 14% said they would no longer take a serious criminal case due to their apprehension of receiving a subpoena compelling information from them. . . .

The ethical and practical concerns discussed above have led a number of jurisdictions to adopt ethical rules limiting the issuance of attorney subpoenas. The most well-known is the rule adopted by the Massachusetts Supreme Court in October of 1985. That rule, known as "PF-15" makes it unprofessional conduct for a prosecutor to issue a grand jury subpoena to an attorney without prior judicial approval. . . .

. . . Moreover, since the Massachusetts Supreme Court's adoption of PF-15, New Hampshire, Tennessee, Virginia and the Air Force Judge Advocate General have adopted similar ethical rules limiting the issuance of attorney subpoenas. And, similar rules are being considered in the District of Columbia, Pennsylvania (where the adoption of the rule is being contested by Federal prosecutors), Rhode Island and New York.

The Report relied heavily on a study by Professor William Genego, Reports from the Field: Prosecutorial Practices Comprising Effective Criminal Defense (Champion, May 1986) at 7-18. The Report also quoted liberally from United States v. Klubock, 639 F. Supp. 117 (D. Mass 1986), aff'd, 832 F.2d 664 (1st Cir. 1987) (en banc); In re Grand Jury Matters, 593 F. Supp. 103 (D.N.H. 1984), aff'd sub nom. United States v. Hodes, 751 F.2d 13 (1st Cir. 1985); and In re Grand Jury Investigation (Sturgis), 412 F. Supp. 943 (E.D. Pa. 1976).

Selected State Variations

California: See Rule 5-110 (Performing the Duty of Member in Government Service) and Rule 5-220 (Suppression of Evidence).

District of Columbia: Rule 3.8 is almost entirely different from the ABA version. The D.C. version of Rule 3.8 provides:

The prosecutor in a criminal case shall not:

(a) in exercising discretion to investigate or to prosecute, improperly favor or invidiously discriminate against any person;

(b) file in court or maintain a charge that the prosecutor knows is not supported by probable cause;

(c) prosecute to trial a charge that the prosecutor knows is not supported by evidence sufficient to establish a prima facie showing of guilt;

(d) intentionally avoid pursuit of evidence or information because it may damage the prosecution's case or aid the defense;

(e) intentionally fail to disclose to the defense, upon request and at a time when use by the defense is reasonably feasible, any evidence or information that the prosecutor knows or reasonably should know tends to negate the guilt of the accused or to mitigate the offense, or, in connection with sentencing, intentionally fail to disclose to the defense upon request any unprivileged mitigating information known to the prosecutor and not reasonably available to the defense, except when the prosecutor is relieved of this responsibility by a protective order of the tribunal;

(f) except for statements which are necessary to inform the public of the nature and extent of the prosecutor's action and which serve a legitimate law enforcement purpose, make extrajudicial comments which serve to heighten condemnation of the accused;

(g) in presenting a case to a grand jury, intentionally interfere with the independence of the grand jury, preempt a function of the grand jury, abuse the processes of the grand jury, or fail to bring to the attention of the grand jury material facts tending substantially to negate the existence of probable cause; or

(h) peremptorily strike jurors on grounds of race, religion, national or ethnic background, or sex.

District of Columbia also *rejected* a proposed subparagraph of Rule 3.8 that would have made it unethical for a prosecutor to "condition a dismissal of charges, nolle prosequi, or similar action on the accused's relinquishment of the right to seek civil redress." However, D.C. Rule 8.4(g), based on DR 7-105, provides that no lawyer may "seek or threaten to seek criminal charges or disciplinary charges solely to obtain an advantage in a civil matter."

Illinois is in the midst of an ongoing struggle over Rule 3.8(f). In 1987, the Illinois legislature passed a law requiring judicial approval of subpoenas issued to lawyers seeking testimony against their clients, but Governor Thompson (a former U.S. Attorney) vetoed the law. Soon after the veto, the Illinois State Bar Association proposed the following rule, which the Illinois Supreme Court rejected without opinion in 1988:

A public prosecutor or other government lawyer shall not subpoena nor cause a subpoena to be issued to an attorney without prior judicial approval after an opportunity for an adversarial proceeding in circumstances where the prosecutor seeks to compel the attorney to provide evidence obtained as a result of the attorney-client relationship concerning a person who is or was represented by the attorney.

In 1990, when Illinois adopted its new Rules of Professional Conduct, it omitted Rule 3.8(f). However, effective November 20, 1991, the Illinois Supreme Court added the language of Rule 3.8(f) by court order. (Justice Heiple dissented.) The Illinois version of Rule 3.8(f) (which is numbered 3.8(c) in Illinois) applies not only to a "public prosecutor" but also to any "other government lawyer." Immediately, the Cook County State's Attorney, the Attorney General of Illinois, and other prosecutors submitted an "emergency motion" to stay enforcement of the new rule, and on December 27, 1991, the Illinois Supreme Court issued an order staying enforcement of the rule.

Maryland's version of subparagraph (e) extends only to an "employee or other person under the control of a prosecutor."

Massachusetts: Supreme Court Rule 3:08 (also designated PF-15) provides: "It is unprofessional conduct for a prosecutor to subpoena an attorney to a grand jury without prior judicial approval in circumstances where the prosecutor seeks to compel the attorney/witness to provide evidence concerning a person who is represented by the attorney/witness."

New Jersey deletes Rule 3.8(e) and changes Rule 3.8(c) to read "not seek to obtain from an unrepresented accused a waiver of important post-indictment pretrial rights."

New York: Same or substantially the same as the ABA Model Code – see Model Code Comparison above.

North Carolina: Rule 7.3 applies to criminal or "quasi-criminal" cases. Rule 7.3(A) prohibits prosecution not supported by probable cause "unless otherwise directed by statutory mandate."

Virginia: DR 8-102 provides that a prosecutor "or other government lawyer in criminal litigation" shall not "induce an unrepresented defendant to surrender important procedural rights" or "discourage a person from giving relevant information to the defendants." DR 8-102(A)(5), a shortened version of Model Rule 3.8(f), prohibits a prosecutor from issuing a subpoena to an attorney "without prior judicial approval in circumstances where the prosecutor seeks to compel the attorney/witness to provide evidence" concerning a past or present client.

Related Materials

ABA Canons: Canon 5 provided:

5. The Defense or Prosecution of Those Accused of Crime

The primary duty of a lawyer engaged in public prosecution is not to convict, but to see that justice is done. The suppression of facts or the secreting of witnesses capable of establishing the innocence of the accused is highly reprehensible.

ABA Standards for Criminal Justice: See Prosecution Function Standard 3-3.9(a) (Discretion in the Charging Decision), Standard 3-3.11 (Disclosure of Evidence by the Prosecutor), and Standard 3-4.1 (Availability for Plea Discussions).

ABA Standards for Imposing Lawyer Discipline: See Standard 5.2 printed in the Related Materials following Model Rule 8.4.

American Lawyer's Code of Conduct: Chapter 9 of the ALCC, entitled "Responsibilities of Government Lawyers," provides as follows:

9.1. A lawyer serving as public prosecutor shall not seek evidence to support a prosecution against a particular individual unless that individual is identified as a suspect in the course of a good faith investigation into suspected criminal conduct.

9.2. In exercising discretion to investigate or to prosecute, a lawyer serving as public prosecutor shall not show favoritism for, or invidiously discriminate against, one person among others similarly situated.

9.3. A lawyer serving as public prosecutor shall not seek or sign formal charges, or proceed to trial, unless a fair-minded juror could conclude beyond a reasonable doubt that the accused is guilty, on the basis of all of the facts that are known to the prosecutor and likely to be admissible into evidence.

Comment to Rule 9.3

Rule 9.3 forbids a prosecutor to seek an indictment or proceed to trial unless a fair-minded juror could conclude that the accused is guilty beyond a reasonable doubt, on the basis of the facts known to the prosecutor and likely to be admissible at trial. A further ethical obligation is assumed by many conscientious prosecutors; they will not seek an indictment or proceed to trial unless they are satisfied that the accused is guilty beyond a reasonable doubt, on the basis of all the facts known to them, regardless of admissibility. That rule should be followed in all cases, but is not here made the basis of a disciplinary violation, because the subjective nature of the standard makes it impossible to enforce.

9.4. A lawyer serving as public prosecutor before a grand jury shall not interfere with the independence of the grand jury, preempt a function of the grand jury, or use the processes of the grand jury for purposes not approved by the grand jury.

Comment to Rule 9.4

[T]he American grand jury has been criticized as a "rubber stamp for the prosecutor," because some prosecutors have used it improperly as an investigative tool and as a device for obtaining unwarranted indictments. Prosecutors have had grand juries dissolved because they would not indict, or because they wished to indict, quite properly, persons the prosecutor did not want indicted. Prosecutors have routinely issued "grand jury subpoenas" for documents they wished to examine, without obtaining the consent of "their" grand juries, or even consulting the grand jury.

Rule 9.4 proscribes such abuses by prosecutors of the extraordinary powers of grand juries, when it is read in conjunction with other applicable rules in this Chapter. . . . [T]hese rules should substantially contribute to returning the grand jury to its constitutional role as a bulwark between the citizen and the power of the state, and reducing its use as a cat's paw for the overzealous prosecutor.

9.5. A lawyer serving as public prosecutor shall not use unconscionable pressures in plea bargaining, such as charging an accused in several counts for what is essentially a single offense, or charging an accused with a more serious offense than is warranted under Rule 9.3.

9.6. A lawyer serving as public prosecutor shall not condition a dismissal, nolle prosequi, or similar action on an accused's relinquishment of constitutional rights, or of rights against the government, a public official, or any other person, other than relinquishment of those rights inherent in pleading not guilty and proceeding to trial.

9.7. A lawyer serving as public prosecutor shall promptly make available to defense counsel, without request for it, any information that the prosecutor knows is likely to be useful to the defense.

Comment to Rule 9.7

Defense counsel has special professional responsibilities deriving from the importance of confidentiality between attorney and client, the presumption of innocence, the constitutional right to counsel, and the constitutional privilege against self-incrimination. The prosecutor, who does not represent a private client, is not affected by those considerations in the same way.

Thus a defense attorney may be professionally bound to withhold evidence. There is nothing unethical in keeping a guilty defendant off the stand and putting the government to its proof; the Constitution guarantees the defendant nothing less. Obviously, however, the prosecutor is not similarly privileged to withhold material evidence; the constitutional command is precisely the contrary.

9.8. A lawyer serving as public prosecutor shall not strike jurors on grounds of race, religion, national or ethnic background, or sex, except to counteract the use of such tactics initiated by the defense.

9.9. A lawyer serving as public prosecutor, who knows that a defendant is not receiving or has not received effective assistance of counsel, shall promptly advise the court, on the record when possible.

9.10. A lawyer representing the government before a court or other tribunal shall inform the tribunal of any facts or legal authorities that might materially affect the decision in the case, and that have not been brought to the attention of the tribunal by other counsel.

9.11. A lawyer in public service shall not engage in publicity regarding a criminal investigation or proceeding, or an administrative investigation or proceeding involving charges of wrongdoing, until after the announcement of a disposition of the case. However, the lawyer may publicize information that is (a) necessary to protect the public from an accused who is at large and reasonably believed to be dangerous; (b) necessary to help in apprehending a suspect; or (c) necessary to rebut publicized allegations of improper conduct on the part of the lawyer or the lawyer's staff.

Comment to Rule 9.11

Along with other unique powers of office, a prosecutor is privileged, in an indictment, to publish severely defamatory information against a private person. Despite their inherent harmfulness, indictments must be publicly available to prevent the abuses of secret proceedings. There is no similar justification, however, for a prosecutor to engage in press conferences, press releases, and other publicity efforts that have the effect of impairing or destroying the reputation of an accused without the due process of a trial or hearing. Yet, on the other hand, an accused may never be more in need of the First Amendment rights to freedom of speech than when officially labeled a wrongdoer before family, friends, neighbors, and business associates. Many defendants are inarticulate; almost all need the special skills of a lawyer as spokesperson. That is why this Code places restrictions on preconviction publicity by public officials, who act under color of law, but recognizes that the First Amendment precludes such restrictions on the speech of private persons and their attorneys.

9.12. A lawyer in public service shall not knowingly violate the rights of any person, or knowingly tolerate the violation of any person's rights by any other public employee.

9.13. A lawyer in public service shall not use the powers of public office for personal advantage, favoritism, or retaliation.

Attorney Fee Forfeitures: A topic often intertwined with subpoenas to defense attorneys is attorney fee forfeiture — seizing an attorney's fees when the government can prove that they are the fruit of federal drug crimes or RICO violations. In 1989, the Supreme Court decided two cases on fee forfeiture, Caplin & Drysdale v. United States, 491 U.S. 617 (1989), and United States v. Monsanto, 491 U.S. 600 (1989).

Department of Justice Guidelines: The United States Department of Justice maintains internal guidelines limiting the circumstances under which Justice Department lawyers may issue subpoenas to criminal defense lawyers. See D.O.J. Subpoenas Guidelines §9-2.161(B) and (F).

Guidelines for the Issuance of Search Warrants: In July 1990, the ABA's Criminal Justice Section issued Guidelines for the Issuance of Search Warrants, many of which directly or indirectly apply to prosecutors.

Model Rules of Professional Conduct for Federal Lawyers: Rule 3.8(a) mandates that a prosecutor shall "[r]efrain from prosecuting a charge that the prosecutor knows is not supported by probable cause, or if not authorized to decline the prosecution of a charge to recommend to the appropriate authority that any charge not warranted by the evidence be withdrawn." Rule 3.8(d) requires timely disclosure only to the defense, not to the tribunal. Rule 3.8(f) obligates a prosecutor to "[r]espect the attorney-client privilege of defendants and not diminish the privilege through investigative or judicial processes." (The Rules for Federal Lawyers do not adopt the ABA version of Rule 3.8(f) requiring prior judicial approval of subpoenas directed to lawyers in criminal cases.)

Supreme Court Cases: The constitutional basis for the disclosure obligations in Rule 3.8(d) is found in Brady v. Maryland, 373 U.S. 83, 87 (1963), which held that "the suppression by the prosecution of evidence favorable to an accused upon request violates due process where the evidence is material. . . ."

18 U.S.C. §3500(b) provides:

§3500. Demands for Production of Statements and Reports of Witnesses

(b) After a witness called by the United States has testified on direct examination, the court shall, on motion of the defendant, order the United States to produce any statement (as hereinafter defined) of the witness in the possession of the United States which relates to the subject matter as to which the witness has testified. If the entire contents of any such statement relate to the subject matter of the testimony of the witness, the court shall order it to be delivered directly to the defendant for his examination and use.

Rule 3.9 Advocate in Nonadjudicative Proceedings

A lawyer representing a client before a legislative or administrative tribunal in a nonadjudicative proceeding shall disclose that the appearance is in a representative capacity and shall conform to the provisions of Rules 3.3(a) through (c), 3.4(a) through (c), and 3.5.

COMMENT

[1] In representation before bodies such as legislatures, municipal councils, and executive and administrative agencies acting in a rule-making or policy-making capacity, lawyers present facts, formulate issues and advance argument

in the matters under consideration. The decision-making body, like a court, should be able to rely on the integrity of the submissions made to it. A lawyer appearing before such a body should deal with the tribunal honestly and in conformity with applicable rules of procedure.

[2] Lawyers have no exclusive right to appear before nonadjudicative bodies, as they do before a court. The requirements of this Rule therefore may subject lawyers to regulations inapplicable to advocates who are not lawyers. However, legislatures and administrative agencies have a right to expect lawyers to deal with them as they deal with courts.

[3] This Rule does not apply to representation of a client in a negotiation or other bilateral transaction with a governmental agency; representation in such a transaction is governed by Rules 4.1 through 4.4.

Model Code Comparison

EC 7-15 stated that a lawyer "appearing before an administrative agency, regardless of the nature of the proceeding it is conducting, has the continuing duty to advance the cause of his client within the bounds of the law." EC 7-16 stated that "[w]hen a lawyer appears in connection with proposed legislation, he ... should comply with applicable laws and legislative rules." EC 8-5 stated that "[f]raudulent, deceptive, or otherwise illegal conduct by a participant in a proceeding before a ... legislative body ... should never be participated in ... by lawyers." DR 7-106(B)(1) provided that "[i]n presenting a matter to a tribunal, a lawyer shall disclose ... [u]nless privileged or irrelevant, the identity of the clients he represents and of the persons who employed him."

Cross-References in Rules

None.

Legislative History

1980 Draft (then Rule 3.12) provided as follows:

(a) A lawyer representing a client before a legislative or administrative tribunal in a nonadjudicative proceeding shall deal fairly with the body conducting the proceeding and with other persons making presentations therein and their counsel.

(b) A lawyer in such a proceeding shall:

(1) identify the client on whose behalf the lawyer appears, unless the identity of the client is privileged;

(2) conform to the provisions of Rules 3.1 and 3.4.

1981 and 1982 Drafts were the same as adopted.

Selected State Variations

California has no direct counterpart.
Illinois omits Rule 3.9.
New Jersey deletes the cross-reference to Rule 3.5(b) in Rule 3.9.
New York: Same or substantially the same as the ABA Model Code — see Model
Code Comparison above.
North Carolina omits Rule 3.9.
Pennsylvania does not incorporate Rule 3.4(c) in Rule 3.9.
Virginia omits Rule 3.9.

Related Materials

ABA Canons: Canon 26 provided:

26. Professional Advocacy Other Than Before Courts

   A lawyer openly, and in his true character may render professional services before legislative or other bodies, regarding proposed legislation and in advocacy of claims before departments of government, upon the same principles of ethics which justify his appearance
before the Courts; but it is unprofessional for a lawyer so engaged to conceal his attorney-
ship, or to employ secret personal solicitations, or to use means other than those addressed to
the reason and understanding, to influence action.

ABA Standards for Criminal Justice: See Prosecution Function Standards 3-3.1, 3-
3.9, 3-3.11.

ARTICLE 4. TRANSACTIONS WITH PERSONS
OTHER THAN CLIENTS

Rule 4.1 Truthfulness in Statements to Others

In the course of representing a client a lawyer shall not knowingly:
   (a) make a false statement of material fact or law to a third person; or
   (b) fail to disclose a material fact to a third person when disclosure is
necessary to avoid assisting a criminal or fraudulent act by a client, unless
disclosure is prohibited by Rule 1.6.

COMMENT

Misrepresentation

[1] A lawyer is required to be truthful when dealing with others on a client's behalf, but generally has no affirmative duty to inform an opposing party of relevant facts. A misrepresentation can occur if the lawyer incorporates or affirms a statement of another person that the lawyer knows is false. Misrepresentations can also occur by failure to act.

Statements of Fact

[2] This Rule refers to statements of fact. Whether a particular statement should be regarded as one of fact can depend on the circumstances. Under generally accepted conventions in negotiation, certain types of statements ordinarily are not taken as statements of material fact. Estimates of price or value placed on the subject of a transaction and a party's intentions as to an acceptable settlement of a claim are in this category, and so is the existence of an undisclosed principal except where nondisclosure of the principal would constitute fraud.

Fraud by Client

[3] Paragraph (b) recognizes that substantive law may require a lawyer to disclose certain information to avoid being deemed to have assisted the client's crime or fraud. The requirement of disclosure created by this paragraph is, however, subject to the obligations created by Rule 1.6.

Model Code Comparison

Paragraph (a) is substantially similar to DR 7-102(A)(5), which stated that "[i]n his representation of a client, a lawyer shall not . . . [k]nowingly make a false statement of law or fact."

With regard to paragraph (b), DR 7-102(A)(3) provided that a lawyer shall not "[c]onceal or knowingly fail to disclose that which he is required by law to reveal."

Cross-References in Rules

Rule 1.6, Comment 20: "The Rules of Professional Conduct in various circumstances permit or require a lawyer to disclose information relating to the representation. See **Rules** 2.2, 2.3, 3.3 and **4.1.**"

Rule 1.13, Comment 6: "[T]his Rule does not limit or expand the lawyer's responsibilities under **Rules** 1.6, 1.8, and 1.16, 3.3, or **4.1.**"

Rule 3.9, Comment 3: "This Rule does not apply to representation of a client in a negotiation or other bilateral transaction with a governmental agency; representation in such a transaction is governed by **Rules 4.1** through 4.4."

Legislative History

1980 Discussion Draft contained the following Introduction:

Negotiator

As negotiator a lawyer seeks agreement concerning matters of interest to a client and another party. Negotiation may concern dispute settlement, settlement of a contract, labor relations, government regulatory activity, custody and support in a family matter, and other legally significant relationships. A lawyer's function in negotiation can include presenting a bargaining position, exploring bases of common interest, reconciling differences, persuading other parties of the merits of the client's position, ironing out details, and formalizing the terms of an agreement.

A negotiator should seek the most advantageous result for the client that is consistent with the requirements of law and the lawyer's responsibilities under the Rules of Professional Conduct. As negotiator, a lawyer should consider not only the client's short-run advantage but also his or her long-run interests, such as the state of future relations between the parties. The lawyer should help the client appreciate the interests and position of the other party and should encourage concessions that will effectuate the client's larger objectives. A lawyer should not transform a bargaining situation into a demonstration of toughness or hypertechnicality or forget that the purely legal aspects of an agreement are often subordinate to its practical aspects. When the alternative to reaching agreement is likely to be litigation, the lawyer should be aware that, although litigation is wholly legitimate as a means of resolving controversy, a fairly negotiated settlement generally yields a better conclusion. A lawyer should also recognize that the lawyer's own interest in resorting to litigation may be different from a client's interest in doing so.

A lawyer's style in negotiations can have great influence on the character of the negotiations — whether they are restrained, open, and business-like, or acrimonious and permeated with distrust. Whatever their outcome, negotiations should be conducted in a civil and forthright manner. Nevertheless, it must be recognized that in negotiations a lawyer is the agent for the client and not an arbitrator or mediator. Negotiation is in part a competition for advantage between parties who have the legal competence to settle their own affairs. A lawyer as negotiator should not impose an agreement on the client, even if the lawyer believes the agreement is in the client's best interests. By the same token, a lawyer does not necessarily endorse the substance of an agreement arrived at through his or her efforts.

1980 Discussion Draft of Rule 4.1 (then called Rule 4.2) provided as follows:

Fairness to Other Participants

(a) In conducting negotiations a lawyer shall be fair in dealing with other participants.

(b) A lawyer shall not make a knowing misrepresentation of fact or law, or fail to disclose a material fact known to the lawyer, even if adverse, when disclosure is:

(1) required by law or the Rules of Professional Conduct; or

(2) necessary to correct a manifest misapprehension of fact or law resulting from a previous representation made by the lawyer or known by the lawyer to have been made by the client. . . .

1980 Discussion Draft also contained the following provision (then called Rule 4.3) that has no equivalent in the Rules as adopted:

Illegal, Fraudulent, or Unconscionable Transactions

A lawyer shall not conclude an agreement, or assist a client in concluding an agreement, that the lawyer knows or reasonably should know is illegal, contains legally prohibited terms, would work a fraud, or would be held to be unconscionable as a matter of law.

1981 Draft: Subparagraph (a) was substantially the same as adopted. Subparagraph (b) provided that a lawyer must not:

(b) knowingly fail to disclose a fact to a third person when:
(1) in the circumstances failure to make the disclosure is equivalent to making a material misrepresentation;
(2) disclosure is necessary to prevent assisting a criminal or fraudulent act, as required by Rule 1.2(d); or
(3) disclosure is necessary to comply with other law.

1982 Draft: Substantially the same as adopted, except that Rule 4.1(b) provided: "The duties stated in this Rule apply even if compliance requires disclosure of information otherwise protected by Rule 1.6."

Selected State Variations

California: See B & P Code §6128(a).

Illinois Rule 4.1(a) prohibits a lawyer from making "a statement of material fact or law to a third person which statement the lawyer knows or reasonably should know to be false."

Kansas states the final clause of Rule 4.1(b) as follows: "unless disclosure is prohibited by or made discretionary under Rule 1.6."

Maryland adds a separate subparagraph providing: "The duties stated in this Rule apply even if compliance requires disclosure of information otherwise protected by Rule 1.6."

Michigan has not adopted Rule 4.1(b). See also Michigan's version of Rule 1.6(c)(3), which is noted in the Comment to Michigan's Rule 4.1.

Mississippi deletes the wording in Rule 4.1(b), "unless disclosure is prohibited by Rule 1.6."

New Jersey Rule 4.1 applies the duties of that Rule even if it requires revelation of information protected by Rule 1.6.

New York: Same or substantially the same as the ABA Model Code — see Model Code Comparison above — except see New York Materials for New York's versions of DR 7-102(B)(1), EC 4-7, and DR 4-101(C)(5).

North Carolina: Rule 7.2(A) is substantially the same as the Model Code.

Texas: Rule 4.1(b) provides in full that a lawyer shall not "fail to disclose a material fact to a third party when disclosure is necessary to avoid making the lawyer a party to a criminal act or knowingly assisting a fraudulent act perpetrated by a client."

Virginia: Substantially the same as the Model Code.

Related Materials

American Academy of Matrimonial Lawyers: The "Bounds of Advocacy" drafted by the American Academy of Matrimonial Lawyers contains the following provisions and commentary:

3.2 An attorney should never deceive or intentionally mislead opposing counsel.

Comment to Rule 3.2

Attorneys are entitled to believe statements by opposing counsel. They should be able to assume that the matrimonial lawyer will correct any misimpression caused by an inaccurate or misleading prior statement by counsel or her client. Although an attorney must maintain the client's confidences, the duty of confidentiality does not require the attorney to deceive, or permit the client to deceive, opposing counsel. When the opposing party or counsel specifically requests information which the attorney is not required to provide and which the attorney has been instructed to withhold or which may be detrimental to the client's interests, the attorney should refuse to provide the information, but should not mislead opposing counsel.

3.3 An attorney should not induce or rely on a mistake by opposing counsel as to matters agreed upon to obtain an unfair benefit for the client.

Comment to Rule 3.3

The need for trust between attorneys, even those representing opposing sides in a dispute, requires more than simply avoiding fraudulent and intentionally deceitful conduct. Misunderstandings should be corrected and not relied upon in the hope they will benefit the client. Thus, for example, the attorney reducing an oral agreement to writing not only should avoid misstating the understanding, but should correct inadvertent errors by opposing counsel that do not reflect prior understandings or agreements. Whether or not conduct or statements by opposing counsel that are not necessarily in her client's best interests should be corrected may not always be clear and will depend on the particular facts of a case. The crucial consideration should be whether the attorney induced the misunderstanding or is aware that opposing counsel's statements do not accurately reflect any prior agreement. It is thus unlikely that tactical, evidentiary or legal errors made by opposing counsel at trial require correction.

3.4 An attorney should not overstate his authority to settle nor represent that he has authority which he does not have.

Comment to Rule 3.4

In either case presented in the Standard, the attorney has improperly induced reliance by opposing counsel that could damage the attorney-client relationship. A matrimonial lawyer who is uncertain of his authority—or simply does not believe that opposing counsel is entitled to such information—should either truthfully disclose his uncertainty, or state that he is unwilling or unable to respond at all.

Rule 4.2 Communication with Person Represented by Counsel

In representing a client, a lawyer shall not communicate about the subject of the representation with a party the lawyer knows to be represented by another lawyer in the matter, unless the lawyer has the consent of the other lawyer or is authorized by law to do so.

COMMENT

[1] This Rule does not prohibit communication with a party, or an employee or agent of a party, concerning matters outside the representation. For example, the existence of a controversy between a government agency and a private party, or between two organizations, does not prohibit a lawyer for either from communicating with nonlawyer representatives of the other regarding a separate matter. Also, parties to a matter may communicate directly with each other and a lawyer having independent justification for communicating with the other party is permitted to do so. Communications authorized by law include, for example, the right of a party to a controversy with a government agency to speak with government officials about the matter.

[2] In the case of an organization, this Rule prohibits communications by a lawyer for one party concerning the matter in representation with persons having a managerial responsibility on behalf of the organization, and with any other person whose act or omission in connection with that matter may be imputed to the organization for purposes of civil or criminal liability or whose statement may constitute an admission on the part of the organization. If an agent or employee of the organization is represented in the matter by his or her own counsel, the consent by that counsel to a communication will be sufficient for purposes of this Rule. Compare Rule 3.4(f).

[3] This rule also covers any person, whether or not a party to a formal proceeding, who is represented by counsel concerning the matter in question.

Model Code Comparison

This Rule is substantially identical to DR 7-104(A)(1).

Cross-References in Rules

Rule 3.4, Comment 4: "Paragraph (f) permits a lawyer to advise employees of a client to refrain from giving information to another party, for the employees may identify their interests with those of the client. See also **Rule 4.2.**"

Rule 3.9, Comment 3: "This Rule does not apply to representation of a client in a negotiation or other bilateral transaction with a governmental agency; representation in such a transaction is governed by **Rules 4.1 through 4.4.**"

Legislative History

1980 Discussion Draft (then Rule 3.2(b)(5)) provided that a lawyer shall not "interview or otherwise communicate with a party who the lawyer knows is represented by other counsel concerning the subject matter of the representation, except with the consent of that party's counsel or as authorized by law."

1981 Draft was substantially the same as adopted.

1982 Draft was adopted.

Selected State Variations

California: See Rule 2-100 (Communication with a Represented Party).

District of Columbia: Rule 4.2 provides:

(b) During the course of representing a client, a lawyer may communicate about the subject of the representation with a nonparty employee of the opposing party without obtaining the consent of that party's lawyer. However, prior to communicating with any such nonparty employee, a lawyer must disclose to such employee both the lawyer's identity and the fact that the lawyer represents a party with a claim against the employee's employer.

(c) For purposes of this rule, the term "party" includes any person, including an employee of a party organization, who has the authority to bind a party organization as to the representation to which the communication relates.

(d) This rule does not prohibit communication by a lawyer with government officials who have the authority to redress the grievances of the lawyer's client, whether or not those grievances or the lawyer's communications relate to matters that are the subject of the representation, provided that in the event of such communications the disclosures specified in (b) are made to the government official to whom the communication is made.

Illinois provides that a lawyer shall not communicate "or cause another to communicate" with a represented party.

New Mexico adds the following sentence to Rule 4.2: "Except for persons having a managerial responsibility on behalf of the organization, an attorney is not prohibited from communicating directly with employees of a corporation, partnership or other entity about the subject matter of the representation even though the corporation, partnership or entity itself is represented by counsel."

New York: Same or substantially the same as the ABA Model Code — see Model Code Comparison above.

North Carolina: Rule 7.4(A) is substantially the same as the Model Code.

Texas Rule 4.02 provides:

(a) In representing a client, a lawyer shall not communicate or cause or encourage another to communicate about the subject of the representation with a person, organization or entity of government the lawyer knows to be represented by another lawyer regarding that subject, unless the lawyer has the consent of the other lawyer or is authorized by law to do so.

(b) In representing a client a lawyer shall not communicate or cause another to communicate about the subject of representation with a person or organization a lawyer knows to be employed or retained for the purpose of conferring with or advising another lawyer about the subject of the representation, unless the lawyer has the consent of the other lawyer or is authorized by law to do so.

(c) For the purpose of this rule, "organization or entity of government" includes: (1) those persons presently having a managerial responsibility with an organization or entity of government that relates to the subject of the representation, or (2) those persons presently employed by such organization or entity and whose act or omission in connection with the subject of representation may make the organization or entity of government vicariously liable for such act or omission.

(d) When a person, organization, or entity of government that is represented by a lawyer in a matter seeks advice regarding that matter from another lawyer, the second lawyer is not prohibited by paragraph (a) from giving such advice without notifying or seeking consent of the first lawyer.

Virginia: Substantially the same as the Model Code.

Related Materials

ABA Canons: Canon 9 provided:

9. Negotiations with Opposite Party

A lawyer should not in any way communicate upon the subject of controversy with a party represented by counsel; much less should he undertake to negotiate or compromise the matter with him, but should deal only with his counsel.

ABA Standards for Criminal Justice: See Prosecution Function Standard 3-4.1(b).
ABA Standards for Imposing Lawyer Discipline:

6.3. Improper Communications with Individuals in the Legal System

6.31. Disbarment is generally appropriate when a lawyer:

(a) intentionally tampers with a witness and causes serious or potentially serious injury to a party, or causes significant or potentially significant interference with the outcome of the legal proceeding; or . . .

(c) improperly communicates with someone in the legal system other than a witness, judge, or juror with the intent to influence or affect the outcome of the proceeding, and causes significant or potentially significant interference with the outcome of the legal proceeding.

6.32. Suspension is generally appropriate when a lawyer engages in communication with an individual in the legal system when the lawyer knows that such communication is improper, and causes injury or potential injury to a party or causes interference or potential interference with the outcome of the legal proceeding.

6.33. Reprimand is generally appropriate when a lawyer is negligent in determining whether it is proper to engage in communication with an individual in the legal system, and causes injury or potential injury to a party or interference or potential interference with the outcome of the legal proceeding.

American Lawyer's Code of Conduct: Rule 3.9 provides: "[A] lawyer may send a written offer of settlement directly to an adverse party, seven days or more after that party's attorney has received the same offer of settlement in writing."

Federal Rules of Civil Procedure: Rule 5(b) provides: "Whenever under these rules service is required or permitted to be made upon a party represented by an attorney the service shall be made upon the attorney unless service on the party is ordered by the court."

Model Rules of Professional Conduct for Federal Lawyers: Rule 4.2 provides as follows:

> (a) In representing a client, a Federal lawyer shall not communicate about the subject of the representation with a party the lawyer knows to be represented by another lawyer in the matter, unless the Federal lawyer has the consent of the other lawyer; [or] in a criminal matter, the individual initiates the communication with the Government lawyer and voluntarily and knowingly waives the right to counsel for the purposes of that communication; or the Federal lawyer otherwise is authorized by law to do so.
>
> (b) This Rule does not prohibit communications by a Non-Government lawyer with Federal Agency officials who have the authority to resolve a matter affecting the lawyer's client, whether or not the lawyer's communications relate to matters that are the subject of the representation, provided that the lawyer discloses the lawyer's identity; the fact that the lawyer represents a client in a matter involving the official's Federal Agency; and that the matter is being handled for the Federal Agency by a Government lawyer.

The Comment explains:

> In a criminal case there may be times when communications between a defendant and a Federal Agency without notice to defense counsel is in the interest of the defendant. Some communications will serve to protect the defendant and to identify sham representations. For example, in certain criminal enterprises, such as organized crime or drug rings, a defendant may wish to cooperate with a Federal Agency, but the counsel may also be the counsel of others involved in the enterprise. To insure that in such instances there is no abuse, this rule would permit communications by the defendant with the Government lawyer, as long as the defendant voluntarily and knowingly waives the right to counsel.

Rule 4.3 Dealing with Unrepresented Person

In dealing on behalf of a client with a person who is not represented by counsel, a lawyer shall not state or imply that the lawyer is disinterested. When the lawyer knows or reasonably should know that the unrepresented person misunderstands the lawyer's role in the matter, the lawyer shall make reasonable efforts to correct the misunderstanding.

COMMENT

An unrepresented person, particularly one not experienced in dealing with legal matters, might assume that a lawyer is disinterested in loyalties or is a disinterested authority on the law even when the lawyer represents a client. During the course of a lawyer's representation of a client, the lawyer should not give advice to an unrepresented person other than the advice to obtain counsel.

Model Code Comparison

There was no direct counterpart to this Rule in the Model Code. DR 7-104(A)(2) provided that a lawyer shall not "[g]ive advice to a person who is not represented by a lawyer, other than the advice to secure counsel. . . ."

Cross-References in Rules

Rule 3.9, Comment 3: "This Rule does not apply to representation of a client in a negotiation or other bilateral transaction with a governmental agency; representation in such a transaction is governed by **Rules 4.1 through 4.4.**"

Legislative History

1980 Discussion Draft (then Rule 3.6) provided as follows:

Appearing Against an Unrepresented Party

When an opposing party is unrepresented, a lawyer shall refrain from unfairly exploiting that party's ignorance of the law or the practices of the tribunal.

1981 Draft was substantially the same as adopted.
1982 Draft was adopted.

Selected State Variations

California: No comparable provision.
District of Columbia: Rule 4.3(a) adds the language of DR 7-104(A)(2) that a lawyer dealing with an unrepresented person shall give no advice "other than the advice to secure counsel."
Louisiana: Rule 4.3 provides:

A lawyer shall assume that an unrepresented person does not understand the lawyer's role in a matter and the lawyer shall carefully explain to the unrepresented person the lawyer's role in the matter.

During the course of a lawyer's representation of a client, the lawyer should not give advice to a non-represented person other than the advice to obtain counsel.

New York: Same or substantially the same as the ABA Model Code — see Model Code Comparison above.
Pennsylvania adds the text of DR 7-104(A)(2) to Rule 4.3.

Related Materials

ABA Canons: Canon 9 provided:

9. Negotiations with Opposite Party

It is incumbent upon the lawyer most particularly to avoid everything that may tend to mislead a party not represented by counsel, and he should not undertake to advise him as to the law.

ABA Standards for Criminal Justice: Prosecution Function Standards 3-3.2(b), 3-3.9(b), and 3-3.10(c).

American Academy of Matrimonial Lawyers: The "Bounds of Advocacy" drafted by the American Academy of Matrimonial Lawyers contains the following provision and commentary:

2.21 An attorney should not advise an unrepresented party.

Comment to Rule 2.21

Once it becomes apparent that an opposing party intends to proceed without a lawyer, the attorney should, at the earliest opportunity, inform the opposing party in writing as follows:

1. I am your spouse's lawyer.
2. I do not and will not represent you.
3. I will at all times look out for your spouse's interests, not yours.
4. Any statements I make to you about this case should be taken by you as negotiation or argument on behalf of your spouse and not as advice to you as to your best interest.
5. I urge you to obtain your own lawyer.

Rule 4.4 Respect for Rights of Third Persons

In representing a client, a lawyer shall not use means that have no substantial purpose other than to embarrass, delay, or burden a third person, or use methods of obtaining evidence that violate the legal rights of such a person.

COMMENT

Responsibility to a client requires a lawyer to subordinate the interests of others to those of the client, but that responsibility does not imply that a lawyer may disregard the rights of third persons. It is impractical to catalogue all such rights, but they include legal restrictions on methods of obtaining evidence from third persons.

Model Code Comparison

DR 7-106(C)(2) provided that a lawyer shall not "[a]sk any question that he has no reasonable basis to believe is relevant to the case and that is intended to degrade a witness or other person." DR 7-102(A)(1) provided that a lawyer shall not "take . . . action on behalf of his client when he knows or when it is obvious that such action would serve merely to harass or maliciously injure another." DR 7-108(D) provided that "[a]fter discharge of the jury . . . the lawyer shall not ask questions or make comments to a member of that jury that are calculated merely to harass or embarrass the juror. . . ." DR 7-108(E) provided that a lawyer "shall not conduct . . . a vexatious or harassing investigation of either a venireman or a juror."

Cross-References in Rules

Rule 3.9, Comment 3: "This Rule does not apply to representation of a client in a negotiation or other bilateral transaction with a governmental agency; representation in such a transaction is governed by **Rules 4.1** through **4.4.**"

Legislative History

1980 Discussion Draft (then Rule 3.4) provided as follows:

(a) In preparing and presenting a cause, a lawyer shall respect the interests of third persons, including witnesses, jurors, and persons incidentally concerned with the proceeding. . . .

1981 and 1982 Drafts were the same as adopted.

Selected State Variations

California: See Rule 3-200(A) (Prohibited Objectives of Employment); Rule 5-100 (Threatening Criminal, Administrative, or Disciplinary Charges); Rule 5-310(B) (Prohibited Contact with Witnesses); B & P Code §§6068(c), 6068(f), 6068(g), and 6128(b).

Missouri: The Interprofessional Code for Physicians and Attorneys (Supreme Court Rule 4, Appendix 2) provides in part:

Physician Called as Witness. The attorney and the physician should treat one another with dignity and respect in the courtroom. The physician should testify solely as to the medical facts in the case and should frankly state his medical opinion. He should never be an advocate and should realize that his testimony is intended to enlighten rather than to impress or prejudice the court or the jury.

It is improper for the attorney to abuse a medical witness or to seek to influence his medical opinion. Established rules of evidence afford ample opportunity to test the qualifications, competence and credibility of a medical witness; and it is always improper and unnecessary for the attorney to embarrass or harass the physician.

Consideration and Disposition of Complaints. The public airing of any complaint or criticism by a member of one profession against the other profession or any of its members is to be deplored. Such complaints or criticism, including complaints of the violation of the principles of this Code, should be referred by the complaining doctor or lawyer through his own association to the appropriate association of the other profession; and all such complaints or criticism should be promptly and adequately processed by the association receiving them.

New York: Same or substantially the same as the ABA Model Code — see Model Code Comparison above.

North Carolina: Rules 7.2, 7.6, and 7.8 are substantially the same as the Model Code.

Texas Rule 4.04(b) forbids lawyers to present or threaten disciplinary or criminal charges "solely to gain an advantage in a civil matter" or civil, criminal, or disciplinary charges "solely" to prevent participation by a complainant or witness in a disciplinary matter.

Virginia: Substantially the same as the Model Code.

Related Materials

ABA Canons: Canon 18 provided:

18. Treatment of Witnesses and Litigants

A lawyer should always treat adverse witnesses and suitors with fairness and due consideration, and he should never minister to the malevolence or prejudices of a client in the trial or conduct of a cause. The client cannot be made the keeper of the lawyer's conscience in professional matters. He has no right to demand that his counsel shall abuse the opposite party or indulge in offensive personalities. Improper speech is not excusable on the ground that it is what the client would say if speaking in his own behalf.

ABA Standards for Criminal Justice: See Prosecution Function Standards 3-2.9(b), 3-3.1(c), and 3-5.7(a); Defense Function Standards 4-1.2(b) and (d), 4-4.2, 4-7.1(e), and 4-7.6(a).

ARTICLE 5. LAW FIRMS AND ASSOCIATIONS

Editors' Note. In the 1980 Discussion Draft, the Article entitled "Law Firms and Associations" (then beginning with Rule 7.1) had the following Introduction:

A majority of American lawyers practice in law firms or the law departments of government or private organizations. In the legal and ethical rules governing lawyers' conduct, a law firm or law department generally is treated as though it were a single practitioner. Thus, the rules prohibiting representation of opposing parties in litigation or suing one's own client apply not only to a single practitioner but also to a law firm or law department. So also, the rule that prohibits a lawyer from revealing the confidences of a client requires that all lawyers in a firm refrain from revealing confidences of a client served by any lawyer in the firm. However, a law firm or organization is in fact comprised of individual lawyers who work in association with each other. In certain circumstances, that fact is significant for purposes of professional ethics. These circumstances include the question of vicarious disqualification of lawyers in law firms and legal departments, a supervising lawyer's responsibility for ethical misconduct by a subordinate lawyer, and a subordinate lawyer's responsibility for misconduct committed at the direction of a supervisor. . . .

Rule 5.1 Responsibilities of a Partner or Supervisory Lawyer

(a) A partner in a law firm shall make reasonable efforts to ensure that the firm has in effect measures giving reasonable assurance that all lawyers in the firm conform to the rules of professional conduct.

(b) A lawyer having direct supervisory authority over another lawyer shall make reasonable efforts to ensure that the other lawyer conforms to the rules of professional conduct.

(c) A lawyer shall be responsible for another lawyer's violation of the rules of professional conduct if:

(1) the lawyer orders or, with knowledge of the specific conduct, ratifies the conduct involved; or

(2) the lawyer is a partner in the law firm in which the other lawyer practices, or has direct supervisory authority over the other lawyer, and knows of the conduct at a time when its consequences can be avoided or mitigated but fails to take reasonable remedial action.

COMMENT

[1] Paragraphs (a) and (b) refer to lawyers who have supervisory authority over the professional work of a firm or legal department of a government agency. This includes members of a partnership and the shareholders in a law firm organized as a professional corporation; lawyers having supervisory authority in the law department of an enterprise or government agency; and lawyers who have intermediate managerial responsibilities in a firm.

[2] The measures required to fulfill the responsibility prescribed in paragraphs (a) and (b) can depend on the firm's structure and the nature of its practice. In a small firm, informal supervision and occasional admonition ordinarily might be sufficient. In a large firm, or in practice situations in which intensely difficult ethical problems frequently arise, more elaborate procedures may be necessary. Some firms, for example, have a procedure whereby junior lawyers can make confidential referral of ethical problems directly to a designated senior partner or special committee. See Rule 5.2. Firms, whether large or small, may also rely on continuing legal education in professional ethics. In any event, the ethical atmosphere of a firm can influence the conduct of all its members and a lawyer having authority over the work of another may not assume that the subordinate lawyer will inevitably conform to the Rules.

[3] Paragraph (c)(1) expresses a general principle of responsibility for acts of another. See also Rule 8.4(a).

[4] Paragraph (c)(2) defines the duty of a lawyer having direct supervisory authority over performance of specific legal work by another lawyer. Whether a lawyer has such supervisory authority in particular circumstances is a question of fact. Partners of a private firm have at least indirect responsibility for all work

being done by the firm, while a partner in charge of a particular matter ordinarily has direct authority over other firm lawyers engaged in the matter. Appropriate remedial action by a partner would depend on the immediacy of the partner's involvement and the seriousness of the misconduct. The supervisor is required to intervene to prevent avoidable consequences of misconduct if the supervisor knows that the misconduct occurred. Thus, if a supervising lawyer knows that a subordinate misrepresented a matter to an opposing party in negotiation, the supervisor as well as the subordinate has a duty to correct the resulting misapprehension.

[5] Professional misconduct by a lawyer under supervision could reveal a violation of paragraph (b) on the part of the supervisory lawyer even though it does not entail a violation of paragraph (c) because there was no direction, ratification or knowledge of the violation.

[6] Apart from this Rule and Rule 8.4(a), a lawyer does not have disciplinary liability for the conduct of a partner, associate or subordinate. Whether a lawyer may be liable civilly or criminally for another lawyer's conduct is a question of law beyond the scope of these Rules.

Model Code Comparison

There was no direct counterpart to this Rule in the Model Code. DR 1-103(A) provided that a lawyer "possessing unprivileged knowledge of a violation of DR 1-102 shall report such knowledge to . . . authority empowered to investigate or act upon such violation."

Cross-References in Rules

Rule 1.5, Comment 4: For purposes of sharing fees under Rule 1.5(e): "Joint responsibility for the representation entails the obligations stated in **Rule 5.1** for purposes of the matter involved."

Legislative History

1980 Discussion Draft of Rule 5.1 (then Rule 7.2) provided as follows:

Responsibilities of a Supervisory Lawyer

(a) A lawyer having supervisory authority over another lawyer shall make a reasonable effort to see that the conduct of the lawyer under supervision conforms to the Rules of Professional Conduct.

(b) A lawyer is chargeable with another lawyer's violation of the Rules of Professional Conduct if:

(1) the lawyer orders or ratifies the conduct involved; or

(2) the lawyer has supervisory responsibility over the other lawyer and has knowledge of the conduct at a time when its consequences can be avoided or mitigated but fails to take appropriate remedial action.

1981 Draft was substantially the same as adopted, except that Rule 5.2(a) applied to "all lawyers in the firm, *including other partners. . . .*"
1982 Draft was adopted.

Selected State Variations

California: See Rule 1-100(B) (defining "law firm" and "associate").
Illinois provides that "[e]ach" partner or lawyer shall make the reasonable efforts specified in Rule 5.1(a) and (b).
New Jersey Rule 5.1(c)(2) applies only to lawyers having "direct supervisory authority"; it deletes the phrase "is a partner in the law firm in which the other lawyer practices."
New York: Amendment partially adopts language from Rule 5.1. See EC 1-8 and DR 1-104 of the New York Code.
North Carolina omits Rule 5.1.
Texas has no equivalent to Rule 5.1(a) and (b).
Virginia omits Rule 5.1.

Related Materials

American Lawyer's Code of Conduct: Rule 8.15 provides:

A lawyer shall take reasonable care to assure that none of the lawyer's partners, associates, or employees commits an act that would be a disciplinary violation if committed by the lawyer.

Model Rules of Professional Conduct for Federal Lawyers add the following new subparagraphs to Rule 5.1:

(c) A Federal lawyer, who is a supervisory lawyer, is responsible for ensuring that the subordinate lawyer is properly trained and is competent to perform the duties to which the subordinate lawyer is assigned.

(d) A Government lawyer, who is a supervisory lawyer, should encourage subordinate lawyers to participate in pro bono publico service activities and the activities of bar associations and law reform organizations.

Rule 5.2 Responsibilities of a Subordinate Lawyer

(a) A lawyer is bound by the rules of professional conduct notwithstanding that the lawyer acted at the direction of another person.

(b) A subordinate lawyer does not violate the rules of professional conduct if that lawyer acts in accordance with a supervisory lawyer's reasonable resolution of an arguable question of professional duty.

COMMENT

[1] Although a lawyer is not relieved of responsibility for a violation by the fact that the lawyer acted at the direction of a supervisor, that fact may be relevant in determining whether a lawyer had the knowledge required to render conduct a violation of the Rules. For example, if a subordinate filed a frivolous pleading at the direction of a supervisor, the subordinate would not be guilty of a professional violation unless the subordinate knew of the document's frivolous character.

[2] When lawyers in a supervisor-subordinate relationship encounter a matter involving professional judgment as to ethical duty, the supervisor may assume responsibility for making the judgment. Otherwise a consistent course of action or position could not be taken. If the question can reasonably be answered only one way, the duty of both lawyers is clear and they are equally responsible for fulfilling it. However, if the question is reasonably arguable, someone has to decide upon the course of action. That authority ordinarily reposes in the supervisor, and a subordinate may be guided accordingly. For example, if a question arises whether the interests of two clients conflict under Rule 1.7, the supervisor's reasonable resolution of the question should protect the subordinate professionally if the resolution is subsequently challenged.

Model Code Comparison

There was no counterpart to this Rule in the Model Code.

Cross-References in Rules

Rule 5.1, Comment 2: "Some firms . . . have a procedure whereby junior lawyers can make confidential referral of ethical problems directly to a designated senior partner or special committee. See **Rule 5.2.**"

Legislative History

1980 Discussion Draft (then Rule 7.3) provided as follows:

(a) A lawyer acting under the supervisory authority of another person is bound by the Rules of Professional Conduct notwithstanding the fact that the lawyer's conduct was ordered by the supervisor.

1981 Draft was substantially the same as adopted.
1982 Draft was adopted.

Selected State Variations

California: No comparable provision.
New York: No comparable provision.
North Carolina omits Rule 5.2.
Virginia omits Rule 5.2.

Rule 5.3 Responsibilities Regarding Nonlawyer Assistants

With respect to a nonlawyer employed or retained by or associated with a lawyer:

(a) a partner in a law firm shall make reasonable efforts to ensure that the firm has in effect measures giving reasonable assurance that the person's conduct is compatible with the professional obligations of the lawyer;

(b) a lawyer having direct supervisory authority over the nonlawyer shall make reasonable efforts to ensure that the person's conduct is compatible with the professional obligations of the lawyer; and

(c) a lawyer shall be responsible for conduct of such a person that would be a violation of the rules of professional conduct if engaged in by a lawyer if:

(1) the lawyer orders or, with the knowledge of the specific conduct, ratifies the conduct involved; or

(2) the lawyer is a partner in the law firm in which the person is employed, or has direct supervisory authority over the person, and knows of the conduct at a time when its consequences can be avoided or mitigated but fails to take reasonable remedial action.

COMMENT

Lawyers generally employ assistants in their practice, including secretaries, investigators, law student interns, and paraprofessionals. Such assistants, whether employees or independent contractors, act for the lawyer in rendition of the lawyer's professional services. A lawyer should give such assistants appropriate instruction and supervision concerning the ethical aspects of their employment, particularly regarding the obligation not to disclose information relating to representation of the client, and should be responsible for their work product. The measures employed in supervising nonlawyers should take account of the fact that they do not have legal training and are not subject to professional discipline.

Model Code Comparison

There was no direct counterpart to this Rule in the Model Code. DR 4-101(D) provided that a lawyer "shall exercise reasonable care to prevent his employees, associates, and others whose services are utilized by him from disclosing or using confidences or secrets of a client."

Cross-References in Rules

Rule 5.5, Comment: "Paragraph (b) does not prohibit a lawyer from employing the services of paraprofessionals and delegating functions to them, so long as the lawyer supervises the delegated work and retains responsibility for their work. See **Rule 5.3.**"

Legislative History

1980 Discussion Draft (then Rule 7.4) provided:

Supervision of Nonlawyer Assistants

A lawyer shall use reasonable effort to ensure that nonlawyers employed or retained by the lawyer conduct themselves in a manner compatible with the professional obligations of the lawyer.

1981 Draft was substantially the same as adopted.
1982 Draft was adopted.

Selected State Variations

California: No comparable provision.

Illinois Rule 5.3(a) applies to "[t]he lawyer, and, in a law firm, each partner," and refers to the professional obligations of the lawyer "and the firm." Illinois Rule 5.3(b) applies to "each" lawyer having direct supervisory authority.

New Hampshire has adopted a detailed set of rules and a lengthy commentary, accompanying Rule 5.3, to govern the use of legal assistants.

New Jersey Rule 5.3(a) provides that "every lawyer or organization authorized by the Court Rules to practice law in this jurisdiction shall adopt and maintain reasonable efforts to ensure that the conduct of nonlawyers retained or employed by the lawyer, law firm or organization is compatible with the professional obligations of the lawyer." In addition, New Jersey has added Rule 5.3(c)(3), which provides that a lawyer is responsible for the conduct of a nonlawyer employee if "the lawyer has failed to make reasonable investigation of circumstances that would disclose past instances of conduct by the nonlawyer incompatible with the professional obligations of a lawyer, which evidence a propensity for such conduct."

New York: In addition to the Model Code Comparison above, see EC 1-8 and DR 1-104 of the New York Code for counterparts to Rule 5.3.

Virginia: DR 3-104 provides:

(A) A lawyer or law firm may employ non-lawyer personnel to perform delegated functions under the direct supervision of a licensed attorney, but shall not permit such non-lawyer personnel to:

(1) counsel clients about legal matters;

(2) appear as counsel in court or in proceedings which are part of the judicial process; or

(3) engage in the unauthorized practice of law.

(B) A lawyer or law firm that employs non-lawyer personnel shall not permit any representation that such non-lawyer is a lawyer.

Related Materials

ABA Standards for Criminal Justice: See Prosecution Function Standards 3-3.1(a) and (c); Defense Function Standard 4-4.2.

American Lawyer's Code of Conduct: See Rule 9.12. In addition, Rule 8.15 provides:

A lawyer shall take reasonable care to assure that none of the lawyer's partners, associates, or employees commits an act that would be a disciplinary violation if committed by the lawyer.

Rule 5.4 Professional Independence of a Lawyer

(a) A lawyer or law firm shall not share legal fees with a nonlawyer, except that:

(1) an agreement by a lawyer with the lawyer's firm, partner, or associate may provide for the payment of money, over a reasonable period of time after the lawyer's death, to the lawyer's estate or to one or more specified persons;

> **Editors' Note.** The following subparagraph, (a)(2), was substantially rewritten by the ABA in 1990 to bring Rule 5.4 into line with the changes brought about by the addition of Rule 1.17 (permitting the sale of a law practice) at the ABA's February 1990 Mid-Year Meeting.

(2) a lawyer who purchases the practice of a deceased, disabled, or disappeared lawyer may, pursuant to the provisions of Rule 1.17, pay to the estate or other representative of that lawyer the agreed-upon purchase price; and

(3) a lawyer or law firm may include nonlawyer employees in a compensation or retirement plan, even though the plan is based in whole or in part on a profit-sharing arrangement.

(b) A lawyer shall not form a partnership with a nonlawyer if any of the activities of the partnership consist of the practice of law.

(c) A lawyer shall not permit a person who recommends, employs, or pays the lawyer to render legal services for another to direct or regulate the lawyer's professional judgment in rendering such legal services.

(d) A lawyer shall not practice with or in the form of a professional corporation or association authorized to practice law for a profit, if:

(1) a nonlawyer owns any interest therein, except that a fiduciary representative of the estate of a lawyer may hold the stock or interest of the lawyer for a reasonable time during administration;

(2) a nonlawyer is a corporate director or officer thereof; or

(3) a nonlawyer has the right to direct or control the professional judgment of a lawyer.

COMMENT

The provisions of this Rule express traditional limitations on sharing fees. These limitations are to protect the lawyer's professional independence of judgment. Where someone other than the client pays the lawyer's fee or salary, or recommends employment of the lawyer, that arrangement does not modify the lawyer's obligation to the client. As stated in paragraph (c), such arrangements should not interfere with the lawyer's professional judgment.

Model Code Comparison

Paragraph (a) is substantially identical to DR 3-102(A).
Paragraph (b) is substantially identical to DR 3-103(A).
Paragraph (c) is substantially identical to DR 5-107(B).
Paragraph (d) is substantially identical to DR 5-107(C).

Cross-References in Rules

Rule 1.17, Comment 1 provides that "when a lawyer or an entire firm ceases to practice and another lawyer or firm takes over the representation, the selling lawyer or firm may obtain compensation for the reasonable value of the practice as may withdrawing partners of law firms. See Rules 5.4 and 5.6."

Legislative History

1980 Discussion Draft (then Rule 7.5) provided as follows:

Professional Independence of a Firm

A lawyer shall not practice with a firm in which an interest is owned or managerial authority is exercised by a nonlawyer, unless services can be rendered in conformity with the Rules of Professional Conduct. The terms of the relationship shall expressly provide that:

(a) there is no interference with the lawyer's independence of professional judgment or with the client-lawyer relationship; and

(b) the confidences of clients are protected as required by Rule 1.7; and

(c) the arrangement does not involve advertising or solicitation prohibited by Rules 9.2 and 9.3; and

(d) the arrangement does not result in charging a client a fee which violates Rule 1.6.

1981 Draft:

Professional Independence of a Firm

A lawyer may be employed by an organization in which a financial interest is held or managerial authority is exercised by a non-lawyer, or by a lawyer acting in a capacity other than that of representing clients, such as a business corporation, insurance company, legal services organization or government agency, but only if the terms of the relationship provide in writing that:

(a) there is no interference with the lawyer's independence of professional judgment or with the client-lawyer relationship;

(b) information relating to representation of a client is protected as required by Rule 1.6;

(c) the arrangement does not involve advertising or personal contract with prospective clients prohibited by Rules 7.2 and 7.3; and

(d) the arrangement does not result in charging a fee that violates Rule 1.5.

The *1982 Draft* was substantially the same as 1981 Draft.

Editors' Note. The version of Rule 5.4 finally adopted in 1983 was proposed as an amendment by the General Practice Section as a substitute for the Kutak Commission's draft. Rule 5.4 was the only proposed rule from the 1982 Draft that was completely rejected and rewritten by the House of Delegates in 1983.

1990 Amendment: At its February 1990 Mid-Year Meeting, the ABA House of Delegates amended Rule 5.4(a)(2) to conform to Rule 1.17 (permitting the sale of a law practice), which was added to the Rules at the same meeting. (There was no Committee Report to explain the change, but the reason for the change is obvious.) The former version of Rule 5.4(a)(2) provided that "a lawyer who undertakes to complete unfinished legal business of a deceased lawyer may pay to the estate of the deceased lawyer that proportion of the total compensation which fairly represents the services rendered by the deceased lawyer."

Selected State Variations

California: See Rule 1-310 (Forming a Partnership with a Non-Lawyer) and Rule 1-320 (Financial Arrangements with Non-Lawyers).

District of Columbia: On March 1, 1990, in a development thus far unique in the nation, the District of Columbia adopted a version of Rule 5.4 (which became effective on January 1, 1991) that allows lawyers to share fees with nonlawyers and to form partnerships with nonlawyers under certain conditions. Because of the importance of this Rule, we reprint here both the pertinent provisions of the Rule and the entire D.C. Comment. Rule 5.4(a)(4) and (b) and the Comment provide:

(a)(4) Sharing of fees is permitted in a partnership or other form of organization which meets the requirements of Paragraph (b).

(b) A lawyer may practice law in a partnership or other form of organization in which a financial interest is held or managerial authority is exercised by an individual nonlawyer who performs professional services which assist the organization in providing legal services to clients, but only if:

(1) The partnership or organization has as its sole purpose providing legal services to clients;

(2) All persons having such managerial authority or holding a financial interest undertake to abide by these Rules of Professional Conduct;

(3) The lawyers who have a financial interest or managerial authority in the partnership or organization undertake to be responsible for the nonlawyer participants to the same extent as if nonlawyer participants were lawyers under Rule 5.1;

(4) The foregoing conditions are set forth in writing.

Comment to Rule 5.4

[1] The provisions of this Rule express traditional limitations on sharing fees with nonlawyers. (On sharing fees among lawyers not in the same firm, see Rule 1.5(e).) These limitations are to protect the lawyer's professional independence of judgment. Where someone other than the client pays the lawyer's fee or salary, or recommends employment of the lawyer, that arrangement does not modify the lawyer's obligation to the client. As stated in paragraph (c), such arrangements should not interfere with the lawyer's professional judgment.

[2] Traditionally, the canons of legal ethics and disciplinary rules prohibited lawyers from practicing law in a partnership that includes nonlawyers or in any other organization where a nonlawyer is a shareholder, director, or officer. Notwithstanding these strictures, the profession implicitly recognized exceptions for lawyers who work for corporate law departments, insurance companies, and legal service organizations.

[3] As the demand increased for a broad range of professional services from a single source, lawyers employed professionals from other disciplines to work for them. So long as the nonlawyers remained employees of the lawyers, these relationships did not violate the disciplinary rules. However, when lawyers and nonlawyers considered forming partnerships and professional corporations to provide a combination of legal and other services to the public, they faced serious obstacles under the former rules.

[4] This Rule rejects an absolute prohibition against lawyers and nonlawyers joining together to provide collaborative services, but continues to impose traditional ethical requirements with respect to the organization thus created. Thus, a lawyer may practice law in an organization where nonlawyers hold a financial interest or exercise managerial authority, but only if the conditions set forth in subparagraphs (b)(1), (b)(2) and (b)(3) are satisfied, and, pursuant to subparagraph (b)(4), satisfaction of these conditions is set

forth in a written instrument. The requirement of a writing helps ensure that these important conditions are not overlooked in establishing the organizational structure of entities in which nonlawyers enjoy an ownership or managerial role equivalent to that of a partner in a traditional law firm.

[5] Nonlawyer participants under Rule 5.4 ought not be confused with nonlawyer assistants under Rule 5.3. Nonlawyer participants are persons having managerial authority or financial interests in organizations which provide legal services. Within such organizations, lawyers with financial interests or managerial authority are held responsible for ethical misconduct by nonlawyer participants about which the lawyers know or reasonably should know. This is the same standard of liability contemplated by Rule 5.1, regarding the responsibilities of lawyers with direct supervisory authority over other lawyers.

[6] Nonlawyer assistants under Rule 5.3 do not have managerial authority or financial interests in the organization. Lawyers having direct supervisory authority over nonlawyer assistants are held responsible only for ethical misconduct by assistants about which the lawyers actually know.

[7] As the introductory portion of subparagraph (b) makes clear, the purpose of liberalizing the rules regarding the possession of a financial interest or the exercise of management authority by a nonlawyer is to permit nonlawyer professionals to work with lawyers in the delivery of legal services without being relegated to the role of an employee. For example, the Rule permits economists to work in a firm with antitrust or public utility practitioners, psychologists or psychiatric social workers to work with family law practitioners to assist in counseling clients, nonlawyer lobbyists to work with lawyers who perform legislative services, certified public accountants to work in conjunction with tax lawyers or others who use accountants' services in performing legal services, and professional managers to serve as office managers, executive directors, or in similar positions. In all of these situations, the professionals may be given financial interests or managerial responsibility, so long as all of the requirements of subparagraph (c) are met.

[8] Subparagraph (b) does not permit an individual or entity to acquire all or any part of the ownership of a law partnership or other form of law practice organization for investment or other purposes. It thus does not permit a corporation, an investment banking firm, an investor, or any other person or entity to entitle itself to all or any portion of the income or profits of a law firm or other similar organization. Since such an investor would not be an individual performing professional services within the law firm or other organization, the requirements of subparagraph (b) would not be met.

[9] The term "individual" in subparagraph (b) is not intended to preclude the participation in a law firm or other organization by an individual professional corporation in the same manner as lawyers who have incorporated as a professional corporation currently participate in partnerships which include professional corporations.

[10] Some sharing of fees is likely to occur in the kinds of organizations permitted by paragraph (b). Subparagraph (a)(4) makes it clear that such fee-sharing is not prohibited.

Illinois: Rule 5.4(a)(2) applies only to a deceased lawyer, not to a "disabled or disappeared" lawyer. Illinois Rule 5.4(d)(2) permits a nonlawyer to serve as secretary for a professional corporation or for-profit association authorized to practice law "if such secretary performs only ministerial duties."

Massachusetts, which retains a modified version of the Code, has deleted DR 2-103. DR 2-103 in the Massachusetts Code deals with solicitation.

New York: Same or substantially the same as the ABA Model Code — see Model Code Comparison above — except see New York Materials for New York's version of DR 3-102(A)(3). The New York Code deletes DR 2-103(D)(4)(a).

North Carolina: Rule 3.2 is substantially the same as the Model Code, but permits payment of fees to a "disbarred lawyer" in proportion to work actually done by the disbarred lawyer before disbarment. North Carolina has no equivalent to Rule 5.4(b)-(d).

North Dakota: In 1987, the North Dakota Supreme Court *rejected* the following proposal from the State Bar:

> Except as prohibited or restricted by law, a lawyer may provide legal services to a client in association with a nonlawyer if:
> (a) The association does not permit any interference with the lawyer's independent professional judgment or with the client-lawyer relationship;
> (b) Information relating to representation of a client is protected as required by these rules;
> (c) The association does not result in communication about the lawyer, a person professionally associated with the lawyer or their services which violates these rules; and
> (d) The association does not result in the client being charged a fee that violates these rules.

Virginia: Substantially the same as the Model Code.

Related Materials

ABA Canons: Canons 33, 34, and 35 provided:

33. Partnerships — Names

Partnerships between lawyers and members of other professions or non-professional persons should not be formed or permitted where any part of the partnership's employment consists of the practice of law.

34. Division of Fees

No division of fees for legal services is proper, except with another lawyer, based upon a division of service or responsibility.

35. Intermediaries

The professional services of a lawyer should not be controlled or exploited by any lay agency, personal or corporate, which intervenes between client and lawyer. A lawyer's responsibilities and qualifications are individual. He should avoid all relations which direct the performance of his duties by or in the interest of such intermediary. A lawyer's relation to his client should be personal, and the responsibility should be direct to the client. Charitable societies rendering aid to the indigents are not deemed such intermediaries.

A lawyer may accept employment from any organization, such as an association, club or trade organization, to render legal services in any matter in which the organization, as an entity, is interested, but this employment should not include the rendering of legal services to the members of such an organization in respect to their individual affairs.

American Lawyer's Code of Conduct: Rule 4.7 provides:

If a lawyer forms a partnership with a nonlawyer for the purpose of more effectively serving clients' interests, the terms of the partnership shall be consistent with the lawyer's obligations under this Code, with particular reference to Rule 2.1, requiring undivided fidelity to the client.

Model Rules of Professional Conduct for Federal Lawyers insert a substantially different version of Rule 5.4, which provides:

(a) A Federal lawyer is expected to exercise professional independence of judgment during the representation of a client, consistent with these Rules.

(b) Notwithstanding a Government lawyer's status as a Government employee, a Government lawyer detailed or assigned to represent an individual Government employee or another person as the client is expected to exercise loyalty and professional independence during the representation, consistent with these Rules and to the same extent as required by a Non-Government lawyer in private practice.

(c) A Supervisory Government lawyer may not base an adverse evaluation or other prejudicial action against a Subordinate Government lawyer on the Subordinate Government lawyer's exercise of professional independence under (b) above.

(d) A Government lawyer shall obey the lawful orders of superiors when representing the United States and individual clients, but a Government lawyer shall not permit a nonlawyer to direct or regulate the Government lawyer's professional judgment in rendering legal services.

(e) A Non-Government lawyer shall not permit a nonlawyer who recommends, employs, or pays the Non-Government lawyer to render legal services for another to direct or regulate the Non-Government lawyer's professional judgment in rendering legal services.

(f) A Non-Government lawyer shall comply with the Rules of Professional Conduct or other applicable laws of the jurisdiction in which the Non-Government lawyer is licensed or is practicing law concerning the limitations on sharing fees and the organizational form of their practice.

The Comment, which has no parallel in the ABA Model Rules, states (with headings omitted):

A Federal lawyer subjected to outside pressures that might impair or give the appearance of impairing the effectiveness of the representation should make full disclosure of the pressures to the client. If the Federal lawyer or the client believes the effectiveness of the representation has been or will be impaired thereby, the lawyer should take proper steps to withdraw from representation of the client.

This Rule recognizes that a Government lawyer is a Government employee required by law to obey the lawful orders of superiors. Nevertheless, the practice of law requires the exercise of judgment solely for the benefit of the client and free of compromising influences and loyalties. Thus, when a Government lawyer is assigned to represent an individual client, neither the lawyer's personal interests, the interests of other clients, nor the interests of third persons should affect the loyalty to the individual client.

Rather than adopting specific rules on the sharing of fees or the organizational makeup of law practices that would apply only to Non-Government lawyers practicing before the Federal Agency, the Federal Agency defers on this matter to the rules and applicable laws of the jurisdictions in which these Non-Government lawyers are licensed.

Rule 5.5 Unauthorized Practice of Law

A lawyer shall not:

(a) practice law in a jurisdiction where doing so violates the regulation of the legal profession in that jurisdiction; or

(b) assist a person who is not a member of the bar in the performance of activity that constitutes the unauthorized practice of law.

COMMENT

The definition of the practice of law is established by law and varies from one jurisdiction to another. Whatever the definition, limiting the practice of law to members of the bar protects the public against rendition of legal services by unqualified persons. Paragraph (b) does not prohibit a lawyer from employing the services of paraprofessionals and delegating functions to them, so long as the lawyer supervises the delegated work and retains responsibility for their work. See Rule 5.3. Likewise, it does not prohibit lawyers from providing professional advice and instruction to nonlawyers whose employment requires knowledge of law; for example, claims adjusters, employees of financial or commercial institutions, social workers, accountants and persons employed in government agencies. In addition, a lawyer may counsel nonlawyers who wish to proceed pro se.

Model Code Comparison

With regard to paragraph (a), DR 3-101(B) of the Model Code provided that "[a] lawyer shall not practice law in a jurisdiction where to do so would be in violation of regulations of the profession in that jurisdiction."

With regard to paragraph (b), DR 3-101(A) of the Model Code provided that "[a] lawyer shall not aid a non-lawyer in the unauthorized practice of law."

Cross-References in Rules

Rule 8.5, Comment 1: "If their activity in another jurisdiction is substantial and continuous, it may constitute practice of law in that jurisdiction. See **Rule 5.5.**"

Legislative History

1980 Discussion Draft (then Rule 10.4(d) and (e)) provided that it was "professional misconduct" for a lawyer to "(d) practice law in a jurisdiction in violation of the regulation of the legal profession in that jurisdiction; or (e) aid a person who is not a member of the bar in the performance of activity that constitutes the practice of law."

1981 and 1982 Drafts (then Rule 8.4(d) and (e)) were the same as adopted.

Selected State Variations

California: See Rule 1-300 (Unauthorized Practice of Law) and B & P Code §§6125-6127.

Florida: Supreme Court Rule 3-6.1 expressly permits lawyers and law firms to employ suspended, disbarred, or resigned attorneys on the same terms as other lay persons, provided the employing lawyer or firm gives notice and reports periodically to the Bar's staff counsel, and provided that "[n]o suspended or disbarred attorney shall have direct contact with any client or receive, disburse, or otherwise handle funds or property of a client."

Missouri: Rule 5.5(c) prohibits the practice of law by a lawyer reported for failure to comply with Missouri Continuing Legal Education requirements.

New Jersey expressly permits nonprofit corporations to practice law, and permits attorneys to assist them, provided certain conditions are met. Supreme Court Rule 1:21-1(d) provides:

> *Charitable and Legal Services Corporation.* Nonprofit corporations incorporated in this or any other state for the purpose, among others, of functioning as a public interest law firm, may practice law provided (i) the matter in controversy directly involves the corporate purpose, (ii) the attorney responsible for the matter is a member of the bar of New Jersey who shall sign all papers above the corporate name, and (iii) the professional relationship between the attorney and client shall not be subject to interference, control, or direction by the corporation.

New York: Same or substantially the same as the ABA Model Code — see Model Code Comparison above. In addition, New York Judiciary Law §495 generally prohibits corporations from practicing law, but exempts "non-profit organizations whether incorporated or unincorporated . . . which furnish legal services as an incidental activity in furtherance of their primary purpose" and "organizations which have as their primary purpose the furnishing of legal services to indigent persons."

North Carolina: Rule 3.1 tracks DR 3-102, but Rules 3.1(C) and (D) add that a law firm "shall not employ a disbarred or suspended lawyer as a law clerk or legal assistant" at any time after the acts leading to disbarment or suspension occurred, and that a law firm employing a disbarred or suspended lawyer "shall not represent any client [who was] represented by the disbarred or suspended lawyer" or by any of his former partners or associates after the acts leading to discipline occurred.

Virginia retains the language of DR 3-101, but adds two new paragraphs (similar to North Carolina's) prohibiting a law firm from continuing to employ disbarred or suspended lawyers who were previously associated with the firm as lawyers, or from representing the former clients of any suspended or disbarred lawyer that the firm employs.

Related Materials

ABA Canons: Canon 47 provided:

47. Aiding the Unauthorized Practice of Law

No lawyer shall permit his professional services, or his name, to be used in aid of, or to make possible, the unauthorized practice of law by any lay agency, personal or corporate.

ABA Model Rules for Advisory Opinions on Unauthorized Practice of Law: In 1984, the ABA House of Delegates adopted Model Rules for Advisory Opinions on Unauthorized Practice of Law, which set forth model procedures for committees and courts to follow in issuing opinions on unauthorized practice. These rules, according to their Preamble, recognize the need "to prevent harm to the public from the unauthorized practice of law and to make public a clear and timely understanding of what is the unauthorized practice of law." The rules can be found in the ABA/BNA Lawyers' Manual on Professional Conduct.

Model Rules of Professional Conduct for Federal Lawyers: Rule 5.5(a) provides that "[e]xcept as authorized by law," a federal lawyer shall not practice in a jurisdiction where doing so violates the regulation of the legal profession in that jurisdiction.

Unauthorized Practice Laws: Most states have enacted statutes making it a crime to engage in the unauthorized practice of law. California B & P Code §6126 is typical:

> *§6126. Unauthorized Practice or Advertising as Misdemeanor*
>
> Any person advertising or holding himself or herself out as practicing or entitled to practice law or otherwise practicing law who is not an active member of the State Bar, is guilty of a misdemeanor.

In many states, the state bar has authority to enforce the unauthorized practice laws. In Florida, for example, the board of governors of the state bar acts "as an arm of the Supreme Court of Florida for the purpose of seeking to prohibit the unauthorized practice of law by investigating, prosecuting, and reporting" incidents involving unlicensed practice. See Florida Supreme Court Rule 1-8.2 and Chapter 10 of those Rules (setting forth detailed procedures for investigating and prosecuting unauthorized practice cases).

Rule 5.6 Restrictions on Right to Practice

A lawyer shall not participate in offering or making:

(a) a partnership or employment agreement that restricts the rights of a lawyer to practice after termination of the relationship, except an agreement concerning benefits upon retirement; or

(b) an agreement in which a restriction on the lawyer's right to practice is part of the settlement of a controversy between private parties.

COMMENT

[1] An agreement restricting the right of partners or associates to practice after leaving a firm not only limits their professional autonomy but also limits the freedom of clients to choose a lawyer. Paragraph (a) prohibits such agreements except for restrictions incident to provisions concerning retirement benefits for service with the firm.

[2] Paragraph (b) prohibits a lawyer from agreeing not to represent other persons in connection with settling a claim on behalf of a client.

[3] This Rule does not apply to prohibit restrictions that may be included in the terms of the sale of a law practice pursuant to Rule 1.17.

Model Code Comparison

This Rule is substantially similar to DR 2-108.

Cross-References in Rules

Rule 1.17, Comment 1: "Pursuant to this Rule, when a lawyer or an entire firm ceases to practice and another lawyer or firm takes over the representation, the selling lawyer or firm may obtain compensation for the reasonable value of the practice as may withdrawing partners of law firms. See Rules 5.4 and 5.6."

Legislative History

1980 and 1981 Drafts had no equivalent to Rule 5.6.
1982 Draft was adopted.

Selected State Variations

California: See Rule 1-500 (Agreement Restricting a Member's Practice).
Georgia permits a lawyer on settling a case to agree not to "accept any other representation arising out of a transaction or event embraced in the subject matter of the controversy or suit thus settled." DR 2-108(B).
New York: Same or substantially the same as the ABA Model Code — see Model Code Comparison above.
North Carolina: Rule 2.7 retains the language of DR 2-108.
Virginia: Substantially the same as the Model Code.

Related Materials

American Lawyer's Code of Conduct: Rule 8.13 provides:

A lawyer shall not enter into an agreement that unreasonably restricts a lawyer's right to practice law or to communicate with members of the public, and which thereby interferes with the freedom of clients to obtain counsel of their choice. However, lawyers in a partnership or similar professional relationship may make reasonable agreements regarding the allocation of fees among themselves with respect to clients who elect to continue with one or another lawyer upon termination of the professional relationship between the lawyers.

Rule 5.7 Provision of Ancillary Services [deleted]

> **Editors' Note.**   At its 1992 Annual Meeting, by a vote of 190-183, the ABA House of Delegates deleted Rule 5.7. Rule 5.7 thus became the first Model Rule of Professional Conduct to be deleted. Rule 5.7 had been adopted only a year earlier, by a vote of 197-186, at the ABA's 1991 Annual Meeting. The unique history of Rule 5.7 is contained in several documents reprinted following the rule.

(a) A lawyer shall not practice law in a law firm which owns a controlling interest in, or operates, an entity which provides non-legal services which are ancillary to the practice of law, or otherwise provides such ancillary non-legal services, except as provided in paragraph (b).

(b) A lawyer may practice law in a law firm which provides non-legal services which are ancillary to the practice of law if:

(1) The ancillary services are provided solely to clients of the law firm and are incidental to, in connection with and concurrent to, the provision of legal services by the law firm to such clients;

(2) Such ancillary services are provided solely by employees of the law firm itself and not by a subsidiary or other affiliate of the law firm;

(3) The law firm makes appropriate disclosure in writing to its clients; and

(4) The law firm does not hold itself out as engaging in any non-legal activities except in conjunction with the provision of legal services, as provided in this rule.

(c) One or more lawyers who engage in the practice of law in a law firm shall neither own a controlling interest in, nor operate, an entity which provides non-legal services which are ancillary to the practice of law, nor otherwise provide such ancillary non-legal services, except that their firms may provide such services as provided in paragraph (b).

(d) Two or more lawyers who engage in the practice of law in separate law firms shall neither own a controlling interest in, nor operate, an entity which provides non-legal services which are ancillary to the practice of law, nor otherwise provide such ancillary non-legal services.

COMMENT

General

[1] For many years, lawyers have provided to their clients non-legal services which are ancillary to the practice of law. Such services included title insurance, trust services and patent consulting. In most instances, these ancillary non-legal services were provided to law firm clients in connection with, and concurrent to, the provision of legal services by the lawyer or law firm. The provision of such

services afforded benefits to clients, including making available a greater range of services from one source and maintaining technical expertise in various fields within a law firm. However, the provision of both legal and ancillary non-legal services raises ethical concerns, including conflicts of interest, confusion on the part of clients and possible loss (or inapplicability) of the attorney-client privilege, which may not have been addressed adequately by the other Model Rules of Professional Conduct.

[2] Eventually, law firms began to form affiliates, largely staffed by non-lawyers, to provide ancillary non-legal services to both clients and customers who were not clients for legal services. In addition to exacerbating the ethical problems of conflicts of interest, confusion and threats to confidentiality, the large-scale movement of law firms into ancillary non-legal businesses raised serious professionalism concerns, including compromising lawyers' independent judgment, the loss of the bar's right to self-regulation and the provision of legal services by entities controlled by non-lawyers.

[3] Rule 5.7 addresses both the ethical and professionalism concerns implicated by the provision of ancillary non-legal services by lawyers and law firms. It preserves the ability of lawyers to provide additional services to their clients and maintain within the law firm a broad range of technical expertise. However, Rule 5.7 restricts the ability of law firms to provide ancillary non-legal services through affiliates to non-client customers and clients alike, the rendition of which raises serious ethical and professionalism concerns.

Limitations on the Provision of Non-Legal Services Which Are Ancillary to the Practice of Law

[4] Paragraph (a) attempts to forestall the ethical and professional concerns which are raised when law firms own or operate non-legal businesses which are ancillary to the practice of law or otherwise provide such services. The provision of such ancillary services by law firms has the potential of compromising a lawyer's independent professional judgment and otherwise causing harm to law firm clients (e.g., creating conflicts of interest, jeopardizing clients' expectations of confidentiality and causing confusion on the part of clients). Additionally, serious threats to lawyers' professionalism are also posed when law firms own or operate ancillary businesses which provide services to persons who are not concurrently seeking legal services from the law firm.

[5] Paragraph (a) prohibits lawyers from practicing in a law firm which owns a controlling interest in, or operates, an entity which provides non-legal services which are ancillary to the practice of law, or which provides such ancillary services from within the law firm, unless such services are incidental to the law firm's provision of legal services as set forth in Paragraph (b).

[6] The term "non-legal services which are ancillary to the practice of law" refers to those services which satisfy all or most of the following indicia: (1) are

provided to clients of a law firm (or customers of a business owned or controlled by a law firm); (2) clearly do not constitute the practice of law; (3) are readily available from those not licensed to practice law; (4) are functionally connected to the provision of legal services, i.e., services which are often sought or needed in connection with (and in addition to) legal services; (5) involve intellectual ability or learning; and (6) have the potential for creating serious ethical problems in the lawyer-client relationship, such as compromising the independent professional judgment of lawyers; creating conflicts of interest; threatening the clients' (or customers') expectations of confidentiality and/or causing confusion on the part of clients or customers.

[7] Among those activities which are not included in the term "non-legal services which are ancillary to the practice of law" because they do not pose serious ethical problems in the lawyer-client relationship are:

(1) law firms or lawyers owning, for example, restaurants, shops or taxi services (since these services are not functionally connected to the practice of law);

(2) law firms providing copying services or other clerical services incidental to the practice of law;

(3) law firms owning and managing the buildings in which their offices are located or other property (since owning and managing property — even through a subsidiary or affiliate — is not functionally connected to the provision of legal services to clients);

(4) a law firm providing services or products intended for use by other lawyers, such as publications, software programs, or legal malpractice insurance (since such services or products are not functionally connected to the provision of legal services to clients);

(5) lawyers serving as fiduciaries of trusts or corporate directors or lawyers serving in quasi-judicial positions such as mediators or arbitrators.

[8] When services provided by a law firm are performed by non-lawyers, there should be an initial presumption that the services do not constitute the practice of law and may be a "non-legal service which is ancillary to the practice of law." In addition, a presumption that a service is "ancillary to the practice of law" should exist if the service is normally provided by non-lawyers in discrete professions or occupations, e.g., doctors, architects, engineers, real estate brokers, investment bankers or financial consultants.

[9] Note that Paragraph (a) does not prohibit a lawyer from practicing in a law firm which acquires a passive financial interest in an entity which provides non-legal ancillary services (i.e., purchasing shares of an investment banking firm or a consulting company), provided that the interest is not a controlling one. This rule does not define the concept of control, which is generally a fact-based inquiry dependent on the particular facts and circumstances. However, the existence of an ownership interest by lawyers in other entities (especially clients) may implicate conflict of interest concerns (see

238

Model Rules of Professional Conduct 1.7 and 1.8) and may require disclosure by the lawyers pursuant to these rules.

Connection Between the Provision of Legal and Ancillary Non-Legal Services

[10] Paragraph (b) preserves the ability of law firms to provide non-legal services which are ancillary to the practice of law, but under conditions designed to ensure that such services are closely related to the firms' provision of legal services and not independent of, and unrelated to, such legal services.

[11] Subsection (1) of Paragraph (b) requires that ancillary non-legal services be provided solely to law firm clients (as opposed to persons who are not currently seeking legal services from a law firm) and be incidental to, in connection with, and concurrent to, the provision of legal services by the law firm. The requirement that ancillary services be "incidental to" and "in connection with" the firm's provision of legal services seeks to ensure that any non-legal services be secondary to, strictly related to, and under the supervision of those responsible for, the provision of legal services.

[12] Paragraph (b) permits law firms to employ the services of other professionals if their services are connected to the firm's provision of legal services. For example, an architect on staff at a law firm would be permitted to help clients and lawyers understand the technical issues in a construction contract negotiation, a building accident litigation or the like. However, the requirement in Paragraph (b) that such services be "incidental to" and "in connection with" the provision of legal services would proscribe a law firm from employing architects to design buildings for law firm clients or for non-client customers who do not use the law firm's legal services. Similarly, an investment banker on staff at a law firm would be permitted to assist lawyers in the negotiation of a transaction or the litigation of valuation issues or the like, as well as to consult with law firm clients when the firm is providing legal services to them, but a law firm would be prohibited from employing investment bankers to seek out acquisitions, sell securities (or otherwise secure financing) or perform other investment banking services unrelated to a pending legal representation. Likewise, a corporation pursuing an acquisition might need the assistance of non-lawyer lobbyists before a state legislature considering anti-takeover legislation. Such lobbying designed to forestall (or attain) a change in the law, if provided by non-lawyers within a law firm, could reasonably be construed to be incidental to the firm's provision of legal services.

[13] Paragraph (b) also requires that the provision of non-legal services be concurrent with the provision of legal services. In essence, law firm clients (like non-legal services customers generally) may not obtain ancillary non-legal services from the law firm (e.g., investment banking services or medical tests), and the firm may not provide them, at a time when the client is not obtaining legal services from the law firm on a related matter.

Provision of Ancillary Non-Legal Services by
Employees of Law Firms

[14] Subsection (2) of Paragraph (b), in an effort to vitiate risks of compromise to lawyers' professional judgment, conflicts of interest, client confusion and potential loss of confidentiality, provides that any ancillary services provided by a law firm must be performed within the law firm by employees of the law firm itself (who work together with, and are supervised by, the firm's lawyers), and not through a subsidiary or affiliate of the law firm. This requirement closely unites the provision of legal and non-legal services under the supervision of lawyers and thereby affords lawyers the opportunity to ensure that their non-lawyer employees are acting responsibly and in accordance with the rules of legal ethics. Such a requirement minimizes the risks of non-legal employees either providing advice with which the firm's lawyers will disagree and/or engaging in improper behavior for which the firm's lawyers would be responsible. In addition, structuring the provision of non-legal services in such a way forestalls confusion on the part of clients as to whether the non-legal services are provided subject to the limitations of the Model Rules (and will prevent lawyers from seeking to provide services outside of the protections afforded to clients by the Model Rules). Finally, if lawyers are present (or otherwise involved) in the provision of non-legal services ancillary to the practice of law, there is a greater likelihood that client confidences will be protected and a client will be able to maintain evidentiary privileges with respect to communications made by the client to the providers of non-legal ancillary services. Paragraph (b)(2) is not designed to limit the ability of lawyers to retain outside (i.e., non-affiliated) consultants such as experts, private investigators or accountants to help them provide legal services to clients.

Disclosure Requirements Relating to the Provision of
Ancillary Non-Legal Services

[15] Subsection (3) of Paragraph (b) requires that before providing ancillary services to a client, a law firm must comply with appropriate disclosure requirements (as mandated in Model Rule of Professional Conduct 1.8, relevant case law and other authorities) and fully disclose in writing the firm's interest in the providers of non-legal services employed by the firm and the potential conflicts of interest inherent in the provision of such services. The law firm should also consider, in appropriate circumstances, recommending that the client seek the advice of independent counsel (or independent providers of non-legal services) before obtaining non-legal services from the firm.

Representations Concerning Ancillary and Non-Legal Services

[16] Subsection (4) of Paragraph (b) ensures that when law firms deal with clients (whether prospective or actual) or the public, they do not represent themselves as providing any ancillary non-legal services independent of the firm's provision of legal services. This proscription attempts to obviate the risks of confusion on the part of clients and the public, actual or apparent overreaching by attorneys and improper solicitation. It ensures that clients and the public are aware that they are dealing with a law firm and can therefore assume that representatives of the firm are bound by the rules of legal ethics; prospective or actual clients do not feel compelled to use the firm's ancillary services; and law firms do not engage in improper solicitation by seeking business for the firm's non-legal services with an expectation that these non-legal services will serve as a "feeder" for the firm's legal services. Paragraph (b)(4) also seeks to preserve the unique and independent status of the legal profession in the public's perception by preventing law firms from representing themselves to clients and the public as multidisciplinary conglomerates or otherwise emphasizing their non-legal activities.

[17] Paragraph (b)(4) is not intended to preclude law firms from making the existence of their non-legal businesses known to clients who have retained the firm for legal services, and who, in the attorney's opinion, might have a need for the firm's ancillary services in addition to legal services (subject to appropriate disclosure requirements). In addition, Paragraph (b)(4) is not intended to prevent individual lawyers from indicating that they are qualified or licensed in other professions, e.g., accounting, where relevant jurisdictions so permit.

Provision of Ancillary Non-Legal Services by One or More Lawyers in a Law Firm

[18] Paragraph (c) prevents one or more lawyers in a single law firm from owning or operating an entity which provides non-legal services which are ancillary to the practice of law. Paragraph (c) attempts to prevent lawyers or law firms from circumventing the restrictions on law firm ownership and operation of ancillary businesses by vesting ownership not in the entire law firm, but in one or more of the attorneys in a law firm. The ethical and professional concerns inherent in the ownership of ancillary businesses are not vitiated when ownership or operation is vested in several partners in a law firm (as opposed to an entire law firm). However, a law firm itself may provide such ancillary non-legal services in accordance with Paragraph (b).

Provision of Ancillary Non-Legal Services by Lawyers from Different Law Firms

[19] Paragraph (d) addresses the concerns which may result when lawyers in separate law firms own or operate an entity which provides non-legal services which are ancillary to the practice of law. The ethical and professional concerns inherent in the ownership and operation of such ancillary businesses by law firms (or one or more lawyers in a firm) are also present (or may be exacerbated) when lawyers in different firms own or operate such businesses.

Model Code Comparison

Rule 5.7 has no direct counterpart in the Disciplinary Rules or Ethical Considerations of the Model Code. — EDS.

Cross-References in Rules

None.

Legislative History

1980, 1981, and 1982 Drafts: None of the Kutak Commission drafts had any provision equivalent to Rule 5.7.

1991 Addition: Rule 5.7 was added to the Model Rules at the ABA's 1991 Annual Meeting. The rule as adopted was proposed by the ABA's Litigation Section, which had been intensively studying ancillary businesses for several years. Before the House of Delegates voted on the Litigation Section's proposal, it rejected by voice vote an alternative version of Rule 5.7 that had been proposed by the ABA's Standing Committee on Ethics and Professional Responsibility. (Some members of the Standing Committee did not want to add any new rule to govern ancillary business activities, but they also believed that the Litigation Section's proposal was too strict. As a compromise, the Standing Committee proposed its own version of Rule 5.7, which was more permissive than the Litigation Section's version. This alternative proposal is reprinted below.) After rejecting the Standing Committee's proposal, the House of Delegates voted 197-186 to adopt the Litigation Section's version of Rule 5.7.

1992 Deletion: Rule 5.7 was deleted from the ABA Model Rules at the ABA's 1992 Annual Meeting. The report urging deletion of the rule was jointly submitted by the Illinois State Bar Association, the ABA Standing Committee on Lawyers Title Guaranty Funds, and six ABA sections. The House of Delegates voted 190-183 to delete the rule. Rule 5.7 is the first rule to be deleted from the Model Rules.

We document below the unique legislative history of Rule 5.7. First, we reprint the alternative version of Rule 5.7 that was proposed by the Standing Committee on Ethics and Professional Responsibility and rejected by the House of Delegates in 1991. We then reprint excerpts from three ABA committee reports relating to Rule 5.7. The first excerpt, from the 1991 Litigation Section report, argues in favor of Rule 5.7 as adopted. The second excerpt, from a 1991 minority report of a member of the Standing Committee, argues against any rule. The third excerpt, from a 1992 report by the Illinois State Bar Association, an ABA standing committee, and six ABA sections, argues for deletion of Rule 5.7.

Standing Committee on Ethics and Professional Responsibility Proposal for Rule 5.7 (Rejected by ABA House of Delegates)

Rule 5.7 Provision of Ancillary Services

(a) A lawyer who provides, or whose law firm provides, representation to clients, and who is also associated, or whose law firm is also associated, with an ancillary business entity:

(1) shall initially disclose in writing to all customers of the ancillary business entity the nature of the relationship between the lawyer or law firm and the ancillary business entity; and

(2) shall treat a customer of the ancillary business entity in all respects as a client under the Rules of Professional Conduct, unless:

(i) the ancillary service is unrelated to any matter in which representation is provided by the lawyer or the law firm to the customer as a client of the lawyer or law firm; and

(ii) the lawyer or law firm, directly or through the ancillary business entity, has first clearly communicated to that customer, by means including written disclosure, that the relationship between the ancillary business entity and the customer is that of non-legal business and customer, not that of lawyer and client.

(b) In the circumstances in which a customer of an ancillary business entity is required to be treated as a client pursuant to paragraph (a)(2):

(1) a lawyer who is a partner in the law firm associated with the ancillary business entity shall make reasonable efforts to ensure that the entity has in effect measures giving reasonable assurance that the conduct with respect to that customer of all those employed or retained by or associated with the entity conforms to the Rules of Professional Conduct;

(2) a practicing lawyer associated with the ancillary business entity who has direct supervisory authority over persons employed or retained by or associated with the entity shall make reasonable efforts to assure that their conduct with respect to that customer is compatible with the professional obligations of the lawyer;

(3) a practicing lawyer associated with the ancillary business entity shall be responsible for conduct with respect to that customer of a person employed or retained by or associated with the entity that would be a violation of the Rules of Professional Conduct if engaged in by a lawyer and if:

(i) the lawyer orders or, with knowledge of the relevant facts and the specific conduct, ratifies the conduct involved; or

(ii) the lawyer is a partner in a law firm associated with that entity or has direct supervisory authority over the person and knows of the conduct at a time when its consequences can be avoided or mitigated but fails to take remedial action; and

(4) if the lawyer reasonably should know that the ancillary business entity is not complying with any obligation imposed by the Rules of Professional Conduct with respect to the provision of ancillary services to such customers, the lawyer shall dissociate from the entity unless the entity immediately rectifies the situation.

243

*Excerpt from Litigation Section's 1991 Report Urging the ABA to Adopt
the Litigation Section's Version of Rule 5.7*

Ethical and Professional Concerns Arising from Non-Legal Businesses

While proponents of diversification claim that the interests of both clients and lawyers are strongly promoted through law firm diversification, both clients and the legal profession stand to lose a great deal through this practice. These risks warrant a detailed examination.

A. THREAT TO INDEPENDENT PROFESSIONAL JUDGMENT

Many legal scholars have observed that when a number of professional services are united in one entity and are bound together economically, the lawyers' (and others') professional judgment may be improperly compromised (or may appear to be improperly compromised), and the lawyers may be faced with insurmountable conflicts of interest. . . . Professor Stephen Gillers of the New York University School of Law illustrates the conflict of interest problems when the professionals retained by a client serve different roles and have different interests. When a law firm owns, or also serves as, a broker on a deal, "The broker, who earns a fee for putting the deal together has an interest in seeing the deal go through, whereas the lawyer should keep the deal from going through if he feels the client is not going to be adequately protected."

Many of the diversified firms attempt to forestall conflicts by advising clients that they have the right to use a different investment bank (consulting firm, broker, etc.) than the one provided by the firm, or for that matter, a different law firm than the one connected to the investment bank or consulting firm. However, in practice, the specter of overreaching and a division in the lawyer's loyalties may never be overcome by informed consent. A law firm's client may feel impelled to use the firm's ancillary business either for fear of insulting the firm's attorneys and becoming a second-class client on legal matters or from an expectation that the client will receive preferential treatment from the business managed by the attorneys. . . .

B. THREAT TO THE QUALITY OF LEGAL WORK

[A]nother problem for clients of diversified law firms is the threat that when lawyers are involved in ancillary business activities, the quality of their legal work will suffer. . . . [T]he Stanley Report raised this issue: "It seems clear to the Commission that the greater the participation by lawyers in the activities other than the practice of law, the less likely it is that the lawyer can capably discharge the obligations which our profession demands."

Phyllis Weiss Haserot, a consultant who advises law firms on how to create subsidiaries which provide ancillary services, reports that many lawyers choose to diversify their practices out of boredom with the practice of law. . . . When lawyers determine that real estate brokering or investment banking is more lucrative or otherwise more satisfying than the practice of law, their legal clients will suffer. What may begin as an ancillary means of generating income and alleviating boredom may become the lawyer's primary concern.

C. THREAT TO THE REPUTATION OF THE PROFESSION

Clients may also suffer when the inevitable but probably unforeseen results of at least some attempts at diversification — namely financial failure, discipline and scandal — disrupt firms' legal practices and cause even further erosion of trust in the bar on the part of the public. Law firms' increasing involvement in business activities in recent years has resulted in financial scandals, disciplinary action, criminal investigations of law firm behavior, civil suits against lawyers and law firms, mass defections and an unprecedented amount of critical media attention. . . .

The ramifications of financial failure and scandal will seriously harm law firm clients whether they be large corporations or *pro bono* litigants. It may be difficult for lawyers to zealously represent their clients or fulfill their professional obligations while they themselves are embroiled in investigations and lawsuits concerning their own behavior. Additionally, the scandals deriving from law firm business activities will make the public more distrustful of the legal profession at a time when the public increasingly view lawyers as more interested in wealth than in public service, and at a time when the bar is earnestly striving to preserve professionalism.

D. THREAT TO THE PROFESSION'S OBLIGATIONS TO SOCIETY

[T]he proponents of the law firm diversification propound a view of the legal profession, which, if adopted by a significant segment of the bar and accepted by the public, could lead to further distrust towards the bar; a widespread belief on the part of the public that the legal profession offers no unique contribution to society; and justification for increased governmental interference with, or regulation of, the bar.

In the words of a leading proponent of law firm diversification,

[T]he time has come for lawyers to ask themselves the question, "What business are we in?" As the year 2000 approaches, the answer to this question may no longer be a simple one for many lawyers and the firms in which they work. . . . Indeed, in many of the large law firms . . . the range of client services and the roles often played by the firms' attorneys in client affairs might lead the attorneys to visualize themselves more accurately as "professional problem solvers" operating on a nationwide, or even a worldwide basis.

. . . The primary and perhaps most dangerous tenet of this philosophy underpinning the law firm diversification movement is the notion that lawyers need to redefine themselves. According to proponents of diversification, lawyers should no longer view themselves as a unique profession, but should imagine themselves as "professional problem-solvers" who work together with other professionals to service a client's needs. . . .

This view fails to admit a truth perhaps obvious to most citizens: the profession of law is a unique profession with special obligations different from any other profession or occupation. . . .

Aside from downplaying or rejecting the unique nature of the legal profession *vis-à-vis* bankers, realtors or the producers of video tapes, proponents of law firm diversification fail to realize that lawyers have obligations to others, and not just to clients. These obligations include duties to society, third parties, their profession and even themselves.

[The Report here included a lengthy discussion of the relationship between ancillary business activities and Model Rule 5.4, which prohibits fee-sharing or partnerships between lawyers and nonlawyers.]

Conclusion

The threat to professionalism brought about by law firm diversification is one of the most important ever to face the American legal profession. If law firm diversification is allowed to continue in its present state, or expands as proponents advocate, vast and adverse changes will likely occur. The Litigation Section believes that if the ancillary business phenomenon is not addressed immediately and forcefully by the ABA, the practice of law will not continue to be a unique and independent profession, and the traditions, concerns, ethical standards and methods of analysis of the legal profession will be jeopardized, and likely will be abandoned or modified beyond recognition, in order to make the practice of law consistent with other occupations. The legal profession will no longer be primarily devoted to public service and, as a consequence, legal practice will be under tight state regulation (jeopardizing the ability of the legal profession to serve as an independent force for preserving government under the rule of law); interests in law firms may ultimately be bought and sold like any other business; and corporations and other entities whose non-legal businesses find themselves in competition for customers with law firm ancillary business subsidiaries will seek and may well obtain the right to hire lawyers who sell legal services to client. If and when law firms are indistinguishable from any other profit-seeking enterprises, more so than ever, legal services will be available only to the wealthy, and the unique professionalism of the law will become indistinguishable from the mores of any other businesses.

Excerpt from 1991 Minority Report of Ralph G. Elliot, a Member of the
ABA Standing Committee on Ethics and Professional Responsibility,
Opposing All Proposals to Add Rule 5.7

Asked to explain her antipathy to one of America's great cities, Gertrude Stein replied, "There's no there there." The same may with justice be said of the great Non-Issue of 1990-1991, ancillary business activities of lawyers. An exhaustive examination of the history of such services thus far discloses not a hint of a perceived problem. There have been no complaints to disciplinary bodies. There have been no lawsuits. There has not even been a low growling murmur of complaint from consumers of those services that they have received less than they expected, or have been confused or misled as to expectations of confidentiality or other incidents simply because lawyers had an ownership interest in the ancillary business, or else performed the service out of their law offices.

Despite this total absence of any perceived problem, the fecund imagination of the Litigation Section has conjured up a parade of horribles that *might* or theoretically *could* happen if ancillary services were permitted to be performed by lawyer-owned or lawyer-controlled businesses. The Section talks about a loss of something vaguely called "professionalism" and a fear that lawyers could face regulation by non-lawyers if they were to engage in such extra-practice activities. Its report evokes remembrance of a pristine professional past that never was and fears of a subjugated future that never will be. Indeed, many purport to see in the Section's report simply a "save-our-turf" concern, with a subtext of anti-competitive restraints upon trade. . . .

While the Litigation Section would prohibit ancillary services performed outside the four walls of a law firm and for non-clients, the Committee would permit lawyer-owned free-standing ancillary business entities, but would regulate their activities by imposing provisions of the Rules of Professional Conduct on lawyers associated with such entities in ownership or provider capacities, absent certain clear warnings to potential consumers.

[N]either approach should be adopted. Rather, the ABA should stay its hand from premature and promiscuous rule-making, and wait to see if any problem develops. If, as and when a problem develops, it will be time enough to devise a response that addresses that problem directly. The sort of in-the-blind regulation represented by both the Section's and the Committee's approaches is inconsistent with that narrowly-tailored approach to specific and documented harms which ought to inform the rule-making judgment of this Association.

Where, as here, no demonstrable problem or harm has surfaced after all these years, the only logical, foreseeable effect of the willy-nilly promulgation of yet more rules to burden the profession will be to inspire in contented clients and consumers of ancillary services doubts, fears and suspicions where none had previously existed or been warranted. Indeed, the compulsory disclosure by lawyers to consumers of ancillary businesses' services about their economic relationship to those businesses, required by the Committee's rule, bids fair to *create* the very confusion and suspicion which the rule is intended to dispel or avoid. That is not the proper office of rules of professional conduct.

Excerpt from 1992 Recommendation to Delete Rule 5.7, Jointly Signed by
the Illinois State Bar Association, the Standing Committee on Lawyers Title
Guaranty Funds, and Six Separate ABA Sections

Lawyers all over the country, in both urban and rural areas from New England to Nebraska, for generations have been providing trust, real estate, title, abstract and a variety of other services to both clients and non-clients. Many lawyers in small towns and rural areas have depended on ancillary business activities for economic survival since long before large firms in metropolitan areas established affiliated business ventures. As the current Vice-Chair of the General Practice Section commented in 1990, "there has never been a time when lawyers in the United States were not engaged in ancillary business activities. . . . [T]o assume a time when lawyers only practiced law is to ignore the facts of American legal history." If Rule 5.7 of the Model Rules of Professional Conduct (MRPC) were adopted at the state level, lawyers would be severely restricted from having any interest in a wide variety of traditional activities they have conducted as adjunct to or separate from their law practices, including *but not limited to* trust services; title insurance; real estate; financial planning services; general insurance; joint ventures with other professionals in connection with personal injury practice, family law practice, and environmental consulting; accountancy; and legislative lobbying.

The Model Rules of Professional Conduct should be amended by deleting Rule 5.7 concerning the provision of ancillary business activities. The Rule has many implications which were not considered at the time of its adoption by the House of Delegates in 1991.

. . . Rule 5.7 has not been adopted by even a single jurisdiction. Indeed, ABA President D'Alemberte has acknowledged that the rule is "unlikely to be adopted anywhere." But even if this Rule is never adopted by any state, its existence as a statement of the Association's view and policy of professional conduct creates an opprobrium, a sweeping condemnation of traditional activities, adversely affecting all practitioners engaged in any "ancillary" services, which by virtue of Rule 5.7 are now deemed inappropriate and unprofessional.

In its consideration of Rule 5.7, the House heard no evidence requiring the adoption of the Rule. . . .

. . . There was (and is) no evidence, for example, that lawyers in firms with ancillary services provided to clients or to non-clients make more money than lawyers in firms which do not; or provide fewer pro bono services than comparable firms or practices which do not; or have a higher incidence of grievances alleging failure to uphold the standards of the profession under the Model Rules of Professional Conduct; or, as a class, are any less devoted to the highest aspirations of professionalism — integrity, competence, fairness, independence, courage and devotion to public interest than others as a class.

The House was urged to adopt Rule 5.7 on the ground that ancillary business activities will lead to the loss of "self-regulation" and lawyer independence. However, in a forum at the 1991 ABA Annual Meeting, the audience was properly reminded[11] that the profession is not really self-regulating at all. In fact, it is and historically has been regulated extensively by the judicial branch of government. Thus for the profession to lose its role in "self-regulation" would require that the courts abdicate judicial regulation of the bar, a highly unlikely prospect.

Rule 5.7 also is based on the flawed premise that if lawyers are allowed to engage in other occupations or ventures, non-lawyers engaged in those occupations and businesses will somehow have a claim to a reciprocal right to practice law. The argument is a chimera for several reasons: it ignores the fact that for decades lawyers have engaged in other occupations and have owned ancillary businesses without prompting reciprocal entry into the practice of law. It also ignores the reality that we risk losing our role as lawyers unless we become more competitive and expand our services to meet the increasing intrusions of other service providers — e.g., accountants, insurance executives, bankers, title companies — into the activities which we would like to believe are the practice of law. Finally, the proponents of Rule 5.7 ignore the reality that the practice of law is and always has been limited to those who satisfy the rigorous requirements of professional licensure.

Perhaps most important, by *requiring* all ancillary business activities to be conducted *within* the law firm and made available only to clients of the law firm in connection with the

---

[11] Speech by Professor Steve Gillers at a Litigation Section program, 1991 Annual Meeting.

delivery of legal services (rather than outside and apart from the law firm), we make it far more likely that the attention of state and federal regulators will be attracted to those activities and to the law firm.

Moreover, by mandating that all ancillary activities be conducted within the law firm, Rule 5.7 would make *every* claim regarding inadequate or incompetent ancillary service a malpractice claim against the law firm itself! This problem is not ameliorated by the requirement that ancillary services be undertaken only for "clients" of the law firm or "in connection with the provision of legal services." Arguably, every activity which falls within the reach of Rule 5.7 is, by definition, ancillary to the provision of legal services, and the lawyer who wants the business can readily relate it to the provision of some legal service to that consumer as a client. Thus, if there are any evils inherent in the delivery of ancillary services, the rule merges those evils directly into the law firm's practice rather than keeping them separate and at arm's length. . . .

Rule 5.7 is not a proper part of the Model Rules of Professional Conduct. Its prohibition of otherwise legal activity is an overreaction to legitimate concerns about the legal profession. There is no demonstrable harm to justify this Rule. At present, existing rules of professional conduct are capable of addressing the ethical concerns which Rule 5.7 purports to address. If the need for something more becomes evident, we can consider the evidence and, if necessary, fashion an appropriate remedy at that time. Rule 5.7 which brands ancillary business as unethical and unprofessional should be deleted from the Model Rules.

Selected State Variations

No state has yet adopted a rule expressly intended to govern the ancillary businesses of law firms. However, the District of Columbia has adopted a version of Rule 5.4 that permits nonlawyers to become full partners in law firms under certain conditions. The D.C. version of Rule 5.4 is reprinted in the State Variations section following Model Rule 5.4.

Related Materials

Professionalism Report: The ABA's Stanley Commission Report on Professionalism, 112 F.R.D. 243 (1986), called the trend toward law firm involvement in nonlegal services "disturbing" and urged the ABA to "initiate a study to see what, if any, controls or prohibitions should be imposed."

ARTICLE 6. PUBLIC SERVICE

Rule 6.1 Pro Bono Publico Service

A lawyer should render public interest legal service. A lawyer may discharge this responsibility by providing professional services at no fee or a reduced fee to persons of limited means or to public service or charitable groups or organizations, by service in activities for improving the law, the legal sys-

tem or the legal profession, and by financial support for organizations that provide legal services to persons of limited means.

COMMENT

[1] The ABA House of Delegates has formally acknowledged "the basic responsibility of each lawyer engaged in the practice of law to provide public interest legal services" without fee, or at a substantially reduced fee, in one or more of the following areas: poverty law, civil rights law, public rights law, charitable organization representation and the administration of justice. This Rule expresses that policy but is not intended to be enforced through disciplinary process.

[2] The rights and responsibilities of individuals and organizations in the United States are increasingly defined in legal terms. As a consequence, legal assistance in coping with the web of statutes, rules and regulations is imperative for persons of modest and limited means, as well as for the relatively well-to-do.

[3] The basic responsibility for providing legal services for those unable to pay ultimately rests upon the individual lawyer, and personal involvement in the problems of the disadvantaged can be one of the most rewarding experiences in the life of a lawyer. Every lawyer, regardless of professional prominence or professional workload, should find time to participate in or otherwise support the provision of legal services to the disadvantaged. The provision of free legal services to those unable to pay reasonable fees continues to be an obligation of each lawyer as well as the profession generally, but the efforts of individual lawyers are often not enough to meet the need. Thus, it has been necessary for the profession and government to institute additional programs to provide legal services. Accordingly, legal aid offices, lawyer referral services and other related programs have been developed, and others will be developed by the profession and government. Every lawyer should support all proper efforts to meet this need for legal services.

Model Code Comparison

There was no counterpart of this Rule in the Disciplinary Rules of the Model Code. EC 2-25 stated that the "basic responsibility for providing legal services for those unable to pay ultimately rests upon the individual lawyer. . . . Every lawyer, regardless of professional prominence or professional work load, should find time to participate in serving the disadvantaged." EC 8-9 stated that "[t]he advancement of our legal system is of vital importance in maintaining the rule of law . . . [and] lawyers should encourage, and should aid in making, needed changes and improvements." EC 8-3 stated that "[t]hose persons unable to pay for legal services should be provided needed services."

Cross-Reference in Rules

Rule 6.2, Comment 1: "All lawyers have a responsibility to assist in providing pro bono publico service. See Rule 6.1."

Legislative History

1980 Discussion Draft of Rule 6.1 (then Rule 8.1) provided as follows: "A lawyer *shall* render unpaid public interest legal services. . . . A lawyer shall make an annual report concerning such service to appropriate regulatory authority."

1981 and 1982 Drafts were the same as adopted, except that neither draft contained the final clause, "by financial support for organizations that provide legal services to persons of limited means."

1992 Proposal: In March of 1992, the ABA Standing Committee on Lawyers' Public Service Responsibility ("SCLPSR") circulated for public comment a proposed amendment to Rule 6.1. The main features of the proposal recommended that: (a) a lawyer should render at least fifty hours of pro bono service each year; (b) at least forty of these pro bono hours should be provided without a fee to poor people or to charitable, religious, civic, community, governmental, or educational organizations in activities that serve poor people; (c) a lawyer should also contribute money to such organizations — but a lawyer cannot "buy out" of the obligation to render fifty hours of personal service per year. (This proposal did not represent ABA policy.)

Hearings on the March 1992 proposal were held in Texas in April 1992 and in San Francisco in August 1992. As we went to press, SCLPSR was revising the proposal based on these hearings and on other comments. The main areas of debate concerned: (a) whether Rule 6.1 should recommend a specific number of hours of public service or should instead use a phrase like "substantial" public service; (b) whether a lawyer should be able to buy out of the obligation of individual service by contributing money; and (c) whether lawyers could fulfill their public service obligation through other lawyers in their firms. A final proposal was expected in November 1992, and SCLIPSR expected to formally submit the proposal to the ABA House of Delegates at its 1993 Mid-Year Meeting.

Selected State Variations

Arizona: In October 1990, Arizona amended its version of Rule 6.1 so that it now contains the following key provisions:

(a) A lawyer should voluntarily render public interest legal service. A lawyer may discharge this responsibility by rendering a minimum of fifty hours of service per calendar year. . . .

(c) A law firm or other group of lawyers may satisfy their responsibility under this Rule, if they desire, collectively. For example, the designation of one or more lawyers to work on pro bono publico matters may be attributed to other lawyers within the firm or group who support the representation. . . .

(d) The efforts of individual lawyers are not enough to meet the needs of the poor. The profession and government have instituted programs to provide direct delivery of legal services to the poor. The direct support of such programs is an alternative expression of support to provide law in the public interest, and a lawyer is encouraged to provide financial support for organizations that provide legal services to persons of limited means or to the Arizona Bar Foundation for the direct delivery of legal services to the poor.

California: No comparable provision.

District of Columbia: Rule 6.1 provides:

> A lawyer should participate in serving those persons, or groups of persons, who are unable to pay all or a portion of reasonable attorneys' fees or who are otherwise unable to obtain counsel. A lawyer may discharge this responsibility by providing professional services at no fee, or at a substantially reduced fee, to persons and groups who are unable to afford or obtain counsel, or by active participation in the work of organizations that provide legal services to them. When personal representation is not feasible, a lawyer may discharge this responsibility by providing financial support for organizations that provide legal representation to those unable to obtain counsel.

Florida clarifies Rule 6.1 by referring to service "without compensation" in "public interest" activities that improve the law, the legal system, or the legal profession. In addition, Chapter 12 of the Florida Supreme Court Rules establishes and regulates an "Emeritus Attorneys Pro Bono Participation Program" that allows retired Florida attorneys to render legal services to indigents under the auspices of legal aid organizations and under the direct supervision of an active licensed attorney.

In February of 1992, pursuant to comprehensive recommendations by a Joint Commission on the Delivery of Legal Services to the Indigent in Florida, the Florida Supreme Court adopted an extensive new plan relating to the implementation of Rule 6.1. The principal features of the plan are: (1) a narrow definition of the kind of pro bono work that can fulfill a lawyer's obligation under Rule 6.1, restricted to legal services to the poor (as opposed to non-legal activities that generally affect conditions of poverty); (2) an individual obligation (albeit voluntary) either to render at least 20 hours of pro bono legal services per year, or, alternatively, to contribute at least $350 annually to organizations providing legal services to the poor; (3) application of the 20 hour pro bono obligation to all licensed attorneys, including government attorneys, judges, and professors (excluding only those who are retired, inactive, or unable to practice due to illness); (4) mandatory reporting of each year's pro bono hours and activities (or monetary contributions) by each attorney as part of the filing of the annual Florida Bar dues form (which is mandatory for all Florida lawyers). A dissenter urged the court to institute a mandatory pro bono requirement of 20 hours per year of legal services to the poor and recommended an additional 30 hours of public service per year on a voluntary basis.

Illinois omits Rule 6.1 and explains why in its Preamble:

> It is the responsibility of those licensed as officers of the court to use their training, experience and skills to provide services in the public interest for which compensation may not be available. It is the responsibility of those who manage law firms to create an environment that is hospitable to the rendering of a reasonable amount of uncompensated service by lawyers practicing in that firm.
>
> Service in the public interest may take many forms. These include but are not limited to *pro bono* representation of persons unable to pay for legal services and assistance in the organized bar's efforts at law reform. An individual lawyer's efforts in these areas is evidence of the lawyer's good character and fitness to practice law, and the efforts of the bar as a whole are essential to the bar's maintenance of professionalism.
>
> The absence from the proposed new rules of ABA Model Rule 6.1 regarding *pro bono* and public service therefore should not be interpreted as limiting the responsibility of attorneys to

render uncompensated service in the public interest. Rather, the rationale for the absence of ABA Model Rule 6.1 is that this concept is not appropriate for a disciplinary code, because an appropriate disciplinary standard regarding *pro bono* and public service is difficult, if not impossible, to articulate. That ABA Model Rule 6.1 itself uses the word "should" instead of "shall" in describing this duty reflects the uncertainty of the ABA on this issue.

Kentucky: In July 1992, Kentucky amended its version of Rule 6.1 to read as follows:

> A lawyer is encouraged to voluntarily render public interest legal service. A lawyer is encouraged to accept and fulfill this responsibility to the public by rendering a minimum of fifty (50) hours of service per calendar year by providing professional services at no fee or a reduced fee to persons of limited means, and/or by financial support for organizations that provide legal services to persons of limited means. Pro bono services may be reported on the annual dues statement furnished by the Kentucky Bar Association. Lawyers rendering a minimum of fifty (50) hours of pro bono service shall receive a recognition award for such service from the Kentucky Bar Association.

New York: Same or substantially the same as the ABA Model Code — see Model Code Comparison above. See also EC 2-25 of the New York Code.
North Carolina omits Rule 6.1.
Virginia omits Rule 6.1.

Related Materials

American Lawyer's Code of Conduct: The Comment to Chapter 8 of the ALCC states:

> This Code has no rule requiring each lawyer to do a particular amount of uncompensated public interest or *pro bono publico* work, on pain of professional discipline. That does not mean that the attorney members of the Commission are unwilling to perform such services or that the non-lawyer members do not want to share in the benefits of *pro bono* work. Rather, it is apparent to the Commission that such a rule would be inherently so vague as to be unenforceable and unenforced, and therefore hypocritical.
>
> All lawyers should do work in the public interest. But some lawyers should not be telling other lawyers how much *pro bono* work they should be doing, and for whom, and disciplining them if they do not. Nor should codes of conduct purport to impose disciplinary requirements that the codifiers know will not be enforced.

Mandatory Pro Bono Plans: A growing number of courts and local bar associations are adopting mandatory pro bono plans.
Model Rules of Professional Conduct for Federal Lawyers add a new subparagraph (b) providing that government lawyers "should provide pro bono legal services consistent with applicable law." In addition, Rule 5.1(d) provides that a supervisory government lawyer "should encourage subordinate lawyers to participate in pro bono publico service activities and the activities of bar associations and law reform organizations." However, the Comment to Rule 6.1 explains that "18 U.S.C. §205 and §209 and other laws, including those governing off-duty employment by members of the Armed Forces, may regulate a Government lawyer's ability to provide legal services on a pro bono basis outside the scope of the Government lawyer's official duties."
Statement of Principles by Chicago Law Firms: In September of 1991, 31 major Chicago law firms formally adopted the following Statement of Principles relating to pro bono work:

In response to the unmet legal needs of the poor and other unrepresented and disadvantaged members of our community, and in the hope that our actions will encourage similar actions by other lawyers throughout the state of Illinois, the undersigned Chicago law firms endorse and commit themselves to these principles:

1. It is the obligation of lawyers and law firms generally to use their training, experience and skills to provide services in the public interest for which compensation may not be available.

2. Those lawyers who manage law firms should take the lead in encouraging other lawyers to provide pro bono legal services and in providing an environment which is hospitable to the rendition of such services.

3. Law firms should adopt written statements of policy which encourage their partners and associates to handle legal matters on a voluntary, pro bono basis and in the public interest, with credit toward annual hourly requirements or goals.

4. Law firms should assign to one or more of their members specific responsibility for encouraging, coordination and supervising pro bono work as a regular part of the firm's practice.

5. Work done on a pro bono basis should be handled with the same care and supervision as work done for a firm's paying clients.

6. Law firms should make it a goal to contribute an average of at least 30 hours of legal services per lawyer per year to representing the poor or other persons and organizations who are unable to retain legal counsel and which serve the public interest.

7. Law firms should contribute financially to organizations, programs and agencies which provide free legal assistance. Such contributions should be commensurate with law firms' special status within the community.

Student Practice Programs: Most states have established student practice programs that allow law students who meet certain criteria to represent indigents or government agencies, provided the students are supervised by licensed attorneys.

Rule 6.2 Accepting Appointments

A lawyer shall not seek to avoid appointment by a tribunal to represent a person except for good cause, such as:

(a) representing the client is likely to result in violation of the rules of professional conduct or other law;

(b) representing the client is likely to result in an unreasonable financial burden on the lawyer; or

(c) the client or the cause is so repugnant to the lawyer as to be likely to impair the client-lawyer relationship or the lawyer's ability to represent the client.

COMMENT

[1] A lawyer ordinarily is not obliged to accept a client whose character or cause the lawyer regards as repugnant. The lawyer's freedom to select clients is, however, qualified. All lawyers have a responsibility to assist in providing pro bono publico service. See Rule 6.1. An individual lawyer ful-

fills this responsibility by accepting a fair share of unpopular matters or indigent or unpopular clients. A lawyer may also be subject to appointment by a court to serve unpopular clients or persons unable to afford legal services.

Appointed Counsel

[2] For good cause a lawyer may seek to decline an appointment to represent a person who cannot afford to retain counsel or whose cause is unpopular. Good cause exists if the lawyer could not handle the matter competently, see Rule 1.1, or if undertaking the representation would result in an improper conflict of interest, for example, when the client or the cause is so repugnant to the lawyer as to be likely to impair the client-lawyer relationship or the lawyer's ability to represent the client. A lawyer may also seek to decline an appointment if acceptance would be unreasonably burdensome, for example, when it would impose a financial sacrifice so great as to be unjust.

[3] An appointed lawyer has the same obligations to the client as retained counsel, including the obligations of loyalty and confidentiality, and is subject to the same limitations on the client-lawyer relationship, such as the obligation to refrain from assisting the client in violation of the Rules.

Model Code Comparison

There was no counterpart to this Rule in the Disciplinary Rules of the Model Code. EC 2-29 stated that when a lawyer is "appointed by a court or requested by a bar association to undertake representation of a person unable to obtain counsel, whether for financial or other reasons, he should not seek to be excused from undertaking the representation except for compelling reasons. Compelling reasons do not include such factors as the repugnance of the subject matter of the proceeding, the identity or position of a person involved in the case, the belief of the lawyer that the defendant in a criminal proceeding is guilty, or the belief of the lawyer regarding the merits of the civil case." EC 2-30 stated that "a lawyer should decline employment if the intensity of his personal feelings, as distinguished from a community attitude, may impair his effective representation of a prospective client."

Cross-References in Rules

Rule 1.1, Comment 4: "A lawyer may accept representation where the requisite level of competence can be achieved by reasonable preparation. This applies as well to a lawyer who is appointed as counsel for an unrepresented person. See also **Rule 6.2.**"

Rule 1.16, Comment 3: "When a lawyer has been appointed to represent a client, withdrawal ordinarily requires approval of the appointing authority. See also **Rule 6.2.**"

Legislative History

1980 Discussion Draft and 1981 Draft were substantially the same as adopted, with only minor changes in phrasing.

1982 Draft was the same as adopted *except* that it completely omitted subparagraph (c).

Selected State Variations

California: See B & P Code §6068(h). (California's Rules of Professional Conduct have no comparable provision.)

New York: Same or substantially the same as the ABA Model Code — see Model Code Comparison above.

North Carolina omits Rule 6.2.

Virginia omits Rule 6.2.

Related Materials

ABA Canons: Canon 4 provided:

4. When Counsel for an Indigent Prisoner

A lawyer assigned as counsel for an indigent prisoner ought not to ask to be excused for any trivial reason, and should always exert his best efforts in his behalf.

Rule 6.3 Membership in Legal Services Organization

A lawyer may serve as a director, officer or member of a legal services organization, apart from the law firm in which the lawyer practices, notwithstanding that the organization serves persons having interests adverse to a client of the lawyer. The lawyer shall not knowingly participate in a decision or action of the organization:

(a) if participating in the decision or action would be incompatible with the lawyer's obligations to a client under Rule 1.7; or

(b) where the decision or action could have a material adverse effect on the representation of a client of the organization whose interests are adverse to a client of the lawyer.

COMMENT

[1] Lawyers should be encouraged to support and participate in legal service organizations. A lawyer who is an officer or a member of such an organi-

zation does not thereby have a client-lawyer relationship with persons served by the organization. However, there is potential conflict between the interests of such persons and the interests of the lawyer's clients. If the possibility of such conflict disqualified a lawyer from serving on the board of a legal services organization, the profession's involvement in such organizations would be severely curtailed.

[2] It may be necessary in appropriate cases to reassure a client of the organization that the representation will not be affected by conflicting loyalties of a member of a board. Established, written policies in this respect can enhance the credibility of such assurances.

Model Code Comparison

There was no counterpart to this Rule in the Model Code.

Cross-References in Rules

None.

Legislative History

1980 Discussion Draft (then Rule 8.2(c)) provided as follows:

(c) A lawyer may serve as a director, member or officer of an organization involved in reform of the law or its administration notwithstanding the fact that the reform may affect interests of a client of the lawyer if:

(1) when the interests of the client could be affected, the fact is disclosed in the course of deliberations on the matter, but the identity of the client need not be disclosed;

(2) when the client could be adversely affected, the lawyer complies with Rule 1.8 with respect to the client; and

(3) the lawyer takes no part in any decision that could result in a direct material benefit or detriment to the client.

1981 Draft was similar to the adopted version of Rule 6.3, except that it contained an additional requirement that "the organization complies with Rule 5.4 concerning the professional independence of its legal staff."

1982 Draft was adopted.

Selected State Variations

California: See Rule 1-600 (Legal Service Programs).

Illinois: Rule 6.3 applies only to a "not-for-profit" legal services organization.

New Jersey Rule 6.3 requires that the organization comply with Rule 5.4 and states the limitation in (b) to include adverse effect on the interest of "a client or class of clients of the organization or upon the independence of professional judgment of a lawyer representing such a client."

New York: See DR 5-110 of the New York Code.

North Carolina omits Rule 6.3.

Virginia omits Rule 6.3.

Rule 6.4 Law Reform Activities Affecting Client Interests

A lawyer may serve as a director, officer or member of an organization involved in reform of the law or its administration not withstanding that the reform may affect the interests of a client of the lawyer. When the lawyer knows that the interests of a client may be materially benefitted by a decision in which the lawyer participates, the lawyer shall disclose that fact but need not identify the client.

COMMENT

Lawyers involved in organization seeking law reform generally do not have a client-lawyer relationship with the organization. Otherwise, it might follow that a lawyer could not be involved in a bar association law reform program that might indirectly affect a client. See also Rule 1.2(b). For example, a lawyer specializing in antitrust litigation might be regarded as disqualified from participating in drafting revisions of rules governing that subject. In determining the nature and scope of participation in such activities, a lawyer should be mindful of obligations to clients under other Rules, particularly Rule 1.7. A lawyer is professionally obligated to protect the integrity of the program by making an appropriate disclosure within the organization when the lawyer knows a private client might be materially benefitted.

Model Code Comparison

There was no counterpart to this Rule in the Model Code.

Cross-References in Rules

None.

Legislative History

1980 Discussion Draft (then Rule 8.2(a) and (b)) provided as follows:

Conflict of Interest in Pro Bono Publico Service

(a) A lawyer engaged in service pro bono publico shall avoid improper conflicts of interest therein.

(b) A lawyer may serve as a director, officer, or member of an organization providing legal services to persons of limited means notwithstanding that such services are provided to persons having interests adverse to a client of the lawyer if:

(1) the organization complies with Rule 7.5 [now Rule 5.4(c)] concerning the professional independence of its legal staff;

(2) when the interests of a client of the lawyer could be affected, the lawyer takes no part in any decision by the organization that could have a material adverse effect on the interest of a client of the organization or upon the independence of professional judgment of a lawyer representing such a client; and

(3) the lawyer otherwise complies with Rule 1.8 with respect to the lawyer's client.

1981 Draft:

A lawyer may serve as a director, officer or member of an organization involved in reform of the law or its administration notwithstanding the fact that the reform may affect the interests of a client of the lawyer if the lawyer takes no part in any decision that could have a direct material effect on the client.

1982 Draft was adopted.

Selected State Variations

California: No comparable provision.

District of Columbia adds the following new subparagraph to Rule 6.4:

(a) A lawyer should assist in improving the administration of justice. A lawyer may discharge this requirement by rendering services in activities for improving the law, the legal system, or the legal profession.

Florida replaces "materially benefitted" with "materially affected" in the second sentence of Rule 6.4.

Illinois: Rule 6.4 applies when the "actions" of the organization may affect a client's interests, rather than when the "reform" may affect the client's interests.

New York: Same or substantially the same as the ABA Model Code — see Model Code Comparison above. See also EC 8-4 of the New York Code.

North Carolina omits Rule 6.4.

Virginia omits Rule 6.4.

Related Materials

Model Rules of Professional Conduct for Federal Lawyers: Rule 6.4 adds a sentence providing that a federal lawyer "shall not knowingly participate in a decision or action of the organization if participating in the decision would be incompatible with the Federal lawyer's obligations to the client under Rule 1.7."

ARTICLE 7. INFORMATION ABOUT LEGAL SERVICES

Rule 7.1 Communications Concerning a Lawyer's Services

A lawyer shall not make a false or misleading communication about the lawyer or the lawyer's services. A communication is false or misleading if it:

(a) contains a material misrepresentation of fact or law, or omits a fact necessary to make the statement considered as a whole not materially misleading;

(b) is likely to create an unjustified expectation about results the lawyer can achieve, or states or implies that the lawyer can achieve results by means that violate the rules of professional conduct or other law; or

(c) compares the lawyer's services with other lawyers' services, unless the comparison can be factually substantiated.

COMMENT

This Rule governs all communications about a lawyer's services, including advertising permitted by Rule 7.2. Whatever means are used to make known a lawyer's services, statements about them should be truthful. The prohibition in paragraph (b) of statements that may create "unjustified expectations" would ordinarily preclude advertisements about results obtained on behalf of a client, such as the amount of a damage award or the lawyer's record in obtaining favorable verdicts, and advertisements containing client endorsements. Such information may create the unjustified expectation that similar results can be obtained for others without reference to the specific factual and legal circumstances.

Model Code Comparison

DR 2-101 provided that "[a] lawyer shall not . . . use . . . any form of public communication containing a false, fraudulent, misleading, deceptive, self-laudatory or unfair statement or claim." DR 2-101(B) provided that a lawyer "may publish or broadcast . . . the following information . . . in the geographic area or areas in which the lawyer resides or maintains offices or in which a significant part of the lawyer's clientele resides, provided that the information . . . complies with DR 2-101(A), and is presented in a dignified manner. . . ." DR 2-101(B) then specified 25 categories of information that may be disseminated. DR 2-101(C) provided that "[a]ny person desiring to expand the information authorized for disclosure in DR 2-101(B), or to provide for its dissemination through other forums may apply to [the agency having jurisdiction under state law]. . . . The relief granted in response to any such application shall be promulgated as an amendment to DR 2-101(B), universally applicable to all lawyers."

Cross-References in Rules

Rule 7.2(a): "Subject to the requirements of **Rule 7.1,** a lawyer may advertise services. . . ."

Rule 7.3, Comment 3: Informal public review of advertising "is itself likely to help guard against statements and claims that might constitute false and misleading communications, in violation of **Rule 7.1.**"

Rule 7.3, Comment 5: "[A]ny solicitation which contains information which is false or misleading within the meaning of **Rule 7.1** . . . is prohibited."

Rule 7.3, Comment 8: "Lawyers who participate in a legal service plan must reasonably assure that the plan sponsors are in compliance with **Rules 7.1,** 7.2, and 7.3(b)."

Rule 7.4, Comment 1: Communications claiming specialization "are subject to the 'false and misleading' standard applied in Rule 7.1 to communications concerning a lawyer's services."

Rule 7.5(a): "A lawyer shall not use a firm name, letterhead or other professional designation that violates **Rule 7.1.** A trade name may be used by a lawyer in private practice if it does not imply a connection with a government agency or with a public or charitable legal services organization and is not otherwise in violation of **Rule 7.1.**"

Legislative History

1980 Discussion Draft of Rule 7.1 (then Rule 9.1) was substantially the same as adopted, except that the first sentence prohibited a lawyer from making any "false, *fraudulent,* or misleading statement. . . ."

1981 and 1982 Drafts were the same as adopted.

Selected State Variations

California: See Rule 1-400 (Advertising and Solicitation) and the accompanying Standards showing presumptive violations of Rule 1-400.

Florida: Rule 7.1 provides that a lawyer shall not make "or permit to be made" a false, misleading, "deceptive or unfair" communication about the lawyer or the lawyer's services. Florida adds a new subparagraph (d) providing that a communication violates Rule 7.1 if it "[c]ontains a testimonial." The Comment explaining Rule 7.1(d) states:

> The prohibition in paragraph (d) would preclude endorsements or testimonials because they are inherently misleading to a layman untrained in the law. Potential clients are likely to infer from the testimonial that the lawyer will reach similar results in future cases. Because the lawyer cannot directly make this assertion, the lawyer is not permitted to indirectly make that assertion through the use of testimonials.

Georgia forbids legal advertising that "makes a claim as to the quality of legal services the lawyer can provide." DR 2-101(A)(4). DR 2-101(B) requires particular language in the event the fee will be contingent. The language must include mention of the fact that such fees are not always permitted and that when they are the client will usually be responsible for other expenses. Written communications to prospective clients must contain the word "Advertisement" on the envelope and the top of each page in a typesize no smaller than the largest typesize in the body of the letter. DR 2-101(C)(2). A lawyer may not send an advertisement to a client about a specific matter if the lawyer knows or reasonably should know that the recipient has counsel on the matter. DR 2-101(C)(4)(a). Targeted mailing is not permitted in connection with personal injury or wrongful death cases. DR 2-101(C)(4)(d). DR 2-103(B) and (C) permit a lawyer to accept referrals from, and pay reasonable fees to, a "bona fide lawyer referral service operated by an organization authorized by law and qualified to do business in this state." The service must comply with certain filing and disclosure requirements. DR 2-103(D) and (E) provide:

> (D) A lawyer may assist in, cooperate with, or offer any qualified legal services plan, or assist in or cooperate with any insurer providing legal services insurance as authorized by law, to promote the use of his services, his partner or association so long as his assistance, cooperation or offer and communications of the organization are not false, fraudulent, deceptive or misleading.
>
> (E) A lawyer may assist and cooperate with a non-profit organization which provides without charge legal services to others as a form of political or associational expression in the promotion of the use of his services or those of his partner or associate provided that his assistance or the communications of the organization on his behalf are not false, fraudulent, deceptive or misleading.

Iowa has among the most restrictive rules in the country on advertising and solicitation. Iowa prohibits not only false or misleading communications but also any "self-laudatory statement" or "any statement or claim ... which appeals to the emotions, prejudices, or likes or dislikes of a person. . . ." Iowa also continues to specify the precise categories of information a lawyer may advertise, basically along the lines of DR 2-101(B), and prohibits use of "any information not hereinafter specifically permitted." Iowa also requires all information to be "presented in a dignified manner." Iowa permits advertising "in words and numbers only," and expressly prohibits "all signs and symbols such as, but not limited to, logos, trademarks, graphics, design work, and pictures." With respect to legal fees, Iowa expressly prohibits use of "all subjective characterizations," including terms such as "cut-rate," "lowest," "reasonable," "moderate," "very reasonable," "give-away," "below-cost," or "special."

Missouri: Rule 7.1 adds that a communication is false or misleading if it:

> (e) contains a representation of, or implication of, fact regarding the quality of legal services which is not susceptible to reasonable verification by the public;
>
> (f) contains any statistical data or other information based on past performance which is not susceptible to reasonable verification by the public;
>
> (g) contains any paid testimonial about, or paid endorsement of, the lawyer, without identifying the fact that payment has been made or, if the testimonial or endorsement is not made by an actual client, without identifying that fact;
>
> (h) contains a simulated description of the lawyer, his partners or associates, his offices or facilities, or his services without identifying the fact that the description is a simulation;
>
> (i) contains any simulated representation or visualization of the lawyer, his partners or associates, his office or facilities, without identifying the fact that the representation or visualization is a simulation.

New Jersey adds a Rule 7.1(a)(4) specifying what a legal advertisement can say about fees.

New Mexico adds Rule 7.1(d), which provides that a communication is false or misleading if it "states or implies that the lawyer is a specialist in any field of law other than as specifically permitted by Rule 7.4."

New York: See New York Materials for New York's version of DR 2-101.

Texas Rule 7.01(c) contains limits on advertising that mentions an area of legal practice depending on whether Texas certifies practitioners in that area.

Related Materials

ABA Canons: Canons 27 and 43 provided:

27. Advertising, Direct or Indirect

It is unprofessional to solicit professional employment by circulars, advertisements, through touters or by personal communications or interviews not warranted by personal relations. Indirect advertisements for professional employment such as furnishing or inspiring newspaper comments, or procuring his photograph to be published in connection with causes in which the lawyer has been or is engaged or concerning the manner of their conduct, the magnitude of the interest involved, the importance of the lawyers's position, and all other like self-laudation, offend the traditions and lower the tone of our profession and are reprehensible; but the customary use of simple professional cards is not improper.

Publication in reputable law lists in a manner consistent with the standards of conduct imposed by these canons of brief biographical and informative data is permissible. Such data must not be misleading and may include only a statement of the lawyer's name and the names of his professsional associates; addresses, telephone numbers, cable addresses; branches of the profession practiced; date and place of birth and admission to the bar; schools attended; with dates of graduation, degrees and other educational distinctions; public or quasi-public offices; posts of honor; legal authorships; legal teaching positions; memberships and offices in bar associations and committees thereof, in legal and scientific societies and legal fraternities; foreign language ability; the fact of listings in other reputable law lists; the names and addresses of references; and, with their written consent, the names of clients regularly represented. A certificate of compliance with the Rules and Standards issued by the Standing Committee on Law Lists may be treated as evidence that such list is reputable.

It is not improper for a lawyer who is admitted to practice as a proctor in admiralty to use that designation on his letterhead or shingle or for a lawyer who has complied with the statutory requirements of admission to practice before the patent office, to so use the designation "patent attorney" or "patent lawyer" or "trademark attorney" or "trademark lawyer" or any combination of those terms.

43. Approved Law Lists

It shall be improper for a lawyer to permit his name to be published in a law list the conduct, management or contents of which are calculated or likely to deceive or injure the public or the profession, or to lower the dignity or standing of the profession.

ABA Aspirational Goals for Lawyer Advertising: In August of 1988, the ABA's House of Delegates endorsed the following goals written by the ABA's Commission on Advertising. These goals are nonbinding and are not grounds for discipline. They are intended to permit lawyers to advertise "effectively yet with dignity."*

Preamble

During the past decade, the courts have sought to define the nature and extent of permissible advertising by lawyers. In a series of decisions, the U.S. Supreme Court has held that lawyer advertising which is not false or misleading is commercial speech entitled to protection under the First Amendment of the U.S. Constitution.

Pending further clarification by the courts, some advertising practices exist which may be detrimental. Some forms of advertising may adversely affect public perceptions about the justice system itself. For example, empirical evidence suggests that undignified advertising can detract from the public's confidence in the legal profession and respect for the justice system.

Under present case law, the matter of dignity is widely believed to be so subjective as to be beyond the scope of constitutionally permitted regulation. Nevertheless, it seems entirely proper for the organized bar to suggest non-binding aspirational goals urging lawyers who wish to advertise to do so in a dignified manner. Although only aspirational, such goals must be scrupulously sensitive to fundamental constitutional rights of lawyers and the needs of the public.

It is the role and responsibility of lawyers to provide legal services to the public. It has been demonstrated by responsible studies that people sometimes do not receive needed legal services, either because they are unaware of available services, don't understand how they can benefit from those services or don't understand how to obtain them. Therefore, it is also the legal profession's responsibility to inform the public about the availability of legal services and how to obtain and use them.

Advertising is one of many methods by which lawyers can inform the public about legal services. Although most people find a lawyer through word-of-mouth networks of family, friends and work associates, when properly done, advertising can help people to better understand the legal services available to them and how to obtain those services.

When properly done, advertising can also be a productive way for lawyers to build and maintain their client bases. Advertising and other forms of marketing can enable lawyers to attain efficiencies of scale which may help make legal services more affordable. As the Supreme Court pointed out in Bates v. State Bar of Arizona, 433 U.S. 350, 377 (1977), it is "entirely possible that advertising will serve to reduce, not advance, the cost of legal services to the consumer."

Lawyers are at all times officers of the court, and as such, they have a special obligation to assure that their conduct conforms to the highest ideals of the legal profession. Thus, lawyers who advertise should be mindful not only of the effect their advertising may have on their own professional image but also of the effect it may have on the public's overall perception of the judicial system.

If lawyer advertising avoids false, misleading or deceptive representations, or coercive or misleading solicitation, it advances the goal of bringing needed legal services to more people than are now being served.

However, if advertising employs false, misleading or deceptive messages or degenerates into undignified and unprofessional presentations, the public is not served, the lawyer who advertised does not benefit and the image of the judicial system may be harmed.

Accordingly, lawyer advertising should exemplify the inherent dignity and professionalism of the legal community. Dignified lawyer advertising tends to inspire public confidence in the professional competence and ability of lawyers and portrays the commitment of lawyers to serve clients' legal needs in accordance with the ethics and public service tradition of a learned profession.

Lawyer advertising is a key facet of the marketing and delivery of legal services to the public. The professional conduct rules for lawyers adopted by the states regulate some aspects of lawyer advertising, but they also leave lawyers much latitude to decide how to advertise. The following Aspirational Goals are presented in an effort to suggest how lawyers can achieve the beneficial goals of advertising while minimizing or eliminating altogether its negative implications.

The ABA does not regulate the conduct of lawyers. Absent adoption by state regulatory bodies, these Aspirational Goals have no binding effect on members of the legal profession.

Aspirational Goals

1. Lawyer advertising should encourage and support the public's confidence in the individual lawyer's competence and integrity as well as the commitment of the legal profession to serve the public's legal needs in the tradition of the law as a learned profession.

2. Since advertising may be the only contact many people have with lawyers, advertising by lawyers should help the public understand its legal rights and the judicial process and should uphold the dignity of the legal profession.

3. While "dignity" and "good taste" are terms open to subjective interpretation, lawyers should consider that advertising which reflects the ideas stated in these Aspirational Goals is likely to be dignified and suitable to the profession.

4. Since advertising must be truthful and accurate, and not false or misleading, lawyers should realize that ambiguous or confusing advertising can be misleading.

5. Particular care should be taken in describing fees and costs in advertisements. If an advertisement states a specific fee for a particular service, it should make clear whether or not all problems of that type can be handled for that specific fee. Similar care should be taken in describing the lawyer's areas of practice.

6. Lawyers should consider that the use of inappropriately dramatic music, unseemly slogans, hawkish spokespersons, premium offers, slapstick routines or outlandish settings in advertising does not instill confidence in the lawyer or the legal profession and undermines the serious purpose of legal services and the judicial system.

7. Advertising developed with a clear identification of its potential audience is more likely to be understandable, respectful and appropriate to that audience, and, therefore, more effective. Lawyers should consider using advertising and marketing professionals to assist in identifying and reaching an appropriate audience.

8. How advertising conveys its message is as important as the message itself. Again, lawyers should consider using professional consultants to help them develop and present a clear message to the audience in an effective and appropriate way.

9. Lawyers should design their advertising to attract legal matters which they are competent to handle.

10. Lawyers should be concerned with making legal services more affordable to the public. Lawyer advertising may be designed to build up client bases so that efficiencies of scale may be achieved that will translate into more affordable legal services.

American Lawyer's Code of Conduct: Rules 7.2 through 7.5 provide:

7.2. A lawyer shall not advertise for or solicit clients in a way that violates a valid law imposing reasonable restrictions regarding time or place.

7.3. A lawyer shall not advertise for or solicit clients through another person when the lawyer knows, or could reasonably ascertain, that such conduct violates a contractual or other legal obligation of that other person.

7.4. A lawyer shall not solicit a member of the public when the lawyer has been told by that person or someone acting on that person's behalf that he or she does not want to receive communications from the lawyer.

7.5. A lawyer who advertises for or solicits clients through another person shall be as responsible for that person's representations to and dealings with potential clients as if the lawyer acted personally.

Comment to Rules 7.2-7.5

Access to the legal system is essential to the exercise of fundamental rights, particularly those rights relating to personal autonomy, freedom of expression, counsel, due process, and equal protection of the laws. Yet members of the public are frequently unaware of their need for legal assistance and of its availability. It is thus important for lawyers to provide members of the public with information regarding the availability of lawyers to serve them, the ways in which legal services can be useful, and the costs of legal services. Lawyers are therefore encouraged to advertise and to solicit clients, subject only to restrictions relating to false and misleading representations, harassment, violation of reasonable time and place regulations, and inducing violations by others of contractual or other legal obligations.

Solicitation refers to spoken communication, in person or by telephone, intended to induce the other person to become a client.

Rule 7.2 Advertising

Editors' Note. At its February 1989 Mid-Year Meeting, the ABA House of Delegates approved minor amendments to Rule 7.2 and far more substantial amendments to Rule 7.3 to conform to the Supreme Court's decision in Shapero v. Kentucky Bar Association, 486 U.S. 466 (1988), which held a blanket prohibition against "targeted" mail unconstitutional. At its 1990 Mid-Year Meeting, the ABA added subparagraph (c)(3) to harmonize with the addition of Rule 1.17. An extensive report explaining the 1989 amendments to Rules 7.2 and 7.3 appears in the Legislative History following Rule 7.3.

(a) Subject to the requirements of Rules 7.1 and 7.3, a lawyer may advertise services through public media, such as a telephone directory, legal directory, newspaper or other periodical, outdoor advertising, radio or television, or through written or recorded communication.

(b) A copy or recording of an advertisement or written communication shall be kept for two years after its last dissemination along with a record of when and where it was used.

(c) A lawyer shall not give anything of value to a person for recommending the lawyer's services except that a lawyer may

(1) pay the reasonable costs of advertisements or communications permitted by this Rule;

(2) pay the usual charges of a not-for-profit lawyer referral service or legal service organization; and

(3) pay for a law practice in accordance with Rule 1.17.

(d) Any communication made pursuant to this rule shall include the name of at least one lawyer responsible for its content.

COMMENT

Editors' Note.   When the text of Rule 7.2 was amended in 1989, the Comment was not amended. However, when Rule 1.17 was added to the Model Rules in 1990, the ABA amended Comment 6 to Rule 7.2 to include a reference to Rule 1.17.

[1] To assist the public in obtaining legal services, lawyers should be allowed to make known their services not only through reputation but also through organized information campaigns in the form of advertising. Advertising involves an active quest for clients, contrary to the tradition that a lawyer should not seek clientele. However, the public's need to know about legal services can be fulfilled in part through advertising. This need is particularly acute in the case of persons of moderate means who have not made extensive use of legal services. The interest in expanding public information about legal services ought to prevail over considerations of tradition. Nevertheless, advertising by lawyers entails the risk of practices that are misleading or overreaching.

[2] This Rule permits public dissemination of information concerning a lawyer's name or firm name, address and telephone number; the kinds of services the lawyer will undertake; the basis on which the lawyer's fees are determined, including prices for specific services and payment and credit arrangements; a lawyer's foreign language ability; names of references and, with their consent, names of clients regularly represented; and other information that might invite the attention of those seeking legal assistance.

[3] Questions of effectiveness and taste in advertising are matters of speculation and subjective judgment. Some jurisdictions have had extensive prohibitions against television advertising, against advertising going beyond specified facts about a lawyer, or against "undignified" advertising. Television is now one of the most powerful media for getting information to the public, particularly persons of low and moderate income; prohibiting television advertising, therefore, would impede the flow of information about legal services to many sectors of the public. Limiting the information that may be advertised has a similar effect and assumes that the bar can accurately forecast the kind of information that the public would regard as relevant.

[4] Neither this Rule nor Rule 7.3 prohibits communications authorized by law, such as notice to members of a class in class action litigation.

Record of Advertising

[5] Paragraph (b) requires that a record of the content and use of advertising be kept in order to facilitate enforcement of this Rule. It does not require that advertising be subject to review prior to dissemination. Such a requirement would be burdensome and expensive relative to its possible benefits, and may be of doubtful constitutionality.

Paying Others to Recommend a Lawyer

[6] A lawyer is allowed to pay for advertising permitted by this Rule and for the purchase of a law practice in accordance with the provisions of Rule 1.17, but otherwise is not permitted to pay another person for channeling professional work. This restriction does not prevent an organization or person other than the lawyer from advertising or recommending the lawyer's services. Thus, a legal aid agency or prepaid legal services plan may pay to advertise legal services provided under its auspices. Likewise, a lawyer may participate in not-for-profit lawyer referral programs and pay the usual fees charged by such programs. Paragraph (c) does not prohibit paying regular compensation to an assistant, such as a secretary, to prepare communications permitted by this Rule.

Model Code Comparison

With regard to paragraph (a), DR 2-101(B) provided that a lawyer "may publish or broadcast, subject to DR 2-103, . . . in print media . . . or television or radio. . . ."

With regard to paragraph (b), DR 2-101(D) provided that if the advertisement is "communicated to the public over television or radio, . . . a recording of the actual transmission shall be retained by the lawyer."

With regard to paragraph (c), DR 2-103(B) provided that a lawyer "shall not compensate or give anything of value to a person or organization to recommend or secure his employment . . . except that he may pay the usual and reasonable fees or dues charged by any of the organizations listed in DR 2-103(D)." (DR 2-103(D) referred to legal aid and other legal services organizations.) DR 2-101(I) provided that a lawyer "shall not compensate or give anything of value to representatives of the press, radio, television, or other communication medium in anticipation of or in return for professional publicity in a news item."

There was no counterpart to paragraph (d) in the Model Code.

Cross-References in Rules

Rule 7.1, Comment: "This Rule governs all communications about a lawyer's services, including advertising permitted by **Rule 7.2**."

Rule 7.3, Comment 2: "This potential for abuse inherent in direct in-person or telephone solicitation of prospective clients justifies its prohibition, particularly since lawyer advertising and written and recorded communication permitted under **Rule 7.2** offer alternative means of conveying necessary information to those who may be in need of legal services."

Rule 7.3, Comment 3: "The contents of advertisements and communications permitted under **Rule 7.2** are permanently recorded so that they cannot be disputed and may be shared with others who know the lawyer."

Rule 7.3, Comment 5: "[I]f after sending a letter or other communication to a client as permitted by **Rule 7.2** the lawyer receives no response, any further effort to communicate with the prospective client may violate the provisions of Rule 7.3(b)."

Rule 7.3, Comment 6: Rule 7.3 does not prohibit lawyers from communicating with representatives of organizations or groups regarding group or prepaid legal service plans because such communications "are functionally similar to and serve the same purpose as advertising permitted under **Rule 7.2.**"

Rule 7.3, Comment 8: "Lawyers who participate in a legal service plan must reasonably assure that the plan sponsors are in compliance with **Rules** 7.1, **7.2,** and 7.3(b)."

Legislative History

1980 Discussion Draft (then Rule 9.2) provided as follows:

> . . . (b) A copy or record of an advertisement in its entirety shall be kept for one year after its dissemination.
>
> (c) A lawyer shall not give anything of value to a person for recommending the lawyer's services, except that a lawyer may pay the reasonable cost of advertising permitted by this rule.

1981 and 1982 Drafts were substantially the same as adopted, except that subparagraph (a) permitted any "written communication not involving personal contract."

1989 Amendments: In 1989, the ABA House of Delegates made minor amendments to Rule 7.2(a) and (c). The ABA did not amend the Comment to Rule 7.2.

1990 Amendment: At its 1990 Mid-Year Meeting, the ABA House of Delegates added subparagraph 7.2(c)(3) to reflect the addition of Rule 1.17.

Selected State Variations

Arizona: Rule 7.2(e)(1) provides that all "written communications to prospective clients for the purpose of obtaining professional employment" must "be plainly marked 'Advertisement' on the face of the envelope and at the top of each page of the written communication in type no smaller than the largest type used in the written communication." In addition, Arizona forbids a lawyer to send a written communication to a prospective client about a specific matter if the lawyer knows or reasonably should know that the recipient has a lawyer in the matter. Rule 7.2(f)(1). Finally, Rule 7.2(g) retains the language of DR 2-103(D) with some expansion.

California: See Rule 1-400 (Advertising and Solicitation) and B & P Code §6129.

District of Columbia omits Rule 7.2, but its Rule 7.1(c) provides:

> A lawyer shall not knowingly assist an organization that furnishes or pays for legal services to others to promote the use of the lawyer's services or those of the lawyer's partner or associate, or any other lawyer affiliated with the lawyer or the lawyer's firm, as a private practitioner, if the promotional activity involves the use of coercion, duress, compulsion, intimidation, threats, or vexation or harassing conduct.

Florida: Rule 7.2(a) permits lawyers to advertise through "recorded messages the public may access by dialing a telephone number," and provides that Florida's Rules do not apply to any advertisement in another jurisdiction "if such advertisement complies with the rules governing lawyer advertising in that jurisdiction and is not intended for broadcast or dissemination within the State of Florida." Florida adds the following new language to Rule 7.2(b):

> Advertisements on the electronic media such as television and radio . . . shall be articulated by a single voice, with no background sound other than instrumental music. The voice may be that of a full-time employee of the firm whose services are advertised; it shall not be that of a celebrity whose voice is recognizable to the public. The lawyer or full-time employee of the firm whose services are being advertised may appear on screen or on radio.

Florida also adds the following new subparagraphs to Rule 7.2:

> (d) Except as provided in this paragraph, all advertisements shall contain the following disclosure: "The hiring of a lawyer is an important decision that should not be based solely upon advertisements. Before you decide, ask us to send you free written information about our qualifications and experience." This disclosure need not appear in electronic advertisements or advertisements in the public print media that contain no illustrations and no information other than that listed in paragraph (n)(1)-(8) of this rule.
>
> (e) There shall be no dramatization in any advertisement in any medium.
>
> (f) Illustrations used in advertisements shall present information which can be factually substantiated and is not merely self-laudatory. . . .
>
> (j) A lawyer shall not make statements which are merely self-laudatory or statements describing or characterizing the quality of the lawyer's services [except for] information furnished to a prospective client at that person's request or to . . . existing clients. . . .
>
> (m) No lawyer shall, directly or indirectly, pay all or a part of the cost of an advertisement by a lawyer not in the same firm unless the advertisement discloses the name and address of the nonadvertising lawyer, the relationship between the advertising lawyer and the nonadvertising lawyer, and whether the advertising lawyer may refer any case received through the advertisement to the nonadvertising lawyer.
>
> (n) [Florida sets forth nine categories of information "presumed not to violate" Rule 7.1, including names, addresses, phone numbers, dates of bar admission, and "[a]cceptance of credit cards."] . . .
>
> (p) A copy or recording of an advertisement or written or recorded communication shall be submitted to the Standing Committee on Advertising. . . .

Florida also adds the following new Rule 7.3:

> (a) Each lawyer or law firm that advertises . . . shall have available in written form for delivery to any potential client:
>
>   (1) A factual statement detailing the background, training and experience of each lawyer or law firm. . . .
>
> (c) Whenever a potential client shall request information regarding a lawyer or law firm for the purpose of making a decision regarding employment of the lawyer or law firm:
>
>   (1) The lawyer or law firm shall promptly furnish (by mail if requested) the written information described in paragraph (a). . . .
>
>   (4) If the information furnished to the client includes a fee contract, the top of each page of the contract shall be marked "SAMPLE" in red ink . . . and the words "DO NOT SIGN" shall appear on the client signature line.
>
> (g) Upon reasonable request by The Florida Bar, a lawyer shall promptly provide proof that any statement or claim made in any advertisement or written communication, as well as the information furnished to a prospective client . . . [is not directly, impliedly, or potentially false, misleading, unfair, or deceptive].

Florida also adds the following Rule 7.8 governing lawyer referral services:

> (a) A lawyer shall not accept referrals from a lawyer referral service unless the service:

(1) Engages in no communication with the public and in no direct contact with prospective clients in a manner that would violate the Rules of Professional Conduct if the communication or contact were made by the lawyer;

(2) Receives no fee or charge that constitutes a division or sharing of fees, unless the service is a not-for-profit service approved by The Florida Bar pursuant to chapter 8 of these rules;

(3) Refers clients only to persons lawfully permitted to practice law in Florida when the services to be rendered constitute the practice of law in Florida;

(4) Requires the lawyer to waive confidentiality for the purpose of enabling The Florida Bar to inform the service of the lawyer's grievance history and the status of each complaint against the lawyer in which there has been a finding of probable cause;

(5) Carries or requires each lawyer participating in the service to carry professional liability insurance in an amount not less than $100,000 per claim or occurrence;

(6) Furnishes The Florida Bar with the names of all lawyers participating in the service; and

(7) Neither represents nor implies to the public that the service is endorsed or approved by The Florida Bar, unless the service is operated by or has been expressly approved by The Florida Bar.

(b) A "lawyer referral service" is any person, group of persons, association, organization, or entity that receives a fee or charge for referring or causing the direct or indirect referral of a potential client to a lawyer drawn from a specific group or panel of lawyers.

In addition, Chapter 8 of the Florida Supreme Court Rules sets forth detailed and extensive requirements for the operation of lawyer referral services by local bar associations, and no local bar association may operate a referral service without the express approval of the state bar. Chapter 9 of the Florida Supreme Court Rules provides detailed regulations governing group and prepaid legal service plans, and defines such plans as follows in Rule 9-1.2 (entitled "Definitions"):

(a) "Group legal services." A plan, program, or insurance intended to cover two (2) or more persons, which assists a participant in obtaining a lawyer and pursuant to which a member of The Florida Bar is paid by the plan, the sponsor, the participant, in whole or in part, legal fees for services rendered to the participant.

(b) "Prepaid legal services." A legal service plan that contains the assumption of a contractual obligation to provide specified legal services, or to reimburse for specified legal expense in consideration of a specified payment in advance for an interval of time. . . .

Georgia: For Georgia's version of Rule 7.2 see Selected State Variations following Rule 7.1.

Illinois prohibits giving anything of value for recommending "or having recommended" the lawyer's services.

Iowa: DR 2-101 permits written advertising in "newspapers or periodicals of general circulation. . . ." Iowa does not expressly permit advertising through "outdoor advertising" or through "public media" in general. In addition, Iowa restricts both written and broadcast advertising to "the geographic area in which the lawyer maintains offices or in which a significant part of the lawyer's clientele resides or in reputable legal directories only." With respect to radio and television, Iowa permits information to be "articulated only by a single non-dramatic voice, not that of the lawyer, and with no other background sound," and on television, "no visual display shall be allowed except that allowed in print as articulated by the announcer." Moreover, Iowa adds DR 2-101(I), which provides that a lawyer shall not give anything of value "to representatives of the press, radio, television or other communication medium in anticipation of or in return for professional publicity in a news item nor voluntarily give any information to such representatives which, if published in a news item, would be in violation of" the basic prohibition on false, deceptive, or misleading communications.

Maryland adds Rule 7.2(e), which provides:

> A lawyer, including a participant in an advertising group or lawyer referral service or other program involving communications concerning the lawyer's services, shall be personally responsible for compliance with the provisions of Rules 7.1, 7.2, 7.3, 7.4 & 7.5 and shall be prepared to substantiate such compliance.

Massachusetts: See selected state variations under Rule 7.3.

Michigan's Rule 7.2(a) ends after the word "advertise" without listing the advertising media.

Mississippi adds subparagraphs (e) and (f), which provide:

> (e) If a public commmunication quotes a fixed fee to be charged for a legal service, it shall contain immediately after the quoted fee the following statement: "The Rules of Professional Conduct of the Mississippi State Bar require that the above services be performed by this lawyer (or firm) for not more than the advertised fee." Any public communication through a written medium shall contain such statement in type no smaller than the largest size type used to quote the fee. Any public communication through an electronic medium shall contain such statement at a time and in a tone and manner so as clearly to convey the required information to the listener or viewer.
>
> (f) If a public communication, other than an approved law list or law directory, refers to an area(s) of law in which a lawyer performs or wishes to perform professional services, except those areas specifically governed by Rule 7.4(b), the public communication must include immediately after the listing the following statement: "Listing of these previously mentioned area(s) of practice does not indicate any certification of expertise therein." Any public communication through a written medium shall contain such statement in type no smaller than the largest size type used to list the areas of practice. Any public communication through an electronic medium shall contain such statement at a time and in a tone and manner so as clearly to convey the required information to the listener or viewer.

New Jersey: As part of its opinion in the case of Felmeister & Isaacs, 518 A.2d 188, 208 (1986), the New Jersey Supreme Court adopted the following version of Rule 7.2:

> Subject to the requirements of RPC 7.1 a lawyer may advertise services through public media, such as a telephone directory, legal directory, newspaper or other periodical, radio, or television, or through mailed written communication. All advertisements shall be predominantly informational. No drawings, animations, dramatizations, music, or lyrics shall be used in connection with televised advertising. No advertisement shall rely in any way on techniques to obtain attention that depend upon absurdity and that demonstrate a clear and intentional lack of relevance to the selection of counsel; included in this category are all advertisements that contain any extreme portrayal of counsel exhibiting characteristics clearly unrelated to legal competence.

New York: See New York Materials for New York's versions of DR 2-101 and 2-103.

North Carolina: Rule 2.2 generally follows Model Rule 7.2, but North Carolina adds the following provisions to govern private, for-profit lawyer referral services:

> (C) . . . A lawyer may participate in and share the cost of a private lawyer referral service so long as the following conditions are met:
>> (1) Only compensation for administrative service may be paid to a lawyer or layman incident to the operation of the private referral service, which compensation shall be reasonable in amount;
>> (2) All advertisements shall be paid for by the participants in the service;

(3) No profit in specie or kind may be received other than from legal fees earned from representation of referred clients;

(4) Employees of the referral service may not initiate contact with prospective clients; and

(5) All advertisements shall (a) state that the referral service is privately operated; (b) state that a list of all participating members will be mailed free of charge to members and to the public; and (c) indicate that the service is not operated or endorsed by any public agency or any disinterested organization.

Any lawyer participating in a private lawyer referral service shall be professionally responsible for its operation.

Pennsylvania omits Rule 7.2(d).

Virginia retains the language of DR 2-101(A) from the Model Code, but omits the prohibitions on "self laudatory" statements and omits all of DR 2-101(B)-(I). DR 2-101(B) requires that a paid advertisement "be identified as such unless it is apparent from the context that it is such a communication." Any electronic communication "must be prerecorded and the prerecorded communication shall be approved by the lawyer before it is broadcast." DR 2-103(D) provides that a lawyer may not compensate a person "as a reward for having made a recommendation resulting in his employment by a client," other than the usual and reasonable fees of "a lawyer referral service and any qualified legal services plan or contract of legal services insurance as authorized by law. . . ."

Related Materials

ABA Canons: Canons 28, 40, and 46 provided:

28. Stirring Up Litigation, Directly or Through Agents

It is unprofessional for a lawyer to volunteer advice to bring a lawsuit, except in rare cases where ties of blood, relationship or trust make it his duty to do so. Stirring up strife and litigation is not only unprofessional, but it is indictable at common law. It is disreputable to hunt up defects in titles or other causes of action and inform thereof in order to be employed to bring suit or collect judgment, or to breed litigation by seeking out those with claims for personal injuries or those having any other grounds of action in order to secure them as clients, or to employ agents or runners for like purposes, or to pay or reward, directly or indirectly, those who bring or influence the bringing of such cases to his office, or to remunerate policemen, court or prison officials, physicians, hospital *attachés* or others who may succeed, under the guise of giving disinterested friendly advice, in influencing the criminal, the sick and the injured, the ignorant or others, to seek his professional services. A duty to the public and to the profession devolves upon every member of the Bar having knowledge of such practices upon the part of any practitioner immediately to inform thereof, to the end that the offender may be disbarred.

40. Newspapers

A lawyer may with propriety write articles for publications in which he gives information upon the law; but he should not accept employment from such publications to advise inquirers in respect to their individual rights.

46. Notice to Local Lawyers

A lawyer available to act as an associate of other lawyers in a particular branch of the law or legal service may send to local lawyers only and publish in his local journal, a brief and dignified announcement of his availability to serve other lawyers in connection therewith. The announcement should be in a form which does not constitute a statement or representation of special experience or expertness.

ABA Recommendation for Minimum State Standards: At its 1989 Annual Meeting, the ABA House of Delegates adopted a recommendation urging states to develop minimum quality standards for lawyer referral services in the following seven areas:

1. Admission criteria for participating panel attorneys;
2. A requirement that all participating panel attorneys maintain malpractice insurance coverage;
3. Minimum experience requirements for lawyer participation on specialty panels, where appropriate;
4. A procedure for determining client satisfaction with the referral process and for addressing client complaints;
5. Procedures for suspension and removal of participating panel attorneys who fail to handle referred clients in a diligent and responsible manner;
6. Maintenance of a minimum number of participating panel attorneys; and
7. A prohibition that any attorney who owns, governs or operates a lawyer referral service may not accept referral cases from that service.*

Rule 7.3 Direct Contact with Prospective Clients

> **Editors' Note.** In Shapero v. Kentucky State Bar, 486 U.S. 466 (1988), reviewing a Kentucky rule identical to Model Rule 7.3, the Supreme Court held that Rule 7.3's blanket prohibition on mailings to people "known to need legal services of the kind provided by the lawyer in the particular matter" violated the First Amendment. At its February 1989 Mid-Year Meeting, the ABA House of Delegates substantially amended Rule 7.3 Comment to conform to *Shapero*. A thorough report in the Legislative History section below explains the amendments and sets out deleted material from the Comment.

(a) A lawyer shall not by in-person or live telephone contact solicit professional employment from a prospective client with whom the lawyer has no family or prior professional relationship when a significant motive for the lawyer's doing so is the lawyer's pecuniary gain.

(b) A lawyer shall not solicit professional employment from a prospective client by written or recorded communication or by in-person or telephone contact even when not otherwise prohibited by paragraph (a), if:

(1) the prospective client has made known to the lawyer a desire not to be solicited by the lawyer; or

(2) the solicitation involves coercion, duress or harassment.

(c) Every written or recorded communication from a lawyer soliciting professional employment from a prospective client known to be in need of legal services in a particular matter, and with whom the lawyer has no family or prior professional relationship, shall include the words "Advertising Material" on the outside envelope and at the beginning and ending of any recorded communication.

(d) Notwithstanding the prohibitions in paragraph (a), a lawyer may participate with a prepaid or group legal service plan operated by an organization not owned or directed by the lawyer which uses in-person or telephone contact to solicit memberships or subscriptions for the plan from persons who are not known to need legal services in a particular matter covered by the plan.

COMMENT

[1] There is a potential for abuse inherent in direct in-person or live telephone contact by a lawyer with a prospective client known to need legal services. These forms of contact between a lawyer and a prospective client subject the lay person to the private importuning of the trained advocate in a direct interpersonal encounter. The prospective client, who may already feel overwhelmed by the circumstances giving rise to the need for legal services, may find it difficult fully to evaluate all available alternatives with reasoned judgment and appropriate self-interest in the face of the lawyer's presence and insistence upon being retained immediately. The situation is fraught with the possibility of undue influence, intimidation, and overreaching.

[2] This potential for abuse inherent in direct in-person or live telephone solicitation of prospective clients justifies its prohibition, particularly since lawyer advertising and written and recorded communication permitted under Rule 7.2 offer alternative means of conveying necessary information to those who may be in need of legal services. Advertising and written and recorded communications which may be mailed or autodialed make it possible for a prospective client to be informed about the need for legal services, and about the qualifications of available lawyers and law firms, without subjecting the prospective client to direct in-person or telephone persuasion that may overwhelm the client's judgment.

[3] The use of general advertising and written and recorded communications to transmit information from lawyer to prospective client, rather than direct in-person or live telephone contact, will help to assure that the information flows cleanly as well as freely. The contents of advertisements and communications permitted under Rule 7.2 are permanently recorded so that they cannot be disputed and may be shared with others who know the lawyer. This potential for informal review is itself likely to help guard against statements and claims that might constitute false and misleading communications, in violation of Rule 7.1. The contents of direct, in-person or live telephone conversations between a law-

yer and a prospective client can be disputed and are not subject to third-party scrutiny. Consequently, they are much more likely to approach (and occasionally cross) the dividing line between accurate representations and those that are false and misleading.

[4] There is far less likelihood that a lawyer would engage in abusive practices against an individual with whom the lawyer has a prior personal or professional relationship or where the lawyer is motivated by considerations other than the lawyer's pecuniary gain. Consequently, the general prohibition in Rule 7.3(a) and the requirements of Rule 7.3(c) are not applicable in those situations.

[5] But even permitted forms of solicitation can be abused. Thus, any solicitation which contains information which is false or misleading within the meaning of Rule 7.1, which involves coercion, duress, or harassment within the meaning of Rule 7.3(b)(2), or which involves contact with a prospective client who has made known to the lawyer a desire not to be solicited by the lawyer within the meaning of Rule 7.3(b)(1), is prohibited. Moreover, if after sending a letter or other communication to a client as permitted by Rule 7.2 the lawyer receives no response, any further effort to communicate with the prospective client may violate the provisions of Rule 7.3(b).

[6] This Rule is not intended to prohibit a lawyer from contacting representatives of organizations or groups that may be interested in establishing a group or prepaid legal plan for their members, insureds, beneficiaries or other third parties for the purpose of informing such entities of the availability of and details concerning the plan or arrangement which the lawyer or lawyer's firm is willing to offer. This form of communication is not directed to a prospective client. Rather, it is usually addressed to an individual acting in a fiduciary capacity seeking a supplier of legal services for others who may, if they choose, become prospective clients of the lawyer. Under these circumstances, the activity which the lawyer undertakes in communicating with such representatives and the type of information transmitted to the individual are functionally similar to and serve the same purpose as advertising permitted under Rule 7.2.

[7] The requirement in Rule 7.3(c) that certain communications be marked "Advertising Material" does not apply to communications sent in response to requests of potential clients or their spokespersons or sponsors. General announcements by lawyers, including changes in personnel or office location, do not constitute communications soliciting professional employment from a prospective client known to be in need of legal services within the meaning of this Rule.

[8] Paragraph (d) of this Rule would permit an attorney to participate with an organization which uses personal contact to solicit members for its group or prepaid legal services plan, provided that the personal contact is not undertaken by any lawyer who would be a provider of legal services through the plan. The organization referred to in paragraph (d) must not be owned or directed (whether as manager or otherwise) by any lawyer or law firm that participates in the plan. For example, paragraph (d) would not permit a lawyer to create an

organization controlled directly or indirectly by the lawyer and use the organization for the in-person or telephone solicitation of legal employment of the lawyer through memberships in the plan or otherwise. The communication permitted by these organizations also must not be directed to a person known to need legal services in a particular matter, but is to be designed to inform potential plan members generally of another means of affordable legal services. Lawyers who participate in a legal service plan must reasonably assure that the plan sponsors are in compliance with Rules 7.1, 7.2, and 7.3(b). See Rule 8.4(a).

Model Code Comparison

DR 2-104(A) provided with certain exceptions that "[a] lawyer who has given in-person unsolicited advice to a layperson that he should obtain counsel or take legal action shall not accept employment resulting from that advice...." The exceptions include DR 2-104(A)(1), which provided that a lawyer "may accept employment by a close friend, relative, former client (if the advice is germane to the former employment), or one whom the lawyer reasonably believes to be a client." DR 2-104(A)(2) through DR 2-104(A)(5) provided other exceptions relating, respectively, to employment resulting from public educational programs, recommendation by a legal assistance organization, public speaking or writing, and representing members of a class in class action litigation.

Cross-References in Rules

Rule 7.2(a): "Subject to the requirements of **Rules** 7.1 and **7.3**, a lawyer may advertise through public media ... or through written or recorded communication."

Rule 7.2, Comment 4: "Neither this Rule nor **Rule 7.3** prohibits communications authorized by law, such as notice to members of a class in class action litigation."

Legislative History

1980 Discussion Draft (then Rule 9.3) provided as follows:

Solicitation

(a) A lawyer shall not initiate contact with a prospective client if:

(1) the lawyer reasonably should know that the physical, emotional, or mental state of the person solicited is such that the person could not exercise reasonable judgment in employing a lawyer;

(2) the person solicited has made known a desire not to receive communications from the lawyer; or

(3) the solicitation involves coercion, duress, or harassment.

(b) subject to the requirements of paragraph (a), a lawyer may initiate contact with a prospective client in the following circumstances:

(1) if the prospective client is a close friend or relative of the lawyer;

276

(2) by a letter concerning a specific event or transaction if the letter is followed up only upon positive response from the addressee;

(3) under the auspices of a public or charitable legal services organization or a bona fide political, social, civic, fraternal, employee, or trade organization whose purposes include but are not limited to providing or recommending legal services.

(c) A lawyer shall not give another person anything of value to initiate contact with a prospective client on behalf of the lawyer.

1981 and 1982 Drafts both provided as follows:

Personal Contact with Prospective Clients

(a) A lawyer may initiate personal contact with a prospective client for the purpose of obtaining professional employment only in the following circumstances and subject to the requirements of paragraph (b):

(1) if the prospective client is a close friend, relative, former client or one whom the lawyer reasonably believes to be a client;

(2) under the auspices of a public or charitable legal services organization; or

(3) under the auspices of a bona fide political, social, civic, fraternal, employee or trade organization whose purposes include but are not limited to providing or recommending legal services, if the legal services are related to the principal purposes of the organization.

(b) A lawyer shall not contact, or send a written communication to, a prospective client for the purpose of obtaining professional employment if:

(1) the lawyer knows or reasonably should know that the physical, emotional or mental state of the person is such that the person could not exercise reasonable judgment in employing a lawyer;

(2) the person has made known to the lawyer a desire not to receive communications from the lawyer; or

(3) the communication involves coercion, duress or harassment.

1989 Amendments: At its February 1989 Mid-Year Meeting, the ABA House of Delegates substantially amended Rule 7.3 and its Comment. As originally promulgated, before its language was declared unconstitutional in Shapero v. Kentucky State Bar, 486 U.S. 466 (1988), Rule 7.3 provided:

A lawyer may not solicit professional employment from a prospective client with whom the lawyer has no family or prior professional relationship, by mail, in person or otherwise, when a significant motive for the lawyer's doing so is the lawyer's pecuniary gain. The term "solicit" includes contact in person, by telephone or telegraph, by letter or other writing, or by other communications directed to a specific recipient, but does not include letters addressed or advertising circulars distributed generally to persons not known to need legal services of the kind provided by the lawyer in a particular matter, but who are so situated that they might in general find such services useful.

When the ABA amended Rule 7.3 in 1989, it *completely deleted* the following two paragraphs from the Comment to Rule 7.3:

These dangers [of false and misleading representations] attend direct solicitation whether in-person or by mail. Direct mail solicitation cannot be effectively regulated by means less drastic than outright prohibition. One proposed safeguard is to require that the designation "Advertising" be stamped on any envelope containing a solicitation letter. This would do nothing to assure the accuracy and reliability of the contents. Another suggestion is that solicitation letters be filed with a state regulatory agency. This would be ineffective as a practical matter. State lawyer discipline agencies struggle for resources to investigate specific complaints, much less for those necessary to screen lawyers' mail solicitation material. Even if they could examine such materials, agency staff members are unlikely to know anything about the lawyer or about the prospective client's underlying problem. Without such knowledge they cannot determine whether the lawyer's representations are misleading. In any event, such review would be after the fact, potentially too late to avert the undesirable consequences of disseminating false and misleading material.

General mailings not speaking to a specific matter do not pose the same danger of abuse as targeted mailings, and therefore are not prohibited by this Rule. The representations made in such mailings are necessarily general rather than tailored, less importuning than informative. They are addressed to recipients unlikely to be specially vulnerable at the time, hence who are likely to be more skeptical about unsubstantiated claims. General mailings not addressed to recipients involved in a specific legal matter or incident, therefore, more closely resemble permissible advertising rather than prohibited solicitation.

The reasons for these deletions and for other amendments to Rules 7.2 and 7.3 are explained by the ABA's Standing Committee on Ethics and Professional Responsibility in the following report that was submitted to the House of Delegates in 1989.

Excerpts from ABA Committee Report

Explanation

The Supreme Court of the United States, in Shapero v. Kentucky Bar Association, 486 U.S. 466 (1988), ruled that the First Amendment does not allow states to impose blanket bans on targeted mail solicitation by lawyers of prospective clients. Held unconstitutional was a Kentucky Supreme Court rule identical to Model Rule 7.3. The principal purpose of the amendments proposed here is to bring the Model Rules into compliance with the *Shapero* decision.

The proposed amendments would make five changes in the Model Rules. The *first change,* contained in Rule 7.2(a), adds recorded communications to the types of communications covered by the advertising and solicitation Rules.

The *second change,* purely technical, would change the third and fourth words in Model Rule 7.3 from "may not" to "shall not." The purpose for the amendment is to substitute the mandatory "shall not" as used in all other provisions of the Model Rules which proscribe lawyer conduct.

The *third change* would prohibit any solicitation even when otherwise permitted under present Model Rule 7.3 if "[t]he prospective client has made known to the lawyer a desire not to be solicited by the lawyer; or [t]he solicitation involves coercion, duress or harassment." Solicitation in-person or by telephone is permitted under present Rule 7.3, if the lawyer has a family or prior professional relationship with the prospective client or when no significant motive for the lawyer's doing so is the lawyer's pecuniary gain. The prospective client should be protected from solicitation, even under these circumstances, if the prospective client has made known a desire not to be solicited by the lawyer or if the solicitation involves coercion, duress or harassment; but there is no present provision in the Rules prohibiting such solicitation. The amendment now proposed would restrict otherwise permissible in-person or telephone solicitation as well as written or recorded communication with a prospective client to that extent. A similar provision was proposed by the Commission on Evaluation of Professional Standards (the "Kutak Commission") in 1983, but was deleted as part of other amendments made by the House of Delegates when the Model Rules were adopted.

The *fourth change* would permit solicitation of professional employment by written and recorded communications with a prospective client known to need legal services of the kind provided by the lawyer in a particular matter (not involving in-person or telephone contact), as is required by the *Shapero* decision.

The *fifth change* requires that written or recorded communications initiated by a lawyer seeking professional employment in a particular legal matter be labelled "Advertising Material." This new requirement was suggested by the Supreme Court in *Shapero*.

The Comment to Rule 7.3 is amended to conform to the black letter Rule as amended.

Selected State Variations

Arizona: Targeted direct mail advertising must contain the following language on the envelope and on the first page: "Advertising Material: This commercial solicitation has not been approved by the State Bar of Arizona." Rule 7.3(b). The rule continues: "Said notification shall be printed in red ink, in all capital letters, in type size at least double that used in the body of the communication."

Arkansas requires that "written communications shall be clearly marked 'advertising' and copies thereof must be kept for 5 years."

California: See Rule 1-400 (Advertising and Solicitation) and B & P Code §6152 (Prohibition of Solicitation).

Connecticut, Maryland, and *Missouri* have adopted versions of Rule 7.3 substantially the same as the Kutak Commission's 1981 and 1982 Drafts.

District of Columbia omits Rule 7.3. Rule 7.1(b) allows *in-person* solicitation, as follows:

> (b) A lawyer shall not seek by in-person contact, or through an intermediary, employment (or employment of a partner of associate) by a non-lawyer who has not sought the lawyer's advice regarding employment of a lawyer, if:
> (1) The solicitation involves use of a statement or claim that is false or misleading, within the meaning of paragraph (a);
> (2) The solicitation involves the use of undue influence;
> (3) The potential client is apparently in a physical or mental condition which would make it unlikely that the potential client could exercise reasonable, considered judgment as to the selection of a lawyer;
> (4) The solicitation involves use of an intermediary and the lawyer knows or could reasonably ascertain that such conduct violates the intermediary's contractual or other legal obligations; or
> (5) The solicitation involves the use of an intermediary and the lawyer has not taken all reasonable steps to ensure that the potential client is informed of (a) the consideration, if any, paid or to be paid by the lawyer to the intermediary, and (b) the effect, if any, of the payment to the intermediary on the total fee to be charged.

Florida adds to its solicitation rule that a lawyer "shall not permit employees or agents of the lawyer to solicit in the lawyer's behalf." Florida also covers solicitation by "facsimile." Florida also provides that a lawyer shall not send a communication to a prospective client or a prospective client's relative if the communication "concerns an action for personal injury or wrongful death or otherwise relates to an accident or disaster . . . unless the accident or disaster occurred more than thirty days prior to the mailing of the communication." Finally, Florida imposes the following stringent requirements on all written communications to prospective clients (see Florida Rule 4-7.4(b)(2)):

> a. Each page of such written communications [and the envelope] shall be plainly marked "advertisement" in red ink. . . .

b. A copy of each such written communication and a sample of the envelopes in which the communications are enclosed shall be filed with the Standing Committee on Advertising either prior to or concurrently with the mailing. . . . If the lawyer periodically sends the identical communication to additional prospective clients, lists of the additional names and addresses shall be filed with the committee no less frequently than monthly.

c. Written communications mailed to prospective clients shall be sent only by regular U.S. mail, not by registered mail or any other forms of restricted delivery.

d. No reference shall be made in the communication about having received any kind of approval from The Florida Bar. . . .

g. The first sentence of any written communication concerning a specific matter shall be: "If you have already retained a lawyer for this matter, please disregard this letter." . . .

j. Any written communication prompted by a specific occurrence involving or affecting the intended recipient of the communication or a family member shall disclose how the lawyer obtained the information prompting the communication.

k. A written communication seeking employment by a specific prospective client in a specific matter shall not reveal on the envelope . . . the nature of the client's legal problem.

Florida also provides a mechanism for obtaining advisory opinions according to the following new rule (Florida Rule 4-7.5):

(a) A lawyer may obtain an advisory opinion concerning the compliance of a contemplated advertisement or written communication with these rules . . . by submitting the material and fee . . . to the Standing Committee on Advertising at least fifteen days prior to such dissemination. . . .

(e) The committee shall evaluate all advertisements and written communications filed with it pursuant to this rule for compliance with the applicable rules. . . . If the committee does not send any communication to the lawyer within fifteen days, the advertisement will be deemed approved.

(f) If requested to do so by the committee, the filing lawyer shall submit information to substantiate representations made or implied in that lawyer's advertisement or written communication.

(g) When the committee determines that an advertisement or written communication is not in compliance with the applicable rules, the committee shall advise the lawyer that dissemination or continued dissemination . . . may result in professional discipline.

(h) A finding by the committee of either compliance or noncompliance shall not be binding in a grievance proceeding, but may be offered as evidence.

A full description of the powers, duties, and composition of Florida's advertising committee is found in Chapter 15 of the Florida Supreme Court Rules.

Georgia: For Georgia's version of Rule 7.3 see Selected State Variations following Rule 7.1.

Illinois permits solicitation "under the auspices of a public or charitable legal services organization or a *bona fide* political, social, civic, charitable, religious, fraternal, employee or trade organization whose purposes include, but are not limited to, providing or recommending legal services." Illinois prohibits solicitation when the conditions in ABA Model Rule 7.3(b)(1)-(2) exist or when "the lawyer reasonably should know that the physical or mental state of the person is such that the person could not exercise reasonable judgment in employing a lawyer."

Massachusetts retains a modified version of the Code. But the advertising and solicitation provisions borrow markedly from the Rules. DR 2-101 and DR2-102 forbid "a deceptive statement or claim" in advertisements and listings. A targeted solicitation must be "clearly labeled 'advertising' on its face and on any envelope or container." DR 2-103(C). In-person solicitation of employment for a fee is forbidden. DR 2-103(D).

Minnesota provides:

> A lawyer may not solicit professional employment from a prospective client with whom the lawyer has no family or prior professional relationship, by in-person or telephone contact, when a significant motive for the lawyer's doing so is the lawyer's pecuniary gain.

Missouri's version of Rule 7.3 follows the Kutak Commission's 1981 and 1982 drafts. *Montana* provides:

Rule 7.3 Direct Contact with Prospective Clients

> A lawyer shall not contact, or send a written communication to, a prospective client for the purpose of obtaining professional employment, if:
>   (a) the lawyer knows or reasonably should know that the physical, emotional, or mental state of the person is such that the person cannot exercise reasonable judgment in employing a lawyer;
>   (b) the person has made known to the lawyer a desire not to receive a communication from the lawyer;
>   (c) the lawyer reasonably should know that the communication involves coercion, duress or harassment; or
>   (d) the lawyer reasonably should know that the person is already represented by another lawyer.

New Jersey: Targeted direct mail letters must carry the word ADVERTISEMENT "prominently displayed in capital letters at the top of the first page of text." In addition, the following notice must appear at the bottom of the text: "Before making your choice of attorney, you should give this matter careful thought. The selection of an attorney is an important decision." Rule 7.3(b)(4).

New York: See New York Materials for New York's version of DR 2-103.

North Carolina: Rule 2.4 generally follows Model Rule 7.3 as amended, but also permits in-person solicitation of strangers unless "the solicitation involves coercion, duress, harassment, compulsion, intimidation or threats." Rule 2.4(D) also permits a lawyer to participate in a prepaid or group legal service plan that uses in-person or telephone contact to solicit memberships "so long as such contact does not involve coercion, duress or harassment and is not false, deceptive or misleading."

Pennsylvania has not adopted Rule 7.3(a).

Texas Rule 7.03 provides:

> A lawyer shall not accept or continue employment when the lawyer knows or reasonably should know that the person who seeks the lawyer's services does so as a result of conduct prohibited by these Rules.

Virginia: DR 2-103 permits telephone or in-person solicitation of strangers unless the solicitation is false, fraudulent, misleading, or deceptive, or if the solicitation

> has a substantial potential for or involves the use of coercion, duress, compulsion, intimidation, threats, unwarranted promises of benefits, overpersuasion, overreaching, vexatious or harassing conduct, taking into account the sophistication regarding legal matters, the physical, emotional or mental state of the person to whom the communication is directed and the circumstances in which the communication is made.

However, Virginia DR 2-103(F) provides that, notwithstanding the quoted language, a lawyer "shall not initiate in person solicitation of professional employment for compensation in a personal injury or wrongful death claim of a prospective client with whom the lawyer has no family or prior professional relationship."

Related Materials

ABA Canons: Canon 28 provided:

28. Stirring Up Litigation, Directly or Through Agents

It is unprofessional for a lawyer to volunteer advice to bring a lawsuit, except in rare cases where ties of blood, relationship or trust make it his duty to do so. Stirring up strife and litigation is not only unprofessional, but it is indictable at common law. It is disreputable to hunt up defects in titles or other causes of action and inform thereof in order to be employed to bring suit or collect judgment, or to breed litigation by seeking out those with claims for personal injuries or those having any other grounds of action in order to secure them as clients, or to employ agents or runners for like purposes, or to pay or reward, directly or indirectly, those who bring or influence the bringing of such cases to his office, or to remunerate policemen, court or prison officials, physicians, hospital *attachés* or others who may succeed, under the guise of giving disinterested friendly advice, in influencing the criminal, the sick and the injured, the ignorant or others, to seek his professional services. A duty to the public and to the profession devolves upon every member of the Bar having knowledge of such practices upon the part of any practitioner immediately to inform thereof, to the end that the offender may be disbarred.

ATLA Code of Conduct: In July 1988, following unfavorable press coverage of lawyer solicitation at various mass disaster sites, the membership of the Association of Trial Lawyers of America (ATLA), which consists largely of plaintiffs' personal injury lawyers, adopted the following Code of Conduct:

1. No ATLA member shall personally, or through a representative, contact any party, or an aggrieved survivor in an attempt to solicit a potential client when there has been no request for such contact from the injured party, an aggrieved survivor, or a relative of either, or the injured parties' union representative.
2. No ATLA member shall go to the scene of an event which caused injury unless requested to do so by an interested party, an aggrieved survivor, a relative of either, or by an attorney representing an injured party or survivor.
3. No ATLA member shall initiate a television appearance or initiate any comment to any news media concerning an event causing injury within 10 days of the event unless the member forgoes any financial return from the compensation of those injured or killed, provided, however, that an individual designated by a bar association to state the official position of such bar association may initiate such media contact to communicate such position.
4. No ATLA member shall personally, or through an associate attorney, file a complaint with a specific *ad damnum* amount unless required by local rules of court. If such amount is stated, it shall be based upon good faith evaluation of facts which the member can demonstrate.
5. No ATLA member shall personally, or through a representative, make representations of trial experience or past results of litigation either of which is in any way false or misleading.
6. No ATLA member shall personally, or through a representative, initiate personal contact with a potential client (who is not a client, former client, relative or close personal friend

of the attorney) for the purpose of advising that individual of the possibility of an unrecognized legal claim for damages unless the member forgoes any financial interest in the compensation of the injured party.

7. No ATLA member shall file or maintain a frivolous suit, issue, or position. However, no ATLA member should refrain from urging or arguing any suit, issue or position that he believes in good faith to have merit.

8. The ATLA Board of Governors has condemned attorneys or legal clinics who advertise for clients in personal injury cases and who have no intention of handling the cases themselves, but do so for the sole purpose of brokering the case to other attorneys. Any ATLA member who enters a contract of representation on behalf of a claimant shall, at the time of retention, fully advise the client, in writing, of all relationships with other attorneys who will be involved in the presentation, the role each attorney shall play, and the proposed division of fees among them. The client shall also be promptly advised of all changes affecting the representation.

9. No ATLA member shall knowingly accept a referral from a person, whether an ATLA member or not, who obtained the representation by conduct which this code prohibits.

Victim's Bill of Rights: In January 1986, shortly after the disaster in Bhopal, India, the Board of Governors of ATLA adopted the following Victim's Bill of Rights:

> We condemn the conduct of any attorney who, uninvited, personally, or through a representative, contacts the injured party or aggrieved survivors in an attempt to solicit a potential client.
>
> We condemn the conduct of attorneys or representatives of insurers or companies who potentially may become defendants who, uninvited, contact the injured party or aggrieved survivors in an attempt to gain some advantage or to discourage them from contacting counsel of their choice.
>
> We condemn the conduct of attorneys or their representatives who go, uninvited, to the scene of a disaster, set up temporary quarters and advertise for prospective clients from among the injured or the survivors of those killed in the incident.
>
> We condemn the conduct of attorneys or legal clinics who advertise for clients in personal injury cases and who have no intention of handling the cases themselves, but do so for the sole purpose of brokering the cases to other attorneys.
>
> We condemn false or misleading legal advertising. We condemn legal advertising that goes beyond the bounds of good taste and common decency or which creates, or attempts to create, an impression in the public's mind of an expertise or experience that does not in fact exist.

Editors' Note. At its 1992 Annual Meeting, the ABA House of Delegates substantially amended Rule 7.4 and its Comment. (The ABA had amended the Comment, but not the text, in 1989.) The 1992 amendments bring Rule 7.4 in line with Peel v. Attorney Registration and Disciplinary Commission, 496 U.S. 91 (1990). In *Peel*, the Supreme Court held that a lawyer had a First Amendment right to advertise the truthful claim that he was "certified" as a "civil trial specialist" by the National Board of Trial Advocacy, a nationally respected organization. The Court also said, however, that a state could require a lawyer to include any disclaimers necessary to avoid confusion. The amended version of Rule 7.4 responds to the *Peel* holding. In both the rule and the Comment, we have underlined new language and stricken out language deleted from the former version of the rule.

Rule 7.4 Communication of Fields of Practice and Certification

A lawyer may communicate the fact that the lawyer does or does not practice in particular fields of law. A lawyer shall not state or imply that the lawyer ~~is~~ has been recognized or certified as a specialist in a particular field of law except as follows:

(a) a lawyer admitted to engage in patent practice before the United States Patent and Trademark Office may use the designation "Patent Attorney" or a substantially similar designation;

(b) a lawyer engaged in admiralty practice may use the designation "Admiralty," "Proctor in Admiralty" or a substantially similar designation; and

(c) ~~(provisions on designation of specialization of the particular state)~~ [for jurisdictions where there is a regulatory authority granting certification or approving organizations that grant certification] a lawyer may communicate the fact that the lawyer has been certified as a specialist in a field of law by a named organization or authority but only if:

(1) such certification is granted by the appropriate regulatory authority or by an organization which has been approved by the appropriate regulatory authority to grant such certification; or

(2) such certification is granted by an organization that has not yet been approved by, or has been denied the approval from, the appropriate regulatory authority, and the absence or denial of approval is clearly stated in the communication, and in any advertising subject to Rule 7.2, such statement appears in the same sentence that communicates the certification.

(c) [for jurisdictions where there is no procedure either for certification or specialities or for approval of organizations granting certification] a lawyer may communicate the fact that the lawyer has been certified as a specialist in a field of law by a named organization, provided that the communication clearly states that there is no procedure in this jurisdiction for approving certifying organizations.

COMMENT

[1] This Rule permits a lawyer to indicate areas of practice in communications about the lawyer's services~~, for example, in a telephone directory or other advertising~~. If a lawyer practices only in certain fields, ~~or will not accept matters except in such fields,~~ the lawyer is permitted to so indicate. A lawyer is generally permitted to state that the lawyer is a "specialist," practices a "specialty," or "specializes in" particular fields, but such communications are subject to the "false and misleading" standard applied in Rule 7.1 to communications concerning a lawyer's services. ~~However, a lawyer is not permitted to state that the~~

~~lawyer is a "specialist," practices a "specialty," or "specializes in" particular fields. These terms have acquired a secondary meaning implying formal recognition as a specialist and, therefore, use of these terms is misleading. [An exception would apply in those states which provide procedures for certification or recognition of specialization and the lawyer has complied with such procedures.]~~

[2] However, a lawyer may not communicate that the lawyer has been recognized or certified as a specialist in a particular field of law, except as provided by this Rule. Recognition of specialization in patent matters is a matter of long-established policy of the Patent and Trademark Office, as reflected in paragraph (a). Paragraph (b) recognizes that Ddesignation of admiralty practice has a long historical tradition associated with maritime commerce and the federal courts.

[3] Paragraph (c) provides for certification as a specialist in a field of law when a state authorizes an appropriate regulatory authority to grant such certification or when the state grants other organizations the right to grant certification. Certification procedures imply that an objective entity has recognized a lawyer's higher degree of specialized ability than is suggested by general licensure to practice law. Those objective entities may be expected to apply standards of competence, experience and knowledge to insure that a lawyer's recognition as a specialist is meaningful and reliable. In order to insure that consumers can obtain access to useful information about an organization granting certification, the name of the certifying organization or agency must be included in any communication regarding the certification.

[4] Lawyers may also be certified as specialists by organizations that either have not yet been approved to grant such certification or have been disapproved. In such instances, the consumer may be misled as to the significance of the lawyer's status as a certified specialist. The Rule therefore requires that a lawyer who chooses to communicate recognition by such an organization also clearly state the absence or denial of the organization's authority to grant such certification. Since lawyer advertising through public media and written or recorded communications invites the greatest danger of misleading consumers, the absence or denial of the organization's authority to grant certification must be clearly stated in such advertising in the same sentence that communicates the certification.

[5] In jurisdictions where no appropriate regulatory authority has a procedure for approving organizations granting certification, the Rule requires that a lawyer clearly state such lack of procedure.

Model Code Comparison

DR 2-105(A) provided that a lawyer

shall not hold himself out publicly as a specialist, as practicing in certain areas of law or as limiting his practice . . . except as follows:

(1) A lawyer admitted to practice before the United States Patent and Trademark Office may use the designation "Patents," "Patent Attorney," "Patent Lawyer," or "Registered Patent Attorney" or any combination of those terms, on his letterhead and office sign.

(2) A lawyer who publicly discloses fields of law in which the lawyer . . . practices or states that his practice is limited to one or more fields of law shall do so by using designations and definitions authorized and approved by [the agency having jurisdiction of the subject under state law].

(3) A lawyer who is certified as a specialist in a particular field of law or law practice by [the authority having jurisdiction under state law over the subject of specialization by lawyers] may hold himself out as such, but only in accordance with the rules prescribed by that authority.

EC 2-14 stated that "In the absence of state controls to insure the existence of special competence, a lawyer should not be permitted to hold himself out as a specialist, . . . other than in the fields of admiralty, trademark, and patent law where a holding out as a specialist historically has been permitted."

Cross-References in Rules

None.

Legislative History

1979 Unofficial Pre-Circulation Draft (then Rule 9.3) provided, in pertinent part, as follows:

(a) A lawyer whose practice is limited to specified types of legal matters may communicate that fact except as otherwise provided by regulations governing specialization. A lawyer may indicate that he or she is a specialist only as permitted by paragraphs (b) and (c) and as follows: [Insert applicable provisions on designation of specialization.]

The remainder of the 1979 Draft was substantially the same as adopted.

1980 Discussion Draft was substantially the same as adopted.

1981 and 1982 Drafts were the same as adopted.

1989 Amendments: At its February 1989 Mid-Year Meeting, the ABA House of Delegates substantially amended the Comment (but not the text) to Rule 7.4. The changes were explained in the following report jointly submitted to the House of Delegates by the ABA Standing Committee on Ethics and Professional Responsibility, the ABA Standing Committee on Specialization, and the ABA Section of Taxation.

Reasons for Amendment

. . . The proposed amendment makes no change in the black-letter of Rule 7.4., but deletes from the Comment the prohibition against a lawyer stating that his or her practice is "limited to" or "concentrated in" particular fields. The proposed amendment to the Comment is consistent with Supreme Court decisions that lawyers' truthful advertising about their practices is protected by the First Amendment. Arguably, the present language in the Comment is not consistent with these decisions. . . .

B. Analysis of Rule 7.4

Rule 7.4 prohibits a lawyer from stating or implying that he or she is a "specialist," with certain limited exceptions. The Rule further provides for designation of specialty in accordance with the rules of the particular jurisdiction. Rule 7.4(c). This rule operates only to prohibit factually inaccurate or misleading information, and appears consistent with both the letter and spirit of *In re R.M.J.* and *Zauderer*.

As presently written, however, the Comment to Rule 7.4 *also* prohibits statements that the lawyer's practice is "limited to" or "concentrated in" certain fields, under the theory that these terms also connote formal recognition of the lawyer as a "specialist." This language is called into question in light of the Court's decisions in *R.M.J.* and *Zauderer*. These cases make clear that a state may not prohibit truthful descriptions of a lawyer's practice merely because the terms raise an inference for a reader that the lawyer has some expertise in the designated fields of practice. The use of the words "limited to" or "concentrated in" in denoting areas of practice do not clearly imply *formal* recognition as a "specialist" and simply do not pose sufficient danger of misleading to warrant a proscription of their use.

Policy Considerations

In view of the desirability of promoting accurate communication by lawyers concerning their services and experience, absolute prohibition of the phrases "limited to" and "concentrated in" is unwarranted. These phrases can provide valuable information to a consumer. Unlike the terms "specialist," "practices a specialty" and "specializes in," the phrases "limited to" and "concentrated in" lack the clear implication of formal recognition of a specialist. Therefore, the Comment to Rule 7.4 should not prohibit statements that a lawyer's practice is "limited to" or "concentrated in" a particular field.

1992 Amendments: At its 1992 Annual Meeting, the ABA House of Delegates substantially amended Rule 7.4 and its Comment to conform the rule to the holding of Peel v. Attorney Registration and Disciplinary Commission, 496 U.S. 91 (1990). The amendments are explained in the following committee report, which was jointly submitted by the ABA Standing Committee on Specialization and the ABA Standing Committee on Ethics and Professional Responsibility.

Excerpt from Joint Report Explaining 1992 Amendment to Rule 7.4

Background

For decades, many lawyers have limited their practices to certain fields of the law. The spiraling complexity of the law and the demand of the public for enhanced expertise on the part of the lawyer has resulted in specialization on an increasing scale. As a matter of practical necessity, most lawyers specialize to some degree by limiting the range of matters they handle.

The findings in a recent survey conducted by the ABA Young Lawyers Division confirmed this reality of de facto specialization in the legal profession. The survey revealed that 64% of all lawyers in private practice spend at least 50% of their time in one substantive field of law. Further, this phenomenon is not limited to large firms. Fifty-five percent of sole practitioners responding to the survey were found to spend half or more of their time in just one field.

Lawyer specialization has proliferated largely without formal recognition by the organized bar or state and federal regulators. An ABA committee concluded in 1967 that in spite of the apparent unwillingness of the bar either to control lawyer specialization or to accept its regulation, "the fact of specialization persists and expands and the need to recognize the fact and regulate its existence and growth becomes steadily more apparent."

After several years of study, the ABA concluded in 1969 that it should not promulgate a national plan to regulate voluntary specialization. Instead, the House of Delegates resolved that the determination whether to adopt a national plan should not be made until experimental programs were conducted at the state level and their results observed.

Twelve states have adopted state-sponsored certification programs which certify lawyers as specialists if they are found to possess a certain level of skill and expertise in a given field of law.[5] These programs are managed by agencies and boards which operate under the jurisdiction of the state's bar or highest court.

The various state plans require applicants to meet certain minimum educational and experience qualifications, and recertification is necessary after a certain period of time. All plans allow certified lawyers to advertise the fact that they are certified. The state certification plans are voluntary. In addition, lawyers who are not certified in a particular field may still handle matters in that field, while certified lawyers are free to practice outside their field of certification.

The *Peel* Decision

In 1990 the legal specialization issue was addressed again by the Supreme Court in *Peel v. Attorney Registration and Disciplinary Commission.* . . .

The *Peel* decision invalidated the broad prohibition of ABA Model Rule 7.4 on lawyers' communications about their specialties, holding that states may not categorically ban a truthful communication by a lawyer that he or she is certified as a specialist by a bona fide private certifying organization.

The National Board of Trial Advocacy, whose certification was at issue in the *Peel* case, had certified lawyers as civil and criminal trial specialists for many years. The *Peel* decision has now spurred other private organizations to establish lawyer certification programs. The American Bankruptcy Board of Certification, a nonprofit organization sponsored by the American Bankruptcy Institute, is beginning to certify qualified lawyers as specialists, offering separate certification in business and consumer bankruptcy. The Commercial Law League of America recently announced its lawyer certification program in bankruptcy and creditors' rights law.

Other private groups such as the National Organization of Social Security Claimants Representatives and the National Academy of Elder Law Attorneys are contemplating certification plans. It is conceivable that even law schools, CLE providers and ABA Sections will become certifiers.

To date, Alabama, Connecticut, Georgia and Minnesota have mechanisms to screen private certifiers for approval, and a number of other states currently studying this issue are similarly inclined.[9]

The proposed amendment of Model Rule 7.4 would bring the ABA Model Rules of Professional Conduct into compliance with the *Peel* decision. Although a few states have now amended their rules to comply with *Peel*, most jurisdictions will be looking to the ABA for guidance and leadership on this issue. Amending Model Rule 7.4 as we have proposed will

---

[5]The states which have adopted certification plans to date are Arizona, Arkansas, California, Florida, Louisiana, Minnesota, New Jersey, New Mexico, North Carolina, South Carolina, Texas and Utah. In addition to its certification plan, Florida has also adopted a specialization program that identifies 18 fields of law in which lawyers may designate themselves as specialists. Although the designations must be approved by a regulatory board, less stringent standards apply than to certification.

[9]The Indiana and Wisconsin state bars have recently recommended to their respective state supreme courts plans for approving private certifying organizations. Committees in Illinois and Tennessee have made similar recommendations to their state bars.

help to insure protection of the users of legal services while authorizing legitimate, truthful advertising claims of lawyer specialists.

Selected State Variations

Arkansas provides: "A lawyer who has been recognized as a specialist under the Arkansas Plan of Specialization approved by the Arkansas Supreme Court may communicate the fact during the period he or she is a 'Board Recognized Specialist in [insert field] of law."

California: See Rule 1-400(D)(6) (regarding specialization).

Connecticut provides:

Rule 7.4A Certification as Specialist

(a) Except as provided in Rule 7.4 [which tracks the pre-1992 version of ABA Model Rule 7.4], a lawyer shall not state or imply that he is a specialist in a field of law unless the lawyer is currently certified as a specialist in that field of law by a board or other entity which is approved by the Rules Committee of the Superior Court of this state. Among the criteria to be considered by the Rules Committee in determining upon application whether to approve a board or entity as an agency which may certify lawyers practicing in this state as being specialists shall be the requirement that the board or entity certify specialists on the basis of published standards and procedures which (1) do not discriminate against any lawyer properly qualified for such certification, (2) provide a reasonable basis for the representation that lawyers so certified possess special competence, and (3) require redetermination of the special qualifications of certified specialists after a period of not more than five years.

(b) A lawyer shall not state that he is a certified specialist if the lawyer's certification has terminated, or if the statement is otherwise contrary to the terms of such certification.

(c) Certification as a specialist may not be attributed to a law firm.

(d) Lawyers may be certified as specialists in [25 fields of law described in detail in the remaining subparagraphs of Rule 7.4A].

Delaware Rule 7.5(a) provides, in part:

(2) A lawyer engaged in a full-time practice, who devotes at least 25 percent of his total practice time to each of 1 or more fields of law, may hold out publicly that the lawyer's practice is limited, or primarily limited, to such fields; provided, however, that in holding himself out as conducting a limited practice the lawyer shall expressly state that he is neither certified nor recognized as a specialist in any field of law.

(3) A lawyer conducting a limited practice authorized by Rule 7.5(a)(2) shall:

(a) Retain in a separate, identifiable file a copy of each public announcement or advertisement with respect to the lawyer's practice. . . .

(b) File with the Board on Professional Responsibility [annually] a certificate, which may be in letter form (i) stating that the lawyer has read and is acting in compliance with Rule 7.5 and (ii) specifying the field or fields of law to which his practice is limited, or primarily limited.

(4) A lawyer may publicly list the fields of law in which he is engaged in practice at the time of such publication but without stating or implying that he specializes in, limits his practice to or emphasizes any of the listed fields of law, except as provided above.

(5) A lawyer who is certified as a specialist in a particular field of law or law practice, under rules which may be prescribed in the future by the Delaware Supreme Court, may hold himself out as such, but only in accordance with such rules.

District of Columbia omits Rule 7.4.
Florida provides:

> (b) A lawyer who complies with the Florida Certification Plan as set forth in chapter 6, Rules Regulating The Florida Bar, or who is certified by a national group which has standards for certification substantially the same as those set out in chapter 6, may inform the public and other lawyers of his or her certified areas of legal practice and may state in communications to the public that the lawyer is a "specialist in (area of certification)";
> (c) A lawyer who complies with the Florida Designation Plan as set forth in chapter 6, Rules Regulating The Florida Bar, may inform the public and other lawyers of his or her designated areas of legal practice.

Pursuant to Supreme Court Rule 6-1.2, the Florida Bar has promulgated the following notice to the public:

> Attorneys indicating they are "board certified" have been identified by The Florida Bar as having special knowledge, skills, and proficiency in their areas of practice. "Florida Bar Designated" attorneys have met minimum experience and educational requirements under the Florida Designation Plan. "Florida Bar Members" may list their areas of practice in the Yellow Pages without meeting any specific criteria.

The rules governing Florida's designation and certification plans are detailed and elaborate, taking up 45 double-spaced typed pages and covering special criteria for some 25 separate fields of law practice.

Illinois, whose old rule on specialization (DR 2-105) was struck down in Peel v. Attorney Registration and Disciplinary Commission of Illinois, 496 U.S. 91 (1990), promulgated a new rule six weeks after the *Peel* decision. The new rule requires that any lawyer advertisement using the terms "certified," "specialist," "expert," or similar terms must meet two conditions:

> (1) the reference must be truthful and verifiable and may not be misleading in violation of Rule 7.1;
> (2) the reference must state that the Supreme Court of Illinois does not recognize certifications of specialties in the practice of law and that the certificate, award or recognition is not a requirement to practice law in Illinois.

Iowa prohibits lawyers from advertising "[f]ixed fees or range of fees for specific legal services" except in the following twelve specified areas of law: (1) abstract examinations and title opinions, (2) uncontested divorces "involving no disagreement concerning custody of children, alimony, child support, or property settlement," (3) wills "leaving all property outright to one beneficiary and contingently to one beneficiary or class or beneficiaries," (4) income tax returns for wage earners, (5) uncontested personal bankruptcies, (6) changes of name, (7) simple residential deeds, (8) residential purchase and sale agreements, (9) residential leases, (10) residential mortgages and notes, (11) powers of attorney, and (12) bills of sale. In addition, Iowa prohibits a lawyer from advertising fixed fees for these services "as an indirect means of attracting clients for whom he performs other legal services not related to the specific legal services publicized."

Michigan Rule 7.4 stops after the first sentence.
Minnesota provides:

> (a) A lawyer may communicate the fact that the lawyer does or does not practice in particular fields of law. A lawyer shall not use any false, fraudulent, misleading or deceptive

statement, claim or designation in describing the lawyer's or the lawyer's firm's practice or in indicating its nature or limitations.

(b) Except as provided in this rule, a lawyer shall not state or imply that the lawyer is a specialist in a field of law unless the lawyer is currently certified as a specialist in that field by a board or other entity which is approved by the State Board of Legal Certification. Among the criteria to be considered by the Board in determining upon application whether to approve a board or entity as an agency which may certify lawyers practicing in this state as being specialists shall be the requirement that the board or entity certify specialists on the basis of published standards and procedures which (1) do not discriminate against any lawyer properly qualified for such certification, (2) provide a reasonable basis for the representation that lawyers so certified possess special competency, and (3) require redetermination of the special qualifications of certified specialists after a period of not more than five years.

(c) A lawyer shall not state that the lawyer is a certified specialist if the lawyer's certification has terminated, or if the statement is otherwise contrary to the terms of such certification.

Montana provides:

(c) A lawyer who is a specialist in a certain field of law by experience in the field, by specialized training or education in the field, or by certification by an authoritative professional entity in the field may communicate the fact of his or her specialty where such communication is not false or misleading under Rule 7.1. A lawyer may communicate that his or her practice is limited to or concentrated in a particular field of law, if such communication does not imply an unwarranted expertise in the field so as to be false or misleading under Rule 7.1

New Hampshire provides:

A lawyer who publicly discloses fields of law in which the lawyer or the law firm practices or states that his or her practice is limited to one or more fields of law shall do so by using descriptive language that is accurate, straightforward, truthful and dignified.

New York: See New York Materials for New York's version of DR 2-101.

North Carolina: Rule 2.5 provides that a lawyer may not say that he is a "specialist" unless he is "certified as a specialist by the North Carolina State Bar" or unless he "includes the following disclaimer or language which is substantially similar: REPRESENTATIONS OF SPECIALTY DO NOT INDICATE STATE CERTIFICATION OR EXPERTISE." Other North Carolina court rules set forth an extensive plan for certification by the state that the lawyer is a specialist.

Texas provides that a lawyer who advertises an "area of the law in which the lawyer practices shall . . . :"

If the lawyer has not been awarded a Certificate of Special Competence by the Texas Board of Legal Specialization in the area so advertised, state with the respect to such area, "Not certified by the Texas Board of Legal Specialization," but if the area of law so advertised has not been designated as an area in which a lawyer may be awarded a Certificate of Special Competence by the Texas Board of Legal Specialization, the lawyer may also state, "No designation has been made by the Texas Board of Legal Specialization for a Certificate of Special Competence in this area."

Virginia generally follows the substance of DR 2-104, but expressly allows a lawyer to "state, announce or hold himself out as limiting his practice to a particular area or field of law" as long as the communication is not false, misleading, or deceptive.

Related Materials

ABA Canons: Canons 45 and 46 provided:

45. Specialists

The canons of the American Bar Association apply to all branches of the legal profession; specialists in particular branches are not to be considered as exempt from the application of these principles.

46. Notice to Local Lawyers

A lawyer available to act as an associate of other lawyers in a particular branch of the law or legal service may send to local lawyers only and publish in his local legal journal, a brief and dignified announcement of his availability to serve other lawyers in connection therewith. The announcement should be in a form which does not constitute a statement or representation of special experience or expertness.

ABA Model Plan of Specialization: In 1979, the ABA House of Delegates adopted the Model Plan of Specialization proposed by the ABA Standing Committee on Specialization. The plan is reprinted in the ABA/BNA Lawyers' Manual on Professional Conduct.

Rule 7.5 Firm Names and Letterheads

(a) A lawyer shall not use a firm name, letterhead or other professional designation that violates Rule 7.1. A trade name may be used by a lawyer in private practice if it does not imply a connection with a government agency or with a public or charitable legal services organization and is not otherwise in violation of Rule 7.1.

(b) A law firm with offices in more than one jurisdiction may use the same name in each jurisdiction, but identification of the lawyers in an office of the firm shall indicate the jurisdictional limitations on those not licensed to practice in the jurisdiction where the office is located.

(c) The name of a lawyer holding a public office shall not be used in the name of a law firm, or in communications on its behalf, during any substantial period in which the lawyer is not actively and regularly practicing with the firm.

(d) Lawyers may state or imply that they practice in a partnership or other organization only when that is the fact.

COMMENT

[1] A firm may be designated by the names of all or some of its members, by the names of deceased members where there has been a continuing succession in the firm's identity or by a trade name such as the "ABC Legal Clinic." Although the United States Supreme Court has held that legislation may prohibit

the use of trade names in professional practice, use of such names in law practice is acceptable so long as it is not misleading. If a private firm uses a trade name that includes a geographical name such as "Springfield Legal Clinic," an express disclaimer that it is a public legal aid agency may be required to avoid a misleading implication. It may be observed that any firm name including the name of a deceased partner is, strictly speaking, a trade name. The use of such names to designate law firms has proven a useful means of identification. However, it is misleading to use the name of a lawyer not associated with the firm or a predecessor of the firm.

[2] With regard to paragraph (d), lawyers sharing office facilities, but who are not in fact partners, may not denominate themselves as, for example, "Smith and Jones," for that title suggests partnership in the practice of law.

Model Code Comparison

With regard to paragraph (a), DR 2-102(A) provided that "[a] lawyer . . . shall not use . . . professional cards . . . letterheads, or similar professional notices or devices, [except] if they are in dignified form. . . ." DR 2-102(B) provided that "[a] lawyer in private practice shall not practice under a trade name, a name that is misleading as to the identity of the lawyer or lawyers practicing under such name, or a firm name containing names other than those of one or more of the lawyers in the firm, except that . . . a firm may use as . . . its name the name or names of one or more deceased or retired members of the firm or of a predecessor firm in a continuing line of succession."

With regard to paragraph (b), DR 2-102(D) provided that a partnership "shall not be formed or continued between or among lawyers licensed in different jurisdictions unless all enumerations of the members and associates of the firm on its letterhead and in other permissible listings make clear the jurisdictional limitations on those members and associates of the firm not licensed to practice in all listed jurisdictions; however, the same firm name may be used in each jurisdiction."

With regard to paragraph (c), DR 2-102(B) provided that "[a] lawyer who assumes a judicial, legislative, or public executive or administrative post or office shall not permit his name to remain in the name of a law firm . . . during any significant period in which he is not actively and regularly practicing law as a member of the firm. . . ."

Paragraph (d) is substantially identical to DR 2-102(C).

Cross-References in Rules

None.

Legislative History

1980 Discussion Draft (then Rule 9.5) did not include the clause in subparagraph (b) requiring lawyers to indicate their jurisdictional limitations, and did not contain subparagraph (d).

1981 Draft was generally the same as adopted, except that Rule 7.5(d) provided: "Lawyers shall not hold themselves out as practicing in a law firm unless the association is in fact a firm."

1982 Draft was adopted.

Selected State Variations

Arizona deletes the clause in subparagraph (a) beginning, "if it does not imply a connection . . . ."

California: See Rule 1-400(E), Standards 6-9.

Florida permits a lawyer to practice under a trade name if the name is "not deceptive" and "does not imply that the firm is something other than a private law firm," and permits a lawyer to use the term "legal clinic" or "legal services" in conjunction with the lawyer's own name "if the lawyer's practice is devoted to providing routine legal services for fees that are lower than the prevailing rate in the community for those services." Florida also adds a new subparagraph to its version of Rule 7.5 (see Florida Rule 4-7.7) stating:

> (c) . . . A lawyer who advertises under a trade or fictitious name shall be in violation of this rule unless the same name is the law firm name that appears on the lawyer's letterhead, business cards, office sign, and fee contracts, and appears with the lawyer's signature on pleadings and other legal documents.

Illinois amplifies Rule 7.5(c) as follows:

> (a) A lawyer who assumes a judicial, legislative, or public executive or administrative post or office shall not permit the lawyer's name to remain in the name of a law firm or to be used in professional notices of the firm during any substantial period in which the lawyer is not actively and regularly practicing law as a member of the firm. . . .

Iowa: DR 2-101(F) prohibits a lawyer from using the word "clinic" in any public communication "unless the practice of the lawyer or his firm is limited to routine matters for which the costs of rendering the service can be substantially reduced because of the repetitive nature of the services performed and the use of standardized forms and office procedures."

Missouri deletes the second sentence of Rule 7.5(a), and adds two new subparagraphs providing as follows:

> (b) A lawyer's firm name shall include the name of the lawyer, the name of another lawyer in the firm or the name of a deceased or retired member of the firm in a continuing line of succession.
>
> (c) A lawyer's firm name shall not include the name of any person other than a present member of the firm or a deceased or retired member of the firm in a continuing line of succession.

New Jersey provides:

> (a) A lawyer shall not use a firm name, letterhead or other professional designation that violates RPC 7.1. Except for nonprofit legal aid or public interest law firms, the name under which a lawyer or law firm practices shall contain only the full or last names of one or more of the lawyers in the firm or office or the names of a person or persons who have ceased to be associated with the firm through death or retirement.

(b) A law firm with offices in more than one jurisdiction may use the same name in each jurisdiction. In New Jersey, identification of all lawyers of the firm, in advertisements, on letterheads or anywhere else that the firm name is used, shall indicate the jurisdictional limitations on those not licensed to practice in New Jersey. Where the name of an attorney not licensed to practice in this State is used in a firm name, any advertisement, letterhead or other communication containing the firm name must include the name of at least one licensed New Jersey attorney who is responsible for the firm's New Jersey practice or the local office thereof.

(c) A firm name shall not contain the name of any person not actively associated with the firm as an attorney, other than that of a person or persons who have ceased to be associated with the firm through death or retirement.

(d) Lawyers may state or imply that they practice in a partnership or other organization only when that is the fact.

(e) In any case where a nonprofit legal aid or public interest law firm practices under a trade name as permitted by paragraph (a) above, the name or names of one or more of its principally responsible attorneys, licensed to practice in this State, shall be displayed on all letterheads, signs, advertisements and cards or other places where the trade name is used.

New York: Substantially the same as the ABA Model Code — see Model Code Comparison above.

North Carolina: Rule 2.5 generally follows Model Rule 7.5, but adds that every trade name must be registered with the State Bar, and "upon a determination by the Council that such name is potentially misleading, a remedial disclaimer or an appropriate identification of the firm's composition or connection may be required." Rule 2.5(C) adds that a "law firm maintaining offices only in North Carolina may not list any person not licensed to practice law in North Carolina as affiliated with the firm." Rule 2.5(F) reinforces this prohibition by providing:

> No lawyer may maintain a permanent professional relationship with any lawyer not licensed to practice law in North Carolina unless law offices are maintained in North Carolina and in a state where such other lawyer is licensed and practices and a certificate of registration authorizing said professional relationship is first obtained from the Secretary of the North Carolina State Bar.

Ohio DR 2-102(G) specifically provides rules for use of the term "legal clinic" in a firm name. The Rule envisions that a legal clinic will provide "standardized and multiple legal services."

Virginia combines the language of DR 2-102 and Model Rule 7.5.

Washington provides, in subparagraph (a):

> A trade name may not be used by a lawyer in private practice except that the use of the words "legal clinic" may be used alone or in conjunction with a geographical designation or the name of one or more of the lawyers connected with the practice so long as the name is not otherwise in violation of Rule 7.1 and except if otherwise lawful a firm may use as, or continue to include in, its name the name or names of one or more deceased or retired members of the firm or of a predecessor firm in a continuing line of succession.

Related Materials

ABA Canons: Canon 33 provided:

33. Partnerships — Names

Partnerships among lawyers for the practice of their profession are very common and are not to be condemned. In the formation of partnerships and the use of partnership names care should be taken not to violate any law, custom, or rule of court locally applicable. Where partnerships are formed between lawyers who are not all admitted to practice in the courts of the state, care should be taken to avoid any misleading name or representation which would create a false impression as to the professional position or privileges of the member not locally admitted. In the formation of partnerships for the practice of law, no person should be admitted or held out as a practitioner or member who is not a member of the legal profession duly authorized to practice, and amenable to professional discipline. In the selection and use of a firm name, no false, misleading, assumed or trade name should be used. The continued use of the name of a deceased or former partner, when permissible by local custom, is not unethical, but care should be taken that no imposition or deception is practiced through this use. When a member of the firm, on becoming a judge, is precluded from practicing law, his name should not be continued in the firm name.

ARTICLE 8. MAINTAINING THE INTEGRITY OF THE PROFESSION

Editors' Note.   In the 1980 Discussion Draft, the Article on Maintaining the Integrity of the Profession (then Rules 10.1 through 10.5) began with the following Introduction:

The legal profession is largely self-governing. Although other professions also have been granted powers of self-government, the legal profession is unique in this respect because of the close relationship between the profession and the processes of government and law enforcement. This connection is manifested in the fact that ultimate authority over the legal profession is vested largely in the courts.

Self-government of the legal profession serves important social purposes. One is reduction of the need for governmental interference in private sector activity. To the extent that the legal profession can secure conformity of its members to the obligations of their professional calling, the occasion for government regulation is obviated. Another objective of self-government is the maintenance of the legal profession's independence from government domination. An independent legal profession is an important force in preserving government under law, for abuse of legal authority is more readily challenged by a profession whose members are not dependent on government for the right to practice.

The legal profession's relative autonomy carries with it special responsibilities of self-government. From a substantive viewpoint, the profession is responsible for seeing that its regulations are conceived in the public interest and not in furtherance of parochial or self-interested concerns of the bar. From a procedural viewpoint, every lawyer is responsible for observance of the Rules of Professional Conduct; a lawyer must not only conform his or her conduct to the Rules, but also must aid in securing their observance by other lawyers. This duty involves irksome and sometimes onerous responsibilities. However, neglect of these responsibilities will compromise the independence of the profession and the public interest which it serves.

Rule 8.1 Bar Admission and Disciplinary Matters

An applicant for admission to the bar, or a lawyer in connection with a bar admission application or in connection with a disciplinary matter, shall not:
(a) knowingly make a false statement of material fact; or
(b) fail to disclose a fact necessary to correct a misapprehension known by the person to have arisen in the matter, or knowingly fail to respond to a lawful demand for information from an admissions or disciplinary authority, except that this Rule does not require disclosure of information otherwise protected by Rule 1.6.

COMMENT

[1] The duty imposed by this Rule extends to persons seeking admission to the bar as well as to lawyers. Hence, if a person makes a material false statement in connection with an application for admission, it may be the basis for subsequent disciplinary action if the person is admitted, and in any event may be relevant in a subsequent admission application. The duty imposed by this Rule applies to a lawyer's own admission or discipline as well as that of others. Thus, it is a separate professional offense for a lawyer to knowingly make a misrepresentation or omission in connection with a disciplinary investigation of the lawyer's own conduct. This Rule also requires affirmative clarification of any misunderstanding on the part of the admissions or disciplinary authority of which the person involved becomes aware.

[2] This Rule is subject to the provisions of the Fifth Amendment of the United States Constitution and corresponding provisions of state constitutions. A person relying on such a provision in reponse to a question, however, should do so openly and not use the right of nondisclosure as a justification for failure to comply with this Rule.

[3] A lawyer representing an applicant for admission to the bar, or representing a lawyer who is the subject of a disciplinary inquiry or proceeding, is governed by the rules applicable to the client-lawyer relationship.

Model Code Comparison

DR 1-101(A) provided that a lawyer is "subject to discipline if he has made a materially false statement in, or if he has deliberately failed to disclose a material fact requested in connection with, his application for admission to the bar." DR 1-101(B) provided that a lawyer "shall not further the application for admission to the bar of another person known by him to be unqualified in respect to character, education, or other relevant attribute." With respect to paragraph (b), DR 1-102(A)(5) provided that a lawyer shall not engage in "conduct that is prejudicial to the administration of justice."

None.

Legislative History

1980 Discussion Draft of Rule 8.1 was substantially the same as adopted, except that subparagraph (a) prohibited a lawyer from making "a knowing misrepresentation of fact," and subparagraph (b) did not include the clause beginning "or knowingly fail to respond. . . ."

1981 and 1982 Drafts were substantially the same as adopted.

Selected State Variations

California: See Rule 1-200 (False Statement Regarding Admission to the State Bar).

Illinois: Rule 8.1(b) provides:

> A lawyer shall not further the application for admission to the bar of another person known by the lawyer to be unqualified in respect to character, education, or any other relevant attribute.

New York: Same or substantially the same as the ABA Model Code — see Model Code Comparison above.

Virginia retains the language of DR 1-101(A), but in place of DR 1-101(B) provides that a lawyer "is subject to discipline if he has made a materially false statement in any certification required to be filed as a condition of maintaining or renewing his license to practice law."

Related Materials

ABA Model Rules for Lawyer Disciplinary Enforcement: At its 1989 Annual Meeting, the ABA adopted a revised set of Model Rules for Lawyer Disciplinary Enforcement. These replaced the 1985 version of the Model Rules for Lawyer Disciplinary Enforcement, which had themselves replaced the 1979 Standards for Lawyer Discipline Proceedings.

Model Rules of Professional Conduct for Federal Lawyers: Rule 8.1 also applies to an "applicant for admission to a bar or employment as a lawyer with a Federal Agency, [and] a Federal lawyer seeking the right to practice before a Federal Agency. . . ."

Rule 8.2 Judicial and Legal Officials

(a) A lawyer shall not make a statement that the lawyer knows to be false or with reckless disregard as to its truth or falsity concerning the qualifications or

integrity of a judge, adjudicatory officer or public legal officer, or of a candidate for election or appointment to judicial or legal office.

(b) A lawyer who is a candidate for judicial office shall comply with the applicable provisions of the code of judicial conduct.

COMMENT

[1] Assessments by lawyers are relied on in evaluating the professional or personal fitness of persons being considered for election or appointment to judicial office and to public legal offices, such as attorney general, prosecuting attorney and public defender. Expressing honest and candid opinions on such matters contributes to improving the administration of justice. Conversely, false statements by a lawyer can unfairly undermine public confidence in the administration of justice.

[2] When a lawyer seeks judicial office, the lawyer should be bound by applicable limitations on political activity.

[3] To maintain the fair and independent administration of justice, lawyers are encouraged to continue traditional efforts to defend judges and courts unjustly criticized.

Model Code Comparison

With regard to paragraph (a), DR 8-102(A) provided that a lawyer "shall not knowingly make false statements of fact concerning the qualifications of a candidate for election or appointment to a judicial office." DR 8-102(B) provided that a lawyer "shall not knowingly make false accusations against a judge or other adjudicatory officer."

Paragraph (b) is substantially identical to DR 8-103.

Cross-References in Rules

None.

Legislative History

1980 Discussion Draft (then Rule 10.2): Subparagraph (a) provided: "A lawyer who is a candidate for judicial office shall comply with the applicable provisions of the code of judicial conduct." Subparagraph (b) was the same as adopted.

1981 and 1982 Drafts were substantially the same as adopted.

Selected State Variations

California: See B & P Code §6068(b).
District of Columbia omits Rule 8.2.
Maryland provides:

> (b) A candidate for judicial position should not make or suffer others to make for him, promises of conduct in office which appeal to the cupidity or prejudices of the appointing or electing powers; he should not announce in advance his conclusions of law on disputed issues to secure class support, and he should do nothing while a candidate to create the impression that if chosen, he will administer his office with bias, partiality or improper discrimination.

New York: Same or substantially the same as the ABA Model Code — see Model Code Comparison above.

North Carolina: Rule 8.2 retains the language of DR 8-102, but adds the language of Model Rule 8.2(b).

Virginia omits Rule 8.2.

Related Materials

ABA Canons: Canons 1 and 2 provided:

1. The Duty of the Lawyer to the Courts

It is the duty of the lawyer to maintain towards the Courts a respectful attitude, not for the sake of the temporary incumbent of the judicial office, but for the maintenance of its supreme importance. Judges, not being wholly free to defend themselves, are peculiarly entitled to receive the support of the Bar against unjust criticism and clamor. Whenever there is proper ground for serious complaint of a judicial officer, it is the right and duty of the lawyer to submit his grievances to the proper authorities. In such cases, but not otherwise, such charges should be encouraged and the person making them should be protected.

2. The Selection of Judges

It is the duty of the Bar to endeavor to prevent political considerations from outweighing judicial fitness in the selections of Judges. It should protest earnestly and actively against the appointment or election of those who are unsuitable for the Bench; and it should strive to have elevated thereto only those willing to forego other employments, whether of a business, political or other character, which may embarrass their free and fair consideration of questions before them for decision. The aspiration of lawyers for judicial position should be governed by an impartial estimate of their ability to add honor to the office and not by a desire for the distinction the position may bring to themselves.

Rule 8.3 Reporting Professional Misconduct

(a) A lawyer having knowledge that another lawyer has committed a violation of the rules of professional conduct that raises a substantial question as to

that lawyer's honesty, trustworthiness or fitness as a lawyer in other respects, shall inform the appropriate professional authority.

(b) A lawyer having knowledge that a judge has committed a violation of applicable rules of judicial conduct that raises a substantial question as to the judge's fitness for office shall inform the appropriate authority.

(c) This rule does not require disclosure of information otherwise protected by Rule 1.6 or information gained by a lawyer or judge while serving as a member of an approved lawyers assistance program to the extent that such information would be confidential if it were communicated subject to the attorney-client privilege.

Editors' Note.   At its August 1991 Annual Meeting, the ABA House of Delegates amended Rule 8.3(c) to protect information gained by a lawyer workng with a lawyer assistance program. The ABA also added Comment 5 to explain the amendment. Excerpts from the Committee Report proposing the amendment are set out in the Legislative History section following this Rule.

COMMENT

[1] Self-regulation of the legal profession requires that members of the profession initiate disciplinary investigation when they know of a violation of the Rules of Professional Conduct. Lawyers have a similar obligation with respect to judicial misconduct. An apparently isolated violation may indicate a pattern of misconduct that only a disciplinary investigation can uncover. Reporting a violation is especially important where the vicitm is unlikely to discover the offense.

[2] A report about misconduct is not required where it would involve violation of Rule 1.6. However, a lawyer should encourage a client to consent to disclosure where prosecution would not substantially prejudice the client's interests.

[3] If a lawyer were obliged to report every violation of the Rules, the failure to report any violation would itself be a professional offense. Such a requirement existed in many jurisdictions but proved to be unenforceable. This Rule limits the reporting obligation to those offenses that a self-regulating profession must vigorously endeavor to prevent. A measure of judgment is, therefore, required in complying with the provisions of this Rule. The term "substantial" refers to the seriousness of the possible offense and not the quantum of evidence of which the lawyer is aware. A report should be made to the bar disciplinary agency unless some other agency, such as a peer review agency, is more appropriate in the circumstances. Similar considerations apply to the reporting of judicial misconduct.

[4] The duty to report professional misconduct does not apply to a lawyer retained to represent a lawyer whose professional conduct is in question. Such a situation is governed by the rules applicable to the client-lawyer relationship.

| **Editors' Note.** The next paragraph of the Comment was added by the ABA at its 1991 Annual Meeting. |

[5] Information about a lawyer's or judge's misconduct or fitness may be received by a lawyer in the course of that lawyer's participation in an approved lawyers' or judges' assistance program. In that circumstance, providing for the confidentiality of such information encourages lawyers and judges to seek treatment through such programs. Conversely, without such confidentiality, lawyers and judges may hesitate to seek assistance from these programs, which may then result in additional harm to their professional careers and additional injury to the welfare of clients and the public. The Rule therefore exempts the lawyer from the reporting requirements of paragraphs (a) and (b) with respect to information that would be privileged if the relationship between the impaired lawyer or judge and the recipient of the information were that of a client and a lawyer. On the other hand, a lawyer who receives such information would nevertheless be required to comply with the Rule 8.3 reporting provisions to report misconduct if the impaired lawyer or judge indicates an intent to engage in illegal activity, for example, the conversion of client funds to his or her use.

Model Code Comparison

DR 1-103(A) provided that "[a] lawyer possessing unprivileged knowledge of a violation of [a Disciplinary Rule] shall report such knowledge to . . . authority empowered to investigate or act upon such violation."

Cross-References in Rules

None.

Legislative History

1980 Discussion Draft (then Rule 10.3) provided:

> A lawyer having information indicating that another lawyer has committed a substantial violation of the Rules of Professional Conduct shall report the information to the appropriate disciplinary authority.

1981 Draft was substantially the same as adopted, except that it did not include any equivalent to Rule 8.3(b).

1982 Draft was adopted.

1991 Amendments: At its August 1991 Annual Meeting, the ABA House of Delegates added the clause beginning "or information gained . . ." to Rule 8.3(c). The following excerpts from the Report of the ABA Standing Committee on Ethics and Professional Responsibility explain the rationale and scope of the amendments.

Excerpts from ABA Ethics Committee Report

The serious concerns that have arisen recently as a result of "lawyer impairment" have led to the creation of special programs throughout the nation to assist lawyers and judges who face alcohol or drug addiction or other serious problems which threaten to affect or have already affected the performance of their professional responsibilities. More than forty-four such programs, commonly known as "Lawyer and Judge Assistance Programs" have been established by state courts or state and local bar associations.

. . . The Committee believes that it is in the interest of the legal profession and the public that the ABA Model Rules be amended to provide for the confidentiality of information that is furnished by the impaired lawyer or judge.

Under the amendment to Model Rule 8.3, the protection of information obtained in the circumstances of a lawyer's or judge's participation in an assistance program is similar to the protection ordinarily provided by the attorney-client privilege. Where the attorney-client privilege would not apply because the information relates to the intention to commit a crime, for example where a lawyer indicates the intention to continue to convert client funds to his or her own use, such information may be disclosed to the appropriate authority, permitting the recipient of the information to comply with the obligation imposed upon him or her by paragraphs (a) or (b). In such situations concerns other than the recovery of the impaired lawyer or judge necessarily outweigh the impaired lawyer's or judge's right to confidentiality. . . . Although the Committee recognizes that disclosure of such information by one member of the profession to the detriment of a professional colleague is painful and difficult, it considers such a situation indistinguishable from other situations in which important public policy considerations require disclosure of confidential information. To extend the confidentiality protection to a lawyer's or judge's intention to commit a crime likely to result in significant harm to others, moreover, would lend support to claims that the profession is unable or unwilling to live up to its obligation to regulate itself in the public interest.

Selected State Variations

California: No comparable provision.

Illinois: Rule 8.3(a) requires a lawyer to report knowledge "not otherwise protected as a confidence by these Rules or by law" that a lawyer has committed specified violations. Rule 8.3(c) provides that upon proper request of a tribunal or disciplinary authority, "a lawyer possessing information not otherwise protected as a confidence by these Rules or by law concerning another lawyer or a judge shall fully reveal such information." Rule 8.3(d) provides:

> A lawyer who has been disciplined as a result of a lawyer disciplinary action brought before any body other than the Illinois Attorney Registration and Disciplinary Commission shall report that fact to the Commission.

Kansas adds the following to Rule 8.3(c):

> In addition, a lawyer is not required to disclose information concerning any such violation which is discovered through participation in a Substance Abuse Committee, Service to the Bar Committee, or similar committees sponsored by a state or local bar association, or by participation in a self-help organization such as Alcoholics Anonymous, through which aid is rendered to another lawyer who may be impaired in the practice of law.

Michigan adds the word "significant" before "violation" in Rule 8.3(a) and Rule 8.3(b).

New York: Amendments to the New York Code substantially adopt the language of Rule 8.3(a). See EC 1-4 and DR 1-103.

Ohio DR 1-103(C) extends a privilege if a lawyer obtains knowledge of another lawyer's wrongdoing while working for a Bar Association substance abuse committee.

Virginia: DR 1-103(A) requires reporting of information "indicating that another lawyer has committed a violation of the Disciplinary Rules that raises a substantial question as to that lawyer's fitness to practice law in other respects" *unless* the information is protected by DR 4-101 (Virginia's basic rule on confidentiality). DR 1-103(B) exempts members of the Virginia Bar's Committee on Substance Abuse, or "a trained intervenor" for the Committee, from any reporting duties regarding information obtained in connection with work for the Substance Abuse Committee.

Washington uses the phrase "should promptly inform" instead of "shall inform."

Related Materials

ABA Canons: Canon 29 provided:

29. Upholding the Honor of the Profession

Lawyers should expose without fear or favor before the proper tribunals corrupt or dishonest conduct in the profession, and should accept without hesitation employment against a member of the Bar who has wronged his client. The counsel upon the trial of a cause in which perjury has been committed owe it to the profession and to the public to bring the matter to the knowledge of the prosecuting authorities. The lawyer should aid in guarding the Bar against the admission to the profession of candidates unfit or unqualified because deficient in either moral character or education. He should strive at all times to uphold the honor and to maintain the dignity of the profession and to improve not only the law but the administration of justice.

Rule 8.4 Misconduct

It is professional misconduct for a lawyer to:

(a) violate or attempt to violate the rules of professional conduct, knowingly assist or induce another to do so, or do so through the acts of another;

(b) commit a criminal act that reflects adversely on the lawyer's honesty, trustworthiness or fitness as a lawyer in other respects;

(c) engage in conduct involving dishonesty, fraud, deceit or misrepresentation;

(d) engage in conduct that is prejudicial to the administration of justice;

(e) state or imply an ability to influence improperly a government agency or official; or

(f) knowingly assist a judge or judicial officer in conduct that is a violation of applicable rules of judicial conduct or other law.

COMMENT

[1] Many kinds of illegal conduct reflect adversely on fitness to practice law, such as offenses involving fraud and the offense of willful failure to file an income tax return. However, some kinds of offense carry no such implication. Traditionally, the distinction was drawn in terms of offenses involving "moral turpitude." That concept can be construed to include offenses concerning some matters of personal morality, such as adultery and comparable offenses, that have no specific connection to fitness for the practice of law. Although a lawyer is personally answerable to the entire criminal law, a lawyer should be professionally answerable only for offenses that indicate lack of those characteristics relevant to law practice. Offenses involving violence, dishonesty, or breach of trust, or serious interference with the administration of justice are in that category. A pattern of repeated offenses, even ones of minor significance when considered separately, can indicate indifference to legal obligation.

[2] A lawyer may refuse to comply with an obligation imposed by law upon a good faith belief that no valid obligation exists. The provisions of Rule 1.2(d) concerning a good faith challenge to the validity, scope, meaning or application of the law apply to challenges of legal regulation of the practice of law.

[3] Lawyers holding public office assume legal responsibilities going beyond those of other citizens. A lawyer's abuse of public office can suggest an inability to fulfill the professional role of attorney. The same is true of abuse of positions of private trust such as trustee, executor, administrator, guardian, agent and officer, director or manager of a corporation or other organization.

Model Code Comparison

With regard to paragraphs (a) through (d), DR 1-102(A) provided that a lawyer shall not:

    (1) Violate a Disciplinary Rule.
    (2) Circumvent a Disciplinary Rule through actions of another.
    (3) Engage in illegal conduct involving moral turpitude.
    (4) Engage in conduct involving dishonesty, fraud, deceit, or misrepresentation.
    (5) Engage in conduct that is prejudicial to the administration of justice.
    (6) Engage in any other conduct that adversely reflects on his fitness to practice law.

Paragraph (e) is substantially similar to DR 9-101(C).

There was no direct counterpart to paragraph (f) in the Disciplinary Rules of the Model Code. EC 7-34 stated in part that "[a] lawyer . . . is never justified in making a gift or a loan to a [judicial officer] except as permitted by . . . the Code of Judicial Conduct."

EC 9-1 stated that a lawyer "should promote public confidence in our [legal] system and in the legal profession."

Cross-References in Rules

Rule 3.3, Comment 2: "Regarding compliance with Rule 1.2(d), see the Comment to that Rule. See also the Comment to **Rule 8.4(b).**"

Rule 3.8, Comment 1: "Applicable law may require other measures by the prosecutor and knowing disregard of those obligations or a systematic abuse of prosecutorial discretion could constitute a violation of **Rule 8.4.**"

Rule 5.1, Comment 3: "Paragraph (c)(1) expresses a general principle of responsibility for acts of another. See also **Rule 8.4(a).**"

Rule 5.1, Comment 6: "Apart from this Rule and **Rule 8.4(a),** a lawyer does not have disciplinary liability for the conduct of a partner, associate or subordinate."

Legislative History

1980 Discussion Draft (then Rule 10.4) provided:

It is professional misconduct for a lawyer to:
  (a) violate the Rules of Professional Conduct or knowingly aid another to do so;
  (b) commit a crime or other deliberately wrongful act that reflects adversely on the lawyer's honesty, trustworthiness, or fitness in other respects to practice law;
  (c) state or imply an ability to influence improperly a government agency or official;
  (d) practice law in a jurisdiction in violation of the regulation of the legal profession in that jurisdiction; or
  (e) aid a person who is not a member of the bar in the performance of activity that constitutes the practice of law.

1981 and 1982 Drafts: Subparagraph (b) of both drafts provided that it was misconduct for a lawyer to "commit a criminal *or fraudulent* act that reflects adversely . . . ," and neither draft included subparagraphs (c) and (d) of the rule as adopted. Subparagraphs (e) and (f) of both drafts were moved to Rule 5.5 of the Rules as adopted.

Selected State Variations

California: See B & P Code §§6101-6106.1.
District of Columbia: Rules 8.4(d) and (g) provide:

(d) engage in conduct that seriously interferes with the administration of justice; . . .
(g) seek or threaten to seek criminal charges or disciplinary charges solely to obtain an advantage in a civil matter.

District of Columbia also adds Rule 9.1, which provides:

A lawyer shall not discriminate against any individual in conditions of employment because of the individual's race, color, religion, national origin, sex, age, marital status, sexual orientation, family responsibility or physical handicap.

Florida: In addition to adopting Model Rule 8.4, the Florida Supreme Court has promulgated Rule 3-4.7, which provides:

> Violation of the oath taken by an attorney to support the constitutions of the United States and the State of Florida is ground for disciplinary action. Membership in, alliance with, or support of any organization, group, or party advocating or dedicated to the overthrow of the government by violence or by any means in violation of the Constitution of the United States or constitution of this state shall be a violation of the oath.

Illinois: Rule 8.4(a)(8) provides that a lawyer shall not "avoid in bad faith the repayment of an education loan guaranteed by the Illinois Student Assistance Commission or other governmental entity." Subparagraph (a)(8) does not prohibit a lawyer from discharging a student loan in a bankruptcy proceeding, but does provide that "the discharge shall not preclude a review of the attorney's conduct to determine if it constitutes bad faith." (A parallel Illinois statute, originally passed in 1986 and amended in 1989, provides that the state shall not issue or renew a law license for a person who has defaulted on a student loan, unless the person has established a satisfactory repayment plan and payment record.) Rule 8.4(b) provides:

> (b) A lawyer who holds public office shall not:
> (1) use that office to obtain, or attempt to obtain, a special advantage in a legislative matter for a client under circumstances where the lawyer knows or reasonably should know that such action is not in the public interest;
> (2) use that office to influence, or attempt to influence, a tribunal to act in favor of a client; or
> (3) represent any client, including a municipal corporation or other public body, in the promotion or defeat of legislative or other proposals pending before the public body of which such lawyer is a member or by which such lawyer is employed.

Louisiana adds Rule 8.4(g), which forbids a lawyer "except upon the expressed assertion of a constitutional privilege, to fail to cooperate with the Committee on Professional Responsibility in its investigation of alleged misconduct."

New Mexico adds that it is professional misconduct for a lawyer to:

> (e) willfully violate the Supreme Court Rules on Minimum Continuing Legal Education or the New Mexico Plan of Specialization, or the Board regulations promulgated under the authority of the Rules or the Plan.

New Jersey: New Jersey has adopted Rule 8.4(g), which makes it professional misconduct for a lawyer to "engage, in a professional capacity, in conduct involving discrimination (except employment discrimination unless resulting in a final agency or judicial determination) because of race, color, religion, age, sex, sexual orientation, national origin, marital status, socio-economic status, or handicap, where the conduct is intended or likely to cause harm." The Supreme Court's comment states that the rule

> would, for example, cover activities in the court house, such as a lawyer's treatment of court support staff, as well as conduct more directly related to litigation; activities related to practice outside of the court house, whether or not related to litigation, such as treatment of other attorneys and their staff; bar association and similar activities; and activities in the lawyer's office and firm. Except to the extent that they are closely related to the foregoing, purely private activities are not intended to be covered by this rule amendment, although they may possibly constitute a violation of some other ethical rule. Nor is employment discrimination in hiring, firing, promotion, or partnership status intended to be covered unless it has resulted in either an agency or judicial determination of discriminatory conduct.

New York: Same or substantially the same as the ABA Model Code — see Model Code Comparison above — except see New York Materials for New York's version of DR 7-102(B)(1). See EC 1-7 and DR 1-102(A)(6) of the New York Code for provisions, having no counterpart in the Model Rules, prohibiting lawyers from unlawfully discriminating in the practice of law "including in hiring, promoting or otherwise determining conditions of employment on the basis of age, race, creed, color, national origin, sex, disability or marital status."

Virginia retains the language of DR 1-102(A), but adds that a lawyer shall not violate a Disciplinary Rule "or knowingly aid another to do so," and replaces the phrase "illegal conduct involving moral turpitude" with the phrase "a crime or other deliberately wrongful act." Virginia also retains the language of DR 9-101(C) (which is comparable to Model Rule 8.4(e)).

Related Materials

ABA Canons: Canon 29 provided:

29. *Upholding the Honor of the Profession*

Lawyers should expose without fear or favor before the proper tribunals corrupt or dishonest conduct in the profession, and should accept without hesitation employment against a member of the Bar who has wronged his client. The counsel upon the trial of a cause in which perjury has been committed owe it to the profession and to the public to bring the matter to the knowledge of the prosecuting authorities. The lawyer should aid in guarding the Bar against the admission to the profession of candidates unfit or unqualified because deficient in either moral character or education. He should strive at all times to uphold the honor and to maintain the dignity of the profession and to improve not only the law but the administration of justice.

ABA Standards for Imposing Lawyer Discipline:

5.1. Failure to Maintain Personal Integrity

5.11. *Disbarment is generally appropriate when:*
   (a) a lawyer engages in serious criminal conduct a necessary element of which includes intentional interference with the administration of justice, false swearing, misrepresentation, fraud, extortion, misappropriation, or theft; or the sale, distribution or importation of controlled substances; or the intentional killing of another; or an attempt or conspiracy or solicitation of another to commit any of these offenses; or
   (b) a lawyer engages in any other intentional conduct involving dishonesty, fraud, deceit, or misrepresentation that seriously adversely reflects on the lawyer's fitness to practice.

5.12. *Suspension* is generally appropriate when a lawyer knowingly engages in criminal conduct which does not contain the elements listed in Standard 5.11 and that seriously adversely reflects on the lawyer's fitness to practice.

5.13. *Reprimand* is generally appropriate when a lawyer knowingly engages in any other conduct that involves dishonesty, fraud, deceit, or misrepresentation and that adversely reflects on the lawyer's fitness to practice law.

5.14. *Admonition* is generally appropriate when a lawyer engages in any other conduct that reflects adversely on the lawyer's fitness to practice law.

5.2. Failure to Maintain the Public Trust

5.21. Disbarment is generally appropriate when a lawyer in an official or governmental position knowingly misuses the position with the intent to obtain a significant benefit or advantage for himself or another, or with the intent to cause serious or potentially serious injury to a party or to the integrity of the legal process.

5.22. Suspension is generally appropriate when a lawyer in an official or governmental position knowingly fails to follow proper procedures or rules and causes injury or potential injury to a party or to the integrity of the legal process.

8.0. Prior Discipline Orders

8.1. Disbarment is generally appropriate when a lawyer:

(a) intentionally or knowingly violates the terms of a prior disciplinary order and such violation causes injury or potential injury to a client, the public, the legal system, or the profession; or

(b) has been suspended for the same or similar misconduct, and intentionally or knowingly engages in further acts of misconduct that cause injury or potential injury to a client, the public, the legal system, or the profession.

8.2. Suspension is generally appropriate when a lawyer has been reprimanded for the same or similar misconduct and engages in further acts of misconduct that cause injury or potential injury to a client, the public, the legal system, or the profession.

Federal Rules of Appellate Procedure: Fed. R. App. P. 46(b) and (c) give federal courts of appeals power to suspend or disbar or "take any appropriate disciplinary action against any attorney who practices before it for conduct unbecoming a member of the bar or for failure to comply with these rules or any rule of court."

Limitations on Jurisdiction: A state's willingness to exercise jurisdiction over a lawyer licensed only in other states may depend on whether the alleged misconduct was directly related to the practice of law. Florida, for example, provides in Supreme Court Rule 3-4.1 that "[j]urisdiction over an attorney of another state who is not a member of The Florida Bar shall be limited to conduct as an attorney in relation to the business for which the attorney was permitted to practice in this state. . . ."

Rule 8.5 Jurisdiction

A lawyer admitted to practice in this jurisdiction is subject to the disciplinary authority of this jurisdiction although engaged in practice elsewhere.

COMMENT

[1] In modern practice lawyers frequently act outside the territorial limits of the jurisdiction in which they are licensed to practice, either in another state or outside the United States. In doing so, they remain subject to the governing authority of the jurisdiction in which they are licensed to practice. If their activity in another jurisdiction is substantial and continuous, it may constitute practice of law in that jurisdiction. See Rule 5.5.

[2] If the rules of professional conduct in the two jurisdictions differ, principles of conflict of laws may apply. Similar problems can arise when a lawyer is licensed to practice in more than one jurisdiction.

[3] Where the lawyer is licensed to practice law in two jurisdictions which impose conflicting obligations, applicable rules of choice of law may govern the situation. A related problem arises with respect to practice before a federal tribunal, where the general authority of the states to regulate the practice of law must be reconciled with such authority as federal tribunals may have to regulate practice before them.

Model Code Comparison

There was no counterpart to this Rule in the Model Code.

Cross-References in Rules

None.

Legislative History

1980 Discussion Draft had no comparable provision.
1981 Draft was substantially the same as adopted.
1982 Draft was adopted.

Selected State Variations

California: See B & P Code §§6002.1(a)(4), 6106.
New York: No comparable provision.
North Carolina omits Rule 8.5.
Virginia: DR 1-102(B) tracks Model Rule 8.5, but adds an exception if "Disciplinary Rules of the foreign jurisdiction permit the activity."

Related Materials

Federal Rules of Appellate Procedure: Fed. R. App. P. 46(b) provides:

> When it is shown to the court that any member of its bar has been suspended or disbarred from practice in any other court of record, or has been guilty of conduct unbecoming a member of the bar of the court, the member will be subject to suspension or disbarment by the court.

Model Rules of Professional Conduct for Federal Lawyers: Rule 8.5 provides:

(a) A Federal lawyer shall comply with the rules of professional conduct applicable to the Federal Agency that employs the Government lawyer or the Federal Agency before which the Federal lawyer practices.

(b) If the Federal Agency has not adopted or promulgated rules of professional conduct, the Federal lawyer shall comply with the rules of professional conduct of the state bars in which the Federal lawyer is admitted to practice.

The Comment to this rule states:

While the Federal lawyer may remain subject to the governing authority of their licensing jurisdiction, the Federal lawyer is also subject to these Rules. However, when a Government lawyer is engaged in the conduct of Federal Agency legal functions, whether servicing the Federal Agency as a client or serving an individual client in the course of official duties, these Rules are regarded as superseding any conflicting rules applicable in the jurisdictions in which the Government lawyer may be licensed.

INDEX TO THE MODEL RULES

Editors' Note. The following index was prepared by the ABA. We have revised it to reflect the 1989 amendments that renumbered some sections of Model Rules 1.9 and 1.10, to reflect the addition of Model Rules 1.17 and 3.8(f) in 1990, to reflect the amendment to Model Rule 8.3 and the addition of Model Rule 5.7 in 1991, and to reflect the amendment of Rule 7.4 in 1992. (Rule 5.7 was deleted in 1992, but we continue to reference it in this index.) In addition to this index, cross-reference tables relating the ABA Model Code to the Model Rules are found following each set of Disciplinary Rules and Ethical Considerations in the Model Code in this volume, and a table relating the old ABA Canons of Professional Ethics to the Model Rules will be found at pages 723-725.

Opposing party raises, Rule 1.7 (Comment)
Third person, interest adverse to client,
    Rule 1.7(b)
Unrelated matters, Rule 1.7 (Comment)
Withdrawal because of, Rule 1.7
    (Comment)
Constitutional law,
    Governing authority of government lawyer,
        Scope
Consult,
    Defined, Terminology
Consultation,
    Defined, Terminology
Contingent fee,
    Expert witness, Rule 3.4 (Comment)
    Prohibited representations, Rule 1.5(d)
    Requirements of, Rule 1.5(c)
Continuing legal education,
    Competence, to maintain, Rule 1.1
        (Comment)
Corporate representation, *See* Organization,
    representation of
Corporation,
    Communicating with employees and officers
        of, Rule 4.2 (Comment)
Court,
    Authority over legal profession, Preamble
    Candor, duty of, Rule 3.3
    Offering false evidence to, Rule 3.3(a)(4)
Creditors of client,
    Claim funds of client, Rule 1.15 (Comment)
Criminal conduct,
    Counselling or assisting a client to engage
        in, Rule 1.2(d); Rule 3.3(a)(2)
    Disclosure of client's, Rule 1.2 (Comment)
Criminal representation,
    Aggregate plea bargain on behalf of
        multiple defendants, Rule 1.8(g)
    Co-defendants, representation of, Rule 1.7
        (Comment)
    Contingent fee for, Rule 1.5(d)(2)
    Decisionmaking authority, Rule 1.2(a)
    Frivolous defense, Rule 3.1
    Perjury by client, Rule 3.3 (Comment)

D

Deceased lawyer,
    Payments to estate of, Rule 5.4(a)(2)
Derivative actions, Rule 1.13 (Comment)
Dilatory practices,
    Prohibited, Rule 3.2 (Comment)
Diligence,
    Duty of, Preamble, Rule 1.3
Disciplinary proceedings,
    Disclosure of client confidences in
        connection with, Rule 1.6
        (Comment)

Failure to comply with requests for
    information, Rule 8.1(b)
Jurisdiction, Rule 8.5
Reporting professional misconduct, Rule
    8.3
Discipline,
    Violation of Rules as basis for,
        Scope
Discovery,
    Obstructive tactics, Rule 3.4(d)
    Refusing to comply, Rule 3.4(d)
Discretion of lawyer,
    Where Rule cast in "may," Scope
Disqualification,
    Former judge, Rule 1.12(a)
    Imputed, *see* Imputed disqualification
    Vicarious, *see* Imputed disqualification
    Waiver by client, Rule 1.9 (Comment);
        Rule 1.10(c)
Division of fees,
    Requirements of, Rule 1.5(e)
    With nonlawyer, Rule 5.4(a)
Domestic relations matters,
    Contingent fee in, Rule 1.5(d)(1)

E

Employees of lawyer,
    Responsibility for, Rule 5.3
Estate planning,
    Conflicts of interest in, Rule 1.7
        (Comment)
Evaluation,
    Confidential information used in preparing,
        Rule 2.3(b)
    Third person, prepared at client's request
        for, Rule 2.3
Evaluator,
    Lawyer as, Preamble
Evidence,
    Destruction of, Rule 3.4(a)
    Obstructing opposing party's access to,
        Rule 3.4(a)
    Offering false, Rule 3.3(a)(4)
Ex parte proceedings, Rule 3.3(d)
Expediting litigation, Rule 3.2
Expenses of litigation,
    Client's right to determine, Rule 1.2
        (Comment)
    Indigent client, paying on behalf of, Rule
        1.8(e)(2)
    Lawyer advancing to client, Rule
        1.8(e)(1)
Expert witness, *See* Witness
Expertise,
    As relating to competent representation,
        Rule 1.1

313

F

Fairness to opposing party and counsel, Rule 3.4
False statement,
  Made to tribunal, Rule 3.3(a)(1)
Fees,
  Acquiring ownership interest in enterprise as, Rule 1.5 (Comment)
  Advance fee payments, Rule 1.5 (Comment)
  Advertising of, Rule 7.2 (Comment)
  Arbitration of, Rule 1.5 (Comment)
  Communication of to client, Rule 1.5(b)
  Contingent fee,
    Prohibited representations, Rule 1.5(d)
    Requirements of, Rule 1.5(c)
  Determination of, Rule 1.5(a)
  Disclosure of confidential information to collect, Rule 1.6(b)(2)
  Division of, Rule 1.5(e)
  Paid by one other than client, Rule 1.7 (Comment); Rule 1.8(f); Rule 5.4(c)
Firm,
  Defined, Terminology
  Disqualification, Rule 1.9 (Comment)
Firm name, Rule 7.5(a)
Former client, *see* Conflict of interest
Former government lawyer,
  "Confidential government information" defined, Rule 1.11(e)
  "Matter" defined, Rule 1.11(d)
  Successive government and private employment, Rule 1.11
Former judge, *see* Judges.
Fraud,
  Defined, Terminology
Fraudulent,
  Defined, Terminology
Fraudulent conduct,
  Counseling or assisting client to engage in, Rule 1.2(d)
  Disclosure of client's, Rule 1.2 (Comment)
Frivolous claims and defenses, Rule 3.1
Funds of client,
  Handling of, Rule 1.15(b)
  Lawyer claims interest in, Rule 1.15(c)

G

Gift,
  To lawyer by client, Rule 1.8(c)
Government agency,
  Representation of, Rule 1.13 (Comment)
Government lawyer,
  Authority established by constitution, statutes and common law, Scope

Conflict of interest, Rule 1.7 (Comment)
Duty of confidentiality, Rule 1.6 (Comment)
Representing multiple clients, Scope
Subject to rules, Rule 1.11 (Comment)

H

Harass,
  Law's procedures used to, Preamble

I

Impartiality and decorum of the tribunal, Rule 3.5
Imputed disqualification,
  General rule, Rule 1.10
  Government lawyers, Rule 1.11 (Comment)
  Witness, when member of firm serves as, Rule 3.7(b)
Incompetent client,
  Appointment of guardian for, Rule 1.14(b)
  Representation of, Rule 1.14(a)
Independence of the legal profession, Preamble
Independent professional judgment,
  Duty to exercise, Rule 2.1; Rule 5.4
Indigent client,
  Paying court costs and expenses on behalf of, Rule 1.8(e)(2)
Insurance representation,
  Conflict of interest, Rule 1.7 (Comment)
Intermediary,
  Between clients, Rule 2.2
  Lawyer as, Preamble
  Withdrawal as, Rule 2.2(c)
Intimidate,
  Law's procedures used to, Preamble

J

Judges,
  Duty to show respect for, Preamble
  Ex parte communication with, Rule 3.5(b)
  Former judge, disqualification, Rule 1.12
  Improper influence on, Rule 3.5(a)
  Lawyers assistance program, confidentiality, Rule 8.3(c)
  Misconduct by, Rule 8.3(b)
  Statements about, Rule 8.2
Juror,
  Improper influence on, Rule 3.5(a)
Jury trial,
  Client's right to waive, Rule 1.2(a)

L

Law clerk,
Negotiating for private employment, Rule 1.12(b)
Law firm,
Defined, Terminology
Nonlawyer assistants, responsibility for, Rule 5.3
Responsibility of partner or supervisory lawyer, Rule 5.1
Subordinate lawyer, responsibility of, Rule 5.2
Law practice, sale of, Rule 1.17
Law reform activities,
Affecting clients' interests, Rule 6.4
Lawyer referral service, Rule 6.1 (Comment)
Cost of, Rule 7.2(c)
Lawyers assistance program, confidentiality, Rule 8.3(c)
Legal education,
Duty to work to strengthen, Preamble
Legislature,
Appearance before on behalf of client, Rule 3.8
Letterheads,
False or misleading, Rule 7.5(a)
Jurisdictional limitations of members, Rule 7.5(b)
Public officials, Rule 7.5(c)
Liability to client,
Agreements limiting, Rule 1.8(h)
Lien,
To secure fees and expenses, Rule 1.8(j) (1)
Literary rights,
Acquiring concerning representation, Rule 1.8(d)
Litigation,
Expedite, duty to, Rule 3.2
Loyalty,
Duty of to client, Rule 1.7 (Comment)

M

Malpractice,
Limiting liability to client for, Rule 1.8(h)
Meritorious claims and contentions, Rule 3.1
Military lawyers,
Adverse interests, representation of, Rule 1.9 (Comment)
Misconduct,
Forms of, Rule 8.4
Misleading legal argument, Rule 3.3 (Comment)
Misrepresentation,
In advertisements, Rule 7.1
To court, Rule 3.3 (Comment)
Multiple representation, *see* Conflict of interest; Intermediary

N

Negotiation,
Conflicting interest, representation of, Rule 1.7 (Comment)
Statements made during, Rule 4.1 (Comment)
Negotiator,
Lawyer as, Preamble
Nonlawyers,
Division of fees with, Rule 5.4(a)
Partnership with, Rule 5.4(b)
Non-legal services,
Provision of, Rule 5.7

O

Objectives of the representation,
Client's right to determine, Rule 1.2(a)
Lawyer's right to limit, Rule 1.2(c)
Opposing party,
Communications with represented party, Rule 4.2
Duty of fairness to, Rule 3.4
Organization, representation of,
Board of directors, lawyer for serving on, Rule 1.7 (Comment)
Communication with, Rule 1.4 (Comment)
Conflict of interest, Rule 1.7 (Comment)
Conflicting interests among officers and employees, Rule 1.7 (Comment)
Constituents, representing, Rule 1.13(e)
Identity of client, Rule 1.13(a); Rule 1.13(d)
Misconduct, client engaged in, Rule 1.13(b)

P

Partner,
Defined, Terminology
Patent practice,
Advertising, Rule 7.4(a)
Perjury,
Criminal defendant, Rule 3.3 (Comment)
Disclosure of, Rule 3.3(b)
Personal affairs of lawyer,
Duty to conduct in compliance with law, Preamble
Plea bargain,
Client's right to accept or reject, Rule 1.2(a)
Pleadings,
Verification of, Rule 3.3 (Comment)
Precedent,
Failure to disclose to court, Rule 3.3(a)(3)
Prepaid legal services,
Advertising for, Rule 7.2 (Comment)
Pro bono publico service, Rule 6.1

ABA Model Code of
Professional Responsibility*
In effect as of August 1983

Editors' Introduction. From 1908 to 1969, the ABA's formal position on matters of legal ethics was embodied in the ABA's Canons of Professional Ethics. In 1964, however, amidst growing dissatisfaction with the Canons, the ABA appointed a Special Committee on the Evaluation of Ethical Standards (the "Wright Committee") to study the Canons. The Wright Committee drafted a proposed Code of Professional Responsibility, which was ultimately approved by the ABA House of Delegates in August of 1969. By 1980, nearly every state had adopted a Code of Professional Responsibility modeled on the ABA Code. Since 1983, however, more than 35 states have revised their ethical rules to conform, in some degree, to the Model Rules of Professional Conduct. Today, fewer than 15 states retain the Model Code, and many of these are currently considering adoption of the Model Rules. Many of the Model Rules, however, closely parallel their counterparts in the Code.

Our version of the Code differs slightly from the versions found in most other supplements. First, after each set of Ethical Considerations, and after each set of Disciplinary Rules, we have included a table relating Code provisions to the comparable provisions in the Model Rules. Second, we have eliminated or edited many of the footnotes, whose primary purpose was to relate the Code to the Canons of Professional Ethics. We have indicated all deletions of substantive matter from the footnotes (but not the deletion of mere citations) by using ellipses.

The Canons themselves are reprinted in the Related Materials section following each Model Rule. Anyone wishing to read a Canon relating to a particular Code provision should simply go to the comparable Model Rule (indicated by our cross-reference table) and look at the Related Materials, which will include the Canon counterpart.

The Code was amended a number of times during the 1970s, principally in response to Supreme Court opinions concerning advertising and group legal services. The version of the Code reprinted here is the version that was in effect at the time the ABA adopted the Model Rules in August 1983. The ABA has not amended the Model Code since the adoption of the Model Rules and does not intend to amend the Code in the future.

Contents

ABA Model Code of Professional Responsibility

PREAMBLE[1]

The continued existence of a free and democratic society depends upon recognition of the concept that justice is based upon the rule of law grounded in respect for the dignity of the individual and his capacity through reason for enlightened self-government. Law so grounded makes justice possible, for only through such law does the dignity of the individual attain respect and protection. Without it, individual rights become subject to unrestrained power, respect for law is destroyed, and rational self-government is impossible.

Lawyers, as guardians of the law, play a vital role in the preservation of society. The fulfillment of this role requires an understanding by lawyers of their

1. The footnotes are intended merely to enable the reader to relate the provisions of this Model Code to the ABA Canons of Professional Ethics adopted in 1908, as amended, the Opinions of the ABA Committee on Professional Ethics, and a limited number of other sources; they are not intended to be an annotation of the views taken by the ABA Special Committee on Evaluation of Ethical Standards. . . .

relationship with and function in our legal system. A consequent obligation of lawyers is to maintain the highest standards of ethical conduct.

In fulfilling his professional responsibilities, a lawyer necessarily assumes various roles that require the performance of many difficult tasks. Not every situation which he may encounter can be foreseen, but fundamental ethical principles are always present to guide him. Within the framework of these principles, a lawyer must with courage and foresight be able and ready to shape the body of the law to the ever-changing relationships of society.[5]

The Model Code of Professional Responsibility points the way to the aspiring and provides standards by which to judge the transgressor. Each lawyer must find within his own conscience the touchstone against which to test the extent to which his actions should rise above minimum standards. But in the last analysis it is the desire for the respect and confidence of the members of his profession and of the society which he serves that should provide to a lawyer the incentive for the highest possible degree of ethical conduct. The possible loss of that respect and confidence is the ultimate sanction. So long as its practitioners are guided by these principles, the law will continue to be a noble profession. This is its greatness and its strength, which permit of no compromise.

PRELIMINARY STATEMENT

In furtherance of the principles stated in the Preamble, the American Bar Association has promulgated this Model Code of Professional Responsibility, consisting of three separate but interrelated parts: Canons, Ethical Considerations, and Disciplinary Rules. The Model Code is designed to be adopted by appropriate agencies both as an inspirational guide to the members of the profession and as a basis for disciplinary action when the conduct of a lawyer falls below the required minimum standards stated in the Disciplinary Rules.

Obviously the Canons, Ethical Considerations, and Disciplinary Rules cannot apply to non-lawyers; however, they do define the type of ethical conduct that the public has a right to expect not only of lawyers but also of their non-professional employees and associates in all matters pertaining to professional employment. A lawyer should ultimately be responsible for the conduct of his employees and associates in the course of the professional representation of the client.

5. "The law and its institutions change as social conditions change. They must change if they are to preserve, much less advance, the political and social values from which they derive their purposes and their life. This is true of the most important of legal institutions, the profession of law. The profession, too, must change when conditions change in order to preserve and advance the social values that are its reasons for being." Cheatham, Availability of Legal Services: The Responsibility of the Individual Lawyer and the Organized Bar, 12 U.C.L.A. L. Rev. 438, 440 (1965).

The Canons are statements of axiomatic norms, expressing in general terms the standards of professional conduct expected of lawyers in their relationships with the public, with the legal system, and with the legal profession. They embody the general concepts from which the Ethical Considerations and the Disciplinary Rules are derived.

The Ethical Considerations are aspirational in character and represent the objectives toward which every member of the profession should strive. They constitute a body of principles upon which the lawyer can rely for guidance in many specific situations.

The Disciplinary Rules, unlike the Ethical Considerations, are mandatory in character. The Disciplinary Rules state the minimum level of conduct below which no lawyer can fall without being subject to disciplinary action. Within the framework of fair trial,[8] the Disciplinary Rules should be uniformly applied to all lawyers,[9] regardless of the nature of their professional activities.[10] The Model Code makes no attempt to prescribe either disciplinary procedures or penalties[11] for violation of a Disciplinary Rule,[12] nor does it undertake to define standards for civil liability of lawyers for professional conduct. The severity of judgment against one found guilty of violating a Disciplinary Rule should be determined by the character of the offense and the attendant circumstances.[13] An enforcing agency, in applying the Disciplinary Rules, may find interpretive guidance in the basic principles embodied in the Canons and in the objectives reflected in the Ethical Considerations.

8. "Disbarment, designed to protect the public, is a punishment or penalty imposed on the lawyer.... He is accordingly entitled to procedural due process, which includes fair notice of the charge." In re Ruffalo, 390 U.S. 544, 550, rehearing denied, 391 U.S. 961 (1968).

"A State cannot exclude a person from the practice of law or from any other occupation in a manner or for reasons that contravene the Due Process or Equal Protection Clause of the Fourteenth Amendment.... A State can require high standards of qualification ... but any qualification must have a rational connection with the applicant's fitness or capacity to practice law." Schware v. Bd. of Bar Examiners, 353 U.S. 232, 239 (1957)....

9. "The canons of professional ethics must be enforced by the Courts and must be respected by members of the Bar if we are to maintain public confidence in the integrity and impartiality of the administration of justice." In re Meeker, 76 N. M. 354, 357, 414 P.2d 862, 864 (1966), appeal dismissed, 385 U.S. 449 (1967).

10. "The Canons of this Association govern all its members, irrespective of the nature of their practice, and the application of the Canons is not affected by statutes or regulations governing certain activities of lawyers which may prescribe less stringent standards." ABA Opinion 203 (1940).

11.... "There is generally no prescribed discipline for any particular type of improper conduct. The disciplinary measures taken are discretionary with the courts, which may disbar, suspend, or merely censure the attorney as the nature of the offense and past indicia of character may warrant." Note, 43 Cornell L.Q. 489, 495 (1958).

12. The Model Code seeks only to specify conduct for which a lawyer should be disciplined by courts and governmental agencies which have adopted it. Recommendations as to the procedures to be used in disciplinary actions are within the jurisdiction of the American Bar Association Standing Committee on Professional Discipline.

13. "The severity of the judgment of this court should be in proportion to the gravity of the offenses, the moral turpitude involved, and the extent that the defendant's acts and conduct affect his professional qualifications to practice law." Louisiana State Bar Assn. v. Steiner, 204 La. 1073, 1092-93, 16 So. 2d 843, 850 (1944) (Higgins, J., concurring in decree)....

CANON 1. A LAWYER SHOULD ASSIST IN MAINTAINING THE INTEGRITY AND COMPETENCE OF THE LEGAL PROFESSION

Ethical Considerations

EC 1-1 A basic tenet of the professional responsibility of lawyers is that every person in our society should have ready access to the independent professional services of a lawyer of integrity and competence. Maintaining the integrity and improving the competence of the bar to meet the highest standards is the ethical responsibility of every lawyer.

EC 1-2 The public should be protected from those who are not qualified to be lawyers by reason of a deficiency in education or moral standards[2] or of other relevant factors[3] but who nevertheless seek to practice law. To assure the maintenance of high moral and educational standards of the legal profession, lawyers should affirmatively assist courts and other appropriate bodies in promulgating, enforcing, and improving requirements for admission to the bar.[4] In like manner, the bar has a positive obligation to aid in the continued improvement of all phases of pre-admission and post-admission legal education.

EC 1-3 Before recommending an applicant for admission, a lawyer should satisfy himself that the applicant is of good moral character. Although a lawyer should not become a self-appointed investigator or judge of applicants for admission, he should report to proper officials all unfavorable information he possesses relating to the character or other qualifications of an applicant.

EC 1-4 The integrity of the profession can be maintained only if conduct of lawyers in violation of the Disciplinary Rules is brought to the attention of the proper officials. A lawyer should reveal voluntarily to those officials all unprivileged knowledge of conduct of lawyers which he believes clearly to be in

2. "Every state in the United States, as a prerequisite for admission to the practice of law, requires that applicants possess 'good moral character.' Although the requirement is of judicial origin, it is now embodied in legislation in most states." Comment, Procedural Due Process and Character Hearings for Bar Applicants, 15 Stan. L. Rev. 500 (1963). . . .

3. "Proceedings to gain admission to the bar are for the purpose of protecting the public and the courts from the ministrations of persons unfit to practice the profession. Attorneys are officers of the court appointed to assist the court in the administration of justice. Into their hands are committed the property, the liberty and sometimes the lives of their clients. This commitment demands a high degree of intelligence, knowledge of the law, respect for its function in society, sound and faithful judgment and, above all else, integrity of character in private and professional conduct." In re Monaghan 126 Vt. 53, 222 A.2d 665, 676 (1966) (Holden, C.J., dissenting).

4. "A bar composed of lawyers of good moral character is a worthy objective but it is unnecessary to sacrifice vital freedoms in order to obtain that goal. It is also important both to society and the bar itself that lawyers be unintimidated — free to think, speak, and act as members of an Independent Bar." Konigsberg v. State Bar, 353 U.S. 252, 273 (1957).

violation of the Disciplinary Rules. A lawyer should, upon request serve on and assist committees and boards having responsibility for the administration of the Disciplinary Rules.

EC 1-5   A lawyer should maintain high standards of professional conduct and should encourage fellow lawyers to do likewise. He should be temperate and dignified, and he should refrain from all illegal and morally reprehensible conduct. Because of his position in society, even minor violations of law by a lawyer may tend to lessen public confidence in the legal profession. Obedience to law exemplifies respect for law. To lawyers especially, respect for the law should be more than a platitude.

EC 1-6   An applicant for admission to the bar or a lawyer may be unqualified, temporarily or permanently, for other than moral and educational reasons, such as mental or emotional instability. Lawyers should be diligent in taking steps to see that during a period of disqualification such person is not granted a license or, if licensed, is not permitted to practice. In like manner, when the disqualification has terminated, members of the bar should assist such person in being licensed, or, if licensed, in being restored to his full right to practice.

	Model Code	*ABA Model Rules*
Model Rules Comparison	EC 1-1	Rules 1.1, 6.1, 8.1(a)
	EC 1-2	Rules 1.1, 6.1, 8.1(a)
	EC 1-3	Rules 8.1(a), 8.3
	EC 1-4	Rules 6.1, 8.3
	EC 1-5	Rule 8.4
	EC 1-6	Rules 1.16(a)(2), 8.4(a)

Disciplinary Rules

**DR 1-101 Maintaining Integrity and Competence of
        the Legal Profession**

(A) A lawyer is subject to discipline if he has made a materially false statement in, or if he has deliberately failed to disclose a material fact requested in connection with, his application for admission to the bar.[10]

10. "This Court has the inherent power to revoke a license to practice law in this State, where such license was issued by this Court, and its issuance was procured by the fraudulent concealment, or by the false and fraudulent representation by the applicant of a fact which was manifestly material to the issuance of the license." North Carolina ex rel. Attorney General v. Gorson, 209 N.C. 320, 326, 183 S.E. 392, 395 (1936), cert. denied, 298 U.S. 662 (1936).

(B) A lawyer shall not further the application for admission to the bar of another person known by him to be unqualified in respect to character, education, or other relevant attribute.

DR 1-102 Misconduct

(A) A lawyer shall not:

(1) Violate a Disciplinary Rule.

(2) Circumvent a Disciplinary Rule through actions of another.[12]

(3) Engage in illegal conduct involving moral turpitude.[13]

(4) Engage in conduct involving dishonesty, fraud, deceit, or misrepresentation.

(5) Engage in conduct that is prejudicial to the administration of justice.

(6) Engage in any other conduct that adversely reflects on his fitness to practice law.[14]

---

12. In ABA Opinion 95 (1933), which held that a municipal attorney could not permit police officers to interview persons with claims against the municipality when the attorney knew the claimants to be represented by counsel, the Committee on Professional Ethics said:

"The law officer is, of course, responsible for the acts of those in his department who are under his supervision and control. Opinion 85. In re Robinson, 136 N.Y.S. 548 (affirmed 209 N. Y. 354-1912) held that it was a matter of disbarment for an attorney to adopt a general course of approving the unethical conduct of employees of his client, even though he did not actively participate therein.

" '. . . The attorney should not advise or sanction acts by his client which he himself should not do.' Opinion 75."

13. "The most obvious non-professional ground for disbarment is conviction for a felony. Most states make conviction for a felony grounds for automatic disbarment. Some of these states, including New York, make disbarment mandatory upon conviction for *any* felony while others require disbarment only for those felonies which involve moral turpitude. There are strong arguments that some felonies, such as involuntary manslaughter, reflect neither on an attorney's fitness, trustworthiness, nor competence and, therefore, should not be grounds for disbarment, but most states tend to disregard these arguments and, following the common law rule, make disbarment mandatory on conviction for any felony." Note, 43 Cornell L.Q. 489, 490 (1958).

"Some states treat conviction for misdemeanors as grounds for automatic disbarment. . . . However, the vast majority, accepting the common law rule, require that the misdemeanor involve moral turpitude. While the definition of moral turpitude may prove difficult, it seems only proper that those minor offenses which do not affect the attorney's fitness to continue in the profession should not be grounds for disbarment. A good example is an assault and battery conviction which would not involve moral turpitude unless done with malice and deliberation." Id. at 491.

". . . Perhaps the best general definition of the term 'moral turpitude' is that it imparts an act of baseness, vileness or depravity in the duties which one person owes to another or to society in general, which is contrary to the usual, accepted and customary rule of right and duty which a person should follow. Although offenses against revenue laws have been held to be crimes of moral turpitude, it has also been held that the attempt to evade the payment of taxes due to the government or any subdivision thereof, while wrong and unlawful, does not involve moral turpitude." Comm. on Legal Ethics v. Scheer, 149 W. Va. 721, 726-27, 143 S.E.2d 141, 145 (1965).

"The right and power to discipline an attorney, as one of its officers, is inherent in the court. . . . This power is not limited to those instances of misconduct wherein he has been employed, or has acted, in a professional capacity; but, on the contrary, this power may be exercised where his misconduct outside the scope of his professional relations shows him to be an unfit person to practice law." In re Wilson, 391 S.W.2d 914, 917-18 (Mo. 1965).

14. "It is a fair characterization of the lawyer's responsibility in our society that he stands 'as a shield,' to quote Devlin, J., in defense of right and to ward off wrong. From a profession charged with

DR 1-103 Disclosure of Information to Authorities

(A) A lawyer possessing unprivileged knowledge of a violation of DR 1-102 shall report such knowledge to a tribunal or other authority empowered to investigate or act upon such violation.

(B) A lawyer possessing unprivileged knowledge or evidence concerning another lawyer or a judge shall reveal fully such knowledge or evidence upon proper request of a tribunal or other authority empowered to investigate or act upon the conduct of lawyers or judges.

	Model Code	*ABA Model Rules*
Model Rules Comparison	DR 1-101	Rule 8.1(a)
	DR 1-102(A)(1)	Rule 8.4(a)
	DR 1-102(A)(2)	Rules 5.1(c), 5.3(b), 8.4(a)
	DR 1-102(A)(3)	Rule 8.4(b), (f)
	DR 1-102(A)(4)	Rules 3.3(a)(1), (2), & (4), 3.4(a), (b), 4.1, 8.4(c), (f)
	DR 1-102(A)(5)	Rules 3.1 through 3.9, Rules 8.1, 8.4(d) & (f)
	DR 1-102(A)(6)	Rules 3.4(b), 8.4(b), (f)
	DR 1-103(A)	Rules 5.1, 8.3
	DR 1-103(B)	Rule 8.1(b)

CANON 2. A LAWYER SHOULD ASSIST THE LEGAL PROFESSION IN FULFILLING ITS DUTY TO MAKE LEGAL COUNSEL AVAILABLE

Ethical Considerations

EC 2-1   The need of members of the public for legal services is met only if they recognize their legal problems, appreciate the importance of seeking assistance, and are able to obtain the services of acceptable legal counsel.[3] Hence,

---

these responsibilities there must be exacted those qualities of truthspeaking, of a high sense of honor, of granite discretion, of the strictest observance of fiduciary responsibility, that have, throughout the centuries, been compendiously described as 'moral character.' " Schware v. Bd. of Bar Examiners, 353 U.S. 232 (1957) (Frankfurter, J., concurring). . . .

3. "This need [to provide legal services] was recognized by . . . Mr. [Lewis F.] Powell [Jr., President, American Bar Association, 1963-64], who said: 'Looking at contemporary America realistically, we must admit that despite all our efforts to date (and these have not been insignificant), far too many persons are not able to obtain equal justice under law. This usually results because their

important functions of the legal profession are to educate laymen to recognize their problems, to facilitate the process of intelligent selection of lawyers, and to assist in making legal services fully available.[4]

Recognition of Legal Problems

EC 2-2 The legal profession should assist laypersons to recognize legal problems because such problems may not be self-revealing and often are not timely noticed. Therefore, lawyers should encourage and participate in educational and public relations programs concerning our legal system with particular reference to legal problems that frequently arise. Preparation of advertisements and professional articles for lay publications[5] and participation in seminars, lectures, and civic programs should be motivated by a desire to educate the public to an awareness of legal needs and to provide information relevant to the selection of the most appropriate counsel rather than to obtain publicity for particular lawyers. The problems of advertising on television require special consideration, due to the style, cost, and transitory nature of such media. If the interests of laypersons in receiving relevant lawyer advertising are not adequately served by print media and radio advertising, and if adequate safeguards to protect the public can reasonably be formulated, television advertising may serve a public interest.

EC 2-3 Whether a lawyer acts properly in volunteering in-person advice to a layperson to seek legal services depends upon the circumstances. The giving of advice that one should take legal action could well be in fulfillment of the duty of the legal profession to assist laypersons in recognizing legal problems.[7] The

---

poverty or their ignorance has prevented them from obtaining legal counsel.' " Address by E. Clinton Bamberger, Association of American Law Schools 1965 Annual Meeting, Dec. 28, 1965, in Proceedings, Part II, 1965, 61, 63-64 (1965).

"A wide gap separates the need for legal services and its satisfaction, as numerous studies reveal. Looked at from the side of the layman, one reason for the gap is poverty and the consequent inability to pay legal fees. Another set of reasons is ignorance of the need for and the value of legal services, and ignorance of where to find a dependable lawyer. There is fear of the mysterious processes and delays of the law, and there is fear of overreaching and overcharging by lawyers, a fear stimulated by the occasional exposure of shysters." Cheatham, Availability of Legal Services: The Responsibility of the Individual Lawyer and of the Organized Bar, 12 U.C.L.A. L. Rev. 438 (1965).

4. "It is not only the right but the duty of the profession as a whole to utilize such methods as may be developed to bring the services of its members to those who need them, so long as this can be done ethically and with dignity." ABA Opinion 320 (1968). . . .

"The obligation to provide legal services for those actually caught up in litigation carries with it the obligation to make preventive legal advice accessible to all. It is among those unaccustomed to business affairs and fearful of the ways of the law that such advice is often most needed. If it is not received in time, the most valiant and skillful representation in court may come too late." Professional Responsibility: Report of the Joint Conference, 44 A.B.A.J. 1159, 1216 (1958).

5. "A lawyer may with propriety write articles for publications in which he gives information upon the law. . . ." ABA Canon 40.

7. This question can assume constitutional dimensions: "We meet at the outset the contention that 'solicitation' is wholly outside the area of freedoms protected by the First Amendment. To this

advice is proper only if motivated by a desire to protect one who does not recognize that he may have legal problems or who is ignorant of his legal rights or obligations. It is improper if motivated by a desire to obtain personal benefit, secure personal publicity, or cause legal action to be taken merely to harass or injure another. A lawyer should not initiate an in-person contact with a nonclient, personally or through a representative, for the purpose of being retained to represent him for compensation.

EC 2-4   Since motivation is subjective and often difficult to judge, the motives of a lawyer who volunteers in-person advice likely to produce legal controversy may well be suspect if he receives professional employment or other benefits as a result.[8] A lawyer who volunteers in-person advice that one should obtain the services of a lawyer generally should not himself accept employment, compensation, or other benefit in connection with that matter. However, it is not improper for a lawyer to volunteer such advice and render resulting legal services to close friends, relatives, former clients (in regard to matters germane to former employment), and regular clients.

EC 2-5   A lawyer who writes or speaks for the purpose of educating members of the public to recognize their legal problems should carefully refrain from giving or appearing to give a general solution applicable to all apparently similar individual problems, since slight changes in fact situations may require a material variance in the applicable advice; otherwise, the public may be misled and misadvised. Talks and writings by lawyers for laypersons should caution them not to attempt to solve individual problems upon the basis of the information contained therein.

Selection of a Lawyer

EC 2-6   Formerly a potential client usually knew the reputations of local lawyers for competency and integrity and therefore could select a practitioner in

---

contention there are two answers. The first is that a State cannot foreclose the exercise of constitutional rights by mere labels. The second is that abstract discussion is not the only species of communication which the Constitution protects; the First Amendment also protects vigorous advocacy, certainly of lawful ends, against governmental intrusion. . . .

"However valid may be Virginia's interest in regulating the traditionally illegal practice of barratry, maintenance and champerty, that interest does not justify the prohibition of the NAACP activities disclosed by this record. Malicious intent was of the essence of the common-law offenses of fomenting or stirring up litigation. And whatever may be or may have been true of suits against governments in other countries, the exercise in our own, as in this case of First Amendment rights to enforce Constitutional rights through litigation, as a matter of law, cannot be deemed malicious." NAACP v. Button, 371 U.S. 415, 429, 439-40 (1963).

8. "It is disreputable for an attorney to breed litigation by seeking out those who have claims for personal injuries or other grounds of action in order to secure them as clients, or to employ agents or runners, or to reward those who bring or influence the bringing of business to his office. . . . Moreover, it tends quite easily to the institution of baseless litigation and the manufacture of perjured testimony. From early times, this danger has been recognized in the law by the condemnation of the crime of common barratry, or the stirring up of suits or quarrels between individuals at law or otherwise." In re Ades, 6 F. Supp. 467, 474-75 (D. Mary. 1934).

whom he had confidence. This traditional selection process worked well because it was initiated by the client and the choice was an informed one.

EC 2-7 Changed conditions, however, have seriously restricted the effectiveness of the traditional selection process. Often the reputations of lawyers are not sufficiently known to enable laypersons to make intelligent choices.[12] The law has become increasingly complex and specialized. Few lawyers are willing and competent to deal with every kind of legal matter, and many laypersons have difficulty in determining the competence of lawyers to render different types of legal services. The selection of legal counsel is particularly difficult for transients, persons moving into new areas, persons of limited education or means, and others who have little or no contact with lawyers. Lack of information about the availability of lawyers, the qualifications of particular lawyers, and the expense of legal representation leads laypersons to avoid seeking legal advice.

EC 2-8 Selection of a lawyer by a layperson should be made on an informed basis. Advice and recommendation of third parties — relatives, friends, acquaintances, business associates, or other lawyers — and disclosure of relevant information about the lawyer and his practice may be helpful. A layperson is best served if the recommendation is disinterested and informed. In order that the recommendation be disinterested, a lawyer should not seek to influence another to recommend his employment. A lawyer should not compensate another person for recommending him, for influencing a prospective client to employ him, or to encourage future recommendations. Advertisements and public communications, whether in law lists, telephone directories, newspapers, other forms of print media, television or radio, should be formulated to convey only information that is necessary to make an appropriate selection. Such information includes: (1) office information, such as, name, including name of law firm and names of professional associates; addresses; telephone numbers; credit card acceptability; fluency in foreign languages; and office hours; (2) relevant biographical information; (3) description of the practice, but only by using designations and definitions authorized by [the agency having jurisdiction of the subject under state law], for example, one or more fields of law in which the lawyer or law firm practices; a statement that practice is limited to one or more fields of law; and/or a statement that the lawyer or law firm specializes in a particular field of law practice, but only by using designations, definitions and standards authorized by [the agency having jurisdiction of the subject under state law]; and (4) permitted fee information. Self-laudation should be avoided.

12. "A group of recent interrelated changes bears directly on the availability of legal services. . . . [One] change is the constantly accelerating urbanization of the country and the decline of personal and neighborhood knowledge of whom to retain as a professional man." Cheatham, Availability of Legal Services: The Responsibility of the Individual Lawyer and of the Organized Bar, 12 U.C.L.A. L. Rev. 438, 440 (1965).

Selection of a Lawyer: Lawyer Advertising

EC 2-9   The lack of sophistication on the part of many members of the public concerning legal services, the importance of the interests affected by the choice of a lawyer and prior experience with unrestricted lawyer advertising, require that special care be taken by lawyers to avoid misleading the public and to assure that the information set forth in any advertising is relevant to the selection of a lawyer. The lawyer must be mindful that the benefits of lawyer advertising depend upon its reliability and accuracy. Examples of information in lawyer advertising that would be deceptive include misstatements of fact, suggestions that the ingenuity or prior record of a lawyer rather than the justice of the claim are the principal factors likely to determine the result, inclusion of information irrelevant to selecting a lawyer, and representations concerning the quality of service, which cannot be measured or verified. Since lawyer advertising is calculated and not spontaneous, reasonable regulation of lawyer advertising designed to foster compliance with appropriate standards serves the public interest without impeding the flow of useful, meaningful, and relevant information to the public.

EC 2-10   A lawyer should ensure that the information contained in any advertising which the lawyer publishes, broadcasts or causes to be published or broadcast is relevant, is disseminated in an objective and understandable fashion, and would facilitate the prospective client's ability to compare the qualifications of the lawyers available to represent him. A lawyer should strive to communicate such information without undue emphasis upon style and advertising stratagems which serve to hinder rather than to facilitate intelligent selection of counsel. Because technological change is a recurrent feature of communications forms, and because perceptions of what is relevant in lawyer selection may change, lawyer advertising regulations should not be cast in rigid, unchangeable terms. Machinery is therefore available to advertisers and consumers for prompt consideration of proposals to change the rules governing lawyer advertising. The determination of any request for such change should depend upon whether the proposal is necessary in light of existing Code provisions, whether the proposal accords with standards of accuracy, reliability and truthfulness, and whether the proposal would facilitate informed selection of lawyers by potential consumers of legal services. Representatives of lawyers and consumers should be heard in addition to the applicant concerning any proposed change. Any change which is approved should be promulgated in the form of an amendment to the Code so that all lawyers practicing in the jurisdiction may avail themselves of its provisions.

EC 2-11   The name under which a lawyer conducts his practice may be a factor in the selection process. The use of a trade name or an assumed name could mislead laypersons concerning the identity, responsibility, and status of those practicing thereunder. Accordingly, a lawyer in private practice should practice only under a designation containing his own name, the name of a lawyer employing him, the name of one or more of the lawyers practicing in a partnership, or, if permitted by law, the name of a professional legal corporation, which should be clearly designated as such. For many years some law firms have used a firm name retaining one or more names of deceased or retired partners and such practice is not improper if the firm is a bona fide successor of a firm in which the deceased or retired person was a member, if the use of the name is authorized by law or by contract, and if the public is not misled thereby. However, the name of a partner who withdraws from a firm but continues to practice law should be omitted from the firm name in order to avoid misleading the public.

EC 2-12   A lawyer occupying a judicial, legislative, or public executive or administrative position who has the right to practice law concurrently may allow his name to remain in the name of the firm if he actively continues to practice law as a member thereof. Otherwise, his name should be removed from the firm name, and he should not be identified as a past or present member of the firm; and he should not hold himself out as being a practicing lawyer.

EC 2-13   In order to avoid the possibility of misleading persons with whom he deals, a lawyer should be scrupulous in the representation of his professional status. He should not hold himself out as being a partner or associate of a law firm if he is not one in fact, and thus should not hold himself out as a partner or associate if he only shares offices with another lawyer.[21]

EC 2-14   In some instances a lawyer confines his practice to a particular field of law.[22] In the absence of state controls to insure the existence of special competence, a lawyer should not be permitted to hold himself out as a specialist or as having official recognition as a specialist, other than in the fields of admiralty, trademark, and patent law where a holding out as a specialist historically has been permitted. A lawyer may, however, indicate in permitted advertising,

21. "The word 'associates' has a variety of meanings. Principally through custom the word when used on the letterheads of law firms has come to be regarded as describing those who are employees of the firm. Because the word has acquired this special significance in connection with the practice of the law the use of the word to describe lawyer relationships other than employer-employee is likely to be misleading." In re Sussman and Tanner, 241 Ore. 246, 248, 405 P.2d 355, 356 (1965).

According to ABA Opinion 310 (1963), use of the term "associates" would be misleading in two situations: (1) where two lawyers are partners and they share both responsibility and liability for the partnership; and (2) where two lawyers practice separately, sharing no responsibility or liability, and only share a suite of offices and some costs.

22. "For a long time, many lawyers have, of necessity, limited their practice to certain branches of law. The increasing complexity of the law and the demand of the public for more expertness on the part of the lawyer has, in the past few years — particularly in the last ten years — brought about specialization on an increasing scale." Report of the Special Committee on Specialization and Specialized Legal Services, 79 A.B.A. Rep. 582, 584 (1954).

if it is factual, a limitation of his practice or one or more particular areas or fields of law in which he practices using designations and definitions authorized for that purpose by [the state agency having jurisdiction]. A lawyer practicing in a jurisdiction which certifies specialists must also be careful not to confuse laypersons as to his status. If a lawyer discloses areas of law in which he practices or to which he limits his practice, but is not certified in [the jurisdiction], he, and the designation authorized in [the jurisdiction], should avoid any implication that he is in fact certified.

EC 2-15   The legal profession has developed lawyer referral systems designed to aid individuals who are able to pay fees but need assistance in locating lawyers competent to handle their particular problems. Use of a lawyer referral system enables a layman to avoid an uninformed selection of a lawyer because such a system makes possible the employment of competent lawyers who have indicated an interest in the subject matter involved. Lawyers should support the principle of lawyer referral systems and should encourage the evolution of other ethical plans which aid in the selection of qualified counsel.

Financial Ability to Employ Counsel: Generally

EC 2-16   The legal profession cannot remain a viable force in fulfilling its role in our society unless its members receive adequate compensation for services rendered, and reasonable fees should be charged in appropriate cases to clients able to pay them. Nevertheless, persons unable to pay all or a portion of a reasonable fee should be able to obtain necessary legal services, and lawyers should support and participate in ethical activities designed to achieve that objective.[25]

Financial Ability to Employ Counsel: Persons Able to Pay Reasonable Fees

EC 2-17   The determination of a proper fee requires consideration of the interests of both client and lawyer. A lawyer should not charge more than a reasonable fee, for excessive cost of legal service would deter laymen from utilizing the legal system in protection of their rights. Furthermore, an excessive charge abuses the professional relationship between lawyer and client. On the other hand, adequate compensation is necessary in order to enable the lawyer to serve

25. "If there is any fundamental proposition of government on which all would agree, it is that one of the highest goals of society must be to achieve and maintain equality before the law. Yet this ideal remains an empty form of words unless the legal profession is ready to provide adequate representation for those unable to pay the usual fees." Professional Representation: Report of the Joint Conference, 44 A.B.A.J. 1159, 1216 (1958).

his client effectively and to preserve the integrity and independence of the profession.[28]

EC 2-18   The determination of the reasonableness of a fee requires consideration of all relevant circumstances, including those stated in the Disciplinary Rules. The fees of a lawyer will vary according to many factors, including the time required, his experience, ability, and reputation, the nature of the employment, the responsibility involved, and the results obtained. It is a commendable and long-standing tradition of the bar that special consideration is given in the fixing of any fee for services rendered a brother lawyer or a member of his immediate family.

EC 2-19   As soon as feasible after a lawyer has been employed, it is desirable that he reach a clear agreement with his client as to the basis of the fee charges to be made. Such a course will not only prevent later misunderstanding but will also work for good relations between the lawyer and the client. It is usually beneficial to reduce to writing the understanding of the parties regarding the fee, particularly when it is contingent. A lawyer should be mindful that many persons who desire to employ him may have had little or no experience with fee charges of lawyers, and for this reason he should explain fully to such persons the reasons for the particular fee arrangement he proposes.

EC 2-20   Contingent fee arrangements[30] in civil cases have long been commonly accepted in the United States in proceedings to enforce claims. The historical bases of their acceptance are that (1) they often, and in a variety of circumstances, provide the only practical means by which one having a claim against another can economically afford, finance, and obtain the services of a competent lawyer to prosecute his claim, and (2) a successful prosecution of the claim produces a *res* out of which the fee can be paid. Although a lawyer generally should decline to accept employment on a contingent fee basis by one who is able to pay a reasonable fixed fee, it is not necessarily improper for a lawyer, where justified by the particular circumstances of a case, to enter into a contingent fee contract in a civil case with any client who, after being fully informed of all relevant factors, desires that arrangement. Because of the human relationships involved and the unique character of the proceedings, contingent fee arrangements in domestic relation cases are rarely justified. In administrative agency proceedings contingent fee contracts should be governed by the same consideration as in other civil cases. Public policy properly condemns contin-

28. "When members of the Bar are induced to render legal services for inadequate compensation, as a consequence the quality of the service rendered may be lowered, the welfare of the profession injured and the administration of justice made less efficient." ABA Opinion 302 (1961).

30. "A contract for a reasonable contingent fee where sanctioned by law is permitted by Canon 13, but the client must remain responsible to the lawyer for expenses advanced by the latter. 'There is to be no barter of the privilege of prosecuting a cause for gain in exchange for the promise of the attorney to prosecute at his own expense.' (Cardozo, C.J. in Matter of Gilman, 251 N.Y. 265, 270-271.)" ABA Opinion 246 (1942).

gent fee arrangements in criminal cases, largely on the ground that legal services in criminal cases do not produce a *res* with which to pay the fee.

EC 2-21 A lawyer should not accept compensation or any thing of value incident to his employment or services from one other than his client without the knowledge and consent of his client after full disclosure.

EC 2-22 Without the consent of his client, a lawyer should not associate in a particular matter another lawyer outside his firm. A fee may properly be divided between lawyers[33] properly associated if the division is in proportion to the services performed and the responsibility assumed by each lawyer[34] and if the total fee is reasonable.

EC 2-23 A lawyer should be zealous in his efforts to avoid controversies over fees with clients and should attempt to resolve amicably any differences on the subject. He should not sue a client for a fee unless necessary to prevent fraud or gross imposition by the client.[37]

Financial Ability to Employ Counsel: Persons Unable to Pay Reasonable Fees

EC 2-24 A layman whose financial ability is not sufficient to permit payment of any fee cannot obtain legal services, other than in cases where a contingent fee is appropriate, unless the services are provided for him. Even a person of moderate means may be unable to pay a reasonable fee which is large because of the complexity, novelty, or difficulty of the problem or similar factors.[38]

33. "Only lawyers may share in . . . a division of fees, but . . . it is not necessary that both lawyers be admitted to practice in the same state, so long as the division was based on the division of services or responsibility." ABA Opinion 316 (1967).
34. "We adhere to our previous rulings that where a lawyer merely brings about the employment of another lawyer *but renders no service and assumes no responsibility in the matter,* a division of the latter's fee is improper. (Opinions 18 and 153.)
"It is assumed that the bar, generally, understands what acts or conduct of a lawyer may constitute 'services' to a client within the intendment of Canon 12. Such acts or conduct invariably, if not always, involve 'responsibility' on the part of the lawyer, whether the word 'responsibility' be construed to denote the possible resultant legal or moral liability on the part of the lawyer to the client or to others, or the onus of deciding what should or should not be done in behalf of the client. The word 'services' in Canon 12 must be construed in this broad sense and may apply to the selection and retainer of associate counsel as well as to other acts or conduct in the client's behalf." ABA Opinion 204 (1940).
37. "Ours is a learned profession, not a mere money-getting trade. . . . Suits to collect fees should be avoided. Only where the circumstances imperatively require, should resort be had to a suit to compel payment. And where a lawyer does resort to a suit to enforce payment of fees which involves a disclosure, he should carefully avoid any disclosure not clearly necessary to obtaining or defending his rights." ABA Opinion 250 (1943). But cf. ABA Opinion 320 (1968).
38. "As a society increases in size, sophistication and technology, the body of laws which is required to control that society also increases in size, scope and complexity. With this growth, the law directly affects more and more facets of individual behavior, creating an expanding need for legal services on the part of the individual members of the society. . . . As legal guidance in social and

EC 2-25   Historically, the need for legal services of those unable to pay reasonable fees has been met in part by lawyers who donated their services or accepted court appointments on behalf of such individuals. The basic responsibility for providing legal services for those unable to pay ultimately rests upon the individual lawyer, and personal involvement in the problems of the disadvantaged can be one of the most rewarding experiences in the life of a lawyer. Every lawyer, regardless of professional prominence or professional workload, should find time to participate in serving the disadvantaged. The rendition of free legal services to those unable to pay reasonable fees continues to be an obligation of each lawyer, but the efforts of individual lawyers are often not enough to meet the need.[39] Thus it has been necessary for the profession to institute additional programs to provide legal services.[40] Accordingly, legal aid offices lawyer referral services, and other related programs have been developed, and others will be developed, by the profession.[42] Every lawyer should support all proper efforts to meet this need for legal services.

Acceptance and Retention of Employment

EC 2-26   A lawyer is under no obligation to act as adviser or advocate for every person who may wish to become his client; but in furtherance of the objec-

---

commercial behavior increasingly becomes necessary, there will come a concurrent demand from the layman that such guidance be made available to him. This demand will not come from those who are able to employ the best legal talent, nor from those who can obtain legal assistance at little or no cost. It will come from the large 'forgotten middle income class,' who can neither afford to pay proportionately large fees nor qualify for ultra-low-cost services. The legal profession must recognize this inevitable demand and consider methods whereby it can be satisfied. If the profession fails to provide such methods, the laity will." Comment, Providing Legal Services for the Middle Class in Civil Matters: The Problem, the Duty and a Solution, 26 U. Pitt. L. Rev. 811, 811-12 (1965).

"The issue is not whether we shall do something or do nothing. The demand for ordinary everyday legal justice is so great and the moral nature of the demand is so strong that the issue has become whether we devise, maintain, and support suitable agencies able to satisfy the demand or, by our own default, force the government to take over the job, supplant us, and ultimately dominate us." Smith, Legal Service Offices for Persons of Moderate Means, 1949 Wis. L. Rev. 416, 418 (1949).

39. ". . . [A] system of justice that attempts, in mid-twentieth century America, to meet the needs of the financially incapacitated accused through primary or exclusive reliance on the uncompensated services of counsel will prove unsuccessful and inadequate. . . . A system of adequate representation, therefore, should be structured and financed in a manner reflecting its public importance. . . ." Report of the Atty. Gen's Comm. on Poverty and the Administration of Criminal Justice 41-43 (1963).

40. " . . . If those who stand in need of this service know of its availability and their need is in fact adequately met, the precise mechanism by which this service is provided becomes of secondary importance. It is of great importance, however, that both the impulse to render this service, and the plan for making that impulse effective, should arise within the legal profession itself." Professional Responsibility: Report of the Joint Conference, 44 A.B.A.J. 1159, 1216 (1958).

42. "Whereas the American Bar Association believes that it is a fundamental duty of the bar to see to it that all persons requiring legal advice be able to attain it, irrespective of their economic status. . . .

"Resolved, that the Association approves and sponsors the setting up by state and local bar associations of lawyer referral plans and low-cost legal service methods for the purpose of dealing with cases of persons who might not otherwise have the benefit of legal advice. . . ." Proceedings of the House of Delegates of the American Bar Association, Oct. 30, 1946, 71 A.B.A. Rep. 103, 109-10 (1946).

tive of the bar to make legal services fully available, a lawyer should not lightly decline proffered employment. The fulfillment of this objective requires acceptance by a lawyer of his share of tendered employment which may be unattractive both to him and the bar generally.

EC 2-27 History is replete with instances of distinguished and sacrificial services by lawyers who have represented unpopular clients and causes. Regardless of his personal feelings, a lawyer should not decline representation because a client or a cause is unpopular or community reaction is adverse.[45]

EC 2-28 The personal preference of a lawyer to avoid adversary alignment against judges, other lawyers,[46] public officials, or influential members of the community does not justify his rejection of tendered employment.

EC 2-29 When a lawyer is appointed by a court or requested by a bar association to undertake representation of a person unable to obtain counsel, whether for financial or other reasons, he should not seek to be excused from undertaking the representation except for compelling reasons.[47] Compelling reasons do not include such factors as the repugnance of the subject matter of the proceeding, the identity or position of a person involved in the case, the belief of the lawyer that the defendant in a criminal proceeding is guilty, or the belief of the lawyer regarding the merits of the civil case.[50]

EC 2-30 Employment should not be accepted by a lawyer when he is unable to render competent service or when he knows or it is obvious that the person seeking to employ him desires to institute or maintain an action merely for

45. "One of the highest services the lawyer can render to society is to appear in court on behalf of clients whose causes are in disfavor with the general public." Professional Responsibility: Report of the Joint Conference, 44 A.B.A.J. 1159, 1216 (1958).

One author proposes the following proposition to be included in "A Proper Oath for Advocates": "I recognize that it is sometimes difficult for clients with unpopular causes to obtain proper legal representation. I will do all that I can to assure that the client with the unpopular cause is properly represented, and that the lawyer representing such a client receives credit from and support of the bar for handling such a matter." Thode, The Ethical Standard for the Advocate, 39 Texas L. Rev. 575, 592 (1961)....

46. " . . . Unfortunately, there appears to be a widespread feeling among laymen that it is difficult, if not impossible, to obtain justice when they have claims against members of the Bar because other lawyers will not accept employment to proceed against them. The honor of the profession, whose members proudly style themselves officers of the court, must surely be sullied if its members bind themselves by custom to refrain from enforcing just claims of laymen against lawyers." ABA Opinion 144 (1935).

47. ABA Canon 4 uses a slightly different test, saying, "A lawyer assigned as counsel for an indigent prisoner ought not to ask to be excused for any trivial reason. . . ."

50. Dr. Johnson's reply to Boswell upon being asked what he thought of "Supporting a cause which you know to be bad" was: "Sir, you do not know it to be good or bad till the Judge determines it. I have said that you are to state facts fairly; so that your thinking, or what you call knowing, a cause to be bad, must be from reasoning, must be from supposing your arguments to be weak and inconclusive. But, Sir, that is not enough. An argument which does not convince yourself, may convince the Judge to whom you urge it: and if it does convince him, why, then, Sir, you are wrong, and he is right." 2 Boswell, The Life of Johnson 47-48 (Hill ed. 1887).

the purpose of harassing or maliciously injuring another. Likewise, a lawyer should decline employment if the intensity of his personal feeling, as distinguished from a community attitude, may impair his effective representation of a prospective client. If a lawyer knows a client has previously obtained counsel, he should not accept employment in the matter unless the other counsel approves or withdraws, or the client terminates the prior employment.[54]

EC 2-31   Full availability of legal counsel requires both that persons be able to obtain counsel and that lawyers who undertake representation complete the work involved. Trial counsel for a convicted defendant should continue to represent his client by advising whether to take an appeal and, if the appeal is prosecuted, by representing him through the appeal unless new counsel is substituted or withdrawal is permitted by the appropriate court.

EC 2-32   A decision by a lawyer to withdraw should be made only on the basis of compelling circumstances,[55] and in a matter pending before a tribunal he must comply with the rules of the tribunal regarding withdrawal. A lawyer should not withdraw without considering carefully and endeavoring to minimize the possible adverse effect on the rights of his client and the possibility of prejudice to his client as a result of his withdrawal. Even when he justifiably withdraws, a lawyer should protect the welfare of his client by giving due notice of his withdrawal, suggesting employment of other counsel, delivering to the client all papers and property to which the client is entitled, cooperating with counsel subsequently employed, and otherwise endeavoring to minimize the possibility of harm. Further, he should refund to the client any compensation not earned during the employment.

EC 2-33   As a part of the legal profession's commitment to the principle that high quality legal services should be available to all, attorneys are encouraged to cooperate with qualified legal assistance organizations providing prepaid legal services. Such participation should at all times be in accordance with the basic tenets of the profession: independence, integrity, competence and devotion to the interests of individual clients. An attorney so participating should make certain that his relationship with a qualified legal assistance organization in no way interferes with his independent, professional representation of the interests of the individual client. An attorney should avoid situations in which officials of the organization who are not lawyers attempt to direct attorneys concerning the manner in which legal services are performed for individual members, and should also avoid situations in which considerations of

54. "From the facts stated we assume that the client has discharged the first attorney and given notice of the discharge. Such being the case, the second attorney may properly accept employment. Canon 7; Opinions 10, 130, 149." ABA Opinion 209 (1941).

55. "I will carefully consider, before taking a case, whether it appears that I can fully represent the client within the framework of law. If the decision is in the affirmative, then it will take extreme circumstances to cause me to decide later that I cannot so represent him." Thode, The Ethical Standard for the Advocate, 39 Texas L. Rev. 575, 592 (1961) (from "A Proper Oath for Advocates").

economy are given undue weight in determining the attorneys employed by an organization or the legal services to be performed for the member or beneficiary rather than competence and quality of service. An attorney interested in maintaining the historic traditions of the profession and preserving the function of a lawyer as a trusted and independent advisor to individual members of society should carefully assess such factors when accepting employment by, or otherwise participating in, a particular qualified legal assistance organization, and while so participating should adhere to the highest professional standards of effort and competence.

	Model Code	*ABA Model Rules*
Model Rules Comparison	EC 2-1	Rules 6.1, 6.2, 7.2(a), 7.4
	EC 2-2	Rules 6.1, 7.2(a)
	EC 2-3	Rules 4.3, 7.3
	EC 2-4	Rule 7.3
	EC 2-5	Rule 7.1(b)
	EC 2-6	Rule 7.2(a)
	EC 2-7	Rules 7.2(a), 7.4
	EC 2-8	Rules 7.1, 7.2(a), (c), 7.4
	EC 2-9	Rule 7.1
	EC 2-10	Rule 7.1(a), (c)
	EC 2-11	Rule 7.5
	EC 2-12	Rule 7.5(c)
	EC 2-13	Rule 7.5(a), (d)
	EC 2-14	Rule 7.4
	EC 2-15	Rule 7.2(a), (c)
	EC 2-16	Rules 1.5(a), 6.1, 6.2(b)
	EC 2-17	Rule 1.5(a)
	EC 2-18	Rule 1.5(a)
	EC 2-19	Rule 1.5(b)
	EC 2-20	Rule 1.5(c), (d)
	EC 2-21	Rules 1.7(b), 1.8(f)
	EC 2-22	Rule 1.5(e)
	EC 2-23	Rule 1.5 Comment ¶5
	EC 2-24	Rules 6.1, 6.2
	EC 2-25	Rules 6.1, 6.2
	EC 2-26	Rules 1.16(a), 6.2
	EC 2-27	Rule 6.2(a), (c)
	EC 2-28	Rule 6.2(a)
	EC 2-29	Rules 1.16(a), 6.2
	EC 2-30	Rules 1.16(a), (b)(3), 4.2, 6.2
	EC 2-31	Rules 1.3, 1.16, 6.2
	EC 2-32	Rule 1.16
	EC 2-33	Rules 5.4, 6.3, 6.4

Disciplinary Rules

DR 2-101 Publicity

(A) A lawyer shall not, on behalf of himself, his partner, associate or any other lawyer affiliated with him or his firm, use or participate in the use of any form of public communication containing a false, fraudulent, misleading, deceptive, self-laudatory or unfair statement or claim.

(B) In order to facilitate the process of informed selection of a lawyer by potential consumers of legal services, a lawyer may publish or broadcast, subject to DR 2-103, the following information in print media distributed or over television or radio broadcast in the geographic area or areas in which the lawyer resides or maintains offices or in which a significant part of the lawyer's clientele resides, provided that the information disclosed by the lawyer in such publication or broadcast complies with DR 2-101(A), and is presented in a dignified manner:

(1) Name, including name of law firm and names of professional associates; addresses and telephone numbers;

(2) One or more fields of law in which the lawyer or law firm practices, a statement that practice is limited to one or more fields of law, or a statement that the lawyer or law firm specializes in a particular field of law practice, to the extent authorized under DR 2-105;

(3) Date and place of birth;

(4) Date and place of admission to the bar of state and federal courts;

(5) Schools attended, with dates of graduation, degrees and other scholastic distinctions;

(6) Public or quasi-public offices;

(7) Military service;

(8) Legal authorships;

(9) Legal teaching positions;

(10) Memberships, offices, and committee assignments, in bar associations;

(11) Membership and offices in legal fraternities and legal societies;

(12) Technical and professional licenses;

(13) Memberships in scientific, technical and professional associations and societies;

(14) Foreign language ability;

(15) Names and addresses of bank references;

(16) With their written consent, names of clients regularly represented;

(17) Prepaid or group legal services programs in which the lawyer participates;

(18) Whether credit cards or other credit arrangements are accepted;

(19) Office and telephone answering service hours;

(20) Fee for an initial consultation;

(21) Availability upon request of a written schedule of fees and/or an estimate of the fee to be charged for specific services;

(22) Contingent fee rates subject to DR 2-106(C), provided that the statement discloses whether percentages are computed before or after deduction of costs;

(23) Range of fees for services, provided that the statement discloses that the specific fee within the range which will be charged will vary depending upon the particular matter to be handled for each client and the client is entitled without obligation to an estimate of the fee within the range likely to be charged, in print size equivalent to the largest print used in setting forth the fee information;

(24) Hourly rate, provided that the statement discloses that the total fee charged will depend upon the number of hours which must be devoted to the particular matter to be handled for each client and the client is entitled to without obligation an estimate of the fee likely to be charged, in print size at least equivalent to the largest print used in setting forth the fee information;

(25) Fixed fees for specific legal services,* the description of which would not be misunderstood or be deceptive, provided that the statement discloses that the quoted fee will be available only to clients whose matters fall into the services described and that the client is entitled without obligation to a specific estimate of the fee likely to be charged in print size at least equivalent to the largest print used in setting forth the fee information.

(C) Any person desiring to expand the information authorized for disclosure in DR 2-101(B), or to provide for its dissemination through other forums may apply to [the agency having jurisdiction under state law]. Any such application shall be served upon [the agencies having jurisdiction under state law over the regulation of the legal profession and consumer matters] who shall be heard, together with the applicant, on the issue of whether the proposal is necessary in light of the existing provisions of the Code, accords with standards of accuracy, reliability and truthfulness, and would facilitate the process of informed selection of lawyers by potential consumers of legal services. The relief granted in response to any such application shall be promulgated as an amendment to DR 2-101(B), universally applicable to all lawyers.**

(D) If the advertisement is communicated to the public over television or radio, it shall be prerecorded, approved for broadcast by the lawyer, and a recording of the actual transmission shall be retained by the lawyer.

(E) If a lawyer advertises a fee for a service, the lawyer must render that service for no more than the fee advertised.

---

*The agency having jurisdiction under state law may desire to issue appropriate guidelines defining "specific legal services."

**The agency having jurisdiction under state law should establish orderly and expeditious procedures for ruling on such applications.

(F) Unless otherwise specified in the advertisement if a lawyer publishes any fee information authorized under DR 2-101(B) in a publication that is published more frequently than one time per month, the lawyer shall be bound by any representation made therein for a period of not less than 30 days after such publication. If a lawyer publishes any fee information authorized under DR 2-101(B) in a publication that is published once a month or less frequently, he shall be bound by any representation made therein until the publication of the succeeding issue. If a lawyer publishes any fee information authorized under DR 2-101(B) in a publication which has no fixed date for publication of a succeeding issue, the lawyer shall be bound by any representation made therein for a reasonable period of time after publication but in no event less than one year.

(G) Unless otherwise specified, if a lawyer broadcasts any fee information authorized under DR 2-101(B), the lawyer shall be bound by any representation made therein for a period of not less than 30 days after such broadcast.

(H) This rule does not prohibit limited and dignified identification of a lawyer as a lawyer as well as by name:

(1) In political advertisements when his professional status is germane to the political campaign or to a political issue.

(2) In public notices when the name and profession of a lawyer are required or authorized by law or are reasonably pertinent for a purpose other than the attraction of potential clients.

(3) In routine reports and announcements of a bona fide business, civic, professional, or political organization in which he serves as a director or officer.

(4) In and on legal documents prepared by him.

(5) In and on legal textbooks, treatises, and other legal publications, and in dignified advertisements thereof.

(I) A lawyer shall not compensate or give any thing of value to representatives of the press, radio, television, or other communication medium in anticipation of or in return for professional publicity in a news item.

DR 2-102 Professional Notices, Letterheads and Offices

(A) A lawyer or law firm shall not use or participate in the use of professional cards, professional announcement cards, office signs, letterheads, or similar professional notices or devices, except that the following may be used if they are in dignified form:

(1) A professional card of a lawyer identifying him by name and as a lawyer, and giving his addresses, telephone numbers, the name of his law firm, and any information permitted under DR 2-105. A professional card of a law firm may also give the names of members and associates. Such cards may be used for identification.

(2) A brief professional announcement card stating new or changed associations or addresses, change of firm name, or similar matters pertaining to the professional offices of a lawyer or law firm, which may be mailed to lawyers, clients, former clients, personal friends, and relatives. It shall not state biographical data except to the extent reasonably necessary to identify the lawyer or to explain the change in his association, but it may state the immediate past position of the lawyer. It may give the names and dates of predecessor firms in a continuing line of succession. It shall not state the nature of the practice except as permitted under DR 2-105.

(3) A sign on or near the door of the office and in the building directory identifying the law office. The sign shall not state the nature of the practice, except as permitted under DR 2-105.

(4) A letterhead of a lawyer identifying him by name and as a lawyer, and giving his addresses, telephone numbers, the name of his law firm, associates and any information permitted under DR 2-105. A letterhead of a law firm may also give the names of members and associates, and names and dates relating to deceased and retired members. A lawyer may be designated "Of Counsel" on a letterhead if he has a continuing relationship with a lawyer or law firm, other than as a partner or associate. A lawyer or law firm may be designated as "General Counsel" or by similar professional reference on stationery of a client if he or the firm devotes a substantial amount of professional time in the representation of that client. The letterhead of a law firm may give the names and dates of predecessor firms in a continuing line of succession.

(B) A lawyer in private practice shall not practice under a trade name, a name that is misleading as to the identity of the lawyer or lawyers practicing under such name, or a firm name containing names other than those of one or more of the lawyers in the firm, except that the name of a professional corporation of professional association may contain "P.C." or "P.A." or similar symbols indicating the nature of the organization, and if otherwise lawful a firm may use as, or continue to include in, its name the name or names of one or more deceased or retired members of the firm or of a predecessor firm in a continuing line of succession. A lawyer who assumes a judicial, legislative, or public executive or administrative post or office shall not permit his name to remain in the name of a law firm or to be used in professional notices of the firm during any significant period in which he is not actively and regularly practicing law as a member of the firm, during such period other members of the firm shall not use his name in the firm name or in professional notices of the firm.

(C) A lawyer shall not hold himself out as having a partnership with one or more other lawyers or professional corporations unless they are in fact partners.

(D) A partnership shall not be formed or continued between or among lawyers licensed in different jurisdictions unless all enumerations of the members and associates of the firm on its letterhead and in other permissible listings make clear the jurisdictional limitations on those members and associates of the firm not licensed to practice in all listed jurisdictions; however, the same firm name may be used in each jurisdiction.

(E) Nothing contained herein shall prohibit a lawyer from using or permitting the use of, in connection with his name, an earned degree or title derived therefrom indicating his training in the law.

DR 2-103 Recommendation of Professional Employment

(A) A lawyer shall not, except as authorized in DR 2-101(B), recommend employment as a private practitioner, of himself, his partner, or associate to a layperson who has not sought his advice regarding employment of a lawyer.[72]

(B) A lawyer shall not compensate or give anything of value to a person or organization to recommend or secure his employment by a client, or as a reward for having made a recommendation resulting in his employment by a client, except that he may pay the usual and reasonable fees or dues charged by any of the organizations listed in DR 2-103(D).

(C) A lawyer shall not request a person or organization to recommend or promote the use of his services or those of his partner or associate, or any other lawyer affiliated with him or his firm, as a private practitioner,[75] except as authorized in DR 2-101, and except that

(1) He may request referrals from a lawyer referral service operated, sponsored, or approved by a bar association and may pay its fees incident thereto.[76]

(2) He may cooperate with the legal service activities of any of the offices or organizations enumerated in DR 2-103(D) (1) through (4) and may perform legal services for those to whom he was recommended by it to do such work if:

(a) The person to whom the recommendation is made is a member or beneficiary of such office or organization; and

(b) The lawyer remains free to exercise his independent professional judgment on behalf of his client.

(D) A lawyer or his partner or associate or any other lawyer affiliated with him or his firm may be recommended, employed or paid by, or may cooperate

---

72. "[A] lawyer may not seek from persons not his clients the opportunity to perform . . . a [legal] check-up." ABA Opinion 307 (1962).

75. "This Court has condemned the practice of ambulance chasing through the media of runners and touters. In similar fashion we have with equal emphasis condemned the practice of direct solicitation by a lawyer. We have classified both offenses as serious breaches of the Canons of Ethics demanding severe treatment of the offending lawyer." State v. Dawson, 111 So. 2d 427, 431 (Fla. 1959).

76. "Registrants [of a lawyer referral plan] may be required to contribute to the expense of operating it by a reasonable registration charge or by a reasonable percentage of fees collected by them." ABA Opinion 291 (1956).

with, one of the following offices or organizations that promote the use of his services or those of his partner or associate or any other lawyer affiliated with him or his firm if there is no interference with the exercise of independent professional judgment in behalf of his client:

(1) A legal aid office or public defender office:

(a) Operated or sponsored by a duly accredited law school.

(b) Operated or sponsored by a bona fide nonprofit community organization.

(c) Operated or sponsored by a governmental agency.

(d) Operated, sponsored, or approved by a bar association.

(2) A military legal assistance office.

(3) A lawyer referral service operated, sponsored, or approved by a bar association.

(4) Any bona fide organization that recommends, furnishes or pays for legal services to its members or beneficiaries[78] provided the following conditions are satisfied:

(a) Such organization, including any affiliate, is so organized and operated that no profit is derived by it from the rendition of legal services by lawyers, and that, if the organization is organized for profit, the legal services are not rendered by lawyers employed, directed, supervised or selected by it except in connection with matters where such organization bears ultimate liability of its member or beneficiary.

(b) Neither the lawyer, nor his partner, nor associate, nor any other lawyer affiliated with him or his firm, nor any non-lawyer, shall have initiated or promoted such organization for the primary purpose of providing financial or other benefit to such lawyer, partner, associate or affiliated lawyer.

(c) Such organization is not operated for the purpose of procuring legal work or financial benefit for any lawyer as a private practitioner outside of the legal services program of the organization.

(d) The member or beneficiary to whom the legal services are furnished, and not such organization, is recognized as the client of the lawyer in the matter.

(e) Any member or beneficiary who is entitled to have legal services furnished or paid for by the organization may, if such member or beneficiary so desires, select counsel other than that furnished, selected or approved by the organization for the particular matter involved; and the legal service plan of such organization provides appropriate relief for any member or beneficiary who asserts a claim that representation by counsel furnished, selected or approved would be unethical, improper or inadequate under the circumstances of the matter involved and the plan provides an appropriate procedure for seeking such relief.

78. United Mine Workers v. Ill. State Bar Assn., 389 U.S. 217 (1967); Brotherhood of R.R. Trainmen v. Virginia, 371 U.S. 1 (1964); NAACP v. Button, 371 U.S. 415 (1963). Also see ABA Opinion 332 (1973) and 333 (1973).

(f) The lawyer does not know or have cause to know that such organization is in violation of applicable laws, rules of court and other legal requirements that govern its legal service operations.

(g) Such organization has filed with the appropriate disciplinary authority at least annually a report with respect to its legal service plan, if any, showing its terms, its schedule of benefits, its subscription charges, agreements with counsel, and financial results of its legal service activities or, if it has failed to do so, the lawyer does not know or have cause to know of such failure.

(E) A lawyer shall not accept employment when he knows or it is obvious that the person who seeks his services does so as a result of conduct prohibited under this Disciplinary Rule.

DR 2-104 Suggestion of Need of Legal Services

(A) A lawyer who has given in-person unsolicited advice to a layperson that he should obtain counsel or take legal action shall not accept employment resulting from that advice, except that:

(1) A lawyer may accept employment by a close friend, relative, former client (if the advice is germane to the former employment), or one whom the lawyer reasonably believes to be a client.[82]

(2) A lawyer may accept employment that results from his participation in activities designed to educate laypersons to recognize legal problems, to make intelligent selection of counsel, or to utilize available legal services if such activities are conducted or sponsored by a qualified legal assistance organization.

(3) A lawyer who is recommended, furnished or paid by a qualified legal assistance organization enumerated in DR 2-103(D) (1) through (4) may represent a member or beneficiary thereof, to the extent and under the conditions prescribed therein.

(4) Without affecting his right to accept employment, a lawyer may speak publicly or write for publication on legal topics so long as he does not emphasize his own professional experience or reputation and does not undertake to give individual advice.

---

82. "It certainly is not improper for a lawyer to advise his regular clients of new statutes, court decisions, and administrative rulings, which may affect the client's interests, provided the communication is strictly limited to such information. . . .

"When such communications go to concerns or individuals other than regular clients of the lawyer, they are thinly disguised advertisements for professional employment, and are obviously improper." ABA Opinion 213 (1941).

"It is our opinion that where the lawyer has no reason to believe that he has been supplanted by another lawyer, it is not only his right, but it might even be his duty to advise his client of any change of fact or law which might defeat the client's testamentary purpose as expressed in the will.

"Periodic notices might be sent to the client for whom a lawyer has drawn a will, suggesting that it might be wise for the client to reexamine his will to determine whether or not there has been any change in his situation requiring a modification of his will." ABA Opinion 210 (1941).

(5) If success in asserting rights or defenses of his client in litigation in the nature of a class action is dependent upon the joinder of others, a lawyer may accept, but shall not seek, employment from those contacted for the purpose of obtaining their joinder.

DR 2-105 Limitation of Practice

(A) A lawyer shall not hold himself out publicly as a specialist, as practicing in certain areas of law or as limiting his practice permitted under DR 2-101(B), except as follows:

(1) A lawyer admitted to practice before the United States Patent and Trademark Office may use the designation "Patents," "Patent Attorney," "Patent Lawyer," or "Registered Patent Attorney" or any combination of those terms, on his letterhead and office sign.

(2) A lawyer who publicly discloses fields of law in which the lawyer or the law firm practices or states that his practice is limited to one or more fields of law shall do so by using designations and definitions authorized and approved by [the agency having jurisdiction of the subject under state law].

(3) A lawyer who is certified as a specialist in a particular field of law or law practice by [the authority having jurisdiction under state law over the subject of specialization by lawyers] may hold himself out as such, but only in accordance with the rules prescribed by that authority.

DR 2-106 Fees for Legal Services

(A) A lawyer shall not enter into an agreement for, charge, or collect an illegal or clearly excessive fee.

(B) A fee is clearly excessive when, after a review of the facts, a lawyer of ordinary prudence would be left with a definite and firm conviction that the fee is in excess of a reasonable fee. Factors to be considered as guides in determining the reasonableness of a fee include the following:

(1) The time and labor required, the novelty and difficulty of the questions involved, and the skill requisite to perform the legal service properly.

(2) The likelihood, if apparent to the client, that the acceptance of the particular employment will preclude other employment by the lawyer.

(3) The fee customarily charged in the locality for similar legal services.

(4) The amount involved and the results obtained.

(5) The time limitations imposed by the client or by the circumstances.

(6) The nature and length of the professional relationship with the client.

(7) The experience, reputation, and ability of the lawyer or lawyers performing the services.

(8) Whether the fee is fixed or contingent.

(C) A lawyer shall not enter into an arrangement for, charge, or collect a contingent fee for representing a defendant in a criminal case.[90]

DR 2-107 Division of Fees Among Lawyers

(A) A lawyer shall not divide a fee for legal services with another lawyer who is not a partner in or associate of his law firm or law office, unless:

(1) The client consents to employment of the other lawyer after a full disclosure that a division of fees will be made.

(2) The division is made in proportion to the services performed and responsibility assumed by each.

(3) The total fee of the lawyers does not clearly exceed reasonable compensation for all legal services they rendered the client.

(B) This Disciplinary Rule does not prohibit payment to a former partner or associate pursuant to a separation or retirement agreement.

DR 2-108 Agreements Restricting the Practice of a Lawyer

(A) A lawyer shall not be a party to or participate in a partnership or employment agreement with another lawyer that restricts the right of a lawyer to practice law after the termination of a relationship created by the agreement, except as a condition to payment of retirement benefits.[93]

(B) In connection with the settlement of a controversy or suit, a lawyer shall not enter into an agreement that restricts his right to practice law.

DR 2-109 Acceptance of Employment

(A) A lawyer shall not accept employment on behalf of a person if he knows or it is obvious that such person wishes to:

(1) Bring a legal action, conduct a defense, or assert a position in litigation, or otherwise have steps taken for him, merely for the purpose of harassing or maliciously injuring any person.

90. . . . "In criminal cases, the rule is stricter because of the danger of corrupting justice. The second part of Section 542 of the Restatement [of Contracts] reads: 'A bargain to conduct a criminal case . . . in consideration of a promise of a fee contingent on success is illegal. . . .' " Peyton v. Margiotti; 398 Pa. 86, 156 A.2d 865, 967 (1959). . . .

93. "[A] general covenant restricting an employed lawyer, after leaving the employment, from practicing in the community for a stated period, appears to this Committee to be an unwarranted restriction on the right of a lawyer to choose where he will practice and inconsistent with our professional status. Accordingly, the Committee is of the opinion it would be improper for the employing lawyer to require the covenant and likewise for the employed lawyer to agree to it." ABA Opinion 300 (1961).

(2) Present a claim or defense in litigation that is not warranted under existing law, unless it can be supported by good faith argument for an extension, modification, or reversal of existing law.

DR 2-110 Withdrawal from Employment

(A) In general.

(1) If permission for withdrawal from employment is required by the rules of a tribunal, a lawyer shall not withdraw from employment in a proceeding before that tribunal without its permission.

(2) In any event, a lawyer shall not withdraw from employment until he has taken reasonable steps to avoid foreseeable prejudice to the rights of his client, including giving due notice to his client, allowing time for employment of other counsel, delivering to the client all papers and property to which the client is entitled, and complying with applicable laws and rules.

(3) A lawyer who withdraws from employment shall refund promptly any part of a fee paid in advance that has not been earned.

(B) Mandatory withdrawal. A lawyer representing a client before a tribunal, with its permission if required by its rules, shall withdraw from employment, and a lawyer representing a client in other matters shall withdraw from employment, if:

(1) He knows or it is obvious that his client is bringing the legal action, conducting the defense, or asserting a position in the litigation, or is otherwise having steps taken for him, merely for the purpose of harassing or maliciously injuring any person.

(2) He knows or it is obvious that his continued employment will result in violation of a Disciplinary Rule.

(3) His mental or physical condition renders it unreasonably difficult for him to carry out the employment effectively.

(4) He is discharged by his client.

(C) Permissive withdrawal. If DR 2-110 (B) is not applicable, a lawyer may not request permission to withdraw in matters pending before a tribunal, and may not withdraw in other matters, unless such request or such withdrawal is because:

(1) His client:

(a) Insists upon presenting a claim or defense that is not warranted under existing law and cannot be supported by good faith argument for an extension, modification, or reversal of existing law.[98]

(b) Personally seeks to pursue an illegal course of conduct.

(c) Insists that the lawyer pursue a course of conduct that is illegal or that is prohibited under the Disciplinary Rules.

98. Cf. Anders v. California, 386 U.S. 738 (1967), rehearing denied, 388 U.S. 924 (1967).

(d) By other conduct renders it unreasonably difficult for the lawyer to carry out his employment effectively.

(e) Insists, in a matter not pending before a tribunal, that the lawyer engage in conduct that is contrary to the judgment and advice of the lawyer but not prohibited under the Disciplinary Rules.

(f) Deliberately disregards an agreement or obligation to the lawyer as to expenses or fees.

(2) His continued employment is likely to result in a violation of a Disciplinary Rule.

(3) His inability to work with co-counsel indicates that the best interests of the client likely will be served by withdrawal.

(4) His mental or physical condition renders it difficult for him to carry out the employment effectively.

(5) His client knowingly and freely assents to termination of his employment.

(6) He believes in good faith, in a proceeding pending before a tribunal, that the tribunal will find the existence of other good cause for withdrawal.

	Model Code	*ABA Model Rules*
Model Rules Comparison	DR 2-101(A)	Rule 7.1
	DR 2-101(B)	Rules 7.1, 7.2(a)
	DR 2-101(C)	Rules 7.1, 7.2
	DR 2-101(D)	Rule 7.2(b)
	DR 2-101(E)	Rule 7.1(a)
	DR 2-101(F)	Rule 7.1
	DR 2-101(G)	Rule 7.1
	DR 2-101(H)	Rules 7.1, 7.2
	DR 2-101(I)	Rule 7.2(c)
	DR 2-102(A)	Rules 7.2(a), 7.4, 7.5
	DR 2-102(B)	Rules 7.2(a), 7.5(a), (c)
	DR 2-102(C)	Rule 7.5(d)
	DR 2-102(D)	Rule 7.5(a), (b)
	DR 2-102(E)	Rules 7.1(a), 7.4, 7.5(a)
	DR 2-103(A)	Rules 7.2(a), 7.3
	DR 2-103(B)	Rules 5.4(c), 7.2(a), (c)
	DR 2-103(C)	Rules 5.4(a), 7.2(c), 7.3
	DR 2-103(D)	Rules 5.4, 7.2(c), 7.3
	DR 2-103(E)	Rules 1.16(a), 8.4(a)
	DR 2-104	Rules 1.16(a), 7.3
	DR 2-105	Rule 7.4
	DR 2-106(A)	Rule 1.5(a)
	DR 2-106(B)	Rule 1.5(a)
	DR 2-106(C)	Rule 1.5(d)(2)
	DR 2-107(A)	Rule 1.5(e)
	DR 2-107(B)	Rule 5.4(a)(1)

	Model Code	*ABA Model Rules*
Model Rules Comparison	DR 2-108(A)	Rule 5.6(a)
	DR 2-108(B)	Rule 5.6(b)
	DR 2-109(A)	Rules 1.16(a), 3.1, 3.2
	DR 2-110(A)	Rule 1.16(c), (d)
	DR 2-110(B)	Rules 1.16(a), 3.1, 4.4
	DR 2-110(C)	Rules 1.2(e), 1.16(a), (b)

CANON 3. A LAWYER SHOULD ASSIST IN PREVENTING THE UNAUTHORIZED PRACTICE OF LAW

Ethical Considerations

EC 3-1 The prohibition against the practice of law by a layman is grounded in the need of the public for integrity and competence of those who undertake to render legal services. Because of the fiduciary and personal character of the lawyer-client relationship and the inherently complex nature of our legal system, the public can better be assured of the requisite responsibility and competence if the practice of law is confined to those who are subject to the requirements and regulations imposed upon members of the legal profession.

EC 3-2 The sensitive variations in the considerations that bear on legal determinations often make it difficult even for a lawyer to exercise appropriate professional judgment, and it is therefore essential that the personal nature of the relationship of client and lawyer be preserved. Competent professional judgment is the product of a trained familiarity with law and legal processes, a disciplined, analytical approach to legal problems, and a firm ethical commitment.

EC 3-3 A non-lawyer who undertakes to handle legal matters is not governed as to integrity or legal competence by the same rules that govern the conduct of a lawyer. A lawyer is not only subject to that regulation but also is committed to high standards of ethical conduct. The public interest is best served in legal matters by a regulated profession committed to such standards.[1] The Disciplinary Rules protect the public in that they prohibit a lawyer from seeking employment by improper overtures, from acting in cases of divided loyalties, and from submitting to the control of others in the exercise of his judgment. Moreover, a person who entrusts legal matters to a lawyer is protected by

---

1. "The condemnation of the unauthorized practice of law is designed to protect the public from legal services by persons unskilled in the law. The prohibition of lay intermediaries is intended to insure the loyalty of the lawyer to the client unimpaired by intervening and possibly conflicting interests." Cheatham, Availability of Legal Services: The Responsibility of the Individual Lawyer and of the Organized Bar, 12 U.C.L.A. L. Rev. 438, 439 (1965).

the attorney-client privilege and by the duty of the lawyer to hold inviolate the confidences and secrets of his client.

EC 3-4   A layman who seeks legal services often is not in a position to judge whether he will receive proper professional attention. The entrustment of a legal matter may well involve the confidences, the reputation, the property, the freedom, or even the life of the client. Proper protection of members of the public demands that no person be permitted to act in the confidential and demanding capacity of a lawyer unless he is subject to the regulations of the legal profession.

EC 3-5   It is neither necessary nor desirable to attempt the formulation of a single, specific definition of what constitutes the practice of law.[2] Functionally, the practice of law relates to the rendition of services for others that call for the professional judgment of a lawyer. The essence of the professional judgment of the lawyer is his educated ability to relate the general body and philosophy of law to a specific legal problem of a client; and thus, the public interest will be better served if only lawyers are permitted to act in matters involving professional judgment. Where this professional judgment is not involved, non-lawyers, such as court clerks, police officers, abstracters, and many governmental employees, may engage in occupations that require a special knowledge of law in certain areas. But the services of a lawyer are essential in the public interest whenever the exercise of professional legal judgment is required.

EC 3-6   A lawyer often delegates tasks to clerks, secretaries, and other lay persons. Such delegation is proper if the lawyer maintains a direct relationship with his client, supervises the delegated work, and has complete professional responsibility for the work product.[3] This delegation enables a lawyer to render legal service more economically and efficiently.

2. "What constitutes unauthorized practice of the law in a particular jurisdiction is a matter for determination by the courts of that jurisdiction." ABA Opinion 198 (1939).

"In the light of the historical development of the lawyer's functions, it is impossible to lay down an exhaustive definition of 'the practice of law' by attempting to enumerate every conceivable act performed by lawyers in the normal course of their work." State Bar of Arizona v. Arizona Land Title & Trust Co., 90 Ariz., 76, 87, 366 P.2d 1, 8-9 (1961), modified, 91 Ariz. 293, 371 P.2d 1020 (1962).

3. "A lawyer can employ lay secretaries, lay investigators, lay detectives, lay researchers, accountants, lay scriveners, nonlawyer draftsmen or nonlawyer researchers. In fact, he may employ nonlawyers to do any task for him except counsel clients about law matters, engage directly in the practice of law, appear in court or appear in formal proceedings a part of the judicial process, so long as it is he who takes the work and vouches for it to the client and becomes responsible to the client." ABA Opinion 316 (1967).

ABA Opinion 316 (1967) also stated that if a lawyer practices law as part of a law firm which includes lawyers from several states, he may delegate tasks to firm members in other states so long as he "is the person who, on behalf of the firm, vouched for the work of all of the others and, with the client and in the courts, did the legal acts defined by that state as the practice of law.

"A lawyer cannot delegate his professional responsibility to a law student employed in his office. He may avail himself of the assistance of the student in many of the fields of the lawyer's work, such as examination of case law, finding and interviewing witnesses, making collections of claims, examining court records, delivering papers, conveying important messages, and other similar matters. But the

EC 3-7　The prohibition against a non-lawyer practicing law does not prevent a layman from representing himself, for then he is ordinarily exposing only himself to possible injury. The purpose of the legal profession is to make educated legal representation available to the public; but anyone who does not wish to avail himself of such representation is not required to do so. Even so, the legal profession should help members of the public to recognize legal problems and to understand why it may be unwise for them to act for themselves in matters having legal consequences.

EC 3-8　Since a lawyer should not aid or encourage a layman to practice law, he should not practice law in association with a layman or otherwise share legal fees with a layman.[4] This does not mean, however, that the pecuniary value of the interest of a deceased lawyer in his firm or practice may not be paid to his estate or specified persons such as his widow or heirs. In like manner, profit-sharing retirement plans of a lawyer or law firm which include non-lawyer office employees are not improper. These limited exceptions to the rule against sharing legal fees with laymen are permissible since they do not aid or encourage laymen to practice law.

EC 3-9　Regulations of the practice of law is accomplished principally by the respective states. Authority to engage in the practice of law conferred in any jurisdiction is not per se a grant of the right to practice elsewhere, and it is improper for a lawyer to engage in practice where he is not permitted by law or by court order to do so. However, the demands of business and the mobility of our society pose distinct problems in the regulation of the practice of law by the states.[8] In furtherance of the public interest, the legal profession should discourage regulation that unreasonably imposes territorial limitations upon the right of a lawyer to handle the legal affairs to obtain the services of a lawyer of his choice in all matters including the presentation of a contested matter in a tribunal before which the lawyer is not permanently admitted to practice.[9]

---

student is not permitted, until he is admitted to the Bar, to perform the professional functions of a lawyer, such as conducting court trials, giving professional advice to clients or drawing legal documents for them. The student in all his work must act as agent for the lawyer employing him, who must supervise his work and be responsible for his good conduct." ABA Opinion 85 (1932).

4. "No division of fees for legal services is proper, except with another lawyer. . . ." ABA Canon 34. Otherwise, according to ABA Opinion 316 (1967), "[t]he Canons of Ethics do not examine into the method by which such persons are remunerated by the lawyer. . . . They may be paid a salary, a per diem charge, a flat fee, a contract price, etc."

8. "Much of clients' business crosses state lines. People are mobile, moving from state to state. Many metropolitan areas cross state lines. It is common today to have a single economic and social community involving more than one state. The business of a single client may involve legal problems in several states." ABA Opinion 316 (1967).

9. "[W]e reaffirmed the general principle that legal services to New Jersey residents with respect to New Jersey matters may ordinarily be furnished only by New Jersey counsel; but we pointed out that there may be multistate transactions where strict adherence to this thesis would not be in the public interest and that, under the circumstances, it would have been not only more costly to the client but also 'grossly impractical and inefficient' to have had the settlement negotiations conducted by separate lawyers from different states." In re Estate of Waring, 47 N.J. 367, 376, 221 A.2d 193, 197 (1966).

	Model Code	*ABA Model Rules*
Model Rules Comparison	EC 3-1	Rules 5.4, 5.5
	EC 3-2	Rules 5.4, 5.5
	EC 3-3	Rules 5.4, 5.5
	EC 3-4	Rules 5.4, 5.5
	EC 3-5	Rules 5.4, 5.5
	EC 3-6	Rule 5.3
	EC 3-7	Rule 5.5
	EC 3-8	Rules 5.4(a), (b), (d), 5.5(b)
	EC 3-9	Rules 5.5(a), 8.5

Disciplinary Rules

DR 3-101 Aiding Unauthorized Practice of Law[10]

(A) A lawyer shall not aid a non-lawyer in the unauthorized practice of law.

(B) A lawyer shall not practice law in a jurisdiction where to do so would be in violation of regulations of the profession in that jurisdiction.[12]

DR 3-102 Dividing Legal Fees with a Non-Lawyer

(A) A lawyer or law firm shall not share legal fees with a non-lawyer,[13] except that:

(1) An agreement by a lawyer with his firm, partner, or associate may provide for the payment of money, over a reasonable period of time after his death, to his estate or to one or more specified persons.

(2) A lawyer who undertakes to complete unfinished legal business of a deceased lawyer may pay to the estate of the deceased lawyer that proportion of the total compensation which fairly represents the services rendered by the deceased lawyer.

(3) A lawyer or law firm may include nonlawyer employees in a compensation or retirement plan, even though the plan is based in whole or in part on a profit-sharing arrangement, providing such plan does not circumvent another Disciplinary Rule.

10. Conduct permitted by the Disciplinary Rules of Canons 2 and 5 does not violate DR 3-101.

12. It should be noted, however, that a lawyer may engage in conduct, otherwise prohibited by this Disciplinary Rule, where such conduct is authorized by preemptive federal legislation. See Sperry v. Florida, 373 U.S. 379 (1963).

13. "The receiving attorney shall not under any guise or form share his fee for legal services with a lay agency, personal or corporate, without prejudice, however, to the right of the lay forwarder to change and collect from the creditor proper compensation for non-legal services rendered by the law [sic] forwarder which are separate and apart from the services performed by the receiving attorney." ABA Opinion 294 (1958).

DR 3-103 Forming a Partnership with a Non-Lawyer

(A) A lawyer shall not form a partnership with a non-lawyer if any of the activities of the partnership consist of the practice of law.[17]

	Model Code	*ABA Model Rules*
Model Rules Comparison	DR 3-101(A)	Rule 5.5(b)
	DR 3-101(B)	Rule 5.5(a)
	DR 3-102	Rule 5.4(a)
	DR 3-103	Rule 5.4(b)

CANON 4. A LAWYER SHOULD PRESERVE THE CONFIDENCES AND SECRETS OF A CLIENT

Ethical Considerations

EC 4-1   Both the fiduciary relationship existing between lawyer and client and the proper functioning of the legal system require the preservation by the lawyer of confidences and secrets of one who has employed or sought to employ him.[1] A client must feel free to discuss whatever he wishes with his lawyer and a lawyer must be equally free to obtain information beyond that volunteered by his client.[2] A lawyer should be fully informed of all the facts of the matter he is

---

17. ABA Opinion 316 (1967) states that lawyers licensed in different jurisdictions may, under certain conditions, enter "into an arrangement for the practice of law" and that a lawyer licensed in State A is not, for such purpose, a layman in State B.

1. "The reason underlying the rule with respect to confidential communications between attorney and client is well stated in Mechem on Agency, 2d Ed., Vol. 2, §2297, as follows: 'The purposes and necessities of the relation between a client and his attorney require, in many cases, on the part of the client, the fullest and freest disclosures to the attorney of the client's objects, motives and acts. This disclosure is made in the strictest confidence, relying upon the attorney's honor and fidelity. To permit the attorney to reveal to others what is so disclosed, would be not only a gross violation of a sacred trust upon his part, but it would utterly destroy and prevent the usefulness and benefits to be derived from professional assistance. Based upon considerations of public policy, therefore, the law wisely declares that all confidential communications and disclosures, made by a client to his legal adviser for the purpose of obtaining his professional aid or advice, shall be strictly privileged; — that the attorney shall not be permitted, without the consent of his client, — and much less will he be compelled — to reveal or disclose communications made to him under such circumstances." ABA Opinion 250 (1943).

"While it is true that complete revelation of relevant facts should be encouraged for trial purposes, nevertheless an attorney's dealings with his client, if both are sincere, and if the dealings involve more than mere technical matters, should be immune to discovery proceedings. There must be freedom from fear of revealment of matters disclosed to an attorney because of the peculiarly intimate relationship existing." Ellis-Foster Co. v. Union Carbide & Carbon Corp., 159 F. Supp. 917, 919 (D.N.J. 1958).

2. "While it is the great purpose of law to ascertain the truth, there is the countervailing necessity of insuring the right of every person to freely and fully confer and confide in one having knowledge of the law, and skilled in its practice, in order that the former may have adequate advice and a

handling in order for his client to obtain the full advantage of our legal system. It is for the lawyer in the exercise of his independent professional judgment to separate the relevant and important from the irrelevant and unimportant. The observance of the ethical obligation of a lawyer to hold inviolate the confidences and secrets of his client not only facilitates the full development of facts essential to proper representation of the client but also encourages laymen to seek early legal assistance.

EC 4-2 The obligation to protect confidences and secrets obviously does not preclude a lawyer from revealing information when his client consents after full disclosure,[3] when necessary to perform his professional employment, when permitted by a Disciplinary Rule, or when required by law. Unless the client otherwise directs, a lawyer may disclose the affairs of his client to partners or associates of his firm. It is a matter of common knowledge that the normal operation of a law office exposes confidential professional information to non-lawyer employees of the office, particularly secretaries and those having access to the files; and this obligates a lawyer to exercise care in selecting and training his employees so that the sanctity of all confidences and secrets of his clients may be preserved. If the obligation extends to two or more clients as to the same information, a lawyer should obtain the permission of all before revealing the information. A lawyer must always be sensitive to the rights and wishes of his client and act scrupulously in the making of decisions which may involve the disclosure of information obtained in his professional relationship. Thus, in the absence of consent of his client after full disclosure, a lawyer should not associate another lawyer in the handling of a matter; nor should he, in the absence of consent, seek counsel from another lawyer if there is a reasonable possibility that the identity of the client or his confidences or secrets would be revealed to such lawyer. Both social amenities and professional duty should cause a lawyer to shun indiscreet conversations concerning his clients.

EC 4-3 Unless the client otherwise directs, it is not improper for a lawyer to give limited information from his files to an outside agency necessary for statistical, bookkeeping, accounting, data processing, banking, printing, or other legitimate purposes, provided he exercises due care in the selection of the agency and warns the agency that the information must be kept confidential.

EC 4-4 The attorney-client privilege is more limited than the ethical obligation of a lawyer to guard the confidences and secrets of his client. This ethical precept, unlike the evidentiary privilege, exists without regard to the nature or

---

proper defense. This assistance can be made safely and readily available only when the client is free from the consequences of apprehension of disclosure by reason of the subsequent statements of the skilled lawyer." Baird v. Koerner, 279 F.2d 623, 629-30 (9th Cir. 1960).

3. "Where . . . [a client] knowingly and after full disclosure participates in a [legal fee] financing plan which requires the furnishing of certain information to the bank, clearly by his conduct he has waived any privilege as to that information." ABA Opinion 320 (1968).

source of information or the fact that others share the knowledge. A lawyer should endeavor to act in a manner which preserves the evidentiary privilege; for example, he should avoid professional discussions in the presence of persons to whom the privilege does not extend. A lawyer owes an obligation to advise the client of the attorney-client privilege and timely to assert the privilege unless it is waived by the client.

EC 4-5 A lawyer should not use information acquired in the course of the representation of a client to the disadvantage of the client and a lawyer should not use, except with the consent of his client after full disclosure, such information for his own purposes. Likewise, a lawyer should be diligent in his efforts to prevent the misuse of such information by his employees and associates. Care should be exercised by a lawyer to prevent the disclosure of the confidences and secrets of one client to another,[7] and no employment should be accepted that might require such disclosure.

EC 4-6 The obligation of a lawyer to preserve the confidences and secrets of his client continues after the termination of his employment.[8] Thus a lawyer should not attempt to sell a law practice as a going business because, among other reasons, to do so would involve the disclosure of confidences and secrets. A lawyer should also provide for the protection of the confidences and secrets of his client following the termination of the practice of the lawyer, whether termination is due to death, disability, or retirement. For example, a lawyer might provide for the personal papers of the client to be returned to him and for the papers of the lawyer to be delivered to another lawyer or to be destroyed. In determining the method of disposition, the instructions and wishes of the client should be a dominant consideration.

	Model Code	ABA Model Rules
Model Rules Comparison	EC 4-1	Rule 1.6
	EC 4-2	Rules 1.6(a), (b)(1), 2.2(a)(1), 5.3(a)
	EC 4-3	Rule 1.6(a)
	EC 4-4	Rule 1.6(a)
	EC 4-5	Rules 1.8(b), 1.9(b), 1.9(c), 1.10(a), 5.1(a), (b) & (c), 5.3(a)
	EC 4-6	Rules 1.9(c), 1.17

7. "[A]n attorney must not accept professional employment against a client or a former client which will, or even *may* require him to use confidential information obtained by the attorney in the course of his professional relations with such client regarding the subject matter of the employment. . . ." ABA Opinion 165 (1936).

8. "Confidential communications between an attorney and his client, made because of the relationship and concerning the subject-matter of the attorney's employment, are generally privileged from disclosure without the consent of the client, and this privilege outlasts the attorney's employment. Canon 37." ABA Opinion 154 (1936).

Disciplinary Rules

DR 4-101 Preservation of Confidences and Secrets of a Client

(A) "Confidence" refers to information protected by the attorney-client privilege under applicable law, and "secret" refers to other information gained in the professional relationship that the client has requested be held inviolate or the disclosure of which would be embarrassing or would be likely to be detrimental to the client.

(B) Except when permitted under DR 4-101 (C), a lawyer shall not knowingly:

(1) Reveal a confidence or secret of his client.[11]

(2) Use a confidence or secret of his client to the disadvantage of the client.

(3) Use a confidence or secret of his client for the advantage of himself or of a third person, unless the client consents after full disclosure.

(C) A lawyer may reveal:

(1) Confidences or secrets with the consent of the client or clients affected, but only after a full disclosure to them.

(2) Confidences or secrets when permitted under Disciplinary Rules or required by law or court order.[15]

(3) The intention of his client to commit a crime[16] and the information necessary to prevent the crime.

(4) Confidences or secrets necessary to estabish or collect his fee or to defend himself or his employees or associates against an accusation of wrongful conduct.[19]

---

11. . . . "Communications between lawyer and client are privileged (Wigmore on Evidence, 3d Ed., Vol. 8 §§2290-2329). The modern theory underlying the privilege is subjective and is to give the client freedom of apprehension in consulting his legal adviser (ibid., §2290, p.548). The privilege applies to communications made in seeking legal advice for any purpose (ibid., §2294, p.563). The mere circumstance that the advice is given without charge therefor does not nullify the privilege (ibid., §2303)." ABA Opinion 216 (1941).

"It is the duty of an attorney to maintain the confidence and preserve inviolate the secrets of his client. . . ." ABA Opinion 155 (1936).

15. . . . "We held in Opinion 155 that a communication by a client to his attorney in respect to the future commission of an unlawful act or to a continuing wrong is not privileged from disclosure. Public policy forbids that the relation of attorney and client should be used to conceal wrongdoing on the part of the client. . . ." ABA Opinion 156 (1936).

16. ABA Opinion 314 (1965) indicates that a lawyer must disclose even the confidences of his clients if "the facts in the attorney's possession indicate beyond reasonable doubt that a crime will be committed."

19. "[T]he adjudicated cases recognize an exception to the rule [that a lawyer shall not reveal the confidences of his client], where disclosure is necessary to protect the attorney's interests arising out of the relation of attorney and client in which disclosure was made.

"The exception is stated in Mechem on Agency, 2d Ed., Vo. 2, §2313, as follows: 'But the attorney may disclose information received from the client when it becomes necessary for his own protection, as if the client should bring an action against the attorney for negligence or misconduct, and it became necessary for the attorney to show what his instructions were, or what was the nature of the duty which the client expected him to perform. So if it became necessary for the attorney to bring an

(D) A lawyer shall exercise reasonable care to prevent his employees, associates, and others whose services are utilized by him from disclosing or using confidences or secrets of a client, except that a lawyer may reveal the information allowed by DR 4-101 (C) through an employee.

Model Rules Comparison	*Model Code*	*ABA Model Rules*
	DR 4-101(A)	Rule 1.6(a)
	DR 4-101(B)	Rules 1.6(a), (b), 1.8(b), 1.9(c)
	DR 4-101(C)	Rules 1.6, 1.9(c)
	DR 4-101(D)	Rules 5.1(a), (b), 5.3(a), (b)

CANON 5. A LAWYER SHOULD EXERCISE INDEPENDENT PROFESSIONAL JUDGMENT ON BEHALF OF A CLIENT

Ethical Considerations

EC 5-1 The professional judgment of a lawyer should be exercised, within the bounds of the law, solely for the benefit of his client and free of compromising influences and loyalties.[1] Neither his personal interests, the interests of other clients, nor the desires of third persons should be permitted to dilute his loyalty to his client.

Interests of a Lawyer That May Affect His Judgment

EC 5-2 A lawyer should not accept proffered employment if his personal interests or desires will, or there is a reasonable probability that they will, affect adversely the advice to be given or services to be rendered the prospective client.[2] After accepting employment, a lawyer carefully should refrain from ac-

---

action against the client, the client's privilege could not prevent the attorney from disclosing what was essential as a means of obtaining or defending his own rights.' . . ." ABA Opinion 250 (1943).

   1. . . . "When a client engages the services of a lawyer in a given piece of business he is entitled to feel that, until that business is finally disposed of in some manner, he has the undivided loyalty of the one upon whom he looks as his advocate and champion. If, as in this case, he is sued and his home attached by his own attorney, who is representing him in another matter, all feeling of loyalty is necessarily destroyed, and the profession is exposed to the charge that it is interested only in money." Grievance Comm. v. Rattner, 152 Conn. 59, 65, 203 A.2d 82, 84 (1964). . . .

   2. "Attorneys must not allow their private interests to conflict with those of their clients. . . . They owe their entire devotion to the interests of their clients." United States v. Anonymous, 215 F. Supp. 111, 113 (E.D. Tenn. 1963).

quiring a property right or assuming a position that would tend to make his judgment less protective of the interests of his client.

EC 5-3 The self-interest of a lawyer resulting from his ownership of property in which his client also has an interest or which may affect property of his client may interfere with the exercise of free judgment on behalf of his client. If such interference would occur with respect to a prospective client, a lawyer should decline employment proffered by him. After accepting employment, a lawyer should not acquire property rights that would adversely affect his professional judgment in the representation of his client. Even if the property interests of a lawyer do not presently interfere with the exercise of his independent judgment, but the likelihood of interference can reasonably be foreseen by him, a lawyer should explain the situation to his client and should decline employment or withdraw unless the client consents to the continuance of the relationship after full disclosure. A lawyer should not seek to persuade his client to permit him to invest in an undertaking of his client nor make improper use of his professional relationship to influence his client to invest in an enterprise in which the lawyer is interested.

EC 5-4 If, in the course of his representation of a client, a lawyer is permitted to receive from his client a beneficial ownership in publication rights relating to the subject matter of the employment, he may be tempted to subordinate the interests of his client to his own anticipated pecuniary gain. For example, a lawyer in a criminal case who obtains from his client television, radio, motion picture, newspaper, magazine, book, or other publication rights with respect to the case may be influenced, consciously or unconsciously, to a course of conduct that will enhance the value of his publication rights to the prejudice of his client. To prevent these potentially differing interests, such arrangements should be scrupulously avoided prior to the termination of all aspects of the matter giving rise to the employment, even though his employment has previously ended.

EC 5-5 A lawyer should not suggest to his client that a gift be made to himself or for his benefit. If a lawyer accepts a gift from his client, he is peculiarly susceptible to the charge that he unduly influenced or over-reached the client. If a client voluntarily offers to make a gift to his lawyer, the lawyer may accept the gift, but before doing so, he should urge that his client secure disinterested advice from an independent, competent person who is cognizant of all the circum-

---

"[T]he court [below] concluded that a firm may not accept any action against a person whom they are presently representing even though there is no relationship between the two cases. In arriving at this conclusion, the court cites an opinion of the Committee on Professional Ethics of the New York County Lawyers' Association which stated in part: 'While under the circumstances . . . there may be no actual conflict of interest . . . "maintenance of public confidence in the Bar requires an attorney who has accepted representation of a client to decline, while representing such client, any employment from an adverse party in any matter even though wholly unrelated to the original retainer." . . .' " Grievance Comm. v. Rattner, 152 Conn. 59, 65, 203 A.2d 82, 84 (1964).

stances.[3] Other than in exceptional circumstances, a lawyer should insist that an instrument in which his client desires to name him beneficially be prepared by another lawyer selected by the client.

EC 5-6   A lawyer should not consciously influence a client to name him as executor, trustee, or lawyer in an instrument. In those cases where a client wishes to name his lawyer as such, care should be taken by the lawyer to avoid even the appearance of impropriety.

EC 5-7   The possibility of an adverse effect upon the exercise of free judgment by a lawyer on behalf of his client during litigation generally makes it undesirable for the lawyer to acquire a proprietary interest in the cause of his client or otherwise to become financially interested in the outcome of the litigation. However, it is not improper for a lawyer to protect his right to collect a fee for his services by the assertion of legally permissible liens, even though by doing so he may acquire an interest in the outcome of litigation. Although a contingent fee arrangement gives a lawyer a financial interest in the outcome of litigation, a reasonable contingent fee is permissible in civil cases because it may be the only means by which a layman can obtain the services of a lawyer of his choice. But a lawyer, because he is in a better position to evaluate a cause of action, should enter into a contingent fee arrangement only in those instances where the arrangement will be beneficial to the client.

EC 5-8   A financial interest in the outcome of litigation also results if monetary advances are made by the lawyer to his client. Although this assistance generally is not encouraged, there are instances when it is not improper to make loans to a client. For example, the advancing or guaranteeing of payment of the costs and expenses of litigation by a lawyer may be the only way a client can enforce his cause of action, but the ultimate liability for such costs and expenses must be that of the client.

EC 5-9   Occasionally a lawyer is called upon to decide in a particular case whether he will be a witness or an advocate. If a lawyer is both counsel and witness, he becomes more easily impeachable for interest and thus may be a less effective witness. Conversely, the opposing counsel may be handicapped in challenging the credibility of the lawyer when the lawyer also appears as an ad-

3. "Courts of equity will scrutinize with jealous vigilance transactions between parties occupying fiduciary relations toward each other. . . . Where a fiduciary relation exists, the burden of proof is on the grantee or beneficiary of an instrument executed during the existence of such relationship to show the fairness of the transaction, that it was equitable and just and that it did not proceed from undue influence. . . . Conversely, an attorney is not prohibited from dealing with his client or buying his property, and such contracts, if open, fair and honest, when deliberately made, are as valid as contracts between other parties. . . . [I]mportant factors in determining whether a transaction is fair include a showing by the fiduciary (1) that he made a full and frank disclosure of all the relevant information that he had; (2) that the consideration was adequate; and (3) that the principal had independent advice before completing the transaction." McFail v. Braden, 19 Ill. 2d 108, 117-18, 166 N.E. 2d 46, 52 (1960).

vocate in the case. An advocate who becomes a witness is in the unseemly and ineffective position of arguing his own credibility. The roles of an advocate and of a witness are inconsistent; the function of an advocate is to advance or argue the cause of another, while that of a witness is to state facts objectively.

EC 5-10 Problems incident to the lawyer-witness relationship arise at different stages; they relate either to whether a lawyer should accept employment or should withdraw from employment.[10] Regardless of when the problem arises, his decision is to be governed by the same basic considerations. It is not objectionable for a lawyer who is a potential witness to be an advocate if it is unlikely that he will be called as a witness because his testimony would be merely cumulative or if his testimony will relate only to an uncontested issue.[11] In the exceptional situation where it will be manifestly unfair to the client for the lawyer to refuse employment or to withdraw when he will likely be a witness on a contested issue, he may serve as advocate even though he may be a witness.[12] In making such decision, he should determine the personal or financial sacrifice of the client that may result from his refusal of employment or withdrawal therefrom, the materiality of his testimony, and the effectiveness of his representation in view of his personal involvement. In weighing these factors, it should be clear that refusal or withdrawal will impose an unreasonable hardship upon the client before the lawyer accepts or continues the employment. Where the question arises, doubts should be resolved in favor of the lawyer testifying and against his becoming or continuing as an advocate.[14]

EC 5-11 A lawyer should not permit his personal interests to influence his advice relative to a suggestion by his client that additional counsel be employed. In like manner, his personal interests should not deter him from suggesting that additional counsel be employed; on the contrary, he should be alert to the desir-

10. "When a lawyer knows, prior to trial, that he will be a necessary witness, except as to merely formal matters such as identification or custody of a document or the like, neither he nor his firm or associates should conduct the trial. If, during the trial, he discovers that the ends of justice require his testimony, he should, from that point on, if feasible and not prejudicial to his client's case, leave further conduct of the trial to other counsel. If circumstances do not permit withdrawal from the conduct of the trial, the lawyer should not argue the credibility of his own testimony." A Code of Trial Conduct: Promulgated by the American College of Trial Lawyers, 43 A.B.A.J. 223, 224-25 (1957).

11. Cf. Canon 19: "When a lawyer is a witness for his client, except as to merely formal matters, such as the attestation or custody of an instrument and the like, he should leave the trial of the case to other counsel."

12. "It is the general rule that a lawyer may not testify in litigation in which he is an advocate unless circumstances arise which could not be anticipated and it is necessary to prevent a miscarriage of justice. In those rare cases where the testimony of an attorney is needed to protect his client's interests, it is not only proper but mandatory that it be forthcoming." Schwartz v. Wenger, 267 Minn. 40, 43-44, 124 N.W. 2d 489, 492 (1963).

14. "[C]ases may arise, and in practice often do arise, in which there would be a failure of justice should the attorney withhold his testimony. In such a case it would be a vicious professional sentiment which would deprive the client of the benefit of his attorney's testimony." Connolly v. Straw, 53 Wis. 645, 649, 11 N.W. 17, 19 (1881).

But see Canon 19: "Except when essential to the ends of justice, a lawyer should avoid testifying in court in behalf of his client."

ability of recommending additional counsel when, in his judgment, the proper representation of his client requires it. However, a lawyer should advise his client not to employ additional counsel suggested by the client if the lawyer believes that such employment would be a disservice to the client, and he should disclose the reasons for his belief.

EC 5-12 Inability of co-counsel to agree on a matter vital to the representation of their client requires that their disagreement be submitted by them jointly to their client for his resolution, and the decision of the client shall control the action to be taken.

EC 5-13 A lawyer should not maintain membership in or be influenced by any organization of employees that undertakes to prescribe, direct, or suggest when or how he should fulfill his professional obligations to a person or organization that employs him as a lawyer. Although it is not necessarily improper for a lawyer employed by a corporation or similar entity to be a member of an organization of employees, he should be vigilant to safeguard his fidelity as a lawyer to his employer, free from outside influences.

Interests of Multiple Clients

EC 5-14 Maintaining the independence of professional judgment required of a lawyer precludes his acceptance or continuation of employment that will adversely affect his judgment on behalf of or dilute his loyalty to a client. This problem arises whenever a lawyer is asked to represent two or more clients who may have differing interests, whether such interests be conflicting, inconsistent, diverse, or otherwise discordant.[18]

EC 5-15 If a lawyer is requested to undertake or to continue representation of multiple clients having potentially differing interests, he must weigh carefully the possibility that his judgment may be impaired or his loyalty divided if he accepts or continues the employment. He should resolve all doubts against the propriety of the representation. A lawyer should never represent in litigation multiple clients with differing interests; and there are few situations in which he would be justified in representing in litigation multiple clients with potentially differing interests. If a lawyer accepted such employment and the interests did become actually differing, he would have to withdraw from employment with likelihood of resulting hardship on the clients; and for this reason it is preferable that he refuse the employment initially. On the other hand, there are many instances in which a lawyer may properly serve multi-

18. The ABA Canons speak of "conflicting interests" rather than "differing interests" but make no attempt to define such other than the statement in Canon 6: "Within the meaning of this canon, a lawyer represents conflicting interests when, in behalf of one client, it is his duty to contend for that which duty to another client requires him to oppose."

ple clients having potentially differing interests in matters not involving litigation. If the interests vary only slightly, it is generally likely that the lawyer will not be subjected to an adverse influence and that he can retain his independent judgment on behalf of each client; and if the interests become differing, withdrawal is less likely to have a disruptive effect upon the causes of his clients.

EC 5-16 In those instances in which a lawyer is justified in representing two or more clients having differing interests, it is nevertheless essential that each client be given the opportunity to evaluate his need for representation free of any potential conflict and to obtain other counsel if he so desires.[20] Thus before a lawyer may represent multiple clients, he should explain fully to each client the implications of the common representation and should accept or continue employment only if the clients consent. If there are present other circumstances that might cause any of the multiple clients to question the undivided loyalty of the lawyer, he should also advise all of the clients of those circumstances.

EC 5-17 Typically recurring situations involving potentially differing interests are those in which a lawyer is asked to represent co-defendants in a criminal case, co-plaintiffs in a personal injury case, an insured and his insurer,[23] and beneficiaries of the estate of a decedent. Whether a lawyer can fairly and adequately protect the interests of multiple clients in these and similar situations depends upon an analysis of each case. In certain circum-

20. "Glasser wished the benefit of the undivided assistance of counsel of his own choice. We think that such a desire on the part of an accused should be respected. Irrespective of any conflict of interest, the additional burden of representing another party may conceivably impair counsel's effectiveness.

"To determine the precise degree of prejudice sustained by Glasser . . . is at once difficult and unnecessary. The right to have the assistance of counsel is too fundamental and absolute to allow courts to indulge in nice calculations as to the amount of prejudice arising from its denial." Glasser v. United States, 315 U.S. 60, 75-76 (1942).

23. "When counsel, although paid by the casualty company, undertakes to represent the policyholder and files his notice of appearance, he owes to his client, the assured, an undeviating and single allegiance. His fealty embraces the requirement to produce in court all witnesses, fact and expert, who are available and necessary for the proper protection of the rights of his client. . . .

" . . . The Canons of Professional Ethics make it pellucid that there are not two standards, one applying to counsel privately retained by a client, and the other to counsel paid by an insurance carrier." American Employers Ins. Co. v. Goble Aircraft Specialties, 205 Misc. 1066, 1075, 131 N.Y.S.2d 393, 401 (1954), motion to withdraw appeal granted, 1 App. Div. 2d 1008, 154 N.Y.S.2d 835 (1956).

"[C]ounsel, selected by State Farm to defend Dorothy Walker's suit for $50,000 damages, was apprised by Walker that his earlier version of the accident was untrue and that actually the accident occurred because he lost control of his car in passing a Cadillac just ahead. At that point, Walker's counsel should have refused to participate further in view of the conflict of interest between Walker and State Farm. . . . Instead he participated in the ensuing deposition of the Walkers, even took an *ex parte* sworn statement from Mr. Walker in order to advise State Farm what action it should take, and later used the statement against Walker in the District Court. This action appears to contravene an Indiana attorney's duty 'at every peril to himself, to preserve the secrets of his client'. . . ." State Farm Mut. Auto Ins. Co. v. Walker, 382 F.2d 548, 552 (1967), cert. denied, 389 U.S. 1045 (1968).

stances, there may exist little chance of the judgment of the lawyer being adversely affected by the slight possibility that the interests will become actually differing; in other circumstances, the chance of adverse effect upon his judgment is not unlikely.

EC 5-18 A lawyer employed or retained by a corporation or similar entity owes his allegiance to the entity and not to a stockholder, director, officer, employee, representative, or other person connected with the entity. In advising the entity, a lawyer should keep paramount its interests and his professional judgment should not be influenced by the personal desires of any person or organization. Occasionally a lawyer for an entity is requested by a stockholder, director, officer, employee, representative, or other person connected with the entity to represent him in an individual capacity; in such case the lawyer may serve the individual only if the lawyer is convinced that differing interests are not present.

EC 5-19 A lawyer may represent several clients whose interests are not actually or potentially differing. Nevertheless, he should explain any circumstances that might cause a client to question his undivided loyalty. Regardless of the belief of a lawyer that he may properly represent multiple clients, he must defer to a client who holds the contrary belief and withdraw from representation of that client.

EC 5-20 A lawyer is often asked to serve as an impartial arbitrator or mediator in matters which involve present or former clients. He may serve in either capacity if he first discloses such present of former relationships. After a lawyer has undertaken to act as an impartial arbitrator or mediator, he should not thereafter represent in the dispute any of the parties involved.

Desires of Third Persons

EC 5-21 The obligation of a lawyer to exercise professional judgment solely on behalf of his client requires that he disregard the desires of others that might impair his free judgment.[25] The desires of a third person will seldom adversely affect a lawyer unless that person is in a position to exert strong eco-

25. See ABA Canon 35.

"Objection to the intervention of a lay intermediary, who may control litigation or otherwise interfere with the rendering of legal services in a confidential relationship, . . . derives from the element of pecuniary gain. Fearful of dangers thought to arise from that element, the courts of several States have sustained regulations aimed at these activities. We intimate no view one way or the other as to the merits of those decisions with respect to the particular arrangements against which they are directed. It is enough that the superficial resemblance in form between those arrangements and that at bar cannot obscure the vital fact that here the entire arrangement employs constitutionally privileged means of expression to secure constitutionally guaranteed civil rights." NAACP v. Button, 371 U.S. 415, 441-42 (1963).

nomic, political, or social pressures upon the lawyer. These influences are often subtle, and a lawyer must be alert to their existence. A lawyer subjected to outside pressures should make full disclosure of them to his client, and if he or his client believes that the effectiveness of his representation has been or will be impaired thereby, the lawyer should take proper steps to withdraw from representation of his client.

EC 5-22   Economic, political, or social pressures by third persons are less likely to impinge upon the independent judgment of a lawyer in a matter in which he is compensated directly by his client and his professional work is exclusively with his client. On the other hand, if a lawyer is compensated from a source other than his client, he may feel a sense of responsibility to someone other than his client.

EC 5-23   A person or organization that pays or furnishes lawyers to represent others possesses a potential power to exert strong pressures against the independent judgment of those lawyers. Some employers may be interested in furthering their own economic, political, or social goals without regard to the professional responsibility of the lawyer to his individual client. Others may be far more concerned with establishment or extension of legal principles than in the immediate protection of the rights of the lawyer's individual client. On some occasions, decisions on priority of work may be made by the employer rather than the lawyer with the result that prosecution of work already undertaken for clients is postponed to their detriment. Similarly, an employer may seek, consciously or unconsciously, to further its own economic interests through the action of the lawyers employed by it. Since a lawyer must always be free to exercise his professional judgment without regard to the interests or motives of a third person, the lawyer who is employed by one to represent another must constantly guard against erosion of his professional freedom.[27]

EC 5-24   To assist a lawyer in preserving his professional independence, a number of courses are available to him. For example, a lawyer should not practice with or in the form of a professional legal corporation, even though the corporate form is permitted by law, if any director, officer, or stockholder of it is a non-lawyer. Although a lawyer may be employed by a business corporation with non-lawyers serving as directors or officers, and they necessarily

27. "Certainly it is true that 'the professional relationship between an attorney and his client is highly personal, involving an intimate appreciation of each individual client's particular problem.' And this Committee does not condone practices which interfere with that relationship. However, the mere fact the lawyer is actually paid by some entity other than the client does not affect that relationship, so long as the lawyer is selected by and is directly responsible to the client. See Informal Opinions 469 and 679. Of course, as the latter decision points out, there must be full disclosure of the arrangement by the attorney to the client. . . ." ABA Opinion 320 (1968).

"[A] third party may pay the cost of legal services as long as control remains in the client and the responsibility of the lawyer is solely to the client. Informal Opinions 469 ad [sic] 679. See also Opinion 237." Id.

have the right to make decisions of business policy, a lawyer must decline to accept direction of his professional judgment from any layman. Various types of legal aid offices are administered by boards of directors composed of lawyers and laymen. A lawyer should not accept employment from such an organization unless the board sets only broad policies and there is no interference in the relationship of the lawyer and the individual client he serves. Where a lawyer is employed by an organization, a written agreement that defines the relationship between him and the organization and provides for his independence is desirable since it may serve to prevent misunderstanding as to their respective roles. Although other innovations in the means of supplying legal counsel may develop, the responsibility of the lawyer to maintain his professional independence remains constant, and the legal profession must insure that changing circumstances do not result in loss of the professional independence of the lawyer.

	Model Code	ABA Model Rules
Model Rules Comparison	EC 5-1	Rules 1.7, 1.8(c), (d), (e), (f), (g), (j)
	EC 5-2	Rules 1.7, 1.8(a), (c), (d), (e), (f), (j)
	EC 5-3	Rules 1.7, 1.8(a), (d), (e)
	EC 5-4	Rule 1.8(d)
	EC 5-5	Rule 1.8(a), (c)
	EC 5-6	Rule 1.8(c)
	EC 5-7	Rules 1.5(c), 1.8(e), (j), 1.15
	EC 5-8	Rule 1.8(e)
	EC 5-9	Rules 1.7(b), 3.7
	EC 5-10	Rule 3.7
	EC 5-11	Rules 1.7, 2.1
	EC 5-12	Rule 1.2(a)
	EC 5-13	Rule 1.7(b)
	EC 5-14	Rules 1.7, 2.2(a)
	EC 5-15	Rules 1.7, 2.2(a), (c)
	EC 5-16	Rules 1.2(e), 1.7(b), 1.13(d), (e), 2.2(a), (b)
	EC 5-17	Rule 1.7
	EC 5-18	Rule 1.13
	EC 5-19	Rules 1.7(b), 2.2(c)
	EC 5-20	Rules 1.12, 2.2
	EC 5-21	Rules 1.7, 1.16(a)(1)
	EC 5-22	Rules 1.7, 1.8(f)
	EC 5-23	Rules 1.7(b), 1.8(f), 5.4(c)
	EC 5-24	Rules 1.13, 5.4(a), (d)

Disciplinary Rules

DR 5-101 Refusing Employment When the Interests of the Lawyer May Impair His Independent Professional Judgment

(A) Except with the consent of his client after full disclosure, a lawyer shall not accept employment if the exercise of his professional judgment on behalf of his client will be or reasonably may be affected by his own financial, business, property, or personal interests.[29]

(B) A lawyer shall not accept employment in contemplated or pending litigation if he knows or it is obvious that he or a lawyer in his firm ought to be called as a witness, except that he may undertake the employment and he or a lawyer in his firm may testify:

(1) If the testimony will relate solely to an uncontested matter.

(2) If the testimony will relate solely to a matter of formality and there is no reason to believe that substantial evidence will be offered in opposition to the testimony.

(3) If the testimony will relate solely to the nature and value of legal services rendered in the case by the lawyer or his firm to the client.

(4) As to any matter, if refusal would work a substantial hardship on the client because of the distinctive value of the lawyer or his firm as counsel in the particular case.

DR 5-102 Withdrawal as Counsel When the Lawyer Becomes a Witness

(A) If, after undertaking employment in contemplated or pending litigation, a lawyer learns or it is obvious that he or a lawyer in his firm ought to be called as a witness on behalf of his client, he shall withdraw from the conduct of the trial and his firm, if any, shall not continue representation in the trial, except that he may continue the representation and he or a lawyer in his firm may testify in the circumstances enumerated in DR 5-101(B) (1) through (4).

(B) If, after undertaking employment in contemplated or pending litigation, a lawyer learns or it is obvious that he or a lawyer in his firm may be called as a

29. "In Opinions 72 and 49 this Committee held: The relations of partners in a law firm are such that neither the firm nor any member or associate thereof, may accept any professional employment which any member of the firm cannot properly accept.

"In Opinion 16 this Committee held that a member of a law firm could not represent a defendant in a criminal case which was being prosecuted by another member of the firm who was public prosecuting attorney. The Opinion stated that it was clearly unethical for one member of the firm to oppose the interest of the state while another member represented those interests. . . . Since the prosecutor himself could not represent both the public and the defendant, no member of his law firm could either." ABA Opinion 296 (1959).

witness other than on behalf of his client, he may continue the representation until it is apparent that his testimony is or may be prejudicial to his client.[31]

DR 5-103 Avoiding Acquisition of Interest in Litigation

(A) A lawyer shall not acquire a proprietary interest in the cause of action or subject matter of litigation he is conducting for a client, except that he may:

(1) Acquire a lien granted by law to secure his fee or expenses.

(2) Contract with a client for a reasonable contingent fee in a civil case.

(B) While representing a client in connection with contemplated or pending litigation, a lawyer shall not advance or guarantee financial assistance to his client, except that a lawyer may advance or guarantee the expenses of litigation, including court costs, expenses of investigation, expenses of medical examination, and costs of obtaining and presenting evidence, provided the client remains ultimately liable for such expenses.

DR 5-104 Limiting Business Relations with a Client

(A) A lawyer shall not enter into a business transaction with a client if they have differing interests therein and if the client expects the lawyer to exercise his professional judgment therein for the protection of the client, unless the client has consented after full disclosure.

(B) Prior to conclusion of all aspects of the matter giving rise to his employment, a lawyer shall not enter into any arrangement or understanding with a client or a prospective client by which he acquires an interest in publication rights with respect to the subject matter of his employment or proposed employment.

DR 5-105 Refusing to Accept or Continue
Employment If the Interests of Another
Client May Impair the Independent
Professional Judgment of the Lawyer

(A) A lawyer shall decline proffered employment if the exercise of his independent professional judgment in behalf of a client will be or is likely to be adversely affected by the acceptence of the proffered employment, or if it

---

31. "... Apparently, the object of this precept is to avoid putting a lawyer in the obviously embarrassing predicament of testifying and then having to argue the credibility and effect of his own testimony. It was not designed to permit a lawyer to call opposing counsel as a witness and thereby disqualify him as counsel." Galarowicz v. Ward, 119 Utah 611, 620, 230 P.2d 576, 580 (1951).

would be likely to involve him in representing differing interests, except to the extent permitted under DR 5-105(C).[36]

(B) A lawyer shall not continue multiple employment if the exercise of his independent professional judgment in behalf of a client will be or is likely to be adversely affected by his representation of another client, or if it would be likely to involve him in representing differing interests, except to the extent permitted under DR 5-105(C).

(C) In the situations covered by DR 5-105 (A) and (B), a lawyer may represent multiple clients if it is obvious that he can adequately represent the interest of each and if each consents to the representation after full disclosure of the possible effect of such representation on the exercise of his independent professional judgment on behalf of each.

(D) If a lawyer is required to decline employment or to withdraw from employment under a Disciplinary Rule, no partner, or associate, or any other lawyer affiliated with him or his firm, may accept or continue such employment.

DR 5-106 Settling Similar Claims of Clients

(A) A lawyer who represents two or more clients shall not make or participate in the making of an aggregate settlement of the claims of or against his clients, unless each client has consented to the settlement after being advised of the existence and nature of all the claims involved in the proposed settlement, of the total amount of the settlement, and of the participation of each person in the settlement.

DR 5-107 Avoiding Influence by Others Than the
Client

(A) Except with the consent of his client after full disclosure, a lawyer shall not:

(1) Accept compensation for his legal services from one other than his client.

(2) Accept from one other than his client any thing of value related to his representation of or his employment by his client.[39]

---

36. ABA Opinion 247 (1942) held that an attorney could not investigate a nightclub shooting on behalf of one of the owner's liability insurers, obtaining the cooperation of the owner, and later represent the injured patron in an action against the owner and a different insurance company unless the attorney obtain the "express consent of all concerned given after a full disclosure of the facts," since to do so would be to represent conflicting interests.

39. "A lawyer who receives a commission (whether delayed or not) from a title insurance company or guaranty fund for recommending or selling the insurance to his client, or for work done for the client or the company, without either fully disclosing to the client his financial interest in the

(B) A lawyer shall not permit a person who recommends, employs, or pays him to render legal services for another to direct or regulate his professional judgment in rendering such legal services.[40]

(C) A lawyer shall not practice with or in the form of a professional corporation or association authorized to practice law for a profit, if:

(1) A non-lawyer owns any interest therein,[41] except that a fiduciary representative of the estate of a lawyer may hold the stock or interest of the lawyer for a reasonable time during administration;

(2) A non-lawyer is a corporate director or officer thereof;[42] or

(3) A non-lawyer has the right to direct or control the professional judgment of a lawyer.[43]

	Model Code	*ABA Model Rules*
Model Rules Comparison	DR 5-101(A)	Rules 1.7, 1.8(j), 6.3, 6.4
	DR 5-101(B)	Rules 1.7, 3.7
	DR 5-102(A)	Rules 1.7, 3.7
	DR 5-102(B)	Rules 1.7, 3.7
	DR 5-103(A)	Rules 1.5(c), 1.8(e), (j), 1.15
	DR 5-103(B)	Rule 1.8(e)
	DR 5-104(A)	Rules 1.7(b), 1.8(a)
	DR 5-104(B)	Rule 1.8(d)
	DR 5-105(A)	Rules 1.7, 2.2
	DR 5-105(B)	Rules 1.7, 1.13(e), 2.2
	DR 5-105(C)	Rules 1.7, 1.9, 1.13(e), 2.2
	DR 5-105(D)	Rules 1.10(a), 1.12(c)
	DR 5-106	Rule 1.8(g)
	DR 5-107(A)	Rules 1.7, 1.8(f)

transaction, or crediting the client's bill with the amount thus received, is guilty of unethical conduct." ABA Opinion 304 (1962).

40. "When the lay forwarder, as agent for the creditor, forwards a claim to an attorney, the direct relationship of attorney and client shall then exist between the attorney and the creditor, and the forwarder shall not interpose itself as an intermediary to control the activities of the attorney." ABA Opinion 294 (1958).

41. "Permanent beneficial and voting rights in the organization set up to practice law, whatever its form, must be restricted to lawyers while the organization is engaged in the practice of law." ABA Opinion 303 (1961).

42. "Canon 33 . . . promulgates underlying principles that must be observed no matter in what form of organization lawyers practice law. Its requirements that no person shall be admitted or held out as a practitioner or member who is not a member of the legal profession duly authorized to practice, and amenable to professional discipline, makes it clear that any centralized management must be in lawyers to avoid a violation of this Canon." ABA Opinion 303 (1961).

43. "There is no intervention of any lay agency between lawyer and client when centralized management provided only by lawyers may give guidance or direction to the services being rendered by a lawyer-member of the organization to a client. The language in Canon 35 that a lawyer should avoid all relations which direct the performance of his duties by or in the interest of an intermediary refers to lay intermediaries and not lawyer intermediaries with whom he is associated in the practice of law." ABA Opinion 303 (1961).

DR 5-107(B)   Rules 1.7, 1.8(f), 1.13(b),
                           (c), 2.1, 5.4(c)
DR 5-107(C)   Rule 5.4(d)

CANON 6. A LAWYER SHOULD REPRESENT A CLIENT COMPETENTLY

Ethical Considerations

EC 6-1 Because of his vital role in the legal process, a lawyer should act with competence and proper care in representing clients. He should strive to become and remain proficient in his practice[1] and should accept employment only in matters which he is or intends to become competent to handle.

EC 6-2 A lawyer is aided in attaining and maintaining his competence by keeping abreast of current legal literature and developments, participating in continuing legal education programs[2] concentrating in particular areas of the law, and by utilizing other available means. He has the additional ethical obligation to assist in improving the legal profession, and he may do so by participating in bar activities intended to advance the quality and standards of members of the profession. Of particular importance is the careful training of his younger associates and the giving of sound guidance to all lawyers who consult him. In short, a lawyer should strive at all levels to aid the legal profession in advancing the highest possible standards of integrity and competence and to meet those standards himself.

EC 6-3 While the licensing of a lawyer is evidence that he has met the standards then prevailing for admission to the bar, a lawyer generally should not accept employment in any area of the law in which he is not qualified. However, he may

1. "[W]hen a citizen is faced with the need for a lawyer, he wants, and is entitled to, the best informed counsel he can obtain. Changing times produce changes in our law and legal procedures. The natural complexities of law require continuing intensive study by a lawyer if he is to render his clients a maximum of efficient service. And, in so doing, he maintains the high standards of the legal profession; and he also increases respect and confidence by the general public." Rochelle & Payne, The Struggle for Public Understanding, 25 Texas B.J. 109, 160 (1962). . . .
"To be sure, no client has a right to expect that his lawyer will have all of the answers at the end of his tongue or even in the back of his head at all times. But the client does have the right to expect that the lawyer will have devoted his time and energies to maintaining and improving his competence to know where to look for the answers, to know how to deal with the problems, and to know how to advise to the best of his legal talents and abilities." Levy & Sprague, Accounting and Law: Is Dual Practice in the Public Interest?, 52 A.B.A.J. 1110, 1112 (1966).
2. "The whole purpose of continuing legal education, so enthusiastically supported by the ABA, is to make it possible for lawyers to make themselves better lawyers. . . . To the extent that that work, whether it be in attending institutes or lecture courses, in studying after hours or in the actual day in and day out practice of his profession, can be concentrated within a limited field, the greater the proficiency and expertness that can be developed." Report to the Special Committee on Specialization and Specialized Legal Education, 79 A.B.A. Rep. 582, 588 (1954).

accept such employment if in good faith he expects to become qualified through study and investigation, as long as such preparation would not result in unreasonable delay or expense to his client. Proper preparation and representation may require the association by the lawyer of professionals in other disciplines. A lawyer offered employment in a matter in which he is not and does not expect to become so qualified should either decline the employment or, with the consent of his client, accept the employment and associate a lawyer who is competent in the matter.

EC 6-4   Having undertaken representation, a lawyer should use proper care to safeguard the interests of his client. If a lawyer has accepted employment in a matter beyond his competence but in which he expected to become competent, he should diligently undertake the work and study necessary to qualify himself. In addition to being qualified to handle a particular matter, his obligation to his client requires him to prepare adequately for and give appropriate attention to his legal work.

EC 6-5   A lawyer should have pride in his professional endeavors. His obligation to act competently calls for higher motivation than that arising from fear of civil liability or disciplinary penalty.

EC 6-6   A lawyer should not seek, by contract or other means, to limit his individual liability to his client for his malpractice. A lawyer who handles the affairs of his client properly has no need to attempt to limit his liability for his professional activities and one who does not handle the affairs of his client properly should not be permitted to do so. A lawyer who is a stockholder in or is associated with a professional legal corporation may, however, limit his liability for malpractice of his associates in the corporation, but only to the extent permitted by law.

	Model Code	*ABA Model Rules*
Model Rules Comparison	EC 6-1	Rule 1.1
	EC 6-2	Rules 1.1, 5.1(a), (b), 6.1
	EC 6-3	Rules 1.1, 1.3
	EC 6-4	Rules 1.1, 1.3
	EC 6-5	Rule 1.1
	EC 6-6	Rule 1.8(h)

Disciplinary Rules

DR 6-101 Failing to Act Competently

(A) A lawyer shall not:
 (1) Handle a legal matter which he knows or should know that he is not competent to handle, without associating with him a lawyer who is competent to handle it.

374

(2) Handle a legal matter without preparation adequate in the circumstances.

(3) Neglect a legal matter entrusted to him.

DR 6-102 Limiting Liability to Client

(A) A lawyer shall not attempt to exonerate himself from or limit his liability to his client for his personal malpractice.

	Model Code	ABA Model Rules
Model Rules Comparison	DR 6-101	Rules 1.1, 1.3, 1.4
	DR 6-102	Rule 1.8(h)

CANON 7. A LAWYER SHOULD REPRESENT A CLIENT ZEALOUSLY WITHIN THE BOUNDS OF THE LAW

Ethical Considerations

EC 7-1   The duty of a lawyer, both to his client[1] and to the legal system, is to represent his client zealously within the bounds of the law,[3] which includes Dis-

---

1. "The right to be heard would be, in many cases, of little avail if it did not comprehend the right to be heard by counsel. Even the intelligent and educated layman has small and sometimes no skill in the science of law." Powell v. Alabama, 287 U.S. 45, 68-69 (1932).

3. . . . "Any persuasion or pressure on the advocate which deters him from planning and carrying out the litigation on the basis of 'what, within the framework of the law, is best for my client's interest?' interferes with the obligation to represent the client fully within the law.

"This obligation, in its fullest sense, is the heart of the adversary process. Each attorney, as an advocate, acts for and seeks that which in his judgment is best for his client, within the bounds authoritatively established. The advocate does not *decide* what is just in this case — he would be usurping the function of the judge and jury — he acts for and seeks for his client that which he is entitled to under the law. He can do no less and properly represent the client." Thode, The Ethical Standard for the Advocate, 39 Texas L. Rev. 575, 584 (1961).

"The [Texas public opinion] survey indicates that distrust of the lawyer can be traced directly to certain factors. Foremost of these is a basic misunderstanding of the function of the lawyer as an advocate in an adversary system.

"Lawyers are accused of taking advantage of 'loopholes' and 'technicalities' to win. Persons who make this charge are unaware, or do not understand, that the lawyer is hired to win, and if he does not exercise every legitimate effort in his client's behalf, then he is betraying a sacred trust." Rochelle and Payne, The Struggle for Public Understanding, 25 Texas B.J. 109, 159 (1962). . . .

"[W]hen defense counsel in a truly adverse proceeding, admits that his conscience would not permit him to adopt certain customary trial procedures, this extends beyond the realm of judgment and strongly suggests an invasion of constitutional rights." Johns v. Smyth, 176 F. Supp. 949, 952 (E.D. Va. 1959).

"The adversary system in law administration bears a striking resemblance to the competitive economic system. In each we assume that the individual through partisanship or through self-inter-

ciplinary Rules and enforceable professional regulations.[4] The professional responsibility of a lawyer derives from his membership in a profession which has the duty of assisting members of the public to secure and protect available legal rights and benefits. In our government of laws and not of men, each member of our society is entitled to have his conduct judged and regulated in accordance with the law,[5] to seek any lawful objective[6] through legally permissible means, and to present for adjudication any lawful claim, issue, or defense.

EC 7-2   The bounds of the law in a given case are often difficult to ascertain.[8] The language of legislative enactments and judicial opinions may be uncertain as applied to varying factual situations. The limits and specific meaning of apparently relevant law may be made doubtful by changing or developing constitutional interpretations, inadequately expressed statutes or judicial opinions, and changing public and judicial attitudes. Certainty of law ranges from well-settled rules through areas of conflicting authority to areas without precedent.

EC 7-3   Where the bounds of law are uncertain, the action of a lawyer may depend on whether he is serving as advocate or adviser. A lawyer may serve simultaneously as both advocate and adviser, but the two roles are essentially different.[9] In asserting a position on behalf of his client, an advocate for the most

---

est will strive mightily for his side, and that kind of striving we must have. But neither system would be tolerable without restraints and modifications, and at times without outright departures from the system itself. Since the legal profession is entrusted with the system of law administration, a part of its task is to develop in its members appropriate restraints without impairing the values of partisan striving. An accompanying task is to aid in the modification of the adversary system or departure from it in areas to which the system is unsuited." Cheatham, The Lawyer's Role and Surroundings, 25 Rocky Mt. L. Rev. 405, 410 (1953).

4. . . . "An attorney does not have the duty to do all and whatever he can that may enable him to win his client's cause or to further his client's interest. His duty and efforts in these respects, although they should be prompted by his 'entire devotion' to the interest of his client, must be within and not without the bounds of the law." In re Wines, 370 S.W.2d 328, 333 (Mo. 1963).

5. "[T]o secure for any controversy a truly informed and dispassionate decision is a difficult thing, requiring for its achievement a special summoning and organization of human effort and the adoption of measures to exclude the biases and prejudgments that have free play outside the courtroom. All of this goes for naught if the man with an unpopular cause is unable to find a competent lawyer courageous enough to represent him. His chance to have his day in court loses much of its meaning if his case is handicapped from the outset by the very kind of prejudgment our rules of evidence and procedure are intended to prevent." Professional Responsibility: Report of the Joint Conference, 44 A.B.A.J. 1159, 1216 (1958).

6. "[I]t is . . . [the tax lawyer's] positive duty to show the client how to avail himself to the full of what the law permits. He is not the keeper of the Congressional conscience." Paul, The Lawyer as a Tax Adviser, 25 Rocky Mt. L. Rev. 412, 418 (1953).

8. "[T]he very meaning of a line in the law is that you intentionally may go as close to it as you can if you do not pass it. . . ." Justice Holmes, in Superior Oil Co. v. Mississippi, 280 U.S. 390, 395-96 (1939).

9. "Today's lawyers perform two distinct types of functions, and our ethical standards should, but in the main do not, recognize these two functions. Judge Philbrick McCoy recently reported to

part deals with past conduct and must take the facts as he finds them. By contrast, a lawyer serving as adviser primarily assists his client in determining the course of future conduct and relationships. While serving as advocate, a lawyer should resolve in favor of his client doubts as to the bounds of the law.[10] In serving a client as adviser, a lawyer in appropriate circumstances should give his professional opinion as to what the ultimate decisions of the courts would likely be as to the applicable law.

Duty of the Lawyer to a Client

EC 7-4 The advocate may urge any permissible construction of the law favorable to his client, without regard to his professional opinion as to the likelihood that the construction will ultimately prevail.[11] His conduct is within the bounds of the law, and therefore permissible, if the position taken is supported by the law or is supportable by a good faith argument for an extension, modification, or reversal of the law. However, a lawyer is not justified in asserting a position in litigation that is frivolous.[12]

---

the American Bar Association the need for a reappraisal of the Canons in light of the new and distinct function of counselor, as distinguished from advocate, which today predominates in the legal profession. . . .

"[T]he counselor's obligation should extend to requiring him to inform and to impress upon the client a just solution of the problem, considering all interests involved." Thode, The Ethical Standard for the Advocate, 39 Texas L. Rev. 575, 578-79 (1961).

" . . . The reasons that justify and even require partisan advocacy in the trial of a cause do not grant any license to the lawyer to participate as legal advisor in a line of conduct that is immoral, unfair, or of doubtful legality. In saving himself from this unworthy involvement, the lawyer cannot be guided solely by an unreflective inner sense of good faith; he must be at pains to preserve a sufficient detachment from his client's interests so that he remains capable of a sound and objective appraisal of the propriety of what his client proposes to do." Professional Responsibility: Report of the Joint Conference, 44 A.B.A.J. 1159, 1161 (1958).

10. "[A] lawyer who is asked to advise his client . . . may freely urge the statement of positions most favorable to the client just as long as there is reasonable basis for those positions." ABA Opinion 314 (1965).

11. "The lawyer . . . is not an umpire, but an advocate. He is under no duty to refrain from making every proper argument in support of any legal point because he is not convinced of its inherent soundness. . . . His personal belief in the soundness of his cause or of the authorities supporting it, is irrelevant." ABA Opinion 280 (1949).

"Counsel apparently misconceived his role. It was his duty to honorably present his client's contentions in the light most favorable to his client. Instead he presumed to advise the court as to the validity and sufficiency of prisoner's motion, by letter. We therefore conclude that prisoner had no effective assistance of counsel and remand this case to the District Court with instructions to set aside the Judgment, appoint new counsel to represent the prisoner if he makes no objection thereto, and proceed anew." McCartney v. United States, 343 F. 2d 471, 472 (9th Cir. 1965).

12. . . . "The constitutional requirement of substantial equality and fair process can only be attained where counsel acts in the role of an active advocate in behalf of his client, as opposed to that of *amicus curiae*. The no-merit letter and the procedure it triggers do not reach that dignity. Counsel should, and can with honor and without conflict, be of more assistance to his client and to the court. His role as advocate requires that he support his client's appeal to the best of his ability. Of course, if counsel finds his case to be wholly frivolous, after a conscientious examination of it, he should so advise the court and request permission to withdraw. That request must, however, be accompanied

EC 7-5   A lawyer as adviser furthers the interest of his client by giving his professional opinion as to what he believes would likely be the ultimate decision of the courts on the matter at hand and by informing his client of the practical effect of such decision. He may continue in the representation of his client even though his client has elected to pursue a course of conduct contrary to the advice of the lawyer so long as he does not thereby knowingly assist the client to engage in illegal conduct or to take a frivolous legal position. A lawyer should never encourage or aid his client to commit criminal acts or counsel his client on how to violate the law and avoid punishment therefor.[14]

EC 7-6   Whether the proposed action of a lawyer is within the bounds of the law may be a perplexing question when his client is contemplating a course of conduct having legal consequences that vary according to the client's intent, motive, or desires at the time of the action. Often a lawyer is asked to assist his client in developing evidence relevant to the state of mind of the client at a particular time. He may properly assist his client in the development and preservation of evidence of existing motive, intent, or desire; obviously, he may not do anything furthering the creation or preservation of false evidence. In many cases a lawyer may not be certain as to the state of mind of his client, and in those situations he should resolve reasonable doubts in favor of his client.

EC 7-7   In certain areas of legal representation not affecting the merits of the cause or substantially prejudicing the rights of a client, a lawyer is entitled to make decisions on his own. But otherwise the authority to make decisions is exclusively that of the client and, if made within the framework of the law, such decisions are binding on his lawyer. As typical examples in civil cases, it is for the client to decide whether he will accept a settlement offer or whether he will waive his right to plead an affirmative defense. A defense lawyer in a criminal case has the duty to advise his client fully on whether a particular plea to a

---

by a brief referring to anything in the record that might arguably support the appeal. A copy of counsel's brief should be furnished the indigent and time allowed him to raise any points that he chooses; the court — not counsel — then proceeds, after a full examination of all the proceedings, to decide whether the case is wholly frivolous. If it so finds it may grant counsel's request to withdraw and dismiss the appeal insofar as federal requirements are concerned, or proceed to a decision on the merits, if state law so requires. On the other hand, if it finds any of the legal points arguable on their merits (and therefore not frivolous) it must, prior to decision, afford the indigent the assistance of counsel to argue the appeal." Anders v. California, 386 U.S. 738, 744, rehearing denied, 388 U.S. 924 (1967).

14. "For a lawyer to represent a syndicate notoriously engaged in the violation of the law for the purpose of advising the members how to break the law and at the same time escape it, is manifestly improper. While a lawyer may see to it that anyone accused of crime, no matter how serious and flagrant, has a fair trial, and present all available defenses, he may not cooperate in planning violations of the law. There is a sharp distinction, of course, between advising what can lawfully be done and advising how unlawful acts can be done in a way to avoid conviction. Where a lawyer accepts a retainer from an organization, known to be unlawful, and agrees in advance to defend its members when from time to time they are accused of crime arising out of its unlawful activities, this is equally improper." ABA Opinion 281 (1952).

charge appears to be desirable and as to the prospects of success on appeal, but it is for the client to decide what plea should be entered and whether an appeal should be taken.

EC 7-8   A lawyer should exert his best efforts to insure that decisions of his client are made only after the client has been informed of relevant considerations. A lawyer ought to initiate this decision-making process if the client does not do so. Advice of a lawyer to his client need not be confined to purely legal considerations.[16] A lawyer should advise his client of the possible effect of each legal alternative.[17] A lawyer should bring to bear upon this decision-making process the fullness of his experience as well as his objective viewpoint.[18] In assisting his client to reach a proper decision, it is often desirable for a lawyer to point out those factors which may lead to a decision that is morally just as well as legally permissible.[19] He may emphasize the possibility of harsh consequences that might result from assertion of legally permissible positions. In the final analysis, however, the lawyer should always remember that the decision whether to forego legally available objectives or methods because of nonlegal factors is ultimately for the client and not for himself. In the event that the client in a non-adjudicatory matter insists upon a course of conduct that is contrary to the judgment and advice of the lawyer but not prohibited by Disciplinary Rules, the lawyer may withdraw from the employment.[20]

16. "First of all, a truly great lawyer is a wise counselor to all manner of men in the varied crises of their lives when they most need disinterested advice. Effective counseling necessarily involves a thoroughgoing knowledge of the principles of the law not merely as they appear in the books but as they actually operate in action." Vanderbilt, The Five Functions of the Lawyer: Service to Clients and the Public, 40 A.B.A.J. 31 (1954).

17. "A lawyer should endeavor to obtain full knowlege of his client's cause before advising thereon. . . ." ABA Canon 8.

18. "[T]he the good lawyer does not serve merely as a legal conduit for his client's desires, but as a wise counselor, experienced in the art of devising arrangements that will put in workable order the entangled affairs and interests of human beings." Professional Responsibility: Report of the Joint Conference, 44 A.B.A.J. 1149, 1162 (1958).

19. "Vital as is the lawyer's role in adjudication, it should not be thought that it is only as an advocate pleading in open court that he contributes to the administration of the law. The most effective realization of the law's aims often takes place in the attorney's office, where litigation is forestalled by anticipating its outcome, where the lawyer's quiet counsel takes the place of public force. Contrary to popular belief, the compliance with the law thus brought about is not generally lip-serving and narrow, for by reminding him of its long-run costs the lawyer often deters his client from a course of conduct technically permissible under existing law, though inconsistent with its underlying spirit and purpose." Professional Responsibility: Report of the Joint Conference, 44 A.B.A.J. 1159, 1161 (1958).

20. "My summation of Judge Sharswood's view of the advocate's duty to the client is that he owes to the client the duty to use all legal means in support of the client's case. However, at the same time Judge Sharswood recognized that many advocates would find this obligation unbearable if applicable without exception. Therefore, the individual lawyer is given the choice of representing his client fully within the bounds set by the law *or of telling his client that he cannot do so,* so that the client may obtain another attorney if he wishes." Thode, The Ethical Standard for the Advocate, 39 Texas L. Rev. 575, 582 (1961).

EC 7-9 In the exercise of his professional judgment on those decisions which are for his determination in the handling of a legal matter, a lawyer should always act in a manner consistent with the best interests of his client. However, when an action in the best interest of his client seems to him to be unjust, he may ask his client for permission to forego such action.

EC 7-10 The duty of a lawyer to represent his client with zeal does not militate against his concurrent obligation to treat with consideration all persons involved in the legal process and to avoid the infliction of needless harm.

EC 7-11 The responsibilities of a lawyer may vary according to the intelligence, experience, mental condition or age of a client, the obligation of a public officer, or the nature of a particular proceeding. Examples include the representation of an illiterate or an incompetent, service as a public prosecutor or other government lawyer, and appearances before administrative and legislative bodies.

EC 7-12 Any mental or physical condition of a client that renders him incapable of making a considered judgment on his own behalf casts additional responsibilities upon his lawyer. Where an incompetent is acting through a guardian or other legal representative, a lawyer must look to such representative for those decisions which are normally the prerogative of the client to make. If a client under disability has no legal representative, his lawyer may be compelled in court proceedings to make decisions on behalf of the client. If the client is capable of understanding the matter in question or of contributing to the advancement of his interests, regardless of whether he is legally disqualified from performing certain acts, the lawyer should obtain from him all possible aid. If the disability of a client and the lack of a legal representative compel the lawyer to make decisions for his client, the lawyer should consider all circumstances then prevailing and act with care to safeguard and advance the interests of his client. But obviously a lawyer cannot perform any act or make any decision which the law requires his client to perform or make, either acting for himself if competent, or by a duly constituted representative if legally incompetent.

EC 7-13 The responsibility of a public prosecutor differs from that of the usual advocate; his duty is to seek justice, not merely to convict.[24] This special

24. "The public prosecutor cannot take as a guide for the conduct of his office the standards of an attorney appearing on behalf of an individual client. The freedom elsewhere wisely granted to a partisan advocate must be severely curtailed if the prosecutor's duties are to be properly discharged. The public prosecutor must recall that he occupies a dual role, being obligated, on the one hand, to furnish that adversary element essential to the informed decision of any controversy, but being possessed, on the other, of important governmental powers that are pledged to the accomplishment of one objective only, that of impartial justice. When the prosecutor is recreant to the trust implicit in his office, he undermines confidence, not only in his profession, but in government and the very ideal of justice itself." Professional Responsibility: Report of the Joint Conference, 44 A.B.A.J. 1159, 1218 (1958).

duty exists because: (1) the prosecutor represents the sovereign and therefore should use restraint in the discretionary exercise of governmental powers, such as in the selection of cases to prosecute; (2) during trial the prosecutor is not only an advocate but he also may make decisions normally made by an individual client, and those affecting the public interest should be fair to all; and (3) in our system of criminal justice the accused is to be given the benefit of all reasonable doubts. With respect to evidence and witnesses, the prosecutor has responsibilities different from those of a lawyer in private practice: the prosecutor should make timely disclosure to the defense of available evidence, known to him, that tends to negate the guilt of the accused, mitigate the degree of the offense, or reduce the punishment. Further, a prosecutor should not intentionally avoid pursuit of evidence merely because he believes it will damage the prosecutor's case or aid the accused.

EC 7-14 A governmental lawyer who has discretionary power relative to litigation should refrain from instituting or continuing litigation that is obviously unfair. A government lawyer not having such discretionary power who believes there is lack of merit in a controversy submitted to him should so advise his superiors and recommend the avoidance of unfair litigation. A government lawyer in a civil action or administrative proceeding has the responsibility to seek justice and to develop a full and fair record, and he should not use his position or the economic power of the government to harass parties or to bring about unjust settlements or results.

EC 7-15 The nature and purpose of proceedings before administrative agencies vary widely. The proceedings may be legislative or quasi-judicial, or a combination of both. They may be *ex parte* in character, in which event they may originate either at the instance of the agency or upon motion of an interested party. The scope of an inquiry may be purely investigative or it may be truly adversary looking toward the adjudication of specific rights of a party or of classes of parties. The foregoing are but examples of some of the types of proceedings conducted by administrative agencies. A lawyer appearing before an administrative agency, regardless of the nature of the proceeding it is conducting, has the continuing duty to advance the cause of his client within the bounds of the law. Where the applicable rules of the agency impose specific obligations upon a lawyer, it is his duty to comply therewith, unless the lawyer has a legitimate basis for challenging the validity thereof. In all appearances before administrative agencies, a lawyer should identify himself, his client if identity of his client is not privileged, and the representative nature of his appearance. It is not improper, however, for a lawyer to seek from an agency information available to the public without identifying his client.

"The prosecuting attorney is the attorney for the state, and it is his primary duty not to convict but to see that justice is done." ABA Opinion 150 (1936).

EC 7-16   The primary business of a legislative body is to enact laws rather than to adjudicate controversies, although on occasion the activities of a legislative body may take on the characteristics of an adversary proceeding, particularly in investigative and impeachment matters. The role of a lawyer supporting or opposing proposed legislation normally is quite different from his role in representing a person under investigation or on trial by a legislative body. When a lawyer appears in connection with proposed legislation, he seeks to affect the lawmaking process, but when he appears on behalf of a client in investigatory or impeachment proceedings, he is concerned with the protection of the rights of his client. In either event, he should identify himself and his client, if identity of his client is not privileged, and should comply with applicable laws and legislative rules.

EC 7-17   The obligation of loyalty to his client applies only to a lawyer in the discharge of his professional duties and implies no obligation to adopt a personal viewpoint favorable to the interests or desires of his client.[29] While a lawyer must act always with circumspection in order that his conduct will not adversely affect the rights of a client in a matter he is then handling, he may take positions on public issues and espouse legal reforms he favors without regard to the individual views of any client.

EC 7-18   The legal system in its broadest sense functions best when persons in need of legal advice or assistance are represented by their own counsel. For this reason a lawyer should not communicate on the subject matter of the representation of his client with a person he knows to be represented in the matter by a lawyer, unless pursuant to law or rule of court or unless he has the consent of the lawyer for that person. If one is not represented by counsel, a lawyer representing another may have to deal directly with the unrepresented person; in such an instance, a lawyer should not undertake to give advice to the person who is attempting to represent himself, except that he may advise him to obtain a lawyer.

Duty of the Lawyer to the Adversary System of Justice

EC 7-19   Our legal system provides for the adjudication of disputes governed by the rules of substantive, evidentiary, and procedural law. An adversary presentation counters the natural human tendency to judge too swiftly in

---

29. . . . "No doubt some tax lawyers feel constrained to abstain from activities on behalf of a better tax system because they think that their clients may object. Clients have no right to object if the tax adviser handles their affairs competently and faithfully and independently of his private views as to tax policy. They buy his expert services, not his private opinions or his silence on issues that gravely affect the public interest." Paul, The Lawyer as a Tax Adviser, 25 Rocky Mt. L. Rev. 412, 434 (1953).

terms of the familiar that which is not yet fully known, the advocate, by his zealous preparation and presentation of facts and law, enables the tribunal to come to the hearing with an open and neutral mind and to render impartial judgments. The duty of a lawyer to his client and his duty to the legal system are the same: to represent his client zealously within the bounds of the law.

EC 7-20   In order to function properly, our adjudicative process requires an informed, impartial tribunal capable of administering justice promptly and efficiently according to procedures that command public confidence and respect. Not only must there be competent, adverse presentation of evidence and issues, but a tribunal must be aided by rules appropriate to an effective and dignified process. The procedures under which tribunals operate in our adversary system have been prescribed largely by legislative enactments, court rules and decisions, and administrative rules. Through the years certain concepts of proper professional conduct have become rules of law applicable to the adversary adjudicative process. Many of these concepts are the bases for standards of professional conduct set forth in the Disciplinary Rules.

EC 7-21   The civil adjudicative process is primarily designed for the settlement of disputes between parties, while the criminal process is designed for the protection of society as a whole. Threatening to use, or using, the criminal process to coerce adjustment of private civil claims or controversies is a subversion of that process; further, the person against whom the criminal process is so misused may be deterred from asserting his legal rights and thus the usefulness of the civil process in settling private disputes is impaired. As in all cases of abuse of judicial process, the improper use of criminal process tends to diminish public confidence in our legal system.

EC 7-22   Respect for judicial rulings is essential to the proper administration of justice; however, a litigant or his lawyer may, in good faith and within the framework of the law, take steps to test the correctness of a ruling of a tribunal.[38]

EC 7-23   The complexity of law often makes it difficult for a tribunal to be fully informed unless the pertinent law is presented by the lawyers in the cause. A tribunal that is fully informed on the applicable law is better able to make a fair and accurate determination of the matter before it. The adversary system contemplates that each lawyer will present and argue the existing law in the

---

38. . . . "There must be protection, however, in the far more frequent case of the attorney who stands on his rights and combats the order in good faith and without disrespect believing with good cause that it is void, for it is here that the independence of the bar becomes valuable." Note, 39 Colum. L. Rev. 433, 438 (1939).

light most favorable to his client.[39] Where a lawyer knows of legal authority in the controlling jurisdiction directly adverse to the position of his client, he should inform the tribunal of its existence unless his adversary has done so; but, having made such disclosure, he may challenge its soundness in whole or in part.[40]

EC 7-24 In order to bring about just and informed decisions, evidentiary and procedural rules have been established by tribunals to permit the inclusion of relevant evidence and argument and the exclusion of all other considerations. The expression by a lawyer of his personal opinion as to the justness of a cause, as to the credibility of a witness, as to the culpability of a civil litigant, or as to the guilt or innocence of an accused is not a proper subject for argument to the trier of fact. It is improper as to factual matters because admissible evidence possessed by a lawyer should be presented only as sworn testimony. It is improper as to all other matters because, were the rule otherwise, the silence of a lawyer on a given occasion could be construed unfavorably to his client. However, a lawyer may argue, on his analysis of the evidence, for any position or conclusion with respect to any of the foregoing matters.

EC 7-25 Rules of evidence and procedures are designed to lead to just decisions and are part of the framework of the law. Thus while a lawyer may take steps in good faith and within the framework of the law to test the validity of rules, he is not justified in consciously violating such rules and he should be diligent in his efforts to guard against his unintentional violation of them. As examples, a lawyer should subscribe to or verify only those pleadings that he believes are in compliance with applicable law and rules; a lawyer should not make any prefatory statement before a tribunal in regard to the purported facts of the case on trial unless he believes that his statement will be supported by admissible evidence; a lawyer should not ask a witness a question solely for the purpose of harassing or embarrassing him; and a lawyer should not by subterfuge put before a jury matters which it cannot properly consider.

EC 7-26 The law and Disciplinary Rules prohibit the use of fraudulent, false, or perjured testimony or evidence. A lawyer who knowingly participates in introduction of such testimony or evidence is subject to discipline. A lawyer should, however, present any admissible evidence his client desires to have pre-

39. "Too many do not understand that accomplishment of the layman's abstract ideas of justice is the function of the judge and jury, and that it is the lawyer's sworn duty to portray his client's case in its most favorable light." Rochelle and Payne, The Struggle for Public Understanding, 25 Texas B.J. 109, 159 (1962).

40. "We are of the opinion that this Canon requires the lawyer to disclose such decisions [that are adverse to his client's contentions] to the court. He may, of course, after doing so, challenge the soundness of the decisions or present reasons which he believes would warrant the court in not following them in the pending case." ABA Opinion 146 (1935).

sented unless he knows, or from facts within his knowledge should know, that such testimony or evidence is false, fraudulent, or perjured.[45]

EC 7-27 Because it interferes with the proper administration of justice, a lawyer should not suppress evidence that he or his client has a legal obligation to reveal or produce. In like manner, a lawyer should not advise or cause a person to secrete himself or to leave the jurisdiction of a tribunal for the purpose of making him unavailable as a witness therein.

EC 7-28 Witnesses should always testify truthfully and should be free from any financial inducements that might tempt them to do otherwise.[48] A lawyer should not pay or agree to pay a non-expert witness an amount in excess of reimbursement for expenses and financial loss incident to his being a witness; however, a lawyer may pay or agree to pay an expert witness a reasonable fee for his services as an expert. But in no event should a lawyer pay or agree to pay a contingent fee to any witness. A lawyer should exercise reasonable diligence to see that his client and lay associates conform to these standards.[49]

EC 7-29 To safeguard the impartiality that is essential to the judicial process, veniremen and jurors should be protected against extraneous influences. When impartiality is present, public confidence in the judicial system is enhanced. There should be no extrajudicial communication with veniremen prior to trial or with jurors during trial by or on behalf of a lawyer connected with the case. Furthermore, a lawyer who is not connected with the case should not communicate with or cause another to communicate with a venireman or a juror about the case. After the trial, communication by a lawyer with jurors is permitted so long as he refrains from asking questions or making comments that tend

45. "Under any standard of proper ethical conduct an attorney should not sit by silently and permit his client to commit what may have been perjury, and which certainly would mislead the court and the opposing party on a matter vital to the issue under consideration. . . .

"Respondent next urges that it was his duty to observe the utmost good faith toward his client, and therefore he could not divulge any confidential information. This duty to the client of course does not extend to the point of authorizing collaboration with him in the commission of fraud." In re Carroll, 244 S.W.2d 474, 474-75 (Ky. 1951).

48. "The prevalence of perjury is a serious menace to the administration of justice, to prevent which no means have as yet been satisfactorily devised. But there certainly can be no greater incentive to perjury than to allow a party to make payments to its opponents witnesses under any guise or on any excuse, and at least attorneys who are officers of the court to aid it in the administration of justice, must keep themselves clear of any connection which in the slightest degree tends to induce witnesses to testify in favor of their clients." In re Robinson, 151 App. Div. 589, 600, 136 N.Y.S. 548, 556-57 (1912), aff'd, 209 N.Y. 354, 103 N.E. 160 (1913).

49. "It will not do for an attorney who seeks to justify himself against charges of this kind to show that he has escaped criminal responsibility under the Penal Law, nor can he blindly shut his eyes to a system which tends to suborn witnesses, to produce perjured testimony, and to suppress the truth. He has an active affirmative duty to protect the administration of justice from perjury and fraud, and that duty is not performed by allowing his subordinates and assistants to attempt to subvert justice and procure results for his clients based upon false testimony and perjured witnesses." Id., 151 App. Div. at 592, 136 N.Y.S. at 551.

to harass or embarrass the juror or to influence actions of the juror in future cases. Were a lawyer to be prohibited from communicating after trial with a juror, he could not ascertain if the verdict might be subject to legal challenge, in which event the invalidity of a verdict might go undetected.[52] When an extrajudicial communication by a lawyer with a juror is permitted by law, it should be made considerately and with deference to the personal feelings of the juror.

EC 7-30   Vexatious or harassing investigations of veniremen or jurors seriously impair the effectiveness of our jury system. For this reason, a lawyer or anyone on his behalf who conducts an investigation of veniremen or jurors should act with circumspection and restraint.

EC 7-31   Communications with or investigations of members of families of veniremen or jurors by a lawyer or by anyone on his behalf are subject to the restrictions imposed upon the lawyer with respect to his communications with or investigations of veniremen and jurors.

EC 7-32   Because of his duty to aid in preserving the integrity of the jury system, a lawyer who learns of improper conduct by or towards a venireman, a juror, or a member of the family of either should make a prompt report to the court regarding such conduct.

EC 7-33   A goal of our legal system is that each party shall have his case, criminal or civil, adjudicated by an impartial tribunal. The attainment of this goal may be defeated by dissemination of news or comments which tend to influence judge or jury.[53] Such news or comments may prevent prospective jurors from being impartial at the outset of the trial and may also interfere with the obligation of jurors to base their verdict solely upon the evidence admitted in

52. ABA Opinion 319 (1968) points out that "[m]any courts today, and the trend is in this direction, allow the testimony of jurors as to all irregularities in and out of the courtroom except those irregularities whose existence can be determined only by exploring the consciousness of a single particular juror, New Jersey v. Kociolek, 20 N.J. 92 (1955). Model Code of Evidence Rule 301. Certainly as to states in which the testimony and affidavits of jurors may be received in support of or against a motion for new trial, a lawyer, in his obligation to protect his client, must have the tools for ascertaining whether or not grounds for a new trial exist and it is not unethical for him to talk to and question jurors."

53. "[T]he trial court might well have proscribed extrajudicial statements by any lawyer, party, witness, or court official which divulged prejudicial matters. . . . [T]he court could also have requested the appropriate city and county officials to promulgate a regulation with respect to dissemination of information about the case by their employees. In addition, reporters who wrote or broadcast prejudicial stories, could have been warned as to the impropriety of publishing material not introduced in the proceedings. . . . In this manner, Sheppard's right to a trial free from outside interference would have been given added protection without corresponding curtailment of the news media. Had the judge, the other officers of the court, and the police placed the interest of justice first, the news media would have soon learned to be content with the task of reporting the case as it unfolded in the courtroom — not pieced together from extrajudicial statements." Sheppard v. Maxwell, 384 U.S. 333, 361-62 (1966).

the trial.[55] The release by a lawyer of out-of-court statements regarding an anticipated or pending trial may improperly affect the impartiality of the tribunal. For these reasons, standards for permissible and prohibited conduct of a lawyer with respect to trial publicity have been established.

EC 7-34 The impartiality of a public servant in our legal system may be impaired by the receipt of gifts or loans. A lawyer,[57] therefore, is never justified in making a gift or a loan to a judge, a hearing officer, or an official or employee of a tribunal except as permitted by Section C(4) of Canon 5 of the Code of Judicial Conduct, but a lawyer may make a contribution to the campaign fund of a candidate for judicial office in conformity with Section B(2) under Canon 7 of the Code of Judicial Conduct.[58]

EC 7-35 All litigants and lawyers should have access to tribunals on an equal basis. Generally, in adversary proceedings a lawyer should not communicate with a judge relative to a matter pending before, or which is to be brought before, a tribunal over which he presides in circumstances which might have the effect or give the appearance of granting undue advantage to one party. For example, a lawyer should not communicate with a tribunal by a writing unless a copy thereof is promptly delivered to opposing counsel or to the adverse party if he is not represented by a lawyer. Ordinarily an oral communication by a lawyer with a judge or hearing officer should be made only upon adequate no-

55. "The undeviating rule of this Court was expressed by Mr. Justice Holmes over half a century ago in Patterson v. Colorado, 205 U.S. 454, 462 (1907):
The theory of our system is that the conclusions to be reached in a case will be induced only by evidence and argument in open court, and not by any outside influence, whether of private talk or public print."
Sheppard v. Maxwell, 384 U.S. 333, 351 (1966).
"The trial judge has a large discretion in ruling on the issue of prejudice resulting from the reading by jurors of news articles concerning the trial. . . . Generalizations beyond that statement are not profitable, because each case must turn on its special facts. . . ." Marshall v. United States, 360 U.S. 310 (1959).
" . . . Our fundamental concepts of justice and our American sense of fair play require that the petit jury . . . shall determine the issues presented to it solely upon the evidence adduced at the trial and according to the law given in the instructions of the trial judge.
"While we may doubt that the effect of public opinion would sway or bias the judgment of the trial judge in an equity proceeding, the defendant should not be called upon to run that risk and the trial court should not have his work made more difficult by any dissemination of statements to the public that would be calculated to create a public demand for a particular judgment in a prospective or pending case." ABA Opinion 199 (1940).
57. Canon 3 observes that a lawyer "deserves rebuke and denunciation for any device or attempt to gain from a Judge special personal consideration or favor."
58. "Judicial Canon 32 provides:
A judge should not accept any presents or favors from litigants, or from lawyers practicing before him or from others whose interests are likely to be submitted to him for judgment.
The language of this Canon is perhaps broad enough to prohibit campaign contributions by lawyers, practicing before the court upon which the candidate hopes to sit. However, we do not think it was intended to prohibit such contributions when the candidate is obligated, by force of circumstances over which he has no control, to conduct a campaign, the expense of which exceeds that which he should reasonably be expected to personally bear!" ABA Opinion 226 (1941).

tice to opposing counsel, or, if there is none, to the opposing party. A lawyer should not condone or lend himself to private importunities by another with a judge or hearing officer on behalf of himself or his client.

EC 7-36   Judicial hearings ought to be conducted through dignified and orderly procedures designed to protect the rights of all parties. Although a lawyer has the duty to represent his client zealously, he should not engage in any conduct that offends the dignity and decorum of proceedings. While maintaining his independence, a lawyer should be respectful, courteous, and above-board in his relations with a judge or hearing officer before whom he appears. He should avoid undue solicitude for the comfort or convenience of judge or jury and should avoid any other conduct calculated to gain special consideration.

EC 7-37   In adversary proceedings, clients are litigants and though ill feeling may exist between clients, such ill feeling should not influence a lawyer in his conduct, attitude, and demeanor towards opposing lawyers. A lawyer should not make unfair or derogatory personal reference to opposing counsel. Haranguing and offensive tactics by lawyers interfere with the orderly administration of justice and have no proper place in our legal system.

EC 7-38   A lawyer should be courteous to opposing counsel and should accede to reasonable requests regarding court proceedings, settings, continuances, waiver of procedural formalities, and similar matters which do not prejudice the rights of his client. He should follow local customs of courtesy or practice, unless he gives timely notice to opposing counsel of his intention not to do so. A lawyer should be punctual in fulfilling all professional commitments.

EC 7-39   In the final analysis, proper functioning of the adversary system depends upon cooperation between lawyers and tribunals in utilizing procedures which will preserve the impartiality of tribunals and make their decisional processes prompt and just, without impinging upon the obligation of lawyers to represent their clients zealously within the framework of the law.

	Model Code	*ABA Model Rules*
Model Rules Comparison	EC 7-1	Rules 1.2(d), 1.3, 3.1
	EC 7-2	Rule 1.2(d)
	EC 7-3	Rules 1.4(b), 2.1
	EC 7-4	Rule 3.1
	EC 7-5	Rules 1.2(d), 1.4(a), 3.1
	EC 7-6	Rule 3.4(a), (b)
	EC 7-7	Rule 1.2(a)
	EC 7-8	Rules 1.2(a), (c), 1.4, 2.1
	EC 7-9	Rule 1.2(c)
	EC 7-10	Rule 4.4

Disciplinary Rules

DR 7-101 Representing a Client Zealously

(A) A lawyer shall not intentionally:

(1) Fail to seek the lawful objectives of his client through reasonably available means permitted by law and the Disciplinary Rules, except as provided by DR 7-101 (B). A lawyer does not violate this Disciplinary Rule, however, by acceding to reasonable requests of opposing counsel which do not prejudice the rights of his client, by being punctual in fulfilling all professional commitments, by avoiding offensive tactics, or by

treating with courtesy and consideration all persons involved in the legal process.

(2) Fail to carry out a contract of employment entered into with a client for professional services, but he may withdraw as permitted under DR 2-110, DR 5-102, and DR 5-105.

(3) Prejudice or damage his client during the course of the professional relationship, except as required under DR 7-102 (B).

(B) In his representation of a client, a lawyer may:

(1) Where permissible, exercise his professional judgment to waive or fail to assert a right or position of his client.

(2) Refuse to aid or participate in conduct that he believes to be unlawful, even though there is some support for an argument that the conduct is legal.

DR 7-102 Representing a Client Within the Bounds of the Law

(A) In his representation of a client, a lawyer shall not:

(1) File a suit, assert a position, conduct a defense, delay a trial, or take other action on behalf of his client when he knows or when it is obvious that such action would serve merely to harass or maliciously injure another.

(2) Knowingly advance a claim or defense that is unwarranted under existing law, except that he may advance such claim or defense if it can be supported by good faith argument for an extension, modification, or reversal of existing law.

(3) Conceal or knowingly fail to disclose that which he is required by law to reveal.

(4) Knowingly use perjured testimony or false evidence.

(5) Knowingly make a false statement of law or fact.

(6) Participate in the creation or preservation of evidence when he knows or it is obvious that the evidence is false.

(7) Counsel or assist his client in conduct that the lawyer knows to be illegal or fraudulent.

(8) Knowingly engage in other illegal conduct or conduct contrary to a Disciplinary Rule.

(B) A lawyer who receives information clearly establishing that:

(1) His client has, in the course of the representation, perpetrated a fraud upon a person or tribunal shall promptly call upon his client to rectify the same, and if his client refuses or is unable to do so, he shall reveal the fraud to the affected person or tribunal, except when the information is protected as a privileged communication.

(2) A person other than his client has perpetrated a fraud upon a tribunal shall promptly reveal the fraud to the tribunal.

DR 7-103 Performing the Duty of Public Prosecutor or Other Government Lawyer

(A) A public prosecutor or other government lawyer shall not institute or cause to be instituted criminal charges when he knows or it is obvious that the charges are not supported by probable cause.

(B) A public prosecutor or other government lawyer in criminal litigation shall make timely disclosure to counsel for the defendant, or to the defendant if he has no counsel, of the existence of evidence, known to the prosecutor or other government lawyer, that tends to negate the guilt of the accused, mitigate the degree of the offense, or reduce the punishment.

DR 7-104 Communicating with One of Adverse Interest

(A) During the course of his representation of a client a lawyer shall not:

(1) Communicate or cause another to communicate on the subject of the representation with a party he knows to be represented by a lawyer in that matter unless he has the prior consent of the lawyer representing such other party[75] or is authorized by law to do so.

(2) Give advice to a person who is not represented by a lawyer, other than the advice to secure counsel, if the interests of such person are or have a reasonable possibility of being in conflict with the interests of his client.

DR 7-105 Threatening Criminal Prosecution

(A) A lawyer shall not present, participate in presenting, or threaten to present criminal charges solely to obtain an advantage in a civil matter.

DR 7-106 Trial Conduct

(A) A lawyer shall not disregard or advise his client to disregard a standing rule of a tribunal or a ruling of a tribunal made in the course of a proceeding, but he may take appropriate steps in good faith to test the validity of such rule or ruling.

(B) In presenting a matter to a tribunal, a lawyer shall disclose:

---

75. "It is clear from the earlier opinions of this committee that Canon 9 is to be construed literally and does not allow a communication with an opposing party, without the consent of his counsel, though the purpose merely be to investigate the facts." ABA Opinion 187 (1938).

(1) Legal authority in the controlling jurisdiction known to him to be directly adverse to the position of his client and which is not disclosed by opposing counsel.[79]

(2) Unless privileged or irrelevant, the identities of the clients he represents and of the persons who employed him.[80]

(C) In appearing in his professional capacity before a tribunal, a lawyer shall not:

(1) State or allude to any matter that he has no reasonable basis to believe is relevant to the case or that will not be supported by admissible evidence.[81]

(2) Ask any question that he has no reasonable basis to believe is relevant to the case and that is intended to degrade a witness or other person.

(3) Assert his personal knowledge of the facts in issue, except when testifying as a witness.

(4) Assert his personal opinion as to the justness of a cause, as to the credibility of a witness, as to the culpability of a civil litigant, or as to the guilt or innocence of an accused;[83] but he may argue, on his analysis of the evidence, for any position or conclusion with respect to the matters stated herein.

(5) Fail to comply with known local customs of courtesy or practice of the bar or a particular tribunal without giving to opposing counsel timely notice of his intent not to comply.[84]

(6) Engage in undignified or discourteous conduct which is degrading to a tribunal.

79. . . . "The test in every case should be: Is the decision which opposing counsel has overlooked one which the court should clearly consider in deciding the case? Would a reasonable judge properly feel that a lawyer who advanced, as the law, a proposition adverse to the undisclosed decision, was lacking in candor and fairness to him? Might the judge consider himself misled by an implied representation that the lawyer knew of no adverse authority?" ABA Opinion 280 (1949).

80. "The authorities are substantially uniform against any privilege as applied to the fact of retainer or identity of the client. The privilege is limited to confidential communications, and a retainer is not a confidential communication, although it cannot come into existence without some communication between the attorney and the — at that stage prospective — client." United States v. Pape, 144 F.2d 778, 782 (2d Cir. 1944), cert. denied, 323 U.S. 752 (1944).

"To be sure, there may be circumstances under which the identification of a client may amount to the prejudicial disclosure of a confidential communication, as where the substance of a disclosure has already been revealed but not its source." Colton v. United States, 306 F.2d 633, 637 (2d Cir. 1962).

81. "The rule allowing counsel when addressing the jury the widest latitude in discussing the evidence and presenting the client's theories falls far short of authorizing the statement by counsel of matter not in evidence, or indulging in argument founded on no proof, or demanding verdicts for purposes other than the just settlement of the matters at issue between the litigants, or appealing to prejudice or passion. The rule confining counsel to legitimate argument is not based on etiquette, but on justice. . . . " Cherry Creek Nat. Bank v. Fidelity & Cas. Co., 207 App. Div. 787, 790-91, 202 N.Y.S. 611, 614 (1924).

83. "The record in the case at bar was silent concerning the qualities and character of the deceased. It is especially improper, in addressing the jury in a murder case, for the prosecuting attorney to make reference to his knowledge of the good qualities of the deceased where there is no evidence in the record bearing upon his character. . . . A prosecutor should never inject into his argument evidence not introduced at the trial." People v. Dukes, 12 Ill. 2d 334, 341, 146 N.E.2d 14, 17-18 (1957).

84. "A lawyer should not ignore known customs or practice of the Bar or of a particular Court, even when the law permits, without giving timely notice to the opposing counsel." ABA Canon 25.

(7) Intentionally or habitually violate any established rule of procedure or of evidence.

DR 7-107 Trial Publicity[85]

(A) A lawyer participating in or associated with the investigation of a criminal matter shall not make or participate in making an extrajudicial statement that a reasonable person would expect to be disseminated by means of public communication and that does more than state without elaboration:

(1) Information contained in a public record.

(2) That the investigation is in progress.

(3) The general scope of the investigation including a description of the offense and, if permitted by law, the identity of the victim.

(4) A request for assistance in apprehending a suspect or assistance in other matters and the information necessary thereto.

(5) A warning to the public of any dangers.

(B) A lawyer or law firm associated with the prosecution or defense of a criminal matter shall not, from the time of the filing of a complaint, information, or indictment, the issuance of an arrest warrant, or arrest until the commencement of the trial or disposition without trial, make or participate in making an extrajudicial statement that a reasonable person would expect to be disseminated by means of public communication and that relates to:

(1) The character, reputation, or prior criminal record (including arrests, indictments, or other charges of crime) of the accused.

(2) The possibility of a plea of guilty to the offense charged or to a lesser offense.

(3) The existence or contents of any confession, admission, or statement given by the accused or his refusal or failure to make a statement.

(4) The performance or results of any examinations or tests or the refusal or failure of the accused to submit to examinations or tests.

(5) The identity, testimony, or credibility of a prospective witness.

(6) Any opinion as to the guilt or innocence of the accused, the evidence, or the merits of the case.

(C) DR 7-107 (B) does not preclude a lawyer during such period from announcing:

---

85. . . . "From the cases coming here we note that unfair and prejudicial news comment on pending trials has become increasingly prevalent. Due process requires that the accused receive a trial by an impractical jury free from outside influences. Given the pervasiveness of modern communications and the difficulty of effacing prejudicial publicity from the minds of the jurors, the trial courts must take strong measures to ensure that the balance is never weighed against the accused. . . . Of course, there is nothing that proscribes the press from reporting events that transpire in the courtroom. But where there is a reasonable likelihood that prejudicial news prior to trial will prevent a fair trial, the judge should continue the case until the threat abates, or transfer it to another county not so permeated with publicity. . . ." Sheppard v. Maxwell, 384 U.S. 333, 362-63 (1966).

(1) The name, age, residence, occupation, and family status of the accused.

(2) If the accused has not been apprehended, any information necessary to aid in his apprehension or to warn the public of any dangers he may present.

(3) A request for assistance in obtaining evidence.

(4) The identity of the victim of the crime.

(5) The fact, time, and place of arrest, resistance, pursuit, and use of weapons.

(6) The identity of investigating and arresting officers or agencies and the length of the investigation.

(7) At the time of seizure, a description of the physical evidence seized, other than a confession, admission, or statement.

(8) The nature, substance, or text of the charge.

(9) Quotations from or references to public records of the court in the case.

(10) The scheduling or result of any step in the judicial proceedings.

(11) That the accused denies the charges made against him.

(D) During the selection of a jury or the trial of a criminal matter, a lawyer or law firm associated with the prosecution or defense of a criminal matter shall not make or participate in making an extrajudicial statement that a reasonable person would expect to be disseminated by means of public communication and that relates to the trial, parties, or issues in the trial or other matters that are reasonably likely to interfere with a fair trial, except that he may quote from or refer without comment to public records of the court in the case.

(E) After the completion of a trial or disposition without trial of a criminal matter and prior to the imposition of sentence, a lawyer or law firm associated with the prosecution or defense shall not make or participate in making an extrajudicial statement that a reasonable person would expect to be disseminated by public communication and that is reasonably likely to affect the imposition of sentence.

(F) The foregoing provisions of DR 7-107 also apply to professional disciplinary proceedings and juvenile disciplinary proceedings when pertinent and consistent with other law applicable to such proceedings.

(G) A lawyer or law firm associated with a civil action shall not during its investigation or litigation make or participate in making an extrajudicial statement, other than a quotation from or reference to public records, that a reasonable person would expect to be disseminated by means of public communication and that relates to:

(1) Evidence regarding the occurrence or transaction involved.

(2) The character, credibility, or criminal record of a party, witness, or prospective witness.

(3) The performance or results of any examinations or tests or the refusal or failure of a party to submit to such.

(4) His opinion as to the merits of the claims or defenses of a party, except as required by law or administrative rule.

(5) Any other matter reasonably likely to interfere with a fair trial of the action.

(H) During the pendency of an administrative proceeding, a lawyer or law firm associated therewith shall not make or participate in making a statement, other than a quotation from or reference to public records, that a reasonable person would expect to be disseminated by means of public communication if it is made outside the official course of the proceeding and relates to:

(1) Evidence regarding the occurrences or transaction involved.

(2) The character, credibility, or criminal record of a party, witness, or prospective witness.

(3) Physical evidence or the performance or results of any examinations or tests or the refusal or failure of a party to submit to such.

(4) His opinion as to the merits of the claims, defenses, or positions of an interested person.

(5) Any other matter reasonably likely to interfere with a fair hearing.

(I) The foregoing provisions of DR 7-107 do not preclude a lawyer from replying to charges of misconduct publicly made against him or from participating in the proceedings of legislative, administrative, or other investigative bodies.

(J) A lawyer shall exercise reasonable care to prevent his employees and associates from making an extrajudicial statement that he would be prohibited from making under DR 7-107.

DR 7-108 Communication with or Investigation of Jurors

(A) Before the trial of a case a lawyer connected therewith shall not communicate with or cause another to communicate with anyone he knows to be a member of the venire from which the jury will be selected for the trial of the case.

(B) During the trial of a case:

(1) A lawyer connected therewith shall not communicate with or cause another to communicate with any member of the jury.

(2) A lawyer who is not connected therewith shall not communicate with or cause another to communicate with a juror concerning the case.

(C) DR 7-108 (A) and (B) do not prohibit a lawyer from communicating with veniremen or jurors in the course of official proceedings.

(D) After discharge of the jury from further consideration of a case with which the lawyer was connected, the lawyer shall not ask questions of or make comments to a member of that jury that are calculated merely to harass or embarrass the juror or to influence his actions in the future jury service.[87]

---

87. "[I]t would be unethical for a lawyer to harass, entice, induce or exert influence on a juror to obtain his testimony." ABA Opinion 319 (1968).

(E) A lawyer shall not conduct or cause, by financial support or otherwise, another to conduct a vexatious or harassing investigation of either a venireman or a juror.

(F) All restrictions imposed by DR 7-108 upon a lawyer also apply to communications with or investigations of members of a family of a venireman or a juror.

(G) A lawyer shall reveal promptly to the court improper conduct by a venireman or a juror, or by another toward a venireman or a juror or a member of his family, of which the lawyer has knowledge.

DR 7-109 Contact with Witnesses

(A) A lawyer shall not suppress any evidence that he or his client has a legal obligation to reveal or produce.

(B) A lawyer shall not advise or cause a person to secrete himself or to leave the jurisdiction of a tribunal for the purpose of making him unavailable as a witness therein.

(C) A lawyer shall not pay, offer to pay, or acquiesce in the payment of compensation to a witness contingent upon the content of his testimony or the outcome of the case. But a lawyer may advance, guarantee, or acquiesce in the payment of:

(1) Expenses reasonably incurred by a witness in attending or testifying.

(2) Reasonable compensation to a witness for his loss of time in attending or testifying.

(3) A reasonable fee for the professional services of an expert witness.

DR 7-110 Contact with Officials

(A) A lawyer shall not give or lend any thing of value to a judge, official, or employee of a tribunal except as permitted by Section C(4) of Canon 5 of the Code of Judicial Conduct, but a lawyer may make a contribution to the campaign fund of a candidate for judicial office in conformity with Section B(2) under Canon 7 of the Code of Judicial Conduct.

(B) In an adversary proceeding, a lawyer shall not communicate, or cause another to communicate, as to the merits of the cause with a judge or an official before whom the proceeding is pending, except:

(1) In the course of official proceedings in the cause.

(2) In writing if he promptly delivers a copy of the writing to opposing counsel or to the adverse party if he is not represented by a lawyer.

(3) Orally upon adequate notice to opposing counsel or to the adverse party if he is not represented by a lawyer.

(4) As otherwise authorized by law, or by Section A(4) under Canon 3 of the Code of Judicial Conduct.

	Model Code	*ABA Model Rules*
Model Rules Comparison	DR 7-101(A)	Rules 1.2(a), (d), 1.3, 3.2, 3.5(c), 4.4
	DR 7-101(B)	Rules 1.2(a), (c), (d), 1.16(b)
	DR 7-102(A)(1)	Rules 3.1, 3.2, 4.4
	DR 7-102(A)(2)	Rule 3.1
	DR 7-102(A)(3)	Rules 3.3(a)(2), (3), 4.1
	DR 7-102(A)(4)	Rule 3.3(a)(4), (c)
	DR 7-102(A)(5)	Rules 3.3(a)(1), 4.1
	DR 7-102(A)(6)	Rules 1.2(b), 3.4(b)
	DR 7-102(A)(7)	Rules 1.2(d), 3.3(a), 4.1
	DR 7-102(A)(8)	Rules 1.2(d), 8.4(a), (b)
	DR 7-102(B)	Rules 1.6(b), 3.3(a)(4), (b), 4.1(b)
	DR 7-103(A)	Rule 3.8(a)
	DR 7-103(B)	Rule 3.8(d)
	DR 7-104	Rules 3.4(f), 4.2, 4.3
	DR 7-105	None
	DR 7-106(A)	Rules 1.2(d), 3.4(c), (d)
	DR 7-106(B)	Rules 3.3(a)(3), 3.9
	DR 7-106(C)	Rules 3.4(a), (c), (d), (e), 3.5, 4.4
	DR 7-107(A)-(I)	Rule 3.6
	DR 7-107(J)	Rules 5.1(a), (b), 5.3(a), (b)
	DR 7-108(A)	Rule 3.5(a), (b)
	DR 7-108(B)	Rules 3.5(a), (b), 5.1(c), 5.3(a), (b), 8.4(a)
	DR 7-108(C)	Rule 3.5(a), (b)
	DR 7-108(D)	Rules 3.5(b), 4.4
	DR 7-108(E)	Rules 3.5(b), 4.4, 5.1(c), 5.3(a), (b), 8.4(a)
	DR 7-108(F)	Rule 4.4
	DR 7-108(G)	None
	DR 7-109(A)	Rules 3.3(a)(2), 3.4(a)
	DR 7-109(B)	Rule 3.4(a), (f)
	DR 7-109(C)	Rule 3.4(b)
	DR 7-110(A)	Rules 3.5(a), 8.4(f)
	DR 7-110(B)	Rule 3.5(a), (b)

CANON 8. A LAWYER SHOULD ASSIST IN IMPROVING THE LEGAL SYSTEM

Ethical Considerations

EC 8-1   Changes in human affairs and imperfections in human institutions make necessary constant efforts to maintain and improve our legal system.[1] This system should function in a manner that commands public respect and fosters the use of legal remedies to achieve redress of grievances. By reason of education and experience, lawyers are especially qualified to recognize deficiencies in the legal system and to initiate corrective measures therein. Thus they should participate in proposing and supporting legislation and programs to improve the system,[2] without regard to the general interests or desires of clients or former clients.

EC 8-2   Rules of law are deficient if they are not just, understandable, and responsive to the needs of society. If a lawyer believes that the existence or absence of a rule of law, substantive or procedural, causes or contributes to an unjust result, he should endeavor by lawful means to obtain appropriate changes in the law. He should encourage the simplification of laws and the repeal or amendment of laws that are outmoded.[4] Likewise, legal procedures should be improved whenever experience indicates a change is needed.

EC 8-3   The fair administration of justice requires the availability of competent lawyers. Members of the public should be educated to recognize the existence of legal problems and the resultant need for legal services, and should be

---

1. " . . . [Another] task of the great lawyer is to do his part individually and as a member of the organized bar to improve his profession, the courts, and the law. As President Theodore Roosevelt aptly put it, 'Every man owes some of his time to the upbuilding of the profession to which he belongs.' Indeed, this obligation is one of the great things which distinguishes a profession from a business. The soundness and the necessity of President Roosevelt's admonition insofar as it relates to the legal profession cannot be doubted. The advances in natural science and technology are so startling and the velocity of change in business and in social life is so great that the law along with the other social sciences, and even human life itself, is in grave danger of being extinguished by new gods of its own invention if it does not awake from its lethargy." Vanderbilt, The Five Functions of the Lawyer: Service to Clients and the Public, 40 A.B.A.J. 31, 31-32 (1954).

2. "The lawyer tempted by repose should recall the heavy costs paid by his profession when needed legal reform has to be accomplished through the initiative of public-spirited laymen. Where change must be thrust from without upon an unwilling Bar, the public's least flattering picture of the lawyer seems confirmed. The lawyer concerned for the standing of his profession will, therefore, interest himself actively in the improvement of the law. In doing so he will not only help to maintain confidence in the Bar, but will have the satisfaction of meeting a responsibility inhering in the nature of his calling." Professional Responsibility: Report of the Joint Conference, 44 A.B.A.J. 1159, 1217 (1958).

4. "There are few great figures in the history of the Bar who have not concerned themselves with the reform and improvement of the law. The special obligation of the profession with respect to legal reform rests on considerations too obvious to require enumeration. Certainly it is the lawyer who has both the best chance to know when the law is working badly and the special competence to put it in order." Professional Responsibility: Report of the Joint Conference, 44 A.B.A.J. 1159, 1217 (1958).

provided methods for intelligent selection of counsel. Those persons unable to pay for legal services should be provided needed services. Clients and lawyers should not be penalized by undue geographical restraints upon representation in legal matters, and the bar should address itself to improvements in licensing, reciprocity, and admission procedures consistent with the needs of modern commerce.

EC 8-4   Whenever a lawyer seeks legislative or administrative changes, he should identify the capacity in which he appears, whether on behalf of himself, a client, or the public. A lawyer may advocate such changes on behalf of a client even though he does not agree with them. But when a lawyer purports to act on behalf of the public, he should espouse only those changes which he conscientiously believes to be in the public interest.

EC 8-5   Fraudulent, deceptive, or otherwise illegal conduct by a participant in a proceeding before a tribunal or legislative body is inconsistent with fair administration of justice, and it should never be participated in or condoned by lawyers. Unless constrained by his obligation to preserve the confidences and secrets of his client, a lawyer should reveal to appropriate authorities any knowledge he may have of such improper conduct.

EC 8-6   Judges and administrative officials having adjudicatory powers ought to be persons of integrity, competence, and suitable temperament. Generally, lawyers are qualified, by personal observation or investigation, to evaluate the qualifications of persons seeking or being considered for such public offices, and for this reason they have a special responsibility to aid in the selection of only those who are qualified.[6] It is the duty of lawyers to endeavor to prevent political considerations from outweighing judicial fitness in the selection of judges. Lawyers should protest earnestly against the appointment or election of those who are unsuited for the bench and should strive to have elected[7] or appointed thereto only those who are willing to forego pursuits, whether of a business, political, or other nature, that may interfere with the free and fair consideration of questions presented for adjudication. Adjudicatory officials, not being wholly free to defend themselves, are entitled to receive the support of the

6. "Lawyers are better able than laymen to appraise accurately the qualifications of candidates for judicial office. It is proper that they should make that appraisal known to the voters in a proper and dignified manner. A lawyer may with propriety endorse a candidate for judicial office and seek like endorsement from other lawyers. But the lawyer who endorses a judicial candidate or seeks that endorsement from other lawyers should be actuated by a sincere belief in the superior qualifications of the candidate for judicial service and not by personal or selfish motives; and a lawyer should not use or attempt to use the power or prestige of the judicial office to secure such endorsement. . . ." ABA Opinion 189 (1938).

7. "[W]e are of the opinion that, whenever a candidate for judicial office merits the endorsement and support of lawyers, the lawyers may make financial contributions toward the campaign if its cost, when reasonably conducted, exceeds that which the candidate would be expected to bear personally." ABA Opinion 226 (1941).

bar against unjust criticism. While a lawyer as a citizen has a right to criticize such officials publicly,[9] he should be certain of the merit of his complaint, use appropriate language, and avoid petty criticisms, for unrestrained and intemperate statements tend to lessen public confidence in our legal system.[10] Criticisms motivated by reasons other than a desire to improve the legal system are not justified.

EC 8-7   Since lawyers are a vital part of the legal system, they should be persons of integrity, of professional skill, and of dedication to the improvement of the system. Thus a lawyer should aid in establishing, as well as enforcing, standards of conduct adequate to protect the public by insuring that those who practice law are qualified to do so.

EC 8-8   Lawyers often serve as legislators or as holders of other public offices. This is highly desirable, as lawyers are uniquely qualified to make significant contributions to the improvement of the legal system. A lawyer who is a public officer, whether full or part-time, should not engage in activities in which his personal or professional interests are or foreseeably may be in conflict with his official duties.

EC 8-9   The advancement of our legal system is of vital importance in maintaining the rule of law and in facilitating orderly changes; therefore, lawyers should encourage, and should aid in making, needed changes and improvements.

	Model Code	*ABA Model Rules*
Model Rules Comparison	EC 8-1	Rules 1.2(b), 6.1
	EC 8-2	Rule 6.1
	EC 8-3	Rules 6.1, 6.2
	EC 8-4	Rule 3.9
	EC 8-5	Rules 3.3(a)(1), (2), (4), (b), 3.9
	EC 8-6	Rule 8.2(a)
	EC 8-7	Rules 5.5, 8.1
	EC 8-8	Rule 1.11(c)
	EC 8-9	Rule 6.1

9. "Citizens have a right under our constitutional system to criticize governmental officials and agencies, Courts are not, and should not be, immune to such criticism." Konigsberg v. State Bar of California, 353 U.S. 252, 269 (1957).

10. "[E]very lawyer, worthy of respect, realizes that public confidence in our courts is the cornerstone of our governmental structure, and will refrain from unjustified attack on the character of the judge, while recognizing the duty to denounce and expose a corrupt or dishonest judge." Kentucky State Bar Assn. v. Lewis, 287 S.W. 2d 321, 326 (Ky. 1955). . . .

Disciplinary Rules

DR 8-101 Action as a Public Official

(A) A lawyer who holds public office shall not:

(1) Use his public position to obtain, or attempt to obtain, a special advantage in legislative matters for himself or for a client under circumstances where he knows or it is obvious that such action is not in the public interest.

(2) Use his public position to influence, or attempt to influence, a tribunal to act in favor of himself or of a client.

(3) Accept any thing of value from any person when the lawyer knows or it is obvious that the offer is for the purpose of influencing his action as a public official.

DR 8-102 Statements Concerning Judges and Other Adjudicatory Officers

(A) A lawyer shall not knowingly make false statements of fact concerning the qualifications of a candidate for election or appointment to a judicial office.

(B) A lawyer shall not knowingly make false accusations against a judge or other adjudicatory officer.

DR 8-103 Lawyer Candidate for Judicial Office

(A) A lawyer who is a candidate for judicial office shall comply with the applicable provisions of Canon 7 of the Code of Judicial Conduct.

	Model Code	*ABA Model Rules*
Model Rules Comparison	DR 8-101	Rules 1.11(c), 3.5(a), 8.4(e), (f)
	DR 8-102	Rule 8.2(a)
	DR 8-103	Rule 8.2(b)

CANON 9. A LAWYER SHOULD AVOID EVEN THE APPEARANCE OF PROFESSIONAL IMPROPRIETY

Ethical Considerations

EC 9-1 Continuation of the American concept that we are to be governed by rules of law requires that the people have faith that justice can be obtained through our legal system.[1] A lawyer should promote public confidence in our system and in the legal profession.[2]

EC 9-2   Public confidence in law and lawyers may be eroded by irresponsible or improper conduct of a lawyer. On occasion, ethical conduct of a lawyer may appear to laymen to be unethical. In order to avoid misunderstandings and hence to maintain confidence, a lawyer should fully and promptly inform his client of material developments in the matters being handled for the client. While the lawyer should guard against otherwise proper conduct that has a tendency to diminish public confidences in the legal system or in the legal profession, his duty to clients or to the public should never be subordinate merely because the full discharge of his obligation may be misunderstood or may tend to subject him or the legal profession to criticism. When explicit ethical guidance does not exist, a lawyer should determine his conduct by acting in a manner that promotes public confidence in the integrity and efficiency of the legal system and the legal profession.

EC 9-3   After a lawyer leaves judicial office or other public employment, he should not accept employment in connection with any matter in which he had substantial responsibility prior to his leaving, since to accept employment would give the appearance of impropriety even if none exists.

EC 9-4   Because the very essence of the legal system is to provide procedures by which matters can be presented in an impartial manner so that they may be decided solely upon the merits, any statement or suggestion by a lawyer that he can or would attempt to circumvent those procedures is detrimental to the legal system and tends to undermine public confidence in it.

EC 9-5   Separation of the funds of a client from those of his lawyer not only serves to protect the client but also avoids even the appearance of impropriety, and therefore commingling of such funds should be avoided.

EC 9-6   Every lawyer owes a solemn duty to uphold the integrity and honor of his profession; to encourage respect for the law and for the courts and the judges thereof; to observe the Code of Professional Responsibility; to act as a member of a learned profession, one dedicated to public service; to cooperate with his brother lawyers in supporting the organized bar through the devoting of his time, efforts, and financial support as his professional standing and ability

1. "Integrity is the very breath of justice. Confidence in our law, our courts, and in the administration of justice is our supreme interest. No practice must be permitted to prevail which invites towards the administration of justice a doubt or distrust of its integrity." Erwin M. Jennings Co. v. DiGenova, 107 Conn. 491, 499, 141 A. 866, 868 (1928).

2. "A lawyer should never be reluctant or too proud to answer unjustified criticism of his profession, of himself, or of his brother lawyer. He should guard the reputation of his profession and of his brothers as zealously as he guards his own." Rochelle and Payne, The Struggle for Public Understanding, 25 Texas B.J. 109, 162 (1962).

reasonably permit; to conduct himself so as to reflect credit on the legal profession and to inspire the confidence, respect, and trust of his clients and of the public; and to strive to avoid not only professional impropriety but also the appearance of impropriety.[5]

EC 9-7   A lawyer has an obligation to the public to participate in collective efforts of the bar to reimburse persons who have lost money or property as a result of the misappropriation or defalcation of another lawyer, and contribution to a clients' security fund is an acceptable method of meeting this obligation.

Model Rules Comparison	*Model Code*	*ABA Model Rules*
	EC 9-1	Rules 3.1 through 3.8, 4.1, 8.4
	EC 9-2	Rules 1.4, 3.1 through 3.8, 4.1
	EC 9-3	Rules 1.11(a), 1.12(a)
	EC 9-4	Rules 7.1(b), 8.4(c), (e)
	EC 9-5	Rule 1.15
	EC 9-6	Preamble, Rule 8.4(e)
	EC 9-7	Rule 1.15

Disciplinary Rules

DR 9-101   Avoiding Even the Appearance of Impropriety

(A) A lawyer shall not accept private employment in a matter upon the merits of which he has acted in a judicial capacity.[7]

(B) A lawyer shall not accept private employment in a matter in which he had substantial responsibility while he was a public employee.

(C) A lawyer shall not state or imply that he is able to influence improperly or upon irrelevant grounds any tribunal, legislative body, or public official.

---

5. . . . . "The lawyer assumes high duties, and has imposed upon him grave responsibilities. He may be the means of much good or much mischief. Interests of vast magnitude are entrusted to him; confidence is reposed in him; life, liberty, character and property should be protected by him. He should guard, with jealous watchfulness, his own reputation, as well as that of his profession." People ex rel. Cutler v. Ford, 54 Ill. 520, 522 (1870), and also quoted in State Board of Law Examiners v. Sheldon, 43 Wyo. 522, 526, 7 P.2d 226, 227 (1932).

7. . . . . "In our opinion, acceptance of a judgeship with the duties of conducting misdemeanor trials, and examinations in felony cases to determine whether those accused should be bound over for trial in a higher court, ethically bars the judge from acting as attorney for the defendants upon such trial, whether they were examined by him or by some other judge. Such a practice would not only diminish public confidence in the administration of justice in both courts, but would produce serious conflict between the private interests of the judge, as a lawyer, and of his clients, and his duties as a judge in adjudicating important phases of criminal processes in other cases. The public and private duties would be incompatible. The prestige of the judicial office would be diverted to private benefit, and the judicial office would be demeaned thereby." ABA Opinion 242 (1942). . . .

DR 9-102 Preserving Identity of Funds and Property of
           a Client

(A) All funds of clients paid to a lawyer or law firm, other than advances for costs and expenses, shall be deposited in one or more identifiable bank accounts maintained in the state in which the law office is situated and no funds belonging to the lawyer or law firm shall be deposited therein except as follows:

(1) Funds reasonably sufficient to pay bank charges may be deposited therein.

(2) Funds belonging in part to a client and in part presently or potentially to the lawyer or law firm must be deposited therein, but the portion belonging to the lawyer or law firm may be withdrawn when due unless the right of the lawyer or law firm to receive it is disputed by the client, in which event the disputed portion shall not be withdrawn until the dispute is finally resolved.

(B) A lawyer shall:

(1) Promptly notify a client of the receipt of his funds, securities, or other properties.

(2) Identify and label securities and properties of a client promptly upon receipt and place them in a safe deposit box or other place of safekeeping as soon as practicable.

(3) Maintain complete records of all funds, securities, and other properties of a client coming into the possession of the lawyer and render appropriate accounts to his client regarding them.

(4) Promptly pay or deliver to the client as requested by a client the funds, securities, or other properties in the possession of the lawyer which the client is entitled to receive.

	Model Code	ABA Model Rules
Model Rules Comparison	DR 9-101(A)	Rule 1.12
	DR 9-101(B)	Rules 1.11(a), 1.12(a), (b)
	DR 9-101(C)	Rules 1.2(e), 7.1(b), 8.4(e)
	DR 9-102	Rules 1.4, 1.15

DEFINITIONS*

As used in the Disciplinary Rules of the Model Code of Professional Responsibility:

* "Confidence" and "secret" are defined in DR 4-101(A).

(1) "Differing interests" include every interest that will adversely affect either the judgment or the loyalty of a lawyer to a client, whether it be a conflicting, inconsistent, diverse, or other interest.

(2) "Law firm" includes a professional legal corporation.

(3) "Person" includes a corporation, an association, a trust, a partnership, and any other organization or legal entity.

(4) "Professional legal corporation" means a corporation, or an association treated as a corporation, authorized by law to practice law for profit.

(5) "State" includes the District of Columbia, Puerto Rico, and other federal territories and possessions.

(6) "Tribunal" includes all courts and all other adjudicatory bodies.

(7) "A Bar association" includes a bar association of specialists as referred to in DR 2-105 (A) (1) or (4).

(8) "Qualified legal assistance organization" means an office or organization of one of the four types listed in DR 2-103(D) (1)-(4), inclusive that meets all the requirements thereof.

ABA Standards for Criminal Justice*
The Prosecution and Defense Functions
Providing Defense Services
Fair Trial and Free Press

Editors' Introduction. In 1964, ABA President Louis F. Powell, Jr. appointed a Special Committee on Standards for the Administration of Criminal Justice. The Special Committee included many distinguished figures, and was at one time chaired by Judge (later Chief Justice) Warren E. Burger. By 1973, the ABA House of Delegates had approved 17 sets of Standards, governing every phase of the criminal justice system. In 1980, all of the Standards, with commentary, were gathered together in a two-volume set, American Bar Association Standards for Criminal Justice, published by Little, Brown and Company.

In recent years, the ABA has amended many of the Standards. At the ABA's August 1990 Annual Meeting, the House of Delegates approved amendments to Chapter 5, "Providing Defense Services." At the ABA's February 1991 Mid-Year Meeting, the House of Delegates approved a complete revision of Chapter 4, "The Defense Function," and more moderate revisions to Chapter 8, "Fair Trial and Free Press." At the ABA's 1992 Mid-Year Meeting, the House of Delegates approved substantial revisions to Chapter 3, "The Prosecution Function."

The Standards for Criminal Justice have been enormously influential. More than 40 states have revised their criminal codes on the basis of the ABA Standards and the Standards are cited dozens of times in each volume of federal court opinions. Two of the most important sets of Standards are "The Prosecution Function" and "The Defense Function." These Standards are intended to present in an organized way "guidelines that have long been adhered to by the best prosecutors and best defense advocates." We reprint here, without commentary, all of the black letter Standards for "The Prosecution Function" as amended in 1992, and

"The Defense Function" as amended in 1991. In addition, we reprint selections from "Providing Defense Services" as amended in 1990, and from "Fair Trial and Free Press" as amended in 1991.

Contents

Chapter 3. The Prosecution Function

CHAPTER 3. THE PROSECUTION FUNCTION

Editors' Note. Chapter 3 was originally approved by the ABA in 1971. At its 1992 Mid-Year Meeting, the ABA approved substantial revisions to "The Prosecution Function." The version that follows reflects these 1992 revisions. The most significant changes are the addition of new standards 3-1.1, 3-1.5, and 3-2.11, and the deletion of old Standard 3-1.4 (Duty to Improve the Law).

Part I. General Standards

Standard 3-1.1. The Function of the Standards

These standards are intended to be used as a guide to professional conduct and performance. They are not intended to be used as criteria for the judicial evaluation of alleged misconduct of the prosecutor to determine the validity of a conviction. They may or may not be relevant in such judicial evaluation, depending upon all the circumstances.

Standard 3-1.2. The Function of the Prosecutor

(a) The office of prosecutor is charged with responsibility for prosecutions in its jurisdiction.

(b) The prosecutor is an administrator of justice, an advocate, and an officer of the court; the prosecutor must exercise sound discretion in the performance of his or her functions.

(c) The duty of the prosecutor is to seek justice, not merely to convict.

(d) It is an important function of the prosecutor to seek to reform and improve the administration of criminal justice. When inadequacies or injustices in the substantive or procedural law come to the prosecutor's attention, he or she should stimulate efforts for remedial action.

(e) It is the duty of the prosecutor to know and be guided by the standards of professional conduct as defined by applicable professional traditions, ethical codes, and law in the prosecutor's jurisdiction. The prosecutor should make use of the guidance afforded by an advisory council of the kind described in standard 4-1.5.

Standard 3-1.3. Conflicts of Interest

(a) A prosecutor should avoid a conflict of interest with respect to his or her official duties.

(b) A prosecutor should not represent a defendant in criminal proceedings in a jurisdiction where he or she is also employed as a prosecutor.

(c) A prosecutor should not, except as law may otherwise expressly permit, participate in a matter in which he or she participated personally and substantially while in private practice or non-governmental employment unless under applicable law no one is, or by lawful delegation may be, authorized to act in the prosecutor's stead in the matter.

(d) A prosecutor who has formerly represented a client in a matter in private practice should not thereafter use information obtained from that representation to the disadvantage of the former client unless the rules of attorney-client confidentiality do not apply or the information has become generally known.

(e) A prosecutor should not, except as law may otherwise expressly permit, negotiate for private employment with any person who is involved as an accused or as an attorney or agent for an accused in a matter in which the prosecutor is participating personally and substantially.

(f) A prosecutor should not permit his or her professional judgment or obligations to be affected by his or her own political, financial, business, property, or personal interests.

(g) A prosecutor who is related to another lawyer as parent, child, sibling or spouse should not participate in the prosecution of a person who the prosecutor knows is represented by the other lawyer. Nor should a prosecutor who has a significant personal or financial relationship with another lawyer participate in the prosecution of a person who the prosecutor knows is represented by the other lawyer, unless the prosecutor's supervisor, if any, is informed and approves or unless there is no other prosecutor authorized to act in the prosecutor's stead.

(h) A prosecutor should not recommend the services of particular defense counsel to accused persons or witnesses unless requested by the accused person or witness to make such a recommendation, and should not make a referral that is likely to create a conflict of interest. Nor should a prosecutor comment upon the reputation or abilities of defense counsel to an accused person or witness who is seeking or may seek such counsel's services unless requested by such person.

Standard 3-1.4. Public Statements

(a) A prosecutor should not make or authorize the making of an extrajudicial statement that a reasonable person would expect to be disseminated by means of public communication if the prosecutor knows or reasonably should know that it will have a substantial likelihood of prejudicing a criminal proceeding.

(b) A prosecutor should exercise reasonable care to prevent investigators, law enforcement personnel, employees or other persons assisting or associated with the prosecutor from making an extrajudicial statement that the prosecutor would be prohibited from making under this standard.

Standard 3-1.5. Duty to Respond to Misconduct

(a) Where a prosecutor knows that another person associated with the prosecutor's office is engaged in action, intends to act or refuses to act in a manner that is a violation of a legal obligation to the prosecutor's office or a violation of law, the prosecutor should follow the policies of the prosecutor's office concerning such matters. If such policies are unavailing or do not exist, the prosecutor should ask the person to reconsider the action or inaction which is at issue if such a request is aptly timed to prevent such misconduct and is otherwise feasible. If such a request for reconsideration is unavailing, inapt or otherwise not feasible or if the seriousness of the matter so requires, the prosecutor should refer the matter to higher authority in the prosecutor's office, including, if warranted by the seriousness of the matter, referral to the chief prosecutor.

(b) If, despite the prosecutor's efforts in accordance with section (a), the chief prosecutor insists upon action, or a refusal to act, that is clearly a violation of law, the prosecutor may take further remedial action, including revealing the information necessary to remedy this violation to other appropriate governmental officials not in the prosecutor's office.

Part II. Organization of the Prosecution Function

Standard 3-2.1. Prosecution Authority to Be Vested in a Public Official

The prosecution function should be performed by a public prosecutor who is a lawyer subject to the standards of professional conduct and discipline.

414

Standard 3-2.2. Interrelationship of Prosecution Offices
Within a State

(a) Local authority and responsibility for prosecution is properly vested in a district, county, or city attorney. Wherever possible, a unit of prosecution should be designed on the basis of population, caseload, and other relevant factors sufficient to warrant at least one full-time prosecutor and the supporting staff necessary to effective prosecution.

(b) In some states, condition such as geographical areas and population may make it appropriate to create a statewide system of prosecution in which the state attorney general is the chief prosecutor and the local prosecutors are deputies.

(c) In all states, there should be coordination of the prosecution policies of local prosecution offices to improve the administration of justice and assure the maximum practicable uniformity in the enforcement of the criminal law throughout the state. A state association of prosecutors should be established in each state.

(d) To the extent needed, a central pool of supporting resources and personnel, including laboratories, investigators, accountants, special counsel, and other experts, should be maintained by the state government and should be available to assist all local prosecutors.

Standard 3-2.3. Assuring High Standards of
Professional Skill

(a) The function of public prosecution requires highly developed professional skills. This objective can best be achieved by promoting continuity of service and broad experience in all phases of the prosecution function.

(b) Wherever feasible, the offices of chief prosecutor and staff should be full-time occupations.

(c) Professional competence should be the basis for selection for prosecutorial office. Prosecutors should select their personnel without regard to partisan political influence.

(d) Special efforts should be made to recruit qualified women and members of minority groups for prosecutorial office.

(e) In order to achieve the objective of professionalism and to encourage competent lawyers to accept such offices, compensation for prosecutors and their staffs should be commensurate with the high responsibilities of the office and comparable to the compensation of their peers in the private sector.

Standard 3-2.4. Special Assistants, Investigative Resources, Experts

(a) Funds should be provided to enable a prosecutor to appoint special assistants from among the trial bar experienced in criminal cases, as needed for the prosecution of a particular case or to assist generally.

(b) Funds should be provided to the prosecutor for the employment of a regular staff of professional investigative personnel and other necessary supporting personnel, under the prosecutor's direct control, to the extent warranted by the responsibilities and scope of the office; the prosecutor should also be provided with funds for the employment of qualified experts as needed for particular cases.

Standard 3-2.5. Prosecutor's Handbook; Policy Guidelines and Procedures

(a) Each prosecutor's office should develop a statement of (i) general policies to guide the exercise of prosecutorial discretion and (ii) procedures of the office. The objectives of these policies as to discretion and procedures should be to achieve a fair, efficient, and effective enforcement of the criminal law.

(b) In the interest of continuity and clarity, such statement of policies and procedures should be maintained in an office handbook. This handbook should be available to the public, except for subject matters declared "confidential," when it is reasonably believed that public access to their contents would adversely affect the prosecution function.

Standard 3-2.6. Training Programs

Training programs should be established within the prosecutor's office for new personnel and for continuing education of the staff. Continuing education programs for prosecutors should be substantially expanded and public funds should be provided to enable prosecutors to attend such programs.

Standard 3-2.7. Relations with Police

(a) The prosecutor should provide legal advice to the police concerning police functions and duties in criminal matters.

(b) The prosecutor should cooperate with police in providing the services of the prosecutor's staff to aid in training police in the performance of their function in accordance with law.

Standard 3-2.8. Relations with the Courts and Bar

(a) A prosecutor should not intentionally misrepresent matters of fact or law to the court.

(b) A prosecutor's duties necessarily involve frequent and regular official contacts with the judge or judges of the prosecutor's jurisdiction. In such contacts the prosecutor should carefully strive to preserve the appearance as well as the reality of the correct relationship which professional traditions, ethical codes, and applicable law require between advocates and judges.

(c) A prosecutor should not engage in unauthorized ex parte discussions with or submission of material to a judge relating to a particular case which is or may come before the judge.

(d) A prosecutor should not fail to disclose to the tribunal legal authority in the controlling jurisdiction known to the prosecutor to be directly adverse to the prosecutor's position and not disclosed by defense counsel.

(e) A prosecutor should strive to develop good working relationships with defense counsel in order to facilitate the resolution of ethical problems. In particular, a prosecutor should assure defense counsel that if counsel finds it necessary to deliver physical items which may be relevant to a pending case or investigation to the prosecutor, the prosecutor will not offer the fact of such delivery by defense counsel as evidence before a jury for purposes of establishing defense counsel's client's culpability. However, nothing in this Standard shall prevent a prosecutor from offering evidence of the fact of such delivery in a subsequent proceeding for the purpose of proving a crime or fraud in the delivery of the evidence.

Standard 3-2.9. Prompt Disposition of Criminal
                Charges

(a) A prosecutor should avoid unnecessary delay in the disposition of cases. A prosecutor should not fail to act with reasonable diligence and promptness in prosecuting an accused.

(b) A prosecutor should not intentionally use procedural devices for delay for which there is no legitimate basis.

(c) The prosecution function should be so organized and supported with staff and facilities as to enable it to dispose of all criminal charges promptly. The prosecutor should be punctual in attendance in court and in the submission of all motions, briefs, and other papers. The prosecutor should emphasize to all witnesses the importance of punctuality in attendance in court.

(d) A prosecutor should not intentionally misrepresent facts or otherwise mislead the court in order to obtain a continuance.

(e) A prosecutor, without attempting to get more funding for additional staff, should not carry a workload that, by reason of its excessive size, interferes with the rendering of quality representation, endangers the interests of justice in the speedy disposition of charges, or may lead to the breach of professional obligations.

Standard 3-2.10. Supercession and Substitution of Prosecutor

(a) Procedures should be established by appropriate legislation to the end that the governor or other elected state official is empowered by law to suspend and supersede a local prosecutor upon making a public finding, after reasonable notice and hearing, that the prosecutor is incapable of fulfilling the duties of office.

(b) The governor or other elected official should be empowered by law to substitute special counsel in the place of the local prosecutor in a particular case, or category of cases, upon making a public finding that this is required for the protection of the public interest.

Standard 3-2.11. Literary or Media Agreements

A prosecutor, prior to conclusion of all aspects of a matter, should not enter into any agreement or understanding by which the prosecutor acquires an interest in literary or media rights to a portrayal or account based in substantial part on information relating to that matter.

Part III. Investigation for Prosecution Decision

Standard 3-3.1. Investigative Function of Prosecutor

(a) A prosecutor ordinarily relies on police and other investigative agencies for investigation of alleged criminal acts, but the prosecutor has an affirmative responsibility to investigate suspected illegal activity when it is not adequately dealt with by other agencies.

(b) A prosecutor should not invidiously discriminate against or in favor of any person on the basis of race, religion, sex, sexual preference, or ethnicity in exercising discretion to investigate or to prosecute. A prosecutor should not use other improper considerations in exercising such discretion.

(c) A prosecutor should not knowingly use illegal means to obtain evidence or to employ or instruct or encourage others to use such means.

(d) A prosecutor should not discourage or obstruct communication between prospective witnesses and defense counsel. A prosecutor should not advise any person or cause any person to be advised to decline to give to the defense information which such person has the right to give.

(e) A prosecutor should not secure the attendance of persons for interviews by use of any communication which has the appearance or color of a subpoena or similar judicial process unless the prosecutor is authorized by law to do so.

(f) A prosecutor should not promise not to prosecute for prospective criminal activity, except where such activity is part of an officially supervised investigative and enforcement program.

(g) Unless a prosecutor is prepared to forgo impeachment of a witness by the prosecutor's own testimony as to what the witness stated in an interview or to seek leave to withdraw from the case in order to present the impeaching testimony, a prosecutor should avoid interviewing a prospective witness except in the presence of a third person.

Standard 3-3.2. Relations with Victims and Prospective Witnesses

(a) A prosecutor should not compensate a witness, other than an expert, for giving testimony, but it is not improper to reimburse an ordinary witness for the reasonable expenses of attendance upon court, attendance for depositions pursuant to statute or court rule, or attendance for pretrial interviews. Payments to a witness may be for transportation and loss of income, provided there is no attempt to conceal the fact of reimbursement.

(b) A prosecutor should advise a witness who is to be interviewed of his or her rights against self-incrimination and the right to counsel whenever the law so requires. It is also proper for a prosecutor to so advise a witness whenever the prosecutor knows or has reason to believe that the witness may be the subject of a criminal prosecution. However, a prosecutor should not so advise a witness for the purpose of influencing the witness in favor of or against testifying.

(c) The prosecutor should readily provide victims and witnesses who request it information about the status of cases in which they are interested.

(d) The prosecutor should seek to insure that victims and witnesses who may need protections against intimidation are advised of and afforded such protections where feasible.

(e) The prosecutor should insure that victims and witnesses are given notice as soon as practicable of scheduling changes which will affect the victims' or witnesses' required attendance at judicial proceedings.

(f) The prosecutor should not require victims and witnesses to attend judicial proceedings unless their testimony is essential to the prosecution or is required by law. When their attendance is required, the prosecutor should seek to reduce to a minimum the time they must spend at the proceedings.

(g) The prosecutor should seek to insure that victims of serious crimes or their representatives are given timely notice of: (i) judicial proceedings relating to the victims' case; (ii) disposition of the case, including plea bargains, trial and sentencing; and (iii) any decision or action in the case which results in the accused's provisional or final release from custody.

(h) Where practical, the prosecutor should seek to insure that victims of serious crimes or their representatives are given an opportunity to consult with and to provide information to the prosecutor prior to the decision whether or not to prosecute, to pursue a disposition by plea, or to dismiss the charges.

Standard 3-3.3. Relations with Expert Witnesses

(a) A prosecutor who engages an expert for an opinion should respect the independence of the expert and should not seek to dictate the formation of the expert's opinion on the subject. To the extent necessary, the prosecutor should explain to the expert his or her role in the trial as an impartial expert called to aid the fact finders and the manner in which the examination of witnesses is conducted.

(b) A prosecutor should not pay an excessive fee for the purpose of influencing the expert's testimony or to fix the amount of the fee contingent upon the testimony the expert will give or the result in the case.

Standard 3-3.4. Decision to Charge

(a) The decision to institute criminal proceedings should be initially and primarily the responsibility of the prosecutor.

(b) Prosecutors should take reasonable care to ensure that investigators working at their direction or under their authority are adequately trained in the standards governing the issuance of arrest and search warrants and should inform investigators that they should seek the approval of a prosecutor in close or difficult cases.

(c) The prosecutor should establish standards and procedures for evaluating complaints to determine whether criminal proceedings should be instituted.

(d) Where the law permits a citizen to complain directly to a judicial officer or the grand jury, the citizen complainant should be required to present the complaint for prior approval to the prosecutor, and the prosecutor's action or recommendation thereon should be communicated to the judicial officer or grand jury.

Standard 3-3.5. Relations with Grand Jury

(a) Where the prosecutor is authorized to act as legal adviser to the grand jury, the prosecutor may appropriately explain the law and express an opinion on the legal significance of the evidence but should give due deference to its status as an independent legal body.

(b) The prosecutor should not make statements or arguments in an effort to influence grand jury action in a manner which would be impermissible at trial before a petit jury.

(c) The prosecutor's communications and presentations to the grand jury should be on the record.

Standard 3-3.6. Quality and Scope of Evidence Before Grand Jury

(a) A prosecutor should only make statements or arguments to the grand jury and only present evidence to the grand jury which the prosecutor believes is appropriate or authorized under law for presentation to the grand jury. In appropriate cases, the prosecutor may present witnesses to summarize admissible evidence available to the prosecutor which the prosecutor believes he or she will be able to present at trial. The prosecutor should also inform the grand jurors that they have the right to hear any available witnesses, including eyewitnesses.

(b) No prosecutor should knowingly fail to disclose to the grand jury evidence which tends to negate guilt or mitigate the offense.

(c) A prosecutor should recommend that the grand jury not indict if he or she believes the evidence presented does not warrant an indictment under governing law.

(d) If the prosecutor believes that a witness is a potential defendant, the prosecutor should not seek to compel the witness's testimony before the grand jury without informing the witness that he or she may be charged and that the witness should seek independent legal advice concerning his or her rights.

(e) The prosecutor should not compel the appearance of a witness before the grand jury whose activities are the subject of the inquiry if the witness states in advance that if called he or she will exercise the constitutional privilege not to testify, unless the prosecutor intends to judicially challenge the exercise of the privilege or to seek a grant of immunity according to the law.

(f) A prosecutor in presenting a case to a grand jury should not intentionally interfere with the independence of the grand jury, preempt a function of the grand jury, or abuse the processes of the grand jury.

(g) Unless the law of the jurisdiction so permits, a prosecutor should not use the grand jury in order to obtain tangible, documentary or testimonial evidence to assist the prosecutor in preparation for trial of a defendant who has already been charged by indictment or information.

(h) Unless the law of the jurisdiction so permits, a prosecutor should not use the grand jury for the purpose of aiding or assisting in any administrative inquiry.

Standard 3-3.7. Quality and Scope of Evidence for Information

Where the prosecutor is empowered to charge by information, the prosecutor's decisions should be governed by the principles embodied in standards 3-3.6 and 3-3.9, where applicable.

Standard 3-3.8. Discretion as to Noncriminal Disposition

(a) The prosecutor should consider in appropriate cases the availability of noncriminal disposition, formal or informal, in deciding whether to press criminal charges which would otherwise be supported by probable cause; especially in the case of a first offender, the nature of the offense may warrant noncriminal disposition.

(b) Prosecutors should be familiar with the resources of social agencies which can assist in the evaluation of cases for diversion from the criminal process.

Standard 3-3.9. Discretion in the Charging Decision

(a) A prosecutor should not institute, or cause to be instituted, or permit the continued pendency of criminal charges when the prosecutor knows that the charges are not supported by probable cause. A prosecutor should not institute, cause to be instituted, or permit the continued pendency of criminal charges in the absence of sufficient admissible evidence to support a conviction.

(b) The prosecutor is not obliged to present all charges which the evidence might support. The prosecutor may in some circumstances and for good cause consistent with the public interest decline to prosecute, notwithstanding that sufficient evidence may exist which would support a conviction. Illustrative of the factors which the prosecutor may properly consider in exercising his or her discretion are:

(i) the prosecutor's reasonable doubt that the accused is in fact guilty;

(ii) the extent of the harm caused by the offense;

(iii) the disproportion of the authorized punishment in relation to the particular offense or the offender;

(iv) possible improper motives of a complainant;

(v) reluctance of the victim to testify;

(vi) cooperation of the accused in the apprehension or conviction of others; and

(vii) availability and likelihood of prosecution by another jurisdiction.

(c) A prosecutor should not be compelled by his or her supervisor to prosecute a case in which he or she has a reasonable doubt about the guilt of the accused.

(d) In making the decision to prosecute, the prosecutor should give no weight to the personal or political advantages or disadvantages which might be involved or to a desire to enhance his or her record of convictions.

(e) In cases which involve a serious threat to the community, the prosecutor should not be deterred from prosecution by the fact that in the jurisdiction juries have tended to acquit persons accused of the particular kind of criminal act in question.

(f) The prosecutor should not bring or seek charges greater in number or degree than can reasonably be supported with evidence at trial or than are necessary to fairly reflect the gravity of the offense.

(g) The prosecutor should not condition a dismissal of charges, nolle prosequi, or similar action on the accused's relinquishment of the right to seek civil redress unless the accused has agreed to the action knowingly and intelligently, freely and voluntarily, and where such waiver is approved by the court.

Standard 3-3.10. Role in First Appearance and Preliminary Hearing

(a) A prosecutor who is present at the first appearance (however denominated) of the accused before a judicial officer should not communicate with the accused unless a waiver of counsel has been entered, except for the purpose of aiding in obtaining counsel or in arranging for the pretrial release of the accused. A prosecutor should not fail to make reasonable efforts to assure that the accused has been advised of the right to, and the procedure for obtaining, counsel and has been given reasonable opportunity to obtain counsel.

(b) The prosecutor should cooperate in good faith in arrangements for release under the prevailing system for pretrial release.

(c) The prosecutor should not seek to obtain from an unrepresented accused a waiver of important pretrial rights, such as the right to a preliminary hearing.

(d) The prosecutor should not seek a continuance solely for the purpose of mooting the preliminary hearing by securing an indictment.

(e) Except for good cause, the prosecutor should not seek delay in the preliminary hearing after an arrest has been made if the accused is in custody.

(f) The prosecutor should ordinarily be present at a preliminary hearing where such hearing is required by law.

Standard 3-3.11. Disclosure of Evidence by the Prosecutor

(a) A prosecutor should not intentionally fail to make timely disclosure to the defense, at the earliest feasible opportunity, of the existence of all evidence or information which tends to negate the guilt of the accused or mitigate the offense charged or which would tend to reduce the punishment of the accused.

(b) A prosecutor should not fail to make a reasonably diligent effort to comply with a legally proper discovery request.

(c) A prosecutor should not intentionally avoid pursuit of evidence because he or she believes it will damage the prosecution's case or aid the accused.

Part IV. Plea Discussions

Standard 3-4.1. Availability for Plea Discussions

(a) The prosecutor should have and make known a general policy or willingness to consult with defense counsel concerning disposition of charges by plea.

(b) A prosecutor should not engage in plea discussions directly with an accused who is represented by defense counsel, except with defense counsel's approval. Where the defendant has properly waived counsel, the prosecuting attorney may engage in plea discussions with the defendant, although, where feasible, a record of such discussions should be made and preserved.

(c) A prosecutor should not knowingly make false statements or representations as to fact or law in the course of plea discussions with defense counsel or the accused.

Standard 3-4.2. Fulfillment of Plea Discussions

(a) A prosecutor should not make any promise or commitment assuring a defendant or defense counsel that a court will impose a specific sentence or a suspension of sentence; a prosecutor may properly advise the defense what position will be taken concerning disposition.

(b) A prosecutor should not imply a greater power to influence the disposition of a case than is actually possessed.

(c) A prosecutor should not fail to comply with a plea agreement, unless a defendant fails to comply with a plea agreement or other extenuating circumstances are present.

Standard 3-4.3. Record of Reasons for Nolle Prosequi Disposition

Whenever felony criminal charges are dismissed by way of nolle prosequi (or its equivalent), the prosecutor should make a record of the reasons for the action.

424

Part V. The Trial

Standard 3-5.1. Calendar Control

Control over the trial calendar should be vested in the court. The prosecuting attorney should advise the court of facts relevant in determining the order of cases on the court's calendar.

Standard 3-5.2. Courtroom Professionalism

(a) As an officer of the court, the prosecutor should support the authority of the court and the dignity of the trial courtroom by strict adherence to codes of professionalism and by manifesting a professional attitude toward the judge, opposing counsel, witnesses, defendants, jurors, and others in the courtroom.

(b) When court is in session, the prosecutor should address the court, not opposing counsel, on all matters relating to the case.

(c) Prosecutor should comply promptly with all orders and directives of the court, but the prosecutor has a duty to have the record reflect adverse rulings or judicial conduct which the prosecutor considers prejudicial. The prosecutor has a right to make respectful requests for reconsideration of adverse rulings.

(d) Prosecutors should cooperate with courts and the organized bar in developing codes of professionalism for each jurisdiction.

Standard 3-5.3. Selection of Jurors

(a) The prosecutor should prepare himself or herself prior to trial to discharge effectively the prosecution function in the selection of the jury and the exercise of challenges for cause and peremptory challenges.

(b) In those cases where it appears necessary to conduct a pretrial investigation of the background of jurors, investigatory methods of the prosecutor should neither harass nor unduly embarrass potential jurors or invade their privacy and, whenever possible, should be restricted to an investigation of records and sources of information already in existence.

(c) The opportunity to question jurors personally should be used solely to obtain information for the intelligent exercise of challenges. A prosecutor should not intentionally use the voir dire to present factual matter which the prosecutor knows will not be admissible at trial or to argue the prosecution's case to the jury.

Standard 3-5.4. Relations with Jury

(a) A prosecutor should not intentionally communicate privately with persons summoned for jury duty or impaneled as jurors prior to or during trial. The prosecutor should avoid the reality or appearance of any such communications.

(b) The prosecutor should treat jurors with deference and respect, avoiding the reality or appearance of currying favor by a show of undue solicitude for their comfort or convenience.

(c) After discharge of the jury from further consideration of a case, a prosecutor should not intentionally make comments to or ask questions of a juror for the purpose of harassing or embarrassing the juror in any way which will tend to influence judgment in future jury service. If the prosecutor believes that the verdict may be subject to legal challenge, he or she may properly, if no statute or rule prohibits such course, communicate with jurors to determine whether such challenge may be available.

Standard 3-5.5. Opening Statement

The prosecutor's opening statement should be confined to a statement of the issues in the case and the evidence the prosecutor intends to offer which the prosecutor believes in good faith will be available and admissible. A prosecutor should not allude to any evidence unless there is a good faith and reasonable basis for believing that such evidence will be tendered and admitted in evidence.

Standard 3-5.6. Presentation of Evidence

(a) A prosecutor should not knowingly offer false evidence, whether by documents, tangible evidence, or the testimony of witnesses, or fail to seek withdrawal thereof upon discovery of its falsity.

(b) A prosecutor should not knowingly and for the purpose of bringing inadmissible matter to the attention of the judge or jury offer inadmissible evidence, ask legally objectionable questions, or make other impermissible comments or arguments in the presence of the judge or jury.

(c) A prosecutor should not permit any tangible evidence to be displayed in the view of the judge or jury which would tend to prejudice fair consideration by the judge or jury until such time as a good faith tender of such evidence is made.

(d) A prosecutor should not tender tangible evidence in the view of the judge or jury if it would tend to prejudice fair consideration by the judge or jury unless there is a reasonable basis for its admission in evidence. When there is any substantial doubt about the admissibility of such evidence, it should be tendered by an offer of proof and a ruling obtained.

Standard 3-5.7. Examination of Witnesses

(a) The interrogation of all witnesses should be conducted fairly, objectively, and with due regard for the dignity and legitimate privacy of the witness, and without seeking to intimidate or humiliate the witness unnecessarily.

(b) The prosecutor's belief that the witness is telling the truth does not preclude cross-examination, but may affect the method and scope of cross-examination. A prosecutor should not use the power of cross-examination to discredit or undermine a witness if the prosecutor knows the witness is testifying truthfully.

(c) A prosecutor should not call a witness in the presence of the jury who the prosecutor knows will claim a valid privilege not to testify.

(d) A prosecutor should not ask a question which implies the existence of a factual predicate for which a good faith belief is lacking.

Standard 3-5.8. Argument to the Jury

(a) In closing argument to the jury, the prosecutor may argue all reasonable inferences from evidence in the record. The prosecutor should not intentionally misstate the evidence or mislead the jury as to the inferences it may draw.

(b) The prosecutor should not express his or her personal belief or opinion as to the truth or falsity of any testimony or evidence or the guilt of the defendant.

(c) The prosecutor should not use arguments calculated to appeal to the prejudices of the jury.

(d) The prosecutor should refrain from argument which would divert the jury from its duty to decide the case on the evidence.

Standard 3-5.9. Facts Outside the Record

The prosecutor should not intentionally refer to or argue on the basis of facts outside the record whether at trial or on appeal, unless such facts are matters of common public knowledge based on ordinary human experience or matters of which the court may take judicial notice.

Standard 3-5.10. Comments by Prosecutor After Verdict

The prosecutor should not make public comments critical of a verdict, whether rendered by judge or jury.

Part VI. Sentencing

Standard 3-6.1. Role in Sentencing

(a) The prosecutor should not make the severity of sentences the index of his or her effectiveness. To the extent that the prosecutor becomes involved in the sentencing process, he or she should seek to assure that a fair and informed judgment is made on the sentence and to avoid unfair sentence disparities.

(b) Where sentence is fixed by the court without jury participation, the prosecutor should be afforded the opportunity to address the court at sentencing and to offer a sentencing recommendation.

(c) Where sentence is fixed by the jury, the prosecutor should present evidence on the issue within the limits permitted in the jurisdiction, but the prosecutor should avoid introducing evidence bearing on sentence which will prejudice the jury's determination of the issue of guilt.

Standard 3-6.2. Information Relevant to Sentencing

(a) The prosecutor should assist the court in basing its sentence on complete and accurate information for use in the presentence report. The prosecutor should disclose to the court any information in the prosecutor's files relevant to the sentence. If incompleteness or inaccurateness in the presentence report comes to the prosecutor's attention, the prosecutor should take steps to present the complete and correct information to the court and to defense counsel.

(b) The prosecutor should disclose to the defense and to the court at or prior to the sentencing proceeding all unprivileged mitigating information known to the prosecutor, except when the prosecutor is relieved of this responsibility by a protective order of the tribunal.

CHAPTER 4. THE DEFENSE FUNCTION

Editors' Note. Chapter 4 was originally approved by the ABA in 1971. As noted in the Editors' Introduction to this chapter, the ABA approved substantial revisions to "The Defense Function" at its 1991 Mid-Year Meeting. Some new sections were added (§§4-1.1, 4-3.9, and 4-4.6), while others were deleted (former §§4-1.6, 4-3.9, and 4-7.7).

Part I. General Standards

Standard 4-1.1. The Function of the Standards

These standards are intended to be used as a guide to professional conduct and performance. They are not intended to be used as criteria for the judicial evaluation of alleged misconduct of defense counsel to determine the validity of a conviction. They may or may not be relevant in such judicial evaluation, depending upon all the circumstances.

Standard 4-1.2. The Function of Defense Counsel

(a) Counsel for the accused is an essential component of the administration of criminal justice. A court properly constituted to hear a criminal case must be viewed as a tripartite entity consisting of the judge (and jury, where appropriate), counsel for the prosecution, and counsel for the accused.

(b) The basic duty defense counsel owes to the administration of justice and as an officer of the court is to serve as the accused's counselor and advocate with courage and devotion and to render effective, quality representation.

(c) Since the death penalty differs from other criminal penalties in its finality, defense counsel in a capital case should respond to this difference by making extraordinary efforts on behalf of the accused. Defense counsel should comply with the ABA Guidelines for the Appointment and Performance of Counsel in Death Penalty Cases.

(d) Defense counsel should seek to reform and improve the administration of criminal justice. When inadequacies or injustices in the substantive or procedural law come to defense counsel's attention, he or she should stimulate efforts for remedial action.

(e) Defense counsel, in common with all members of the bar, is subject to standards of conduct stated in statutes, rules, decisions of courts, and codes, canons, or other standards of professional conduct. Defense counsel has no duty to execute any directive of the accused which does not comport with law or such standards. Defense counsel is the professional representative of the accused, not the accused's alter ego.

(f) Defense counsel should not intentionally misrepresent matters of fact or law to the court.

(g) Defense counsel should disclose to the tribunal legal authority in the controlling jurisdiction known to defense counsel to be directly adverse to the position of the accused and not disclosed by the prosecutor.

(h) It is the duty of defense counsel to know and be guided by the standards of professional conduct as defined in codes and canons of the legal profession applicable in defense counsel's jurisdiction. Once representation has been undertaken, the functions and duties of defense counsel are the same whether defense counsel is assigned, privately retained, or serving in a legal aid or defender program.

Standard 4-1.3. Delays; Punctuality; Workload

(a) Defense counsel should act with reasonable diligence and promptness in representing a client.

(b) Defense counsel should avoid unnecessary delay in the disposition of cases. Defense counsel should be punctual in attendance upon court and in the submission of all motions, briefs, and other papers. Defense counsel should emphasize to the client and all witnesses the importance of punctuality in attendance in court.

(c) Defense counsel should not intentionally misrepresent facts or otherwise mislead the court in order to obtain a continuance.

(d) Defense counsel should not intentionally use procedural devices for delay for which there is no legitimate basis.

(e) Defense counsel should not carry a workload that, by reason of its excessive size, interferes with the rendering of quality representation, endangers the client's interest in the speedy disposition of charges, or may lead to the breach of professional obligations. Defense counsel should not accept employment for the purpose of delaying trial.

Standard 4-1.4. Public Statements

Defense counsel should not make or authorize the making of an extrajudicial statement that a reasonable person would expect to be disseminated by means of public communication if defense counsel knows or reasonably should know that it will have a substantial likelihood of prejudicing a criminal proceeding.

Standard 4-1.5. Advisory Councils on Professional Conduct

(a) In every jurisdiction, an advisory body of lawyers selected for their experience, integrity, and standing at the trial bar should be established as an advisory council on problems of professional conduct in criminal cases. This council should provide prompt and confidential guidance and advice to lawyers seeking assistance in the application of standards of professional conduct in criminal cases.

(b) Communications between an inquiring lawyer and an advisory council member have the same attorney-client privilege for protection of the client's confidences as ordinarily exists between any other lawyer and client. The council member should be bound by statute or rule of court in the same manner as a lawyer is ordinarily bound in that jurisdiction not to reveal any disclosure of the client. Confidences may also be revealed, however, to the extent necessary:

(i) if the inquiring lawyer's client challenges the effectiveness of the lawyer's conduct of the case and the lawyer relies on the guidance received from the council member, or

(ii) if the inquiring lawyer's conduct is called into question in an authoritative disciplinary inquiry or proceeding.

Standard 4-1.6. Trial Lawyer's Duty to Administration of Justice

(a) The bar should encourage through every available means the widest possible participation in the defense of criminal cases by lawyers. Lawyers should be encouraged to qualify themselves for participation in criminal cases both by formal training and through experience as associate counsel.

(b) All such qualified lawyers should stand ready to undertake the defense of an accused regardless of public hostility toward the accused or personal distaste for the offense charged or the person of the defendant.

(c) Such qualified lawyers should not assert or announce a general unwillingness to appear in criminal cases. Law firms should encourage partners and associates to become qualified and to appear in criminal cases.

(d) Such qualified lawyers should not seek to avoid appointment by a tribunal to represent an accused except for good cause, such as: representing the accused is likely to result in violation of applicable ethical codes or other law, representing the accused is likely to result in an unreasonable financial burden on the lawyer, or the client or crime is so repugnant to the lawyer as to be likely to impair the client-lawyer relationship or the lawyer's ability to represent the client.

Part II. Access to Counsel

Standard 4-2.1. Communication

Every jurisdiction should guarantee by statute or rule of court the right of an accused person to prompt and effective communication with a lawyer and should require that reasonable access to a telephone or other facilities be provided for that purpose.

Standard 4-2.2. Referral Service for Criminal Cases

(a) To assist persons who wish to retain defense counsel privately and who do not know a lawyer or how to engage one, every jurisdiction should have a referral service for criminal cases. The referral service should maintain a list of defense counsel willing and qualified to undertake the defense of a criminal case; it should be so organized that it can provide prompt service at all times.

(b) The availability of the referral service should be publicized. In addition, notices containing the essential information about the referral service and how to contact it should be posted conspicuously in police stations, jails, and wherever else it is likely to give effective notice.

Standard 4-2.3. Prohibited Referrals

(a) Defense counsel should not give anything of value to a person for recommending the lawyer's services.

(b) Defense counsel should not accept a referral from any source, including prosecutors, law enforcement personnel, victims, bondsmen, or court personnel where the acceptance of such a referral is likely to create a conflict of interest.

Part III. Lawyer-Client Relationship

Standard 4-3.1. Establishment of Relationship

(a) Defense counsel should seek to establish a relationship of trust and confidence with the accused and should discuss the objectives of the representation and whether defense counsel will continue to represent the accused if there is an appeal. Defense counsel should explain the necessity of full disclosure of all facts known to the client for an effective defense, and defense counsel should explain the extent to which counsel's obligation of confidentiality makes privileged the accused's disclosures.

(b) To ensure the privacy essential for confidential communication between defense counsel and client, adequate facilities should be available for private discussions between counsel and accused in jails, prisons, courthouses, and other places where accused persons must confer with counsel.

(c) Personnel of jails, prisons, and custodial institutions should be prohibited by law or administrative regulations from examining or otherwise interfering with any communication or correspondence between client and defense counsel relating to legal action arising out of charges or incarceration.

Standard 4-3.2. Interviewing the Client

(a) As soon as practicable, defense counsel should seek to determine all relevant facts known to the accused. In so doing, defense counsel should probe for all legally relevant information without seeking to influence the direction of the client's responses.

(b) Defense counsel should not instruct the client or intimate to the client in any way that the client should not be candid in revealing facts so as to afford defense counsel free rein to take action which would be precluded by counsel's knowing of such facts.

Standard 4-3.3. Fees

(a) Defense counsel should not enter into an agreement for, charge, or collect an illegal or unreasonable fee.

(b) In determining the amount of the fee in a criminal case, it is proper to consider the time and effort required, the responsibility assumed by counsel, the novelty and difficulty of the questions involved, the skill requisite to proper representation, the likelihood that other employment will be precluded, the fee customarily charged in the locality for similar services, the gravity of the charge, the experience, reputation, and ability of defense counsel, and the capacity of the client to pay the fee.

(c) Defense counsel should not imply that his or her compensation is for anything other than professional services rendered by defense counsel or by others for defense counsel.

(d) Defense counsel should not divide a fee with a nonlawyer, except as permitted by applicable ethical codes of conduct.

(e) Defense counsel not in the same firm should not divide fees unless the division is in proportion to the services performed by each counsel or, by written agreement with the client, each counsel assumes joint responsibility for the representation, the client is advised of and does not object to the participation of all counsel involved, and the total fee is reasonable.

(f) Defense counsel should not enter into an arrangement for, charge, or collect a contingent fee for representing a defendant in a criminal case.

(g) When defense counsel has not regularly represented the client, defense counsel should communicate the basis or rate of the fee to the client, preferably in writing, before or within a reasonable time after commencing the representation.

Standard 4-3.4. Obtaining Literary or Media Rights
from the Accused

Defense counsel, prior to conclusion of all aspects of the matter giving rise to his or her employment, should not enter into any agreement or understanding with a client or a prospective client by which defense counsel acquires an interest in literary or media rights to a portrayal or account based in substantial part on information relating to the employment or proposed employment.

Standard 4-3.5. Conflicts of Interest

(a) Defense counsel should not permit his or her professional judgment or obligations to be affected by his or her own political, financial, business, property, or personal interests.

(b) Defense counsel should disclose to the defendant at the earliest feasible opportunity any interest in or connection with the case or any other matter that might be relevant to the defendant's selection of counsel to represent him or her or counsel's continuing representation. Such disclosure should include communication of information reasonably sufficient to permit the client to appreciate the significance of any conflict or potential conflict of interest.

(c) Except for preliminary matters such as initial hearings or applications for bail, defense counsel who are associated in practice should not undertake to defend more than one defendant in the same criminal case if the duty to one of the defendants may conflict with the duty to another. The potential for conflict of interest in representing multiple defendants is so grave that ordinarily defense counsel should decline to act for more than one of several codefendants except in unusual situations when, after careful investigation, it is clear either that no conflict is likely to develop at trial, sentencing, or at any other time in the proceeding or that common representation will be advantageous to each of the codefendants represented and, in either case, that:

(i) the several defendants give an informed consent to such multiple representation; and

(ii) the consent of the defendants is made a matter of judicial record. In determining the presence of consent by the defendants, the trial judge should make appropriate inquiries respecting actual or potential conflicts of interest of counsel and whether the defendants fully comprehend the difficulties that defense counsel sometimes encounters in defending multiple clients.

(d) Defense counsel who has formerly represented a defendant should not thereafter use information related to the former representation to the disadvantage of the former client unless the information has become generally known or the ethical obligation of confidentiality otherwise does not apply.

(e) In accepting payment of fees by one person for the defense of another, defense counsel should be careful to determine that he or she will not be confronted with a conflict of loyalty since defense counsel's entire loyalty is due the accused. Defense counsel should not accept such compensation unless:

(i) the accused consents after disclosure;

(ii) there is no interference with defense counsel's independence of professional judgment or with the client-lawyer relationship; and

(iii) information relating to the representation of the accused is protected from disclosure as required by defense counsel's ethical obligation of confidentiality.

Defense counsel should not permit a person who recommends, employs, or pays defense counsel to render legal services for another to direct or regulate counsel's professional judgment in rendering such legal services.

(f) Defense counsel should not defend a criminal case in which counsel's partner or other professional associate is or has been the prosecutor in the same case.

(g) Defense counsel should not represent a criminal defendant in a jurisdiction in which he or she is also a prosecutor.

(h) Defense counsel who formerly participated personally and substantially in the prosecution of a defendant should not thereafter represent any person in the same or a substantially related matter. Defense counsel who was formerly a prosecutor should not use confidential information about a person acquired when defense counsel was a prosecutor in the representation of a client whose interests are adverse to that person in a matter.

(i) Defense counsel who is related to a prosecutor as parent, child, sibling or spouse should not represent a client in a criminal matter where defense counsel knows that government is represented in the matter by such prosecutor. Nor should defense counsel who has a significant personal or financial relationship with a prosecutor represent a client in a criminal matter where defense counsel knows the government is represented in the matter by such prosecutor, except upon consent by the client after consultation regarding the relationship.

(j) Defense counsel should not act as surety on a bond either for the accused represented by counsel or for any other accused in the same or a related case.

(k) Except as law may otherwise expressly permit, defense counsel should not negotiate to employ any person who is significantly involved as an attorney or employee of the government in a matter in which defense counsel is participating personally and substantially.

Standard 4-3.6. Prompt Action to Protect the Accused

Many important rights of the accused can be protected and preserved only by prompt legal action. Defense counsel should inform the accused of his or her rights at the earliest opportunity and take all necessary action to vindicate such rights. Defense counsel should consider all procedural steps which in good faith may be taken, including, for example, motions seeking pretrial release of the accused, obtaining psychiatric examination of the accused when a need appears, moving for change of venue or continuance, moving for severance from jointly charged defendants, and seeking dismissal of the charges.

Standard 4-3.7. Advice and Service on Anticipated Unlawful Conduct

(a) It is defense counsel's duty to advise a client to comply with the law, but counsel may advise concerning the meaning, scope, and validity of a law.

(b) Defense counsel should not counsel a client in or knowingly assist a client to engage in conduct which defense counsel knows to be illegal or fraudulent but defense counsel may discuss the legal consequences of any proposed course of conduct with a client.

(c) Defense counsel should not agree in advance of the commission of a crime that he or she will serve as counsel for the defendant, except as part of a bona fide effort to determine the validity, scope, meaning, or application of the law, or where the defense is incident to a general retainer for legal services to a person or enterprise engaged in legitimate activity.

(d) Defense counsel should not reveal information relating to representation of a client unless the client consents after consultation, except for disclosures that are impliedly authorized in order to carry out the representation and except that defense counsel may reveal such information to the extent he or she reasonably believes necessary to prevent the client from committing a criminal act that defense counsel believes is likely to result in imminent death or substantial bodily harm.

Standard 4-3.8. Duty to Keep Client Informed

(a) Defense counsel should keep the client informed of the developments in the case and the progress of preparing the defense and should promptly comply with reasonable requests for information.

(b) Defense counsel should explain developments in the case to the extent reasonably necessary to permit the client to make informed decisions regarding the representation.

Standard 4-3.9. Obligations of Hybrid and Standby Counsel

(a) Defense counsel whose duty is to actively assist a pro se accused should permit the accused to make the final decisions on all matters, including strategic and tactical matters relating to the conduct of the case.

(b) Defense counsel whose duty is to assist a pro se accused only when the accused requests assistance may bring to the attention of the accused matters beneficial to him or her, but should not actively participate in the conduct of the defense unless requested by the accused or insofar as directed to do so by the court.

Part IV. Investigation and Preparation

Standard 4-4.1. Duty to Investigate

(a) Defense counsel should conduct a prompt investigation of the circumstances of the case and explore all avenues leading to facts relevant to the merits of the case and the penalty in the event of conviction. The investigation should include efforts to secure information in the possession of the prosecution and law enforcement authorities. The duty to investigate exists regardless of the accused's admissions or statements to defense counsel of facts constituting guilt or the accused's stated desire to plead guilty.

(b) Defense counsel should not seek to acquire possession of physical evidence personally or through use of an investigator where defense counsel's sole purpose is to obstruct access to such evidence.

Standard 4-4.2. Illegal Investigation

Defense counsel should not knowingly use illegal means to obtain evidence or information or to employ, instruct, or encourage others to do so.

Standard 4-4.3. Relations with Prospective Witnesses

(a) Defense counsel, in representing an accused, should not use means that have no substantial purpose other than to embarrass, delay, or burden a third person, or use methods of obtaining evidence that violate the legal rights of such a person.

(b) Defense counsel should not compensate a witness, other than an expert, for giving testimony, but it is not improper to reimburse a witness for the reasonable expenses of attendance upon court, including transportation and loss of income, attendance for depositions pursuant to statute or court rule, or attendance for pretrial interviews, provided there is no attempt to conceal the fact of reimbursement.

(c) It is not necessary for defense counsel or defense counsel's investigator, in interviewing a prospective witness, to caution the witness concerning possible self-incrimination and the need for counsel.

(d) Defense counsel should not discourage or obstruct communication between prospective witnesses and the prosecutor. It is unprofessional conduct to advise any person other than a client, or cause such person to be advised, to decline to give to the prosecutor or defense counsel for codefendants information which such person has a right to give.

(e) Unless defense counsel is prepared to forgo impeachment of a witness by counsel's own testimony as to what the witness stated in an interview or to seek leave to withdraw from the case in order to present such impeaching testimony, defense counsel should avoid interviewing a prospective witness except in the presence of a third person.

Standard 4-4.4. Relations with Expert Witnesses

(a) Defense counsel who engages an expert for an opinion should respect the independence of the expert and should not seek to dictate the formation of the expert's opinion on the subject. To the extent necessary, defense counsel should explain to the expert his or her role in the trial as an impartial witness called to aid the fact finders and the manner in which the examination of witnesses is conducted.

(b) Defense counsel should not pay an excessive fee for the purpose of influencing an expert's testimony or fix the amount of the fee contingent upon the testimony an expert will give or the result in the case.

Standard 4-4.5. Compliance with Discovery Procedure

Defense counsel should make a reasonably diligent effort to comply with a legally proper discovery request.

Standard 4-4.6. Physical Evidence

(a) Defense counsel who receives a physical item under circumstances implicating a client in criminal conduct should disclose the location of or should deliver that item to law enforcement authorities only: (1) if required by law or court order, or (2) as provided in paragraph (d).

(b) Unless required to disclose, defense counsel should return the item to the source from whom defense counsel received it, except as provided in paragraphs (c) and (d). In returning the item to the source, defense counsel should advise the source of the legal consequences pertaining to possession or destruction of the item. Defense counsel should also prepare a written record of these events for his or her file, but should not give the source a copy of such record.

(c) Defense counsel may receive the item for a reasonable period of time during which defense counsel: (1) intends to return it to the owner; (2) reasonably fears that return of the item to the source will result in destruction of the item; (3) reasonably fears that return of the item to the source will result in physical harm to anyone; (4) intends to test, examine, inspect, or use the item in any way as part of defense counsel's representation of the client; or (5) cannot return it to the source. If defense counsel tests or examines the item, he or she should thereafter return it to the source unless there is reason to believe that the evidence might be altered or destroyed or used to harm another or return is otherwise impossible. If defense counsel retains the item, he or she should retain it in his or her law office in a manner that does not impede the lawful ability of law enforcement authorities to obtain the item.

(d) If the item received is contraband, i.e. an item, possession of which is in and of itself a crime, such as narcotics, defense counsel may suggest that the client destroy it where there is no pending case or investigation relating to this evidence and where such destruction is clearly not in violation of any criminal statute. If such destruction is not permitted by law or if in defense counsel's judgment he or she cannot retain the item, whether or not it is contraband, in a way that does not pose an unreasonable risk of physical harm to anyone, defense counsel should disclose the location of or should deliver the item to law enforcement authorities.

(e) If defense counsel discloses the location of or delivers the item to law enforcement authorities under paragraphs (a) or (d), or to a third party under paragraph (c)(1), he or she should do so in the way best designed to protect the client's interests.

Part V. Control and Direction of Litigation

Standard 4-5.1. Advising the Accused

(a) After informing himself or herself fully on the facts and the law, defense counsel should advise the accused with complete candor concerning all aspects of the case, including a candid estimate of the probable outcome.

(b) Defense counsel should not intentionally understate or overstate the risks, hazards, or prospects of the case to exert undue influence on the accused's decision as to his or her plea.

(c) Defense counsel should caution the client to avoid communication about the case with witnesses, except with the approval of counsel, to avoid any contact with jurors or prospective jurors, and to avoid either the reality or the appearance of any other improper activity.

Standard 4-5.2. Control and Direction of the Case

(a) Certain decisions relating to the conduct of the case are ultimately for the accused and others are ultimately for defense counsel. The decisions which are to be made by the accused after full consultation with counsel include:

    (i) what pleas to enter;

    (ii) whether to accept a plea agreement;

    (iii) whether to waive jury trial;

    (iv) whether to testify in his or her own behalf; and

    (v) whether to appeal.

(b) Strategic and tactical decisions should be made by defense counsel after consultation with the client where feasible and appropriate. Such decisions include what witnesses to call, whether and how to conduct cross-examination, what jurors to accept or strike, what trial motions should be made, and what evidence should be introduced.

(c) If a disagreement on significant matters of tactics or strategy arises between defense counsel and the client, defense counsel should make a record of the circumstances, counsel's advice and reasons, and the conclusion reached. The record should be made in a manner which protects the confidentiality of the lawyer-client relationship.

Part VI. Disposition Without Trial

Standard 4-6.1. Duty to Explore Disposition Without Trial

(a) Whenever the law, nature, and circumstances of the case permit, defense counsel should explore the possibility of an early diversion of the case from the criminal process through the use of other community agencies.

(b) Defense counsel may engage in plea discussions with the prosecutor. Under no circumstances should defense counsel recommend to a defendant acceptance of a plea unless appropriate investigation and study of the case has been completed, including an analysis of controlling law and the evidence likely to be introduced at trial.

Standard 4-6.2. Plea Discussions

(a) Defense counsel should keep the accused advised of developments arising out of plea discussions conducted with the prosecutor.

(b) Defense counsel should promptly communicate and explain to the accused all significant plea proposals made by the prosecutor.

(c) Defense counsel should not knowingly make false statements concerning the evidence in the course of plea discussions with the prosecutor.

(d) Defense counsel should not seek concessions favorable to one client by any agreement which is detrimental to the legitimate interests of a client in another case.

(e) Defense counsel representing two or more clients in the same or related cases should not participate in making an aggregated agreement as to guilty or nolo contendre pleas, unless each client consents after consultation, including disclosure of the existence and nature of all the claims or pleas involved.

Part VII. Trial

Standard 4-7.1. Courtroom Professionalism

(a) As an officer of the court, defense counsel should support the authority of the court and the dignity of the trial courtroom by strict adherence to codes of professionalism and by manifesting a professional attitude toward the judge, opposing counsel, witnesses, jurors, and others in the courtroom.

(b) Defense counsel should not engage in unauthorized ex parte discussions with or submission of material to a judge relating to a particular case which is or may come before the judge.

(c) When court is in session, defense counsel should address the court and should not address the prosecutor directly on all matters relating to the case.

(d) Defense counsel should comply promptly with all orders and directives of the court, but defense counsel has a duty to have the record reflect adverse rulings or judicial conduct which counsel considers prejudicial to his or her client's legitimate interests. Defense counsel has a right to make respectful requests for reconsiderations of adverse rulings.

(e) Defense counsel should cooperate with courts and the organized bar in developing codes of professionalism for each jurisdiction.

Standard 4-7.2. Selection of Jurors

(a) Defense counsel should prepare himself or herself prior to trial to discharge effectively his or her function in the selection of the jury, including the raising of any appropriate issues concerning the method by which the jury panel was selected and the exercise of both challenges for cause and peremptory challenges.

(b) In those cases where it appears necessary to conduct a pretrial investigation of the background of jurors, investigatory methods of defense counsel should neither harass nor unduly embarrass potential jurors or invade their privacy and, whenever possible, should be restricted to an investigation of records and sources of information already in existence.

(c) The opportunity to question jurors personally should be used solely to obtain information for the intelligent exercise of challenges. Defense counsel should not intentionally use the voir dire to present factual matter which defense counsel knows will not be admissible at trial or to argue counsel's case to the jury.

Standard 4-7.3. Relations with Jury

(a) Defense counsel should not intentionally communicate privately with persons summoned for jury duty or impaneled as jurors prior to or during the trial. Defense counsel should avoid the reality or appearance of any such communications.

(b) Defense counsel should treat jurors with deference and respect, avoiding the reality or appearance of currying favor by a show of undue solicitude for their comfort or convenience.

(c) After discharge of the jury from further consideration of a case, defense counsel should not intentionally make comments to or ask questions of a juror for the purpose of harassing or embarrassing the juror in any way which will tend to influence judgment in future jury service. If defense counsel believes that the verdict may be subject to legal challenge, he or she may properly, if no statute or rule prohibits such course, communicate with jurors to determine whether such challenge may be available.

Standard 4-7.4. Opening Statement

Defense counsel's opening statement should be confined to a statement of the issues in the case and the evidence defense counsel believes in good faith will be available and admissible. Defense counsel should not allude to any evidence unless there is a good faith and reasonable basis for believing such evidence will be tendered and admitted in evidence.

Standard 4-7.5. Presentation of Evidence

(a) Defense counsel should not knowingly offer false evidence, whether by documents, tangible evidence, or the testimony of witnesses, or fail to take reasonable remedial measures upon discovery of its falsity.

(b) Defense counsel should not knowingly and for the purpose of bringing inadmissible matter to the attention of the judge or jury offer inadmissible evidence, ask legally objectionable questions, or make other impermissible comments or arguments in the presence of the judge or jury.

(c) Defense counsel should not permit any tangible evidence to be displayed in the view of the judge or jury which would tend to prejudice fair con-

442

sideration of the case by the judge or jury until such time as a good faith tender of such evidence is made.

(d) Defense counsel should not tender tangible evidence in the presence of the judge or jury if it would tend to prejudice fair consideration of the case unless there is a reasonable basis for its admission in evidence. When there is any substantial doubt about the admissibility of such evidence, it should be tendered by an offer of proof and a ruling obtained.

Standard 4-7.6. Examination of Witnesses

(a) The interrogation of all witnesses should be conducted fairly, objectively, and with due regard for the dignity and legitimate privacy of the witness, and without seeking to intimidate or humiliate the witness unnecessarily.

(b) Defense counsel's belief or knowledge that the witness is telling the truth does not preclude cross-examination.

(c) Defense counsel should not call a witness in the presence of the jury who the lawyer knows will claim a valid privilege not to testify.

(d) Defense counsel should not ask a question which implies the existence of a factual predicate for which a good faith belief is lacking.

Standard 4-7.7. Argument to the Jury

(a) In closing argument to the jury, defense counsel may argue all reasonable inferences from the evidence in the record. Defense counsel should not intentionally misstate the evidence or mislead the jury as to the inferences it may draw.

(b) Defense counsel should not express a personal belief or opinion in his or her client's innocence or personal belief or opinion in the truth or falsity of any testimony or evidence.

(c) Defense counsel should not make arguments calculated to appeal to the prejudices of the jury.

(d) Defense counsel should refrain from argument which would divert the jury from its duty to decide the case on the evidence.

Standard 4-7.8. Facts Outside the Record

Defense counsel should not intentionally refer to or argue on the basis of facts outside the record whether at trial or on appeal, unless such facts are matters of common public knowledge based on ordinary human experience or matters of which the court can take judicial notice.

Standard 4-7.9. Posttrial Motions

Defense counsel's responsibility includes presenting appropriate posttrial motions to protect the defendant's rights.

Part VIII. After Conviction

Standard 4-8.1. Sentencing

(a) Defense counsel should, at the earliest possible time, be or become familiar with all of the sentencing alternatives available to the court and with community and other facilities which may be of assistance in a plan for meeting for accused's needs. Defense counsel's preparation should also include familiarization with the court's practices in exercising sentencing discretion, the practical consequences of different sentences, and the normal pattern of sentences for the offense involved, including any guidelines applicable at either the sentencing or parole stages. The consequences of the various dispositions available should be explained fully by defense counsel to the accused.

(b) Defense counsel should present to the court any ground which will assist in reaching a proper disposition favorable to the accused. If a presentence report or summary is made available to defense counsel, he or she should seek to verify the information contained in it and should be prepared to supplement or challenge it if necessary. If there is no presentence report or if it is not disclosed, defense counsel should submit to the court and the prosecutor all favorable information relevant to sentencing and in an appropriate case, with the consent of the accused, be prepared to suggest a program of rehabilitation based on defense counsel's exploration of employment, educational, and other opportunities made available by community services.

(c) Defense counsel should also insure that the accused understands the nature of the presentence investigation process, and in particular the significance of statements made by the accused to probation officers and related personnel. Where appropriate, defense counsel should attend the probation officer's interview with the accused.

(d) Defense counsel should alert the accused to the right of allocution, if any, and to the possible dangers of making a statement that might tend to prejudice an appeal.

Standard 4-8.2. Appeal

(a) After conviction, defense counsel should explain to the defendant the meaning and consequences of the court's judgment and defendant's right of appeal. Defense counsel should give the defendant his or her professional judgment as to whether there are meritorious grounds for appeal and as to the probable results of an appeal. Defense counsel should also explain to the defendant the advantages and disadvantages of an appeal. The decision whether to appeal must be the defendant's own choice.

(b) Defense counsel should take whatever steps are necessary to protect the defendant's right of appeal.

Standard 4-8.3. Counsel on Appeal

(a) Appellate counsel should not seek to withdraw from a case solely on the basis of his or her own determination that the appeal lacks merit.

(b) Appellate counsel should give a client his or her best professional evaluation of the questions that might be presented on appeal. Counsel, when inquiring into the case, should consider all issues that might affect the validity of the judgment of conviction and sentence, including any that might require initial presentation in a postconviction proceeding. Counsel should advise on the probable outcome of a challenge to the conviction or sentence. Counsel should endeavor to persuade the client to abandon a wholly frivolous appeal or to eliminate contentions lacking in substance.

(c) If the client chooses to proceed with an appeal against the advice of counsel, counsel should present the case, so long as such advocacy does not involve deception of the court. When counsel cannot continue without misleading the court, counsel may request permission to withdraw.

(d) Appellate counsel has the ultimate authority to decide which arguments to make on appeal. When appellate counsel decides not to argue all of the issues that his or her client desires to be argued, appellate counsel should inform the client or his or her pro se briefing rights.

(e) In a jurisdiction with an intermediate appellate court, counsel for a defendant-appellant or a defendant-appellee should continue to represent the client if the prosecution seeks review in the highest court, unless new counsel is substituted or unless the court permits counsel to withdraw. Similarly, in any jurisdiction, such appellate counsel should continue to represent the client if the prosecution seeks review in the Supreme Court of the United States.

Standard 4-8.4. Conduct of Appeal

(a) Appellate counsel should be diligent in perfecting appeals and expediting their prompt submission to appellate courts.

(b) Appellate counsel should be accurate in referring to the record and the authorities upon which counsel relies in the presentation to the court of briefs and oral argument.

(c) Appellate counsel should not intentionally refer to or argue on the basis of facts outside the record on appeal, unless such facts are matters of common public knowledge based on ordinary human experience or matters of which the court may take judicial notice.

Standard 4-8.5. Post-Conviction Remedies

After a conviction is affirmed on appeal, appellate counsel should determine whether there is any ground for relief under other post-conviction remedies. If there is a reasonable prospect of a favorable result, counsel should explain to the defendant the advantages and disadvantages of taking such action. Appellate counsel is not obligated to represent the defendant in a post-conviction proceeding unless counsel has agreed to do so. In other respects, the responsibility of a lawyer in a post-conviction proceeding should be guided generally by the standards governing the conduct of lawyers in criminal cases.

Standard 4-8.6. Challenges to the Effectiveness of Counsel

(a) If defense counsel, after investigation, is satisfied that another defense counsel who served in an earlier phase of the case did not provide effective assistance, he or she should not hesitate to seek relief for the defendant on that ground.

(b) If defense counsel, after investigation, is satisfied that another defense counsel who served in an earlier phase of the case provided effective assistance, he or she should so advise the client and may decline to proceed further.

(c) If defense counsel concludes that he or she did not provide effective assistance in an earlier phase of the case, defense counsel should explain this conclusion to the defendant and seek to withdraw from representation with an explanation to the court of the reason therefor.

(d) Defense counsel whose conduct of a criminal case is drawn into question is entitled to testify concerning the matters charged and is not precluded from disclosing the truth concerning the accusation to the extent defense counsel reasonably believes necessary, even though this involves revealing matters which were given in confidence.

CHAPTER 5. PROVIDING DEFENSE SERVICES

Editors' Note. Chapter 5 was originally approved by the ABA in 1968. The excerpts below include some of the revisions approved at the ABA's August 1990 Annual Meeting. For reasons of space, only selected portions of some of the black-letter ABA Standards are reprinted here. Deletions reflect the judgment of the editors and not the ABA.

Part I. General Principles

Standard 5-1.1. Objective

The objective in providing counsel should be to assure that quality legal representation is afforded to all persons eligible for counsel pursuant to this chapter. The bar should educate the public to the importance of this objective.

Standard 5-1.2. Systems for Legal Representation

(a) The legal representation plan for each jurisdiction should provide for the services of a full-time defender organization when population and caseload are sufficient to support such an organization. Multi-jurisdictional organizations may be appropriate in rural areas.

(b) Every system should include the active and substantial participation of the private bar. That participation should be through a coordinated assigned-counsel system and may also include contracts for services. No program should be precluded from representing clients in any particular type or category of case.

(c) Conditions may make it preferable to create a statewide system of defense.

(d) Where capital punishment is permitted in the jurisdiction, the plan should take into account the unique and time-consuming demands of appointed representation in capital cases. The plan should comply with the ABA Guidelines for the Appointment and Performance of Counsel in Death Penalty Cases.

Standard 5-1.3. Professional Independence

(a) The legal representation plan for a jurisdiction should be designed to guarantee the integrity of the relationship between lawyer and client. The plan and the lawyers serving under it should be free from political influence and should be subject to judicial supervision only in the same manner and to the same extent as are lawyers in private practice. The selection of lawyers for specific cases should not be made by the judiciary or elected officials, but should be arranged for by the administrators of the defender, assigned-counsel and contract-for-service programs.

(b) An effective means of securing professional independence for defender organizations is to place responsibility for governance in a board of trustees. . . . Boards of trustees should not include prosecutors or judges. The primary function of boards of trustees is to support and protect the independence of the defense services program. . . . Boards of trustees should be precluded from interfering in the conduct of particular cases. . . .

Standard 5-1.4. Supporting Services

The legal representation plan should provide for investigatory, expert, and other services necessary to quality legal representation. These should include not only those services and facilities needed for an effective defense at trial but also those that are required for effective defense participation in every phase of the process. In addition, supporting services necessary for providing quality legal representation should be available to the clients of retained counsel who are financially unable to afford necessary supporting services.

Standard 5-1.5. Training and Professional Development

The legal representation plan should provide for the effective training, professional development and continuing education of all counsel and staff involved in providing defense services. . . .

Standard 5-1.6. Funding

Government has the responsibility to fund the full cost of quality legal representation for all eligible persons, as defined in standard 5-7.1. . . . Under no circumstances should the funding power interfere with or retaliate against professional judgments made in the proper performance of defense services.

Part II. Assigned Counsel

Standard 5-2.1. Systematic Assignment

The plan for legal representation should include substantial participation by assigned counsel. That participation should include a systematic and publicized method of distributing assignments. . . .

Standard 5-2.2. Eligibility to Serve

Assignments should be distributed as widely as possible among the qualified members of the bar. . . . Each jurisdiction should adopt specific qualification standards for attorney eligibility, and the private bar should be encouraged to become qualified pursuant to such standards. . . .

Standard 5-2.3. Rotation of Assignments and Revision of Roster

(a) As nearly as possible, assignments should be made in an orderly way to avoid patronage and its appearance, and to assure fair distribution of assignments among all whose names appear on the roster of eligible lawyers. Ordinarily, assignments should be made in the sequence that the names appear on the roster of eligible lawyers. Where the nature of the charges or other circumstances require, a lawyer may be selected because of his or her special qualifications to serve in the case, without regard to the established sequence.

(b) The roster of lawyers should periodically be revised to remove those who have not provided quality legal representation or who have refused to accept appointments on enough occasions to evidence lack of interest. Specific criteria for removal should be adopted in conjunction with qualification standards.

Standard 5-2.4. Compensation and Expenses

Assigned counsel should receive prompt compensation at a reasonable hourly rate and should be reimbursed for their reasonable out-of-pocket expenses. Assigned counsel should be compensated for all hours necessary to provide quality legal representation. . . .

Part III. Contract Defense Services

Standard 5-3.1. Use of Contracts for Services

Contracts for services of defense counsel may be a component of the legal representation plan. Such contracts should ensure quality legal representation. The contracting authority should not award a contract primarily on the basis of cost.

Standard 5-3.2. Contracting Parties and Procedures

. . . (c) The contracting parties should avoid provisions that create conflicts of interest between the contractor and clients.

Standard 5-3.3. Elements of the Contract for Services

(a) Contracts should include provisions which ensure quality legal representation and fully describe the rights and duties of the parties, including the compensation of the contractor. . . .

Part IV. Defender Systems

Standard 5-4.1. Chief Defender and Staff

Selection of the chief defender and staff should be made on the basis of merit. Recruitment of attorneys should include special efforts to employ women and members of minority groups. . . . The chief defender should be appointed for a fixed term of years and be subject to renewal. Neither the chief defender nor staff should be removed except upon a showing of good cause. Selection of the chief defender and staff by judges should be prohibited.

Standard 5-4.2. Restrictions on Private Practice

Defense organizations should be staffed with full-time attorneys. All such attorneys should be prohibited from engaging in the private practice of law.

Standard 5-4.3. Facilities; Library

Every defender office should be located in a place convenient to the courts and be furnished in a manner appropriate to the dignity of the legal profession. A library of sufficient size, considering the needs of the office and the accessibility of other libraries, and other necessary facilities and equipment should be provided.

Part V. Types of Proceedings and Quality of Representation

Standard 5-5.1. Criminal Cases

Counsel should be provided in all proceedings for offenses punishable by death or incarceration, regardless of their denomination as felonies, misdemeanors, or otherwise. An offense is also deemed to be punishable by incarceration if the fact of conviction may be established in a subsequent proceeding, thereby subjecting the defendant to incarceration.

Standard 5-5.2. Collateral Proceedings

Counsel should be provided in all proceedings arising from or connected with the initiation of a criminal action against the accused, including but not limited to extradition, mental competency, postconviction relief, and probation and parole revocation, regardless of the designation of the tribunal in which they occur or classification of the proceedings as civil in nature.

Standard 5-5.3. Workload

(a) Neither defender organizations, assigned counsel nor contractors for services should accept workloads that, by reason of their excessive size, interfere with the rendering of quality representation or lead to the breach of professional obligations. Special consideration should be given to the workload created by representation in capital cases.

(b) Whenever . . . the acceptance of additional cases or continued representation in previously accepted cases will lead to the furnishing of representation lacking in quality or to the breach of professional obligations, the defender organization, individual defender, assigned counsel or contractor for services must take such steps as may be appropriate to reduce their pending or projected caseloads, including the refusal of further appointments. Courts should not require individuals or programs to accept workloads that will lead to the furnishing of representation lacking in quality or to the breach of professional obligations.

Standard 5-5.4. Impact Litigation

(a) The legal representation plan should permit pursuit of litigation which affects:

(i) substantial numbers of similarly situated clients of the program, or

(ii) fundamental rights which cannot otherwise be effectively protected.

(b) Any such litigation should be undertaken only when it is in the best interests of the affected clients.

Part VI. Stage of Proceedings

Standard 5-6.1. Initial Provision of Counsel

Upon request, counsel should be provided to persons who have not been charged or taken into custody but who are in need of legal representation arising from criminal proceedings. Counsel should be provided to the accused as soon as feasible and, in any event, after custody begins, at appearance before a committing magistrate, or when formal charges are filed, whichever occurs earliest. In capital cases, two qualified trial attorneys should be assigned to represent the defendant. . . .

Standard 5-6.2. Duration of Representation

Counsel should be provided at every stage of the proceedings, including sentencing, appeal, certiorari and postconviction review. In capital cases, counsel also should be provided in clemency proceedings. Counsel initially provided should continue to represent the defendant throughout the trial court proceedings and should preserve the defendant's right to appeal, if necessary.

Standard 5-6.3. Removal

Representation of an accused establishes an inviolable attorney-client relationship. Removal of counsel from representation of an accused therefore should not occur over the objection of the attorney and the client.

Part VII. Eligibility for Assistance

Standard 5-7.1. Eligibility; Ability to Pay Partial Costs

Counsel should be provided to persons who are financially unable to obtain adequate representation without substantial hardship. Counsel should not be denied because of a person's ability to pay part of the cost of representation, because friends or relatives have resources to retain counsel, or because bond has been or can be posted.

Standard 5-7.2. Reimbursement, Notice and Imposition of Contribution

(a) Reimbursement of counsel or the organization of governmental unit providing counsel should not be required, except on the ground of fraud in obtaining the determination of eligibility. . . .

Standard 5-7.3. Determination of Eligibility

Determination of eligibility should be made by defenders, contractors for services, assigned counsel, a neutral screening agency, or by the court. . . .

Part VIII. Offer and Waiver

Standard 5-8.1. Providing Counsel to Persons in Custody

(a) A person taken into custody or otherwise deprived of liberty should immediately be informed, preferably by defense counsel, of the right to legal representation. . . .

Standard 5-8.2. In-Court Waiver

(a) The accused's failure to request counsel or an announced intention to plead guilty should not of itself be construed to constitute a waiver of counsel in court. An accused should not be deemed to have waived the assistance of counsel until the entire process of offering counsel has been completed before a judge and a thorough inquiry into the accused's comprehension of the offer and capacity to make the choice intelligently and understandingly has been made. . . .

(b) If an accused in a proceeding involving the possibility of incarceration has not seen a lawyer and indicates an intention to waive the assistance of counsel, a lawyer should be provided before any in-court waiver is accepted. No waiver should be accepted unless the accused has at least once conferred with a lawyer. If a waiver is accepted, the offer should be renewed at each subsequent stage of the proceedings at which the accused appears without counsel.

CHAPTER 8. FAIR TRIAL AND FREE PRESS

Editors' Note. Chapter 8 was originally approved by the ABA in 1968. Revisions to "Fair Trial and Free Press" were approved at the ABA's February 1991 Mid-Year Meeting. The excerpts below include some of these revisions. For reasons of space, only selected portions of some of the black-letter ABA Standards are reprinted here. Deletions reflect the judgment of the editors and not the ABA.

Standard 8-1.1 is similar to ABA Model Rule of Professional Conduct 3.6. Paragraphs identical to Rule 3.6 are mostly omitted. Differences between Rule 3.6 and Standard 8-1.1 are noted in italics.

Part I. Conduct of Attorneys in Criminal Cases

Standard 8-1.1. Extrajudicial Statements by Attorneys

(a) A lawyer should not make or authorize the making of an extrajudicial statement that a reasonable person would expect to be disseminated by means of public communication if the lawyer knows or reasonably should know that it will have a substantial likelihood of prejudicing a criminal proceeding.

(b) Statements relating to the following matters are ordinarily likely to have a substantial likelihood of prejudicing a criminal proceeding: . . .

(3) the opinion of the lawyer on the guilt of the defendant, *the merits of the case or the merits of the evidence in the case;* . . .

(c) Notwithstanding paragraphs (a) and (b), statements relating to the following matters may be made:

(1) the general nature of the charges against the accused, *provided that there is included therein a statement explaining that the charge is merely an accusation and that the defendant is presumed innocent until and unless proven guilty;*

(2) the general nature of the defense to the charges or to other public accusations against the accused, *including that the accused has no prior criminal record;* . . .

(8) *the identity of the victim, where the release of that information is not otherwise prohibited by law or would not be harmful to the victim;* . . .

(d) *Nothing in this standard is intended to preclude the formulation or application of more restrictive rules relating to the release of information about juvenile offenders, to preclude the holding of hearings or the lawful issuance of reports by legislative, administrative, or investigative bodies, to preclude any lawyer from replying to charges of misconduct that are publicly made against him or her, or to preclude or inhibit any lawyer from making an otherwise permissible statement which serves to educate or inform the public concerning the operations of the criminal justice system.*

Standard 8-1.2. Rule of Court

Unless adopted by statute or pursuant to the supervisory authority of the highest court in the jurisdiction, the substance of Standard 8-1.1 should be adopted as a rule of court governing the conduct of attorneys.

Part II. Conduct of Law Enforcement Officers, Judges, and Court Personnel in Criminal Cases

Standard 8-2.1. Release of Information by Law Enforcement Agencies

(a) The provisions of Standard 8-1.1 should be applicable to the release of information to the public by law enforcement officers and agencies.

(b) Law enforcement officers and agencies should not exercise their custodial authority over an accused individual in a manner that is likely to result in either:

(1) the deliberate exposure of a person in custody for the purpose of photographing or televising by representatives of the news media, or

(2) the interviewing by representatives of the news media of a person in custody except upon request or consent by that person to an interview after being informed adequately of the right to consult with counsel and of the right to refuse to grant an interview.

(c) Nothing in this standard is intended to preclude any law enforcement officer or agency from replying to charges of misconduct that are publicly made against him or her or from participating in any legislative, administrative, or investigative hearing, nor is this standard intended to supersede more restrictive rules governing the release of information concerning juvenile offenders.

Standard 8-2.2. Disclosures by Court Personnel

Court personnel should not disclose to any unauthorized person information relating to a pending criminal case that is not part of the public records of the court and that may be prejudicial to the right of the prosecution or the defense to a fair trial, particularly with reference to information covered by a closure order issued pursuant to Standard 8-3.2.

Standard 8-2.3. Conduct of Judges

Judges should refrain from any conduct or the making of any statements that may be prejudicial to the right of the prosecution or of the defense to a fair trial.

Part III. *Conduct of Judicial Proceedings in Criminal Cases* [Standards 8-3.3 to 8-3.7 are omitted.]

Standard 8-3.1. Prohibition of Direct Restraints on Media

Absent a clear and present danger to the fairness of a trial or other compelling interest, no rule of court or judicial order should be promulgated that prohibits representatives of the news media from broadcasting or publishing any information in their possession relating to a criminal case.

Standard 8-3.2. Public Access to Judicial Proceedings and Related Documents and Exhibits

(a) In any criminal case, all judicial proceedings and related documents and exhibits, and any record made thereof, not otherwise required to remain confidential, should be accessible to the public, except as provided in section (b).

(b)(1) A court may issue a closure order to deny access to the public to specified portions of a judicial proceeding or related document or exhibit only after reasonable notice of and an opportunity to be heard on such proposed order has been provided to the parties and the public and the court thereafter enters findings that:

(A) unrestricted access would pose a substantial probability of harm to the fairness of the trial or other overriding interest which substantially outweighs the defendant's right to a public trial;

(B) the proposed order will effectively prevent the aforesaid harm; and

(C) there is no less restrictive alternative reasonably available to prevent the aforesaid harm. . . .

Standard 8-3.8. Broadcasting, Televising, Recording and Photographing Courtroom Proceedings

A judge should prohibit broadcasting, televising, recording, or photographing in courtrooms and areas immediately adjacent thereto during sessions of court, or recesses between sessions, except that under rules prescribed by a supervising appellate court or other appropriate authority, a judge may authorize, broadcasting, televising, recording and photographing of judicial proceedings in courtrooms and areas immediately adjacent thereto consistent with the right to a fair trial and subject to express conditions, limitations, and guidelines which allow such coverage in a manner that will be unobtrusive, will not distract or otherwise adversely affect witnesses or other trial participants, and will not otherwise interfere with the administration of justice.

ABA Code of
Judicial Conduct*

Editors' Introduction. The ABA first adopted Canons of Judicial Ethics in 1924. (The original spur for judicial canons was that Kennesaw Mountain Landis, the first Commissioner of Baseball, refused to resign as a federal judge after accepting the job of Commissioner.) With occasional amendments, the Canons of Judicial Ethics served the profession well for nearly 50 years and were adopted by most states. In 1969, however, the ABA created a Special Committee on Standards of Judicial Conduct, chaired by California Supreme Court Justice Roger Traynor, "to draw up modern standards and to replace the Canons of Judicial Ethics." In August 1972, the ABA House of Delegates formally adopted the Code of Judicial Conduct to replace the Canons. The ABA made minor changes in 1982 and 1984.

The ABA Code of Judicial Conduct proved widely influential. Nearly all states (plus the District of Columbia) have adopted codes of judicial conduct closely modeled on the ABA Code. New York and California are good examples. New York's Code of Judicial Conduct follows the ABA Code of Judicial Conduct virtually verbatim, including the Commentary. California also generally follows the ABA Code, although California has revised, added, or deleted some provisions, has written special commentary for some provisions, and has reworked the language of the Code to make it gender neutral.

In August 1990, the ABA revised the Code of Judicial Conduct. Although it is like the 1972 Code in many regards, it also contains many differences, affecting such issues as judicial membership in exclusionary clubs and judicial responsibility to prohibit race and sex discrimination and other kinds of bias in the courtroom. In all likelihood, the 1990 Code will lead to changes in state judicial conduct codes. Principal changes from the 1972 Code are described in Part III of the Report of the Standing Committee on Ethics and Professional Responsibility, which follows. For a legislative history of the 1990 Code, see L. Milord, The Development of the ABA Judicial Code (1992).

Contents

460

AMERICAN BAR ASSOCIATION
STANDING COMMITTEE ON ETHICS AND
PROFESSIONAL RESPONSIBILITY
REPORT TO THE HOUSE OF DELEGATES

RECOMMENDATION

RESOLVED, that the American Bar Association adopts the Model Code of Judicial Conduct (August 1990), including the Preamble, Terminology Section, Canons, text, Commentary and Application Section, to replace the ABA Code of Judicial Conduct (adopted August 1972, as amended August 1982 and August 1984).

REPORT

I. Introduction

The recommended Model Code of Judicial Conduct (1990) (1990 Code) is a comprehensive revision of the ABA Code of Judicial Conduct (1972, amended 1982 and 1984) (1972 Code). The 1990 Code was prepared initially by a Subcommittee of the Standing Committee on Ethics and Professional Responsibility comprised of several members and former members of the Standing Committee and several members of the judiciary. . . .

The Committee believes that every jurisdiction should have an advisory body to interpret the Code on an ongoing basis so that judges may obtain advance guidance on proposed conduct about which questions arise under the Code. Accordingly, an *Appendix* appears immediately following the proposed 1990 Code, containing an example of a rule which may provide helpful guidance in establishing a judicial ethics advisory committee in a jurisdiction that does not have one. Although it is recommended that the Appendix be printed with the 1990 Code, it is not intended that the Appendix be adopted as a part of the Code. . . .

III. Principal Changes from 1972 Code

As noted in the Report accompanying the Midyear 1990 Draft, general guidelines were adopted to govern the revision of the Code. These included the following: the substance of provisions that were well-understood and working

461

effectively should not be changed; the general format of the 1972 Code, consisting of Canons, followed by Sections of text, together with the explanatory Commentary, should be retained; the Code should be gender neutral; and Commentary should be expanded to provide further guidance in application of the Code.

The Preface of the 1972 Code states that the "canons and text establish mandatory standards unless otherwise indicated." The use of the term "should" in the Canons and text to express mandatory standards, however, has been misunderstood at times as expressing aspirational standards only. Moreover, some jurisdictions in adopting the Code omitted the Preface with its explanation that mandatory standards are intended. To avoid misunderstanding in the future, the proposed 1990 Code distinguishes between mandatory standards (by use of "shall" in the text and "must" in the Commentary) and aspirational standards (by use of "should" or "may" in the text and the Commentary), respectively.

Although all of the proposed changes in the text and Commentary merit careful consideration, the Committee sets forth here, in the order in which they appear in the proposed 1990 Code, the changes from the 1972 Code that the Committee believes to be of special note. A more complete statement of the reasons for the changes appears in the Committee Notes, which are interspersed throughout the text and Commentary of the legislative draft of the proposed 1990 Code and the Committee Amendments. In addition, Part IV of this Report reiterates the reasons for changes from the Midyear 1990 Draft.

The *Preamble*, which is to be adopted as part of the Code, is new. It states general principles, sets out the objectives of the Code and describes the relationship between the text and Commentary. The Preamble also notes that the standards embodied in the text are rules of reason and explains that the Code is intended to supplement general ethical standards.

A *Terminology* Section has been added to explain key terms that are used throughout the Code. Reference to the appropriate portion of the Terminology Section is indicated by an asterisk and footnote where an explained term appears in the text.

Canon 1 provides: *A judge shall uphold the integrity and independence of the judiciary.* The Section under this Canon is unchanged from Canon 1 of the 1972 Code, except to distinguish between mandatory and aspirational standards. A paragraph of Commentary has been added to explain the significance and scope of the concept of the independence of the judiciary.

Canon 2 provides: *A judge shall avoid impropriety and the appearance of impropriety in all of the judge's activities.* The Commentary to Canon 2 is expanded to furnish more specific guidance as to conduct that amounts to impropriety or gives the appearance of impropriety. Several commentators noted that the Section 2B Commentary in the Midyear 1990 Draft, relating to recommendations by a judge and responses to requests for information, was ambiguous. Committee Amendment 2.1 is intended to clarify the Section 2B Commentary in this regard.

The Committee has heard extensive criticism of the portions of the Commentary to Canon 2 of the 1972 Code adopted in 1984 relating to membership of judges in organizations that practice invidious discrimination on the basis of race, sex, religion or national origin. Many suggestions regarding that issue also were received following distribution of the Discussion Draft and the Midyear 1990 Draft.

After careful consideration, the Committee recommends adoption of a blackletter standard in a new Section C of Canon 2 to prohibit a judge from holding membership in any organization that practices invidious discrimination on the basis of race, sex, religion or national origin. The term "invidious discrimination," taken from the Commentary to Canon 2 in the 1972 Code, has been retained in new Section 2C as a term that has gained acceptance and usage necessary to describe the type of discrimination to which the provision is directed. The Committee also decided to retain the prohibited categories of discrimination based upon race, sex, religion or national origin because those categories are the only ones universally acknowledged to be constitutionally protected.

The Commentary for new Section 2C explains this standard in language similar to the Commentary on this subject adopted by the ABA House of Delegates in 1984, but with some significant changes. First, the Committee believes it is not appropriate or workable to leave to each individual judge's conscience the determination whether an organization practices invidious discrimination. Second, the Commentary has been revised in Committee Amendment 2.2 to remove any inference that a judge would be prohibited from membership in an organization that had formerly practiced invidious discrimination in its membership policies but had discontinued those practices. Third, the revised Commentary makes it clear that the categories of organizations in which membership is proscribed by the text of Section 2C do not include intimate, purely private organizations whose membership limitations could not be constitutionally prohibited or organizations dedicated to the preservation of religious, ethnic or cultural values of legitimate common interest to their members. Fourth, the Commentary states that membership of a judge in an organization that engages in any discriminatory membership practices prohibited by the law of the jurisdiction gives the appearance of impropriety. Fifth, the revised Commentary states in Committee Amendment 2.2 that any public manifestation by a judge of knowing approval of invidious discrimination on any basis would violate the Canon. This could involve a judge's membership in an intimate, purely private organization, when the organization engages in invidiously discriminatory membership practices and the judge publicly manifests approval of those practices by statements or other conduct that may in some circumstances include continuing to hold membership in the organization. Finally, Committee Amendment 2.2 also states that a judge who is an incumbent at the time of adoption of the applicable provisions of Canon 2 in the judge's jurisdiction and who learns about an organization's invidiously discriminatory practices only after he or she becomes a member of the organization may, in lieu of resigning immediately from the organization, retain membership for a limited time in which to make an effort to have the organization discontinue its invidiously discriminatory practices, provided the judge does not participate in any of the other activities of the organization.

Taken together, these provisions seek to balance a judge's right of private association with the need of the public to be assured that every judge both gives the appearance of impartiality and is capable of fair and unbiased trial conduct and decisions. The changes proposed in Committee Amendment 2.2 accommodate the concerns expressed in the Minority Concurring Report filed with the Midyear 1990 Draft and as a consequence no draft substitute or minority concurring report is filed with this Recommendation and Report.

Canon 3 provides: *A judge shall perform the duties of judicial office impartially and diligently.* The provisions of Canon 3 of the 1972 Code required substantial revision to eliminate ambiguities and to provide more specific guidance. Therefore, some Sections in Canon 3 are amended, new Sections are added, and the Commentary is substantially expanded.

Provisions are added that address the judge's affirmative duty to hear matters and that prohibit manifestation of bias by a judge and improper comment by a judge on a jury's verdict. A provision is added requiring a judge to direct lawyers before the judge to refrain, within the limits of legitimate advocacy, from manifesting bias against parties, witnesses, counsel or others, on the basis of race, sex, religion, national origin, disability, age, sexual orientation or socioeconomic status. A provision is added addressing a supervisory judge's administrative responsibilities. The provision on *ex parte* communications is changed to allow, in certain circumstances and with appropriate restrictions, those communications necessary for scheduling and other limited case management purposes. Refinements are made in the disqualification provision to give further guidance and to obviate the need for disqualification where a judge's financial interest is *de minimis* and would not affect impartiality.

The provision concerning reporting of lawyer or judicial misconduct is modified in Committee Amendment 3.7 to require a judge to report serious violations of which the judge has knowledge to disciplinary authorities; while providing that a judge retains discretion, in less serious matters and in matters in which the judge believes, without having actual knowledge, that there is a substantial likelihood that a violation has been committed, to take such action as may be appropriate. The proposed 1990 Code deletes the Section relating to cameras in the courts because this subject is not directly related to judicial ethics and is more appropriately addressed by administrative rules adopted within each jurisdiction.

Most of the Committee Amendments to Canon 3 and its Commentary are for purposes of clarification and were suggested by comments the Standing Committee received since February 1990. In addition, Commentary relating to sexual harassment is proposed by Committee Amendment 3.2. A requirement that a judge disclose on the record information that the judge believes relevant to disqualification is proposed by Committee Amendment 3.8. Personal bias or prejudice concerning a party's lawyer as well as concerning a party has been added as a further basis for disqualification in Committee Amendment 3.9.

Canon 4 provides: *A judge shall so conduct the judge's extra-judicial activities as to minimize the risk of conflict with judicial obligations.* In the 1972 Code, Canon 4 provides: "A judge may engage in activities to improve the law, the legal system and the administration of justice." Canon 5 provides: "A judge should regulate his extra-judicial activities to minimize the risk of conflict with his judicial duties." Canon 6 provides: "A judge should regularly file reports of compensation received for extra-judicial activity." Because these Canons all relate to a judge's extra-judicial activities, the proposed 1990 Code combines, in a single Canon 4, the subject matter of Canons 4, 5 and 6 of the 1972 Code.

Canon 5 of the 1972 Code has been the subject of conflicting judicial ethics opinions, suggesting the need for greater clarity and additional guidance in certain of its provisions. Those provisions are substantially revised and expanded, and new Commentary is added. For example, the revised provisions distinguish those fundraising activities that lend themselves to abuse from those that do not. The provisions on financial activities are modified to allow for participation in family businesses if consistent with the primary obligations of a judge as a judge. Other Sections in the Canon relating to judges' spouses and family members are revised to acknowledge the reality that such persons often act independently of the judge. Uncompensated personal legal consultation with a judge's family is permitted.

With the exception of Committee Amendment 4.2, which makes more realistic the rule regarding service on the boards of civic or charitable organizations, the Committee Amendments proposed in new Canon 4 and its Commentary result from suggestions received by the Standing Committee for clarification of the provisions in the Midyear 1990 Draft.

Canon 6 of the 1972 Code addresses financial reporting by judges, a subject that is now regulated by law, with wide variation, in most jurisdictions. The provisions of Canon 6 are retained as Section H of Canon 4 of the proposed 1990 Code. Section H provides limitations on compensation and expense reimbursement for a judge's extra-judicial activities and includes financial reporting requirements that can be adopted in jurisdictions that do not otherwise regulate financial reporting.

Canon 5 provides: *A judge or judicial candidate shall refrain from inappropriate political activity.* Canon 5 of the proposed 1990 Code replaces Canon 7 of the 1972 Code. New Canon 5 addresses the conduct of all judges and candidates for judicial office, whether chosen by appointment, nonpartisan election or partisan election. The provisions have been substantially restructured in the proposed

1990 Code to make clear which Sections apply to all judges and candidates regardless of how selected and which Sections apply solely to judges and candidates for judicial office selected by a particular method. The proposed 1990 Code undertakes to deal with the existence of various methods of judicial selection in the jurisdictions. In so doing, the Committee is nonetheless cognizant that American Bar Association policy favors merit selection of judges (see House Report 119, August, 1977). Among the specific changes recommended in Canon 5 are provisions extending the length of time allowed for pre-election fundraising and provisions removing certain restrictions on political speech and other political conduct. In addition, the substance of former Section 7A(4) in the 1972 Code has been revised and relocated as free-standing Section 5D, to make clear that incumbent judges are prohibited from engaging in any political activity that is not conducted on behalf of measures to improve the law, the legal system or the administration of justice, or that is not otherwise authorized by the Code or expressly authorized by law. Furthermore, the Commentary to Canon 5 has been expanded considerably to provide more specific guidance to candidates for judicial office.

Although a number of Committee Amendments are proposed to be made in Canon 5 and its Commentary, most of the changes are to provide added clarity. For example, Committee Amendment 5.7 adding a new Section 5B(2) is intended to make it clear that a candidate for appointment to a judicial office, a judge who is a candidate for reappointment or a judge who is a candidate for appointment to another judicial or governmental office may, notwithstanding the prohibition in Section 5D against political activity except as authorized under any other Section of the Code or as expressly authorized by law, engage in necessary and appropriately limited political activity to obtain the reappointment or appointment. Committee Amendment 5.8 proposes to restructure Section 5C(1) for purposes of clarity and includes permission to engage in specified political conduct when the judge is a candidate for public election. Similarly, political conduct by a candidate's committee is permitted by additional language added to Section 5C(2) by Committee Amendment 5.9. For a more detailed discussion, see Section IV of this Report.

The 1972 Code contains a Section titled "Compliance with the Code of Judicial Conduct." This Section has been revised and titled *Application of the Code of Judicial Conduct*, and appears after the Canons in the proposed 1990 Code. . . .

MODEL CODE OF JUDICIAL CONDUCT
(1990)

PREAMBLE[†]

Our legal system is based on the principle that an independent, fair and competent judiciary will interpret and apply the laws that govern us. The role of the judiciary is central to American concepts of justice and the rule of law. Intrinsic to all sections of this Code are the precepts that judges, individually and collectively, must respect and honor the judicial office as a public trust and strive to enhance and maintain confidence in our legal system. The judge is an arbiter of facts and law for the resolution of disputes and a highly visible symbol of government under the rule of law.

The Code of Judicial Conduct is intended to establish standards for ethical conduct of judges. It consists of broad statements called Canons, specific rules set forth in Sections under each Canon, a Terminology Section, an Application Section and Commentary. The text of the Canons and the Sections, including the Terminology and Application Sections, is authoritative. The Commentary, by explanation and example, provides guidance with respect to the purpose and meaning of the Canons and Sections. The Commentary is not intended as a statement of additional rules. When the text uses "shall" or "shall not," it is intended to impose binding obligations the violation of which can result in disciplinary action. When "should" or "should not" is used, the text is intended as hortatory and as a statement of what is or is not appropriate conduct but not as a binding rule under which a judge may be disciplined. When "may" is used, it denotes permissible discretion or, depending on the context, it refers to action that is not covered by specific proscriptions.

The Canons and Sections are rules of reason. They should be applied consistent with constitutional requirements, statutes, other court rules and decisional law and in the context of all relevant circumstances. The Code is to be construed so as not to impinge on the essential independence of judges in making judicial decisions.

The Code is designed to provide guidance to judges and candidates for judicial office and to provide a structure for regulating conduct through disciplinary agencies. It is not designed or intended as a basis for civil liability or criminal prosecution. Furthermore, the purpose of the Code would be subverted if the Code were invoked by lawyers for mere tactical advantage in a proceeding.

The text of the Canons and Sections is intended to govern conduct of judges and to be binding upon them. It is not intended, however, that every transgression will result in disciplinary action. Whether disciplinary action is appropriate, and the degree of discipline to be imposed, should be determined through a reasonable and reasoned application of the text and should depend on such factors as the serious-

---

[†]For a summary of changes from corresponding provisions of the 1972 Code of Judicial Conduct, see excerpts from the Standing Committee's Report printed at page 462 above. — EDS.

ness of the transgression, whether there is a pattern of improper activity and the effect of the improper activity on others or on the judicial system. See ABA Standards Relating to Judicial Discipline and Disability Retirement.[1]

The Code of Judicial Conduct is not intended as an exhaustive guide for the conduct of judges. They should also be governed in their judicial and personal conduct by general ethical standards. The Code is intended, however, to state basic standards which should govern the conduct of all judges and to provide guidance to assist judges in establishing and maintaining high standards of judicial and personal conduct.

TERMINOLOGY[†]

Terms explained below are noted with an asterisk (*) in the Sections where they appear. In addition, the Sections where terms appear are referred to after the explanation of each term below.

"Appropriate authority" denotes the authority with responsibility for initiation of disciplinary process with respect to the violation to be reported. See Sections 3D(1) and 3D(2).

"Candidate." A candidate is a person seeking selection for or retention in judicial office by election or appointment. A person becomes a candidate for judicial office as soon as he or she makes a public announcement of candidacy, declares or files as a candidate with the election or appointment authority, or authorizes solicitation or acceptance of contributions or support. The term "candidate" has the same meaning when applied to a judge seeking election or appointment to nonjudicial office. See Preamble and Sections 5A, 5B, 5C and 5E.

"Continuing part-time judge." A continuing part-time judge is a judge who serves repeatedly on a part-time basis by election or under a continuing appointment, including a retired judge subject to recall who is permitted to practice law. See Application Section C.

"Court personnel" does not include the lawyers in a proceeding before a judge. See Sections 3B(7)(c) and 3B(9).

"De minimis" denotes an insignificant interest that could not raise reasonable question as to a judge's impartiality. See Sections 3E(1)(c) and 3E(1)(d).

---

1. Judicial disciplinary procedures adopted in the jurisdictions should comport with the requirements of due process. The ABA Standards Relating to Judicial Discipline and Disability Retirement are cited as an example of how these due process requirements may be satisfied.

†For a summary of changes from corresponding provisions of the 1972 Code of Judicial Conduct, see excerpts from the Standing Committee's Report printed at page 462 above. — EDS.

"Economic interest" denotes ownership of a more than de minimis legal or equitable interest, or a relationship as officer, director, advisor or other active participant in the affairs of a party, except that:

(i) ownership of an interest in a mutual or common investment fund that holds securities is not an economic interest in such securities unless the judge participates in the management of the fund or a proceeding pending or impending before the judge could substantially affect the value of the interest;

(ii) service by a judge as an officer, director, advisor or other active participant in an educational, religious, charitable, fraternal or civic organization, or service by a judge's spouse, parent or child as an officer, director, advisor or other active participant in any organization does not create an economic interest in securities held by that organization;

(iii) a deposit in a financial institution, the proprietary interest of a policy holder in a mutual insurance company, of a depositor in a mutual savings association or of a member in a credit union, or a similar proprietary interest, is not an economic interest in the organization unless a proceeding pending or impending before the judge could substantially affect the value of the interest;

(iv) ownership of government securities is not an economic interest in the issuer unless a proceeding pending or impending before the judge could substantially affect the value of the securities.
See Sections 3E(1)(c) and 3E(2).

"Fiduciary" includes such relationships as executor, administrator, trustee, and guardian. See Sections 3E(2) and 4E.

"Knowingly," "knowledge," "known" or "knows" denotes actual knowledge of the fact in question. A person's knowledge may be inferred from circumstances. See Sections 3D, 3E(1), and 5A(3).

"Law" denotes court rules as well as statutes, constitutional provisions and decisional law. See Sections 2A, 3A, 3B(2), 3B(6), 4B, 4C, 4D(5), 4F, 4I, 5A(2), 5A(3), 5B(2), 5C(1), 5C(3) and 5D.

"Member of the candidate's family" denotes a spouse, child, grandchild, parent, grandparent or other relative or person with whom the candidate maintains a close familial relationship. See Section 5A(3)(a).

"Member of the judge's family" denotes a spouse, child, grandchild, parent, grandparent, or other relative or person with whom the judge maintains a close familial relationship. See Sections 4D(3), 4E and 4G.

"Member of the judge's family residing in the judge's household" denotes any relative of a judge by blood or marriage, or a person treated by a judge as a member of the judge's family, who resides in the judge's household. See Sections 3E(1) and 4D(5).

"Nonpublic information" denotes information that, by law, is not available to the public. Nonpublic information may include but is not limited to: information that is sealed by statute or court order, impounded or communicated in camera; and information offered in grand jury proceedings, presentencing reports, dependency cases or psychiatric reports. See Section 3B(11).

"Periodic part-time judge." A periodic part-time judge is a judge who serves or expects to serve repeatedly on a part-time basis but under a separate appointment for each limited period of service or for each matter. See Application Section D.

"Political organization" denotes a political party or other group, the principal purpose of which is to further the election or appointment of candidates to political office. See Sections 5A(1), 5B(2) and 5C(1).

"Pro tempore part-time judge." A pro tempore part-time judge is a judge who serves or expects to serve once or only sporadically on a part-time basis under a separate appointment for each period of service or for each case heard. See Application Section E.

"Public election." This term includes primary and general elections; it includes partisan elections, nonpartisan elections and retention elections. See Section 5C.

"Require." The rules prescribing that a judge "require" certain conduct of others are, like all of the rules in this Code, rules of reason. The use of the term "require" in that context means a judge is to exercise reasonable direction and control over the conduct of those persons subject to the judge's direction and control. See Sections 3B(3), 3B(4), 3B(5), 3B(6), 3B(9) and 3C(2).

"Third degree of relationship." The following persons are relatives within the third degree of relationship: great-grandparent, grandparent, parent, uncle, aunt, brother, sister, child, grandchild, great-grandchild, nephew or niece. See Section 3E(1)(d).

CANON 1. A JUDGE SHALL UPHOLD THE INTEGRITY AND INDEPENDENCE OF THE JUDICIARY[†]

A. An independent and honorable judiciary is indispensable to justice in our society. A judge should participate in establishing, maintaining and enforcing high standards of conduct, and shall personally observe those standards so that the integrity and independence of the judiciary will be

[†]For a summary of changes from corresponding provisions of the 1972 Code of Judicial Conduct, see excerpts from the Standing Committee's Report printed at page 462 above. — EDS.

preserved. The provisions of this Code are to be construed and applied to further that objective.

Commentary

Deference to the judgments and rulings of courts depends upon public confidence in the integrity and independence of judges. The integrity and independence of judges depends in turn upon their acting without fear or favor. Although judges should be independent, they must comply with the law, including the provisions of this Code. Public confidence in the impartiality of the judiciary is maintained by the adherence of each judge to this responsibility. Conversely, violation of this Code diminishes public confidence in the judiciary and thereby does injury to the system of government under law.

CANON 2. A JUDGE SHALL AVOID IMPROPRIETY AND THE APPEARANCE OF IMPROPRIETY IN ALL OF THE JUDGE'S ACTIVITIES[†]

A. A judge shall respect and comply with the law* and shall act at all times in a manner that promotes public confidence in the integrity and impartiality of the judiciary.

Commentary

Public confidence in the judiciary is eroded by irresponsible or improper conduct by judges. A judge must avoid all impropriety and appearance of impropriety. A judge must expect to be the subject of constant public scrutiny. A judge must therefore accept restrictions on the judge's conduct that might be viewed as burdensome by the ordinary citizen and should do so freely and willingly.

The prohibition against behaving with impropriety or the appearance of impropriety applies to both the professional and personal conduct of a judge. Because it is not practicable to list all prohibited acts, the proscription is necessarily cast in general terms that extend to conduct by judges that is harmful although not specifically mentioned in the Code. Actual improprieties under this standard include violations of law, court rules or other specific provisions of this Code. The test for appearance of impropriety is whether the conduct would create in reasonable minds a perception that the judge's ability to carry out judicial responsibilities with integrity, impartiality and competence is impaired.

[†]For a summary of changes from corresponding provisions of the 1972 Code of Judicial Conduct, see excerpts from the Standing Committee's Report printed at pages 462-464 above. — EDS.
 *Asterisked terms are defined in the Terminology Section. — EDS.

See also Commentary under Section 2C.

B. A judge shall not allow family, social, political or other relationships to influence the judge's judicial conduct or judgment. A judge shall not lend the prestige of judicial office to advance the private interests of the judge or others; nor shall a judge convey or permit others to convey the impression that they are in a special position to influence the judge. A judge shall not testify voluntarily as a character witness.

Commentary

Maintaining the prestige of judicial office is essential to a system of government in which the judiciary functions independently of the executive and legislative branches. Respect for the judicial office facilitates the orderly conduct of legitimate judicial functions. Judges should distinguish between proper and improper use of the prestige of office in all of their activities. For example, it would be improper for a judge to allude to his or her judgeship to gain a personal advantage such as deferential treatment when stopped by a police officer for a traffic offense. Similarly, judicial letterhead must not be used for conducting a judge's personal business.

A judge must avoid lending the prestige of judicial office for the advancement of the private interests of others. For example, a judge must not use the judge's judicial position to gain advantage in a civil suit involving a member of the judge's family. In contracts for publication of a judge's writings, a judge should retain control over the advertising to avoid exploitation of the judge's office. As to the acceptance of awards, see Section 4D(5)(a) and Commentary.

Although a judge should be sensitive to possible abuse of the prestige of office, a judge may, based on the judge's personal knowledge, serve as a reference or provide a letter of recommendation. However, a judge must not initiate the communication of information to a sentencing judge or a probation or corrections officer but may provide to such persons information for the record in response to a formal request.

Judges may participate in the process of judicial selection by cooperating with appointing authorities and screening committees seeking names for consideration, and by responding to official inquiries concerning a person being considered for a judgeship. See also Canon 5 regarding use of a judge's name in political activities.

A judge must not testify voluntarily as a character witness because to do so may lend the prestige of the judicial office in support of the party for whom the judge testifies. Moreover, when a judge testifies as a witness, a lawyer who regularly appears before the judge may be placed in the awkward position of cross-examining the judge. A judge may, however, testify when properly summoned. Except in unusual circumstances where the demands of justice require, a judge should discourage a party from requiring the judge to testify as a character witness.

C. A judge shall not hold membership in any organization that practices invidious discrimination on the basis of race, sex, religion or national origin.

Commentary

Membership of a judge in an organization that practices invidious discrimination gives rise to perceptions that the judge's impartiality is impaired. Section 2C refers to the current practices of the organization. Whether an organization practices invidious discrimination is often a complex question to which judges should be sensitive. The answer cannot be determined from a mere examination of an organization's current membership rolls but rather depends on how the organization selects members and other relevant factors, such as that the organization is dedicated to the preservation of religious, ethnic or cultural values of legitimate common interest to its members, or that it is in fact and effect an intimate, purely private organization whose membership limitations could not be constitutionally prohibited. Absent such factors, an organization is generally said to discriminate invidiously if it arbitrarily excludes from membership on the basis of race, religion, sex or national origin persons who would otherwise be admitted to membership. See New York State Club Assn., Inc. v. City of New York, 108 S. Ct. 2225, 101 L. Ed. 2d 1 (1988); Board of Directors of Rotary International v. Rotary Club of Duarte, 481 U.S. 537, 107 S. Ct. 1940 (1987), 95 L. Ed. 2d 474; Roberts v. United States Jaycees, 468 U.S. 609, 104 S. Ct. 3244, 82 L. Ed. 2d 462 (1984).

Although Section 2C relates only to membership in organizations that invidiously discriminate on the basis of race, sex, religion or national origin, a judge's membership in an organization that engages in any discriminatory membership practices prohibited by the law of the jurisdiction also violates Canon 2 and Section 2A and gives the appearance of impropriety. In addition, it would be a violation of Canon 2 and Section 2A for a judge to arrange a meeting at a club that the judge knows practices invidious discrimination on the basis of race, sex, religion or national origin in its membership or other policies, or for the judge to regularly use such a club. Moreover, public manifestation by a judge of the judge's knowing approval of invidious discrimination on any basis gives the appearance of impropriety under Canon 2 and diminishes public confidence in the integrity and impartiality of the judiciary, in violation of Section 2A.

When a person who is a judge in the date this Code becomes effective [in the jurisdiction in which the person is a judge][1] learns that an organization to which the judge belongs engages in invidious discrimination that would preclude membership under Section 2C or under Canon 2 and Section 2A, the judge is permitted, in lieu of resigning, to make immediate efforts to have the organization discontinue its invidiously discriminatory practices, but is required to suspend participation in any other activities of the organization. If the organization fails to discontinue its invidiously discriminatory practices as promptly as possible (and in all events within a year of the judge's first learning of the practices), the judge is required to resign immediately from the organization.

---

1. The language within the brackets should be deleted when the jurisdiction adopts this provision.

CANON 3. A JUDGE SHALL PERFORM THE DUTIES OF JUDICIAL OFFICE IMPARTIALLY AND DILIGENTLY†

A. *Judicial Duties in General.*

The judicial duties of a judge take precedence over all the judge's other activities. The judge's judicial duties include all the duties of the judge's office prescribed by law.* In the performance of these duties, the following standards apply.

B. *Adjudicative Responsibilities.*

(1) A judge shall hear and decide matters assigned to the judge except those in which disqualification is required.

(2) A judge shall be faithful to the law* and maintain professional competence in it. A judge shall not be swayed by partisan interests, public clamor or fear of criticism.

(3) A judge shall require* order and decorum in proceedings before the judge.

(4) A judge shall be patient, dignified and courteous to litigants, jurors, witnesses, lawyers and others with whom the judge deals in an official capacity, and shall require* similar conduct of lawyers, and of staff, court officials and others subject to the judge's direction and control.

Commentary

The duty to hear all proceedings fairly and with patience is not inconsistent with the duty to dispose promptly of the business of the court. Judges can be efficient and businesslike while being patient and deliberate.

(5) A judge shall perform judicial duties without bias or prejudice. A judge shall not, in the performance of judicial duties, by words or conduct manifest bias or prejudice, including but not limited to bias or prejudice based upon race, sex, religion, national origin, disability, age, sexual orientation or socioeconomic status, and shall not permit staff, court officials and others subject to the judge's direction and control to do so.

†For a summary of changes from corresponding provisions of the 1972 Code of Judicial Conduct, see excerpts from the Standing Committee's Report printed at pages 464-465 above. — EDS.
*Asterisked terms are defined in the Terminology Section. — EDS.

Commentary

A judge must refrain from speech, gestures or other conduct that could reasonably be perceived as sexual harassment and must require the same standard of conduct of others subject to the judge's direction and control.

A judge must perform judicial duties impartially and fairly. A judge who manifests bias on any basis in a proceeding impairs the fairness of the proceeding and brings the judiciary into disrepute. Facial expression and body language, in addition to oral communication, can give to parties or lawyers in the proceeding, jurors, the media and others an appearance of judicial bias. A judge must be alert to avoid behavior that may be perceived as prejudicial.

(6) A judge shall require* lawyers in proceedings before the judge to refrain from manifesting, by words or conduct, bias or prejudice based upon race, sex, religion, national origin, disability, age, sexual orientation or socioeconomic status, against parties, witnesses, counsel or others. This Section 3B(6) does not preclude legitimate advocacy when race, sex, religion, national origin, disability, age, sexual orientation or socioeconomic status, or other similar factors, are issues in the proceeding.

(7) A judge shall accord to every person who has a legal interest in a proceeding, or that person's lawyer, the right to be heard according to law.* A judge shall not initiate, permit, or consider ex parte communications, or consider other communications made to the judge outside the presence of the parties concerning a pending or impending proceeding except that:

(a) Where circumstances require, ex parte communications for scheduling, administrative purposes or emergencies that do not deal with substantive matters or issues on the merits are authorized; provided:

(i) the judge reasonably believes that no party will gain a procedural or tactical advantage as a result of the ex parte communication, and

(ii) the judge makes provision promptly to notify all other parties of the substance of the ex parte communication and allows an opportunity to respond.

(b) A judge may obtain the advice of a disinterested expert on the law* applicable to a proceeding before the judge if the judge gives notice to the parties of the person consulted and the substance of the advice, and affords the parties reasonable opportunity to respond.

(c) A judge may consult with court personnel* whose function is to aid the judge in carrying out the judge's adjudicative responsibilities or with other judges.

(d) A judge may, with the consent of the parties, confer separately with the parties and their lawyers in an effort to mediate or settle matters pending before the judge.

(e) A judge may initiate or consider any ex parte communications when expressly authorized by law* to do so.

*Asterisked terms are defined in the Terminology Section. — EDS.

Commentary

The proscription against communications concerning a proceeding includes communications from lawyers, law teachers, and other persons who are not participants in the proceeding, except to the limited extent permitted.

To the extent reasonably possible, all parties or their lawyers shall be included in communications with a judge.

Whenever presence of a party or notice to a party is required by Section 3B(7), it is the party's lawyer, or if the party is unrepresented the party, who is to be present or to whom notice is to be given.

An appropriate and often desirable procedure for a court to obtain the advice of a disinterested expert on legal issues is to invite the expert to file a brief *amicus curiae*.

Certain ex parte communication is approved by Section 3B(7) to facilitate scheduling and other administrative purposes and to accommodate emergencies. In general, however, a judge must discourage ex parte communication and allow it only if all the criteria stated in Section 3B(7) are clearly met. A judge must disclose to all parties all ex parte communications described in Sections 3B(7)(a) and 3B(7)(b) regarding a proceeding pending or impending before the judge.

A judge must not independently investigate facts in a case and must consider only the evidence presented.

A judge may request a party to submit proposed findings of fact and conclusions of law, so long as the other parties are apprised of the request and are given an opportunity to respond to the proposed findings and conclusions.

A judge must make reasonable efforts, including the provision of appropriate supervision, to ensure that Section 3B(7) is not violated through law clerks or other personnel on the judge's staff.

If communication between the trial judge and the appellate court with respect to a proceeding is permitted, a copy of any written communication or the substance of any oral communication should be provided to all parties.

(8) A judge shall dispose of all judicial matters promptly, efficiently and fairly.

Commentary

In disposing of matters promptly, efficiently and fairly, a judge must demonstrate due regard for the rights of the parties to be heard and to have issues resolved without unnecessary cost or delay. Containing costs while preserving fundamental rights of parties also protects the interests of witnesses and the general public. A judge should monitor and supervise cases so as to reduce or eliminate dilatory practices, avoidable delays and unnecessary costs. A judge should encourage and seek to facilitate settlement, but parties should not feel coerced into surrendering the right to have their controversy resolved by the courts.

Prompt disposition of the court's business requires a judge to devote adequate time to judicial duties, to be punctual in attending court and expeditious in determining matters

*Asterisked terms are defined in the Terminology Section. — EDS.

under submission, and to insist that court officials, litigants and their lawyers cooperate with the judge to that end.

(9) A judge shall not, while a proceeding is pending or impending in any court, make any public comment that might reasonably be expected to affect its outcome or impair its fairness or make any nonpublic comment that might substantially interfere with a fair trial or hearing. The judge shall require* similar abstention on the part of court personnel* subject to the judge's direction and control. This Section does not prohibit judges from making public statements in the course of their official duties or from explaining for public information the procedures of the court. This Section does not apply to proceedings in which the judge is a litigant in a personal capacity.

Commentary

The requirement that judges abstain from public comment regarding a pending or impending proceeding continues during any appellate process and until final disposition. This Section does not prohibit a judge from commenting on proceedings in which the judge is a litigant in a personal capacity, but in cases such as a writ of mandamus where the judge is a litigant in an official capacity, the judge must not comment publicly. The conduct of lawyers relating to trial publicity is governed by [Rule 3.6 of the ABA Model Rules of Professional Conduct]. (Each jurisdiction should substitute an appropriate reference to its rule.)

(10) A judge shall not commend or criticize jurors for their verdict other than in a court order or opinion in a proceeding, but may express appreciation to jurors for their service to the judicial system and the community.

Commentary

Commending or criticizing jurors for their verdict may imply a judicial expectation in future cases and may impair a juror's ability to be fair and impartial in a subsequent case.

(11) A judge shall not disclose or use, for any purpose unrelated to judicial duties, nonpublic information* acquired in a judicial capacity.

C. Administrative Responsibilities.

(1) A judge shall diligently discharge the judge's administrative responsibilities without bias or prejudice and maintain professional competence in ju-

*Asterisked terms are defined in the Terminology Section. — EDS.

477

dicial administration, and should cooperate with other judges and court officials in the administration of court business.

(2) A judge shall require* staff, court officials and others subject to the judge's direction and control to observe the standards of fidelity and diligence that apply to the judge and to refrain from manifesting bias or prejudice in the performance of their official duties.

(3) A judge with supervisory authority for the judicial performance of other judges shall take reasonable measures to assure the prompt disposition of matters before them and the proper performance of their other judicial responsibilities.

(4) A judge shall not make unnecessary appointments. A judge shall exercise the power of appointment impartially and on the basis of merit. A judge shall avoid nepotism and favoritism. A judge shall not approve compensation of appointees beyond the fair value of services rendered.

Commentary

Appointees of a judge include assigned counsel, officials such as referees, commissioners, special masters, receivers and guardians and personnel such as clerks, secretaries and bailiffs. Consent by the parties to an appointment or an award of compensation does not relieve the judge of the obligation prescribed by Section 3C(4).

D. Disciplinary Responsibilities.

(1) A judge who receives information indicating a substantial likelihood that another judge has committed a violation of this Code should take appropriate action. A judge having knowledge* that another judge has committed a violation of this Code that raises a substantial question as to the other judge's fitness for office shall inform the appropriate authority.*

(2) A judge who receives information indicating a substantial likelihood that a lawyer has committed a violation of the Rules of Professional Conduct [substitute correct title if the applicable rules of lawyer conduct have a different title] should take appropriate action. A judge having knowledge* that a lawyer has committed a violation of the Rules of Professional Conduct [substitute correct title if the applicable rules of lawyer conduct have a different title] that raises a substantial question as to the lawyer's honesty, trustworthiness or fitness as a lawyer in other respects shall inform the appropriate authority.*

(3) Acts of a judge, in the discharge of disciplinary responsibilities, required or permitted by Sections 3D(1) and 3D(2) are part of a judge's judicial duties and shall be absolutely privileged, and no civil action predicated thereon may be instituted against the judge.

*Asterisked terms are defined in the Terminology Section. — EDS.

Commentary

Appropriate action may include direct communication with the judge or lawyer who has committed the violation, other direct action if available, and reporting the violation to the appropriate authority or other agency or body.

E. Disqualification.

(1) A judge shall disqualify himself or herself in a proceeding in which the judge's impartiality might reasonably be questioned, including but not limited to instances where:

Commentary

Under this rule, a judge is disqualified whenever the judge's impartiality might reasonably be questioned, regardless whether any of the specific rules in Section 3E(1) apply. For example, if a judge were in the process of negotiating for employment with a law firm, the judge would be disqualified from any matters in which that law firm appeared, unless the disqualification was waived by the parties after disclosure by the judge.

A judge should disclose on the record information that the judge believes the parties or their lawyers might consider relevant to the question of disqualification, even if the judge believes there is no real basis for disqualification.

By decisional law, the rule of necessity may override the rule of disqualification. For example, a judge might be required to participate in judicial review of a judicial salary statute, or might be the only judge available in a matter requiring immediate judicial action, such as a hearing on probable cause or a temporary restraining order. In the latter case, the judge must disclose on the record the basis for possible disqualification and use reasonable efforts to transfer the matter to another judge as soon as practicable.

(a) the judge has a personal bias or prejudice concerning a party or a party's lawyer, or personal knowledge* of disputed evidentiary facts concerning the proceeding;

(b) the judge served as a lawyer in the matter in controversy, or a lawyer with whom the judge previously practiced law served during such association as a lawyer concerning the matter, or the judge has been a material witness concerning it;

Commentary

A lawyer in a government agency does not ordinarily have an association with other lawyers employed by that agency within the meaning of Section 3E(1)(b); a judge formerly employed by a government agency, however, should disqualify himself or herself

---

*Asterisked terms are defined in the Terminology Section. — EDS.

in a proceeding if the judge's impartiality might reasonably be questioned because of such association.

   (c) the judge knows* that he or she, individually or as a fiduciary, or the judge's spouse, parent or child wherever residing, or any other member of the judge's family residing in the judge's household,* has an economic interest* in the subject matter in controversy or in a party to the proceeding or has any other more than de minimis* interest that could be substantially affected by the proceeding;

   (d) the judge or the judge's spouse, or a person within the third degree of relationship* to either of them, or the spouse of such a person:

   (i) is a party to the proceeding, or an officer, director or trustee of a party;

   (ii) is acting as a lawyer in the proceeding;

   (iii) is known* by the judge to have a more than de minimis* interest that could be substantially affected by the proceeding;

   (iv) is to the judge's knowledge* likely to be a material witness in the proceeding.

Commentary

   The fact that a lawyer in a proceeding is affiliated with a law firm with which a relative of the judge is affiliated does not of itself disqualify the judge. Under appropriate circumstances, the fact that "the judge's impartiality might reasonably be questioned" under Section 3E(1), or that the relative is known by the judge to have an interest in the law firm that could be "substantially affected by the outcome of the proceeding" under Section 3E(1)(d)(iii) may require the judge's disqualification.

   (2) A judge shall keep informed about the judge's personal and fiduciary* economic interests,* and make a reasonable effort to keep informed about the personal economic interests of the judge's spouse and minor children residing in the judge's household.

F. Remittal of Disqualification.

   A judge disqualified by the terms of Section 3E may disclose on the record the basis of the judge's disqualification and may ask the parties and their lawyers to consider, out of the presence of the judge, whether to waive disqualification. If following disclosure of any basis for disqualification other than personal bias or prejudice concerning a party, the parties and lawyers, without participation by the judge, all agree that the judge should not be disqualified, and the judge is then

   *Asterisked terms are defined in the Terminology Section. — EDS.

willing to participate, the judge may participate in the proceeding. The agreement shall be incorporated in the record of the proceeding.

Commentary

A remittal procedure provides the parties an opportunity to proceed without delay if they wish to waive the disqualification. To assure that consideration of the question of remittal is made independently of the judge, a judge must not solicit, seek or hear comment on possible remittal or waiver of the disqualification unless the lawyers jointly propose remittal after consultation as provided in the rule. A party may act through counsel if counsel represents on the record that the party has been consulted and consents. As a practical matter, a judge may wish to have all parties and their lawyers sign the remittal agreement.

CANON 4. A JUDGE SHALL SO CONDUCT THE JUDGE'S EXTRA-JUDICIAL ACTIVITIES AS TO MINIMIZE THE RISK OF CONFLICT WITH JUDICIAL OBLIGATIONS[†]

A. Extra-Judicial Activities in General.

A judge shall conduct all of the judge's extra-judicial activities so that they do not:

(1) cast reasonable doubt on the judge's capacity to act impartially as a judge;

(2) demean the judicial office; or

(3) interfere with the proper performance of judicial duties.

Commentary

Complete separation of a judge from extra-judicial activities is neither possible nor wise; a judge should not become isolated from the community in which the judge lives.

Expressions of bias or prejudice by a judge, even outside the judge's judicial activities, may cast reasonable doubt on the judge's capacity to act impartially as a judge. Expressions which may do so include jokes or other remarks demeaning individuals on the basis

---

[†]For a summary of changes from corresponding provisions of the 1972 Code of Judicial Conduct, see excerpts from the Standing Committee's Report printed at page 465 above. — EDS.

*Asterisked terms are defined in the Terminology Section. — EDS.

of their race, sex, religion, national origin, disability, age, sexual orientation or socioeconomic status. See Section 2C and accompanying Commentary.

B. Avocational Activities.

A judge may speak, write, lecture, teach and participate in other extrajudicial activities concerning the law,* the legal system, the administration of justice and non-legal subjects, subject to the requirements of this Code.

Commentary

As a judicial officer and person specially learned in the law, a judge is in a unique position to contribute to the improvement of the law, the legal system, and the administration of justice, including revision of substantive and procedural law and improvement of criminal and juvenile justice. To the extent that time permits, a judge is encouraged to do so, either independently or through a bar association, judicial conference or other organization dedicated to the improvement of the law. Judges may participate in efforts to promote the fair administration of justice, the independence of the judiciary and the integrity of the legal profession and may express opposition to the persecution of lawyers and judges in other countries because of their professional activities.

In this and other Sections of Canon 4, the phrase "subject to the requirements of this Code" is used, notably in connection with a judge's governmental, civic or charitable activities. This phrase is included to remind judges that the use of permissive language in various Sections of the Code does not relieve a judge from the other requirements of the Code that apply to the specific conduct.

C. Governmental, Civic or Charitable Activities.

(1) A judge shall not appear at a public hearing before, or otherwise consult with, an executive or legislative body or official except on matters concerning the law,* the legal system or the administration of justice or except when acting pro se in a matter involving the judge or the judge's interests.

Commentary

See Section 2B regarding the obligation to avoid improper influence.

(2) A judge shall not accept appointment to a governmental committee or commission or other governmental position that is concerned with issues of fact or policy on matters other than the improvement of the law,* the legal

*Asterisked terms are defined in the Terminology Section. — EDS.

system or the administration of justice. A judge may, however, represent a country, state or locality on ceremonial occasions or in connection with historical, educational or cultural activities.

Commentary

Section 4C(2) prohibits a judge from accepting any governmental position except one relating to the law, legal system or administration of justice as authorized by Section 4C(3). The appropriateness of accepting extra-judicial assignments must be assessed in light of the demands on judicial resources created by crowded dockets and the need to protect the courts from involvement in extra-judicial matters that may prove to be controversial. Judges should not accept governmental appointments that are likely to interfere with the effectiveness and independence of the judiciary.

Section 4C(2) does not govern a judge's service in a nongovernmental position. See Section 4C(3) permitting service by a judge with organizations devoted to the improvement of the law, the legal system or the administration of justice and with educational, religious, charitable, fraternal or civic organizations not conducted for profit. For example, service on the board of a public educational institution, unless it were a law school, would be prohibited under Section 4C(2), but service on the board of a public law school or any private educational institution would generally be permitted under Section 4C(3).

(3) A judge may serve as an officer, director, trustee or non-legal advisor of an organization or governmental agency devoted to the improvement of the law,* the legal system or the administration of justice or of an educational, religious, charitable, fraternal or civic organization not conducted for profit, subject to the following limitations and the other requirements of this Code.

Commentary

Section 4C(3) does not apply to a judge's service in a governmental position unconnected with the improvement of the law, the legal system or the administration of justice; see Section 4C(2).

See Commentary to Section 4B regarding use of the phrase "subject to the following limitations and the other requirements of this Code." As an example of the meaning of the phrase, a judge permitted by Section 4C(3) to serve on the board of a fraternal institution may be prohibited from such service by Sections 2C or 4A if the institution practices invidious discrimination or if service on the board otherwise casts reasonable doubt on the judge's capacity to act impartially as a judge.

Service by a judge on behalf of a civic or charitable organization may be governed by other provisions of Canon 4 in addition to Section 4C. For example, a judge is prohibited by Section 4G from serving as a legal advisor to a civic or charitable organization.

*Asterisked terms are defined in the Terminology Section. — EDS.

(a) A judge shall not serve as an officer, director, trustee or non-legal advisor if it is likely that the organization

(i) will be engaged in proceedings that would ordinarily come before the judge, or

(ii) will be engaged frequently in adversary proceedings in the court of which the judge is a member or in any court subject to the appellate jurisdiction of the court of which the judge is a member.

Commentary

The changing nature of some organizations and of their relationship to the law makes it necessary for a judge regularly to reexamine the activities of each organization with which the judge is affiliated to determine if it is proper for the judge to continue the affiliation. For example, in many jurisdictions charitable hospitals are now more frequently in court than in the past. Similarly, the boards of some legal aid organizations now make policy decisions that may have political significance or imply commitment to causes that may come before the courts for adjudication.

(b) A judge as an officer, director, trustee or non-legal advisor, or as a member or otherwise:

(i) may assist such an organization in planning fund-raising and may participate in the management and investment of the organization's funds, but shall not personally participate in the solicitation of funds or other fund-raising activities, except that a judge may solicit funds from other judges over whom the judge does not exercise supervisory or appellate authority;

(ii) may make recommendations to public and private fund-granting organizations on projects and programs concerning the law,* the legal system or the administration of justice;

(iii) shall not personally participate in membership solicitation if the solicitation might reasonably be perceived as coercive or, except as permitted in Section 4C(3)(b)(i), if the membership solicitation is essentially a fund-raising mechanism;

(iv) shall not use or permit the use of the prestige of judicial office for fund-raising or membership solicitation.

Commentary

A judge may solicit membership or endorse or encourage membership efforts for an organization devoted to the improvement of the law, the legal system or the administration of justice or a nonprofit educational, religious, charitable, fraternal or civic organization as long as the solicitation cannot reasonably be perceived as coercive and is not

*Asterisked terms are defined in the Terminology Section. — EDS.

essentially a fund-raising mechanism. Solicitation of funds for an organization and solicitation of memberships similarly involve the danger that the person solicited will feel obligated to respond favorably to the solicitor if the solicitor is in a position of influence or control. A judge must not engage in direct, individual solicitation of funds or memberships in person, in writing or by telephone except in the following cases: 1) a judge may solicit for funds or memberships other judges over whom the judge does not exercise supervisory or appellate authority, 2) a judge may solicit other persons for membership in the organizations described above if neither those persons nor persons with whom they are affiliated are likely ever to appear before the court on which the judge serves and 3) a judge who is an officer of such an organization may send a general membership solicitation mailing over the judge's signature.

Use of an organization letterhead for fund-raising or membership solicitation does not violate Section 4C(3)(b) provided the letterhead lists only the judge's name and office or other position in the organization, and, if comparable designations are listed for other persons, the judge's judicial designation. In addition, a judge must also make reasonable efforts to ensure that the judge's staff, court officials and others subject to the judge's direction and control do not solicit funds on the judge's behalf for any purpose, charitable or otherwise.

A judge must not be a speaker or guest of honor at an organization's fund-raising event, but mere attendance at such an event is permissible if otherwise consistent with this Code.

D. Financial Activities.

(1) A judge shall not engage in financial and business dealings that:

(a) may reasonably be perceived to exploit the judge's judicial position, or

(b) involve the judge in frequent transactions or continuing business relationships with those lawyers or other persons likely to come before the court on which the judge serves.

Commentary

The Time for Compliance provision of this Code (Application, Section F) postpones the time for compliance with certain provisions of this Section in some cases.

When a judge acquires in a judicial capacity information, such as material contained in filings with the court, that is not yet generally known, the judge must not use the information for private gain. See Section 2B; see also Section 3B(11).

A judge must avoid financial and business dealings that involve the judge in frequent transactions or continuing business relationships with persons likely to come either before the judge personally or before other judges in the judge's court. In addition, a judge should discourage members of the judge's family from engaging in dealings that would reasonably appear to exploit the judge's judicial position. This rule is necessary to avoid creating an appearance of exploitation of office or favoritism and to minimize the potential for disqualification. With respect to affiliation of relatives of judges with law firms appearing before the judge, see Commentary to Section 3E(1) relating to disqualification.

Participation by a judge in financial and business dealings is subject to the general prohibitions in Section 4A against activities that tend to reflect adversely on impartiality, demean the judicial office, or interfere with the proper performance of judicial duties. Such participation is also subject to the general prohibition in Canon 2 against activities involving impropriety or the appearance of impropriety and the prohibition in Section 2B against the misuse of the prestige of judicial office. In addition, a judge must maintain high standards of conduct in all of the judge's activities, as set forth in Canon 1. See Commentary for Section 4B regarding use of the phrase "subject to the requirements of this Code."

(2) A judge may, subject to the requirements of this Code, hold and manage investments of the judge and members of the judge's family,* including real estate, and engage in other remunerative activity.

Commentary

This Section provides that, subject to the requirements of this Code, a judge may hold and manage investments owned solely by the judge, investments owned solely by a member or members of the judge's family, and investments owned jointly by the judge and members of the judge's family.

(3) A judge shall not serve as an officer, director, manager, general partner, advisor or employee of any business entity except that a judge may, subject to the requirements of this Code, manage and participate in:

(a) a business closely held by the judge or members of the judge's family,* or

(b) a business entity primarily engaged in investment of the financial resources of the judge or members of the judge's family.

Commentary

Subject to the requirements of this Code, a judge may participate in a business that is closely held either by the judge alone, by members of the judge's family, or by the judge and members of the judge's family.

Although participation by a judge in a closely-held family business might otherwise be permitted by Section 4D(3), a judge may be prohibited from participation by other provisions of this Code when, for example, the business entity frequently appears before the judge's court or the participation requires significant time away from judicial duties. Similarly, a judge must avoid participating in a closely-held family business if the judge's participation would involve misuse of the prestige of judicial office.

*Asterisked terms are defined in the Terminology Section. — EDS.

(4) A judge shall manage the judge's investments and other financial interests to minimize the number of cases in which the judge is disqualified. As soon as the judge can do so without serious financial detriment, the judge shall divest himself or herself of investments and other financial interests that might require frequent disqualification.

(5) A judge shall not accept, and shall urge members of the judge's family residing in the judge's household* not to accept, a gift, bequest, favor or loan from anyone except for:

Commentary

Section 4D(5) does not apply to contributions to a judge's campaign for judicial office, a matter governed by Canon 5.

Because a gift, bequest, favor or loan to a member of the judge's family residing in the judge's household might be viewed as intended to influence the judge, a judge must inform those family members of the relevant ethical constraints upon the judge in this regard and discourage those family members from violating them. A judge cannot, however, reasonably be expected to know or control all of the financial or business activities of all family members residing in the judge's household.

(a) a gift incident to a public testimonial, books, tapes and other resource materials supplied by publishers on a complimentary basis for official use, or an invitation to the judge and the judge's spouse or guest to attend a bar-related function or an activity devoted to the improvement of the law,* the legal system or the administration of justice;

Commentary

Acceptance of an invitation to a law-related function is governed by Section 4D(5)(a); acceptance of an invitation paid for by an individual lawyer or group of lawyers is governed by Section 4D(5)(h).

A judge may accept a public testimonial or a gift incident thereto only if the donor organization is not an organization whose members comprise or frequently represent the same side in litigation, and the testimonial and gift are otherwise in compliance with other provisions of this Code. See Sections 4A(1) and 2B.

(b) a gift, award or benefit incident to the business, profession or other separate activity of a spouse or other family member of a judge residing in the judge's household, including gifts, awards and benefits for the use of both the spouse or other family member and the judge (as spouse or family member), provided the gift, award or benefit could not reasonably be per-

*Asterisked terms are defined in the Terminology Section. — EDS.

ceived as intended to influence the judge in the performance of judicial
duties;

(c) ordinary social hospitality;

(d) a gift from a relative or friend, for a special occasion, such as a wed-
ding, anniversary or birthday, if the gift is fairly commensurate with the
occasion and the relationship;

Commentary

A gift to a judge, or to a member of the judge's family living in the judge's household,
that is excessive in value raises questions about the judge's impartiality and the integrity
of the judicial office and might require disqualification of the judge where disqualification would not otherwise be required. See, however, Section 4D(5)(e).

(e) a gift, bequest, favor or loan from a relative or close personal friend
whose appearance or interest in a case would in any event require disqualification under Section 3E;

(f) a loan from a lending institution in its regular course of business on
the same terms generally available to persons who are not judges;

(g) a scholarship or fellowship awarded on the same terms and based on
the same criteria applied to other applicants; or

(h) any other gift, bequest, favor or loan, only if: the donor is not a party
or other person who has come or is likely to come or whose interests have
come or are likely to come before the judge; and, if its value exceeds
$150.00, the judge reports it in the same manner as the judge reports com-
pensation in Section 4H.

Commentary

Section 4D(5)(h) prohibits judges from accepting gifts, favors, bequests or loans from
lawyers or their firms if they have come or are likely to come before the judge; it also
prohibits gifts, favors, bequests or loans from clients of lawyers or their firms when the
clients' interests have come or are likely to come before the judge.

E. Fiduciary Activities.

(1) A judge shall not serve as executor, administrator or other personal
representative, trustee, guardian, attorney in fact or other fiduciary,* except
for the estate, trust or person of a member of the judge's family,* and then
only if such service will not interfere with the proper performance of judicial
duties.

*Asterisked terms are defined in the Terminology Section. — EDS.

488

(2) A judge shall not serve as a fiduciary* if it is likely that the judge as a fiduciary will be engaged in proceedings that would ordinarily come before the judge, or if the estate, trust or ward becomes involved in adversary proceedings in the court on which the judge serves or one under its appellate jurisdiction.

(3) The same restrictions on financial activities that apply to a judge personally also apply to the judge while acting in a fiduciary* capacity.

Commentary

The Time for Compliance provision of this Code (Application, Section F) postpones the time for compliance with certain provisions of this Section in some cases.

The restrictions imposed by this Canon may conflict with the judge's obligation as a fiduciary. For example, a judge should resign as trustee if detriment to the trust would result from divestiture of holdings the retention of which would place the judge in violation of Section 4D(4).

F. Service as Arbitrator or Mediator.

A judge shall not act as an arbitrator or mediator or otherwise perform judicial functions in a private capacity unless expressly authorized by law.*

Commentary

Section 4F does not prohibit a judge from participating in arbitration, mediation or settlement conferences performed as part of judicial duties.

G. Practice of Law.

A judge shall not practice law. Notwithstanding this prohibition, a judge may act pro se and may, without compensation, give legal advice to and draft or review documents for a member of the judge's family.*

Commentary

This prohibition refers to the practice of law in a representative capacity and not in a pro se capacity. A judge may act for himself or herself in all legal matters, including matters involving litigation and matters involving appearances before or other dealings with legislative and other governmental bodies. However, in so doing, a judge must not abuse

*Asterisked terms are defined in the Terminology Section. — EDS.

the prestige of office to advance the interests of the judge or the judge's family. See Section 2(B).

The Code allows a judge to give legal advice to and draft legal documents for members of the judge's family, so long as the judge receives no compensation. A judge must not, however, act as an advocate or negotiator for a member of the judge's family in a legal matter.

=========

Canon 6, new in the 1972 Code, reflected concerns about conflicts of interest and appearances of impropriety arising from compensation for off-the-bench activities. Since 1972, however, reporting requirements that are much more comprehensive with respect to what must be reported and with whom reports must be filed have been adopted by many jurisdictions. The Committee believes that although reports of compensation for extra-judicial activities should be required, reporting requirements preferably should be developed to suit the respective jurisdictions, not simply adopted as set forth in a national model code of judicial conduct. Because of the Committee's concern that deletion of this Canon might lead to the misconception that reporting compensation for extra-judicial activities is no longer important, the substance of Canon 6 is carried forward as Section 4H in this Code for adoption in those jurisdictions that do not have other reporting requirements. In jurisdictions that have separately established reporting requirements, Section 4H(2) (Public Reporting) may be deleted and the caption for Section 4H modified appropriately.

H. Compensation, Reimbursement and Reporting.

(1) Compensation and Reimbursement. A judge may receive compensation and reimbursement of expenses for the extra-judicial activities permitted by this Code, if the source of such payments does not give the appearance of influencing the judge's performance of judicial duties or otherwise give the appearance of impropriety.

(a) Compensation shall not exceed a reasonable amount nor shall it exceed what a person who is not a judge would receive for the same activity.

(b) Expense reimbursement shall be limited to the actual cost of travel, food and lodging reasonably incurred by the judge and, where appropriate to the occasion, by the judge's spouse or guest. Any payment in excess of such an amount is compensation.

(2) Public Reports. A judge shall report the date, place and nature of any activity for which the judge received compensation, and the name of the payor and the amount of compensation so received. Compensation or income of a spouse attributed to the judge by operation of a community property law is not extra-judicial compensation to the judge. The judge's report shall be made at least annually and shall be filed as a public document in the office of the clerk of the court on which the judge serves or other office designated by law.*

*Asterisked terms are defined in the Terminology Section. — EDS.

Commentary

See Section 4D(5) regarding reporting of gifts, bequests and loans.

The Code does not prohibit a judge from accepting honoraria or speaking fees provided that the compensation is reasonable and commensurate with the task performed. A judge should ensure, however, that no conflicts are created by the arrangement. A judge must not appear to trade on the judicial position for personal advantage. Nor should a judge spend significant time away from court duties to meet speaking or writing commitments for compensation. In addition, the source of the payment must not raise any question of undue influence or the judge's ability or willingness to be impartial.

I. [Disclosure of Judge's Assets]

Disclosure of a judge's income, debts, investments or other assets is required only to the extent provided in this Canon and in Sections 3E and 3F, or as otherwise required by law.*

Commentary

Section 3E requires a judge to disqualify himself or herself in any proceeding in which the judge has an economic interest. See "economic interest" as explained in the Terminology Section. Section 4D requires a judge to refrain from engaging in business and from financial activities that might interfere with the impartial performance of judicial duties; Section 4H requires a judge to report all compensation the judge received for activities outside judicial office. A judge has the rights of any other citizen, including the right to privacy of the judge's financial affairs, except to the extent that limitations established by law are required to safeguard the proper performance of the judge's duties.

---

*Asterisked terms are defined in the Terminology Section. — EDS.

CANON 5. A JUDGE OR JUDICIAL CANDIDATE SHALL REFRAIN FROM INAPPROPRIATE POLITICAL ACTIVITY[2,†]

A. All Judges and Candidates.

(1) Except as authorized in Sections 5B(2), 5C(1) and 5C(3), a judge or a candidate* for election or appointment to judicial office shall not:

(a) act as a leader or hold an office in a political organization;*

(b) publicly endorse or publicly oppose another candidate for public office;

(c) make speeches on behalf of a political organization;

(d) attend political gatherings; or

(e) solicit funds for, pay an assessment to or make a contribution to a political organization or candidate, or purchase tickets for political party dinners or other functions.

Commentary

A judge or candidate for judicial office retains the right to participate in the political process as a voter.

Where false information concerning a judicial candidate is made public, a judge or another judicial candidate having knowledge of the facts is not prohibited by Section 5A(1) from making the facts public.

2. Introductory Note to Canon 5: There is wide variation in the methods of judicial selection used, both among jurisdictions and within the jurisdictions themselves. In a given state, judges may be selected by one method initially, retained by a different method, and selected by still another method to fill interim vacancies.

According to figures compiled in 1987 by the National Center for State Courts, 32 states and the District of Columbia use a merit selection method (in which an executive such as a governor appoints a judge from a group of nominees selected by a judicial nominating commission) to select judges in the state either initially or to fill an interim vacancy. Of those 33 jurisdictions, a merit selection method is used in 18 jurisdictions to choose judges of courts of last resort, in 13 jurisdictions to choose judges of intermediate appellate courts, in 12 jurisdictions to choose judges of general jurisdiction courts and in 5 jurisdictions to choose judges of limited jurisdiction courts.

Methods of judicial selection other than merit selection include nonpartisan election (10 states use it for initial selection at all court levels, another 10 states use it for initial selection for at least one court level) and partisan election (8 states use it for initial selection at all court levels, another 7 states use it for initial selection for at least one level). In a small minority of the states, judicial selection methods include executive or legislative appointment (without nomination of a group of potential appointees by a judicial nominating commission) and court selection. In addition, the federal judicial system utilizes an executive appointment method. See State Court Organization 1987 (National Center for State Courts, 1988).

†For a summary of changes from corresponding provisions of the 1972 Code of Judicial Conduct, see excerpts from the Standing Committee's Report printed at pages 465-466 above. — EDS.

*Asterisked terms are defined in the Terminology Section. — EDS.

Section 5A(1)(a) does not prohibit a candidate for elective judicial office from retaining during candidacy a public office such as county prosecutor, which is not "an office in a political organization."

Section 5A(1)(b) does not prohibit a judge or judicial candidate from privately expressing his or her views on judicial candidates or other candidates for public office.

A candidate does not publicly endorse another candidate for public office by having that candidate's name on the same ticket.

(2) A judge shall resign from judicial office upon becoming a candidate* for a non-judicial office either in a primary or in a general election, except that the judge may continue to hold judicial office while being a candidate for election to or serving as a delegate in a state constitutional convention if the judge is otherwise permitted by law* to do so.

(3) A candidate* for a judicial office:

(a) shall maintain the dignity appropriate to judicial office and act in a manner consistent with the integrity and independence of the judiciary, and shall encourage members of the candidate's family* to adhere to the same standards of political conduct in support of the candidate as apply to the candidate;

Commentary

Although a judicial candidate must encourage members of his or her family to adhere to the same standards of political conduct in support of the candidate that apply to the candidate, family members are free to participate in other political activity.

(b) shall prohibit employees and officials who serve at the pleasure of the candidate,* and shall discourage other employees and officials subject to the candidate's direction and control from doing on the candidate's behalf what the candidate is prohibited from doing under the Sections of this Canon;

(c) except to the extent permitted by Section 5C(2), shall not authorize or knowingly* permit any other person to do for the candidate* what the candidate is prohibited from doing under the Sections of this Canon;

(d) shall not:

(i) make pledges or promises of conduct in office other than the faithful and impartial performance of the duties of the office;

(ii) make statements that commit or appear to commit the candidate with respect to cases, controversies or issues that are likely to come before the court; or

(iii) knowingly* misrepresent the identity, qualifications, present position or other fact concerning the candidate or an opponent;

*Asterisked terms are defined in the Terminology Section. — EDS.

Commentary

Section 5A(3)(d) prohibits a candidate for judicial office from making statements that appear to commit the candidate regarding cases, controversies or issues likely to come before the court. As a corollary, a candidate should emphasize in any public statement the candidate's duty to uphold the law regardless of his or her personal views. See also Section 3B(9), the general rule on public comment by judges. Section 5A(3)(d) does not prohibit a candidate from making pledges or promises respecting improvements in court administration. Nor does this Section prohibit an incumbent judge from making private statements to other judges or court personnel in the performance of judicial duties. This Section applies to any statement made in the process of securing judicial office, such as statements to commissions charged with judicial selection and tenure and legislative bodies confirming appointment. See also Rule 8.2 of the ABA Model Rules of Professional Conduct.

(e) may respond to personal attacks or attacks on the candidate's record as long as the response does not violate Section 5A(3)(d).

B. Candidates Seeking Appointment to Judicial or Other Governmental Office.

(1) A candidate* for appointment to judicial office or a judge seeking other governmental office shall not solicit or accept funds, personally or through a committee or otherwise, to support his or her candidacy.

(2) A candidate* for appointment to judicial office or a judge seeking other governmental office shall not engage in any political activity to secure the appointment except that:

(a) such persons may:

(i) communicate with the appointing authority, including any selection or nominating commission or other agency designated to screen candidates;

(ii) seek support or endorsement for the appointment from organizations that regularly make recommendations for reappointment or appointment to the office, and from individuals to the extent requested or required by those specified in Section 5B(2)(a); and

(iii) provide to those specified in Sections 5B(2)(a)(i) and 5B(2)(a)(ii) information as to his or her qualifications for the office;

(b) a non-judge candidate* for appointment to judicial office may, in addition, unless otherwise prohibited by law:*

(i) retain an office in a political organization,*

(ii) attend political gatherings, and

---

*Asterisked terms are defined in the Terminology Section. — EDS.

(iii) continue to pay ordinary assessments and ordinary contributions to a political organization or candidate and purchase tickets for political party dinners or other functions.

Commentary

Section 5B(2) provides a limited exception to the restrictions imposed by Sections 5A(1) and 5D. Under Section 5B(2), candidates seeking reappointment to the same judicial office or appointment to another judicial office or other governmental office may apply for the appointment and seek appropriate support.

Although under Section 5B(2) non-judge candidates seeking appointment to judicial office are permitted during candidacy to retain office in a political organization, attend political gatherings and pay ordinary dues and assessments, they remain subject to other provisions of this Code during candidacy. See Sections 5B(1), 5B(2)(a), 5E and Application Section.

C. Judges and Candidates Subject to Public Election.

(1) A judge or a candidate* subject to public election* may, except as prohibited by law:*
 (a) at any time
  (i) purchase tickets for and attend political gatherings;
  (ii) identify himself or herself as a member of a political party; and
  (iii) contribute to a political organization;*
 (b) when a candidate for election
  (i) speak to gatherings on his or her own behalf;
  (ii) appear in newspaper, television and other media advertisements supporting his or her candidacy;
  (iii) distribute pamphlets and other promotional campaign literature supporting his or her candidacy; and
  (iv) publicly endorse or publicly oppose other candidates for the same judicial office in a public election in which the judge or judicial candidate is running.

Commentary

Section 5C(1) permits judges subject to election at any time to be involved in limited political activity. Section 5D, applicable solely to incumbent judges, would otherwise bar this activity.

*Asterisked terms are defined in the Terminology Section. — EDS.

(2) A candidate* shall not personally solicit or accept campaign contributions or personally solicit publicly stated support. A candidate may, however, establish committees of responsible persons to conduct campaigns for the candidate through media advertisements, brochures, mailings, candidate forums and other means not prohibited by law. Such committees may solicit and accept reasonable campaign contributions, manage the expenditure of funds for the candidate's campaign and obtain public statements of support for his or her candidacy. Such committees are not prohibited from soliciting and accepting reasonable campaign contributions and public support from lawyers. A candidate's committee may solicit contributions and public support for the candidate's campaign no earlier than [one year] before an election and no later than [90] days after the last election in which the candidate participates during the election year. A candidate shall not use or permit the use of campaign contributions for the private benefit of the candidate or others.

Commentary

Section 5C(2) permits a candidate, other than a candidate for appointment, to establish campaign committees to solicit and accept public support and reasonable financial contributions. At the start of the campaign, the candidate must instruct his or her campaign committees to solicit or accept only contributions that are reasonable under the circumstances. Though not prohibited, campaign contributions of which a judge has knowledge, made by lawyers or others who appear before the judge, may be relevant to disqualification under Section 3E.

Campaign committees established under Section 5C(2) should manage campaign finances responsibly, avoiding deficits that might necessitate post-election fund-raising, to the extent possible.

Section 5C(2) does not prohibit a candidate from initiating an evaluation by a judicial selection commission or bar association, or, subject to the requirements of this Code, from responding to a request for information from any organization.

(3) Except as prohibited by law,* a candidate* for judicial office in a public election* may permit the candidate's name: (a) to be listed on election materials along with the names of other candidates for elective public office, and (b) to appear in promotions of the ticket.

Commentary

Section 5C(3) provides a limited exception to the restrictions imposed by Section 5A(1).

*Asterisked terms are defined in the Terminology Section. — EDS.

D. Incumbent Judges.

A judge shall not engage in any political activity except (i) as authorized under any other Section of this Code, (ii) on behalf of measures to improve the law,* the legal system or the administration of justice, or (iii) as expressly authorized by law.

Commentary

Neither Section 5D nor any other section of the Code prohibits a judge in the exercise of administrative functions from engaging in planning and other official activities with members of the executive and legislative branches of government. With respect to a judge's activity on behalf of measures to improve the law, the legal system and the administration of justice, see Commentary to Section 4B and Section 4C(1) and its Commentary.

E. Applicability.

Canon 5 generally applies to all incumbent judges and judicial candidates.* A successful candidate, whether or not an incumbent, is subject to judicial discipline for his or her campaign conduct; an unsuccessful candidate who is a lawyer is subject to lawyer discipline for his or her campaign conduct. A lawyer who is a candidate for judicial office is subject to [Rule 8.2(b) of the ABA Model Rules of Professional Conduct]. (An adopting jurisdiction should substitute a reference to its applicable rule.)

APPLICATION OF THE CODE OF JUDICIAL CONDUCT

A. [Definition of a Judge]

Anyone, whether or not a lawyer, who is an officer of a judicial system[3] and who performs judicial functions, including an officer such as a magistrate,

---

*Asterisked terms are defined in the Terminology Section. — EDS.

3. Applicability of this Code to administrative law judges should be determined by each adopting jurisdiction. Administrative law judges generally are affiliated with the executive branch of government rather than the judicial branch and each adopting jurisdiction should consider the unique characteristics of particular administrative law judge positions in adopting and adapting the Code for administrative law judges. See, e.g., Model Code of Judicial Conduct for Federal Administrative Law Judges, endorsed by the National Conference of Administrative Law Judges in February 1989.

court commissioner, special master or referee, is a judge within the meaning of this Code. All judges shall comply with this Code except as provided below.

Commentary

The four categories of judicial service in other than a full-time capacity are necessarily defined in general terms because of the widely varying forms of judicial service. For the purposes of this Section, as long as a retired judge is subject to recall the judge is considered to "perform judicial functions." The determination of which category and, accordingly, which specific Code provisions apply to an individual judicial officer, depend upon the facts of the particular judicial service.

B. *Retired Judge Subject to Recall.*

A retired judge subject to recall who by law is not permitted to practice law is not required to comply:
(1) except while serving as a judge, with Section 4F; and
(2) at any time with Section 4E.

C. *Continuing Part-Time Judge.*

A continuing part-time judge:*
(1) is not required to comply
    (a) except while serving as a judge, with Section 3B(9); and
    (b) at any time with Sections 4C(2), 4D(3), 4E(1), 4F, 4G, 4H, 5A(1), 5B(2) and 5D.
(2) shall not practice law in the court on which the judge serves or in any court subject to the appellate jurisdiction of the court on which the judge serves, and shall not act as a lawyer in a proceeding in which the judge has served as a judge or in any other proceeding related thereto.

Commentary

When a person who has been a continuing part-time judge is no longer a continuing part-time judge, including a retired judge no longer subject to recall, that person may act as a lawyer in a proceeding in which he or she has served as a judge or in any other proceeding related thereto only with the express consent of all parties pursuant to [Rule 1.12(a) of the ABA Model Rules of Professional Conduct]. (An adopting jurisdiction should substitute a reference to its applicable rule.)

*Asterisked terms are defined in the Terminology Section. — EDS.

498

D. Periodic Part-Time Judge.

A periodic part-time judge:*
(1) is not required to comply
  (a) except while serving as a judge, with Section 3B(9);
  (b) at any time, with Sections 4C(2), 4C(3)(a), 4D(1)(b), 4D(3), 4D(4), 4D(5), 4E, 4F, 4G, 4H, 5A(1), 5B(2) and 5D.
(2) shall not practice law in the court on which the judge serves or in any court subject to the appellate jurisdiction of the court on which the judge serves, and shall not act as a lawyer in a proceeding in which the judge has served as a judge or in any other proceeding related thereto.

Commentary

When a person who has been a periodic part-time judge is no longer a periodic part-time judge (no longer accepts appointments), that person may act as a lawyer in a proceeding in which he or she has served as a judge or in any other proceeding related thereto only with the express consent of all parties pursuant to [Rule 1.12(a) of the ABA Model Rules of Professional Conduct]. (An adopting jurisdiction should substitute a reference to its applicable rule.)

E. Pro Tempore Part-Time Judge.

A pro tempore part-time judge:*
(1) is not required to comply
  (a) except while serving as a judge, with Sections 2A, 2B, 3B(9) and 4C(1);
  (b) at any time with Sections 2C, 4C(2), 4C(3)(a), 4C(3)(b), 4D(1)(b), 4D(3), 4D(4), 4D(5), 4E, 4F, 4G, 4H, 5A(1), 5A(2), 5B(2) and 5D.
(2) A person who has been a pro tempore part-time judge* shall not act as a lawyer in a proceeding in which the judge has served as a judge or in any other proceeding related thereto except as otherwise permitted by [Rule 1.12(a) of the ABA Model Rules of Professional Conduct]. (An adopting jurisdiction should substitute a reference to its applicable rule.)

F. Time for Compliance.

A person to whom this Code becomes applicable shall comply immediately with all provisions of this Code except Sections 4D(2), 4D(3) and 4E and shall

*Asterisked terms are defined in the Terminology Section. — EDS.

comply with these Sections as soon as reasonably possible and shall do so in any event within the period of one year.

Commentary

If serving as a fiduciary when selected as judge, a new judge may, notwithstanding the prohibitions in Section 4E, continue to serve as fiduciary but only for that period of time necessary to avoid serious adverse consequences to the beneficiary of the fiduciary relationship and in no event longer than one year. Similarly, if engaged at the time of judicial selection in a business activity, a new judge may, notwithstanding the prohibitions in Section 4D(3), continue in that activity for a reasonable period but in no event longer than one year.

APPENDIX. JUDICIAL ETHICS COMMITTEE

A. The [chief judge of the highest court of the jurisdiction] shall appoint a Judicial Ethics Committee consisting of [nine] members. [Five] members shall be judges; [two] members shall be non-judge lawyers; and [two] members shall be public members. Of the judicial members, one member shall be appointed from each of [the highest court, the intermediate levels of courts, and the trial courts]. The remaining judicial members shall be judges appointed from any of the above courts, but not from the [highest court of the jurisdiction]. The [chief judge] shall designate one of the members as chairperson. Members shall serve three-year terms; terms shall be staggered; and no individual shall serve for more than two consecutive terms.

B. The Judicial Ethics Committee so established shall have authority to:

(1) by the concurrence of a majority of its members, express its opinion on proper judicial conduct with respect to the provisions of [the code of judicial conduct adopted by the jurisdiction and any other specified sections of law of the jurisdiction regarding the judiciary, such as financial reporting requirements], either on its own initiative, at the request of a judge or candidate for judicial office, or at the request of a court or an agency charged with the administration of judicial discipline in the jurisdiction, provided that an opinion may not be issued on a matter that is pending before a court or before such an agency except on request of the court or agency;

(2) make recommendations to [the highest court of the jurisdiction] for amendment of the Code of Judicial Conduct [of the jurisdiction]; and

(3) adopt rules relating to the procedures to be used in expressing opinions, including rules to assure a timely response to inquiries.

500

C. A judge or candidate for judicial office as defined in the Terminology Section of this Code who has requested and relied upon an opinion may not be disciplined for conduct conforming to that opinion.

D. An opinion issued pursuant to this rule shall be filed with [appropriate official of the judicial conference of the jurisdiction]. Such an opinion is confidential and not public information unless [the highest court of the jurisdiction] otherwise directs. However, the [appropriate official of the judicial conference of the jurisdiction] shall cause an edited version of each opinion to be prepared, in which the identity and geographic location of the person who has requested the opinion, the specific court involved, and the identity of other individuals, organizations or groups mentioned in the opinion are not disclosed. Opinions so edited shall be published periodically in the manner [the appropriate official of the judicial conference of the jurisdiction] deems proper.

Specialized Ethical Codes

Editors' Introduction. The ABA Model Rules of Professional Conduct are intended to govern the conduct of lawyers in all types of practice. Because the Rules cover such a wide range of conduct, they are often general. They do not give detailed guidance about problems that arise in specialized types of practice (such as matrimonial practice or federal government service), or that confront lawyers serving in nontraditional roles (such as arbitrator or mediator). To fill this gap, various private organizations and specialized bar associations have developed their own codes. Excerpts from and cross-references to some of these appear under Related Materials following each Model Rule.

In addition, the European Community has adopted a Code of Conduct for European lawyers engaged in "cross-border activities," and the Association of American Law Schools (the AALS) has adopted a Statement of Good Practices by Law Professors.

The documents that follow are but a few examples of the specialized codes that various groups have drafted to guide lawyers in particular types of practice or in particular law-related professions.

Contents

ABA STANDARDS OF PRACTICE FOR LAWYER MEDIATORS
IN FAMILY DISPUTES

Standards
- I. The mediator has a duty to define and describe the process of mediation and its cost before the parties reach an agreement to mediate.
- II. The mediator shall not voluntarily disclose information obtained through the mediation process without the prior consent of both participants.
- III. The mediator has a duty to be impartial.
- IV. The mediator has a duty to assure that the mediation participants make decisions based upon sufficient information and knowledge.

V. The mediator has a duty to suspend or terminate mediation whenever continuation of the process would harm one or more of the participants.

VI. The mediator has a continuing duty to advise each of the mediation participants to obtain legal review prior to reaching any agreement.

CODE OF ETHICS OF THE AMERICAN ARBITRATION ASSOCIATION FOR ARBITRATORS IN COMMERCIAL DISPUTES

Preamble

Canons

I. An Arbitrator Should Uphold the Integrity and Fairness of the Arbitration Process

II. An Arbitrator Should Disclose Any Interest or Relationship Likely to Affect Impartiality or Which Might Create an Appearance of Partiality or Bias

III. An Arbitrator in Communicating with the Parties Should Avoid Impropriety or the Appearance of Impropriety

IV. An Arbitrator Should Conduct the Proceedings Fairly and Diligently

V. An Arbitrator Should Make Decisions in a Just, Independent and Deliberate Manner

VI. An Arbitrator Should Be Faithful to the Relationship of Trust and Confidentiality Inherent in That Office

VII. Ethical Considerations Relating to Arbitrators Appointed by One Party

ETHICAL STANDARDS OF PROFESSIONAL CONDUCT OF THE SOCIETY OF PROFESSIONALS IN DISPUTE RESOLUTION

Introduction
Application of Standards
Scope
General Responsibilities
Responsibilities of the Parties
    1. Impartiality
    2. Informed Consent
    3. Confidentiality
    4. Conflict of Interest
    5. Promptness
    6. The Settlement and Its Consequences
Unrepresented Interests
Use of Multiple Procedures
Background and Qualifications
Disclosure of Fees
Support of the Profession
Responsibilities of Neutrals Working on the Same Case
Advertising and Solicitation

Specialized Ethical Codes

III. Responsibilities To Colleagues
IV. Responsibilities To The Law School and University
 V. Responsibilities To The Bar and General Public

ABA STANDARDS OF PRACTICE FOR
LAWYER MEDIATORS IN FAMILY DISPUTES*

Editors' Note. Model Rule 2.2 governs the lawyer as "intermediary" but Comment 2 to that Rule makes clear that Rule 2.2 "does not apply to a lawyer acting as arbitrator or mediator between or among parties who are not clients of the lawyer. . . ." The Model Rules thus give no specific guidance to the lawyer acting as a mediator. In August 1984, however, the ABA House of Delegates adopted Standards of Practice for Lawyer Mediators in Family Disputes, which were developed by a Task Force of the ABA Family Law Section's Mediation and Arbitration Committees. Although these Standards are specifically designed to govern family disputes, they contain many useful guidelines for lawyers acting as mediators in all types of disputes. The Standards do not contain comments, but an unofficial introductory commentary can be found in the December 1984 Dispute Resolution Forum (published by the National Institute for Dispute Resolution), in which the Standards were first published.

ABA Note: For the purposes of these standards, family mediation is defined as a process in which a lawyer helps family members resolve their disputes in an informative and consensual manner. This process requires that the mediator be qualified by training, experience, and temperament; that the mediator be impartial; that the participants reach decisions voluntarily; that their decisions be based on sufficient factual data; and that each participant understands the information upon which decisions are reached. While family mediation may be viewed as an alternative means of conflict resolution, it is not a substitute for the benefit of independent legal advice.

Standard I.   The mediator has a duty to define and describe the process of mediation and its cost before the parties reach an agreement to mediate.

SPECIFIC CONSIDERATIONS

Before the actual mediation sessions begin, the mediator shall conduct an orientation session to give an overview of the process and to assess the appropriateness of mediation for the participants. Among the topics covered, the mediator shall discuss the following:

*Copyright © 1984. Reprinted by permission of the American Bar Association.

A. The mediator shall define the process in context so that the participants understand the differences between mediation and other means of conflict resolution available to them. In defining the process, the mediator shall also distinguish it from therapy or marriage counseling.

B. The mediator shall obtain sufficient information from the participants so they can mutually define the issues to be resolved in mediation.

C. It should be emphasized that the mediator may make suggestions for the participants to consider, such as alternative ways of resolving problems, and may draft proposals for the participants' consideration, but that all decisions are to be made voluntarily by the participants themselves, and the mediator's views are to be given no independent weight or credence.

D. The duties and responsibilities that the mediator and the participants accept in the mediation process shall be agreed upon. The mediator shall instruct the participants that either of them or the mediator has the right to suspend or terminate the process at any time.

E. The mediator shall assess the ability and willingness of the participants to mediate. The mediator has a continuing duty to assess his or her own ability and willingness to undertake mediation with the particular participants and the issues to be mediated. The mediator shall not continue and shall terminate the process, if in his or her judgment, one of the parties is not able or willing to participate in good faith.

F. The mediator shall explain the fees for mediation. It is inappropriate for a mediator to charge a contingency fee or to base the fee on the outcome of the mediation process.

G. The mediator shall inform the participants of the need to employ independent legal counsel for advice throughout the mediation process. The mediator shall inform the participants that the mediator cannot represent either or both of them in a marital dissolution or in any legal action.

H. The mediator shall discuss the issue of separate sessions. The mediator shall reach an understanding with the participants as to whether and under what circumstances the mediator may meet alone with either of them or with any third party. [**ABA Commentary to Paragraph H:** The mediator cannot act as lawyer for either party or for them jointly and should make that clear to both parties.]

I. It should be brought to the participants' attention that emotions play a part in the decision-making process. The mediator shall attempt to elicit from each of the participants a confirmation that each understands the connection between one's own emotions and the bargaining process.

Standard II.   The mediator shall not voluntarily disclose information obtained through the mediation process without the prior consent of both participants.

SPECIFIC CONSIDERATIONS

A. At the outset of mediation, the parties should agree in writing not to require the mediator to disclose to any third party any statements made in the course of mediation. The mediator shall inform the participants that the mediator will not voluntarily disclose to any third party any of the information obtained through the mediation process, unless such disclosure is required by law, without the prior consent of the participants. The mediator also shall inform the parties of the limitations of confidentiality such as statutory or judicially mandated reporting.

B. If subpoenaed or otherwise noticed to testify, the mediator shall inform the participants immediately so as to afford them an opportunity to quash the process.

C. The mediator shall inform the participants of the mediator's inability to bind third parties to an agreement not to disclose information furnished during the mediation in the absence of any absolute privilege.

Standard III.   The mediator has a duty to be impartial.

SPECIFIC CONSIDERATIONS

A. The mediator shall not represent either party during or after the mediation process in any legal matters. In the event the mediator has represented one of the parties beforehand, the mediator shall not undertake the mediation.

B. The mediator shall disclose to the participants any biases or strong views relating to the issues to be mediated, both in the orientation session, and also before these issues are discussed in mediation.

C. The mediator must be impartial as between the mediation participants. The mediator's task is to facilitate the ability of the participants to negotiate their own agreement, while raising questions as to the fairness, equity and feasibility of proposed options for settlement.

D. The mediator has a duty to ensure that the participants consider fully the best interests of the children, that they understand the consequences of any decision they reach concerning the children. The mediator also has a duty to assist parents to examine the separate and individual needs of their children and to consider those needs apart from their own desires for any particular parenting formula. If the mediator believes that any proposed agreement of the parent does not protect the best interests of the children, the mediator has a duty to inform them of this belief and its basis.

E. The mediator shall not communicate with either party alone or with any third party to discuss mediation issues without the prior consent of the mediation participants. The mediator shall obtain an agreement from the participants during the orientation session as to whether and under what circumstances the mediator may speak directly and separately with each of their lawyers during the mediation process.

Standard IV.   The mediator has a duty to assure that the mediation participants make decisions based upon sufficient information and knowledge.

SPECIFIC CONSIDERATIONS

A. The mediator shall assure that there is full financial disclosure, evaluation and development of relevant factual information in the mediation process, such as each would reasonably receive in the discovery process, or that the parties have sufficient information to intelligently waive the right to such disclosure.

B. In addition to requiring this disclosure, evaluation and development of information, the mediator shall promote the equal understanding of such information before any agreement is reached. This consideration may require the mediator to recommend that either or both obtain expert consultation in the event that it appears that additional knowledge or understanding is necessary for balanced negotiations.

C. The mediator may define the legal issues, but shall not direct the decision of the mediation participants based upon the mediator's interpretation of the law as applied to the facts of the situation. The mediator shall endeavor to assure that the participants have a sufficient understanding of appropriate statutory and case law as well as local judicial tradition, before reaching an agreement by recommending to the participants that they obtain independent legal representation during the process.

Standard V.   The mediator has a duty to suspend or terminate mediation whenever continuation of the process would harm one or more of the participants.

SPECIFIC CONSIDERATIONS

A. If the mediator believes that the participants are unable or unwilling to meaningfully participate in the process or that reasonable agreement is unlikely, the mediator may suspend or terminate mediation and should encourage the parties to seek appropriate professional help. The mediator shall recognize that the decisions are to be made by the parties on the basis of adequate information. The mediator shall not, however, participate in a process that the mediator believes will result in harm to a participant.

B. The mediator shall assure that each person has had the opportunity to understand fully the implications and ramifications of all options available.

C. The mediator has a duty to assure a balanced dialogue and must attempt to diffuse any manipulative or intimidating negotiation techniques utilized by either of the participants.

D. If the mediator has suspended or terminated the process, the mediator should suggest that the participants obtain additional professional services as may be appropriate.

Standard VI. The mediator has a continuing duty to advise each of the mediation participants to obtain legal review prior to reaching any agreement.

SPECIFIC CONSIDERATIONS

A. Each of the mediation participants should have independent legal counsel before reaching final agreement. At the beginning of the mediation process, the mediator should inform the participants that each should employ independent legal counsel for advice at the beginning of the process and that the independent legal counsel should be utilized throughout the process and before the participants have reached any accord to which they have made an emotional commitment. In order to promote the integrity of the process, the mediator shall not refer either of the participants to any particular lawyers. When an attorney referral is requested, the parties should be referred to a Bar Association list if available. In the absence of such a list, the mediator may only provide a list of qualified family law attorneys in the community.

B. The mediator shall inform the participants that the mediator cannot represent either or both of them in a marital dissolution.

C. The mediator shall obtain an agreement from the husband and the wife that each lawyer, upon request, shall be entitled to review all the factual documentation provided by the participants in the mediation process.

D. Any memo of understanding or proposed agreement which is prepared in the mediation process should be separately reviewed by independent counsel for each participant before it is signed. While a mediator cannot insist that each participant have separate counsel, they should be discouraged from signing any agreement which has not been so reviewed. If the participants, or either of them, choose to proceed without independent counsel, the mediator shall warn them of any risk involved in not being represented, including where appropriate, the possibility that the agreement they submit to a court may be rejected as unreasonable in light of both parties' legal rights or may not be binding on them.

CODE OF ETHICS OF THE AMERICAN ARBITRATION ASSOCIATION FOR ARBITRATORS IN COMMERCIAL DISPUTES*

Editors' Note. The American Arbitration Association is the nation's most prominent private sponsor of dispute resolution through arbitration and other techniques. Many private contracts specifically require that disputes arising

*Reprinted with permission of the American Arbitration Association.

under them be resolved before the AAA. The AAA Code that follows was adopted in 1977. The Code is intended as a guide for commercial arbitrators but it is not an official part of the Association's rules.

PREAMBLE

The use of commercial arbitration to resolve a wide variety of disputes has grown extensively and forms a significant part of the system of justice which our society relies upon for the fair determination of legal rights. Persons who act as commercial arbitrators therefore undertake serious responsibilities to the public as well as to the parties. These responsibilities include important ethical obligations.

Few cases of unethical behavior by commercial arbitrators have arisen. Nevertheless, the American Bar Association and the American Arbitration Association believe that it is in the public interest to set forth generally accepted standards of ethical conduct for the guidance of arbitrators and parties in commercial disputes. By establishing this Code, the sponsors hope to contribute to the maintenance of high standards and continued confidence in the process of arbitration.

There are many different types of commercial arbitration. Some cases are conducted under arbitration rules established by various organizations and trade associations, while others are carried on without such rules. Although most cases are arbitrated pursuant to voluntary agreement of the parties, certain types of disputes are submitted to arbitration by reason of particular laws. This Code is intended to apply to all such proceedings in which disputes or claims are submitted for decision to one or more arbitrators appointed in a manner provided by an agreement of the parties, by applicable arbitration rules or by law. In all such cases the persons who have the power to decide should observe fundamental standards of ethical conduct. In this Code all such persons are called "arbitrators," although in some types of cases they may be called "umpires" or may have some other title.

Various aspects of the conduct of arbitrators, including some matters covered by this Code, may be governed by agreements of the parties, by arbitration rules to which the parties have agreed, or by applicable law. This Code does not take the place of, or supersede, any such agreements, rules and laws and does not establish any new or additional grounds for judicial review of arbitration awards.

While this Code is intended to provide ethical guidelines in many types of arbitration, it does not form part of the arbitration rules of the American Arbitration Association or of any other organization, nor is it intended to apply to mediation or conciliation. Labor arbitrations are governed by the "Code of Professional Responsibility for Arbitrators of Labor-Management Disputes," not by this Code.

Arbitrators, like judges, have the power to decide cases. However, unlike full-time judges, arbitrators are usually engaged in other occupations before, during and after the time they serve as arbitrators. Often arbitrators are purposely chosen from the same trade or industry as the parties in order to bring special knowledge to the task of deciding. This Code recognizes these fundamental differences between arbitrators and judges.

In some types of arbitration there are three, or more, arbitrators. In these cases, it is sometimes the practice for each party, acting alone, to appoint one arbitrator and for the other arbitrator(s) to be designated by those two, or by the parties, or by an independent institution or individual. The sponsors of this Code believe that it is preferable for parties to agree that all arbitrators should comply with the same ethical standards. However, it is recognized that there is a long-established practice in some types of arbitration for those arbitrators who are appointed by one party, acting alone, to be governed by special ethical considerations. Those special considerations are set forth in the last section of the Code, headed "Ethical Considerations Relating to Arbitrators Appointed By One Party."

Although this Code is sponsored by the American Arbitration Association and the American Bar Association, its use is not limited to arbitrations administered by the AAA or to cases in which the arbitrators are lawyers. Rather, it is presented as a public service to provide guidance in all types of commercial arbitration.

CANON I. AN ARBITRATOR SHOULD UPHOLD THE INTEGRITY AND FAIRNESS OF THE ARBITRATION PROCESS

A. Fair and just processes for resolving disputes are indispensable in our society. Commercial arbitration is an important method for deciding many types of disputes. In order for commercial arbitration to be effective, there must be broad public confidence in the integrity and fairness of the process. Therefore, an arbitrator has a responsibility not only to the parties but also to the process of arbitration itself, and must observe high standards of conduct so that the integrity and fairness of the process will be preserved. Accordingly, an arbitrator should recognize a responsibility to the public, to the parties whose rights will be decided, and to all other participants in the proceeding. The provisions of this Code should be construed and applied to further these objectives.

B. It is inconsistent with the integrity of the arbitration process for persons to solicit appointment for themselves. However, a person may indicate a general willingness to serve as an arbitrator.

C. Persons should accept appointment as arbitrators only if they believe that they can be available to conduct the arbitration promptly.

D. After accepting appointment and while serving as an arbitrator, a person should avoid entering into any financial, business, professional, family or social relationship, or acquiring any financial or personal interest, which is

likely to affect impartiality or which might reasonably create the appearance of partiality or bias. For a reasonable period of time after the decision of a case, persons who have served as arbitrators should avoid entering into any such relationship, or acquiring any such interest, in circumstances which might reasonably create the appearance that they had been influenced in the arbitration by the anticipation or expectation of the relationship or interest.

E. Arbitrators should conduct themselves in a way that is fair to all parties and should not be swayed by outside pressure, by public clamor, or fear of criticism or by self-interest.

F. When an arbitrator's authority is derived from an agreement of the parties, the arbitrator should neither exceed that authority nor do less than is required to exercise that authority completely. Where the agreement of the parties sets forth procedures to be followed in conducting the arbitration or refers to rules to be followed, it is the obligation of the arbitrator to comply with such procedures or rules.

G. An arbitrator should make all reasonable efforts to prevent delaying tactics, harassment of parties or other participants, or other abuse or disruption of the arbitration process.

H. The ethical obligations of an arbitrator begin upon acceptance of the appointment and continue throughout all stages of the proceeding. In addition, wherever specifically set forth in this Code, certain ethical obligations begin as soon as a person is requested to serve as an arbitrator and certain ethical obligations continue even after the decision in the case has been given to the parties.

CANON II. AN ARBITRATOR SHOULD DISCLOSE ANY INTEREST OR RELATIONSHIP LIKELY TO AFFECT IMPARTIALITY OR WHICH MIGHT CREATE AN APPEARANCE OF PARTIALITY OR BIAS

Introductory Note:

This Code reflects the prevailing principle that arbitrators should disclose the existence of any interests or relationships which are likely to affect their impartiality or which might reasonably create the appearance that they are biased against one party or favorable to another. These provisions of the Code are intended to be applied realistically so that the burden of detailed disclosure does not become so great that it is impractical for persons in the business world to be arbitrators, thereby depriving parties of the services of those who might be best informed and qualified to decide particular types of cases.*

This Code does not limit the freedom of parties to agree on anyone they choose as an arbitrator. When parties, with knowledge of a person's interests and relationships, nevertheless desire that individual to serve as an arbitrator, that person may properly serve.

Disclosure:

A. Persons who are requested to serve as arbitrators should, before accepting, disclose:

(1) Any direct or indirect financial or personal interest in the outcome of the arbitration;

(2) Any existing or past financial, business, professional, family or social relationships which are likely to affect impartiality or which might reasonably create an appearance of partiality or bias. Persons requested to serve as arbitrators should disclose any such relationships which they personally have with any party or its lawyer, or with any individual whom they have been told will be a witness. They should also disclose any such relationships involving members of their families or their current employers, partners or business associates.

B. Persons who are requested to accept appointment as arbitrators should make a reasonable effort to inform themselves of any interests or relationships described in Paragraph A above.

C. The obligation to disclose interests or relationships described in Paragraph A above is a continuing duty which requires a person who accepts appointment as an arbitrator to disclose, at any stage of the arbitration, any such interests or relationships which may arise, or which are recalled or discovered.

D. Disclosure should be made to all parties unless other procedures for disclosure are provided in the rules or practices of an institution which is administering the arbitration. Where more than one arbitrator has been appointed, each should inform the others of the interests and relationships which have been disclosed.

E. In the event that an arbitrator is requested by all parties to withdraw, the arbitrator should do so. In the event that an arbitrator is requested to with-

*In applying the provisions of this Code relating to disclosure, it may be helpful to recall the words of the concurring opinion in a case decided by the United States Supreme Court, that arbitrators "should err on the side of disclosure" because "it is better that the relationship be disclosed at the outset when the parties are free to reject the arbitrator or accept him with knowledge of the relationship." At the same time, it must be recognized that "an arbitrator's business relationships may be diverse indeed, involving more or less remote commercial connections with great numbers of people." Accordingly, an arbitrator "cannot be expected to provide the parties with his complete and unexpurgated business biography," nor is an arbitrator called upon to disclose interests or relationships which are merely "trivial." (Concurring opinion in Commonwealth Coatings Corp. v. Continental Casualty Co., 393 U.S. 145, 151-152 (1968).)

draw by less than all of the parties because of alleged partiality or bias, the arbitrator should withdraw unless either of the following circumstances exists:

(1) If an agreement of the parties, or arbitration rules agreed to by the parties, establishes procedures for determining challenges to arbitrators, then those procedures should be followed; or

(2) If the arbitrator, after carefully considering the matter, determines that the reason for the challenge is not substantial, and that he or she can nevertheless act and decide the case impartially and fairly, and that withdrawal would cause unfair delay or expense to another party or would be contrary to the ends of justice.

CANON III. AN ARBITRATOR IN COMMUNICATING WITH THE PARTIES SHOULD AVOID IMPROPRIETY OR THE APPEARANCE OF IMPROPRIETY

A. If an agreement of the parties, or any applicable arbitration rules referred to in that agreement, establishes the manner or content of communications between the arbitrator and the parties, the arbitrator should follow those procedures notwithstanding any contrary provisions of the following Paragraphs B and C.

B. Unless otherwise provided in applicable arbitration rules or in an agreement of the parties, arbitrators should not discuss a case with any party in the absence of each other party, except in any of the following circumstances:

(1) Discussions may be had with a party concerning such matters as setting the time and place of hearings or making other arrangements for the conduct of the proceedings. However, the arbitrator should promptly inform each other party of the discussion and should not make any final determination concerning the matter discussed before giving each absent party an opportunity to express its views.

(2) If a party fails to be present at a hearing after having been given due notice, the arbitrator may discuss the case with any party who is present.

(3) If all parties request or consent that such discussion take place.

C. Unless otherwise provided in applicable arbitration rules or in an agreement of the parties, whenever an arbitrator communicates in writing with one party, the arbitrator should at the same time send a copy of the communication to each other party. Whenever an arbitrator receives any written communication concerning the case from one party which has not already been sent to each other party, the arbitrator should do so.

CANON IV. AN ARBITRATOR SHOULD
CONDUCT THE PROCEEDINGS
FAIRLY AND DILIGENTLY

A. An arbitrator should conduct the proceedings in an evenhanded manner and treat all parties with equality and fairness at all stages of the proceedings.

B. An arbitrator should perform duties diligently and conclude the case as promptly as the circumstances reasonably permit.

C. An arbitrator should be patient and courteous to the parties, to their lawyers and to the witnesses and should encourage similar conduct by all participants in the proceedings.

D. Unless otherwise agreed by the parties or provided in arbitration rules agreed to by the parties, an arbitrator should accord to all parties the right to appear in person and to be heard after due notice of the time and place of hearing.

E. An arbitrator should not deny any party the opportunity to be represented by counsel.

F. If a party fails to appear after due notice, an arbitrator should proceed with the arbitration when authorized to do so by the agreement of the parties, the rules agreed to by the parties or by law. However, an arbitrator should do so only after receiving assurance that notice has been given to the absent party.

G. When an arbitrator determines that more information than has been presented by the parties is required to decide the case, it is not improper for the arbitrator to ask questions, call witnesses, and request documents or other evidence.

H. It is not improper for an arbitrator to suggest to the parties that they discuss the possibility of settlement of the case. However, an arbitrator should not be present or otherwise participate in the settlement discussions unless requested to do so by all parties. An arbitrator should not exert pressure on any party to settle.

I. Nothing in this Code is intended to prevent a person from acting as a mediator or conciliator of a dispute in which he or she has been appointed as arbitrator, if requested to do so by all parties or where authorized or required to do so by applicable laws or rules.

J. When there is more than one arbitrator, the arbitrators should afford each other the full opportunuty to participate in all aspects of the proceedings.

CANON V. AN ARBITRATOR SHOULD MAKE DECISIONS IN A JUST, INDEPENDENT AND DELIBERATE MANNER

A. An arbitrator should, after careful deliberation, decide all issues submitted for determination. An arbitrator should decide no other issues.

B. An arbitrator should decide all matters justly, exercising independent judgment, and should not permit outside pressure to affect the decision.

C. An arbitrator should not delegate the duty to decide to any other person.

D. In the event that all parties agree upon a settlement of the issues in dispute and request an arbitrator to embody that agreement in an award, an arbitrator may do so, but is not required to do so unless satisfied with the propriety of the terms of settlement. Whenever an arbitrator embodies a settlement by the parties in an award, the arbitrator should state in the award that it is based on an agreement of the parties.

CANON VI. AN ARBITRATOR SHOULD BE FAITHFUL TO THE RELATIONSHIP OF TRUST AND CONFIDENTIALITY INHERENT IN THAT OFFICE

A. An arbitrator is in a relationship of trust to the parties and should not, at any time, use confidential information acquired during the arbitration proceeding to gain personal advantage or advantage for others, or to affect adversely the interest of another.

B. Unless otherwise agreed by the parties, or required by applicable rules or law, an arbitrator should keep confidential all matters relating to the arbitration proceedings and decision.

C. It is not proper at any time for an arbitrator to inform anyone of the decision in advance of the time it is given to all parties. In a case in which there is more than one arbitrator, it is not proper at any time for an arbitrator to inform anyone concerning the deliberations of the arbitrators. After an arbitration award has been made, it is not proper for an arbitrator to assist in any post-arbitration proceedings, except as may be required by law.

D. In many types of arbitration it is customary practice for the arbitrators to serve without pay. However, in some types of cases it is customary for arbitrators to receive compensation for their services and reimbursement for their expenses. In cases in which any such payments are to be made, all persons

517

who are requested to serve, or who are serving as arbitrators, should be governed by the same high standards of integrity and fairness as apply to their other activities in the case. Accordingly, such persons should srcupulously avoid bargaining with parties over the amount of payments or engaging in any communications concerning payments which would create an appearance of coercion or other impropriety. In the absence of governing provisions in the agreement of the parties or in rules agreed to by the parties or in applicable law, certain practices relating to payments are generally recognized as being preferable in order to preserve the integrity and fairness of the arbitration process. These practices include:

(1) It is preferable that before the arbitrator finally accepts appointment the basis of payment be established and that all parties be informed therof in writing.

(2) In cases conducted under the rules or administration of an institution which is available to assist in making arrangements for payments, the payments should be arranged by the institution to avoid the necessity for communication by the arbitrators directly with the parties concerning the subject.

(3) In cases where no institution is available to assist in making arrangements for payments, it is preferable that any discussions with arbitrators concerning payments should take place in the presence of all parties.

CANON VII. ETHICAL CONSIDERATIONS RELATING TO ARBITRATORS APPOINTED BY ONE PARTY

Editors' Note. As of February 1990, the American Arbitration Association and American Bar Association began considering a proposal to replace the third paragraph of the Introductory Note to Canon VII with the following:

Many commercial arbitrations now involve parties from different countries, sometimes including governmental trading or other organizations. While these arbitrations often are similar to arbitrations between two American parties and involve the same considerations of arbitrator ethics, in international proceedings there may be a heightened need to assure impartiality of all the decisionmakers. Whether these arbitrations occur in the United States or elsewhere, the standards of arbitrator neutrality applied may affect international enforceability of the award. Arbitrators in all international commercial matters should, to the extent practicable in the circumstances, serve as neutrals.

Introductory Note:

In some types of arbitration in which there are three arbitrators it is customary for each party, acting alone, to appoint one arbitrator. The third arbitrator is then appointed either by agreement of the parties or of the two arbitrators, or, failing such agreement, by an independent institution or individual. In some of these types of arbitration, all three arbitrators are customarily considered to be neutral and are expected to observe the same standards of ethical conduct. However, there are also many types of tripartite arbitration in which it has been the practice that the two arbitrators appointed by the parties are not considered to be neutral and are expected to observe many — but not all — of the same ethical standards as the neutral third arbitrator. For the purposes of this Code, an arbitrator appointed by one party who is not expected to observe all of the same standards as the third arbitrator is referred to as a "non-neutral arbitrator." This Canon VII describes the ethical obligations which non-neutral party-appointed arbitrators should observe and those which are not applicable to them.

In all arbitrations in which there are two or more party-appointed arbitrators, it is important for everyone concerned to know from the start whether the party-appointed arbitrators are expected to be neutrals or non-neutrals. In such arbitrations, the two party-appointed arbitrators should be considered non-neutrals unless both parties inform the arbitrators that all three arbitrators are to be neutral, or unless the contract, the applicable arbitration rules, or any governing law requires that all three arbitrators are to be neutral.

It should be noted that in cases where the arbitration is conducted outside the United States the applicable law may require that all arbitrators be neutral. Accordingly, in such cases the governing law should be considered before applying any of the following provisions relating to non-neutral party-appointed arbitrators.

A. Obligations Under Canon I

Non-neutral party-appointed arbitrators should observe all of the obligations of Canon I to uphold the integrity and fairness of the arbitration process, subject only to the following provisions:

(1) Non-neutral arbitrators may be predisposed toward the party who appointed them but in all other respects are obligated to act in good faith and with integrity and fairness. For example, non-neutral arbitrators should not engage in delaying tactics or harassment of any party or witness and should not knowingly make untrue or misleading statements to the other arbitrators.

(2) The provisions of Canon I-D relating to relationships and interests are not applicable to non-neutral arbitrators.

B. Obligations Under Canon II

Non-neutral party-appointed arbitrators should disclose to all parties, and to the other arbitrators, all interests and relationships which Canon II requires be disclosed. Disclosure as required by Canon II is for the benefit not only of the party who appointed the non-neutral arbitrator, but also for the benefit of the other parties and arbitrators so that they may know of any bias which may exist or appear to exist. However, this obligation is subject to the following provisions:

(1) Disclosure by non-neutral arbitrators should be sufficient to describe the general nature and scope of any interest or relationship, but need not include as detailed information as is expected from persons appointed as neutral arbitrators.

(2) Non-neutral arbitrators are not obligated to withdraw if requested to do so by the party who did not appoint them, notwithstanding the provisions of Canon II-E.

C. Obligations Under Canon III

Non-neutral party-appointed arbitrators should observe all of the obligations of Canon III concerning communications with the parties, subject only to the following provisions:

(1) In an arbitration in which the two party-appointed arbitrators are expected to appoint the third arbitrator, non-neutral arbitrators may consult with the party who appointed them concerning the acceptability of persons under consideration for appointment as the third arbitrator.

(2) Non-neutral arbitrators may communicate with the party who appointed them concerning any other aspect of the case, provided they first inform the other arbitrators and the parties that they intend to do so. If such communication occurred prior to the time the person was appointed as arbitrator, or prior to the first hearing or other meeting of the parties with the arbitrators, the non-neutral arbitrator should at the first hearing or meeting, disclose the fact that such communication has taken place. In complying with the provisions of this paragraph, it is sufficient that there be disclosure of the fact that such communication has occurred without disclosing the content of the communication. It is also sufficient to disclose at any time the intention to follow the procedure of having such communications in the future and there is no requirement thereafter that there be disclosure before each separate occasion on which such a communication occurs.

(3) When non-neutral arbitrators communicate in writing with the party who appointed them concerning any matter as to which communication is permitted under this Code, they are not required to send copies of any such written communications to any other party or arbitrator.

D. Obligations Under Canon IV

Non-neutral party-appointed arbitrators should observe all of the obligations of Canon IV to conduct the proceedings fairly and diligently.

E. Obligations Under Canon V

Non-neutral party-appointed arbitrators should observe all of the obligations of Canon V concerning making decisions, subject only to the following provision:

(1) Non-neutral arbitrators are permitted to be predisposed toward deciding in favor of the party who appointed them.

F. Obligations Under Canon VI

Non-neutral party-appointed arbitrators should observe all of the obligations of Canon VI to be faithful to the relationship of trust inherent in the office of arbitrator, subject only to the following provision:

(1) Non-neutral arbitrators are not subject to the provisions of Canon VI-D with respect to any payments by the party who appointed them.

ETHICAL STANDARDS OF PROFESSIONAL CONDUCT OF THE SOCIETY OF PROFESSIONALS IN DISPUTE RESOLUTION*

> **Editors' Note.** The Society of Professionals in Dispute Resolution (SPIDR) was formed in 1973 and consists of about 1,700 members (called "neutrals") who have at least three years of experience in various forms of dispute resolution. SPIDR's ethical standards were adopted in 1986, effective January 1989. SPIDR's goals include furthering the dispute resolution skills of its members and increasing the public's understanding and acceptance of the role of neutrals in dispute resolution.

INTRODUCTION

The Society for Professionals in Dispute Resolution was established in 1973 to promote the peaceful resolution of disputes. Members of the society believe that

*Copyright © 1986 by the Society of Professionals in Dispute Resolution, Inc. Reprinted with permission of the Society of Professionals in Dispute Resolution, Inc.

resolving disputes through negotiation, mediation, arbitration, and other neutral interventions can be of great benefit to disputing parties and to society. In 1983, the SPIDR Board charged the Ethics Committee with the task of developing ethical standards of professional responsibility. The committee membership represented all the various sectors and disciplines within SPIDR. This document, adopted by the Board on June 2, 1986, is the result of that charge.

The purpose of this document is to promote among SPIDR members and associates ethical conduct and a high level of competency among SPIDR members, including honesty, integrity, impartiality, and the exercise of good judgment in their dispute resolution efforts. It is hoped that this document also will help to (1) define the profession of dispute resolution, (2) educate the public, and (3) inform users of dispute resolution services.

APPLICATION OF STANDARDS

Adherence to these ethical standards by SPIDR members and associates is basic to professional responsibility. SPIDR members and associates commit themselves to be guided in their professional conduct by these standards. The SPIDR Board of Directors or its designee is available to advise members and associates about interpretation of these standards. Other neutral practitioners and organizations are welcome to follow these standards.

SCOPE

It is recognized that SPIDR members and associates resolve disputes in various sectors within the disciplines of dispute resolution and have their own codes of professional conduct. These standards have been developed as general guidelines of practice for neutral disciplines represented in the SPIDR membership. Ethical considerations relevant to some, but not to all, of these disciplines are not covered by these standards.

GENERAL RESPONSIBILITIES

Neutrals have a duty to the parties, to the profession, and to themselves. They should be honest and unbiased, act in good faith, be diligent, and not seek to advance their own interests at the expense of the parties.

Neutrals must act fairly in dealing with the parties, have no personal interest in the terms of the settlement, show no bias toward individuals and institutions involved in the dispute, be reasonably available as requested by the parties, and be certain that the parties are informed of the process in which they are involved.

RESPONSIBILITIES TO THE PARTIES

1. Impartiality

The neutral must maintain impartiality toward all parties. Impartiality means freedom from favoritism or bias either by word or by action, and a commitment to serve all parties as opposed to a single party.

2. Informed Consent

The neutral has an obligation to assure that all parties understand the nature of the process, the procedures, the particular role of the neutral, and the parties' relationship to the neutral.

3. Confidentiality

Maintaining confidentiality is critical to the dispute resolution process. Confidentiality encourages candor, a full exploration of the issues, and a neutral's acceptability. There may be some types of cases, however, in which confidentiality is not protected. In such cases, the neutral must advise the parties, when appropriate in the dispute resolution process, that the confidentiality of the proceedings cannot necessarily be maintained. Except in such instances, the neutral must resist all attempts to cause him or her to reveal any information outside the process. A commitment by the neutral to hold information in confidence within the process also must be honored.

4. Conflict of Interest

The neutral must refrain from entering or continuing in any dispute if he or she believes or perceives the participation as a neutral would be a clear conflict of interest. The neutral also must disclose any circumstances that may create or give the appearance of a conflict of interest and any circumstances that may reasonably raise a question as to the neutral's impartiality.

The duty to disclose is a continuing obligation throughout the process.

5. Promptness

The neutral shall exert every reasonable effort to expedite the process.

6. The Settlement and Its Consequences

The dispute resolution process belongs to the parties. The neutral has no vested interest in the terms of a settlement, but must be satisfied that agreements in which he or she has participated will not impugn the integrity of the process. The neutral has a responsibility to see that the parties consider the terms of a settlement. If the neutral is concerned about the possible consequences of a proposed agreement, and the needs of the parties dictate, the neutral must inform the parties of that concern. In adhering to this standard, the neutral may find it advisable to educate the parties, to refer one or more parties for specialized advice, or to withdraw from the case. In no case, however, shall the neutral violate section 3 above, Confidentiality, of these standards.

UNREPRESENTED INTERESTS

The neutral must consider circumstances where interests are not represented in the process. The neutral has an obligation, where in his or her judgment the needs of the parties dictate, to assure that such interests have been considered by the principal parties.

USE OF MULTIPLE PROCEDURES

The use of more than one dispute resolution procedure by the same neutral involves additional responsibilities. Where the use of more than one procedure is initially contemplated, the neutral must take care at the outset to advise the parties of the nature of the procedures and the consequences of revealing information during any one procedure which the neutral may later use for decision making or may share with another decision maker. Where the use of more than one procedure is contemplated after the initiation of the dispute resolution process, the neutral must explain the consequences and afford the parties an opportunity to select another neutral for the subsequent procedures. It is also incumbent upon the neutral to advise the parties of the transition from one dispute resolution process to another.

BACKGROUND AND QUALIFICATIONS

A neutral should accept responsibility only in cases where the neutral has sufficient knowledge regarding the appropriate process and subject matter to be effective. A neutral has a responsibility to maintain and improve his or her professional skills.

DISCLOSURE OF FEES

It is the duty of the neutral to explain to the parties at the outset of the process, the bases of compensation, fees, and charges, if any.

SUPPORT OF THE PROFESSION

The experienced neutral should participate in the development of new practitioners in the field and engage in efforts to educate the public about the value and use of neutral dispute resolution procedures. The neutral should provide pro bono services, as appropriate.

RESPONSIBILITIES OF NEUTRALS WORKING
ON THE SAME CASE

In the event that more than one neutral is involved in the resolution of a dispute, each has an obligation to inform the others regarding his or her entry in the case. Neutrals working with the same parties should maintain an open and professional relationship with each other.

ADVERTISING AND SOLICITATION

A neutral must be aware that some forms of advertising and solicitations are inappropriate and in some conflict resolution disciplines, such as labor arbitration, are impermissible. All advertising must honestly represent the services to be rendered. No claims of specific results or promises which imply favor of one side over another for the purpose of obtaining business should be made. No commissions, rebates, or other similar forms of remuneration should be given or received by a neutral for the referral of clients.

CODE OF CONDUCT FOR LAWYERS IN THE EUROPEAN COMMUNITY

Editors' Note. In 1988, twelve national delegations representing the bars and law societies of the European Community unanimously adopted a Code of Conduct for Lawyers in the European Community. The Code is based on the 1977 Declaration of Perugia and applies to the "cross-border" activities of all lawyers in the twelve member states of the European community — Belgium, Denmark, France, Germany, Greece, Ireland, Italy, Luxembourg, the Netherlands, Portugal, Spain, and the United Kingdom. (Lawyers in these countries go by various names, including advocates, barristers, solicitors, "Rechtsanwalt," "dikogoros," and "procuratore.") In addition, observer delegations from Austria, Norway, Sweden, Switzerland, Finland, and Cyprus, which are not members of the EEC, participated in the work of the Code. A comment to the Code expresses hope that the Code can be applied "by appropriate conventions" to lawyers in these observer countries and in "other non-Member States in Europe and elsewhere. . . ."

The Code does not replace or supersede the internal rules and regulations governing lawyers in any of the signatory states. It applies only to "cross-border" activities of lawyers. "Cross-border" activities include all contacts, whether in person, by telephone, or by written communication, between lawyers of two or more different countries, and all professional activities of a lawyer in a country other than his own. The Code does not govern contacts between two or more lawyers of the same country concerning the law of another country.

1. Preamble

1.1. The Function of the Lawyer in Society

In a society founded on respect for the rule of law the lawyer fulfils a special role. His duties do not begin and end with the faithful performance of what he is instructed to do so far as the law permits. A lawyer must serve the interests of justice as well as those whose rights and liberties he is trusted to assert and defend and it is his duty not only to plead his client's cause but to be his adviser.

A lawyer's function therefore lays on him a variety of legal and moral obligations (sometimes appearing to be in conflict with each other) towards:

the client;

the courts and other authorities before whom the lawyer pleads his client's cause or acts on his behalf;

the legal profession in general and each fellow member of it in particular; and

the public for whom the existence of a free and independent profession, bound together by respect for rules made by the profession itself, is an essential means of safeguarding human rights in face of the power of the state and other interests in society.

1.2. The Nature of Rules of Professional Conduct

1.2.1. Rules of professional conduct are designed through their willing acceptance by those to whom they apply to ensure the proper performance by the lawyer of a function which is recognised as essential in all civilised societies. The failure of the lawyer to observe these rules must in the last resort result in a disciplinary sanction.

1.2.2. The particular rules of each Bar or Law Society arise from its own traditions. They are adapted to the organisation and sphere of activity of the profession in the Member State concerned and to its judicial and administrative procedures and to its national legislation. It is neither possible nor desirable that they should be taken out of their context nor that an attempt should be made to give general application to rules which are inherently incapable of such application.

The particular rules of each Bar and Law Society nevertheless are based on the same values and in most cases demonstrate a common foundation.

1.3. The Purpose of the Code

1.3.1. The continued integration of the European Community and the increasing frequency of the cross-border activities of lawyers within the Community have made necessary in the public interest the statement of the common rules which apply to all lawyers from the Community whatever Bar or Law Society they belong to in relation to their cross-border practice. A particular purpose of the statement of those rules is to mitigate the difficulties which result from the application of "double deontology" as set out in Article 4 of the E.C. Directive 77/249 of 22nd March 1977.

1.3.2. The organisations representing the legal profession through the CCBE propose that the rules codified in the following articles:

be recognised at the present time as the expression of a consensus of all the Bars and Law Societies of the European Community;

be adopted as enforceable rules as soon as possible in accordance with national or Community procedures in relation to the cross-border activities of the lawyer in the European Community;

be taken into account in all revisions of national rules of deontology or professional practice with a view to their progressive harmonisation.

They further express the wish that the national rules of deontology or professional practice be interpreted and applied whenever possible in a way consistent with the rules of this Code.

After the rules in this Code have been adopted as enforceable rules in relation to his cross-border activities the lawyer will remain bound to observe the rules of the Bar or Law Society to which he belongs to the extent that they are consistent with the rules in this Code.

1.4. Field of Application Ratione Personae

The following rules shall apply to lawyers of the European Community as they are defined by the Directive 77/249 of 22nd March 1977.

1.5. Field of Application Ratione Materiae

Without prejudice to the pursuit of a progressive harmonisation of rules of deontology or professional practice which apply only internally within a Member State, the following rules shall apply to the cross-border activities of the lawyer within the European Community. Cross-border activities shall mean:

(a) all professional contacts with lawyers of Member States other than his own; and

(b) the professional activities of the lawyer in a Member State other than his own, whether or not the lawyer is physically present in that Member State.

1.6. Definitions

In these rules:

"Home Member State" means the Member State of the Bar or Law Society to which the lawyer belongs.

"Host Member State" means any other Member State where the lawyer carries on cross-border activities.

"Competent authority" means the professional organisation(s) or authority(ies) of the Member State concerned responsible for the laying down of rules of professional conduct and the administration of discipline of lawyers.

2. *General Principles*

2.1. Independence

2.1.1. The many duties to which a lawyer is subject require his absolute independence, free from any other influence, especially such as may arise from his personal interests or external pressure. Such independence is as necessary to trust in the process of justice as the impartiality of the judge. A lawyer must therefore avoid any impairment of his independence and be careful not to compromise his professional standards in order to please his client, the court or third parties.

2.1.2. This independence is necessary in non-contentious matters as well as in litigation. Advice given by a lawyer to his client has no value if it is given only to ingratiate himself, to serve his personal interests or in response to outside pressure.

2.2. Trust and Personal Integrity

Relationships of trust can only exist if a lawyer's personal honour, honesty and integrity are beyond doubt. For the lawyer these traditional virtues are professional obligations.

2.3. Confidentiality

2.3.1. It is of the essence of a lawyer's function that he should be told by his client things which the client would not tell to others, and that he should be the recipient of other information on a basis of confidence. Without the certainty of confidentiality there cannot be trust. Confidentiality is therefore a primary and fundamental right and duty of the lawyer.

2.3.2. A lawyer shall accordingly respect the confidentiality of all information given to him by his client, or received by him about his client or others in the course of rendering services to his client.

2.3.3. The obligation of confidentiality is not limited in time.

2.3.4. A lawyer shall require his associates and staff and anyone engaged by him in the course of providing professional services to observe the same obligation of confidentiality.

2.4. Respect for the Rules of Other Bars and Law Societies

Under Community Law (in particular under the Directive 77/249 of 22nd March 1977) a lawyer from another Member State may be bound to comply

529

with the rules of the Bar or Law Society of the host Member State. Lawyers have a duty to inform themselves as to the rules which will affect them in the performance of any particular activity.

2.5. Incompatible Occupations

2.5.1. In order to perform his functions with due independence and in a manner which is consistent with his duty to participate in the administration of justice a lawyer is excluded from some occupations.

2.5.2. A lawyer who acts in the representation of the defence of a client in legal proceedings or before any public authorities in a host Member State shall there observe the rules regarding incompatible occupations as they are applied to lawyers of the host Member State.

2.5.3. A lawyer established in a host Member State in which he wishes to participate directly in commercial or other activities not connected with the practice of the law shall respect the rules regarding forbidden or incompatible occupations as they are applied to lawyers of that Member State.

2.6. Personal Publicity

2.6.1. A lawyer should not advertise or seek personal publicity where this is not permitted.

In other cases a lawyer should only advertise or seek personal publicity to the extent and in the manner permitted by the rules to which he is subject.

2.6.2. Advertising and personal publicity shall be regarded as taking place where it is permitted, if the lawyer concerned shows that it was placed for the purpose of reaching clients or potential clients located where such advertising or personal publicity is permitted and its communication elsewhere is incidental.

2.7. The Client's Interests

Subject to due observance of all rules of law and professional conduct, a lawyer must always act in the best interests of his client and must put those interests before his own interests or those of fellow members of the legal profession.

3. Relations with Clients

3.1. Acceptance and Termination of Instructions

3.1.1. A lawyer shall not handle a case for a party except on his instructions. He may, however, act in a case in which he has been instructed by another lawyer who himself acts for the party or where the case has been assigned to him by a competent body.

3.1.2. A lawyer shall advise and represent his client promptly, conscientiously and diligently. He shall undertake personal responsibility for the discharge of the instructions given to him. He shall keep his client informed as to the progress of the matter entrusted to him.

3.1.3. A lawyer shall not handle a matter which he knows or ought to know he is not competent to handle, without co-operating with a lawyer who is competent to handle it.

A lawyer shall not accept instructions unless he can discharge those instructions promptly having regard to the pressure of other work.

3.1.4. A lawyer shall not be entitled to exercise his right to withdraw from a case in such a way or in such circumstances that the client may be unable to find other legal assistance in time to prevent prejudice being suffered by the client.

3.2. Conflict of Interest

3.2.1. A lawyer may not advise, represent or act on behalf of two or more clients in the same matter if there is a conflict, or a significant risk of a conflict, between the interests of those clients.

3.2.2. A lawyer must cease to act for both clients when a conflict of interests arises between those clients and also whenever there is a risk of a breach of confidence or where his independence may be impaired.

3.2.3. A lawyer must also refrain from acting for a new client if there is a risk of a breach of confidences entrusted to the lawyer by a former client or if the knowledge which the lawyer possesses of the affairs of the former client would give an undue advantage to the new client.

3.2.4. Where lawyers are practising in association, paragraphs 3.2.1 to 3.2.3 above shall apply to the association and all its members.

3.3. Pactum de Quota Litis

3.3.1. A lawyer shall not be entitled to make a pactum de quota litis.

3.3.2. By "pactum de quota litis" is meant an agreement between a lawyer and his client entered into prior to the final conclusion of a matter to which the client is a party, by virtue of which the client undertakes to pay the lawyer a share of the result regardless of whether this is represented by a sum of money or by any other benefit achieved by the client upon the conclusion of the matter.

3.3.3. The pactum de quota litis does not include an agreement that fees be charged in proportion to the value of a matter handled by the lawyer if this is in accordance with an officially approved fee scale or under the control of competent authority having jurisdiction over the lawyer.

3.4. Regulation of Fees

3.4.1. A fee charged by a lawyer shall be fully disclosed to his client and shall be fair and reasonable.

3.4.2. Subject to any proper agreement to the contrary between a lawyer and his client fees charged by a lawyer shall be subject to regulation in accordance with the rules applied to members of the Bar or Law Society to which he belongs. If he belongs to more than one Bar or Law Society the rules applied shall be those with the closest connection to the contract between the lawyer and his client.

3.5. Payment on Account

If a lawyer requires a payment on account of his fees and/or disbursements such payment should not exceed a reasonable estimate of the fees and probable disbursements involved.

Failing such payment, a lawyer may withdraw from the case or refuse to handle it, but subject always to paragraph 3.1.4 above.

3.6. Fee Sharing with Non-Lawyers

3.6.1. Subject as after-mentioned a lawyer may not share his fees with a person who is not a lawyer.

3.6.2. The provisions of 3.6.1 above shall not preclude a lawyer from paying a fee, commissions or other compensation to a deceased lawyer's heirs or to a retired lawyer in respect of taking over the deceased or retired lawyer's practice.

3.7. Legal Aid

A lawyer shall inform his client of the availability of legal aid where applicable.

532

3.8. Client's Funds

3.8.1. When lawyers at any time in the course of their practice come into possession of funds on behalf of their clients or third parties (hereinafter called "client's funds") it shall be obligatory:

3.8.1.1. That client's funds shall always be held in an account in a bank or similar institution subject to supervision of Public Authority and that all client's funds received by a lawyer should be paid into such an account unless the client explicitly or by implication agrees that the funds should be dealt with otherwise.

3.8.1.2. That any account in which the client's funds are held in the name of the lawyer should indicate in the title or designation that the funds are held on behalf of the client or clients of the lawyer.

3.8.1.3. That any account or accounts in which client's funds are held in the name of the lawyer should at all times contain a sum which is not less than the total of the client's funds held by the lawyer.

3.8.1.4. That all client's funds should be available for payment to clients on demand or upon such conditions as the client may authorise.

3.8.1.5. That payments made from client's funds on behalf of a client to any other person including

a) payments made to or for one client from funds held for another client and

b) payment of the lawyer's fees

be prohibited except to the extent that they are permitted by law or have the express or implied authority of the client for whom the payment is being made.

3.8.1.6. That the lawyer shall maintain full and accurate records, available to each client on request, showing all his dealings with his client's funds and distinguishing client's funds from other funds held by him.

3.8.1.7. That the competent authorities in all Member States should have powers to allow them to examine and investigate on a confidential basis the financial records of lawyer's client's funds to ascertain whether or not the rules which they make are being complied with and to impose sanctions upon lawyers who fail to comply with those rules.

3.8.2. Subject as aftermentioned, and without prejudice to the rules set out in 3.8.1 above, a lawyer who holds client's funds in the course of carrying on practice in any Member State must comply with the rules relating to holding and accounting for client's funds which are applied by the competent authorities of the Home Member State.

3.8.3. A lawyer who carries on practice or provides services in a Host Member State may with agreement of the competent authorities of the Home and Host Member State concerned comply with the requirements of the Host Member State to the exclusion of the requirements of the Home Member State. In that event he shall take reasonable steps to inform his clients that he complies with the requirements in force in the Host Member State.

3.9. Professional Indemnity Insurance

3.9.1. Lawyers shall be insured at all times against claims based on professional negligence to an extent which is reasonable having regard to the nature and extent of the risks which lawyers incur in practice.

3.9.2.1. Subject as aftermentioned, a lawyer who provides services or carries on practice in a Member State must comply with any Rules relating to his obligation to insure against his professional liability as a lawyer which are in force in his Home Member State.

3.9.2.2. A lawyer who is obliged so to insure in his Home Member State and who provides services or carries on practice in any Host Member State shall use his best endeavours to obtain insurance cover on the basis required in his Home Member State extended to services which he provides or practice which he carries on in a Host Member State.

3.9.2.3. A lawyer who fails to obtain the extended insurance cover referred to in paragraph 3.9.2.2 above or who is not obliged to so insure in his Home Member State and who provides services or carries on practice in a Host Member State shall in so far as possible obtain insurance cover against his professional liability as a lawyer whilst acting for clients in that Host Member State on at least an equivalent basis to that required of lawyers in the Host Member State.

3.9.2.4. To the extent that a lawyer is unable to obtain the insurance cover required by the foregoing rules, he shall take reasonable steps to draw that fact to the attention of such of his clients as might be affected in the event of a claim against him.

3.9.2.5. A lawyer who carries on practice or provides services in a Host Member State may with the agreement of the competent authorities of the Home and Host Member States concerned comply with such insurance requirements as are in force in the Host Member State to the exclusion of the insurance requirements of the Home Member State. In this event he shall take reasonable steps to inform his clients that he is insured according to the requirements in force in the Host Member State.

4. Relations with the Courts

4.1. Applicable Rules of Conduct in Court

A lawyer who appears, or takes part in a case, before a court or tribunal in a Member State must comply with the rules of conduct applied before that court or tribunal.

4.2. Fair Conduct of Proceedings

A lawyer must always have due regard for the fair conduct of proceedings. He must not, for example, make contact with the judge without first informing the lawyer acting for the opposing party or submit exhibits, notes or documents to the judge without communicating them in good time to the lawyer on the other side unless such steps are permitted under the relevant rules of procedure.

4.3. Demeanour in Court

A lawyer shall while maintaining due respect and courtesy towards the court defend the interests of his client honourably and in a way which he considers will be to the client's best advantage within the limits of the law.

4.4. False or Misleading Information

A lawyer shall never knowingly give false or misleading information to the court.

4.5. Extension to Arbitrators Etc.

The rules governing a lawyer's relations with the courts apply also to his relations with arbitrators and any other persons exercising judicial or quasijudicial functions even on an occasional basis.

5. Relations Between Lawyers

5.1. Corporate Spirit of the Profession

5.1.1. The corporate spirit of the profession requires a relationship of trust and co-operation between lawyers for the benefit of their clients and in order to avoid unnecessary litigation. It can never justify setting the interests of the profession against those of justice or of those who seek it.

5.1.2. A lawyer should recognise all other lawyers of Member States as professional colleagues and act fairly and courteously towards them.

5.2. Co-operation Among Lawyers of Different Member States

5.2.1. It is the duty of a lawyer who is approached by a colleague from another Member State not to accept instructions in a matter which he is not competent to undertake. He should be prepared to help his colleague to obtain the information necessary to enable him to instruct a lawyer who is capable of providing the service asked for.

5.2.2. Where a lawyer of a Member State co-operates with a lawyer from another Member State, both have a general duty to take into account the differences which may exist between their respective legal systems and the professional organisations' competences and obligations of lawyers in the Member States concerned.

5.3. Correspondence Between Lawyers

5.3.1. If a lawyer sending a communication to a lawyer in another Member State wishes it to remain confidential or without prejudice he should clearly express this intention when communicating the document.

5.3.2. If the recipient of the communication is unable to ensure its status as confidential or without prejudice he should return it to the sender without revealing the contents to others.

5.4. Referral Fees

5.4.1. A lawyer may not demand or accept from another lawyer or any other person a fee commission or any other compensation for referring or recommending a client.

5.4.2. A lawyer may not pay anyone a fee commission or any other compensation as a consideration for referring a client to himself.

5.5. Communication with Opposing Parties

A lawyer shall not communicate about a particular case or matter directly with any person whom he knows to be represented or advised in the case or matter by another lawyer, without the consent of that other lawyer (and shall keep the other lawyer informed of any such communications).

5.6. Change of Lawyer

5.6.1. A lawyer who is instructed to represent a client in substitution for another lawyer in relation to a particular matter should inform that other lawyer and, subject to 5.6.2 below, should not begin to act until he has ascertained that arrangements have been made for the settlement of the other lawyer's fees and disbursements. This duty does not, however, make the new lawyer personally responsible for the former lawyer's fees and disbursements.

5.6.2. If urgent steps have to be taken in the interests of the client before the conditions in 5.6.1 above can be complied with, the lawyer may take such steps provided he informs the other lawyer immediately.

5.7. Responsibility for Fees

In professional relations between members of Bars of different Member States, where a lawyer does not confine himself to recommending another lawyer or introducing him to the client but himself entrusts a correspondent with a particular matter or seeks his advice, he is personally bound, even if the client is insolvent, to pay the fees, costs and outlays which are due to the foreign correspondent. The lawyers concerned may, however, at the outset of the relationship between them make special arrangements on this matter. Further, the instructing lawyer may at any time limit his personal responsibility to the amount of the fees, costs and outlay incurred before intimation to the foreign lawyer of his disclaimer of responsibility for the future.

5.8. Training Young Lawyers

In order to improve trust and co-operation amongst lawyers of different Member States for the clients' benefit there is a need to encourage a better knowledge of the laws and procedures in different Member States. Therefore, when considering the need for the profession to give good training to young lawyers, lawyers should take into account the need to give training to young lawyers from other Member States.

5.9. Disputes Amongst Lawyers in Different Member States

5.9.1. If a lawyer considers that a colleague in another Member State has acted in breach of a rule of professional conduct he shall draw the matter to the attention of his colleague.

5.9.2. If any personal dispute of a professional nature arises amongst lawyers in different Member States they should if possible first try to settle it in a friendly way.

5.9.3. A lawyer shall not commence any form of proceedings against a colleague in another Member State on matters referred to in 5.9.1 or 5.9.2 above without first informing the Bars or Law Societies to which they both belong for the purpose of allowing both Bars or Law Societies concerned an opportunity to assist in reaching a settlement.

STATEMENT OF GOOD PRACTICES BY LAW PROFESSORS IN THE DISCHARGE OF THEIR ETHICAL AND PROFESSIONAL RESPONSIBILITIES*

Editors' Note. At its November 1989 meeting, the Executive Committee of the Association of American Law Schools adopted the following "Statement of Good Practices of Law Professors in the Discharge of Their Ethical and Professional Responsibilities." According to the February 1990 AALS Newsletter, in which this Statement of Good Practices was first published, the Statement "is not intended to be a disciplinary code but instead, to provide guidance to law professors concerning their ethical and professional responsibilities. Thus the Statement is couched in aspirational terms."

American law professors typically are members of two professions and thus should comply with the requirements and standards of each. Law professors who are lawyers are subject to the law of professional ethics in force in the relevant jurisdictions. Non-lawyers, in turn, should be guided by the norms associated with their disciplines. In addition, as members of the teaching profession, all law faculty members are subject to the regulations of the institutions at which they teach and to guidelines that are more generally applicable, such as the Statement of Professional Ethics of the American Association of University Professors.

This statement does not diminish the commands of other sources of ethical and professional conduct. Instead, it is intended to provide general guidance to law professors concerning ethical and professional standards both because of the intrinsic importance of those standards and because law professors serve as important role models for law students. In the words of the American Bar Association's Commission on Professionalism, since "the law school experience provides the student's first exposure to the profession and . . . professors inevitably serve as important role models for students, . . . the highest standards of ethics and professionalism should be adhered to within law schools."

Law professors' responsibilities extend beyond the classroom to include out of class associations with students and other professional activities. Members of the law teaching profession should have a strong sense of the special obligations that attach to their calling. They should recognize their responsibility to serve others and not be limited to pursuit of self interest. This general aspiration cannot be achieved by edict, for moral integrity and dedication to the welfare of others cannot be legislated. Nevertheless, a public statement of good practices concerning ethical and professional responsibility can enlighten newcomers and remind experienced teachers about the basic ethical and professional tenets — the *ethos* — of their profession.

Although the norms of conduct set forth in this Statement may be relevant when questions concerning propriety of conduct arise in a particular institutional context, the statement is not promulgated as a disciplinary code. Rather, the primary purpose of the Statement — couched for the most part in general aspirational terms — is to provide guidance to law professors concerning their responsibilities (1) to students, (2) as scholars, (3) to colleagues, (4) to the law school and university at which they teach and (5) to the bar and the general public.

I. Responsibilities to Students

As teachers, scholars, counselors, mentors and friends, law professors can profoundly influence students' attitudes concerning professional competence and responsibility. Professors should assist students to recognize the responsibility of lawyers to advance individual and social justice.

Because of their inevitable function as role models, professors should be guided by the most sensitive ethical and professional standards.

Law professors should aspire to excellence in teaching and to mastery of the doctrines and theories of their subjects. They should prepare conscientiously for class and employ teaching methods appropriate for the subject matters and objectives of their courses. The objectives and requirements of their courses, including applicable attendance and grading rules, should be clearly stated. Classes should be met as scheduled or, when this is impracticable, classes should be rescheduled at a time reasonably convenient for students, or alternative means of instruction should be provided.

Law professors have an obligation to treat students with civility and respect and to foster a stimulating and productive learning enironment in which the pros and cons of debatable issues are fairly acknowledged. Teachers should nurture and protect intellectual freedom for their students and colleagues. If a professor expresses views in class that were espoused in representing a client or in consulting, the professor should make appropriate disclosure.

Evaluation of student work is one of the fundamental obligations of law professors. Examinations and assignments should be conscientiously designed and all student work should be evaluated with impartiality. Grading should be done in a timely fashion and should be consistent with standards recognized as legitimate within the university and the profession. A student who so requests should be given an explanation of the grade assigned.

Law professors should be reasonably available to counsel students about academic matters, career choices, and professional interests. In performing this function, professors should make every reasonable effort to ensure that the information they transmit is timely and accurate. When in the course of counseling a law professor receives information that the student may reasonably expect to be confidential, the professor should not disclose that information unless required to do so by university rule or applicable law. Professors should inform students concerning the possibility of such disclosure.

Professors should be as fair and complete as possible when communicating evaluative recommendations for students and should not permit invidious or irrelevant considerations to infect these recommendations. If information disclosed in confidence by the student to the professor makes it impossible for the professor to write a fair and complete recommendation without revealing the information, the professor should so inform the student and refuse to provide the recommendation unless the student consents to full disclosure.

Discriminatory conduct based on such factors as race, color, religion, national origin, sex, sexual orientation, disability or handicap, age, or political beliefs is unacceptable in the law school community. Law professors should seek to make the law school a hospitable community for all students and should be sensitive to the harmful consequences of professorial or student conduct or comments in classroom discussions or elsewhere that perpetuate stereotypes or prejudices involving such factors. Law professors should not sexually harass students and should not use their role or position to induce a student to enter into a sexual relationship, or to subject a student to a hostile academic environment based on any form of sexual harassment.

Sexual relationships between a professor and a student who are not married to each other or who do not have a preexisting analogous relationship are inappropriate whenever the professor has a professional responsibility for the student in such matters as teaching a course or in otherwise evaluating, supervising or advising a student as part of a school program. Even when a professor has no professional responsibility for a student, the professor should be sensitive to the perceptions of other students that a student who has a sexual relationship with a professor may receive preferential treatment from the professor or the professor's colleagues. A professor who is closely related to a student by blood or marriage, or who has a preexisting analogous relationship with a student, normally should eschew roles involving a professional responsibility for the student.

II. Responsibilities as Scholars

A basic responsibility of the community of higher education in the United States is to refine, extend and transmit knowledge. As members of that community, law professors share with their colleagues in the other disciplines the obligation to discharge that responsibility. Law schools are required by accreditation standards to limit the burden of teaching so that professors will have the time to do research and to share its results with others. Law schools also have a responsibility to maintain an atmosphere of freedom and tolerance in which knowledge can be sought and shared without hindrance. Law professors are obligated, in turn, to make the best and fullest use of that freedom to fulfill their scholarly responsibilities.

In teaching, as well as in research, writing and publication, the scholarship of others is indispensable to one's own. A law professor thus has a responsibility to be informed concerning the relevant scholarship of others in the fields in which the professor writes and teaches. To keep current in any field of law requires continuing study. To this extent the professor, as a scholar, must remain a student. As a corollary, law professors have a responsibility to engage in their own research and publish their conclusions. In this way, law professors participate in an intellectual exchange that tests and improves their knowledge of the field, to the ultimate benefit of their students, the profession, and society.

The scholar's commitment to truth requires intellectual honesty and open-mindedness. Although a law professor should feel free to criticize another's work, distortion or misrepresentation is always unacceptable. Relevant evidence and arguments should be addressed. Conclusions should be frankly stated, even if unpopular.

When another's scholarship is used — whether that of another professor or that of a student — it should be fairly summarized and candidly acknowledged. Significant contributions require acknowledgement in every context in which ideas are exchanged. Publication permits at least three ways of doing this: shared authorship, attribution by footnote or endnote, and discussion of another's contribution within the main text. Which of these will suffice to acknowledge scholarly contributions by others will, of course, depend on the extent of the contribution.

A law professor has a responsibility to preserve the integrity and independence of legal scholarship. Sponsored or remunerated research should always be acknowledged with full disclosure of the interests of the parties. If views expressed in an article were also espoused in the course of representation of a client or in consulting, this should be acknowledged.

III. Responsibilities to Colleagues

Law professors should treat colleagues and staff members with civility and respect. Senior law professors should be particularly sensitive to the terms of any debate involving their junior colleagues and should so conduct themselves that junior colleagues will understand that no adverse professional consequences would follow from expression of, or action based upon, beliefs or opinions contrary to those held by the senior professor.

Matters of law school governance deserve the exercise of independent judgment by each voting member of the faculty. It is therefore inappropriate for a law professor to apply any sort of pressure other than persuasion on the merits in an effort to influence the vote of another member of the faculty.

Law professors should comply with institutional rules or policies requiring confidentiality concerning oral or written communications. Such rules or policies frequently will exist with respect to personnel matters and evaluations of student performance. If there is doubt whether such a rule or policy is in effect, a law professor should seek clarification.

An evaluation made of any colleague for purposes of promotion or tenure should be based exclusively upon appropriate academic and service criteria fairly weighted in accordance with standards understood by the faculty and communicated to the subject of the evaluation.

Law professors should make themselves reasonably available to colleagues for purposes of discussing teaching methods, content of courses, possible topics of scholarship, scholarly work in progress and related matters. Except in rare cases and for compelling reasons, professors should always honor requests from their own law schools for evaluation of scholarship in connection with promotion or tenure decisions. Law professors should also give sympathetic consideration to similar requests from other law schools.

As is the case with respect to students (Part I), sexual harassment or discriminatory conduct involving colleagues or staff members on the basis of race, color, religion, national origin, sex, sexual orientation, disability or handicap, age, or political beliefs is unacceptable.

IV. Responsibilities to the Law School and University

Law professors have a responsibility to participate in the governance of their university and particularly the law school itself. Although many duties within modern universities are assumed by professional administrators, the faculty retains substantial collective responsibility to provide institutional leadership. Individual professors have a responsibility to assume a fair share of that leadership, including the duty to serve on faculty committees and to participate in faculty deliberations.

Law professors are frequently in demand to participate in activities outside the law school. Such involvement may help bring fresh insights to the professor's classes and writing. Excessive involvement in outside activities, however, tends to reduce the time that the professor has to meet obligations to students, colleagues and the law school. A professor thus has a responsibility both to adhere to a university's specific limitations on outside activity and to assure that outside activities do not significantly diminish the professor's availability to meet institutional obligations. Professors should comply with applicable laws and university regulations and policies concerning the use of university funds, personnel, and property in connection with such activities.

When a law professor resigns from the university to assume another position, or seeks a leave of absence to teach at another institution or assumes a temporary position in practice or government, the professor should provide reasonable advance notice. Absent unusual circumstances, a professor should adhere to the dates established in the Statement of Good Practices for the Recruitment of and Resignation by Full-Time Faculty Members of the Association of American Law Schools.

Although all law professors have the right as citizens to take positions on public questions, each professor has a duty not to imply that he or she speaks on behalf of the law school or university. Thus, a professor should take steps to assure that any designation of the professor's institution in connection with the professor's name is for identification only.

V. Responsibilities to the Bar and General Public

A law professor occupies a unique role as a bridge between the bar and students preparing to become members of the bar. It is important that professors accept the responsibilities of professional status. At a minimum, a law professor should adhere to the Code or Rules of Professional Conduct of the state bars to which the law professor may belong. A law professor may responsibly test the limits of professional rules in an effort to determine their constitutionality or proper application. Other conduct warranting discipline as a lawyer should be a matter of serious concern to the professor's law school and university.

One of the traditional obligations of members of the bar is to engage in uncompensated public service or pro bono legal activities. As role models for students and as members of the legal profession, law professors share this responsibility. This responsibility can be met in a variety of ways, including direct client contact through legal aid or public defender offices (whether or not through the law school), participating in the legal work of public interest organizations, lecturing in continuing legal education programs, educating public school pupils or other groups concerning the legal system, advising local, state and national government officials on legal issues, engaging in legislative drafting or other law reform activities.

The fact that a law professor's income does not depend on serving the interests of private clients permits a law professor to take positions on issues as to which practicing lawyers may be more inhibited. With that freedom from economic pressure goes an enhanced obligation to pursue individual and social justice.

Selected Attorney-Client Privilege and Work Product Provisions

Editors' Introduction. The ethical obligation of confidentiality is closely related to the evidentiary rules governing the attorney-client privilege and the procedural rules protecting attorney work product. The materials in this chapter show how the attorney-client privilege and the work product doctrine are treated in the Federal Rules of Evidence, the Federal Rules of Civil Procedure, New York's Civil Practice Law and Rules, the California Evidence Code, and tentative drafts of the American Law Institute's Restatement of the Law Governing Lawyers.

The Restatement provisions concerning work product are especially interesting. They were the subject of vigorous debate at the ALI's 1992 Annual Meeting; so many members objected to the proposed definition of work product in §136 that the membership voted to withdraw §136 and send it back to committee for redrafting.

Contents

546

FEDERAL RULES OF EVIDENCE

Rule 501. General Rule

Except as otherwise required by the Constitution of the United States or provided by Act of Congress or in rules prescribed by the Supreme Court pursuant to statutory authority, the privilege of a witness, person, government, State, or political subdivision thereof shall be governed by the principles of the common law as they may be interpreted by the courts of the United States in the light of reason and experience. However, in civil actions and proceedings, with respect to an element of a claim or defense as to which State law supplies the rule of decision, the privilege of a witness, person, government, State, or political subdivision thereof shall be determined in accordance with State law.

Proposed Rule 503 (not enacted)

(a) Definitions. As used in this rule:

(1) A "client" is a person, public officer, or corporation, association, or other organization or entity, either public or private, who is rendered professional legal services by a lawyer, or who consults a lawyer with a view to obtaining professional legal services from him.

(2) A "lawyer" is a person authorized, or reasonably believed by the client to be authorized, to practice law in any state or nation.

(3) A "representative of the lawyer" is one employed to assist the lawyer in the rendition of professional legal services.

(4) A communication is "confidential" if not intended to be disclosed to third persons other than those to whom disclosure is in furtherance of the rendition of professional legal services to the client or those reasonably necessary for the transmission of the communication.

(b) General rule of privilege. A client has a privilege to refuse to disclose and to prevent any other person from disclosing confidential communications made for the purpose of facilitating the rendition of professional legal services to the client, (1) between himself or his representative and his lawyer or his lawyer's representative, or (2) between his lawyer and the lawyer's representative, or (3) by him or his lawyer to a lawyer representing another in a matter of common

547

interest, or (4) between representatives of the client or between the client and a representative of the client, or (5) between lawyers representing the client.

(c) Who may claim the privilege? The privilege may be claimed by the client, his guardian or conservator, the personal representative of a deceased client, or the successor, trustee, or similar representative of a corporation, association, or other organization, whether or not in existence. The person who was the lawyer at the time of the communication may claim the privilege but only on behalf of the client. His authority to do so is presumed in the absence of evidence to the contrary.

(d) Exceptions. There is no privilege under this rule:

(1) *Furtherance of crime or fraud.* If the services of the lawyer were sought or obtained to enable or aid anyone to commit or plan to commit what the client knew or reasonably should have known to be a crime or fraud; or

(2) *Claimants through same deceased client.* As to a communication relevant to an issue between parties who claim through the same deceased client, regardless of whether the claims are by testate or intestate succession or by inter vivos transaction; or

(3) *Breach of duty by lawyer or client.* As to a communication relevant to an issue of breach of duty by the lawyer to his client or by the client to his lawyer; or

(4) *Document attested by lawyer.* As to a communication relevant to an issue concerning an attested document to which the lawyer is an attesting witness; or

(5) *Joint clients.* As to a communication relevant to a matter of common interest between two or more clients if the communication was made by any of them to a lawyer retained or consulted in common, when offered in an action between any of the clients.

FEDERAL RULES OF CIVIL PROCEDURE

Editors' Note. In federal courts, the work product doctrine is codified in Rules 26(b)(3)-(4) of the Federal Rules of Civil Procedure. These provisions were added to the rules by amendment in 1970 to resolve confusion and disagreements over the judicially created work product doctrine stemming from Hickman v. Taylor, 329 U.S. 495 (1947). Rule 26(b)(3) governs work product generally, including the mental opinions and impressions of lawyers, and Rule 26(b)(4) governs work product relating to experts.

Rule 26. General Provisions Governing Discovery

... **(b)(3)** *Trial Preparation: Materials.* **Subject to the provisions of subdivision (b)(4) of this rule, a party may obtain discovery of documents and tangi-**

ble things otherwise discoverable under subdivision (b)(1) of this rule and prepared in anticipation of litigation or for trial by or for another party or by or for that other party's representative (including the other party's attorney, consultant, surety, indemnitor, insurer, or agent) only upon a showing that the party seeking discovery has substantial need of the materials in the preparation of the party's case and that the party is unable without undue hardship to obtain the substantial equivalent of the materials by other means. In ordering discovery of such materials when the required showing has been made, the court shall protect against disclosure of the mental impressions, conclusions, opinions, or legal theories of an attorney or other representative of a party concerning the litigation.

A party may obtain without the required showing a statement concerning the action or its subject matter previously made by that party. Upon request, a person not a party may obtain without the required showing a statement concerning the action or its subject matter previously made by that person. If the request is refused, the person may move for a court order. The provisions of Rule 37(a)(4) apply to the award of expenses incurred in relation to the motion. For purposes of this paragraph, a statement previously made is (A) a written statement signed or otherwise adopted or approved by the person making it, or (B) a stenographic, mechanical, electrical, or other recording, or a transcription thereof, which is a substantially verbatim recital of an oral statement by the person making it and contemporaneously recorded.

(4) *Trial Preparation: Experts.* Discovery of facts known and opinions held by experts, otherwise discoverable under the provisions of subdivision (b)(1) of this rule and acquired or developed in anticipation of litigation or for trial, may be obtained only as follows:

(A)(i) A party may through interrogatories require any other party to identify each person whom the other party expects to call as an expert witness at trial, to state the subject matter on which the expert is expected to testify, and to state the substance of the facts and opinions to which the expert is expected to testify and a summary of the grounds for each opinion. (ii) Upon motion, the court may order further discovery by other means, subject to such restrictions as to scope and such provisions, pursuant to subdivision (b)(4)(C) of this rule, concerning fees and expenses as the court may deem appropriate.

(B) A party may discover facts known or opinions held by an expert who has been retained or specially employed by another party in anticipation of litigation or preparation for trial and who is not expected to be called as a witness at trial, only as provided in Rule 35(b) or upon a showing of exceptional circumstances under which it is impracticable for the party seeking discovery to obtain facts or opinions on the same subject by other means.

(C) Unless manifest injustice would result, (i) the court shall require that the party seeking discovery pay the expert a reasonable fee for time spent in responding to discovery under subdivisions (b)(4)(A)(ii) and (b)(4)(B) of this rule; and (ii) with respect to discovery obtained under subdivision (b)(4)(A)(ii) of this rule the court may require, and with respect to discovery obtained under subdivision (b)(4)(B) of this rule the court shall require, the party seeking discovery to pay the other party a fair portion of the fees and expenses reasonably incurred by the latter party in obtaining facts and opinions from the expert.

NEW YORK CIVIL PRACTICE LAW AND RULES

§4503. Attorney

(a) Confidential communication privileged; non-judicial proceedings. Unless the client waives the privilege, an attorney or his employee, or any person who obtains without the knowledge of the client evidence of a confidential communication made between the attorney or his employee and the client in the course of professional employment, shall not disclose, or be allowed to disclose such communication, nor shall the client be compelled to disclose such communication, in any action, disciplinary trial or hearing, or administrative action, proceeding or hearing conducted by or on behalf of any state, municipal or local governmental agency or by the legislature or any committee or body thereof. Evidence of any such communication obtained by any such person, and evidence resulting therefrom, shall not be disclosed by any state, municipal or local governmental agency or by the legislature or any committee or body thereof. The relationship of an attorney and client shall exist between a professional service corporation organized under article fifteen of the business corporation law to practice as an attorney and counselor-at-law and the clients to whom it renders legal services.

(b) Wills. In any action involving the probate, validity or construction of a will, an attorney or his employee shall be required to disclose information as to the preparation, execution or revocation of any will or other relevant instrument, but he shall not be allowed to disclose any communication privileged under subdivision (a) which would tend to disgrace the memory of the decedent.

CALIFORNIA EVIDENCE CODE

§950. "Lawyer"

As used in this article, "lawyer" means a person authorized, or reasonably believed by the client to be authorized, to practice law in any state or nation.

§951. "Client"

As used in this article, "client" means a person who, directly or through an authorized representative, consults a lawyer for the purpose of retaining the lawyer or securing legal service or advice from him in his professional capacity, and includes an incompetent (a) who himself so consults the lawyer or (b) whose guardian or conservator so consults the lawyer in behalf of the incompetent.

§952. "Confidential communication between client and lawyer"

As used in this article, "confidential communication between client and lawyer" means information transmitted between a client and his lawyer in the course of that relationship and in confidence by a means which, so far as the client is aware, discloses the information to no third persons other than those who are present to further the interest of the client in the consultation or those to whom disclosure is reasonably necessary for the transmission of the information or the accomplishment of the purpose for which the lawyer is consulted, and includes a legal opinion formed and the advice given by the lawyer in the course of that relationship.

§953. "Holder of the privilege"

As used in this article, "holder of the privilege" means:
    (a) The client when he has no guardian or conservator.
    (b) A guardian or conservator of the client when the client has a guardian or conservator.
    (c) The personal representative of the client if the client is dead.
    (d) A successor, assign, trustee in dissolution, or any similar representative of a firm, association, organization, partnership, business trust, corporation, or public entity that is no longer in existence.

§954. Lawyer-Client Privilege

Subject to Section 912 and except as otherwise provided in this article, the client, whether or not a party, has a privilege to refuse to disclose, and to prevent another from disclosing, a confidential communication between client and lawyer if the privilege is claimed by:
    (a) The holder of the privilege;
    (b) A person who is authorized to claim the privilege by the holder of the privilege; or

(c) The person who was the lawyer at the time of the confidential communication, but such person may not claim the privilege if there is no holder of the privilege in existence or if he is otherwise instructed by a person authorized to permit disclosure.

The relationship of attorney and client shall exist between a law corporation as defined in Article 10 (commencing with Section 6160) of Chapter 4 of Division 3 of the Business and Professions Code and the persons to whom it renders professional services, as well as between such persons and members of the State Bar employed by such corporation to render services to such persons. The word "persons" as used in this subdivision includes partnerships, corporations, associations and other groups and entities.

§955. When Lawyer Required to Claim Privilege

The lawyer who received or made a communication subject to the privilege under this article shall claim the privilege whenever he is present when the communication is sought to be disclosed and is authorized to claim the privilege under subdivision (c) of Section 954.

§956. Exception: Crime or Fraud

There is no privilege under this article if the services of the lawyer were sought or obtained to enable or aid anyone to commit or plan to commit a crime or a fraud.

§957. Exception: Parties Claiming Through Deceased Client

There is no privilege under this article as to a communication relevant to an issue between parties all of whom claim through a deceased client, regardless of whether the claims are by testate or intestate succession or by inter vivos transaction.

§958. Exception: Breach of Duty Arising out of Lawyer-Client Relationship

There is no privilege under this article as to a communication relevant to an issue of breach, by the lawyer or by the client, of a duty arising out of the lawyer-client relationship.

§959. Exception: Lawyer as Attesting Witness

There is no privilege under this article as to a communication relevant to an issue concerning the intention or competence of a client executing an attested document of which the lawyer is an attesting witness, or concerning the execution or attestation of such a document.

§960. Exception: Intention of Deceased Client Concerning Writing Affecting Property Interest

There is no privilege under this article as to a communication relevant to an issue concerning the intention of a client, now deceased, with respect to a deed of conveyance, will, or other writing, executed by the client, purporting to affect an interest in property.

§961. Exception: Validity of Writing Affecting Property Interest

There is no privilege under this article as to a communication relevant to an issue concerning the validity of a deed of conveyance, will, or other writing, executed by a client, now deceased, purporting to affect an interest in property.

§962. Exception: Joint Clients

Where two or more clients have retained or consulted a lawyer upon a matter of common interest, none of them, nor the successor in interest of any of them, may claim a privilege under this article as to a communication made in the course of that relationship when such communication is offered in a civil proceeding between one of such clients (or his successor in interest) and another of such clients (or his successor in interest).

RESTATEMENT OF THE LAW GOVERNING
LAWYERS*
(TENTATIVE DRAFT NO. 2)

Editors' Note. The American Law Institute has tentatively approved the following provisions concerning the attorney-client privilege.

§118. The Attorney-Client Privilege

Except as otherwise provided in this Restatement, the attorney-client privilege may be invoked as provided in §135 with respect to:
  (1) A communication
  (2) Made between privileged persons
  (3) In confidence
  (4) For the purpose of obtaining or providing legal assistance for the client.

§119. Communications Covered by the Privilege

A communication within the meaning of §118 is any expression through which a privileged person, as defined in §120, undertakes to convey information to another privileged person and any document or other record that embodies such an expression.

§120. Privileged Persons

Within the meaning of §118, privileged persons are the client (including a prospective client), the client's lawyer, communicating agents of either of them, and representing agents of the lawyer.

§121. Definition of "In Confidence"

Within the meaning of §118, a communication is in confidence if, at the time of the communication, the communicating person intends that no one learn of the contents of the communication except privileged persons as defined in §120 or persons to whom communications are protected under a similar evidentiary privilege.

§122. Legal Assistance as the Object of Privileged
Communications

Within the meaning of §118, a communication is made for the purpose of obtaining or providing legal assistance for a client if:

(1) It involves legal advice or other legal assistance that a lawyer renders to a client or is made for the purpose of enabling the client and lawyer to consult initially about whether the lawyer will provide such assistance; and

(2) It is made to or by a person or the privileged agent of such a person as defined in §120:

(a) Who is functioning in the professional capacity of lawyer or the client believes the person to be so functioning; and

(b) Who is consulted for the purpose of obtaining legal assistance for the client in the matter that is the subject of the communication.

§123. Scope of the Privilege for Organizations

Where a client is a corporation, unincorporated association, partnership, sole proprietorship, or other for-profit or not-for-profit organization, the attorney-client privilege extends to a communication if:

(1) The communication otherwise qualifies as privileged under §§118-122;

(2) The communication is between a person communicating pursuant to an agency relationship with the organization and a privileged person within the meaning of §120;

(3) The communication concerns a legal matter of interest to the organization; and

(4) The communication is shared only with:

(a) Privileged persons as defined in §§120 and 123(2); and

(b) Other agents of the organization who reasonably need to know of the communication in order to act for the organization.

§124. Privilege for Governmental Clients

Unless applicable law otherwise provides, the attorney-client privilege extends to a communication involving a client that is a governmental organization to the extent stated in §§118-123 and to a communication involving an individual officer or other client who is an employee or other agent of a governmental organization to the extent stated in §§118-122.

§125. The Limited Privilege for Co-Clients

If two or more persons are jointly represented by the same lawyer in a matter, the communications of each co-client with the lawyer or other privileged person that otherwise qualify as privileged under §§118-122:

(1) Are privileged as against a third person, and any co-client may assert the privilege; but

(2) Unless the co-clients have explicitly agreed otherwise, are not privileged as between the co-clients in subsequent litigation between them.

§126. Pooled-Information Arrangements

If two or more clients represented by separate lawyers share a common interest in a matter, the communications of each separately represented client that otherwise qualify as privileged under §§118-122:

(1) Are privileged as against a third person, and any such client may assert the privilege, if the communication is made in confidence between such a client, the client's communicating agents, the client's lawyer, or the lawyer's representing agent, and another commonly interested client or such a client's communicating agent, lawyer, or representing agent; but

(2) Unless the affected clients in the pooled-information arrangement have explicitly agreed otherwise, a communication within subsection (1) is not privileged as between such clients in subsequent litigation between two or more of the clients when it is offered against the client who originally made the communication, or on whose behalf it was made, by a client who learned of the communication in the circumstances described in subsection (1).

§127. Duration of the Privilege

Unless it is waived (§§128-130) or is subject to an exception (§§131-134), the attorney-client privilege may be invoked as provided in §135 at any time during and after the termination of the client-lawyer relationship.

§128. Waiver by Consent, Disclaimer, or Defective Assertion

The attorney-client privilege of a client is waived if the client, the client's lawyer, or another authorized agent of the client:

(1) Consents to waive the privilege;

(2) Disclaims the protection of the privilege and:

(a) Another person reasonably relied on the disclaimer to that person's detriment; or

(b) Reasons of judicial administration require that the client not be permitted to revoke the disclaimer; or

(3) In a proceeding before a tribunal, fails properly to object to an attempt by another person to give or exact testimony or other evidence of a privileged communication.

§129. Waiver by Subsequent Disclosure

The attorney-client privilege of a client is waived if the client, the client's lawyer, or another authorized agent of the client substantially discloses the communication in a non-privileged communication.

§130. Waiver by Putting Assistance or Communication
       in Issue

(1) The attorney-client privilege is waived if the client asserts as to a material issue in a proceeding that:

(a) The client acted upon the advice of a lawyer or that the advice was otherwise relevant to the legal significance of the client's conduct; or

(b) A lawyer's assistance was ineffective, negligent, or for some other reason wrongful.

(2) The attorney-client privilege is waived with respect to a recorded communication if:

(a) A witness employs the communication to aid the witness's testimony while testifying; or

(b) A witness employed the communication to refresh recollection prior to testifying and the tribunal finds that the witness's testimony is based on the communication and not on the witness's memory.

§131. Exception for Disputes Concerning Decedent's
       Disposition of Property

The attorney-client privilege does not apply to a communication when it becomes relevant to an issue between parties who claim an interest through the same deceased client, either by testate or intestate succession or by an inter vivos transaction.

§132. Exception for Client Crimes and Frauds

The attorney-client privilege does not apply to a communication occurring when a client consults a lawyer for the purpose of obtaining assistance in engaging in conduct or aiding a third person in engaging in conduct if the client, at the time of the communication, knows or reasonably should know that the conduct is a crime or fraud.

§133. Exceptions for Lawyer Self-Protection

The attorney-client privilege does not apply to a communication that is relevant and appropriate for a lawyer to employ in a proceeding:

(1) To resolve a dispute with a client concerning compensation or reimbursement that the lawyer reasonably claims is due to the lawyer from the client; or

(2) To defend the lawyer against an allegation by any person that the lawyer, an agent of the lawyer, or another person for whose conduct the lawyer is responsible acted wrongfully during the course of representing a client.

§134. Exception for Organizational Fiduciaries

In a proceeding involving a dispute between an organizational client and shareholders, members, or other constituents of the organization toward whom the controlling directors or officers of the organization bear fiduciary responsibilities, the attorney-client privilege of the organization does not apply to a communication if:

(1) Directors or officers of the organization are charged with breach of their obligations toward the shareholders, members, or other beneficial owners or toward the organization itself;

(2) The communication occurred prior to the suit and relates directly to those charges; and

(3) The tribunal concludes that the need of the requesting party to discover or introduce the communication is sufficiently compelling and the threat to confidentiality sufficiently confined to justify setting the privilege aside.

§135. Invoking the Privilege and Its Exceptions

(1) When an attempt is made to discover or introduce in evidence a communication privileged under §118:

(A) Either personally or through counsel or another authorized agent, a client, a personal representative of an incompetent or deceased client, or a person succeeding to the interest of a client may invoke or waive the privilege;

(B) When called upon to present evidence, a lawyer, an agent of the lawyer for the purpose of communicating with or representing the client, or a communicating agent of a client from whom a privileged communication is sought must invoke the privilege, unless the client has waived the privilege or authorized the lawyer or agent to waive it; and

(C) In the absence of an objection by a person with standing to do so, the presiding officer may order that a communication not be disclosed if it is privileged and not subject to waiver or an exception.

(2) A person entitled to assert the privilege must ordinarily object contemporaneously on the ground that the evidence is privileged and, if the objection is contested, demonstrate each element of the privilege under §118.

(3) A person seeking to establish a waiver of or exception to the attorney-client privilege under §§128-134 must assert the waiver or exception and, if the assertion is contested, demonstrate each of its elements.

RESTATEMENT OF THE LAW GOVERNING LAWYERS*
(TENTATIVE DRAFT NO. 5)

Editors' Note. At its 1992 Annual Meeting, the American Law Institute approved all of the following sections governing attorney work product, with the exception of §136, which was withdrawn and sent back to committee for redrafting.

§136. Work Product Immunity (withdrawn)

(1) Work product immunity applies to material or its intangible equivalent if:

(a) The material records or reflects litigation investigation or analysis, but work product does not include facts;

(b) The material was prepared by or for a party or party's representative, including a party's lawyer, consultant, surety, indemnitor, insurer, or agent; and

(c) The material was prepared in anticipation of litigation, that is, it was prepared for litigation then in progress or its preparation was primarily motivated by the prospect of future litigation.

(2) Except as stated in §137 for ordinary work product, in §138 for opinion work product, in §§140-142, and in Subsection (3) for witness statements, the work product of a party or a party's representatives is immune from discovery or other compelled disclosure when work-product immunity is invoked as described in §139.

(3) A witness statement, although ordinary work product and thus immune from discovery by another party as stated in §137, may be obtained by the person or party who gave the statement.

§137. Ordinary Work Product

A tribunal may order discovery of ordinary work product, that is, material defined in §136 other than opinion work product as defined in §138, if the material is otherwise discoverable and the inquiring party demonstrates either that an exception recognized in §§140-142 applies or that:

(1) The party has a substantial need for the material in order to prepare for trial; and

(2) The party is unable without due hardship to obtain the substantial equivalent of the material by other means.

§138. Opinion Work Product

Unless an exception recognized in §§140-142 applies, work product consisting of the opinions or mental impressions of a party or a party's lawyer or other representative is not subject to discovery or other disclosure.

§139. Invoking Work Product Immunity and Its Exceptions

(1) Work product immunity may be invoked by or for the client on whose behalf it was prepared. In order to be timely, objection based on the immunity must be asserted when responding to a discovery request or, in other circumstances when an attempt to gain access to work product material is made, with reasonable promptness. A person invoking the immunity must demonstrate each of its elements.

(2) When the elements of work product immunity have been established, a person seeking access to the material on the ground of need under §§137(1) and (2) or of waiver or exception under §§140-142 must demonstrate the elements of the need, waiver or exception invoked.

§140. Waiver of Work Product Immunity by Voluntary Acts

Work product immunity is waived if a party entitled to assert the immunity or the party's lawyer or other authorized representative:

(1) Agrees with the party seeking discovery not to assert the immunity;

(2) Unilaterally disclaims protection of the immunity and:

(a) Another person reasonably and to that person's detriment relies on the disclaimer; or

(b) Considerations of judicial administration require that the party making the disclaimer not be permitted to change position;

(3) During discovery or in a proceeding before a tribunal, fails to object properly to an attempt by another person to give or elicit testimony or other matter containing work product;

(4) Discloses the material to third persons in circumstances in which there is a significant likelihood that an adversary or potential adversary will obtain it.

§141. Waiver of Work Product Immunity by Use in Litigation or Removal Through Direct Relevance

(1) Work product immunity for material is waived if, in a proceeding pending before a tribunal, the party asserting the immunity introduces the material into evidence, shows the material to a witness while the witness is testifying, or directly employs the material to prepare a non-party witness to testify.

(2) Work product immunity is waived as to materials directly relevant to the issue if a party asserts as to a material issue in a proceeding pending before a tribunal that:

(a) The party acted upon the advice of a lawyer or that the advice was otherwise relevant in determining the legal significance of the party's conduct; or

(b) A lawyer's assistance to that party was ineffective, negligent, or for some other reason wrongful and fairly determining the truth of that assertion requires disclosure of the work product.

(3) Work product immunity is removed for materials directly and substantially in issue in a proceeding pending before a tribunal.

§142. Exception for Crime or Fraud

Work product immunity does not apply to material when a client consults a lawyer for the purpose of obtaining assistance in engaging in conduct or aiding a third person in engaging in conduct if the client, at the time the asserted work product is produced, knows or reasonably should know that the conduct is a crime or fraud.

§143. Access to Predecessor Lawyer's Work Product

When a predecessor lawyer is disqualified or withdraws from representing a client, a lawyer who succeeds the predecessor lawyer in representing the client may have access to the predecessor lawyer's work product except to the extent necessary to protect against improper disclosure of confidential information, including work product of another client of the predecessor lawyer.

Creeds of Courtesy and Professionalism

Editors' Introduction. In 1984, Chief Justice Warren Burger recommended that the ABA study the question of professionalism. In 1985, ABA President John Shepherd of St. Louis appointed a Commission on Professionalism. In 1986, the Commission on Professionalism issued a highly influential report. Many state and local bar associations have since taken up the study of professionalism, and some have issued their own reports or codes of professionalism. In this section of the book, we are reprinting several items relating to professionalism. Each item is introduced separately.

Contents

MISSION AND GOALS OF THE AMERICAN BAR ASSOCIATION*

Editors' Note. At its 1981 Annual Meeting, the ABA for the first time adopted a set of goals "as the framework on which association programs should be developed." Originally, there were only seven goals. More goals have been added over the years, and today there are eleven goals. We reprint them all here, together with the ABA's own brief introduction.

The mission of the American Bar Association is to be the national representative of the legal profession, serving the public and the profession by promoting justice, professional excellence and respect for the law.

The goals of the ABA reflect our commitment to these principles, as well as our determination to remain responsive to the challenges of a changing world. Each of the programs and activities of the ABA is intended to further one of the following goals:

I. To promote improvements in the American system of justice

II. To promote meaningful access to legal representation and the American system of justice for all persons regardless of their economic or social condition

III. To provide ongoing leadership in improving the law to serve the changing needs of society

IV. To increase public understanding of and respect for the law, the legal process, and the role of the legal profession

V. To achieve the highest standards of professionalism, competence and ethical conduct

VI. To serve as the national representative of the legal profession

VII. To provide benefits, programs and services which promote professional growth and enhance the quality of life of the members

VIII. To advance the rule of law in the world

IX. To promote full and equal participation in the legal profession by minorities and women

X. To preserve and enhance the ideals of the legal profession as a common calling and its dedication to public service

XI. To preserve the independence of the legal profession and the judiciary as fundamental to a free society

ABA CREED AND PLEDGE OF PROFESSIONALISM*

Editors' Note. At the ABA's annual meeting in August 1988, the ABA Tort and Insurance Practice Section (TIPS) proposed a Creed of Professionalism. Part of the Creed recommends that state and local bar associations encourage their members to accept and comply with a creed of professionalism as a guide for their individual conduct. The ABA House of Delegates by voice vote urged state and local bar groups to adopt a creed of professionalism. TIPS then disseminated its own Creed to state and local bars, urging its adoption. To avoid any misunderstanding, however, the House of Delegates stated that "nothing in such a creed shall be deemed to supersede or in any way amend the Model Rules of Professional Conduct or other disciplinary codes, or alter existing standards of conduct against which lawyer negligence might be judged or become a basis for the imposition of civil liability of any kind."

At the same 1988 annual meeting, the House of Delegates reviewed a Pledge of Professionalism formulated by the ABA Young Lawyers Division. The ABA authorized its "dissemination to the profession." We reprint both the Creed of Professionalism and the Pledge of Professionalism here.

Lawyer's Creed of Professionalism

Preamble

As a lawyer I must strive to make our system of justice work fairly and efficiently. In order to carry out that responsibility, not only will I comply with the letter and spirit of the disciplinary standards applicable to all lawyers, but I will also conduct myself in accordance with the following Creed of Professionalism when dealing with my client, opposing parties, their counsel, the courts and the general public.

A. With respect to my client:

1. I will be loyal and committed to my client's cause, but I will not permit that loyalty and commitment to interfere with my ability to provide my client with objective and independent advice;

2. I will endeavor to achieve my client's lawful objectives in business transactions and in litigation as expeditiously and economically as possible;

3. In appropriate cases, I will counsel my client with respect to mediation, arbitration and other alternative methods of resolving disputes;

4. I will advise my client against pursuing litigation (or any other course of action) that is without merit and against insisting on tactics which are intended to delay resolution of the matter or to harass or drain the financial resources of the opposing party;

5. I will advise my client that civility and courtesy are not to be equated with weakness;

6. While I must abide by my client's decision concerning the objectives of the representation, I nevertheless will counsel my client that a willingness to initiate or engage in settlement discussions is consistent with zealous and effective representation.

B. With respect to opposing parties and their counsel:

1. I will endeavor to be courteous and civil, both in oral and in written communications;

2. I will not knowingly make statements of fact or of law that are untrue;

3. In litigation proceedings I will agree to reasonable requests for extensions of time or for waiver of procedural formalities when the legitimate interests of my client will not be adversely affected;

4. I will endeavor to consult with opposing counsel before scheduling depositions and meetings and before re-scheduling hearings, and I will cooperate with opposing counsel when scheduling changes are requested;

5. I will refrain from utilizing litigation or any other course of conduct to harass the opposing party;

6. I will refrain from engaging in excessive and abusive discovery, and I will comply with all reasonable discovery requests;

7. I will refrain from utilizing delaying tactics;

8. In depositions and other proceedings, and in negotiations, I will conduct myself with dignity, avoid making groundless objections and refrain from engaging in acts of rudeness or disrespect;

9. I will not serve motions and pleadings on the other party, or his counsel, at such a time or in such a manner as will unfairly limit the other party's opportunity to respond;

10. In business transactions I will not quarrel over matters of form or style, but will concentrate on matters of substance and content;

11. I will clearly identify, for other counsel or parties, all changes that I have made in documents submitted to me for review.

C. With respect to the courts and other tribunals:

1. I will be a vigorous and zealous advocate on behalf of my client, while recognizing, as an officer of the court, that excessive zeal may be detrimental to my client's interests as well as to the proper functioning of our system of justice;

2. Where consistent with my client's interests, I will communicate with opposing counsel in an effort to avoid litigation and to resolve litigation that has actually commenced;

3. I will voluntarily withdraw claims or defenses when it becomes apparent that they do not have merit or are superfluous;

4. I will refrain from filing frivolous motions;

5. I will make every effort to agree with other counsel, as early as possible, on a voluntary exchange of information and on a plan for discovery;

6. I will attempt to resolve, by agreement, my objections to matters contained in my opponent's pleadings and discovery requests;

7. When scheduling hearings or depositions have to be canceled, I will notify opposing counsel, and, if appropriate, the court (or other tribunal) as early as possible;

8. Before dates for hearings or trials are set — or if that is not feasible, immediately after such dates have been set — I will attempt to verify the availability of key participants and witnesses so that I can promptly notify the court (or other tribunal) and opposing counsel of any likely problem in that regard;

9. In civil matters, I will stipulate to facts as to which there is no genuine dispute;

10. I will endeavor to be punctual in attending court hearings, conferences and depositions;

11. I will at all times be candid with the court.

D. With respect to the public and to our system of justice:

1. I will remember that, in addition to commitment to my client's cause, my responsibilities as a lawyer include a devotion to the public good.

2. I will endeavor to keep myself current in the areas in which I practice and, when necessary, will associate with, or refer my client to, counsel knowledgeable in another field of practice;

3. I will be mindful of the fact that, as a member of a self-regulating profession, it is encumbent on me to report violations by fellow lawyers of any disciplinary rule;

4. I will be mindful of the need to protect the image of the legal profession in the eyes of the public and will be so guided when considering methods and content of advertising.

5. I will be mindful that the law is a learned profession and that among its desirable goals are devotion to public service, improvement of administration of justice, and the contribution of uncompensated time and civic influence on behalf of those persons who cannot afford adequate legal assistance.

Lawyers' Pledge of Professionalism

1. I will remember that the practice of law is first and foremost a profession, and I will subordinate business concerns to professionalism concerns.

2. I will encourage respect for the law and our legal system through my words and actions.

3. I will remember my responsibilities to serve as an officer of the court and protector of individual rights.

4. I will contribute time and resources to public service, public education, charitable, and *pro bono* activities in my community.

5. I will work with the other participants in the legal system, including judges, opposing counsel and those whose practices are different from mine, to make our legal system more accessible and responsive.

6. I will resolve matters expeditiously and without unnecessary expense.

7. I will resolve disputes through negotiation whenever possible.

8. I will keep my clients well-informed and involved in making the decisions that affect them.

9. I will continue to expand my knowledge of the law.

10. I will achieve and maintain proficiency in my practice.

11. I will be courteous to those with whom I come into contact during the course of my work.

12. I will honor the spirit and intent, as well as the requirements, of the applicable rules or code of professional conduct for my jurisdiction, and I will encourage others to do the same.

KENTUCKY BAR ASSOCIATION CODE OF
PROFESSIONAL COURTESY

Editors' Note. In 1989, the Kentucky Bar Association adopted a Code of Professional Courtesy. The Code has since been amended, and in July 1992, the Kentucky Bar petitioned the Kentucky Supreme Court to approve the Code as an aspirational guideline. At press time, the court had not yet acted on the petition.

1. A lawyer should avoid taking action adverse to the interests of a litigant known to be represented without timely notice to opposing counsel unless ex parte proceedings are allowed.

2. A lawyer should promptly return telephone calls and correspondence from other lawyers.

3. A lawyer should respect opposing counsel's schedule by seeking agreement on deposition dates and court appearances (other than routine motions) rather than merely serving notice.

4. A lawyer should avoid making ill-considered accusations of unethical conduct toward an opponent.

5. A lawyer should not engage in intentionally discourteous behavior.

6. A lawyer should never intentionally embarrass another attorney and should avoid personal criticism of other counsel.

7. A lawyer should not seek sanctions against or disqualification of another attorney unless necessary for the protection of a client and fully justified by the circumstances, not for the mere purpose of obtaining tactical advantage.

8. A lawyer should strive to maintain a courteous tone in correspondence, pleadings and other written communications.

9. A lawyer should not intentionally mislead or deceive an adversary and should honor promises or commitments made.

10. A lawyer should recognize that the conflicts within a legal matter are professional and not personal and should endeavor to maintain a friendly and professional relationship with other attorneys in the matter — "leave the matter in the courtroom."

11. A lawyer should express professional courtesy to the Court and has the right to expect professional courtesy from the Court.

STANDARDS OF PRACTICE FOR THE
NORTHERN DISTRICT OF TEXAS

> **Editors' Note.** In July 1988, sitting en banc, the United States District Court for the Northern District of Texas adopted standards of practice to be observed by all lawyers appearing in civil actions in that district. The standards were based largely on "Guidelines of Professional Courtesy" and a "Lawyer's Creed" that had been adopted earlier in 1988 by the Dallas Bar Association.
>
> The court's decision to adopt standards was prompted by the contentious practices of opposing lawyers in Dondi Properties Corp. v. Commerce Savings & Loan Assn., 121 F.R.D. 284, 287-288 (N.D. Tex. 1988) (en banc). The court adopted the standards pursuant to its inherent power but warned lawyers that violation of these standards would prompt sanctions of the type imposed under Fed. R. Civ. P. 11, which could include a friendly discussion on the record, a reprimand in open court, compulsory legal education, monetary sanctions, and other appropriate measures.

(A) In fulfilling his or her primary duty to the client, a lawyer must be ever conscious of the broader duty to the judicial system that serves both attorney and client.

(B) A lawyer owes, to the judiciary, candor, diligence and utmost respect.

(C) A lawyer owes, to opposing counsel, a duty of courtesy and cooperation, the observance of which is necessary for the efficient administration of our system of justice and the respect of the public it serves.

(D) A lawyer unquestionably owes, to the administration of justice, the fundamental duties of personal dignity and professional integrity.

(E) Lawyers should treat each other, the opposing party, the court, and members of the court staff with courtesy and civility and conduct themselves in a professional manner at all times.

(F) A client has no right to demand that counsel abuse the opposite party or indulge in offensive conduct. A lawyer shall always treat the adverse witnesses and suitors with fairness and due consideration.

(G) In adversary proceedings, clients are litigants and though ill feeling may exist between clients, such ill feeling should not influence a lawyer's conduct, attitude, or demeanor towards opposing lawyers.

(H) A lawyer should not use any form of discovery, or the scheduling of discovery, as a means of harassing opposing counsel or counsel's client.

(I) Lawyers will be punctual in communications with others and in honoring scheduled appearances, and will recognize that neglect and tardiness are demeaning to the lawyer and to the judicial system.

(J) If a fellow member of the Bar makes a just request for cooperation, or seeks scheduling accommodation, a lawyer will not arbitrarily or unreasonably withhold consent.

(K) Effective advocacy does not require antagonistic or obnoxious behavior and members of the bar will adhere to the higher standard of conduct which judges, lawyers, clients, and the public may rightfully expect.

LAW FIRM CREDO

> **Editors' Note.** The law firm of Ryan, Swanson & Cleveland in Seattle, Washington has formally adopted a law firm creed. It was reprinted in the ABA Journal, January 1989. We include it here because we are intrigued by the concept of a law firm creed of professionalism.

We are a firm of professionals whose goal is to provide excellent legal services to our clients for fair and reasonable compensation. We practice as a firm, not as individuals. We seek to earn and maintain the respect of our clients, our colleagues and the legal community, as well as enhance self-respect by providing outstanding professional services to our clients.

Our goal is to be the best law firm possible, not necessarily the biggest or most profitable.

In all matters, we shall undertake to represent each of our clients as we would want to be represented. As lawyers, each of us commits to excel in our individual area of expertise and provide our clients the full benefit of our knowledge, ability and effort.

We recognize that our continued success requires a firm investment in human and technical resources. We commit to the investment of time, energy and money as an integral part of our practice so that the quality of our organization can be continually improved. We recognize our accountability to each other and mutual responsibility for the implementation of this credo.

We strive to enable our employees to grow to their highest potential while rewarding their personal efforts and contributions.

We shall provide a quality working environment for our employees and accord them the recognition which they deserve.

We recognize our obligations to our families and to the community in which we live and work. We support civic activities and encourage our members to participate in them.

We intend to conduct this firm in a businesslike manner, employing all the benefits and economies of technology and efficient organization. We reject, however, the concept that the practice of law is to be shaped by a profit orientation which diverts and obstructs us from the achievement of our professional goals.

We view our ultimate objective as the rendering of service, and the making of profit is only a component, albeit an important component, in the pursuit of that objective.

Federal Materials

Federal Conflict and Confidentiality Provisions

Editors' Introduction. Lawyers who work (or have worked) for the federal government are subject not only to rules of legal ethics but also to various federal statutes and regulations governing confidentiality and conflicts of interest. The statutes and regulations that follow contain detailed restrictions on the use or revelation of confidential information and on the propriety of a former government lawyer's representation of private clients in matters relating to work the lawyer did while in government service. Violation of the statutory provisions is a crime.

Contents

SELECTED PROVISIONS FROM 18 U.S.C.

SELECTED PROVISIONS FROM 28 C.F.R. PARTS 45 AND 50

SELECTED PROVISIONS FROM 18 U.S.C.
(As Amended Effective January 1, 1991)

§202. Definitions

... **(b) For the purposes of sections 205 and 207 of this title, the term "official responsibility" means the direct administrative or operating authority, whether intermediate or final, and either exercisable alone or with others, and either personally or through subordinates, to approve, disapprove, or otherwise direct Government action.**

(c) Except as otherwise provided in such sections, the terms "officer" and "employee" in sections 203, 205, 207 through 209, and 218 of this title shall not include the President, the Vice President, a Member of Congress, or a Federal judge.

§207. Restrictions on Former Officers, Employees, and Elected Officials of the Executive and Legislative Branches

(a) *Restrictions on all officers and employees of the executive branch and certain other agencies.* —

(1) *Permanent restrictions on representation on particular matters.* — **Any person who is an officer or employee (including any special Government employee) of the executive branch of the United States (including any independent agency of the United States), or of the District of Columbia, and who, after the termination of his or her service or employment with the United States or the District of Columbia, knowingly makes, with the intent to influence, any communication to or appearance before any officer or employee of any department, agency, court, or court-martial of the United States or the District of Columbia, on behalf of any other person (except the United States or the District of Columbia) in connection with a particular matter —**

(A) in which the United States or the District of Columbia is a party or has a direct and substantial interest,

(B) in which the person participated personally and substantially as such officer or employee, and

(C) which involved a specific party or specific parties at the time of such participation,

shall be punished as provided in section 216 of this title.

(2) *Two-year restrictions concerning particular matters under official responsibility.* — Any person subject to the restrictions contained in paragraph (1) who, within 2 years after the termination of his or her service or employment with the United States or the District of Columbia, knowingly makes, with the intent to influence, any communication to or appearance before any officer or employee of any department, agency, court, or court-martial of the United States or the District of Columbia, on behalf of any other person (except the United States or the District of Columbia), in connection with a particular matter —

(A) in which the United States or the District of Columbia is a party or has a direct and substantial interest,

(B) which such person knows or reasonably should know was actually pending under his or her official responsibility as such officer or employee within a period of 1 year before the termination of his or her service or employment with the United States or the District of Columbia, and

(C) which involved a specific party or specific parties at the time it was so pending,

shall be punished as provided in section 216 of this title.

(3) *Clarification of restrictions.* — The restrictions contained in paragraphs (1) and (2) shall apply —

(A) in the case of an officer or employee of the executive branch of the United States (including any independent agency), only with respect to communications to or appearances before any officer or employee of any department, agency, court, or court-martial of the United States on behalf of any other person (except the United States), and only with respect to a matter in which the United States is a party or has a direct and substantial interest; and

(B) in the case of an officer or employee of the District of Columbia, only with respect to communications to or appearances before any officer or employee of any department, agency, or court of the District of Columbia on behalf of any other person (except the District of Columbia), and only with respect to a matter in which the District of Columbia is a party or has a direct and substantial interest.

(b) *One-year restrictions on aiding or advising.* —

(1) *In general.* — Any person who is a former officer or employee of the executive branch of the United States (including any independent agency) and is subject to the restrictions contained in subsection (a)(1), or any person who is a former officer or employee of the legislative branch or a former Member of Congress, who personally and substantially participated in any ongoing trade or treaty negotiation on behalf of the United States

within the 1-year period preceding the date on which his or her service or employment with the United States terminated, and who had access to information concerning such trade or treaty negotiation which is exempt from disclosure under section 552 of title 5, which is so designated by the appropriate department or agency, and which the person knew or should have known was so designated, shall not, on the basis of that information, knowingly represent, aid, or advise any other person (except the United States) concerning such ongoing trade or treaty negotiation for a period of 1 year after his or her service or employment with the United States terminates. Any person who violates this subsection shall be punished as provided in section 216 of this title.

(2) *Definition.* — For purposes of this paragraph —

(A) the term "trade negotiation" means negotiations which the President determines to undertake to enter into a trade agreement pursuant to section 1102 of the Omnibus Trade and Competitiveness Act of 1988, and does not include any action taken before that determination is made; and

(B) the term "treaty" means an international agreement made by the President that requires the advice and consent of the Senate.

(c) *One-year restrictions on certain senior personnel of the executive branch and independent agencies.* —

(1) *Restrictions.* — In addition to the restrictions set forth in subsections (a) and (b), any person who is an officer or employee (including any special Government employee) of the executive branch of the United States (including an independent agency), who is referred to in paragraph (2), and who, within 1 year after the termination of his or her service or employment as such officer or employee, knowingly makes, with the intent to influence, any communication to or appearance before any officer or employee of the department or agency in which such person served within 1 year before such termination, on behalf of any other person (except the United States), in connection with any matter on which such person seeks official action by any officer or employee of such department or agency, shall be punished as provided in section 216 of this title.

(2) *Persons to whom restrictions apply.* — (A) Paragraph (1) shall apply to a person (other than a person subject to the restrictions of subsection (d)) —

(i) employed at a rate of pay specified in or fixed according to subchapter II of chapter 53 of title 5,

(ii) employed in a position which is not referred to in clause (i) and for which the basic rate of pay, exclusive of any locality-based pay adjustment under section 5302 of title 5 (or any comparable adjustment pursuant to interim authority of the President), is equal to or greater than the rate of basic pay payable for level V of the Executive Schedule;

(iii) appointed by the President to a position under section 105(a)(2)(B) of title 3 or by the Vice President to a position under section 106(a)(1)(B) of title 3, or

(iv) employed in a position which is held by an active duty commissioned officer of the uniformed services who is serving in a grade or rank for which the pay grade (as specified in section 201 of title 37) is pay grade O-7 or above.

(B)Paragraph (1) shall not apply to a special Government employee who serves less than 60 days in the 1-year period before his or her service or employment as such employee terminates.

(C) At the request of a department or agency, the Director of the Office of Government Ethics may waive the restrictions contained in paragraph (1) with respect to any position, or category of positions, referred to in clause (ii) or (iv) of subparagraph (A), in such department or agency if the Director determines that —

(i) the imposition of the restrictions with respect to such position or positions would create an undue hardship on the department or agency in obtaining qualified personnel to fill such position or positions, and

(ii) granting the waiver would not create the potential for use of undue influence or unfair advantage.

(d) *Restrictions on very senior personnel of the executive branch and independent agencies.* —

(1) *Restrictions.* — In addition to the restrictions set forth in subsections (a) and (b), any person who —

(A) serves in the position of Vice President of the United States,

(B) is employed in a position in the executive branch of the United States (including any independent agency) at a rate of pay payable for level I of the Executive Schedule or employed in a position in the Executive Office of the President at a rate of pay payable for level II of the Executive Schedule, or

(C) is appointed by the President to a position under section 105(a)(2)(A) of title 3 or by the Vice President to a position under section 106(a)(1)(A) of title 3,

and who, within 1 year after the termination of that person's service in that position, knowingly makes, with the intent to influence, any communication to or appearance before any person described in paragraph (2), on behalf of any other person (except the United States), in connection with any matter on which such person seeks official action by any officer or employee of the executive branch of the United States, shall be punished as provided in section 216 of this title.

(2) *Persons who may not be contacted.* — The persons referred to in paragraph (1) with respect to appearances or communications by a person in a position described in subparagraph (A), (B), or (C) of paragraph (1) are —

(A) any officer or employee of any department or agency in which such person served in such position within a period of 1 year before such person's service or employment with the United States Government terminated, and

(B) any person appointed to a position in the executive branch which is listed in sections 5312, 5313, 5314, 5315, or 5316 of title 5.

(e) *Restrictions on members of Congress and officers and employees of the legislative branch.* —

(1) *Members of congress and elected officers.* — (A) Any person who is a Member of Congress or an elected officer of either House of Congress and who, within 1 year after that person leaves office, knowingly makes, with the intent to influence, any communication to or appearance before any of the persons described in subparagraph (B) or (C), on behalf of any other person (except the United States) in connection with any matter on which such former Member of Congress or elected officer seeks action by a Member, officer, or employee of either House of Congress, in his or her official capacity, shall be punished as provided in section 216 of this title.

(B) The persons referred to in subparagraph (A) with respect to appearances or communications by a former Member of Congress are any Member, officer, or employee of either House of Congress, and any employee of any other legislative office of the Congress.

(C) The persons referred to in subparagraph (A) with respect to appearances or communications by a former elected officer are any Member, officer, or employee of the House of Congress in which the elected officer served.

(2) *Personal staff.* — (A) Any person who is an employee of a Senator or an employee of a Member of the House of Representatives and who, within 1 year after the termination of that employment, knowingly makes, with the intent to influence, any communication to or appearance before any of the persons described in subparagraph (B), on behalf of any other person (except the United States) in connection with any matter on which such former employee seeks action by a Member, officer, or employee of either House of Congress, in his or her official capacity, shall be punished as provided in section 216 of this title.

(B) The persons referred to in subparagraph (A) with respect to appearances or communications by a person who is a former employee are the following:

(i) the Senator or Member of the House of Representatives for whom that person was an employee; and

(ii) any employee of that Senator or Member of the House of Representatives.

(3) *Committee staff.* — Any person who is an employee of a committee of Congress and who, within 1 year after the termination of that person's employment on such committee, knowingly makes, with the intent to influ-

ence, any communication to or appearance before any person who is a Member or an employee of that committee or who was a Member of the committee in the year immediately prior to the termination of such person's employment by the committee, on behalf of any other person (except the United States) in connection with any matter on which such former employee seeks action by a Member, officer, or employee of either House of Congress, in his or her official capacity, shall be punished as provided in section 216 of this title.

(4) *Leadership staff.* — (A) Any person who is an employee on the leadership staff of the House of Representatives or an employee on the leadership staff of the Senate and who, within 1 year after the termination of that person's employment on such staff, knowingly makes, with the intent to influence, any communication to or appearance before any of the persons described in subparagraph (B), on behalf of any other person (except the United States) in connection with any matter on which such former employee seeks action by a Member, officer, or employee of either House of Congress, in his or her official capacity, shall be punished as provided in section 216 of this title.

(B) The persons referred to in subparagraph (A) with respect to appearances or communications by a former employee are the following:

(i) in the case of a former employee on the leadership staff of the House of Representatives, those persons are any Member of the leadership of the House of Representatives and any employee on the leadership staff of the House of Representatives; and

(ii) in the case of a former employee on the leadership staff of the Senate, those persons are any Member of the leadership of the Senate and any employee on the leadership staff of the Senate.

(5) *Other legislative offices.* — (A) Any person who is an employee of any other legislative office of the Congress and who, within 1 year after the termination of that person's employment in such office, knowingly makes, with the intent to influence, any communication to or appearance before any of the persons described in subparagraph (B), on behalf of any other person (except the United States) in connection with any matter on which such former employee seeks action by any officer or employee of such office, in his or her official capacity, shall be punished as provided in section 216 of this title.

(B) The persons referred to in subparagraph (A) with respect to appearances or communications by a former employee are the employees and officers of the former legislative office of the Congress of the former employee.

(6) *Limitation on restrictions.* — (A) The restrictions contained in paragraphs (2), (3), and (4) apply only to acts by a former employee who, for at least 60 days, in the aggregate, during the 1-year period before that former employee's service as such employee terminated, was paid a rate of

basic pay equal to or greater than an amount which is 75 percent of the basic rate of pay payable for a Member of the House of Congress in which such employee was employed.

(B) The restrictions contained in paragraph (5) apply only to acts by a former employee who, for at least 60 days, in the aggregate, during the 1-year period before that former employee's service as such employee terminated, was employed in a position for which the rate of basic pay, exclusive of any locality-based pay adjustment under section 5302 of title 5 (or any comparable adjustment pursuant to interim authority of the President), is equal to or greater than the basic rate of pay payable for level V of the Executive Schedule.

(7) *Definitions.* — As used in this subsection —

(A) the term "committee of Congress" includes standing committees, joint committees, and select committees;

(B) a person is an employee of a House of Congress if that person is an employee of the Senate or an employee of the House of Representatives;

(C) the term "employee of the House of Representatives" means an employee of a Member of the House of Representatives, an employee of a committee of the House of Representatives, an employee of a joint committee of the Congress whose pay is disbursed by the Clerk of the House of Representatives, and an employee on the leadership staff of the House of Representatives;

(D) the term "employee of the Senate" means an employee of a Senator, an employee of a committee of the Senate, an employee of a joint committee of the Congress whose pay is disbursed by the Secretary of the Senate, and an employee on the leadership staff of the Senate;

(E) a person is an employee of a Member of the House of Representatives if that person is an employee of a Member of the House of Representatives under the clerk hire allowance;

(F) a person is an employee of a Senator if that person is an employee in a position in the office of a Senator;

(G) the term "employee of any other legislative office of the Congress" means an officer or employee of the Architect of the Capitol, the United States Botanic Garden, the General Accounting Office, the Government Printing Office, the Library of Congress, the Office of Technology Assessment, the Congressional Budget Office, the Copyright Royalty Tribunal, the United States Capitol Police, and any other agency, entity, or office in the legislative branch not covered by paragraph (1), (2), (3), or (4) of this subsection;

(H) the term "employee on the leadership staff of the House of Representatives" means an employee of the office of a Member of the leadership of the House of Representatives described in subparagraph (L), and any elected minority employee of the House of Representatives;

(I) the term "employee on the leadership staff of the Senate" means an employee of the office of a Member of the leadership of the Senate described in subparagraph (M);

(J) the term "Member of Congress" means a Senator or a Member of the House of Representatives;

(K) the term "Member of the House of Representatives" means a Representative in, or a Delegate or Resident Commissioner to, the Congress;

(L) the term "Member of the leadership of the House of Representatives" means the Speaker, majority leader, minority leader, majority whip, minority whip, chief deputy majority whip, chief deputy minority whip, chairman of the Democratic Steering Committee, chairman and vice chairman of the Democratic Caucus, chairman, vice chairman, and secretary of the Republican Conference, chairman of the Republican Research Committee, and chairman of the Republican Policy Committee, of the House of Representatives (or any similar position created on or after the effective date set forth in section 102(a) of the Ethics Reform Act of 1989);

(M) the term "Member of the leadership of the Senate" means the Vice President, and the President pro tempore, Deputy President pro tempore, majority leader, minority leader, majority whip, minority whip, chairman and secretary of the Conference of the Majority, chairman and secretary of the Conference of the Minority, chairman and co-chairman of the Majority Policy Committee, and chairman of the Minority Policy Committee, of the Senate (or any similar position created on or after the effective date set forth in section 102(a) of the Ethics Reform Act of 1989).

(f) *Restrictions relating to foreign entities.* —

(1) *Restrictions.* — Any person who is subject to the restrictions contained in subsection (c), (d), or (e) and who knowingly, within 1 year after leaving the position, office, or employment referred to in such subsection —

(A) represents a foreign entity before any officer or employee of any department or agency of the United States with the intent to influence a decision of such officer or employee in carrying out his or her official duties, or

(B) aids or advises a foreign entity with the intent to influence a decision of any officer or employee of any department or agency of the United States, in carrying out his or her official duties,

shall be punished as provided in section 216 of this title.

(2) *Definition.* — For purposes of this subsection, the term "foreign entity" means the government of a foreign country as defined in section 1(e) of the Foreign Agents Registration Act of 1938, as amended, or a foreign political party as defined in section 1(f) of that Act.

(g) *Special rules for detailees.* — For purposes of this section, a person who is detailed from one department, agency, or other entity to another department, agency, or other entity shall, during the period such person is detailed, be deemed to be an officer or employee of both departments, agencies, or such entities.

(h) *Designations of separate statutory agencies and bureaus. —*

(1) *Designations. —* For purposes of subsection (c) and except as provided in paragraph (2), whenever the Director of the Office of Government Ethics determines that an agency or bureau within a department or agency in the executive branch exercises functions which are distinct and separate from the remaining functions of the department or agency and that there exists no potential for use of undue influence or unfair advantage based on past Government service, the Director shall by rule designate such agency or bureau as a separate department or agency. On an annual basis the Director of the Office of Government Ethics shall review the designations and determinations made under this subparagraph and, in consultation with the department or agency concerned, make such additions and deletions as are necessary. Departments and agencies shall cooperate to the fullest extent with the Director of the Office of Government Ethics in the exercise of his or her responsibilities under this paragraph.

(2) *Inapplicability of designations. —* No agency or bureau within the Executive Office of the President may be designated under paragraph (1) as a separate department or agency. No designation under paragraph (1) shall apply to persons referred to in subsection (c)(2)(A)(i) or (iii).

(i) *Definitions. —* For purposes of this section —

(1) the term "officer or employee", when used to describe the person to whom a communication is made or before whom an appearance is made, with the intent to influence, shall include —

    (A) in subsections (a), (c), and (d), the President and the Vice President; and

    (B) in subsection (f), the President, the Vice President, and Members of Congress;

(2) the term "participated" means an action taken as an officer or employee through decision, approval, disapproval, recommendation, the rendering of advice, investigation, or other such action; and

(3) the term "particular matter" includes any investigation, application, request for a ruling or determination, rulemaking, contract, controversy, claim, charge, accusation, arrest, or judicial or other proceeding.

§208. Acts Affecting a Personal Financial Interest

(a) Except as permitted by subsection (b) hereof, whoever, being an officer or employee of the executive branch of the United States Government, or of any independent agency of the United States, a Federal Reserve bank director, officer, or employee, or an officer or employee of the District of Columbia, including a special Government employee, participates personally and substantially as a Government officer or employee, through decision, approval, disapproval, recommendation, the rendering of advice, investigation, or otherwise, in a judicial or other proceeding, application, request for a ruling or other determination, contract, claim, controversy, charge, accusation, arrest, or other particular matter in which, to his knowledge, he, his spouse, minor child, general partner, organization in which he is serving as officer, director, trustee, general partner or employee, or any person or organization with whom he is negotiating or has any arrangement concerning prospective employment, has a financial interest —

Shall be subject to the penalties set forth in section 216 of this title.

(b) Subsection (a) shall not apply —

(1) if the officer or employee first advises the Government official responsible for appointment to his or her position of the nature and circumstances of the judicial or other proceeding, application, request for a ruling or other determination, contract, claim, controversy, charge, accusation, arrest, or other particular matter and makes full disclosure of the financial interest and receives in advance a written determination made by such official that the interest is not so substantial as to be deemed likely to affect the integrity of the services which the Government may expect from such officer or employee;

(2) if, by regulation issued by the Director of the Office of Government Ethics, applicable to all or a portion of all officers and employees covered by this section, and published in the Federal Register, the financial interest has been exempted from the requirements of paragraph (a) as being too remote or too inconsequential to affect the integrity of the services of the Government officers or employees to which such regulation applies;

(3) in the case of a special Government employee serving on an advisory committee within the meaning of the Federal Advisory Committee Act (including an individual being considered for an appointment to such a position), the official responsible for the employee's appointment, after review of the financial disclosure report filed by the individual pursuant to section 107 of the Ethics in Government Act of 1978, certifies in writing that the need for the individual's services outweighs the potential for a conflict of interest created by the financial interest involved. . . .

(d)(1) Upon request, a copy of any determination granting an exemption under subsection (b)(1) or (b)(3) shall be made available to the public by the agency granting the exemption pursuant to the procedures set forth in section 105 of the Ethics in Government Act of 1978. In making such determination available, the agency may withhold from disclosure any information contained in the determination that would be exempt from disclosure under section 552 of title 5. For purposes of determinations under subsection (b)(3), the information describing each financial interest shall be no more extensive than that required of the individual in his or her financial disclosure report under the Ethics in Government Act of 1978.

(2) The Office of Government Ethics, after consultation with the Attorney General, shall issue uniform regulations for the issuance of waivers and exemptions under subsection (b) which shall —

(A) list and describe exemptions; and

(B) provide guidance with respect to the types of interests that are not so substantial as to be deemed likely to affect the integrity of the services the Government may expect from the employee.

§1905. Disclosure of Confidential Information
          Generally

Whoever, being an officer or employee of the United States or of any department or agency thereof, or agent of the Department of Justice as defined in the Antitrust Civil Process Act (15 U.S.C. 1311-1314), publishes, divulges, discloses, or makes known in any manner or to any extent not authorized by law any information coming to him in the course of his employment or official duties or by reason of any examination or investigation made by, or return, report or record made to or filed with, such department or agency or officer or employee thereof, which information concerns or relates to the trade secrets, processes, operations, style of work, or apparatus, or to the identity, confidential statistical data, amount or source of any income, profits, losses, or expenditures of any person, firm, partnership, corporation, or association; or permits any income return or copy thereof or any book containing any abstract or particulars thereof to be seen or examined by any person except as provided by law; shall be fined not more than $1,000, or imprisoned not more than one year, or both; and shall be removed from office or employment.

SELECTED PROVISIONS FROM 28 C.F.R.
PARTS 45 AND 50

§45.735-4. Disqualification Arising from Personal or
            Political Relationship

(a) Unless authorized under paragraph (b) of this section, no employee shall participate in a criminal investigation or prosecution if he has a personal or political relationship with:

(1) Any person or organization substantially involved in the conduct that is the subject of the investigation or prosecution; or

(2) Any person or organization which he knows has a specific and substantial interest that would be directly affected by the outcome of the investigation or prosecution.

(b) An employee assigned to or otherwise participating in a criminal investigation or prosecution who believes that his participation may be prohibited by paragraph (a) of this section shall report the matter and all attendant facts and circumstances to his supervisor at the level of section chief or the equivalent or higher. If the supervisor determines that a personal or political relationship exists between the employee and a person or organization described in paragraph (a) of this section, he shall relieve the employee from participation unless he determines further, in writing, after full consideration of all the facts and circumstances, that:

(1) The relationship will not have the effect of rendering the employee's service less than fully impartial and professional; and

(2) The employee's participation would not create an appearance of a conflict of interest likely to affect the public perception of the integrity of the investigation or prosecution.

(c) For the purposes of this section:

(1) "Political relationship" means a close identification with an elected official, a candidate (whether or not successful) for elective public office, a political party, or a campaign organization, arising from service as a principal adviser thereto or a principal official thereof; and

(2) "Personal relationship" means a close and substantial connection of the type normally viewed as likely to induce partiality. An employee is presumed to have a personal relationship with his father, mother, brother, sister, child and spouse. Whether relationships (including friendships) of an employee to other persons or organizations are "personal" must be judged on an individual basis with due regard given to the subjective opinion of the employee.

(d) This section pertains to agency management and is not intended to create rights enforceable by private individuals or organizations.

§45.735-5. Disqualification Arising from Private Financial Interests

(a) No employee shall participate personally and substantially as a Government employee, through decision, approval, disapproval, recommendation, the rendering of advice, investigation or otherwise, in a judicial or other proceeding, application, request for a ruling or other determination, contract, claim, controversy, charge, accusation, arrest or other particular matter in which, to his knowledge, he, his spouse, minor child, partner, organization in which he is serving as officer, director, trustee, partner or employee, or any person or organization with whom he is negotiating or has any arrangement concerning prospective employment, has a financial interest, unless authorized to do so in accordance with the following described procedure:

(1) The employee shall inform the head of his division of the nature and circumstances of the matter and of the financial interest involved and shall

request a determination as to the propriety of his participation in the matter.

(2) The head of the division, after examining the information submitted, may relieve the employee from participation in the matter, or he may submit the matter to the Deputy Attorney General with recommendations for appropriate action. In cases so referred to him, the Deputy Attorney General may relieve the employee from participation in the matter or may approve the employee's participation in the matter upon determining in writing that the interest involved is not so substantial as to be likely to affect the integrity of the services which the Government may expect from such employee.

(b) The financial interests described below are hereby exempted from the prohibition of 18 U.S.C. 208(a) as being too remote or too inconsequential to affect the integrity of an employee's services in a matter:

> The stock, bond, or policy holdings of an employee in a mutual fund, investment company, bank or insurance company which owns an interest in an entity involved in the matter, provided that in the case of a mutual fund, investment company or bank the fair value of such stock or bond holding does not exceed 1 percent of the value of the reported assets of the mutual fund, investment company, or bank [quoting 18 U.S.C. §208(a)].

§45.735-7. Disqualification of Former Employees; Disqualification of Partners of Current Employees

(a) No individual who has been an employee shall, after his employment has ceased, knowingly act as agent or attorney for, or otherwise represent, any other person (except the United States) in any formal or informal appearance before, or, with the intent to influence, make any oral or written communication on behalf of any other person (except the United States)

(1) To any department, agency, court, court-martial, or any civil, military, or naval commission of the United States or the District of Columbia, or any officer or employee thereof,

(2) In connection with any judicial or other proceeding, application, request for a ruling or other determination, contract, claim, controversy, investigation, charge, accusation, arrest, or other particular matter involving a specific party or parties in which the United States or the District of Columbia is a party or has a direct and substantial interest, and

(3) In which he participated personally and substantially as an employee through decision, approval, disapproval, recommendation, the rendering of advice, investigation or otherwise, while so employed. (18 U.S.C. 207(a))

(b) No individual who has been an employee shall, within two years after his employment has ceased, knowingly act as agent or attorney for, or otherwise represent, any other person (except the United States) in any formal or informal appearance before, or with intent to influence, make any oral or written communication on behalf of any other person (except the United States)

(1) To an organization enumerated in paragraph (a)(1) of this section, or any officer or employee thereof,

(2) In connection with any matter enumerated and described in paragraph (a)(2) of this section, and

(3) Which was actually pending under his official responsibility as an employee within a period of one year prior to the termination of such responsibility. (18 U.S.C. 207(b)(i))

(c) No individual who has been an employee in an executive level position, in a position with a comparable or greater rate of pay, or in a position that involved significant decisionmaking or supervisory responsibility as designated by the Director of the Office of Government Ethics under 18 U.S.C. 207(d)(1)(C), shall, within two years after his employment in such position has ceased, knowingly represent or aid, counsel, advise, consult, or assist in representing any other person (except the United States) by personal presence at any formal or informal appearance before (1) an organization enumerated in paragraph (a)(1) of this section, or an officer or employee thereof, (2) in connection with any matter enumerated and described in paragraph (a)(2) of this section, and (3) in which he participated personally or substantially as an employee. (18 U.S.C. 207(b)(ii))

(d) No individual (other than one who was a special Government employee with service of less than sixty days in a given calendar year) who has been an employee in an executive level position or a position with a comparable or greater rate of pay, or in a position which involved significant decisionmaking or supervisory responsibility as designated by the Director of the Office of Government Ethics under 18 U.S.C. 207(d)(1)(C), shall, within one year after such employment has ceased, knowingly engage in conduct described in the next sentence. The prohibited knowing conduct is that of acting as attorney or agent for, or otherwise representing, anyone other than the United States in any formal or informal appearance before, or with the intent to influence, making any oral or written communication on behalf of anyone other than the United States (1) to the Department of Justice, or any employee thereof, (2) in connection with any rulemaking or any matter enumerated and described in paragraph (a)(2) of this section, and (3) which is pending before this Department or in which it has a direct and substantial interest. (18 U.S.C. 207(c); but see 5 CFR 737.13, 737.31 and 737.32)

(e) No partner of an employee shall act as agent or attorney for anyone other than the United States before an organization enumerated in paragraph (a)(1) of this section, or any officer or employee thereof, in connection with any matter enumerated and described in paragraph (a)(2) of this section in which such Government employee is participating or has participated personally and substantially as a Government employee through decision, approval, disapproval, recommendation, the rendering of advice, investigation or otherwise, or which is the subject of his official responsibility.

§45.735-10. Improper Use of Official Information

No employee shall use for financial gain for himself or for another person, or make any other improper use of, whether by direct action on his part or by counsel, recommendation, or suggestion to another person, information which comes to the employee by reason of his status as a Department of Justice employee and which has not become part of the body of public information.

§45.735-11. Investments

No employee shall make investments: (a) In enterprises which it is reasonable to believe will be involved in decisions to be made by him, (b) on the basis of information which comes to him by reason of his status as a Department of Justice employee and which has not become part of the body of public information or (c) which are reasonably likely to create any conflict in the proper discharge of his official duties.

§45.735-12. Speeches, Publications and Teaching

(a) No employee shall accept a fee from an outside source on account of a public appearance, speech, lecture, or publication if the public appearance or the preparation of the speech, lecture, or publication was a part of the official duties of the employee.

(b) No employee shall receive compensation or anything of monetary value for any consultation, lecture, teaching, discussion, writing, or appearance the subject matter of which is devoted substantially to the responsibilities, programs or operations of the Department, or which draws substantially on official data or ideas which have not become part of the body of public information.

(c) No employee shall engage, whether with or without compensation, in teaching, lecturing or writing that is dependent on information obtained as a result of his Government employment except when that information has been made available to the general public or when the Deputy Attorney General gives written authorization for the use of nonpublic information on the basis that the use is in the public interest.

(d)(1) The Attorney General, Deputy Attorney General, Associate Attorney General, and the heads of divisions shall not make speeches or otherwise lend their names or support in a prominent fashion to a fundraising drive or a fundraising event or similar event intended for the benefit of any person. No Department of Justice employee or special Government employee shall engage in any of these activities if the invitation was extended primarily because of his official position with the Department or if the fact of his official position with the Department has been or will be used in the promotion of the event to any significant degree.

(2) For purposes of this subsection, an event will be regarded as a fundraising event if any portion of the ticket or other cost of admission is designated as a charitable contribution for tax purposes, if one of its purposes is to produce net proceeds for the benefit of any person, or if it is a "kickoff" dinner or similar occasion that is part of a broader fundraising effort.

(3) Nothing in this subsection shall apply to the Combined Federal Campaign or any other authorized fundraising drive directed primarily at Federal employees, or to a fundraising event of an organization which is exempt from taxation under 26 U.S.C. 501(c)(3).

(4) Nothing in this subsection shall apply to a meeting, seminar, or conference sponsored by a professional or other appropriate organization where a tuition or other fee is charged for attendance if such tuition or fee is reasonable under the circumstances.

(e) When an employee is prohibited by this section from accepting compensation for an activity, he is also prohibited from suggesting that the person offering such compensation donate it to a particular charity or other third party.

§50.2. Release of Information by Personnel of the Department of Justice Relating to Criminal and Civil Proceedings

(a) General. (1) The availability to news media of information in criminal and civil cases is a matter which has become increasingly a subject of concern in the administration of justice. The purpose of this statement is to formulate specific guidelines for the release of such information by personnel of the Department of Justice.

(2) While the release of information for the purpose of influencing a trial is, of course, always improper, there are valid reasons for making available to the public information about the administration of the law. The task of striking a fair balance between the protection of individuals accused of crime or involved in civil proceedings with the Government and public understandings of the problems of controlling crime and administering government depends largely on the exercise of sound judgment by

589

those responsible for administering the law and by representatives of the press and other media.

(3) Inasmuch as the Department of Justice has generally fulfilled its responsibilities with awareness and understanding of the competing needs in this area, this statement, to a considerable extent, reflects and formalizes the standards to which representatives of the Department have adhered in the past. Nonetheless, it will be helpful in ensuring uniformity of practice to set forth the following guidelines for all personnel of the Department of Justice.

(4) Because of the difficulty and importance of the questions they raise, it is felt that some portions of the matters covered by this statement, such as the authorization to make available Federal conviction records and a description of items seized at the time of arrest, should be the subject of continuing review and consideration by the Department on the basis of experience and suggestions from those within and outside the Department.

(b) Guidelines to criminal actions. (1) These guidelines shall apply to the release of information to news media from the time a person is the subject of a criminal investigation until any proceeding resulting from such an investigation has been terminated by trial or otherwise.

(2) At no time shall personnel of the Department of Justice furnish any statement or information for the purpose of influencing the outcome of a defendant's trial, nor shall personnel of the Department furnish any statement or information, which could reasonably be expected to be disseminated by means of public communication, if such a statement or information may reasonably be expected to influence the outcome of a pending or future trial.

(3) Personnel of the Department of Justice, subject to specific limitations imposed by law or court rule or order, may make public the following information:

(i) The defendant's name, age, residence, employment, marital status, and similar background information.

(ii) The substance or text of the charge, such as a complaint, indictment, or information.

(iii) The identity of the investigating and/or arresting agency and the length or scope of an investigation.

(iv) The circumstances immediately surrounding an arrest, resistance, pursuit, possession and use of weapons, and a description of physical items seized at the time of arrest.

Disclosures should include only incontrovertible, factual matters, and should not include subjective observations. In addition, where background information or information relating to the circumstances of an arrest or investigation would be highly prejudicial or where the release thereof would serve no law enforcement function, such information should not be made public.

(4) Personnel of the Department shall not disseminate any information concerning a defendant's prior criminal record.

(5) Because of the particular danger of prejudice resulting from statements in the period approaching and during trial, they ought strenuously to be avoided during that period. Any such statement or release shall be made only on the infrequent occasion when circumstances absolutely demand a disclosure of information and shall include only information which is clearly not prejudicial.

(6) The release of certain types of information generally tends to create dangers of prejudice without serving a significant law enforcement function. Therefore, personnel of the Department should refrain from making available the following:

(i) Observations about a defendant's character.

(ii) Statements, admissions, confessions, or alibis attributable to a defendant, or the refusal or failure of the accused to make a statement.

(iii) Reference to investigative procedures such as fingerprints, polygraph examinations, ballistic tests, or laboratory tests, or to the refusal by the defendant to submit to such tests or examinations.

(iv) Statements concerning the identity, testimony, or credibility of prospective witnesses.

(v) Statements concerning evidence or argument in the case, whether or not it is anticipated that such evidence or argument will be used at trial.

(vi) Any opinion as to the accused's guilt, or the possibility of a plea of guilty to the offense charged, or the possibility of a plea to a lesser offense.

(7) Personnel of the Department of Justice should take no action to encourage or assist news media in photographing or televising a defendant or accused person being held or transported in Federal custody. Departmental representatives should not make available photographs of a defendant unless a law enforcement function is served thereby.

(8) This statement of policy is not intended to restrict the release of information concerning a defendant who is a fugitive from justice.

(9) Since the purpose of this statement is to set forth generally applicable guidelines, there will, of course, be situations in which it will limit the release of information which would not be prejudicial under the particular circumstances. If a representative of the Department believes that in the interest of the fair administration of justice and the law enforcement process information beyond these guidelines should be released, in a particular case, he shall request the permission of the Attorney General or the Deputy Attorney General to do so.

(c) Guidelines to civil actions. Personnel of the Department of Justice associated with a civil action shall not during its investigation or litigation make or participate in making an extrajudicial statement, other than a quotation from or reference to public records, which a reasonable person would expect to be disseminated by means of public communication if there is a reasonable likelihood that such dissemination will interfere with a fair trial and which relates to:

(1) Evidence regarding the occurrence or transaction involved.

(2) The character, credibility, or criminal records of a party, witness, or prospective witness.

(3) The performance or results of any examinations or tests or the refusal or failure of a party to submit to such.

(4) An opinion as to the merits of the claims or defenses of a party, except as required by law or administrative rule.

(5) Any other matter reasonably likely to interfere with a fair trial of the action.

§50.19. Procedures to Be Followed by Government
         Attorneys Prior to Filing Recusal or
         Disqualification Motions

The determination to seek for any reason the disqualification or recusal of a justice, judge, or magistrate is a most significant and sensitive decision. This is particularly true for government attorneys, who should be guided by uniform procedures in obtaining the requisite authorization for such a motion. This statement is designed to establish a uniform procedure.

(a) No motion to recuse or disqualify a justice, judge, or magistrate *(see, e.g.,* 28 U.S.C. 144, 455) shall be made or supported by any Department of Justice attorney, U.S. Attorney (including Assistant U.S. Attorneys) or agency counsel conducting litigation pursuant to agreement with or authority delegated by the Attorney General, without the prior written approval of the Assistant Attorney General having ultimate supervisory power over the action in which recusal or disqualification is being considered.

(b) Prior to seeking such approval, Justice Department lawyer(s) handling the litigation shall timely seek the recommendations of the U.S. Attorney for the district in which the matter is pending, and the views of the client agencies, if any. Similarly, if agency attorneys are primarily handling any such suit, they shall seek the recommendations of the U.S. Attorney and provide them to the Department of Justice with the request for approval. In actions where the United States Attorneys are primarily handling the litigation in question, they shall seek the recommendation of the client agencies, if any, for submission to the Assistant Attorney General.

(c) In the event that the conduct and pace of the litigation does not allow sufficient time to seek the prior written approval by the Assistant Attorney General, prior oral authorization shall be sought and a written record fully reflecting that authorization shall be subsequently prepared and submitted to the Assistant Attorney General.

(d) Assistant Attorneys General may delegate the authority to approve or deny requests made pursuant to this section, but only to Deputy Assistant Attorneys General or an equivalent position.

(e) This policy statement does not create or enlarge any legal obligations upon the Department of Justice in civil or criminal litigation, and it is not intended to create any private rights enforceable by private parties in litigation with the United States.

Selected Federal Statutes Regarding Bias and Disqualification of Federal Judges and Judicial Discipline

Editors' Introduction. The Code of Judicial Conduct prohibits judges from presiding over cases in which they have conflicts of interest or in which they are biased. However, the Code of Judicial Conduct does not by itself give parties the right to disqualify judges who fail to heed those prohibitions. In federal court, the right to disqualify judges derives from two federal statutes, 28 U.S.C. §§144 and 455, which we reprint below.

Federal judges appointed under Article III of the Constitution enjoy life tenure and can only be removed from office through impeachment by Congress. Provisions for discipline short of removal are contained in 28 U.S.C. §372(c), which follows the disqualification statutes below.

Contents

28 U.S.C. §144. Bias or Prejudice of Judges

Whenever a party to any proceeding in a district court makes and files a timely and sufficient affidavit that the judge before whom the matter is pending has a personal bias or prejudice either against him or in favor of any adverse party, such judge shall proceed no further therein, but another judge shall be assigned to hear such proceeding.

The affidavit shall state the facts and the reasons for the belief that bias or prejudice exists, and shall be filed not less than ten days before the beginning of the term at which the proceeding is to be heard, or good cause shall be shown for failure to file it within such time. A party may file only one such affidavit in any case. It shall be accompanied by a certificate of counsel of record stating that it is made in good faith.

28 U.S.C. §455. Disqualification of Justice, Judge, or Magistrate

(a) Any justice, judge, or magistrate of the United States shall disqualify himself in any proceeding in which his impartiality might reasonably be questioned.

(b) He shall also disqualify himself in the following circumstances:

(1) Where he has a personal bias or prejudice concerning a party, or personal knowledge of disputed evidentiary facts concerning the proceeding;

(2) Where in private practice he served as lawyer in the matter in controversy, or a lawyer with whom he previously practiced law served during such association as a lawyer concerning the matter, or the judge or such lawyer has been a material witness concerning it;

(3) Where he has served in governmental employment and in such capacity participated as counsel, adviser or material witness concerning the proceeding or expressed an opinion concerning the merits of the particular case in controversy;

(4) He knows that he, individually or as a fiduciary, or his spouse or minor child residing in his household, has a financial interest in the subject matter in controversy or in a party to the proceeding, or any other interest that could be substantially affected by the outcome of the proceeding;

(5) He or his spouse, or a person within the third degree of relationship to either of them, or the spouse of such a person:

(i) Is a party to the proceeding, or an officer, director, or trustee of a party;

(ii) Is acting as a lawyer in the proceeding;

(iii) Is known by the judge to have an interest that could be substantially affected by the outcome of the proceeding;

(iv) Is to the judge's knowledge likely to be a material witness in the proceeding.

(c) A judge should inform himself about his personal and fiduciary financial interests, and make a reasonable effort to inform himself about the personal financial interests of his spouse and minor children residing in his household.

(d) For the purposes of this section the following words or phrases shall have the meaning indicated:

(1) "proceeding" includes pretrial, trial, appellate review, or other stages of litigation;

(2) the degree of relationship is calculated according to the civil law system;

(3) "fiduciary" includes such relationships as executor, administrator, trustee, and guardian;

(4) "financial interest" means ownership of a legal or equitable interest, however small, or a relationship as director, adviser, or other active participant in the affairs of a party, except that:

(i) Ownership in a mutual or common investment fund that holds securities is not a "financial interest" in such securities unless the judge participates in the management of the fund;

(ii) An office in an educational, religious, charitable, fraternal, or civic organization is not a "financial interest" in securities held by the organization;

(iii) The proprietary interest of a policyholder in a mutual insurance company, of a depositor in a mutual savings association, or a similar proprietary interest, is a "financial interest" in the organization only if the outcome of the proceeding could substantially affect the value of the interest;

(iv) Ownership of governmental securities is a "financial interest" in the issuer only if the outcome of the proceeding could substantially affect the value of the securities.

(e) No justice, judge, or magistrate shall accept from the parties to the proceeding a waiver of any ground for disqualification enumerated in subsection (b). Where the ground for disqualification arises only under subsection (a), waiver may be accepted provided it is preceded by a full disclosure on the record of the basis for disqualification.

(f) Notwithstanding the preceding provisions of this section, if any justice, judge, magistrate, or bankruptcy judge to whom a matter has been assigned would be disqualified, after substantial judicial time has been devoted to the matter, because of the appearance or discovery, after the matter was assigned to him or her, that he or she individually or as a fiduciary, or his or her spouse or minor child residing in his or her household, has a financial interest in a party (other than an interest that could be substantially affected by the outcome), disqualification is not required if the justice, judge, magistrate, bankruptcy judge, spouse or minor child, as the case may be, divests himself or herself of the interest that provides the grounds for the disqualification.

Editors' Note. Subsection (f) of §455 was added by Congress in Public Law 100-702, effective November 19, 1988.

28 U.S.C. §372(c). Retirement for Disability;
                    Substitute Judge on Failure to
                    Retire; Judicial Discipline

. . . (c)(1) Any person alleging that a circuit, district, or bankruptcy judge, or a magistrate, has engaged in conduct prejudicial to the effective and expeditious administration of the business of the courts, or alleging that such a judge or magistrate is unable to discharge all the duties of office by reason of mental or physical disability, may file with the clerk of the court of appeals for the circuit a written complaint containing a brief statement of the facts constituting such conduct. In the interests of the effective and expeditious administration of the business of the courts and on the basis of information available to the chief judge of the circuit, the chief judge may, by written order stating reasons therefor, identify a complaint for purposes of this subsection and thereby dispense with filing of a written complaint.

(2) Upon receipt of a complaint filed under paragraph (1) of this subsection, the clerk shall promptly transmit such complaint to the chief judge of the circuit, or, if the conduct complained of is that of the chief judge, to that circuit judge in regular active service next senior in date of commission (hereafter, for purposes of this subsection only, included in the term "chief judge"). The clerk shall simultaneously transmit a copy of the complaint to the judge or magistrate whose conduct is the subject of the complaint.

(3) After expeditiously reviewing a complaint, the chief judge, by written order stating his reasons, may —

(A) dismiss the complaint, if he finds it to be (i) not in conformity with paragraph (1) of this subsection, (ii) directly related to the merits of a decision or procedural ruling, or (iii) frivolous; or

(B) conclude the proceeding if he finds that appropriate corrective action has been taken or that action on the complaint is no longer necessary because of intervening events.

The chief judge shall transmit copies of his written order to the complainant and to the judge or magistrate whose conduct is the subject of the complaint.

(4) If the chief judge does not enter an order under paragraph (3) of this subsection, such judge shall promptly —

(A) appoint himself and equal numbers of circuit and district judges of the circuit to a special committee to investigate the facts and allegations contained in the complaint;

(B) certify the complaint and any other documents pertaining thereto to each member of such committee; and

(C) provide written notice to the complainant and the judge or magistrate whose conduct is the subject of the complaint of the action taken under this paragraph.

A judge appointed to a special committee under this paragraph may continue to serve on that committee after becoming a senior judge or, in the case of the chief judge of the circuit, after his or her term as chief judge terminates under subsection (a)(3) or (c) of section 45 of this title. If a judge appointed to a committee under this paragraph dies, or retires from office under section 371(a) of this title, while serving on the committee, the chief judge of the circuit may appoint another circuit or district judge, as the case may be, to the committee.

(5) Each committee appointed under paragraph (4) of this subsection shall conduct an investigation as extensive as it considers necessary, and shall expeditiously file a comprehensive written report thereon with the judicial council of the circuit. Such report shall present both the findings of the investigation and the committee's recommendations for necessary and appropriate action by the judicial council of the circuit.

(6) Upon receipt of a report filed under paragraph (5) of this subsection, the judicial council —

(A) may conduct any additional investigation which it considers to be necessary;

(B) shall take such action as is appropriate to assure the effective and expeditious administration of the business of the courts within the circuit, including, but not limited to, any of the following actions:

(i) directing the chief judge of the district of the magistrate whose conduct is the subject of the complaint to take such action as the judicial council considers appropriate;

(ii) certifying disability of a judge appointed to hold office during good behavior whose conduct is the subject of the complaint, pursuant to the procedures and standards provided under subsection (b) of this section;

(iii) requesting that any such judge appointed to hold office during good behavior voluntarily retire, with the provision that the length of service requirements under section 371 of this title shall not apply;

(iv) ordering that, on a temporary basis for a time certain, no further cases be assigned to any judge or magistrate whose conduct is the subject of a complaint;

(v) censuring or reprimanding such judge or magistrate by means of private communication;

(vi) censuring or reprimanding such judge or magistrate by means of public announcement; or

(vii) ordering such other action as it considers appropriate under the circumstances, except that (I) in no circumstances may the council order removal from office of any judge appointed to hold office during good behavior, and (II) any removal of a magistrate shall be in accordance with section 631 of this title and any removal of a bankruptcy judge shall be in accordance with section 152 of this title;

(C) may dismiss the complaint; and

(D) shall immediately provide written notice to the complainant and to such judge or magistrate of the action taken under this paragraph.

(7)(A) In addition to the authority granted under paragraph (6) of this subsection, the judicial council may, in its discretion, refer any complaint under this subsection, together with the record of any associated proceedings and its recommendations for appropriate action, to the Judicial Conference of the United States.

(B) In any case in which the judicial council determines, on the basis of a complaint and an investigation under this subsection, or on the basis of information otherwise available to the council, that a judge appointed to hold office during good behavior may have engaged in conduct —

(i) which might constitute one or more grounds for impeachment under article II of the Constitution; or

(ii) which, in the interest of justice, is not amenable to resolution by the judicial council,

the judicial council shall promptly certify such determination, together with any complaint and a record of any associated proceedings, to the Judicial Conference of the United States.

(C) A judicial council acting under authority of this paragraph shall, unless contrary to the interests of justice, immediately submit written notice to the complainant and to the judge or magistrate whose conduct is the subject of the action taken under this paragraph.

(8)(A) Upon referral or certification of any matter under paragraph (7) of this subsection, the Judicial Conference, after consideration of the prior proceedings and such additional investigation as it considers appropriate, shall by majority vote take such action, as described in paragraph (6)(B) of this subsection, as it considers appropriate. If the Judicial Conference concurs in the determination of the council, or makes its own determination, that consideration of impeachment may be warranted, it shall so certify and transmit the determination and the record of proceedings to the House of Representatives for whatever action the House of Representatives considers to be necessary. Upon receipt of the determination and record of proceedings in the House of Representatives, the Clerk of the House of Representatives shall make available to the public the determination and any reasons for the determination.

(B) If a judge or magistrate has been convicted of a felony and has exhausted all means of obtaining direct review of the conviction, or the time for seeking further direct review of the conviction has passed and no such review has been sought, the Judicial Conference may, by majority vote and without referral or certification under paragraph (7), transmit to the House of Representatives a determination that consideration of impeachment may be warranted, together with appropriate court records, for whatever action the House of Representatives considers to be necessary.

(9)(A) In conducting any investigation under this subsection, the judicial council, or a special committee appointed under paragraph (4) of this subsection, shall have full subpoena powers as provided in section 332(d) of this title.

(B) In conducting any investigation under this subsection, the Judicial Conference, or a standing committee appointed by the Chief Justice under section 331 of this title, shall have full subpoena powers as provided in that section.

(10) A complainant, judge, or magistrate aggrieved by a final order of the chief judge under paragraph (3) of this subsection may petition the judicial council for review thereof. A complainant, judge, or magistrate aggrieved by an action of the judicial council under paragraph (6) of this subsection may petition the Judical Conference of the United States for review thereof. The Judicial Conference, or the standing committee established under section 331 of this title, may grant a petition filed by a complainant, judge, or magistrate under this paragraph. Except as expressly provided in this paragraph, all orders and determinations, including denials of petitions for review, shall be final and conclusive and shall not be judicially reviewable on appeal or otherwise.

(11) Each judicial council and the Judicial Conference may prescribe such rules for the conduct of proceedings under this subsection, including the processing of petitions for review, as each considers to be appropriate. Such rules shall contain provisions requiring that —

(A) adequate prior notice of any investigation be given in writing to the judge or magistrate whose conduct is the subject of the complaint;

(B) the judge or magistrate whose conduct is the subject of the complaint be afforded an opportunity to appear (in person or by counsel) at proceedings conducted by the investigating panel, to present oral and documentary evidence, to compel the attendance of witnesses or the production of documents, to cross-examine witnesses, and to present argument orally or in writing; and

(C) the complainant be afforded an opportunity to appear at proceedings conducted by the investigating panel, if the panel concludes that the complainant could offer substantial information.

Any such rule shall be made or amended only after giving appropriate public notice and an opportunity for comment. Any rule promulgated under this subsection shall be a matter of public record, and any such rule promulgated by a judicial council may be modified by the Judicial Conference. No rule promulgated under this subsection may limit the period of time within which a person may file a complaint under this subsection.

(12) No judge or magistrate whose conduct is the subject of an investigation under this subsection shall serve upon a special committee appointed under paragraph (4) of this subsection, upon a judicial council, upon the Judicial Conference, or upon the standing committee established under

section 331 of this title, until all related proceedings under this subsection have been finally terminated.

(13) No person shall be granted the right to intervene or to appear as amicus curiae in any proceeding before a judical council or the Judicial Conference under this subsection.

(14) Except as provided in paragraph (8), all papers, documents, and records of proceedings related to investigations conducted under this subsection shall be confidential and shall not be disclosed by any person in any proceeding except to the extent that —

(A) the judicial council of the circuit in its discretion releases a copy of a report of a special investigative committee under paragraph (5) to the complainant whose complaint initiated the investigation by that special committee and to the judge or magistrate whose conduct is the subject of the complaint;

(B) the judicial council of the circuit, the Judicial Conference of the United States, or the Senate or the House of Representatives by resolution, releases any such material which is believed necessary to an impeachment investigation or trial of a judge under article I of the Constitution; or

(B) such disclosure is authorized in writing by the judge or magistrate who is the subject to the complaint and by the chief judge of the circuit, the Chief Justice, or the chairman of the standing committee established under section 331 of this title.

(15) Each written order to implement any action under paragraph (6)(B) of this subsection, which is issued by a judicial council, the Judicial Conference, or the standing committee established under section 331 of this title, shall be made available to the public through the appropriate clerk's office of the court of appeals for the circuit. Unless contrary to the interests of justice, each such order issued under this paragraph shall be accompanied by written reasons therefor.

(16) Upon the request of a judge or magistrate whose conduct is the subject of a complaint under this subsection, the judicial council may, if the complaint has been finally dismissed under paragraph (6)(C), recommend that the Director of the Administrative Office of the United States Courts award reimbursement, from funds appropriated to the Federal judiciary, for those reasonable expenses, including attorneys' fees, incurred by that judge or magistrate during the investigation which would not have been incurred but for the requirements of this subsection.

(17) Except as expressly provided in this subsection, nothing in this subsection shall be construed to affect any other provision of this title, the Federal Rules of Civil Procedure, the Federal Rules of Criminal Procedure, the Federal Rules of Appellate Procedure, or the Federal Rules of Evidence.

(18) The United States Claims Court, the Court of International Trade, and the Court of Appeals for the Federal Circuit shall each prescribe rules,

consistent with the foregoing provisions of this subsection, establishing procedures for the filing of complaints with respect to the conduct of any judge
of such court and for the investigation and resolution of such complaints.
In investigating and taking action with respect to any such complaint, each
such court shall have the powers granted to a judicial council under this
subsection.

Selected Federal Sanctions Provisions

Editors' Introduction. Various ethical rules admonish lawyers not to assert frivolous claims or defenses, not to knowingly disobey an obligation under the rules of a tribunal, not to make frivolous discovery requests, and to avoid other forms of improper litigation behavior. These ethical prohibitions are reinforced by numerous sanctions provisions in the Federal Rules of Civil Procedure, the Federal Rules of Appellate Procedure, and federal statutes.

Rule 11 of the Federal Rules of Civil Procedure has received the most attention, and the Supreme Court has issued three opinions interpreting Rule 11 — *Business Guides, Inc. v. Chromatic Communications Enterprises, Inc.*, 111 S. Ct. 922 (1991), *Pavelic & LeFlore v. Marvel Entertainment Group*, 493 U.S. 120 (1990), and *Cooter & Gell v. Hartmarx Corp.*, 496 U.S. 384 (1990). In addition, a September 1992 proposal to amend Rule 11 is currently pending before the Supreme Court.

Courts impose sanctions under other provisions as well, and under their "inherent" powers. We reprint here a selection of the most important federal sanctions provisions. In addition, references to these and other rules of civil and appellate procedure are found in the Related Materials sections following ABA Model Rules of Professional Conduct 3.1, 3.2, 3.4, 8.4, and 8.5.

Contents

FEDERAL RULES OF CIVIL PROCEDURE

FEDERAL RULES OF CIVIL PROCEDURE

Rule 11. Signing of Pleadings, Motions, and Other Papers; Sanctions

Every pleading, motion, and other paper of a party represented by an attorney shall be signed by at least one attorney of record in the attorney's individual name, whose address shall be stated. A party who is not represented by an attorney shall sign the party's pleading, motion, or other paper and state the party's address. Except when otherwise specifically provided by rule or statute, pleadings need not be verified or accompanied by affidavit. The rule in equity that the averments of an answer under oath must be overcome by the testimony of two witnesses or of one witness sustained by corroborating circumstances is abolished. The signature of an attorney or party constitutes a certificate by the signer that the signer has read the pleading, motion, or other paper; that to the best of the signer's knowledge, information, and belief formed after reasonable inquiry it is well grounded in fact and is warranted by existing law or a good faith argument for the extension, modification, or reversal of existing law, and that it is not interposed for any improper purpose, such as to harass or to cause unnecessary delay or needless increase in the cost of litigation. If a pleading, motion, or other paper is not signed, it shall be stricken unless it is signed promptly after the omission is called to the attention of the pleader or movant. If a pleading, motion, or other paper is signed in violation of this rule, the court, upon motion or upon its own initiative, shall impose upon the person who signed it, a represented party, or both, an appropriate sanction, which may include an order to pay to the other party or parties the amount of the reasonable expenses incurred because of the filing of the pleading, motion, or other paper, including a reasonable attorney's fee.

Editors' Note. In September 1992, the Judicial Conference of the United States approved a proposed amendment to Rule 11. The proposal, which would significantly change Rule 11, reflects years of study and battle over the rule, which was amended to its present form in 1983. In May 1992, the Advisory Committee on Civil Rules approved a proposal similar to the one reprinted below, but with two significant differences. First, the Advisory Committee's version provided in subsection (b) that a lawyer would violate Rule 11 simply by "pursuing" or "maintaining" an improper pleading. The Judicial Conference proposal took out those words, making clear that a lawyer cannot be sanctioned without some affirmative action, such as "later advocating" an improper pleading. Second, in subsection (c), the Advisory Committee's version provided that a court "shall" impose sanctions for a violation of Rule 11. The Judicial Conference proposal replaces "shall" with "may," thus making Rule 11 sanctions discretionary rather than mandatory.

In June 1992, the Standing Committee on Rules of Practice and Procedure revised the Advisory Committee's proposal by putting it in its present form. The Judicial Conference approved the Standing Committee's proposal without change at its September 1992 meeting. The Judicial Conference proposal will now be forwarded to the United States Supreme Court and, if the Supreme Court approves, to Congress. If the proposed amendment is not blocked or altered by the Supreme Court or Congress, it will take effect on December 1, 1993.

Rule 11. Signing of Pleadings, Motions, and Other Papers; Representations to Court; Sanctions [Proposed]

(a) *Signature.* Every pleading, written motion, and other paper shall be signed by at least one attorney of record in the attorney's individual name, or, if the party is not represented by an attorney, shall be signed by the party. Each paper shall state the signer's address and telephone number, if any. Except when otherwise specifically provided by rule or statute, pleadings need not be verified or accompanied by affidavit. An unsigned paper shall be stricken unless omission of the signature is corrected promptly after being called to the attention of the attorney or party.

(b) *Representations to Court.* By presenting to the court (whether by signing, filing, submitting, or later advocating) a pleading, written motion, or other paper filed with or submitted to the court, an attorney or unrepresented party is certifying that to the best of the person's knowledge, information, and belief, formed after an inquiry reasonable under the circumstances, —

    (1) it is not being presented for any improper purpose, such as to harass or to cause unnecessary delay or needless increase in the cost of litigation;

    (2) the claims, defenses, and other legal contentions therein are warranted by existing law or by a nonfrivolous argument for the extension, modification, or reversal of existing law or the establishment of new law;

    (3) the allegations and other factual contentions have evidentiary support or, if specifically so identified, are likely to have evidentiary support after a reasonable opportunity for further investigation or discovery; and

(4) the denials of factual contentions are warranted on the evidence or, if specifically so identified, are reasonably based on a lack of information or belief.

(c) *Sanctions.* If, after notice and a reasonable opportunity to respond, the court determines that subdivision (b) has been violated, the court may, subject to the conditions stated below, impose an appropriate sanction upon the attorneys, law firms, or parties that have violated subdivision (b) or are responsible for the violation.

(1) *How Initiated.*

(A) *By Motion.* A motion for sanctions under this rule shall be made separately from other motions or requests and shall describe the specific conduct alleged to violate subdivision (b). It shall be served as provided in Rule 5, but shall not be filed with or presented to the court unless, within 21 days after service of the motion (or such other period as the court may prescribe), the challenged paper, claim, defense, contention, allegation, or denial is not withdrawn or appropriately corrected. If warranted, the court may award to the party prevailing on the motion the reasonable expenses and attorney's fees incurred in presenting or opposing the motion. Absent exceptional circumstances, a law firm shall be held jointly responsible for violations committed by its partners, associates, and employees.

(B) *On Court's Initiative.* On its own initiative, the court may enter an order describing the specific conduct that appears to violate subdivision (b) and directing an attorney, law firm, or party to show cause why it has not violated subdivision (b) with respect thereto.

(2) *Nature of Sanction; Limitations.* A sanction imposed for violation of this rule shall be limited to what is sufficient to deter repetition of such conduct or comparable conduct by persons similarly situated. Subject to the limitations in subparagraphs (a) and (b), the sanction may consist of, or include, directives of a non-monetary nature, an order to pay a penalty into court, or, if imposed on motion and warranted for effective deterrence, an order directing payment to the movant of some or all of the reasonable attorneys' fees and other expenses incurred as a direct result of the violation.

(A) Monetary sanctions may not be awarded against a represented party for a violation of subdivision (b)(2).

(B) Monetary sanctions may not be awarded on the court's initiative unless the court issues its order to show cause before a voluntary dismissal or settlement of the claims made by or against the party which is, or whose attorneys are, to be sanctioned.

(3) *Order.* When imposing sanctions, the court shall describe the conduct determined to constitute a violation of this rule and explain the basis for the sanction imposed.

(d) *Inapplicability to Discovery.* Subdivisions (a) through (c) of this rule do not apply to disclosures and discovery requests, responses, objections, and motions that are subject to the provisions of Rules 26 through 37.

Rule 16. Pretrial Conferences; Scheduling; Management

... (f) Sanctions. If a party or party's attorney fails to obey a scheduling or pretrial order, or if no appearance is made on behalf of a party at a scheduling or pretrial conference, or if a party or party's attorney is substantially unprepared to participate in the conference, or if a party or party's attorney fails to participate in good faith, the judge, upon motion or the judge's own initiative, may make such orders with regard thereto as are just, and among others any of the orders provided in Rule 37(b)(2)(B), (C), (D). In lieu of or in addition to any other sanction, the judge shall require the party or the attorney representing the party or both to pay the reasonable expenses incurred because of any noncompliance with this rule, including attorney's fees, unless the judge finds that the noncompliance was substantially justified or that other circumstances make an award of expenses unjust.

Rule 26. General Provisions Governing Discovery

... (g) Signing of Discovery Requests, Responses, and Objections. Every request for discovery or response or objection thereto made by a party represented by an attorney shall be signed by at least one attorney of record in the attorney's individual name, whose address shall be stated. A party who is not represented by an attorney shall sign the request, response, or objection and state the party's address. The signature of the attorney or party constitutes a certification that the signer has read the request, response, or objection, and that to the best of the signer's knowledge, information, and belief formed after a reasonable inquiry it is: (1) consistent with these rules and warranted by existing law or a good faith argument for the extension, modification, or reversal of existing law; (2) not interposed for any improper purpose, such as to harass or to cause unnecessary delay or needless increase in the cost of litigation; and (3) not unreasonable or unduly burdensome or expensive, given the needs of the case, the discovery already had in the case, the amount in controversy, and the importance of the issues at stake in the litigation. If a request, response, or objection is not signed, it shall be stricken unless it is signed promptly after the omission is called to the attention of the party making the request, response or objection and a party shall not be obligated to take any action with respect to it until it is signed.

If a certification is made in violation of the rule, the court, upon motion or upon its own initiative, shall impose upon the person who made the certification, the party on whose behalf the request, response, or objection is made, or both, an appropriate sanction, which may include an order to pay the amount of the reasonable expenses incurred because of the violation, including a reasonable attorney's fee.

Rule 41. Dismissal of Actions

... (b) Involuntary Dismissal: Effect Thereof. For failure of the plaintiff to prosecute or to comply with these rules or any order of court, a defendant may move for dismissal of an action or of any claim against the defendant.... Unless the court in its order for dismissal otherwise specifies, a dismissal under this subdivision and any dismissal not provided for in this rule ... operates as an adjudication upon the merits.

Rule 45. Subpoena

... (e) Contempt. Failure by any person without adequate excuse to obey a subpoena served upon that person may be deemed a contempt of the court from which the subpoena issued.

FEDERAL RULES OF APPELLATE PROCEDURE

Rule 38. Damages for Delay

If a court of appeals shall determine that an appeal is frivolous, it may award just damages and single or double costs to the appellee.

Rule 46. Attorneys

... (b) Suspension or Disbarment. When it is shown to the court that any member of its bar has been suspended or disbarred from practice in any other court of record, or has been guilty of conduct unbecoming a member of the bar of the court, the member will be subject to suspension or disbarment by the court. The member shall be afforded an opportunity to show good cause, within such time as the court shall prescribe, why the member should not be suspended or disbarred....

(c) Disciplinary Power of the Court over Attorneys. A court of appeals may, after reasonable notice and an opportunity to show cause to the contrary, and after hearing, if requested, take any appropriate disciplinary action against any attorney who practices before it for conduct unbecoming a member of the bar or for failure to comply with these rules or any rule of the court.

UNITED STATES CODE

28 U.S.C. §1927. Counsel's Liability for Excessive Costs

Any attorney or other person admitted to conduct cases in any court of the United States or any Territory thereof who so multiplies the proceedings in any case unreasonably and vexatiously may be required by the court to satisfy personally the excess costs, expenses, and attorneys' fees reasonably incurred because of such conduct.

Ethics Rules of Federal District Courts

Editors' Introduction. Most federal district courts have adopted the ethics rules of the state in which they sit. But exceptions exist. Judge Easterbrook catalogues the rules of the various district courts in Rand v. Monsanto, 926 F.2d 596 (7th Cir. 1991) (Appendix).

The district courts have a variety of local rules on attorney discipline. A list follows. Citations to "Rule _____" mean "Local Rule _____."

I. Code Districts, Unilateral

These districts have adopted the ABA Code of Professional Responsibility, without regard to state rules.

D. Hawaii	Rule 110(3)
N.D. Ill.	Rule 3.54(b)
N.D. N.Y.	Rules 2(a) and 4(f)
E.D. Okla.	Rule 4(j)
N.D. Okla.	Rule 4J
M.D. Tenn.	Rule 1(e)(4)
W.D. Tenn.	Rule 1(c)

II. Canons Districts, Unilateral

The following districts announce that the Canons of Professional Ethics apply to attorney discipline in the district. (Because the Code of Professional Responsibility springs from the Canons, these districts are effectively "Code districts.")

S.D. Fla.	Rule 16C
S.D. Ga.	Section IV, Rule 5(d)
D. Mont.	Rule 110(3)

III. Rules Districts, Unilateral

No districts have expressly adopted the ABA Model Rules of Professional Conduct independently of the states in which they sit.

IV. State Rules Districts

The districts below follow whatever disciplinary rules the state in which the district court sits uses. Some of these states have the Code and some the Rules.

A. CODE STATES

N.D. Cal.	Rule 110(3)
C.D. Cal.	Rule 2.5.1
S.D. Cal.	Rule 110(5) (the district also enforces the ABA Code)
E.D. Cal.	Rule 184(b)
D. Colo.	Rule 306 & App. A
N.D. Ga.	Rule 110(3)
D. Mass.	Rule 83.6(4)(B)
D. Neb.	Rule 5B
S.D. N.Y.	Rule 4(f) (the district also enforces the ABA Code)
E.D. N.Y.	Rule 4(f) (the district also enforces the ABA Code)
D. Ore.	Rule 110-6(a)
E.D. Tenn.	Rule 4.1
E.D. Va.	Rule 7(I)

B. RULES STATES

D. Ariz.	Rule 7(d)
D. Conn.	Rule 3(a)1 (with minor alterations in Rule 3(a)2)
D. Del.	Rule 8.2.D(2)
D. D.C.	Rule 706(a)
N.D. Fla.	Rule 4(G)(1) (this rule adopts Florida's version of the ABA Code; as Florida has switched to the ABA Rules, we assume that the district court follows automatically)
M.D. Fla.	Rule 2.04(c)

D. Idaho	Rule 1-107
N.D. Ind.	Rule 1(g)
S.D. Ind.	Rule 1(f) (arguably adopts Model Rules independent of the state's rules)
D. Kan.	Rule 407(a)
E.D. Ky.	Rule 3(b)(2)(E)
W.D. Ky.	Rule 3(b)(2)(E)
E.D. La.	Rule 20.04
M.D. La.	same
W.D. La.	same
E.D. Mo.	Rule 2(G)(2)
D. Nev.	Rule 120.8(a)
D. N.H.	Rule 4(d) & (e)
D. N.J.	Rule 6A (arguably adopts the ABA's Model Rules independent of the state's rules)
D. N.M.	Rule 83.9
M.D. N.C.	Rule 103(b)
E.D. N.C.	Rule 2.10
W.D. Okla.	Rule 4(J)(4)(b)
D. R.I.	Rule 4(d)
D. S.C.	Rule 2.08
E.D. Wash.	Rule 1.2(f)(2)
W.D. Wash.	Rule 2(e)(1)
N.D. W.V.	Rule 1.05(a)

V. Rules *Plus* Code Districts

The following districts have adopted both the Model Rules and the Code in some way (the way is indicated after the district).

N.D. Ala.	Rule 7(a)(4) (adopts Alabama law, the Code, plus the ABA Rules)
S.D. Ala.	Rule 1(A)(4) (same as above)
M.D. Ala.	Rule 1(a)(4) (same as above)
W.D. N.C.	Rule 1A (this is hard to interpret, because it incorporates an oath that refers to both the state's rules and the ABA Canons, which preceded the ABA Code; North Carolina adopted the ABA's Rules in 1985)
W.D. Tex.	Rule AT-4 (adopts Texas law, the Rules, plus the ABA Code)
E.D. Tex.	Rule 3(a) (same as above)
D. Utah	Rule 1(g) (adopts Utah law, the Rules, plus the ABA Code)

S.D. W.V.   Rule 1.03(h) (adopts W.V. law, the Rules, plus the ABA Code)

VI. Federal Rules Districts

The following districts have adopted the Uniform Federal Rules of Disciplinary Enforcement.*

E.D. Ark.	Rule 2(e)
W.D. Ark.	Rule 2(e)
S.D. Ill.	Rules 1(f) and 33
D. Maine	Rule 5
D. Md.	Rule 705
E.D. Mich.	Rule 13
W.D. Mo.	Rule 2
S.D. Ohio	Rule 2.6 (this district does not follow Rules XI and XII)
E.D. Pa.	Rule 14
W.D. Pa.	Rule 22
S.D. Tex.	Rule 1L
D. Vt.	Rule 1D
D. Wyo.	Rules 301-312

VII. Districts Without Rules

The following districts have adopted no discernible body of rules to govern attorney conduct. Most of them have local rules saying that attorneys can be disciplined for "bad conduct" of some sort.

D. Alaska	Rule 3(G) generally governs misconduct
M.D. Ga.	[no rules of conduct]
C.D. Ill.	Rule 2 generally governs
N.D. Iowa	Rule 5.g generally governs
S.D. Iowa	same
W.D. Mich.	Rule 19(c) generally governs
N.D. Miss.	Rule 1(c) generally governs
S.D. Miss.	same
W.D. N.Y.	Rule 3(b)(5)(G) generally, possibly suggests the Code applies
D. N.D.	Rule 2(e)(2) generally governs
N.D. Ohio	Rule 2.09 generally governs

*These rules incorporate by reference the professional conduct rules of the state in which the court sits. — EDS.

D. S.D.	Rule 2 generally governs
N.D. Tex.	Rule 13.2 generally governs
W.D. Va.	Rule [1](6) generally governs
E.D. Wis.	Rule 2.05 generally governs
W.D. Wis.	Rule 1(e) generally governs

VIII. Unknown or Uncounted

The District of Minnesota and the Middle District of Pennsylvania have local rules governing professional conduct, but we could not discover the source or nature of those rules. We also omit the district courts outside the 50 states.

Totals

Category	Number	Percent
Rules	28	31.82%
Adopted Rules unilaterally	0	-
Adopted state's Rules	28	-
Code	23	26.14
Adopted Code unilaterally	10	-
Adopted state's Code	13	-
Rules plus Code	8	9.09
Uniform Federal Rules	13	14.77
No rules	16	18.1
Total	88	100.00%

California Materials

California Rules of Professional Conduct

Editors' Note. On November 28, 1988, the California Supreme Court adopted new Rules of Professional Conduct. These rules, which follow, took effect on May 27, 1989, and represented the first major revision of California's ethics rules since 1975. After the rules, we print a table cross-referencing the old (1975) California rules to the current rules and a proposed rule governing waiver of attorney fees in settlement offers. This proposal was rejected by the California Supreme Court in 1989.

During 1992, there were several significant changes (and some minor changes) to the California Rules of Professional Conduct. On August 13, 1992, the California Supreme Court issued an order amending many of the rules, amending one of the standards governing advertising, adopting a new standard to govern claims of certification or specialization, and adding an entirely new rule (Rule 3-120) governing sexual relationships between lawyers and clients. California is the first state in the nation to adopt a rule of professional conduct expressly addressing the question of sex with clients. All of the amendments took effect in September 1992. We have shown the changes by striking out deletions and underscoring additions to the rules.

Other important changes also occurred during 1992. On July 11, 1992, pursuant to Rule 4-100(C), the California State Bar adopted Trust Account Record Keeping Standards. These Standards will become operative on January 1, 1993. We have reprinted these new Standards immediately following Rule 4-100.

The California State Bar expects further changes in the near future. When we went to press, the State Bar had recently filed with the California Supreme Court proposals to amend Rules 4-100 and 3-700. These proposed amendments would add more explicit provisions regarding legal fees paid in advance of services. The court had not yet acted on these proposals. The State Bar had also approved a new rule on confidences and secrets, to be numbered Rule 3-100, and is expected to file the proposed rule with the California Supreme Court by the end of 1992.

Contents

Chapter 1. Professional Integrity in General

Chapter 2. Relationship Among Members

Chapter 3. Professional Relationship with Clients

Chapter 4. Financial Relationship with Clients

CHAPTER 1. PROFESSIONAL INTEGRITY IN GENERAL

Rule 1-100. Rules of Professional Conduct, in General*

(A) Purpose and Function.

The following rules are intended to regulate professional conduct of members of the State Bar through discipline. They have been adopted by the Board of Governors of the State Bar of California and approved by the Supreme Court of California pursuant to Business and Professions Code sections 6076 and 6077 to protect the public and to promote respect and confidence in the legal profession. These rules together with any standards adopted by the Board of Governors pursuant to these rules shall be binding upon all members of the State Bar.

For a willful breach of any of these rules, the Board of Governors has the power to discipline members as provided by law.

The prohibition of certain conduct in these rules is not exclusive. Members are also bound by applicable law including the State Bar Act (Bus. & Prof. Code, §6000 et seq.) and opinions of California courts. Although not binding, opinions of ethics committees in California should be consulted by members for guidance on proper professional conduct. Ethics opinions and rules and standards promulgated by other jurisdictions and bar associations may also be considered.

*Strike-throughs and underscorings show deletions and additions made by the California Supreme Court on August 13, 1992. The changes became operative in September 1992. — EDS.

These rules are not intended to create new civil causes of action. Nothing in these rules shall be deemed to create, augment, diminish, or eliminate any substantive legal duty of lawyers or the non-disciplinary consequences of violating such a duty.

(B) Definitions.

(1) "Law Firm" means:

(a) two or more lawyers whose activities constitute the practice of law, and who share its profits, expenses, and liabilities; or

(b) a law corporation which employs more than one member lawyer; or

(c) a division, department, office, or group within a business entity, which includes more than one lawyer who performs legal services for the business entity; or

(d) a publicly funded entity which employs more than one lawyer to perform legal services.

(2) "Member" means a member of the State Bar of California.

(3) "Lawyer" means a member of the State Bar of California or a person who is admitted in good standing of and eligible to practice before the bar of any United States court or the highest court of the District of Columbia or any state, territory, or insular possession of the United States, or is licensed to practice law in, or is admitted in good standing and eligible to practice before the bar of the highest court of, a foreign country or any political subdivision thereof.

(4) "Associate" means an employee or fellow employee who is employed as a lawyer.

(5) "Shareholder" means a shareholder in a professional corporation pursuant to Business and Professions Code section 6160 et seq.

(C) Purpose of Discussions.

Because it is a practical impossibility to convey in black letter form all of the nuances of these disciplinary rules, the comments contained in the Discussions of the rules, while they do not add independent basis for imposing discipline, are intended to provide guidance for interpreting the rules and practicing in compliance with them.

(D) Geographic Scope of Rules.

(1) As to members: These rules shall govern the activities of members in and outside this state, except as members lawfully practicing outside this state may be specifically required by a jurisdiction in which they are practicing to follow rules of professional conduct different from these rules.

(2) As to lawyers from other jurisdictions: These rules shall also govern the activities of lawyers while engaged in the performance of lawyer functions in this state; but nothing contained in these rules shall be deemed to authorize the performance of such functions by such persons in this state except as otherwise permitted by law.

(E) These rules may be cited and referred to as "Rules of Professional Conduct of the State Bar of California."

DISCUSSION

The Rules of Professional Conduct are intended to establish the standards for members for purposes of discipline. (See Ames v. State Bar (1973) 8 Cal. 3d 910 [106 Cal. Rptr. 489].) The fact that a member has engaged in conduct that may be contrary to these rules does not automatically give rise to a civil cause of action. (See Noble v. Sears, Roebuck & Co. (1973) 33 Cal. App. 3d 654 [109 Cal. Rptr. 269]; Wilhelm v. Pray, Price, Williams & Russell (1986) 186 Cal. App. 3d 1324 [231 Cal. Rptr. 355].) These rules are not intended to supercede existing law relating to members in non-disciplinary contexts. (See, e.g., Klemm v. Superior Court (1977) 75 Cal. App. 3d 893 [142 Cal. Rptr. 509] (motion for disqualification of counsel due to a conflict of interest); Academy of California Optometrists, Inc. v. Superior Court (1975) 51 Cal. App. 3d 999 [124 Cal. Rptr. 668] (duty to return client files); Chronometrics, Inc. v. Sysgen, Inc. (1980) 110 Cal. App. 3d 597 [168 Cal. Rptr. 196] (disqualification of member appropriate remedy for improper communication with adverse party).)

Law firm, as defined by subparagraph (B)(1), is not intended to include an association of ~~members~~ lawyers who do not share profits, expenses, and liabilities. The subparagraph is not intended to imply that a law firm may include a person who is not a member in violation of the law governing the unauthorized practice of law.

Related Materials

ABA Model Rules: 5.1.
California Business & Professions Code: No equivalent.
Old California Rules of Professional Conduct: No equivalent.

Rule 1-110. Disciplinary Authority of the State Bar

A member shall comply with conditions attached to public or private reprovals or other discipline administered by the State Bar pursuant to Business and Professions Code sections 6077 and 6078 and rule 956, California Rules of Court.

Related Materials

ABA Model Rules: No equivalent.
California Business & Professions Code: §§6077, 6078.
Old California Rules of Professional Conduct: 9-101.

Rule 1-120. Assisting, Soliciting, or Inducing Violations

A member shall not knowingly assist in, solicit, or induce any violation of these rules or the State Bar Act.

Related Materials

ABA Model Rules: 8.4(a).
California Business & Professions Code: No equivalent.
Old California Rules of Professional Conduct: No equivalent.

Rule 1-200. False Statement Regarding Admission to the State Bar

(A) A member shall not knowingly make a false statement regarding a material fact or knowingly fail to disclose a material fact in connection with an application for admission to the State Bar.

(B) A member shall not further an application for admission to the State Bar of a person whom the member knows to be unqualified in respect to character, education, or other relevant attributes.

(C) This rule shall not prevent a member from serving as counsel of record for an applicant for admission to practice in proceedings related to such admission.

DISCUSSION

For purposes of rule 1-200 "admission" includes readmission.

Related Materials

ABA Model Rules: 8.1.
California Business & Professions Code: §6068(b).
Old California Rules of Professional Conduct: No equivalent.

Rule 1-300. Unauthorized Practice of Law

(A) A member shall not aid any person or entity in the unauthorized practice of law.

(B) A member shall not practice law in a jurisdiction where to do so would be in violation of regulations of the profession in that jurisdiction.

Related Materials

ABA Model Rules: 5.5.
California Business & Professions Code: §§6125-6127.
Old California Rules of Professional Conduct: 3-101.

Rule 1-310. Forming a Partnership with a Non-Lawyer*

A member shall not form a partnership with a person ~~not licensed to practice law~~ <u>who is not a lawyer</u> if any of the activities of that partnership consist of the practice of law.

DISCUSSION

Rule 1-310 is not intended to govern members' activities which cannot be considered to constitute the practice of law. It is intended solely to preclude a member from being involved in the practice of law with a person ~~not licensed to practice law~~ <u>who is not a lawyer</u>.

Related Materials

ABA Model Rules: 5.4.
California Business & Professions Code: No equivalent.
Old California Rules of Professional Conduct: 3-103.

Rule 1-320. Financial Arrangements with Non-Lawyers*

(A) Neither a member nor a law firm shall directly or indirectly share legal fees with a person ~~or entity not licensed to practice law,~~ <u>who is not a lawyer,</u> except that:

(1) An agreement between a member and a law firm, partner, or associate may provide for the payment of money after the member's death to the

*Strike-throughs and underscorings show deletions and additions made by the California Supreme Court on August 13, 1992. The changes become operative in September 1992. — EDS.

member's estate or to one or more specified persons over a reasonable period of time; or

(2) A member or law firm undertaking to complete unfinished legal business of a deceased member may pay to the estate of the deceased member or other person legally entitled thereto that proportion of the total compensation which fairly represents the services rendered by the deceased member;

(3) A member or law firm may include non-member employees in a compensation, profit-sharing, or retirement plan even though the plan is based in whole or in part on a profit-sharing arrangement, if such plan does not circumvent these rules or Business and Professions Code section 6000 et seq.; or

(4) A member may pay a prescribed registration, referral, or participation fee to a lawyer referral service established, sponsored, and operated in accordance with the State Bar of California's Minimum Standards for a Lawyer Referral Service in California.

(B) A member shall not compensate, give, or promise anything of value to any person or entity for the purpose of recommending or securing employment of the member or the member's law firm by a client, or as a reward for having made a recommendation resulting in employment of the member or the member's law firm by a client. A member's offering of or giving a gift or gratuity to any person or entity having made a recommendation resulting in the employment of the member or the member's law firm shall not of itself violate this rule, provided that the gift or gratuity was not offered or given in consideration of any promise, agreement, or understanding that such a gift or gratuity would be forthcoming or that referrals would be made or encouraged in the future.

(C) A member shall not compensate, give, or promise anything of value to any representative of the press, radio, television, or other communication medium in anticipation of or in return for publicity of the member, the law firm, or any other member as such in a news item, but the incidental provision of food or beverage shall not of itself violate this rule.

DISCUSSION

Rule 1-320(C) is not intended to preclude compensation to the communications media in exchange for advertising the member's or law firm's availability for professional employment.

Related Materials

ABA Model Rules: 5.4(a), 7.2.
California Business & Professions Code: §§6129, 6154.
Old California Rules of Professional Conduct: 2-101, 3-102.

Rule 1-400. Advertising and Solicitation

(A) For purposes of this rule, "communication" means any message or offer made by or on behalf of a member concerning the availability for professional employment of a member or a law firm directed to any former, present, or prospective client, including but not limited to the following:

(1) Any use of firm name, trade name, fictitious name, or other professional designation of such member or law firm; or

(2) Any stationery, letterhead, business card, sign, brochure, or other comparable written material describing such member, law firm, or lawyers; or

(3) Any advertisement (regardless of medium) of such member or law firm directed to the general public or any substantial portion thereof; or

(4) Any unsolicited correspondence from a member or law firm directed to any person or entity.

(B) For purposes of this rule, a "solicitation" means any communication:

(1) Concerning the availability for professional employment of a member or a law firm in which a significant motive is pecuniary gain; and

(2) Which is;

(a) delivered in person or by telephone, or

(b) directed by any means to a person known to the sender to be represented by counsel in a matter which is a subject of the communication.

(C) A solicitation shall not be made by or on behalf of a member or law firm to a prospective client with whom the member or law firm has no family or prior professional relationship, unless the solicitation is protected from abridgment by the Constitution of the United States or by the Constitution of the State of California. A solicitation to a former or present client in the discharge of a member's or law firm's professional duties is not prohibited.

(D) A communication or a solicitation (as defined herein) shall not:

(1) Contain any untrue statement; or

(2) Contain any matter, or present or arrange any matter in a manner or format which is false, deceptive, or which tends to confuse, deceive, or mislead the public; or

(3) Omit to state any fact necessary to make the statements made, in the light of circumstances under which they are made, not misleading to the public; or

(4) Fail to indicate clearly, expressly, or by context, that it is a communication or solicitation, as the case may be; or

(5) Be transmitted in any manner which involves intrusion, coercion, duress, compulsion, intimidation, threats, or vexatious or harassing conduct; or

(6) State that a member is a "certified specialist" unless the member holds a current certificate as a specialist issued by the California Board of Legal Specialization pursuant to a plan for specialization approved by the Supreme Court.

(E) The Board of Governors of the State Bar shall formulate and adopt standards as to communications which will be presumed to violate this rule 1-400. The standards shall only be used as presumptions affecting the burden of proof in disciplinary proceedings involving alleged violations of these rules. "Presumption affecting the burden of proof" means that presumption defined in Evidence Code sections 605 and 606. Such standards formulated and adopted by the Board, as from time to time amended, shall be effective and binding on all members.

(F) A member shall retain for two years a true and correct copy or recording of any communication made by written or electronic media. Upon written request, the member shall make any such copy or recording available to the State Bar, and, if requested, shall provide to the State Bar evidence to support any factual or objective claim contained in the communication.

STANDARDS*

Pursuant to rule 1-400(E) the Board of Governors of the State Bar has adopted the following standards, effective May 27, 1989 as forms of "communication" defined in rule 1-400(A) which are presumed to be in violation of rule 1-400:

(1) A "communication" which contains guarantees, warranties, or predictions regarding the result of the representation.

(2) A "communication" which contains testimonials about or endorsements of a member unless such communication also contains an express disclaimer such as "this testimonial or endorsement does not constitute a guarantee, warranty, or prediction regarding the outcome of your legal matter."

(3) A "communication" which is delivered to a potential client whom the member knows or should reasonably know is in such a physical, emotional, or mental state that he or she would not be expected to exercise reasonable judgment as to the retention of counsel.

(4) A "communication" which is transmitted at the scene of an accident or at or en route to a hospital, emergency care center, or other health care facility.

(5) A "communication," except professional announcements, seeking professional employment primarily for pecuniary gain which is transmitted by mail or equivalent means which does not indicate clearly ~~identify itself as an advertisement~~, expressly or by context that it is a form of advertising. If such communication, including firm brochures, newsletters, recent legal developments advisories, and similar materials, is transmitted in an envelope, the envelope shall ~~be identified as an advertisement~~ bear the word

*Strike-throughs and underscorings show deletions and additions made by the California Supreme Court on August 13, 1992. The changes became operative in September 1992. — EDS.

"Advertisement," "Newsletter" or a similar identification on the outside thereof.

(6) A "communication" in the form of a firm name, trade name, fictitious name, or other professional designation which states or implies a relationship between any member in private practice and a government agency or instrumentality or a public or non-profit legal services organization.

(7) A "communication" in the form of a firm name, trade name, fictitious name, or other professional designation which states or implies that a member has a relationship to any other ~~member~~ <u>lawyer</u> or a law firm as a partner or associate, or officer or shareholder pursuant to Business and Professions Code sections 6160-6172 unless such relationship in fact exists.

(8) A "communication" which states or implies that a member or law firm is "of counsel" to another ~~member~~ <u>lawyer</u> or a law firm unless the former has a relationship with the latter (other than as a partner or associate, or officer or shareholder pursuant to Business and Professions Code sections 6160-6172) which is close, personal, continuous, and regular.

(9) A "communication" in the form of a firm name, trade name, fictitious name, or other professional designation used by a member or law firm in private practice which differs materially from any other such designation used by such member or law firm at the same time in the same community.

(10) A "communication" which implies that the member or ~~member's~~ law firm is participating in a lawyer referral service which has been certified by the State Bar of California or as having satisfied the Minimum Standards for Lawyer Referral Services in California, when that is not the case.

(11) A "communication" which states or implies that a member is a "certified specialist" unless such communication also states the complete name of the entity which granted the certification as a specialist.

Related Materials

ABA Model Rules: 7.1, 7.2, 7.3, 7.4, 7.5.
California Business & Professions Code: §6129.
Old California Rules of Professional Conduct: 2-101, 3-102.

Rule 1-500. Agreements Restricting a Member's Practice*

(A) A member shall not be a party to or participate in offering or making an agreement, whether in connection with the settlement of a lawsuit or other-

---

*Strike-throughs and underscorings show deletions and additions made by the California Supreme Court on August 13, 1992. The changes became operative in September 1992. — EDS.

wise, if the agreement restricts the right of a member to practice law~, except that this rule shall not prohibit such an agreement which:

~~(B) Nothing in paragraph (A) of this rule shall be construed as prohibiting such a restrictive agreement which:~~

(1) Is a part of an employment, shareholders', or partnership agreement among members provided the restrictive agreement does not survive the termination of the employment, shareholder, or partnership relationship; or

(2) Requires payments to a member upon the member's retirement from the practice of law; or

(3) Is authorized by Business & Professions Code sections 6092.5(i) or 6093.

(B) ~~(C)~~ A member shall not be a party to or participate in offering or making an agreement which precludes the reporting of a violation of these rules.

DISCUSSION

Paragraph (A) makes it clear that the practice, in connection with settlement agreements, of proposing that a member refrain from representing other clients in similar litigation, is prohibited. Neither counsel may demand or suggest such provisions nor may opposing counsel accede or agree to such provisions.

Paragraph ~~(B)~~ (A) permits a restrictive covenant in a law corporation, partnership, or employment agreement. The law corporation shareholder, partner, or associate may agree not to have a separate practice during the existence of the relationship; however, upon termination of the relationship (whether voluntary or involuntary), the member is free to practice law without any contractual restriction except in the case of retirement from the active practice of law.

Related Materials

ABA Model Rules: 5.6.
California Business & Professions Code: No equivalent.
Old California Rules of Professional Conduct: 2-109.

Rule 1-600. Legal Service Programs

(A) A member shall not participate in a nongovernmental program, activity, or organization furnishing, recommending, or paying for legal services, which allows any third person or organization to interfere with the member's independence of professional judgment, or with the client-lawyer relationship, or allows unlicensed persons to practice law, or allows any third person or organization to receive directly or indirectly any part of the consideration paid to the member except as permitted by these rules, or otherwise violates the State Bar Act or these rules.

(B) The Board of Governors of the State Bar shall formulate and adopt Minimum Standards for Lawyer Referral Services, which, as from time to time amended, shall be binding on members.

DISCUSSION

The participation of a member in a lawyer referral service established, sponsored, supervised, and operated in conformity with the Minimum Standards for a Lawyer Referral Service in California is encouraged and is not, of itself, a violation of these rules.

Rule 1-600 is not intended to override any contractual agreement or relationship between insurers and insureds regarding the provision of legal services.

Rule 1-600 is not intended to apply to the activities of a public agency responsible for providing legal services to a government or to the public.

For purposes of paragraph (A), "a nongovernmental program, activity, or organization" includes, but is not limited to group, prepaid, and voluntary legal service programs, activities, or organizations.

Related Materials

ABA Model Rules: 6.3, 7.2.
California Business & Professions Code: §6129.
Old California Rules of Professional Conduct: 2-101, 2-102(A), 3-102.

CHAPTER 2. RELATIONSHIP AMONG
MEMBERS

Rule 2-100. Communication with a Represented Party

(A) While representing a client, a member shall not communicate directly or indirectly about the subject of the representation with a party the member knows to be represented by another lawyer in the matter, unless the member has the consent of the other lawyer.

(B) For purposes of this rule, a "party" includes:

(1) An officer, director, or managing agent of a corporation or association, and a partner or managing agent of a partnership; or

(2) An association member or an employee of an association, corporation, or partnership, if the subject of the communication is any act or omission of such person in connection with the matter which may be binding upon or imputed to the organization for purposes of civil or criminal liability or whose statement may constitute an admission on the part of the organization.

(C) This rule shall not prohibit:

(1) Communications with a public officer, board, committee, or body;

(2) Communications initiated by a party seeking advice or representation from an independent lawyer of the party's choice; or

(3) Communications otherwise authorized by law.

DISCUSSION*

Rule 2-100 is intended to control communications between a member and persons the member knows to be represented by counsel unless a statutory scheme or case law will override the rule. There are a number of express statutory schemes which authorize communications between a member and person who would otherwise be subject to this rule. These statutes protect a variety of other rights such as the right of employees to organize and to engage in collective bargaining, employee health and safety, or equal employment opportunity. Other applicable law also includes the authority of government prosecutors and investigators to conduct criminal investigations, as limited by the relevant decisional law.

Rule 2-100 is not intended to prevent the parties themselves from communicating with respect to the subject matter of the representation, and nothing in the rule prevents a member from advising the client that such communication can be made. Moreover, the rule does not prohibit a member who is also a party to a legal matter from directly or indirectly communicating on his or her own behalf with a represented party. Such a member has independent rights as a party which should not be abrogated because of his or her professional status. To prevent any possible abuse in such situations, the counsel for the opposing party may advise that party (1) about the risks and benefits of communications with a lawyer-party, and (2) not to accept or engage in communications with the lawyer-party.

Rule 2-100 also addresses the situation in which member A is contacted by an opposing party who is represented and, because of dissatisfaction with that party's counsel, seeks A's independent advice. Since A is employed by the opposition, the member cannot give independent advice.

As used in paragraph (A), "the subject of the representation," "matter," and "party" are not limited to a litigation context.

*Strike-throughs and underscorings show deletions and additions made by the California Supreme Court on August 13, 1992. The changes became operative in September 1992. — EDS.

Paragraph (B) is intended to apply only to persons employed at the time of the communication.

Subparagraph (C)(2) is intended to permit a member to communicate with ~~an individual~~ a party seeking to hire new counsel or to obtain a second opinion. A member contacted by such ~~an individual~~ a party continues to be bound by other Rules of Professional Conduct. (See, e.g., rules 1-400 and 3-310.)

Related Materials

ABA Model Rules: 4.2.
California Business & Professions Code: No equivalent.
Old California Rules of Professional Conduct: 7-103.

Rule 2-200. Financial Arrangements Among Lawyers

(A) A member shall not divide a fee for legal services with a lawyer who is not a partner of, associate of, or shareholder with the member unless:

(1) The client has consented in writing thereto after a full disclosure has been made in writing that a division of fees will be made and the terms of such division; and

(2) The total fee charged by all lawyers is not increased solely by reason of the provision for division of fees and is not unconscionable as that term is defined in rule 4-200.

(B) Except as permitted in paragraph (A) of this rule or rule 2-300, a member shall not compensate, give, or promise anything of value to any lawyer for the purpose of recommending or securing employment of the member or the member's law firm by a client, or as a reward for having made a recommendation resulting in employment of the member or the member's law firm by a client. A member's offering of or giving a gift or gratuity to any lawyer who has made a recommendation resulting in the employment of the member or the member's law firm shall not of itself violate this rule, provided that the gift or gratuity was not offered in consideration of any promise, agreement, or understanding that such a gift or gratuity would be forthcoming or that referrals would be made or encouraged in the future.

Related Materials

ABA Model Rules: No equivalent (but see 1.8).
California Business & Professions Code: No equivalent.
Old California Rules of Professional Conduct: 5-103.

Rule 2-300. Sale or Purchase of a Law Practice of a
           Member, Living or Deceased*

All or substantially all of the law practice of a member, living or deceased, including goodwill, may be sold to another member or law firm subject to all the following conditions:

(A) Fees charged to clients shall not be increased solely by reason of such sale.

(B) If the sale contemplates the transfer of responsibility for work not yet completed or responsibility for client files or information protected by Business and Professions Code section 6068, subdivision (e), then;

(1) if the seller is deceased, or has a conservator or other person acting in a representative capacity, and no member has been appointed to act for the seller pursuant to Business and Professions Code section 6180.5, then prior to the transfer;

(a) the purchaser shall cause a written notice to be given to the client stating that the interest in the law practice is being transferred to the purchaser; that the client has the right to retain other counsel; that the client may take possession of any client papers and property, as required by rule 3-700(D); and that if no response is received to the notification within 90 days of the sending of such notice, or in the event the client's rights would be prejudiced by a failure to act during that time, the purchaser may act on behalf of the client until otherwise notified by the client. Such notice shall comply with the requirements as set forth in rule 1-400(D) and any provisions relating to attorney-client fee arrangements, and

(b) the purchaser shall obtain the written consent of the client provided that such consent shall be presumed until otherwise notified by the client if no response is received to the notification specified in subparagraph (a) within 90 days of the date of the sending of such notification to the client's last address as shown on the records of the seller, or the client's rights would be prejudiced by a failure to act during such 90-day period.

(2) in all other circumstances, not less than 90 days prior to the transfer;

(a) the seller, or the member appointed to act for the seller pursuant to Business and Professions code section 6180.5, shall cause a written notice to be given to the client stating that the interest in the law practice is being transferred to the purchaser; that the client has the right to retain other counsel; that the client may take possession of any client papers and property, as required by rule 3-700(D); and that if no response is received to the notification within 90 days of the

---

*Underscorings show additions made by the California Supreme Court on August 13, 1992. The changes became operative in September 1992. — Eds.

sending of such notice, the purchaser may act on behalf of the client until otherwise notified by the client. Such notice shall comply with the requirements as set forth in rule 1-400(D) and any provisions relating to attorney-client fee arrangements, and

(b) the seller, or the member appointed to act for the seller pursuant to Business and Professions Code section 6180.5, shall obtain the written consent of the client prior to the transfer provided that such consent shall be presumed until otherwise notified by the client if no response is received to the notification specified in subparagraph (a) within 90 days of the date of the sending of such notification to the client's last address as shown on the records of the seller.

(C) If substitution is required by the rules of a tribunal in which a matter is pending, all steps necessary to substitute a member shall be taken.

(D) All activity of a purchaser or potential purchaser under this rule shall be subject to compliance with rules 3-300 and 3-310 where applicable.

(E) Confidential information shall not be disclosed to a non-member in connection with a sale under this rule.

(F) Admission to or retirement from a law partnership or law corporation, retirement plans and similar arrangements, or sale of tangible assets of a law practice shall not be deemed a sale or purchase under this rule.

DISCUSSION

Paragraph (A) is intended to prohibit the purchaser from charging the former clients of the seller a higher fee than the purchaser is charging his or her existing clients.

"All or substantially all of the law practice of a member" means, for purposes of rule 2-300, that, for example, a member may retain one or two clients who have such a longstanding personal and professional relationship with the member that transfer of those clients' files is not feasible. Conversely, rule 2-300 is not intended to authorize the sale of a law practice in a piecemeal fashion except as may be required by subparagraph (B)(1)(a) or paragraph (D).

Transfer of individual client matters, where permitted, is governed by rule 2-200. Payment of a fee to a non-lawyer broker for arranging the sale or purchase of a law practice is governed by rule 1-320.

Related Materials

ABA Model Rules: 1.17.
California Business & Professions Code: No equivalent.
Old California Rules of Professional Conduct: No equivalent.

CHAPTER 3. PROFESSIONAL RELATIONSHIP WITH CLIENTS

Rule 3-110. Failing to Act Competently*

(A) A member shall not intentionally, ~~or with reckless disregard~~ recklessly, or repeatedly fail to perform legal services ~~competently~~ with competence.

(B) ~~To perform legal services competently means diligently to apply the learning and skill necessary to perform the member's duties arising from employment or representation.~~ For purposes of this rule, "competence" in any legal service shall mean to apply the 1) diligence, 2) learning and skill, and 3) mental, emotional, and physical ability reasonably necessary for the performance of such service. ~~If the member does not have sufficient learning and skills when the employment or representation is undertaken, or during the course of the employment or representation, the member may nonetheless perform such duties competently by associating or, where appropriate, professionally consulting another member reasonably believed to be competent, or by acquiring sufficient learning and skill before performance is required, if the member has sufficient time, resources, and ability to do so.~~

(C) ~~As used in this rule, the term "ability" means a quality or state of having sufficient learning and skill and being mentally, emotionally, and physically able to perform legal services.~~ If a member does not have sufficient learning and skill when the legal service is undertaken, the member may nonetheless perform such services competently by 1) associating with or, where appropriate, professionally consulting another lawyer reasonably believed to be competent, or 2) by acquiring sufficient learning and skill before performance is required.

DISCUSSION

The duties set forth in rule 3-110 include the duty to supervise the work of subordinate attorney and non-attorney employees or agents. (See, e.g., Waysman v. State Bar (1986) 41 Cal. 3d 452; Trousil v. State Bar (1985) 38 Cal. 3d 337, 342 [211 Cal. Rptr. 525]; Palomo v. State Bar (1984) 36 Cal. 3d 785 [205 Cal. Rptr. 834]; Crane v. State Bar (1981) 30 Cal. 3d 117, 122; Black v. State Bar (1972) 7 Cal. 3d 676, 692 [103 Cal. Rptr. 288; 499 P.2d 968]; Vaughn v. State Bar (1972) 6 Cal. 3d 847, 857-858 [100 Cal. Rptr. 713; 494 P.2d 1257]; Moore v. State Bar (1964) 62 Cal. 2d 74, 81 [41 Cal. Rptr. 161; 396 P.2d 577].)

In an emergency a lawyer may give advice or assistance in a matter in which the lawyer does not have the skill ordinarily required where referral to or consultation with another lawyer would be impractical. Even in an emergency,

*Strike-throughs and underscorings show deletions and additions made by the California Supreme Court on August 13, 1992. The changes became operative in September 1992. — EDS.

however, assistance should be limited to that reasonably necessary in the circumstances.

Related Materials

ABA Model Rules: 1.1, 1.3, 5.3.
California Business & Professions Code: No equivalent.
Old California Rules of Professional Conduct: 3-102(A), 3-103, 6-101(A), (B), and (C).

Rule 3-120. Sexual Relations with Client

Editors' Note. The following new rule is a direct outgrowth of California Business and Professions Code §6106.8 (reprinted in the following chapter), enacted by the California legislature in 1989. That statute found there was "no rule that governs the propriety of sexual relationships between lawyers and clients," and commanded the Bar to submit an appropriate rule to the California Supreme Court. The Bar, slightly tardy, submitted a proposed rule to the California Supreme Court in May 1991. In August 1991, the California Supreme Court remanded the proposal for recirculation. This was done and the proposal was resubmitted to the California Supreme Court unchanged. On August 13, 1992, the California Supreme Court adopted the rule as proposed, except that the court deleted the following proposed subparagraph E:

> (E) A member who engages in sexual relations with his or her client will be presumed to violate rule 3-120, paragraph (B)(3). This presumption shall only be used as a presumption affecting the burden of proof in disciplinary proceedings involving alleged violations of these rules. "Presumption affecting the burden of proof" means that presumption defined in Evidence Code sections 605 and 606.

Thus, violation of Rule 3-120 does not carry a presumption of incompetence in providing legal services.

California is the first state to adopt a rule of legal ethics expressly addressing sexual relationships with clients. For a parallel state statute signed into law in September 1992, see §6106.9 of the California Business and Professions Code below.

(A) For purposes of this rule, "sexual relations" means sexual intercourse or the touching of an intimate part of another person for the purpose of sexual arousal, gratification, or abuse.

(B) A member shall not:

(1) Require or demand sexual relations with a client incident to or as a condition of any professional representation; or

(2) Employ coercion, intimidation, or undue influence in entering into sexual relations with a client; or

(3) Continue representation of a client with whom the member has sexual relations if such sexual relations cause the member to perform legal services incompetently in violation of rule 3-110.

(C) Paragraph (B) shall not apply to sexual relations between members and their spouses or to ongoing consensual lawyer-client sexual relations which pre-date the initiation of the lawyer-client relationship.

(D) Where a lawyer in a firm has sexual relations with a client but does not participate in the representation of that client, the lawyers in the firm shall not be subject to discipline under this rule solely because of the occurrence of such sexual relations.

DISCUSSION

Rule 3-120 is intended to prohibit sexual exploitation by a lawyer in the course of a professional representation. Often, based upon the nature of the underlying representation, a client exhibits great emotional vulnerability and dependence upon the advice and guidance of counsel. Attorneys owe the utmost duty of good faith and fidelity to clients. (See, e.g., Greenbaum v. State Bar (1976) 15 Cal. 3d 893, 903 [126 Cal. Rptr. 785]; Alkow v. State Bar (1971) 3 Cal. 3d 924, 935 [92 Cal. Rptr. 278]; Cutler v. State Bar (1969) 71 Cal. 2d 241, 251 [78 Cal. Rptr. 172]; Clancy v. State Bar (1969) 71 Cal. 2d 140, 146 [77 Cal. Rptr. 657].) The relationship between an attorney and client is a fiduciary relationship of the very highest character and all dealings between an attorney and client that are beneficial to the attorney will be closely scrutinized with the utmost strictness for unfairness. (See, e.g., Giovanazzi v. State Bar (1980) 28 Cal. 3d 465, 472 [169 Cal. Rptr. 581]; Benson v. State Bar (1975) 13 Cal. 3d 581, 586 [119 Cal. Rptr. 297]; Lee v. State Bar (1970) 2 Cal. 3d 927, 939 [88 Cal. Rptr. 361]; Clancy v. State Bar (1969) 71 Cal. 2d 140, 146 [77 Cal. Rptr. 657].) Where attorneys exercise undue influence over clients or take unfair advantage of clients, discipline is appropriate. (See, e.g., Magee v. State Bar (1962) 58 Cal. 2d 423 [24 Cal. Rptr. 839]; Lantz v. State Bar (1931) 212 Cal. 213 [298 P. 497].) In all client matters, a member is advised to keep clients' interests paramount in the course of the member's representation.

For purposes of this rule, if the client is an organization, any individual overseeing the representation shall be deemed to be the client. (See rule 3-600.)

Although paragraph (C) excludes representation of certain clients from the scope of rule 3-120, such exclusion is not intended to preclude the applicability of other Rules of Professional Conduct, including rule 3-110.

Related Materials

ABA Model Rules: No equivalent (but see 1.1 and 1.7(b)).
California Business & Professions Code: §6106.8.
Old California Rules of Professional Conduct: No equivalent.

Rule 3-200. Prohibited Objectives of Employment

A member shall not seek, accept, or continue employment if the member knows or should know that the objective of such employment is:

(A) To bring an action, conduct a defense, assert a position in litigation, or take an appeal, without probable cause and for the purpose of harassing or maliciously injuring any person; or

(B) To present a claim or defense in litigation that is not warranted under existing law, unless it can be supported by a good faith argument for an extension, modification, or reversal of such existing law.

Related Materials

ABA Model Rules: 3.1, 4.4.
California Business & Professions Code: §§6068(c), 6068(f), 6068(g), 6128(a).
Old California Rules of Professional Conduct: 2-101(A)(6), 2-110(A), 7-106(D), 7-106(F).

Rule 3-210. Advising the Violation of Law

A member shall not advise the violation of any law, rule, or ruling of a tribunal unless the member believes in good faith that such law, rule, or ruling is invalid. A member may take appropriate steps in good faith to test the validity of any law, rule, or ruling of a tribunal.

DISCUSSION

Rule 3-210 is intended to apply not only to the prospective conduct of a client but also to the interaction between the member and client and to the specific legal service sought by the client from the member. An example of the former is the handling of physical evidence of a crime in the possession of the client and offered to the member. (See People v. Meredith (1981) 29 Cal. 3d 682 [175 Cal. Rptr. 612].) An example of the latter is a request that the member negotiate the return of stolen property in exchange for the owner's agreement not to report the theft to the police or prosecutorial authorities. (See People v. Pic'l (1982) 31 Cal. 3d 731 [183 Cal. Rptr. 685].)

Related Materials

ABA Model Rules: 1.2(d), 5.4.
California Business & Professions Code: §6068(c).
Old California Rules of Professional Conduct: 3-102(A), 3-103, 7-101.

Rule 3-300.　Avoiding ~~Adverse~~ Interests <u>Adverse to a</u> <u>Client</u>*

A member shall not enter into a business transaction with a client; or knowingly acquire an ownership, possessory, security, or other pecuniary interest adverse to a client, unless each of the following requirements has been satisfied:

(A) The transaction or acquisition and its terms are fair and reasonable to the client and are fully disclosed and transmitted in writing to the client in a manner which should reasonably have been understood by the client; and

(B) The client is advised in writing that the client may seek the advice of an independent lawyer of the client's choice and is given a reasonable opportunity to seek that advice; and

(C) The client thereafter consents in writing to the terms of the transaction or the terms of the acquisition.

DISCUSSION

Rule 3-300 is not intended to apply to the agreement by which the member is retained by the client, unless the agreement confers on the member an ownership, possessory, security, or other pecuniary interest adverse to the client. Such an agreement is governed, in part, by rule 4-200.

Rule 3-300 is not intended to apply where the member and client each make an investment on terms offered to the general public or a significant portion thereof. For example, rule 3-300 is not intended to apply where *A*, a member, invests in a limited partnership syndicated by a third party. *B*, *A*'s client, makes the same investment. Although *A* and *B* are each investing in the same business, *A* did not enter into the transaction "with" *B* for the purposes of the rule.

Rule 3-300 is intended to apply where the member wishes to obtain an interest in client's property in order to secure the amount of the member's past due or future fees.

---

*Strike-throughs and underscorings show deletions and additions made by the California Supreme Court on August 13, 1992. The changes became operative in September 1992. — Eds.

Related Materials

ABA Model Rules: 1.8(a).
California Business & Professions Code: No equivalent; but see §6106.8 (sexual involve-ment with clients).
Old California Rules of Professional Conduct: 5-101.

Rule 3-310. Avoiding the Representation of Adverse Interests*

(~~F~~A) ~~As used in this rule "informed" means full disclosure to the client of the circumstances and advice to the client of any actual or reasonably foresee-able adverse effects of those circumstances upon the representation.~~ For pur-poses of this rule:

(1) "Disclosure" means informing the client or former client of the rele-vant circumstances and of the actual and reasonably foreseeable adverse consequences to the client or former client;

(2) "Informed written consent" means the client's or former client's written agreement to the representation following written disclosure;

(3) "Written means any writing as defined in Evidence Code section 250.

(~~A~~B) ~~If a member has or had a relationship with another party interested in the representation, or has an interest in its subject matter, the member shall not accept or continue such representation without all affected clients' in-formed written consent.~~ A member shall not accept or continue representation of a client without providing written disclosure to the client where:

(1) The member has a legal, business, financial, professional, or per-sonal relationship with a party or witness in the same matter; or

(2) The member knows or reasonably should know that:

(a) the member previously had a legal, business, financial, profes-sional, or personal relationship with a party or witness in the same mat-ter; and

(b) the previous relationship would substantially affect the member's representation; or

(3) The member has or had a legal, business, financial, professional, or personal relationship with another person or entity the member knows or reasonably should know would be affected substantially by resolution of the matter; or

(4) The member has or had a legal, business, financial, or professional interest in the subject matter of the representation.

*Strike-throughs and underscorings show deletions and additions made by the California Supreme Court on August 13, 1992. The changes became operative in September 1992. — EDS.

(BC) ~~A member shall not concurrently represent clients whose interests conflict, except with their informed written consent.~~ A member shall not, without the informed written consent of each client:

(1) Accept representation of more than one client in a matter in which the interests of the clients potentially conflict; or

(2) Accept or continue representation of more than one client in a matter in which the interests of the clients actually conflict; or

(3) Represent a client in a matter and at the same time in a separate matter accept as a client a person or entity whose interest in the first matter is adverse to the client in the first matter.

(CD) A member who represents two or more clients shall not enter into an aggregate settlement of the claims of or against the clients, ~~except with their~~ without the informed written consent of each client.

(DE) A member shall not, without the informed written consent of the client or former client, accept employment adverse to a the client or former client where, by reason of the representation of the client or former client, the member has obtained confidential information material to the employment ~~except with the informed written consent of the client or former client.~~

(EF) A member shall not accept compensation for representing a client from one other than the client unless:

(1) There is no interference with the member's independence of professional judgment or with the client-lawyer relationship; and

(2) Information relating to representation of a the client is protected as required by Business and Professions Code section 6068, subdivision (e); and

(3) The member obtains the client's informed written consent ~~s after disclosure~~, provided that no disclosure or consent is required if;:

(a) such nondisclosure is otherwise authorized by law;; or

(b) the member is rendering legal services on behalf of any public agency which provides legal services to other public agencies or ~~members of~~ the public.

DISCUSSION

Rule 3-310 is not intended to prohibit a member from representing parties having antagonistic positions on the same legal question that has arisen in different cases, unless representation of either client would be adversely affected.

Other rules and laws may preclude making adequate disclosure under this rule. If such disclosure is precluded, informed written consent is likewise precluded. (See, e.g., Business and Professions Code section 6068, subsection (e).)

Paragraph (B) is not intended to apply to the relationship of a member to another party's lawyer. Such relationships are governed by rule 3-320.

Paragraph (B) is not intended to require either the disclosure of the new engagement to a former client or the consent of the former client to the new engagement. However, such disclosure or consent is required if paragraph (E) applies.

While paragraph (B) deals with the issues of adequate disclosure to the present client or clients of the member's present or past relationships to other parties or witnesses or present interest in the subject matter of the representation, paragraph (E) is intended to protect the confidences of another present or former client. These two paragraphs are to apply as complementary provisions.

Paragraph (B) is intended to apply only to a member's own relationships or interests, unless the member knows that a partner or associate in the same firm as the member has or had a relationship with another party or witness or has or had an interest in the subject matter of the representation.

~~Paragraph (A)~~ Subparagraphs (C)(1) and (C)(2) ~~is~~ are intended to apply to all types of legal employment, including the concurrent representation of multiple parties in litigation or in a single transaction or in some other common enterprise or legal relationship. Examples of the latter include the formation of a partnership for several partners or a corporation for several shareholders, the preparation of an ante-nuptial agreement, or joint or reciprocal wills for a husband and wife, or the resolution of an "uncontested" marital dissolution. In such situations, for the sake of convenience or economy, the parties may well prefer to employ a single counsel, but a member must disclose the potential adverse aspects of such multiple representation (e.g., Evid. Code, §962) and must obtain the informed written consent of the clients thereto pursuant to subparagraph (C)(1). Moreover, if the potential adversity should become actual, the member must obtain the further informed written consent of the clients pursuant to subparagraph ~~(B)~~ (C)(2).

Subparagraph (C)(3) is intended to apply to representations of clients in both litigation and transactional matters.

There are some matters in which the conflicts are such that written consent may not suffice for non-disciplinary purposes. (See Woods v. Superior Court (1983) 149 Cal. App. 3d 931 [197 Cal. Rptr. 185]; Klemm v. Superior Court (1977) 75 Cal. App. 3d 893 [142 Cal. Rptr. 509]; Ishmael v. Millington (1966) 241 Cal. App. 2d 520 [50 Cal. Rptr. 592].)

Paragraph (D) is not intended to apply to class action settlements subject to court approval.

Paragraph (~~E~~F) is not intended to abrogate existing relationships between insurers and insureds whereby the insurer has the contractual right to unilaterally select counsel for the insured, where there is no conflict of interest. (See San Diego Navy Federal Credit Union v. Cumis Insurance Society (1984) 162 Cal. App. 3d 358 [208 Cal. Rptr. 494].)

Related Materials

ABA Model Rules: 1.7, 1.8(f), 1.8(g), 1.9.
California Business & Professions Code: §6068(e).

Old California Rules of Professional Conduct: 4-101, 5-102.

Rule 3-320. Relationship with Other Party's Lawyer

A member shall not represent a client in a matter in which another party's lawyer is a spouse, parent, child, or sibling of the member, lives with the member, is a client of the member, or has an intimate personal relationship with the member, unless the member informs the client in writing of the relationship.

DISCUSSION*

Rule 3-320 is not intended to apply to circumstances in which a member fails to advise the client of a relationship with another ~~member~~ <u>lawyer</u> who is merely a partner or associate in the same law firm as the adverse party's counsel, and who has no direct involvement in the matter.

Related Materials

ABA Model Rules: 1.8(i).
California Business & Professions Code: No equivalent.
Old California Rules of Professional Conduct: No equivalent.

Rule 3-400. Limiting Liability to Client*

A member shall not:
    (A) Contract with a client prospectively limiting the member's liability to the client for the member's professional malpractice; or
    (B) Settle a claim or potential claim for ~~such~~ <u>the member's liability to the client for the member's professional malpractice</u> unless the client is informed in writing that the client may seek the advice of an independent lawyer of the client's choice regarding the settlement and is given a reasonable opportunity to seek that advice.

Strike-throughs and underscorings show deletions and additions made by the California Supreme Court on August 13, 1992. The changes became operative in September 1992. — EDS.

DISCUSSION

Rule 3-400 is not intended to apply to customary qualifications and limitations in legal opinions and memoranda, nor is it intended to prevent a member from reasonably limiting the scope of the member's employment or representation.

Related Materials

ABA Model Rules: 1.8(h).
California Business & Professions Code: No equivalent.
Old California Rules of Professional Conduct: 6-102.

Rule 3-500. Communication

A member shall keep a client reasonably informed about significant developments relating to the employment or representation and promptly comply with reasonable requests for information.

DISCUSSION

Rule 3-500 is not intended to change a member's duties to his or her clients. It is intended to make clear that, while a client must be informed of significant developments in the matter, a member will not be disciplined for failing to communicate insignificant or irrelevant information. (See Bus. & Prof. Code, §6068, subd. (m).)

Related Materials

ABA Model Rules: 1.4.
California Business & Professions Code: §6068(m).
Old California Rules of Professional Conduct: 5-105.

Rule 3-510. Communication of Settlement Offer

(A) A member shall promptly communicate to the member's client:

(1) All terms and conditions of any offer made to the client in a criminal matter; and

(2) All amounts, terms, and conditions of any written offer of settlement made to the client in all other matters.

(B) As used in this rule, "client" includes a person who possesses the authority to accept an offer of settlement or plea, or, in a class action, all the named representatives of the class.

DISCUSSION

Rule 3-510 is intended to require that counsel in a criminal matter convey all offers, whether written or oral, to the client, as give and take negotiations are less common in criminal matters, and, even were they to occur, such negotiations should require the participation of the accused.

Any oral offers of settlement made to the client in a civil matter should also be communicated if they are "significant" for the purposes of rule 3-500.

Related Materials

ABA Model Rules: 1.4.
California Business & Professions Code: §6068(m).
Old California Rules of Professional Conduct: 5-105.

Rule 3-600. Organization as Client

(A) In representing an organization, a member shall conform his or her representation to the concept that the client is the organization itself, acting through its highest authorized officer, employee, body, or constituent overseeing the particular engagement.

(B) If a member acting on behalf of an organization knows that an actual or apparent agent of the organization acts or intends or refuses to act in a manner that is or may be a violation of law reasonably imputable to the organization, or in a manner which is likely to result in substantial injury to the organization, the member shall not violate his or her duty of protecting all confidential information as provided in Business and Professions Code section 6068, subdivision (e). Subject to Business and Professions Code section 6068, subdivision (e), the member may take such actions as appear to the member to be in the best lawful interest of the organization. Such actions may include among others:

(1) Urging reconsideration of the matter while explaining its likely consequences to the organization; or

(2) Referring the matter to the next higher authority in the organization, including, if warranted by the seriousness of the matter, referral to the highest internal authority that can act on behalf of the organization.

(C) If, despite the member's actions in accordance with paragraph (B), the highest authority that can act on behalf of the organization insists upon action or a refusal to act that is a violation of law and is likely to result in substantial injury to the organization, the member's response is limited to the member's right, and, where appropriate, duty to resign in accordance with rule 3-700.

(D) In dealing with an organization's directors, officers, employees, members, shareholders, or other constituents, a member shall explain the identity of the client for whom the member acts, whenever it is or becomes apparent that the organization's interests are or may become adverse to those of the constituent(s) with whom the member is dealing. The member shall not mislead such a constituent into believing that the constituent may communicate confidential information to the member in a way that will not be used in the organization's interest if that is or becomes adverse to the constituent.

(E) A member representing an organization may also represent any of its directors, officers, employees, members, shareholders, or other constituents, subject to the provisions of rule 3-310. If the organization's consent to the dual representation is required by rule 3-310, the consent shall be given by an appropriate constituent of the organization other than the individual or constituent who is to be represented, or by the shareholder(s) or organization members.

DISCUSSION

Rule 3-600 is not intended to enmesh members in the intricacies of the entity and aggregate theories of partnership.

Rule 3-600 is not intended to prohibit members from representing both an organization and other parties connected with it, as for instance (as simply one example) in establishing employee benefit packages for closely held corporations or professional partnerships.

Rule 3-600 is not intended to create or to validate artificial distinctions between entities and their officers, employees, or members, nor is it the purpose of the rule to deny the existence or importance of such formal distinctions. In dealing with a close corporation or small association, members commonly perform professional engagements for both the organization and its major constituents. When a change in control occurs or is threatened, members are faced with complex decisions involving personal and institutional relationships and loyalties and have frequently had difficulty in perceiving their correct duty. (See People ex rel. Deukmejian v. Brown (1981) 29 Cal. 3d 150 [172 Cal. Rptr. 478]; Goldstein v. Lees (1975) 46 Cal. App. 3d 614 [120 Cal. Rptr. 253]; Woods v. Superior Court (1983) 149 Cal. App. 3d 931 [197 Cal. Rptr. 185]; In re Banks (1978) 283 Ore. 459 [584 P.2d 284]; 1 A.L.R.4th 1105.) In resolving such multiple relationships, members must rely on case law.

ABA Model Rules: 1.13.
California Business & Professions Code: No equivalent.
Old California Rules of Professional Conduct: No equivalent.

Rule 3-700. Termination of Employment*

(A) In General.

(1) If permission for termination of employment is required by the rules of a tribunal, a member shall not withdraw from employment in a proceeding before that tribunal without its permission.

(2) A member shall not withdraw from employment until the member has taken reasonable steps to avoid reasonably foreseeable prejudice to the rights of the client, including giving due notice to the client, allowing time for employment of other counsel, complying with rule 3-700(D), and complying with applicable laws and rules.

(B) Mandatory Withdrawal.

A member representing a client before a tribunal shall withdraw from employment with the permission of the tribunal, if required by its rules, and a member representing a client in other matters shall withdraw from employment, if:

(1) The member knows or should know that the client is bringing an action, conducting a defense, asserting a position in litigation, or taking an appeal, without probable cause and for the purpose of harassing or maliciously injuring any person; or

(2) The member knows or should know that continued employment will result in violation of these rules or of the State Bar Act; or

(3) The member's mental or physical condition renders it unreasonably difficult to carry out the employment effectively.

(C) Permissive Withdrawal.

If rule 3-700(B) is not applicable, a member may not request permission to withdraw in matters pending before a tribunal, and may not withdraw in other matters, unless such request or such withdrawal is because:

(1) The client

(a) insists upon presenting a claim or defense that is not warranted under existing law and cannot be supported by good faith argument for an extension, modification, or reversal of existing law, or

(b) seeks to pursue an illegal course of conduct, or

(c) insists that the member pursue a course of conduct that is illegal or that is prohibited under these rules or the State Bar Act, or

---

*Strike-throughs and underscorings show deletions and additions made by the California Supreme Court on August 13, 1992. The changes became operative in September 1992. — EDS.

(d) by other conduct renders it unreasonably difficult for the member to carry out the employment effectively, or

(e) insists, in a matter not pending before a tribunal, that the member engage in conduct that is contrary to the judgment and advice of the member but not prohibited under these rules or the State Bar Act, or

(f) breaches an agreement or obligation to the member as to expenses or fees.

(2) The continued employment is likely to result in a violation of these rules or of the State Bar Act; or

(3) The inability to work with co-counsel indicates that the best interests of the client likely will be served by withdrawal; or

(4) The member's mental or physical condition renders it difficult for the member to carry out the employment effectively; or

(5) The client knowingly and freely assents to termination of the employment; or

(6) The member believes in good faith, in a proceeding pending before a tribunal, that the tribunal will find the existence of other good cause for withdrawal.

(D) Papers, Property, and Fees.

A member whose employment has terminated shall:

(1) Subject to any protective order or non-disclosure agreement, promptly release to the client, at the request of the client, all the client papers and property. "Client papers and property" includes correspondence, pleadings, deposition transcripts, exhibits, physical evidence, expert's reports, and other items reasonably necessary to the client's representation, whether the client has paid for them or not; and

(2) Promptly refund any part of a fee paid in advance that has not been earned. This provision is not applicable to a true retainer fee which is paid solely for the purpose of ensuring the availability of the member for the matter.

DISCUSSION

Subparagraph (A)(2) provides that "a member shall not withdraw from employment until the member has taken reasonable steps to avoid reasonably foreseeable prejudice to the rights of the clients." What such steps would include, of course, will vary according to the circumstancs. Absent special circumstances, "reasonable steps" do not include providing additional services to the client once the successor counsel has been employed and rule 3-700(D) has been satisfied.

Paragraph (D) makes clear the member's duties in the recurring situation in which new counsel seeks to obtain client files from a member discharged by the client. It codifies existing case law. (See Academy of California Optometrists v.

Superior Court (1975) 51 Cal. App. 3d 999 [124 Cal. Rptr. 668]; Weiss v. Marcus (1975) 51 Cal. App. 3d 590 [124 Cal. Rptr. 297].) ~~Paragraph (D) also requires that the member "promptly" return unearned fees paid in advance. If a client disputes the amount to be returned, the member shall comply with rule 4-100(A)(2).~~

Subparagraph (D)(2) ~~also~~ requires that the member "promptly" return unearned fees paid in advance. If ~~a client disputes the amount to be returned~~ such fees have been placed in a trust account pursuant to rule 4-100, the member shall comply with the provisions of rule 4-100(A)(2), should the client dispute the amount to be returned. If the written fee agreement expressly provided that the fee paid in advance was nonrefundable and the engagement is not completed, the member may repay the client from the member's own funds. In any event all advances for costs and expenses must be placed in a trust account. (See Stevens v. State Bar (1990) 51 Cal. 3d 283 [272 Cal. Rptr. 167].)

Paragraph (D) is not intended to prohibit a member from making, at the member's own expense, and retaining copies of papers released to the client, nor to prohibit a claim for the recovery of the member's expense in any subsequent legal proceeding.

Related Materials

ABA Model Rules: 1.16.
California Business & Professions Code: No equivalent.
Old California Rules of Professional Conduct: 2-111.

CHAPTER 4. FINANCIAL RELATIONSHIP WITH CLIENTS

Rule 4-100. Preserving Identity of Funds and Property of a Client

(A) All funds received or held for the benefit of clients by a member or law firm, including advances for costs and expenses, shall be deposited in one or more identifiable bank accounts labelled "Trust Account," "Client's Funds Account" or words of similar import, maintained in the State of California, or, with written consent of the client, in any other jurisdiction where there is a substantial relationship between the client or the client's business and the other jurisdiction. No funds belonging to the member or the law firm shall be deposited therein or otherwise commingled therewith except as follows:

(1) Funds reasonably sufficient to pay bank charges.

(2) In the case of funds belonging in part to a client and in part presently or potentially to the member or the law firm, the portion belonging to the

member or law firm must be withdrawn at the earliest reasonable time after the member's interest in that portion becomes fixed. However, when the right of the member or law firm to receive a portion of trust funds is disputed by the client, the disputed portion shall not be withdrawn until the dispute is finally resolved.

(B) A member shall:

(1) Promptly notify a client of the receipt of the client's funds, securities, or other properties.

(2) Identify and label securities and properties of a client promptly upon receipt and place them in a safe deposit box or other place of safekeeping as soon as practicable.

(3) Maintain complete records of all funds, securities, and other properties of a client coming into the possession of the member or law firm and render appropriate accounts to the client regarding them; preserve such records for a period of no less than five years after final appropriate distribution of such funds or properties; and comply with any order for an audit of such records issued pursuant to the Rules of Procedure of the State Bar.

(4) Promptly pay or deliver, as requested by the client, any funds, securities, or other properties in the possession of the member which the client is entitled to receive.

(C) The Board of Governors of the State Bar shall have the authority to formulate and adopt standards as to what "records" shall be maintained by members and law firms in accordance with subparagraph (B)(3). The standards formulated and adopted by the Board, as from time to time amended, shall be effective and binding on all members.

Trust Account Record Keeping Standards as Adopted by the Board of Governors on July 11, 1992 to Become Operative on January 1, 1993*

Pursuant to rule 4-100(C) the Board of Governors of the State Bar has adopted the following standards, effective January 1, 1993, as to what "records" shall be maintained by members and law firms in accordance with subparagraph (B)(3).

(1) A member shall, from the date of receipt of client funds through the period ending five years from the date of appropriate disbursement of such funds, maintain:

(a) a written ledger for each client on whose behalf funds are held that sets forth

(i) the name of such client,

(ii) the date, amount and source of all funds received on behalf of such client,

---

*Underscorings show additions made by the California Supreme Court on August 13, 1992. The changes became operative in September 1992. — EDS.

(iii) the date, amount, payee and purpose of each disbursement made on behalf of such client, and

(iv) the current balance for such client;

(b) a written journal for each bank account that sets forth

(i) the name of such account,

(ii) the date, amount and client affected by each debit and credit, and

(iii) the current balance in such account;

(c) all bank statements and cancelled checks for each bank account; and

(d) each monthly reconciliation (balancing) of (a), (b), and (c).

(2) A member shall, from the date of receipt of all securities and other properties held for the benefit of client through the period ending five years from the date of appropriate disbursement of such securities and other properties, maintain a written journal that specifies:

(a) each item of security and property held;

(b) the person on whose behalf the security or property is held;

(c) the date of receipt of the security or property;

(d) the date of distribution of the security or property; and

(e) person to whom the security or property was distributed.

Related Materials

ABA Model Rules: 1.15.
California Business & Professions Code: No equivalent.
Old California Rules of Professional Conduct: 8-101.

Rule 4-200. Fees for Legal Services*

(A) A member shall not enter into an agreement for, charge, or collect an illegal or unconscionable fee.

(B) Unconscionability of a fee agreement shall be determined on the basis of all the facts and circumstances existing at the time the agreement is entered into except where the parties contemplate that the fee will be affected by later events. Among the factors to be considered, where appropriate, in determining the conscionability of a fee are the following:

(1) The amount of the fee in proportion to the value of the services performed.

(2) The relative sophistication of the member and the client.

(3) The novelty and difficulty of the questions involved and the skill requisite to perform the legal service properly.

(4) The likelihood, if apparent to the client, that the acceptance of the particular employment will preclude other employment by the member.

*Strike-throughs show deletions made by the California Supreme Court on August 13, 1992. The changes became operative in September 1992. — EDS.

(5) The amount involved and the results obtained.

(6) The time limitations imposed by the client or by the circumstances.

(7) The nature and length of the professional relationship with the client.

(8) The experience, reputation, and ability of the member or members performing the services.

(9) Whether the fee is fixed or contingent.

(10) The time and labor required.

(11) The informed consent of the client to the fee agreement.

Related Materials

ABA Model Rules: 1.5, 1.5(e).
California Business & Professions Code: §§6147-6149 and 6200-6206.
Old California Rules of Professional Conduct: 2-107, 2-108(A).

Rule 4-210. Payment of Personal or Business Expenses Incurred by or for a Client

(A) A member shall not directly or indirectly pay or agree to pay, guarantee, represent, or sanction a representation that the member or member's law firm will pay the personal or business expenses of a prospective or existing client, except that this rule shall not prohibit a member:

(1) With the consent of the client, from paying or agreeing to pay such expenses to third persons from funds collected or to be collected for the client as a result of the representation; or

(2) After employment, from lending money to the client upon the client's promise in writing to repay such loan; or

(3) From advancing the costs of prosecuting or defending a claim or action or otherwise protecting or promoting the client's interests, the repayment of which may be contingent on the outcome of the matter. Such costs within the meaning of this subparagraph (3) shall be limited to all reasonable expenses of litigation or reasonable expenses in preparation for litigation or in providing any legal services to the client.

(B) Nothing in rule 4-210 shall be deemed to limit rules 3-300, 3-310, and 4-300.

Related Materials

ABA Model Rules: 1.8(e).
California Business & Professions Code: No equivalent.
Old California Rules of Professional Conduct: 5-101.

Rule 4-300. Purchasing Property at a Foreclosure or a Sale Subject to Judicial Review*

(A) A member shall not directly or indirectly purchase property at a probate, foreclosure, receiver's, trustee's, or judicial sale in an action or proceeding in which such member or any ~~member~~ lawyer affiliated by reason of personal, business, or professional relationship with that member or with that member's law firm is ~~an attorney~~ acting as a lawyer for a party or ~~is acting~~ as executor, receiver, trustee, administrator, guardian, or conservator.

(B) A member shall not represent the seller at a probate, foreclosure, receiver, trustee, or judicial sale in an action or proceeding in which the purchaser is a spouse or relative of the member or of another lawyer in the member's law firm or is an employee of the member or the member's law firm.

Related Materials

ABA Model Rules: 1.5(e), 7.2.
California Business & Professions Code: No equivalent.
Old California Rules of Professional Conduct: 2-108.

Rule 4-400. Gifts from Client

A member shall not induce a client to make a substantial gift, including a testamentary gift, to the member or to the member's parent, child, sibling, or spouse, except where the client is related to the member.

DISCUSSION

A member may accept a gift from a member's client, subject to general standards of fairness and absence of undue influence. The member who participates in the preparation of an instrument memorializing a gift which is otherwise permissible ought not to be subject to professional discipline. On the other hand, where impermissible influence occurred, discipline is appropriate. (See Magee v. State Bar (1962) 58 Cal. 2d 423 [24 Cal. Rptr. 839].)

Related Materials

ABA Model Rules: 1.8(c).
California Business & Professions Code: No equivalent.

*Strike-throughs and underscorings show deletions and additions made by the California Supreme Court on August 13, 1992. The changes became operative in September 1992. – EDS.

Old California Rules of Professional Conduct: No equivalent.

CHAPTER 5. ADVOCACY AND
REPRESENTATION

Rule 5-100. Threatening Criminal, Administrative, or
Disciplinary Charges

(A) A member shall not threaten to present criminal, administrative, or disciplinary charges to obtain an advantage in a civil dispute.

(B) As used in paragraph (A) of this rule, the term "administrative charges" means the filing or lodging of a complaint with a federal, state, or local governmental entity which may order or recommend the loss or suspension of a license, or may impose or recommend the imposition of a fine, pecuniary sanction, or other sanction of a quasi-criminal nature but does not include filing charges with an administrative entity required by law as a condition precedent to maintaining a civil action.

(C) As used in paragraph (A) of this rule, the term "civil dispute" means a controversy or potential controversy over the rights and duties of two or more parties under civil law, whether or not an action has been commenced, and includes an administrative proceeding of a quasi-civil nature pending before a federal, state, or local governmental entity.

DISCUSSION

Rule 5-100 is not intended to apply to a member's threatening to initiate contempt proceedings against a party for a failure to comply with a court order.

Paragraph (B) is intended to exempt the threat of filing an administrative charge which is a prerequisite to filing a civil complaint on the same transaction or occurrence.

For purposes of paragraph (C), the definition of "civil dispute" makes clear that the rule is applicable prior to the formal filing of a civil action.

Related Materials

ABA Model Rules: No equivalent (but see 4.4, 8.4(d)).

California Business & Professions Code: §§6068(c), 6068(f), 6068(g), 6128(a).

Old California Rules of Professional Conduct: 2-101(A)(6), 2-110(A), 7-106(D), 7-106(F).

Rule 5-110. Performing the Duty of Member in Government Service

A member in government service shall not institute or cause to be instituted criminal charges when the member knows or should know that the charges are not supported by probable cause. If, after the institution of criminal charges, the member in government service having responsibility for prosecuting the charges becomes aware that those charges are not supported by probable cause, the member shall promptly so advise the court in which the criminal matter is pending.

Related Materials

ABA Model Rules: 3.8.
California Business & Professions Code: No equivalent.
Old California Rules of Professional Conduct: 7-102.

Rule 5-200. Trial Conduct

In presenting a matter to a tribunal, a member:

(A) Shall employ, for the purpose of maintaining the causes confided to the member such means only as are consistent with truth;

(B) Shall not seek to mislead the judge, judicial officer, or jury by an artifice or false statement of fact or law;

(C) Shall not intentionally misquote to a tribunal the language of a book, statute, or decision;

(D) Shall not, knowing its invalidity, cite as authority a decision that has been overruled or a statute that has been repealed or declared unconstitutional; and

(E) Shall not assert personal knowledge of the facts at issue, except when testifying as a witness.

Related Materials

ABA Model Rules: 3.3, 3.4.
California Business & Professions Code: §§6068(d), 6103, 6128(a).
Old California Rules of Professional Conduct: 7-105, 7-107.

Rule 5-210. Member as Witness

A member shall not act as an advocate before a jury which will hear testimony from the member unless:

(A) The testimony relates to an uncontested matter; or

(B) The testimony relates to the nature and value of legal services rendered in the case; or

(C) The member has the informed, written consent of the client. If the member represents the People or a governmental entity, the consent shall be obtained from the head of the office or a designee of the head of the office by which the member is employed and shall be consistent with principles of recusal.

*DISCUSSION**

Rule 5-210 is intended to apply to situations in which the member knows or should know that he or she ought to be called as a witness in litigation in which there is a jury. This rule is not intended to encompass situations in which the member is representing the client in an adversarial proceeding and is testifying before a judge. In non-adversarial proceedings, as where the ~~lawyer~~ member testifies on behalf of the client in a hearing before a legislative body, rule 5-210 is not applicable.

Rule 5-210 is not intended to apply to circumstances in which a ~~partner or associate~~ lawyer in an advocate's firm will be a witness.

Related Materials

ABA Model Rules: 3.7.
California Business & Professions Code: No equivalent.
Old California Rules of Professional Conduct: 2-111(A).

Rule 5-220. Suppression of Evidence

A member shall not suppress any evidence that the member or the member's client has a legal obligation to reveal or to produce.

Related Materials

ABA Model Rules: 3.4(a), 3.8.

*Strike-throughs and underscorings show deletions and additions made by the California Supreme Court on August 13, 1992. The changes became operative in September 1992. — EDS.

California Business & Professions Code: No equivalent.
Old California Rules of Professional Conduct: 7-102.

Rule 5-300. Contact with Officials*

(A) A member shall not directly or indirectly give or lend anything of value to a judge, official, or employee of a tribunal unless the personal or family relationship between the member and the judge, official, or employee is such that gifts are customarily given and exchanged. Nothing contained in this rule shall prohibit a member from contributing to the campaign fund of a judge running for election or confirmation pursuant to applicable law pertaining to such contributions.

(B) A member shall not directly or indirectly communicate with or argue to a judge or judicial officer upon the merits of a contested matter pending before such judge or judicial officer, except:

(1) In open court; or

(2) With the consent of all other counsel in such matter; or

(3) In the presence of all other counsel in such matter; or

(4) In writing with a copy thereof furnished to such other counsel; or

(5) In ex parte matters.

(C) As used in this rule, ~~the phrase~~ "judge ~~or~~ and judicial officer" shall include law clerks, research attorneys, or other court personnel who participate in the decision-making process.

Related Materials

ABA Model Rules: 3.5.
California Business & Professions Code: No equivalent.
Old California Rules of Professional Conduct: 7-106, 7-108.

Rule 5-310. Prohibited Contact with Witnesses

A member shall not:

(A) Advise or directly or indirectly cause a person to secrete himself or herself or to leave the jurisdiction of a tribunal for the purpose of making that person unavailable as a witness therein.

(B) Directly or indirectly pay, offer to pay, or acquiesce in the payment of compensation to a witness contingent upon the content of the witness's testimony or the outcome of the case. Except where prohibited by law, a member may advance, guarantee, or acquiesce in the payment of:

*Strike-throughs and underscorings show deletions and additions made by the California Supreme Court on August 13, 1992. The changes became operative in September 1992. — EDS.

(1) Expenses reasonably incurred by a witness in attending or testifying.

(2) Reasonable compensation to a witness for loss of time in attending or testifying.

(3) A reasonable fee for the professional services of an expert witness.

Related Materials

ABA Model Rules: 3.4, 4.4.

California Business & Professions Code: §§6068(c), 6068(d), 6068(f), 6068(g), 6103, 6128(a).

Old California Rules of Professional Conduct: 7-105, 7-107, 2-101(A)(6), 2-110(A), 7-106(D), 7-106(F).

Rule 5-320. Contact with Jurors*

(A) A member connected with a case shall not communicate directly or indirectly with anyone the member knows to be a member of the venire from which the jury will be selected for trial of that case.

(B) During trial a member connected with the case shall not communicate directly or indirectly with any ~~member of the jury~~ juror.

(C) During trial a member who is not connected with the case shall not communicate directly or indirectly concerning the case with anyone ~~a~~ the member knows is a juror in the case.

(D) After discharge of the jury from further consideration of a case a member shall not ask questions of or make comments to a member of that jury that are intended to harass or embarrass the juror or to influence the juror's actions in future jury service.

(E) A member shall not ~~conduct~~ directly or indirectly conduct an out of court investigation of a person who is either a ~~venireman~~ member or the venire or a juror ~~of a type~~ in a manner likely to influence the state of mind of such ~~venireman or juror in~~ person in connection with present or future jury service.

(F) All restrictions imposed by this rule ~~5-320 upon a member~~ also apply to communications with, or investigations of, members of the family of a ~~venireman~~ person who is either a member of the venire or a juror.

(G) A member shall reveal promptly to the court improper conduct by a ~~venireman~~ person who is either a member of a venire or a juror, or by another toward a ~~venireman~~ person who is either a member of a venire or a juror or a member of his or her family, of which the member has knowledge.

*Strike-throughs and underscorings show deletions and additions made by the California Supreme Court on August 13, 1992. The changes became operative in September 1992. — EDS.

(H) This ~~Rrule 5-320~~ does not prohibit a member from communicating with ~~veniremen~~ persons who are members of a venire or jurors as a part of the official proceedings.

(I) For purposes of this rule, "juror" means any empaneled, discharged, or excused juror.

Related Materials

ABA Model Rules: 3.5(a).
California Business & Professions Code: No equivalent.
Old California Rules of Professional Conduct: 7-106.

Proposed Rule 2-400. Improper Settlement Offer
[disapproved]

Editors' Note. On August 25, 1988, the Board of Governors of the State Bar of California proposed Rule 2-400 to the California Supreme Court. On March 23, 1989, the California Supreme Court disapproved of Rule 2-400. The proposed rule is reprinted here.

A member shall not make or present a settlement offer in any case involving a request by the opposing party for attorney's fees pursuant to private attorney general statutes which is conditioned on opposing counsel waiving all or substantially all fees. This rule does not preclude a member from making or presenting an offer of a lump sum to settle all claims including attorney's fee.

Cross-Reference Chart from Old Rules to New Rules
Old Rules of Professional Conduct
(Effective January 1, 1975)
to
New Rules of Professional Conduct
(Operative May 27, 1989)

Old Number	New Title of Rule	New Number
1-100	Rules of Professional Conduct, in General.	1-100
1-101	False Statement Regarding Admission to the State Bar.	1-200
2-101	Advertising and Solicitation.	1-400
2-102	Legal Service Programs.	1-600
2-107	Fees for Legal Services.	4-200
2-108	Financial Arrangements Among Lawyers.	2-200

2-109	Agreements Restricting a Member's Practice.	1-500
2-110	Prohibited Objectives of Employment.	3-200
2-111	Termination of Employment.	3-700
2-111(A)(4) & (5)	Member as Witness.	5-210
3-101	Unauthorized Practice of Law.	1-300
3-102	Financial Arrangements with Non-Lawyers.	1-320
3-103	Forming a Partnership with a Non-Lawyer.	1-310
4-101	Avoiding the Representation of Adverse Interests.	3-310(D)
5-101	Avoiding Adverse Interests.	3-300
5-102	Avoiding the Representation of Adverse Interests.	3-310
5-103	Purchasing Property at a Foreclosure or a Sale Subject to Judicial Review.	4-300
5-104	Payment of Personal or Business Expenses Incurred by or for a Client.	4-210
5-105	Communication of Settlement Offer.	3-510
6-101	Failing to Act Competently.	3-110
6-102	Limiting Liability to Client.	3-400
7-101	Advising the Violation of Law.	3-210
7-102	Performing the Duty of Member in Government Service.	5-110
7-103	Communication with a Represented Party.	2-100
7-104	Threatening Criminal, Administrative, or Disciplinary Charges.	5-100
7-105	Trial Conduct.	5-200
7-106	Contact with Jurors.	5-320
7-107	Prohibited Contact with Witnesses.	5-310
7-107(A)	Suppression of Evidence.	5-220
7-108	Contact with Officials.	5-300
8-101	Preserving Identity of Funds and Property of a Client.	4-100
9-101	Disciplinary Authority of the State Bar.	1-110
New	Assisting, Soliciting, or Inducing Violations.	1-120
New	Sale or Purchase of a Law Practice of a Member, Living or Deceased.	2-300
New	Relationship with Other Party's Lawyer.	3-320
New	Sexual Relations with Clients.	3-120
New	Communication.	3-500
New	Organization as Client.	3-600
New	Gifts from Client.	4-400

Selected Provisions of the California Business and Professions Code

Editors' Introduction. More than any other state, California governs the conduct of lawyers by statute. California's provision on confidentiality, for example, is found in §6068, which lists the duties of an attorney. The statutes also contain detailed provisions governing fee agreements, communication of settlement offers, legal services offices, attorney discipline, and many other matters. The Business and Professions Code should therefore be read in conjunction with the California Rules of Professional Conduct (reprinted above), which play an equal role in governing California lawyers.

We have included here the statutory materials that parallel issues usually covered in law school courses on professional responsibility. We have omitted statutes on such things as state bar administration, state bar committees, and bar dues. Our table of contents gives the title of the articles that we have omitted. We have also omitted lengthy procedural rules concerning bar admission and discipline. What remains is a representative collection of the major statutes governing California lawyers.

The statutes here reflect changes through September 1992. The most recent addition to the code is §6106.9, which governs sexual relations between lawyers and clients. It was unanimously passed by the California House and Senate and was signed into law on September 21, 1992. It is the first statute of its kind in the nation and parallels California Rule of Professional Conduct 3-120, the first ethics rule in the nation to govern sex with clients. (See the previous chapter for details.) But the statute goes further than Rule 3-120, because it requires the State Bar to maintain statistical data on the number of complaints to the Bar growing out of sexual relations between lawyers and clients, and to develop standards for implementing §6106.9.

Contents

666

California Business and Professions Code

667

ARTICLE 4. ADMISSION TO THE STATE BAR

§6068. Duties of Attorney

It is the duty of an attorney to do all of the following:

(a) To support the Constitution and laws of the United States and of this state.

(b) To maintain the respect due to the courts of justice and judicial officers.

(c) To counsel or maintain such actions, proceedings, or defenses only as appear to him or her legal or just, except the defense of a person charged with a public offense.

(d) To employ, for the purpose of maintaining the causes confided to him or her such means only as are consistent with truth, and never to seek to mislead the judge or any judicial officer by an artifice or false statement of fact or law.

(e) To maintain inviolate the confidence, and at every peril to himself or herself to preserve the secrets, of his or her client.

(f) To abstain from all offensive personality, and to advance no fact prejudicial to the honor or reputation of a party or witness, unless required by the justice of the cause with which he or she is charged.

(g) Not to encourage either the commencement or the continuance of an action or proceeding from any corrupt motive of passion or interest.

(h) Never to reject, for any consideration personal to himself or herself, the cause of the defenseless or the oppressed.

(i) To cooperate and participate in any disciplinary investigation or other regulatory or disciplinary proceeding pending against the attorney. However, this subdivision shall not be construed to deprive an attorney of any privilege guaranteed by the Fifth Amendment to the Constitution of the United States or any other constitutional or statutory privileges.

(j) To comply with the requirements of Section 6002.1.

(k) To comply with all conditions attached to any disciplinary probation, including a probation imposed with the concurrence of the attorney.

(l) To keep all agreements made in lieu of disciplinary prosecution with the agency charged with attorney discipline.

(m) To respond promptly to reasonable status inquiries of clients and to keep clients reasonably informed of significant developments in matters with regard to which the attorney has agreed to provide legal services.

(n) To provide copies to the client of certain documents under time limits and as prescribed in a rule of professional conduct which the board shall adopt.

(o) To report to the agency charged with attorney discipline, in writing, within 30 days of the time the attorney has knowledge of any of the following:

(1) The filing of three or more lawsuits in a 12-month period against the attorney for malpractice or other wrongful conduct committed in a professional capacity.

(2) The entry of judgment against the attorney in any civil action for fraud, misrepresentation, breach of fiduciary duty, or gross negligence committed in a professional capacity.

(3) The imposition of any judicial sanctions against the attorney, except for sanctions for failure to make discovery or monetary sanctions of less than one thousand dollars ($1,000).

(4) The bringing of an indictment or information charging a felony against the attorney.

(5) The conviction of the attorney, including any verdict of guilty, or plea of guilty or no contest, of any felony, or any misdemeanor committed in the course of the practice of law, or in any manner such that a client of the attorney was the victim, or a necessary element of which, as determined by the statutory or common law definition of the misdemeanor, involves improper conduct of an attorney, including dishonesty or other moral turpitude, or an attempt or a conspiracy or solicitation of another to commit a felony or any such misdemeanor.

(6) The imposition of discipline against the attorney by any professional or occupational disciplinary agency or licensing board, whether in California or elsewhere.

(7) Reversal of judgment in a proceeding based in whole or in part upon misconduct, grossly incompetent representation, or willful misrepresentation by an attorney.

(8) As used in this subdivision, "against the attorney" includes claims and proceedings against any firm of attorneys for the practice of law in which the attorney was a partner at the time of the conduct complained of and any law corporation in which the attorney was a shareholder at the time of the conduct complained of unless the matter has to the attorney's knowledge already been reported by the law firm or corporation.

(9) The State Bar may develop a prescribed form for the making of reports required by this section, usage of which it may require by rule or regulation.

(10) This subdivision is only intended to provide that the failure to report as required herein may serve as a basis of discipline.
(Amended 1985, 1986, 1988, 1990.)

ARTICLE 5. DISCIPLINARY AUTHORITY OF THE BOARD OF GOVERNORS

§6079.4. Exercise by Attorney of Constitutional or Statutory Privileges Not Deemed Failure to Cooperate

The exercise by an attorney of his or her privilege under the Fifth Amendment to the Constitution of the United States, or of any other constitutional or statutory privileges shall not be deemed a failure to cooperate within the meaning of subdivision (i) of Section 6068.
(Added 1990.)

§6086.7. Court Actions, Judgments and Sanctions Against Attorneys; Notification to State Bar

A court shall notify the State Bar of any of the following:
(a) A final order of contempt imposed against an attorney that may involve grounds warranting discipline under this chapter. The court entering the final order shall transmit to the State Bar a copy of the relevant minutes, final order, and transcript, if one exists.
(b) Whenever a modification or reversal of a judgment in a judicial proceeding is based in whole or in part on the misconduct, incompetent representation, or willful misrepresentation of an attorney.
(c) The imposition of any judicial sanctions against an attorney, except sanctions for failure to make discovery or monetary sanctions of less than one thousand dollars ($1,000).
In the event of a notification made under subdivision (a), (b), or (c), the court shall also notify the attorney involved that the matter has been referred to the State Bar.
The State Bar shall investigate any matter reported under this section as to the appropriateness of initiating disciplinary action against the attorney.
(Added 1990.)

§6086.8. Judgments for Actions Committed in a
Professional Capacity; Claims or Actions for
Damages; Reports to State Bar

(a) Within 20 days after a judgment by a court of this state that a member of the State Bar of California is liable for any damages resulting in a judgment against the attorney in any civil action for fraud, misrepresentation, breach of fiduciary duty, or gross negligence committed in a professional capacity, the court which rendered the judgment shall report that fact in writing to the State Bar of California.

(b) Every claim or action of damages against a member of the State Bar of California for fraud, misrepresentation, breach of fiduciary duty, or negligence committed in a professional capacity shall be reported to the State Bar of California within 30 days of receipt by the admitted insurer or licensed surplus brokers providing professional liability insurance to that member of the State Bar.

(c) An attorney who does not possess professional liability insurance shall send a complete written report to the State Bar as to any settlement, judgment, or arbitration award described in subdivision (b), in the manner specified in that subdivision.

(Added 1986, amended 1988.)

ARTICLE 5.5 MISCELLANEOUS DISCIPLINARY PROVISIONS

§6090.5. Settlement of Civil Action for Professional
Misconduct; Agreement Not to File Complaint
with Disciplinary Agency

It is a cause for suspension, disbarment, or other discipline for any member of the State Bar to require as a condition of a settlement of a civil action for professional misconduct brought against the member that the plaintiff agree to not file a complaint with the disciplinary agency concerning that misconduct.

(Added 1986.)

§6094. Privileged Communications; Immunity

(a) Communications to the disciplinary agency relating to lawyer misconduct or disability or competence, or any communication related to an investigation or proceeding and testimony given in the proceeding are privileged, and no lawsuit predicated thereon may be instituted against any person. . . .

Nothing in this subdivision limits or alters the privileges accorded communications to the State Bar or testimony given in investigations or proceedings conducted by it or the immunities accorded complainants, informants, witnesses, the State Bar, its officers, and employees as existed prior to the enactment of this section. This subdivision does not constitute a change in, but is cumulative with the existing law.

(b) Upon application by the disciplinary agency and notice to the appropriate prosecuting authority, the superior court may grant immunity from criminal prosecution to a witness in any disciplinary agency proceeding.

(Added 1986.)

ARTICLE 6. DISCIPLINARY AUTHORITY OF THE COURTS

§6103.5. Written Offers of Settlement; Required Communication to Client; Discovery

(a) A member of the State Bar shall promptly communicate to the member's client all amounts, terms, and conditions of any written offer of settlement made by or on behalf of an opposing party. As used in this section, "client" includes any person employing the member of the State Bar who possesses the authority to accept an offer of settlement, or in a class action, who is a representative of the class.

(b) Any written offer of settlement or any required communication of a settlement offer, as described in subdivision (a), shall be discoverable by either party in any action in which the existence or communication of the offer of settlement is an issue before the trier of fact.

(Added 1986, amended 1987.)

§6105. Permitting Misuse of Name

Lending his name to be used as attorney by another person who is not an attorney constitutes a cause for disbarment or suspension.

§6106. Moral Turpitude, Dishonesty or Corruption Irrespective of Criminal Conviction

The commission of any act involving moral turpitude, dishonesty or corruption, whether the act is committed in the course of his relations as an attorney or otherwise, and whether the act is a felony or misdemeanor or not, constitutes a cause of disbarment or suspension.

If the act constitutes a felony or misdemeanor, conviction thereof in a criminal proceeding is not a condition precedent to disbarment or suspension from practice therefor.

§6106.5. Insurance Claims; Fraud

It shall constitute cause for disbarment or suspension for an attorney to engage in any conduct prohibited under Section 1871.1 or 1871.4 of the Insurance Code.
(Added 1978, amended 1988, 1991.)

Editors' Note. Sections 1871.1 and 1871.4 of the California Insurance Code were enacted in 1989 and 1991 respectively. Violation of these statutes is punishable by a fine, imprisonment, or both. They provide, in pertinent part, as follows:

§1871.1. False or Fraudulent Claim; Penalty; Prior Convictions; Notice of Claim Forms

(a) It is unlawful to do any of the following:

(1) Knowingly present or cause to be presented any false or fraudulent claim for the payment of a loss, including payment of a loss under a contract of insurance.

(2) Knowingly present multiple claims for the same loss or injury, including presentation of multiple claims to more than one insurer, with an intent to defraud.

(3) Knowingly cause or participate in a vehicular collision, or any other vehicular accident, for the purpose of presenting any false or fraudulent claim.

(4) Knowingly present a false or fraudulent claim for the payment of a loss or theft, destruction, damage, or conversion of a motor vehicle, a motor vehicle part, or contents of a motor vehicle.

(5) Knowingly prepare, make, or subscribe any writing, with intent to present or use the same, or to allow it to be presented in support of any false or fraudulent claim.

(6) Knowingly assist, abet, solicit, or conspire with [any person who engages in an unlawful act under this section]. . . .

§1871.4. Unlawful Conduct; Penalties

(a) It is unlawful to do any of the following:

(1) Make or cause to be made any knowingly false or fraudulent material statement or material representation for the purpose of obtaining or denying any compensation, as defined in Section 3207 of the Labor Code.

(2) Present or cause to be presented any knowingly false or fraudulent written or oral material statement in support of, or in opposition to, any claim for compensation for the purpose of obtaining or denying any compensation. . . .

(3) Knowingly assist, abet, solicit, or conspire with any person who engages in an unlawful act under this section. . . .

§6106.8. Sexual Involvement Between Lawyers and Clients; Rule of Professional Conduct

Editors' Note. In May 1991, a few months after the deadline set forth in §6106.8(c), the California State Bar submitted a proposed rule (Rule 3-120) to the California Supreme Court to govern sexual relations with clients. On August 13, 1992, the California Supreme Court adopted the proposed rule with modifications. The rule is reprinted above in the California Rules of Professional Conduct.

(a) The Legislature hereby finds and declares that there is no rule that governs propriety of sexual relationships between lawyers and clients. The Legislature further finds and declares that it is difficult to separate sound judgment from emotion or bias which may result from sexual involvement between a lawyer and his or her client during the period that an attorney-client relationship exists, and that emotional detachment is essential to the lawyer's ability to render competent legal services. Therefore, in order to ensure that a lawyer acts in the best interest of his or her client, a rule of professional conduct governing sexual relations between attorneys and their clients shall be adopted.

(b) With the approval of the Supreme Court, the State Bar shall adopt a rule of professional conduct governing sexual relations between attorneys and their clients in cases involving, but not limited to, probate matters and domestic relations, including dissolution proceedings, child custody cases, and settlement proceedings.

(c) The State Bar shall submit the proposed rule to the Supreme Court for approval no later than January 1, 1991.

(d) Intentional violation of this rule shall constitute a cause for suspension or disbarment.

(Added 1989.)

§6106.9. Attorneys: Sexual Conduct

SEC. 1. (a) It shall constitute cause for the imposition of discipline of an attorney within the meaning of this chapter for an attorney to do any of the following:

(1) Expressly or impliedly condition the performance of legal services for a current or prospective client upon the client's willingness to engage in sexual relations with the attorney.

(2) Employ coercion, intimidation, or undue influence in entering into sexual relations with a client.

(3) Continue representation of a client with whom the attorney has sexual relations if the sexual relations cause the attorney to perform legal services incompetently in violation of Rule 3-110 of the Rules of Professional Conduct of the State Bar of California, or if the sexual relations would, or would be likely to, damage or prejudice the client's case.

(b) Subdivision (a) shall not apply to sexual relations between attorneys and their spouses or persons in an equivalent domestic relationship or to ongoing consensual sexual relationships that predate the initiation of the attorney-client relationship.

(c) Where an attorney in a firm has sexual relations with a client but does not participate in the representation of that client, the attorneys in the firm shall not be subject to discipline under this section solely because of the occurrence of those sexual relations.

(d) For the purposes of this section, "sexual relations" means sexual intercourse or the touching of an intimate part of another person for the purpose of sexual arousal, gratification, or abuse.

(e) Any complaint made to the State Bar alleging a violation of subdivision (a) shall be verified under oath by the person making the complaint.

SEC. 2. Commencing January 1, 1993, the State Bar shall maintain statistical data regarding the number of complaints presented and the disposition or discipline imposed pursuant to Section 6106.9 of the Business and Professions Code. The State Bar shall submit a report to the Legislature regarding the statistical compilation on or before January 1, 1996.

The State Bar shall also develop and implement uniform standards for the implementation of Section 6106.9 of the Business and Professions Code and policies and procedures to ensure that complaints will be handled in a responsive and sensitive manner. The State Bar shall also provide appropriate training to staff on the standards, policies, and practices.

(Added 1992).

§6107. Proceedings upon Court's Own Knowledge or
upon Information

The proceedings to disbar or suspend an attorney, on grounds other than the conviction of a felony or misdemeanor, involving moral turpitude, may be taken by the court for the matters within its knowledge, or may be taken upon the information of another.

ARTICLE 7. UNLAWFUL PRACTICE OF LAW

§6128. Deceit, Collusion, Delay of Suit and Improper Receipt of Money as Misdemeanor

Every attorney is guilty of a misdemeanor who either:

(a) Is guilty of any deceit or collusion, or consents to any deceit or collusion, with intent to deceive the court or any party.

(b) Willfully delays his client's suit with a view to his own gain.

(c) Willfully receives any money or allowance for or on account of any money which he has not laid out or become answerable for.

Any violation of the provisions of this section is punishable by imprisonment in the county jail not exceeding six months, or by a fine not exceeding two thousand five hundred dollars ($2,500), or by both.

§6129. Buying Claim as Misdemeanor

Every attorney who, either directly or indirectly, buys or is interested in buying any evidence of debt or thing in action, with intent to bring suit thereon, is guilty of a misdemeanor.

Any violation of the provisions of this section is punishable by imprisonment in the county jail not exceeding six months, or by a fine not exceeding two thousand five hundred dollars ($2,500), or by both.

§6131. Aiding Defense Where Partner or Self Has Acted as Public Prosecutor; Misdemeanor and Disbarment

Every attorney is guilty of a misdemeanor and, in addition to the punishment prescribed therefor, shall be disbarred:

(a) Who directly or indirectly advises in relation to, or aids, or promotes the defense of any action or proceeding in any court the prosecution of which is carried on, aided or promoted by any person as district attorney or other public prosecutor with whom such person is directly or indirectly connected as a partner.

(b) Who, having himself prosecuted or in any manner aided or promoted any action or proceeding in any court as district attorney or other public prosecutor, afterwards, directly or indirectly, advises in relation to or takes any part in the defense thereof, as attorney or otherwise, or who takes or receives any valuable consideration from or on behalf of any defendant in any such action upon any understanding or agreement whatever having relation to the defense thereof.

This section does not prohibit an attorney from defending himself in person, as attorney or counsel, when prosecuted, either civilly or criminally.

ARTICLE 8.5. FEE AGREEMENTS

§6146. Limitations; Periodic Payments

(a) An attorney shall not contract for or collect a contingency fee for representing any person seeking damages in connection with an action for injury or damage against a health care provider based upon such person's alleged professional negligence in excess of the following limits:

(1) Forty percent of the first fifty thousand dollars ($50,000) recovered.

(2) Thirty-three and one-third percent of the next fifty thousand dollars ($50,000) recovered.

(3) Twenty-five percent of the next five hundred thousand dollars ($500,000) recovered.

(4) Fifteen percent of any amount on which the recovery exceeds six hundred thousand dollars ($600,000).

The limitations shall apply regardless of whether the recovery is by settlement, arbitration, or judgment, or whether the person for whom the recovery is made is a responsible adult, an infant, or a person of unsound mind.

(b) If periodic payments are awarded to the plaintiff pursuant to Section 667.7 of the Code of Civil Procedure, the court shall place a total value on these payments based upon the projected life expectancy of the plaintiff and include this amount in computing the total award from which attorney's fees are calculated under this section. . . .

(Added 1975, amended 1981, 1987.)

§6147. Contingency Fee Contracts; Duplicate Copy; Contents; Effect of Noncompliance; Recovery of Workers' Compensation Benefits

(a) An attorney who contracts to represent a plaintiff on a contingency fee basis shall, at the time the contract is entered into, provide a duplicate copy of the contract, signed by both the attorney and the plaintiff, or his guardian or representative, to the plaintiff, or to the plaintiff's guardian or representative. The contract shall be in writing and shall include, but is not limited to, all of the following:

(1) A statement of the contingency fee rate which the client and attorney have agreed upon.

677

(2) A statement as to how disbursements and costs incurred in connection with the prosecution or settlement of the claim will affect the contingency fee and the client's recovery.

(3) A statement as to what extent, if any, the plaintiff could be required to pay any compensation to the attorney for related matters that arise out of their relationship not covered by their contingency fee contract. This may include any amounts collected for the plaintiff by the attorney.

(4) Unless the claim is subject to the provisions of Section 6146, a statement that the fee is not set by law but is negotiable between attorney and client.

(5) If the claim is subject to the provisions of Section 6146, a statement that the rates set forth in that section are the maximum limits for the contingency fee agreement, and that the attorney and client may negotiate a lower rate.

(b) Failure to comply with any provision of this section renders the agreement voidable at the option of the plaintiff, and the attorney shall thereupon be entitled to collect a reasonable fee.

(c) This section shall not apply to contingency fee contracts for the recovery of workers' compensation benefits.

(Added 1982, amended 1986.)

§6147.5. Contingency Fee Contracts; Recovery of
          Claims Between Merchants

(a) Sections 6147 and 6148 shall not apply to contingency fee contracts for the recovery of claims between merchants as defined in Section 2104 of the Commercial Code, arising from the sale or lease of goods or services rendered, or money loaned for use, in the conduct of a business or profession if the merchant contracting for legal services employs 10 or more individuals.

(b)(1) In the instances in which no written contract for legal services exists as permitted by subdivision (a), an attorney shall not contract for or collect a contingency fee in excess of the following limits:

(A) Twenty percent of the first three hundred dollars ($300) collected.

(B) Eighteen percent of the next one thousand seven hundred dollars ($1,700) collected.

(C) Thirteen percent of sums collected in excess of two thousand dollars ($2,000).

(2) However, the following minimum charges may be charged and collected:

(A) Twenty-five dollars ($25) in collections of seventy-five dollars ($75) to one hundred twenty-five dollars ($125).

(B) Thirty-three and one-third percent of collections less than seventy-five dollars ($75).
(Added 1990.)

§6148. Contracts for Services in Cases Not Coming Within §6147; Bills Rendered by Attorney; Contents; Failure to Comply

(a) In any case not coming within Section 6147 in which it is reasonably foreseeable that total expense to a client, including attorney fees will exceed one thousand dollars ($1,000), the contract for services in the case shall be in writing and shall contain all of the following:

(1) The hourly rate and other standard rates, fees, and charges applicable to the case.

(2) The general nature of the legal services to be provided to the client.

(3) The respective responsibilities of the attorney and the client as to the performance of the contract.

(b) All bills rendered by an attorney to a client shall clearly state the basis thereof. Bills for the fee portion of the bill shall include the amount, rate, basis for calculation, or other method of determination of the attorney's fees and costs. Bills for the cost and expense portion of the bill shall clearly identify the costs and expenses incurred and the amount of the costs and expenses. Upon request by the client, the attorney shall provide a bill to the client no later than 10 days following the request unless the attorney has provided a bill to the client within 31 days prior to the request, in which case the attorney may provide a bill to the client no later than 31 days following the date the most recent bill was provided. The client is entitled to make similar requests at intervals of no less than 30 days following the initial request. In providing responses to client requests for billing information, the attorney may use billing data that is currently effective on the date of the request, or, if any fees or costs to that date cannot be accurately determined, they shall be described and estimated.

(c) Failure to comply with any provision of this section renders the agreement voidable at the option of the client, and the attorney shall, upon the agreement being voided, be entitled to collect a reasonable fee.

(d) This section shall not apply to any of the following:

(1) Services rendered in an emergency to avoid foreseeable prejudice to the rights or interests of the client or where a writing is otherwise impractical.

(2) An arrangement as to the fee implied by the fact that the attorney's services are of the same general kind as previously rendered to and paid for by the client.

(3) If the client knowingly states in writing, after full disclosure of this section, that a writing concerning fees is not required.

(4) If the client is a corporation.

(e) This section applies prospectively only to fee agreements following its operative date.

(Added 1986, amended 1990.)

§6149. Written Fee Contract as Confidential
　　　　Communication

A written fee contract shall be deemed to be a confidential communication within the meaning of subdivision (e) of Section 6068 and of Section 952 of the Evidence Code.

(Added 1986.)

Editors' Note. Section 6068(e) of the Business and Professions Code is reprinted above in this chapter. Section 952 of the Evidence Code is reprinted above in the chapter on the attorney-client privilege and work product.

ARTICLE 9. UNLAWFUL SOLICITATION

§6151. Definitions

As used in this article:

(a) A runner or capper is any person, firm, association or corporation acting for consideration in any manner or in any capacity as an agent for an attorney at law or law firm, whether the attorney or any member of the law firm is admitted in California or any other jurisdiction, in the solicitation or procurement of business for the attorney at law or law firm as provided in this article.

(b) An agent is one who represents another in dealings with one or more third persons.

(Amended 1991.)

§6152. Prohibition of Solicitation

(a) It is unlawful for:

(1) Any person, in his individual capacity or in his capacity as a public or private employee, or for any firm, corporation, partnership or association to act as a runner or capper for any such attorneys or to solicit any business for any such attorneys in and about the state prisons, county jails, city jails, city prisons, or other places of detention of persons, city receiving hospitals, city and county receiving hospitals, county hospitals, justice

courts, municipal courts, superior courts, or in any public institution or in any public place or upon any public street or highway or in and about private hospitals, sanitariums or in and about any private institution or upon private property of any character whatsoever.

(2) Any person to solicit another person to commit or join in the commission of a violation of subdivision (a).

(b) A general release from a liability claim obtained from any person during the period of the first physical confinement, whether as an inpatient or outpatient, in a clinic or health facility ... as a result of the injury alleged to have given rise to such claim and primarily for treatment of such injury, is presumed fraudulent if such release is executed within 15 days after the commencement of such confinement or prior to release from such confinement, whichever occurs first.

(c) Nothing in this section shall be construed to prevent the recommendation of professional employment where such recommendation is not prohibited by the Rules of Professional Conduct of the State Bar of California.

(d) Nothing in this section shall be construed to mean that a public defender or assigned counsel may not make known his or her services as a criminal defense attorney to persons unable to afford legal counsel whether such persons are in custody or otherwise.

(Amended 1976, 1977.)

§6153. Violation as Misdemeanor; Forfeiture of Public Office or Employment

Any person, firm, partnership, association, or corporation violating subdivision (a) of Section 6152 is punishable, upon a first conviction, by imprisonment in a county jail for not more than one year. Upon a second or subsequent conviction, a person, firm, partnership, association, or corporation is punishable by imprisonment in a county jail for not more than one year, or by imprisonment in the state prison for 16 months or 2 or 3 years, or by a fine of up to ten thousand dollars ($10,000), or by both that imprisonment and fine.

Any person employed either as an officer, director, trustee, clerk, servant or agent of this state or of any county or other municipal corporation or subdivision thereof, who is found guilty of violating any of the provisions of this article, shall forfeit the right to his office and employment in addition to any other penalty provided in this article.

(Amended 1976, 1977, 1991).

§6154. Validity of Contract for Services; Civil Penalties

Any contract for professional services secured by any attorney at law or law firm in this state through the services of a runner or capper is void. In any action against any attorney or law firm under the Unfair Practices Act, Chapter 4 (commencing with Section 17000) of Division 7, or Chapter 5 (commencing with Section 17200) of Division 7, any judgment shall include an order divesting the attorney or law firm of any fees and other compensation received pursuant to any such void contract. Those fees and compensation shall be recoverable as additional civil penalties under Chapter 4 (commencing with Section 17000) or Chapter 5 (commencing with Section 17200) of Division 7.

(Amended 1991.)

§6155. Referral Services; Conflicts of Interest; Enforcement; Rules and Regulations; Duration of Section

(a) An individual, partnership, corporation, association, or any other entity shall not use the term "referral service" or similar terms, if the purpose of the individual, partnership, corporation, association, or entity is to refer potential clients to attorneys, unless all of the following requirements are met:

(1) The service is registered with the State Bar of California and . . . is operated in conformity with minimum standards for a lawyer referral service established by the State Bar. . . .

(2) The combined charges to the potential client by the referral service and the attorney to whom the potential client is referred do not exceed the total cost that the client would normally pay if no referral service were involved.

(b) A referral service shall not be owned or operated, in whole or in part, directly or indirectly, by those lawyers to whom, individually or collectively, more than 20 percent of referrals are made. For purposes of this subdivision, a referral service that is owned or operated by a bar association, as defined in the minimum standards, shall be deemed to be owned or operated by its governing committee so long as the governing committee is constituted and functions in the manner prescribed by the minimum standards.

(c) Neither of the following is a lawyer referral service:

(1) A plan of legal insurance as defined in Section 119.6 of the Insurance Code.

(2) A group or prepaid legal plan, whether operated by a union, trust, mutual benefit or aid association, public or private corporation, or other entity or person, which meets both of the following conditions:

(A) It recommends, furnishes, or pays for legal services to its members or beneficiaries.

(B) It provides telephone advice or personal consultation.

(d) The following are in the public interest and do not constitute an unlawful restraint of trade or commerce:

(1) An agreement between a referral service and a participating attorney to eliminate or restrict the attorney's fee for an initial office consultation for each potential client or to provide free or reduced fee services.

(2) Requirements by a referral service that attorneys meet reasonable participation requirements, including experience, education, and training requirements.

(3) Provisions of the minimum standards as approved by the Supreme Court.

(e) A violation or threatened violation of this section may be enjoined by any person.

(f) With the approval of the Supreme Court, the State Bar shall formulate and enforce rules and regulations for carrying out this section, including rules and regulations which do the following:

(1) Establish minimum standards for lawyer referral services. The minimum standards shall include provisions ensuring that panel membership shall be open to all attorneys practicing in the geographical area served who are qualified by virtue of suitable experience, and limiting attorney registration and membership fees to reasonable sums which do not discourage widespread attorney membership.

(2) Require that an entity seeking to qualify as a lawyer referral service register with the State Bar and obtain from the State Bar a certificate of compliance with the minimum standards for lawyer referral services. . . .

(5) Require each lawyer who is a member of a certified lawyer referral service to possess a policy of errors and omissions insurance in an amount not less than one hundred thousand dollars ($100,000) for each occurrence and three hundred thousand ($300,000) aggregate, per year. By rule, the State Bar may provide for alternative proof of financial responsibility to meet this requirement. . . .

(h) This section shall not be construed to prohibit attorneys from jointly advertising their services.

(i) This section shall become inoperative on July 1, 1993, and, as of January 1, 1994, is repealed, unless a later enacted statute, which becomes effective on or before January 1, 1994, deletes or extends the dates on which it becomes inoperative and is repealed.

(Added 1987.)

Editors' Note. Effective October 26, 1989, the California Supreme Court adopted "Minimum Standards for a Lawyer Referral Service in California," which are referred to in §6155. On November 4, 1989, the California State Bar adopted provisions governing "Certification and Renewal Fees for Lawyer Referral Service," and these were amended in January of 1991. Both the minimum standards and the certification and renewal rules can be found in California statute books following §6155. They are too lengthy to reprint here.

ARTICLE 13. ARBITRATION OF ATTORNEYS' FEES

§6200. Establishment of System and Procedure;
Applicability of Article; Voluntary or
Mandatory Nature; Rules; Immunity of
Arbitrator; Powers of Arbitrator

(a) The board of governors shall, by rule, establish, maintain, and administer a system and procedure for the arbitration of disputes concerning fees, costs, or both, charged for professional services by members of the State Bar or by members of the bar of other jurisdictions. The rules may include provision for a filing fee in such amount as the board may, from time to time determine.

(b) This article shall not apply to any of the following:

(1) Disputes where a member of the State Bar of California is also admitted to practice in another jurisdiction or where an attorney is only admitted to practice in another jurisdiction, and he or she maintains no office in the State of California, and no material portion of the services were rendered in the State of California.

(2) Claims for affirmative relief against the attorney for damages or otherwise based upon alleged malpractice or professional misconduct, except as provided in subdivision (a) of Section 6203.

(3) Disputes where the fee or cost to be paid by the client or on his or her behalf has been determined pursuant to statute or court order.

(c) Arbitration under this article shall be voluntary for a client and shall be mandatory for an attorney if commenced by a client. . . .

(e) In adopting or reviewing rules of arbitration under this section the board shall provide that the panel shall include one attorney member whose area of practice is either, at the option of the client, civil or criminal law, as follows:

(1) If the panel is composed of three members the panel shall include one attorney member whose area of practice is either, at the option of the client, civil or criminal law, and shall include one lay member.

(2) If the panel is composed of one member, that member shall be an attorney whose area of practice is either, at the option of the client, civil or criminal law.

(f) . . .

(Amended 1989, 1990.)

§6202. Disclosure of Attorney-Client Communication or Attorney's Work Product; Limitation

The provisions of Article 3 (commencing with Section 950) of Chapter 4 of Division 8 of the Evidence Code shall not prohibit the disclosure of any relevant communication, nor shall the provisions of Section 2016 of the Code of Civil Procedure be construed to prohibit the disclosure of any relevant work product of the attorney in connection with: (1) an arbitration hearing pursuant to this article; (2) a trial after arbitration; or (3) judicial confirmation, correction, or vacation of an arbitration award. In no event shall such disclosure be deemed a waiver of the confidential character of such matters for any other purpose.

§6203. Award; Contents; Damages and Offset; Fees and Costs; Finality of Award; Appellate Fees and Costs

(a) The award shall be in writing and signed by the arbitrators concurring therein. It shall include a determination of all the questions submitted to the arbitrators, the decision of which is necessary in order to determine the controversy. The award shall not include any award to either party for attorney's fees incurred, notwithstanding any contract between the parties providing for such an award or attorney's fees. However, this section shall not preclude an award of attorney's fees to either party by a court pursuant to subdivision (c) of this section or of subdivision (d) of Section 6204. The State Bar, or the local bar association delegated by the State Bar to conduct the arbitration, shall deliver to each of the parties with the award, an original declaration of service of the award.

The arbitrators may receive evidence relating to claims of malpractice and professional misconduct but only to the extent that those claims bear upon the fees to which the attorney is entitled. The arbitrators shall not award affirmative relief, in the form of damages or offset or otherwise, for injuries underlying any such claim. Nothing in this section shall be construed to prevent the arbitrators from awarding a refund of unearned prepaid fees.

(b) Even if the parties to the arbitration have not agreed in writing to be bound, the arbitration award shall become binding upon the passage of 30 days after mailing of notice of the award, unless a party has, within the 30 days, sought a trial after arbitration pursuant to Section 6204. . . .

(c) A court confirming, correcting, or vacating an award under this section may award to the prevailing party reasonable fees and costs including, if applicable, fees or costs on appeal, incurred in obtaining confirmation, correction, or vacation of the award. The party obtaining judgment confirming, correcting, or vacating the award shall be the prevailing party except that, without regard to consideration of who the prevailing party may be, if a party did not appear at the arbitration hearing in the manner provided by the rules

adopted by the board of governors, that party shall not be entitled to attorney's fees or costs upon confirmation, correction, or vacation of the award.
(Added 1978, amended 1982, 1984, 1989, 1990.)

ARTICLE 14. FUNDS FOR THE PROVISION OF LEGAL SERVICES TO INDIGENT PERSONS

Editors' Note. In 1981, California enacted legislation for an Interest on Lawyers' Trust Accounts (IOLTA) program. All IOLTA funds are distributed by the state bar to fund civil legal services for indigents. We reprint here the main sections of the IOLTA legislation, as amended in 1984.

§6210. Legislative Findings; Purpose

The Legislature finds that, due to insufficient funding, existing programs providing free legal services in civil matters to indigent persons, especially underserved client groups, such as the elderly, the disabled, juveniles, and non–English-speaking persons, do not adequately meet the needs of these persons. It is the purpose of this article to expand the availability and improve the quality of existing free legal services in civil matters to indigent persons, and to initiate new programs that will provide services to them. The Legislature finds that the use of funds collected by the State Bar pursuant to this article for these purposes is in the public interest, is a proper use of the funds, and is consistent with essential public and governmental purposes in the judicial branch of government. The Legislature further finds that the expansion, improvement, and initiation of legal services to indigent persons will aid in the advancement of the science of jurisprudence and the improvement of the administration of justice.

§6211. Establishment by Attorney of Demand Trust Account; Interest Earned to Be Paid to State Bar; Other Accounts Not Prohibited; Rules of Professional Conduct, Authority of Supreme Court or State Bar Not Affected

(a) An attorney or law firm, which in the course of the practice of law receives or disburses trust funds, shall establish and maintain an interest bearing demand trust account and shall deposit therein all client deposits that are nominal in amount or are on deposit for a short period of time. All such client funds may be deposited in a single unsegregated account. The interest earned on all such accounts shall be paid to the State Bar of California to be used for the purposes set forth in this article.

(b) Nothing in this article shall be construed to prohibit an attorney or law firm from establishing one or more interest bearing bank accounts or other trust investments as may be permitted by the Supreme Court, with the interest or dividends earned on the accounts payable to clients for trust funds not deposited in accordance with subdivision (a)....

§6216. Distribution of Funds

The State Bar shall distribute all moneys received under the program established by this article for the provision of civil legal services to indigent persons....

§6217. Maintenance of Quality Services, Professional Standards, Attorney-Client Privilege; Funds to Be Expended in Accordance with Article; Interference with Attorney Prohibited

With respect to the provision or legal assistance under this article, each recipient shall ensure all of the following:

(a) The maintenance of quality service and professional standards.

(b) The expenditure of funds received in accordance with the provisions of this article.

(c) The preservation of the attorney-client privilege in any case, and the protection of the integrity of the adversary process from any impairment in furnishing legal assistance to indigent persons.

(d) That no one shall interfere with any attorney funded in whole or in part by this article in carrying out his or her professional responsibility to his or her client as established by the rules of professional responsibility and this chapter.

§6218. Eligibility for Services; Establishment of Guidelines; Funds to Be Expended in Accordance with Article

All legal services projects and support centers receiving funds pursuant to this article shall adopt financial eligibility guidelines for indigent persons.

(a) Qualified legal services programs shall ensure that funds appropriated pursuant to this article shall be used solely to defray the costs of providing legal services to indigent persons or for such other purposes as set forth in this article. . . .

§6219. Provision of Work Opportunities and Scholarships for Disadvantaged Law Students

Qualified legal services projects and support centers may use funds provided under this article to provide work opportunities with pay, and where feasible, scholarships for disadvantaged law students to help defray their law school expenses.

§6220. Private Attorneys Providing Legal Services Without Charge; Support Center Services

Attorneys in private practice who are providing legal services without charge to indigent persons shall not be disqualified from receiving the services of the qualified support centers.

§6221. Services for Indigent Members of Disadvantaged and Underserved Groups

Qualified legal services projects shall make significant efforts to utilize 20 percent of the funds allocated under this article for increasing the availability of services to the elderly, the disabled, juveniles, or other indigent persons who are members of disadvantaged and underserved groups within their service area.

§6223. Expenditure of Funds; Prohibitions

No funds allocated by the State Bar pursuant to this article shall be used for any of the following purposes:

(a) The provision of legal assistance with respect to any fee generating case, except in accordance with guidelines which shall be promulgated by the State Bar.

(b) The provision of legal assistance with respect to any criminal proceeding.

(c) The provision of legal assistance, except to indigent persons or except to provide support services to qualified legal services projects as defined by this article.

New York Materials

New York Code of Professional Responsibility

Editors' Introduction. New York has not adopted the Model Rules of Professional Conduct. It has instead retained a version of the Model Code of Professional Responsibility. The New York Code has always varied somewhat from the Model Code. In the spring of 1990, the four Appellate Divisions of the New York State Supreme Court, which under §90 of the Judiciary Law have responsibility for promulgating rules of conduct for lawyers in the state, adopted amendments to the New York Code effective September 1, 1990. Many of these amendments draw upon the Model Rules. The Appellate Divisions have not adopted the Ethical Considerations of the Code as rules governing the behavior of lawyers, but the New York State Bar Association has and has modified these in response to the Model Rules. Following are those Ethical Considerations and Disciplinary Rules of the New York Code that vary significantly from parallel provisions of the Model Code.

Contents

EC 1-4 The integrity of the profession can be maintained only if conduct of lawyers in violation of the Disciplinary Rules is brought to the attention of the proper officials. A lawyer should reveal voluntarily to those officials all knowledge, other than knowledge protected as a confidence or secret, of conduct of another lawyer which the lawyer believes clearly to be a violation of the Disciplinary Rules that raises a substantial question as to the other lawyer's honesty, trustworthiness or fitness in other respects as a lawyer. A lawyer should, upon request, serve on and assist committees and boards having responsibility for the administration of the Disciplinary Rules.

EC 1-7 A lawyer should avoid bias and condescension toward, and treat with dignity and respect, all parties, witnesses, lawyers, court employees, and other persons involved in the legal process.

EC 1-8 A law firm should adopt measures giving reasonable assurance that all lawyers in the firm conform to the Disciplinary Rules and that the conduct of non-lawyers employed by the firm is compatible with the professional obligations of the lawyers in the firm. Such measures may include information supervision and occasional admonition, a procedure whereby junior lawyers can make confidential referral of ethical problems directly to a designated senior lawyer or special committee, and continuing legal education in professional ethics.

DR 1-102. Misconduct

A. A lawyer shall not: . . .

6. Unlawfully discriminate in the practice of law, including in hiring, promoting or otherwise determining conditions of employment, on the basis of age, race, creed, color, national origin, sex, disability, or marital status. Where there is available a tribunal of competent jurisdiction, other than a Departmental Disciplinary Committee, a complaint of professional misconduct based on unlawful discrimination shall be brought before such tribunal in the first instance. A certified copy of a determination by such a tribunal, which has become final and enforceable, and as to which the right to judicial or appellate review has been exhausted, finding that the lawyer has engaged in an unlawful discriminatory practice shall constitute *prima facie* evidence of professional misconduct in a disciplinary proceeding. . . .

DR 1-103. Disclosure of Information to Authorities

A. A lawyer possessing knowledge, not protected as a confidence or secret, of a violation of DR 1-102 that raises a substantial question as to another lawyer's honesty, trustworthiness or fitness in other respects as a lawyer shall report such knowledge to a tribunal or other authority empowered to investigate or act upon such violation.

B. A lawyer possessing knowledge or evidence, not protected as a confidence or secret, concerning another lawyer or a judge shall reveal fully such knowledge or evidence upon proper request of a tribunal or other authority empowered to investigate or act upon the conduct of lawyers or judges.

DR 1-104. Responsibilities of a Supervisory Lawyer

A. A lawyer shall be responsible for a violation of the Disciplinary Rules by another lawyer or for conduct of a non-lawyer employed or retained by or associated with the lawyer that would be a violation of the Disciplinary Rules if engaged in by a lawyer if:

1. The lawyer orders the conduct; or

2. The lawyer has supervisory authority over the other lawyer or the non-lawyer, and knows or should have known of the conduct at a time

when its consequences can be avoided or mitigated but fails to take reasonable remedial action.

EC 2-22   Without the consent of the client, a lawyer should not associate in a particular matter another lawyer outside the lawyer's firm. A fee may properly be divided between lawyers properly associated if the division is in proportion to the services performed by each lawyer or, by a writing given to the client, each lawyer assumes joint responsibility for the representation and if the total fee is reasonable.

EC 2-25   A lawyer has an obligation to render public interest and pro bono legal service. A lawyer may fulfill this responsibility by providing professional services at no fee or at a reduced fee to individuals of limited financial means or to public service or charitable groups or organizations, or by participation in programs and organizations specifically designed to increase the availability of legal services. In addition, lawyers or law firms are encouraged to supplement this responsibility through the financial and other support of organizations that provide legal services to persons of limited means.

EC 2-27   History is replete with instances of distinguished sacrificial services by lawyers who have represented unpopular clients and causes. Regardless of personal feelings, a lawyer should not decline representation because a client or a cause is unpopular or community reaction is adverse. A lawyer's representation of a client, including representation by appointment, does not constitute an endorsement of the client's political, economic, social or moral views or activities.

DR 2-101. Publicity and Advertising

A. A lawyer on behalf of himself or herself or partners or associates, shall not use or disseminate or participate in the preparation or dissemination of any public communication containing statements or claims that are false, deceptive, misleading or cast reflection on the legal profession as a whole.

B. Advertising or other publicity by lawyers, including participation in public functions, shall not contain puffery, self-laudation, claims regarding the quality of the lawyers' legal services, or claims that cannot be measured or verified.

C. It is proper to include information, provided its dissemination does not violate the provisions of subdivisions (A) and (B) of this section, as to:

1. education, degrees and other scholastic distinctions, dates of admission to any bar; areas of the law in which the lawyer or law firm practices, as authorized by the Code of Professional Responsibility; public offices and teaching positions held; memberships in bar associations or other professional societies or organizations, including offices and committee assignments therein; foreign language fluency;

2. names of clients regularly represented, provided that the client has given prior written consent;

3. bank references; credit arrangements accepted; prepaid or group legal services programs in which the attorney or firm participates; and

4. legal fees for initial consultation; contingent fee rates in civil matters when accompanied by a statement disclosing whether percentages are computed before or after deduction of costs and disbursements; range of fees for services, provided that there be available to the public free of charge a written statement clearly describing the scope of each advertised service; hourly rates; and fixed fees for specified legal services.

D. Advertising and publicity shall be designed to educate the public to an awareness of legal needs and to provide information relevant to the selection of the most appropriate counsel. Information other than that specifically authorized in subdivision (C) of this section that is consistent with these purposes may be disseminated providing that it does not violate any other provisions of this Rule.

E. A lawyer or law firm advertising any fixed fee for specified legal services shall, at the time of fee publication, have available to the public a written statement clearly describing the scope of each advertised service, which statement shall be delivered to the client at the time of retainer for any such service. Such legal services shall include all those services which are recognized as reasonable and necessary under local custom in the area of practice in the community where the services are performed.

F. If the advertisement is broadcast, it shall be prerecorded or taped and approved for broadcast by the lawyer, and a recording or videotape of the actual transmission shall be retained by the lawyer for a period of not less than one year following such transmission. All advertisements of legal services that are mailed, or are distributed other than by radio, television, directory, newspaper, magazine or other periodical, by a lawyer or law firm with an office for the practice of law in this state, shall also be subject to the following provisions:

1. A copy of each advertisement shall at the time of its initial mailing or distribution be filed with the Department Disciplinary Committee of the appropriate judicial department.

2. Such advertisement shall contain no reference to the fact of filing.

3. If such advertisement is directed to a predetermined addressee, a list, containing the names and addresses of all persons to whom the advertisement is being or will thereafter be mailed or distributed, shall be retained by the lawyer or law firm for a period of not less than one year following the last date of mailing or distribution.

4. The advertisements filed pursuant to this subdivision shall be open to public inspection.

5. The requirements of this subdivision shall not apply to such professional cards or other announcements the distribution of which is authorized by DR 2-102(A). . . .

K. All advertisements of legal services shall include the name, office address and telephone number of the attorney or law firm whose services are being offered.

DR 2-103. Solicitation and Recommendation of
Professional Employment

... D. A lawyer or the lawyer's partner or associate or any other affiliated lawyer may be recommended, employed or paid by, or may cooperate with one of the following offices or organizations which promote the use of the lawyer's services or those of a partner or associate or any other affiliated lawyer if there is no interference with the exercise of independent professional judgment on behalf of the client: ...

4. Any bona fide organization which recommends, furnishes or pays for legal services to its members or beneficiaries provided the following conditions are satisfied:

a. Neither the lawyer, nor the lawyer's partner, nor associate, nor any other affiliated lawyer nor any non-lawyer, shall have initiated or promoted such organization for the primary purpose of providing financial or other benefit to such lawyer, partner, associate or affiliated lawyer.

b. Such organization is not operated for the purpose of procuring legal work or financial benefit for any lawyer as a private practitioner outside of the legal services program of the organization.

c. The member or beneficiary to whom the legal services are furnished, and not such organization, is recognized as the client of the lawyer in the matter.

d. Any member or beneficiary who is entitled to have legal services furnished or paid for by the organization may, if such member or beneficiary so desires, select counsel other than that furnished, selected or approved by the organization for the particular matter involved; and the legal service plan of such organization provides appropriate relief for any member or beneficiary who asserts a claim that representation by counsel furnished, selected or approved would be unethical, improper or inadequate under the circumstances of the matter involved; and the plan provides an appropriate procedure for seeking such relief.

e. The lawyer does not know or have cause to know that such organization is in violation of applicable laws, rules of court or other legal requirements that govern its legal service operations.

f. Such organization has filed with the appropriate disciplinary authority, to the extent required by such authority, at least annually a report with respect to its legal service plan, if any, showing its terms, its schedule of benefits, its subscription charges, agreements with counsel and financial results of its legal service activities or, if it has failed to do so, the lawyer does not know or have cause to know of such failure. . . .

DR 2-106. Fee for Legal Services

. . . C. A lawyer shall not enter into an arrangement for, charge or collect:

1. A contingent fee for representing a defendant in a criminal case; or

2. Any fee in a domestic relations matter, the payment or amount of which is contingent upon the securing of a divorce or upon the amount of maintenance, support, equitable distribution, or property settlement; or

3. A fee proscribed by law or rule of court.

D. Promptly after a lawyer has been employed in a contingent fee matter, the lawyer shall provide the client with a writing stating the method by which the fee is to be determined, including the percentage or percentages that shall accrue to the lawyer in the event of settlement, trial or appeal, litigation and other expenses to be deducted from the recovery and whether such expenses are to be deducted before or after the contingent fee is calculated. Upon conclusion of a contingent fee matter, the lawyer shall provide the client with a written statement stating the outcome of the matter, and if there is a recovery, showing the remittance to the client and the method of its determination.

DR 2-107. Division of Fees Among Lawyers

A. A lawyer shall not divide a fee for legal services with another lawyer who is not a partner in or associate of the lawyer's law firm or law office, unless:

1. The client consents to employment of the other lawyer after a full disclosure that a division of fees will be made.

2. The division is in proportion to the services performed by each lawyer or, by a writing given to the client, each lawyer assumes joint responsibility for the representation.

3. The total fee of the lawyers does not exceed reasonable compensation for all legal services they rendered the client.

B. This Disciplinary Rule does not prohibit payment to a former partner or associate pursuant to a separation or retirement agreement.

DR 3-102. Dividing Legal Fees with a Non-Lawyer

A. A lawyer or law firm shall not share legal fees with a non-lawyer, except that:

1. An agreement by a lawyer with his or her firm, partner, or associate may provide for the payment of money, over a reasonable period of time

after the lawyer's death, to the lawyer's estate or to one or more specified persons.

2. A lawyer who undertakes to complete unfinished legal business of a deceased lawyer may pay to the estate of the deceased lawyer that proportion of the total compensation which fairly represents the services rendered by the deceased lawyer.

3. A lawyer or law firm may include non-lawyer employees in a retirement plan, even though the plan is based in whole or in part on a profit-sharing arrangement.

EC 4-7   The lawyer's exercise of discretion to disclose confidences and secrets requires consideration of a wide range of factors and should not be subject to reexamination. A lawyer is afforded the professional discretion to reveal the intention of a client to commit a crime and the information necessary to prevent the crime and cannot be subjected to discipline either for revealing or not revealing such intention or information. In exercising this discretion, however, the lawyer should consider such factors as the seriousness of the potential injury to others if the prospective crime is committed, the likelihood that it will be committed and its imminence, the apparent absence of any other feasible way in which the potential injury can be prevented, the extent to which the client may have attempted to involve the lawyer in the prospective crime, the circumstances under which the lawyer acquired the information of the client's intent, and any other possibly aggravating or extenuating circumstances. In any case, a disclosure adverse to the client's interest should be no greater than the lawyer reasonably believes necessary to the purpose.

DR 4-101.   Preservation of Confidences and Secrets of a Client

... C. A lawyer may reveal:

1. Confidences or secrets with the consent of the client or clients affected, but only after a full disclosure to them.

2. Confidences or secrets when permitted under Disciplinary Rules or required by law or court order.

3. The intention of a client to commit a crime and the information necessary to prevent the crime.

4. Confidences or secrets necessary to establish or collect the lawyer's fee or to defend the lawyer or his or her employees or associates against an accusation of wrongful conduct.

5. Confidences or secrets to the extent implicit in withdrawing a written or oral opinion or representation previously given by the lawyer and believed by the lawyer still to be relied upon by a third person where the lawyer has discovered that the opinion or representation was based on

materially inaccurate information or is being used to further a crime or fraud. . . .

EC 5-18   A lawyer employed or retained by a corporation or similar entity owes allegiance to the entity and not to a stockholder, director, officer, employee, representative, or other person connected with the entity. In advising the entity, a lawyer should keep paramount its interests and the lawyer's professional judgment should not be influenced by the personal desires of any person or organization. Occasionally, the lawyer may learn that an officer, employee or other person associated with the entity is engaged in action, refuses to act, or intends to act or to refrain from acting in a matter related to the representation that is a violation of a legal obligation to the entity, or a violation of law which reasonably might be imputed to the entity, and is likely to result in substantial injury to the entity. In such event, the lawyer should proceed as is reasonably necessary in the best interest of the entity. In determining how to proceed, the lawyer should give due consideration to the seriousness of the violation and its consequences, the scope and nature of the lawyer's representation, the responsibility in the entity and the apparent motivation of the person involved, the policies of the entity concerning such matters and any other relevant considerations. Any measures taken should be designed to minimize disruption of the entity and the risk of revealing confidences and secrets of the entity. Such measures may include, among others: asking reconsideration of the matter, advising that a separate legal opinion on the matter be sought for presentation to appropriate authority in the entity, and referring the matter to higher authority in the entity not involved in the wrongdoing, including, if warranted by the seriousness of the matter, referral to the highest authority that can act in behalf of the entity as determined by applicable law. Occasionally a lawyer for an entity is requested to represent a stockholder, director, officer, employee, representative, or other person connected with the entity in an individual capacity; in such case the lawyer may serve the individual only if the lawyer is convinced that differing interests are not present.

DR 5-101. Refusing Employment When the Interests of the Lawyer May Impair Independent Professional Judgment

   . . . B. A lawyer shall not act, or accept employment that contemplates the lawyer's acting, as an advocate before any tribunal if the lawyer knows or it is obvious that the lawyer ought to be called as a witness on behalf of the client, except that the lawyer may act as an advocate and also testify:
   1. If the testimony will relate solely to an uncontested issue.

2. If the testimony will relate solely to a matter of formality and there is no reason to believe that substantial evidence will be offered in opposition to the testimony.

3. If the testimony will relate solely to the nature and value of legal services rendered in the case by the lawyer or the lawyer's firm to the client.

4. As to any matter, if disqualification as an advocate would work a substantial hardship on the client because of the distinctive value of the lawyer as counsel in the particular case.

C. Neither a lawyer nor the lawyer's firm shall accept employment in contemplated or pending litigation if the lawyer knows or it is obvious that the lawyer or another lawyer in the lawyer's firm may be called as a witness other than on behalf of the client, and it is apparent that the testimony would or might be prejudicial to the client.

DR 5-102. Withdrawal as Counsel When the Lawyer Becomes a Witness

A. If, after undertaking employment in contemplated or pending litigation, a lawyer learns or it is obvious that the lawyer ought to be called as a witness on behalf of the client, the lawyer shall withdraw as an advocate before the tribunal, except that the lawyer may continue as an advocate and may testify in the circumstances enumerated in DR 5-101(B)(1) through (4).

B. If, after undertaking employment in contemplated or pending litigation, a lawyer learns or it is obvious that the lawyer or a lawyer in his firm may be called as a witness other than on behalf of the client, the lawyer may continue the representation until it is apparent that the testimony is or may be prejudicial to the client at which point the lawyer and the firm must withdraw from acting as an advocate before the tribunal.

DR 5-103. Avoiding Acquisition of Interest in Litigation

A. lawyer shall not acquire a proprietary interest in the cause of action or subject matter of litigation he or she is conducting for a client, except that the lawyer may:

1. Acquire a lien granted by law to secure the lawyer's fee or expenses.

2. Except as provided in DR 2-106(C)(2) or (3), contract with a client for a reasonable contingent fee in a civil case.

B. While representing a client in connection with contemplated or pending litigation, a lawyer shall not advance or guarantee financial assistance to the client, except that:

1. A lawyer may advance or guarantee the expenses of litigation, including court costs, expenses of investigation, expenses of medical examination,

and costs of obtaining and presenting evidence, provided the client remains ultimately liable for such expenses.

2. Unless prohibited by law or rule of court, a lawyer representing an indigent client on a pro bono basis may pay court costs and reasonable expenses of litigation on behalf of the client.

DR 5-105. Refusing to Accept or Continue Employment If the Interests of Another Client May Impair the Independent Professional Judgment of the Lawyer

. . . D. While lawyers are associated in a law firm, none of them shall knowingly accept or continue employment when any one of them practicing alone would be prohibited from doing so under DR 5-101(A), DR 5-105(A), (B) or (C), DR 5-108, or DR 9-101(B) except as otherwise provided therein.

DR 5-108. Conflict of Interest — Former Client

A. Except with the consent of a former client after full disclosure a lawyer who has represented the former client in a matter shall not:

1. Thereafter represent another person in the same or a substantially related matter in which that person's interests are materially adverse to the interests of the former client.

2. Use any confidences or secrets of the former client except as permitted by DR 4-101(C) or when the confidence or secret has become generally known.

DR 5-109. Conflict of Interest — Organization as Client

A. When a lawyer employed or retained by an organization is dealing with the organization's directors, officers, employees, members, shareholders or other constituents, and it appears that the organization's interests may differ from those of the constituents with whom the lawyer is dealing, the lawyer shall explain that the lawyer is the lawyer for the organization and not for any of the constituents.

DR 5-110. Membership in Legal Services Organization

A. A lawyer may serve as a director, officer or member of a not-for-profit legal services organization, apart from the law firm in which the lawyer practices, notwithstanding that the organization serves persons having interests that differ from those of a client of the lawyer or the lawyer's firm, provided that the lawyer shall not knowingly participate in a decision or action of the organization:

1. If participating in the decision or action would be incompatible with the lawyer's duty of loyalty to a client under Canon 5; or

2. Where the decision or action could have a material adverse effect on the representation of a client of the organization whose interests differ from those of a client of the lawyer or the lawyer's firm.

DR 6-102. Limiting Liability to Client

A. A lawyer shall not seek, by contract or other means, to limit prospectively the lawyer's individual liability to a client for malpractice, or, without first advising that person that independent representation is appropriate in connection therewith, to settle a claim for such liability with an unrepresented client or former client.

EC 7-14 A government lawyer who has discretionary power relative to litigation should refrain from instituting or continuing litigation that is obviously unfair. A government lawyer not having such discretionary power who believes there is lack of merit in a controversy submitted to the lawyer should so advise his or her superiors and recommend the avoidance of unfair litigation. A government lawyer in a civil action or administrative proceeding has the responsibility to seek justice and to develop a full and fair record, and should not use his or her position or the economic power of the government to harass parties or to bring about unjust settlements or results. The responsibilities of government lawyers with respect to the compulsion of testimony and other information are generally the same as those of public prosecutors.

DR 7-102. Representing a Client Within the Bounds of the Law

. . . B. A lawyer who receives information clearly establishing that:

1. The client has, in the course of the representation, perpetrated a fraud upon a person or tribunal shall promptly call upon the client to rectify the same, and if the client refuses or is unable to do so, the lawyer shall reveal the fraud to the affected person or tribunal, except when the information is protected as a confidence or secret.

2. A person other than the client has perpetrated a fraud upon a tribunal shall promptly reveal the fraud to the tribunal.

DR 7-107. Trial Publicity

A. A lawyer participating in or associated with a criminal or civil matter shall not make an extrajudicial statement that a reasonable person would expect to be disseminated by means of public communication if the lawyer knows or reasonably should know that it will have a substantial likelihood of materially prejudicing an adjudicative proceeding.

B. A statement ordinarily is likely to prejudice materially an adjudicative proceeding when it refers to a civil matter triable to a jury, a criminal matter, or any other proceeding that could result in incarceration, and the statement relates to:

1. The character, credibility, reputation or criminal record of a party, suspect in a criminal investigation or witness, or the identity of a witness, or the expected testimony of a party or witness.

2. In a criminal case or proceeding that could result in incarceration, the possibility of a plea of guilty to the offense or the existence or contents of any confession, admission, or statement given by a defendant or suspect or that person's refusal or failure to make a statement.

3. The performance or results of any examination or test or the refusal or failure of a person to submit to an examination or test, or the identity or nature of physical evidence expected to be presented.

4. Any opinion as to the guilt or innocence of a defendant or suspect in a criminal case or proceeding that could result in incarceration.

5. Information the lawyer knows or reasonably should know is likely to be inadmissible as evidence in a trial and would if disclosed create a substantial risk of prejudicing an impartial trial.

6. The fact that a defendant has been charged with a crime, unless there is included therein a statement explaining that the charge is merely an accusation and that the defendant is presumed innocent until and unless proven guilty.

C. Provided that the statement complies with DR 7-107(A), a lawyer involved with the investigation or litigation of a matter may state the following without elaboration:

1. The general nature of the claim or defense.

2. The information contained in a public record.

3. That an investigation of the matter is in progress.

4. The scheduling or result of any step in litigation.

5. A request for assistance in obtaining evidence and information necessary thereto.

6. A warning of danger concerning the behavior of a person involved, when there is reason to believe that there exists the likelihood of substantial harm to an individual or to the public interest.

7. In a criminal case:

a. The identity, age, residence, occupation and family status of the accused.

b. If the accused has not been apprehended, information necessary to aid in apprehension of that person.

c. The fact, time and place of arrest, resistance, pursuit, use of weapons, and a description of physical evidence seized, other than as contained only in a confession, admission, or statement.

d. The identity of investigating and arresting officers or agencies and the length of the investigation.

EC 8-4   Whenever a lawyer seeks legislative or administrative changes, the lawyer should identify the capacity in which he or she appears, whether on behalf of the lawyer, a client, or the public. A lawyer may advocate such changes on behalf of a client even though the lawyer does not agree with them. But when a lawyer purports to act on behalf of the public, the lawyer should espouse only those changes which the lawyer conscientiously believes to be in the public interest. Lawyers involved in organizations seeking law reform generally do not have a lawyer-client relationship with the organization. In determining the nature and scope of participation in law reform activities, a lawyer should be mindful of obligations under Canon 5, particularly DR 5-101 through DR 5-110. A lawyer is professionally obligated to protect the integrity of the organization by making an appropriate disclosure within the organization when the lawyer knows that a private client might be materially affected.

DR 9-101. Avoiding Even the Appearance of Impropriety

A. A lawyer shall not accept private employment in a matter upon the merits of which the lawyer has acted in a judicial capacity.

B. Except as law may otherwise expressly permit:

1. A lawyer shall not represent a private client in connection with a matter in which the lawyer participated personally and substantially as a public officer or employee, and no lawyer in a firm with which that lawyer is associated may knowingly undertake or continue representation in such a matter unless:

a. The disqualified lawyer is effectively screened from any participation, direct or indirect, including discussion, in the matter and is apportioned no part of the fee therefrom; and

b. There are no other circumstances in the particular representation that create an appearance of impropriety.

2. A lawyer having information that the lawyer knows is confidential government information about a person, acquired when the lawyer was a public officer or employee, may not represent a private client whose interests are adverse to that person in a matter in which the information could be used to the material disadvantage of that person. A firm with which that lawyer is associated may knowingly undertake or continue representation

in the matter only if the disqualified lawyer is effectively screened from any participation, direct or indirect, including discussion, in the matter and is apportioned no part of the fee therefrom.

3. A lawyer serving as a public officer or employee shall not:

a. Participate in a matter in which the lawyer participated personally and substantially while in private practice or non-governmental employment, unless under applicable law no one is, or by lawful delegation may be, authorized to act in the lawyer's stead in the matter; or

b. Negotiate for private employment with any person who is involved as a party or as attorney for a party in a matter in which the lawyer is participating personally and substantially.

C. A lawyer shall not state or imply that the lawyer is able to influence improperly or upon irrelevant grounds any tribunal, legislative body, or public official.

D. A lawyer related to another lawyer as parent, child, sibling or spouse shall not represent in any matter a client whose interests differ from those of another party to the matter who the lawyer knows is represented by the other lawyer unless the client consents to the representation after full disclosure and the lawyer concludes that the lawyer can adequately represent the interests of the client.

DR 9-102.   Preserving Identity of Funds and Property
            of Others; Fiduciary Responsibility;
            Maintenance of Bank Accounts;
            Recordkeeping; Examination of Records

A. Prohibition Against Commingling. A lawyer in possession of any funds or other property belonging to another person, where such possession is incident to his or her practice of law, is a fiduciary, and must not commingle such property with his or her own.

B. Separate Accounts.

1. A lawyer who is in possession of funds belonging to another person incident to the lawyer's practice of law, shall maintain such funds in a banking institution within the State of New York which agrees to provide dishonored check reports in accordance with the provisions of Part 1300 of these rules (22 NYCRR Part 1300).* "Banking institution" means a state or national bank, trust company, savings bank, savings and loan association or credit union. Such funds shall be maintained, in the lawyer's own name, or in the name of a firm of lawyers of which he or she is a member, or in the name of the lawyer or firm of lawyers by whom he or she is employed, in a

---

*Part 1300 contemplates that the bank will inform the Lawyers' Fund for Client Protection "whenever a properly payable instrument is presented against an attorney special, trust, or escrow account which contains insufficient available funds, and the banking institution dishonors the instrument for that reason." After ten days, the Lawyers' Fund must forward the dishonored check report to the appropriate attorney disciplinary committee. —EDS.

special account or accounts, separate from any business or personal accounts of the lawyer or lawyer's firm, and separate from any accounts which the lawyer may maintain as executor, guardian, trustee or receiver, or in any other fiduciary capacity, into which special account or accounts all funds held in escrow or otherwise entrusted to the lawyer or firm shall be deposited; provided, however, that such funds may be maintained in a banking institution located outside the State of New York if such banking institution complies with such Part 1300, and the lawyer has obtained the prior written approval of the person to whom such funds belong which specifies the name and address of the office or branch of the banking institution where such funds are to be maintained.

2. A lawyer or the lawyer's firm shall identify the special bank account or accounts required by subdivision (b)(1) of this section as an "Attorney Special Account," or "Attorney Trust Account," or "Attorney Escrow Account," and shall obtain checks and deposit slips that bear such title. Such title may be accompanied by such other descriptive language as the lawyer may deem appropriate, provided that such additional language distinguishes such special account or accounts from other bank accounts that are maintained by the lawyer or the lawyer's firm.

3. Funds reasonably sufficient to maintain the account or to pay account charges may be deposited therein.

4. Funds belonging in part to a client or third person and in part presently or potentially to the lawyer or law firm shall be kept in such special account or accounts, but the portion belonging to the lawyer or law firm may be withdrawn when due unless the right of the lawyer or law firm to receive it is disputed by the client or third person, in which event the disputed portion shall not be withdrawn until the dispute is finally resolved.

C. Notification of Receipt of Property; Safekeeping; Rendering Accounts; Payment or Delivery of Property. A lawyer shall:

1. Promptly notify a client or third person of the receipt of funds, securities, or other properties in which the client or third person has an interest.

2. Identify and label securities and properties of a client or third person promptly upon receipt and place them in a safe deposit box or other place of safekeeping as soon as practicable.

3. Maintain complete records of all funds, securities, and other properties of a client or third person coming into the possession of the lawyer and render appropriate accounts to the client or third person regarding them.

4. Promptly pay or deliver to the client or third person as requested by the client or third person the funds, securities, or other properties in the possession of the lawyer which the client or third person is entitled to receive.

D. Required Bookkeeping Records. A lawyer shall maintain for seven years after the events which they record:

1. The records of all deposits in and withdrawals from the accounts specified in subdivision (B) of this Disciplinary Rule and of any other bank account which concerns or affects the lawyer's practice of law.

These records shall specifically identify the date, source and description of each item deposited, as well as the date, payee and purpose of each withdrawal or disbursement.

2. A record for special accounts, showing the source of all funds deposited in such accounts, the names of all persons for whom the funds are or were held, the amount of such funds, the description and amounts, and the names of all persons to whom such funds were disbursed.

3. Copies of all retainer and compensation agreements with clients.

4. Copies of all statements to clients or other persons showing the disbursement of funds to them or on their behalf.

5. Copies of all bills rendered to clients.

6. Copies of all records showing payments to lawyers, investigators or other persons, not in the lawyer's regular employ, for services rendered or performed.

7. Copies of all retainer and closing statements filed with the Office of Court Administration.

8. All checkbooks and checkstubs, bank statements, prenumbered cancelled checks and duplicate deposit slips.

Lawyers shall make accurate entries of all financial transactions in their records of receipts and disbursements, in their special accounts, in their ledger books or similar records, and in any other books of account kept by them in the regular course of their practice, which entries shall be made at or near the time of the act, condition or event recorded.

E. Authorized Signatories. All special account withdrawals shall be made only to a named payee and not to cash. Such withdrawals shall be made by check or, with the prior written approval of the party entitled to the proceeds, by bank transfer. Only an attorney admitted to practice law in New York State shall be an authorized signatory of a special account.

F. Missing Clients. Whenever any sum of money is payable to a client and the lawyer is unable to locate the client, the lawyer shall apply to the court in which the action was brought, or, if no action was commenced, to the Supreme Court in the county in which the lawyer has his or her office, for an order directing payment to the lawyer of his or her fee and disbursements and to the clerk of the court of the balance due to the client.

G. Dissolution of a Firm. Upon the dissolution of any firm of lawyers, the former partners or members shall make appropriate arrangements for the maintenance by one of them or by a successor firm of the records specified in subdivision (D) of this Disciplinary Rule.

H. Availability of Bookkeeping Records; Records Subject to Production in Disciplinary Investigations and Proceedings. The financial records required by this Disciplinary Rule shall be located, or made available, at the principal New York State office of the lawyers subject hereto and any such records shall be produced in response to a notice or subpoena duces tecum issued in connection with a complaint before or any investigation by the appropriate grievance or departmental disciplinary committee, or shall be produced at the direction of the appropriate Appellate Division before any person designated by it. All books and records produced pursuant to this subdivision shall be kept confidential, except for the purpose of the particular proceeding, and their contents shall not be disclosed by anyone in violation of the lawyer-client privilege.

I. Disciplinary Action. A lawyer who does not maintain and keep the accounts and records as specified and required by this Disciplinary Rule, or who does not produce any such records pursuant to this Rule, shall be deemed in violation of these Rules and shall be subject to disciplinary proceedings.

DEFINITIONS

. . . 9. "Fraud" does not include conduct, although characterized as fraudulent by statute or administrative rule, which lacks an element of scienter, deceit, intent to mislead, or knowing failure to correct misrepresentations which can be reasonably expected to induce detrimental reliance by another.

Selected Provisions of the New York State Judiciary Law

Editors' Introduction. In New York, as in California, lawyers are heavily regulated by statute. Most of the statutes regulating lawyers are found in the New York State Judiciary Law. We reprint the most important sections of that law.

Contents

§479. Soliciting Business on Behalf of an Attorney

It shall be unlawful for any person or his agent, employee or any person acting on his behalf, to solicit or procure through solicitation either directly or indirectly legal business, or to solicit or procure through solicitation a retainer, written or oral, or any agreement authorizing an attorney to perform or render legal services, or to make it a business so to solicit or procure such business, retainers or agreements.

§480. Entering Hospital to Negotiate Settlement or Obtain Release or Statement

It shall be unlawful for any person to enter a hospital for the purpose of negotiating a settlement or obtaining a general release or statement, written or oral, from any person confined in said hospital or sanitarium as a patient, with reference to any personal injuries for which said person is confined in said hospital or sanitarium within fifteen days after the injuries were sustained, unless at least five days prior to the obtaining or procuring of such general release or statement such injured party has signified in writing his willingness that such general release or statement be given. This section shall not apply to a person entering a hospital for the purpose of visiting a person therein confined, as his attorney or on behalf of his attorney.

§481. Aiding, Assisting or Abetting the Solicitation of Persons or the Procurement of a Retainer for or on Behalf of an Attorney

It shall be unlawful for any person in the employ of or in any capacity attached to any hospital, sanitarium, police department, prison or court, or for a person authorized to furnish bail bonds, to communicate directly or indirectly with any attorney or person acting on his behalf for the purpose of aiding, assisting or abetting such attorney in the solicitation of legal business or the procurement through solicitation of a retainer, written or oral, or any agreement authorizing the attorney to perform or render legal services.

§482. Employment by Attorney of Person to Aid, Assist or Abet in the Solicitation of Business or the Procurement Through Solicitation of a Retainer to Perform Legal Services

It shall be unlawful for an attorney to employ any person for the purpose of soliciting or aiding, assisting or abetting in the solicitation of legal business or the procurement through solicitation either directly or indirectly of a retainer, written or oral, or of any agreement authorizing the attorney to perform or render legal services.

§483. Signs Advertising Services as Attorney at Law

It shall be unlawful for any person to maintain on real property or to permit or allow any other person to maintain, on such property a sign, in any language, to the effect that an attorney-at-law or legal services are available therein unless the full name of the attorney-at-law or the firm rendering such services is set forth thereon. In any prosecution for violation of the provisions of this section the existence of such a sign on real property shall be presumptive evidence that it was placed or permitted to exist thereon with the knowledge and consent of the person or persons in possession of said premises.

§487. Misconduct by Attorneys

An attorney or counselor who:
   1. Is guilty of any deceit or collusion, or consents to any deceit or collusion, with intent to deceive the court or any party; or,
   2. Wilfully delays his client's suit with a view to his own gain; or, wilfully receives any money or allowance for or on account of any money which he has not laid out, or becomes answerable for,
Is guilty of a misdemeanor, and in addition to the punishment prescribed therefor by the penal law, he forfeits to the party injured treble damages, to be recovered in a civil action.

§488. Buying Demands on Which to Bring an Action

An attorney or counselor shall not:
   1. Directly or indirectly, buy, take an assignment of or be in any manner interested in buying or taking an assignment of a bond, promissory note, bill of exchange, book debt, or other thing in action, with the intent and for the purpose of bringing an action thereon.
   2. By himself, or by or in the name of another person, either before or after action brought, promise or give, or procure to be promised or given, a valuable consideration to any person, as an inducement to placing, or in consideration of having placed, in his hands, or in the hands of another person, a demand of any kind, for the purpose of bringing an action thereon, or of representing the claimant in the pursuit of any civil remedy for the recovery thereof. But this subdivision does not apply to an agree-

ment between attorneys and counsellors, or either, to divide between themselves the compensation to be received.

3. An attorney or counselor who violates the provisions of this section is guilty of a misdemeanor.

§489. Purchase of Claims by Corporations or Collection Agencies

No person or co-partnership, engaged directly or indirectly in the business of collection and adjustment of claims, and no corporation or association, directly or indirectly, itself or by or through its officers, agents or employees, shall solicit, buy or take an assignment of, or be in any manner interested in buying or taking an assignment of a bond, promissory note, bill of exchange, book debt, or other thing in action, or any claim or demand, with the intent and for the purpose of bringing an action or proceeding thereon; provided however, that bills receivable, notes receivable, bills of exchange, judgments or other things in action may be solicited, bought, or assignment thereof taken, from any executor, administrator, assignee for the benefit of creditors, trustee or receiver in bankruptcy, or any other person or persons in charge of the administration, settlement or compromise of any estate, through court actions, proceedings or otherwise. Nothing herein contained shall affect any assignment heretofore or hereafter taken by any moneyed corporation authorized to do business in the state of New York or its nominee pursuant to a subrogation agreement or a salvage operation, or by any corporation organized for religious, benevolent or charitable purposes.

Any corporation or association violating the provisions of this section shall be liable to a fine of not more than five thousand dollars; any person or co-partnership, violating the provisions of this section, and any officer, trustee, director, agent or employee of any person, co-partnership, corporation or association violating this section who, directly or indirectly, engages or assists in such violation, is guilty of a misdemeanor.

§491. Sharing of Compensation by Attorneys Prohibited

1. It shall be unlawful for any person, partnership, corporation, or association to divide with or receive from, or to agree to divide with or receive from, any attorney-at-law or group of attorneys-at-law, whether practicing in this state or elsewhere, either before or after action brought, any portion of any fee or compensation, charged or received by such attorney-at-law or any valuable consideration or reward, as an inducement for placing, or in consideration of having placed, in the hands of such attorney-at-law, or in the hands of another person, a claim or demand of any kind for the purpose of collecting such

claim, or bringing an action thereon, or of representing claimant in the pursuit of any civil remedy for the recovery thereof. But this section does not apply to an agreement between attorneys and counsellors-at-law to divide between themselves the compensation to be received.

2. Any person violating any of the provisions of this section is guilty of a misdemeanor.

§492. Use of Attorney's Name by Another

If an attorney knowingly permits any person, not being his general law partner or a clerk in his office, to sue out any process or to prosecute or defend any action in his name, except as authorized by this section, such attorney, and every person who shall so use his name, is guilty of a misdemeanor.

Whenever an action or proceeding is authorized by law to be prosecuted or defended in the name of the people, or of any public officer, board of officers, or municipal corporation, on behalf of another party, the attorney-general, or district attorney, or attorney of such public officer or board or corporation may permit any proceeding therein, to be taken in his name by an attorney to be chosen by the party in interest.

§493. Attorneys Forbidden to Defend Criminal Prosecutions Carried on by Their Partners, or Formerly by Themselves

An attorney, who directly or indirectly advises in relation to, or aids or promotes the defense of any action or proceeding in any court, the prosecution of which is carried on, aided or promoted by a person as district attorney or other public prosecutor, with whom such attorney is directly or indirectly connected as a partner; or who, having himself prosecuted or in any manner aided or promoted any action or proceeding in any court, as district attorney or other public prosecutor, afterwards directly or indirectly advises in relation to, or takes any part in, the defense thereof, as attorney or otherwise; or who takes or receives any valuable consideration from or on behalf of any defendant in any such action, upon any understanding or agreement whatever, express or implied, having relation to the defense thereof, is guilty of a misdemeanor.

§494. Attorneys May Defend Themselves

The last section does not prohibit an attorney from defending himself in person, as attorney or as counsel, when prosecuted either civilly or criminally.

§495. Corporations and Voluntary Associations Not to Practice Law

1. No corporation or voluntary association shall

(a) practice or appear as an attorney-at-law for any person in any court in this state or before any judicial body, nor

(b) make it a business to practice as an attorney-at-law, for any person, in any of said courts, nor

(c) hold itself out to the public as being entitled to practice law, or to render legal services or advice, nor

(d) furnish attorneys or counsel, nor

(e) render legal services of any kind in actions or proceedings of any nature or in any other way or manner, nor

(f) assume in any other manner to be entitled to practice law, nor

(g) assume, use or advertise the title of lawyer or attorney, attorney-at-law, or equivalent terms in any language in such manner as to convey the impression that it is entitled to practice law or to furnish legal advice, services or counsel, nor

(h) advertise that either alone or together with or by or through any person whether or not a duly and regularly admitted attorney-at-law, it has, owns, conducts or maintains a law office or an office for the practice of law, or for furnishing legal advice, services or counsel.

2. No corporation or voluntary association shall itself or by or through its officers, agents or employees, solicit any claim or demand, or take an assignment thereof, for the purpose of representing any person in the pursuit of any civil remedy, nor solicit any claim or demand for the purpose of representing as attorney-at-law, or of furnishing legal advice, services or counsel to, a person sued or about to be sued in any action or proceeding or against whom an action or proceeding has been or is about to be brought, or who may be affected by any action or proceeding which has been or may be instituted in any court or before any judicial body.

Nothing herein contained shall affect any assignment heretofore or hereafter taken by any moneyed corporation authorized to do business in the state of New York or its nominee pursuant to a subrogation agreement or a salvage operation. Any corporation or voluntary association violating the provisions of this subdivision or of subdivision one of this section shall be liable to a fine of not more than five thousand dollars and every officer, trustee, director, agent or employee of such corporation or voluntary association who directly or indirectly engages in any of the acts prohibited in this subdivision or in subdivision one of this section or assists such corporation or voluntary association to do such prohibited acts is guilty of a misdemeanor. The fact that such officer, trustee, director, agent or employee shall be a duly and regularly admitted attorney-at-law, shall not be held to permit or allow any such corporation or voluntary association to do the acts so prohibited nor shall such fact be a defense upon the trial of any of the persons mentioned herein for a violation of the provisions of this subdivision or subdivision one of this section.

3. No voluntary association or corporation shall ask or receive directly or indirectly, compensation for preparing deeds, mortgages, assignments, discharges, leases, or any other instruments affecting real estate, wills, codicils, or any other instruments affecting disposition of property after death or decedents' estates, or pleadings of any kind in actions or proceedings of any nature. Any association or corporation violating the provisions of this subdivision is guilty of a misdemeanor.

4. Subdivisions one and two of this section shall not apply to any corporation or voluntary association lawfully engaged in a business authorized by the provisions of any existing statute.

5. This section shall not apply to a corporation or voluntary association lawfully engaged in the examination and insuring of titles to real property, in the preparation of any deeds, mortgages, assignments, discharges, leases or any other instruments affecting real property insofar as such instruments are necessary to the examination and insuring of titles, and necessary or incidental to loans made by any such corporation or association; nor shall it prohibit a corporation or voluntary association from employing an attorney or attorneys in and about its own immediate affairs or in any litigation to which it is or may be a party. Nothing herein contained shall be construed to prevent a corporation or association from furnishing to any person, lawfully engaged in the practice of law, such information or such clerical services in and about his professional work as, except for the provisions of this section, may be lawful, provided that at all times the lawyer receiving such information or such services shall maintain full professional and direct responsibility to his clients for the information and services so received. But no corporation shall be permitted to render any services which cannot lawfully be rendered by a person not admitted to practice law in this state nor to solicit directly or indirectly professional employment for a lawyer.

6. This section shall not apply to a corporation organized under article fifteen, *or authorized to do business in this state under article fifteen-A,* of the business corporation law.

7. This section does not apply to organizations which offer prepaid legal services; to non-profit organizations whether incorporated or unincorporated, organized and operating primarily for a purpose other than the provision of legal services and which furnish legal services as an incidental activity in furtherance of their primary purpose; or to organizations which have as their primary purpose the furnishing of legal services to indigent persons.

§496. [Prepaid Legal Services Plans; Registration
　　　 Statement]

An organization described in subdivision seven of section four hundred ninety-five of this article shall file with the appellate division department in which its principal office is located a statement describing the nature and purposes of the organization, the composition of its governing body, the type of legal services being made available, and the names and addresses of any attorneys and counselors-at-law employed by the organization or with whom commitments have been made. An updating of this information shall be furnished the appropriate appellate division on or before July first of each year and the names and addresses of attorneys and counselors-at-law who rendered legal services during that year shall be included.

§498. Professional Referrals

1. There shall be no cause of action for damages arising against any association or society of attorneys and counsellors at law authorized to practice in the state of New York for referring any person or persons to a member of the profession for the purpose of obtaining legal services, provided that such referral was made without charge and as a public service by said association or society, and without malice, and in the reasonable belief that such referral was warranted, based upon the facts disclosed.

2. For the purposes of this section, "association or society of attorneys or counsellors at law" shall mean any such organization, whether incorporated or unincorporated, which offers professional referrals as an incidental service in the normal course of business, but which business does not include the providing of legal services.

Selected New York Sanctions Provisions

Editors' Introduction. The following excerpts from the New York Rules of Court represent that jurisdiction's most significant sanctioning provisions. These can be usefully compared with Rule 11 and proposals to amend Rule 11. Most notably, the New York Rules place limits on the amount of a monetary sanction and make the sanction permissive rather than mandatory. The Rules also permit sanctions against a lawyer individually or against the lawyer's firm or office.

Contents

§130-1.1. Costs; Sanctions

(a) **The court, in its discretion, may award to any party or attorney in any civil action or proceeding before the court, except where prohibited by law, costs in the form of reimbursement for actual expenses reasonably incurred and reasonable attorney's fees, resulting from frivolous conduct as defined in this Part. In addition to or in lieu of awarding costs, the court, in its discretion may impose financial sanctions upon any party or attorney in a civil action or proceeding who engages in frivolous conduct** as defined in this Part, which shall be payable as provided in section 130.3 of this Part. . . .

(b) The court, as appropriate, may make such award of costs or impose such financial sanctions against either an attorney or a party to the litigation or against both. Where the award or sanction is against an attorney, it may be against the attorney personally or upon a partnership, firm, corporation, government agency, prosecutor's office, legal aid society or public defender's office with which the attorney is associated and that has appeared as attorney of record. The award or sanctions may be imposed upon any attorney appearing in the action or upon a partnership, firm or corporation with which the attorney is associated.

(c) For purposes of this Part, conduct is frivolous if:

(1) it is completely without merit in law or fact and cannot be supported by a reasonable argument for an extension, modification or reversal of existing law; or

(2) it is undertaken primarily to delay or prolong the resolution of the litigation, or to harass or maliciously injure another.

Frivolous conduct shall include the making of a frivolous motion for costs or sanctions under this section. In determining whether the conduct undertaken was frivolous, the court shall consider, among other issues, (1) the circumstances under which the conduct took place, including the time available for investigating the legal or factual basis of the conduct; and (2) whether or not the conduct was continued when its lack of legal or factual basis was apparent or should have been apparent to counsel.

(d) An award of costs or the imposition of sanctions may be made either upon motion in compliance with CPLR 2214 or 2215 or upon the court's own initiative, after a reasonable opportunity to be heard. The form of the hearing shall depend upon the nature of the conduct and the circumstances of the case.

§130-1.2. Order Awarding Costs or Imposing Sanctions

The court may make an award of costs or impose sanctions or both only upon a written decision setting forth the conduct on which the award or imposition is based, the reasons why the court found the conduct to be frivolous, and the reasons why the court found the amount awarded or imposed to be appropriate. An award of costs or the imposition of sanctions or both shall be entered as a judgment of the court. In no event shall the total amount of costs awarded and sanctions imposed exceed $10,000 in any action or proceeding.

§130-1.3. Payment of Sanctions

Payments of sanctions by an attorney shall be deposited with the Clients' Security Fund established pursuant to section 97-t of the State Finance Law. Payments of sanctions by a party who is not an attorney shall be deposited with the clerk of the court for transmittal to the State Commissioner of Taxation and Finance. . . .

§130-2.1. Sanctions

(a) The court, in its discretion, may impose financial sanctions upon any attorney in a criminal action or proceeding, or in any proceeding in Family Court, who, without good cause, fails to appear at a time and place scheduled for such action or proceeding to be heard before a designated court. . . .

(b) In determining whether an attorney's failure to appear at a scheduled court appearance was without good cause and in determining the measure of sanctions to be imposed, the court shall consider all of the attendant circumstances, including but not limited to: (1) the explanation, if any, offered by the attorney for his or her nonappearance; (2) the adequacy of the notice to the attorney of the time and date of the scheduled appearance; (3) whether the attorney notified the court and opposing counsel in advance that he or she would be unable to appear; (4) whether substitute counsel appeared in court at the time previously scheduled to proffer an explanation of the attorney's nonappearance and whether such substitute counsel was prepared to go forward with the case; (5) whether an affidavit or affirmation of actual engagement was filed in the manner prescribed in Part 125 of the Uniform Rules for the Trial Courts of the Unified Court System; (6) whether the attorney on prior occasions in the same action or proceeding failed to appear at a scheduled court action or proceeding; (7) whether financial sanctions have been imposed upon the attorney pursuant to this section in some other action or proceeding; and (8) the extent and nature of the harm caused by the attorney's failure to appear.

(c) The court, as appropriate, may impose any such financial sanctions upon an attorney personally or upon a partnership, firm, corporation, government agency, prosecutor's office, legal aid society or public defender's office with which the attorney is associated and that has appeared as attorney of record.

(d) The imposition of sanctions may be made either upon motion or upon the court's own initiative, after a reasonable opportunity to be heard. The form of the hearing shall depend upon the nature of the attorney's failure to appear and the totality of the circumstances of the case.

§130-2.2. Order Imposing Sanctions

The court may impose sanctions only upon a written memorandum decision or statement on the record setting forth the conduct on which the award or imposition is based and the reasons why the court found the attorney's failure to appear at a scheduled court appearance to be without good cause. The imposition of sanctions shall be entered as a judgment of the court. In no event shall the amount of sanctions imposed exceed $250 for any single failure to appear at a scheduled court appearance.

§130-2.3. Payment of Sanctions

Payments of sanctions shall be deposited with the Clients' Security Fund established pursuant to section 97-t of the State Finance Law. . . .

Tables

Editors' Introduction. As standards guiding professional conduct have proliferated in recent years, it has become interesting to compare the variety of approaches to similar problems. In this chapter, we have created two original tables showing how to find the ABA Model Rules of Professional Conduct that most nearly correspond to provisions in the ABA Canons of Professional Ethics (Table I) and the Restatement of the Law Governing Lawyers as it stands to date (Table II). Readers starting from any given provision of the Canons or the Restatement can use these tables to locate comparable provisions of the ABA Model Rules. (Readers starting from the ABA Model Rules of Professional Conduct can find the comparable provisions of the ABA Canons and the Restatement simply by referring to the Related Materials section following each Model Rule. No tables are necessary for this purpose. Also, Code-to-Rules tables appear at the conclusion of each Canon of the Model Code of Professional Responsibility.)

Contents

═══════════════════════════

TABLE I: ABA CANONS OF PROFESSIONAL ETHICS CROSS-REFERENCED TO THE ABA MODEL RULES OF PROFESSIONAL CONDUCT

Editors' Note. The ABA Canons of Professional Ethics have been reprinted in the Related Materials corresponding to the ABA Model Rules of Professional Conduct. This table has been prepared by the editors to allow the user to locate each of the ABA Canons.

723

Table I **Tables**

TABLE II: RESTATEMENT OF THE LAW GOVERNING LAWYERS CROSS-REFERENCED TO THE ABA MODEL RULES OF PROFESSIONAL CONDUCT

Editors' Note. Sections of the Restatement of the Law Governing Lawyers have been reprinted in the Related Materials following corresponding ABA Model Rules of Professional Conduct and also in the chapter on attorney-client privileges. This table has been prepared by the editors to allow the user to locate Restatement sections. (References to "AC/WP" are to the chapter on attorney-client privilege and work product.)

Restatement of the Law Governing Lawyers	ABA Model Rules of Professional Conduct
Ch. 2 The Client-Lawyer Relationship	
Topic 1 Creating the Relationship	
§26 Formation of a Client-Lawyer Relationship	1.6
§27 A Lawyer's Duties to a Prospective Client	1.6
Topic 2 Summary of Duties Under the Relationship	
§28 Lawyer's Duties to Client in General	1.1
§29 Client's Duties to Lawyer	1.16
§29A Client-Lawyer Contracts	1.5
§30 Limited Representation and Waiver of Client or Lawyer Duties	1.2
Topic 3 Authority to Make Decisions	
§31 Lawyer's Duty to Inform and Consult with Client	1.2

Table II   Tables

Table II   Tables

The Kaye Scholer File

THE FACTUAL SETTING, THE QUESTIONS
LEFT OPEN

The collapse of many of America's savings and loan institutions in the late 1980s led to claims against professionals who advised the failed thrifts, among them lawyers and accountants. Plaintiffs included creditors of the S&Ls and government agencies. Among the agencies were the Resolution Trust Corporation (RTC), which by operation of law succeeded to the interests of seized banks, and the Office of Thrift Supervision (OTS), created by Congress in 1989 to supervise savings institutions insured under the Federal Deposit Insurance Act. The OTS houses the RTC. Leading law firms, and many smaller ones, settled claims arising out of thrift failures, sometimes with payments in the tens of millions of dollars. See generally M. Mayer, The Greatest Ever Bank Robbery (1990); France, Savings & Loan Lawyers, ABA Journal 52 (May 1991).

The bank failure said to have been most costly to government insurers was that of the Lincoln Savings & Loan Association of Irvine, California. Lincoln was a subsidiary of the American Continental Corporation (ACC), which was controlled by Charles Keating. Its collapse reportedly cost the government more than two billion dollars. The cost was this high in part because outside professionals are alleged to have helped Keating keep Lincoln in operation long after it had ceased to be solvent — enabling it to incur additional obligations covered by government insurance — and because six United States Senators, to whom Keating had made sizeable campaign contributions, interceded on his behalf before the regulators. Lincoln was finally shut down in April 1989. Keating, who failed in his effort to regain control of the bank, see Lincoln Savings & Loan Assn. v. Wall, 743 F. Supp. 901 (D.D.C. 1990), was eventually convicted in California state court of crimes associated with Lincoln's operation. At this writing, he is awaiting trial on a federal indictment.·

Among the major American law firms that have settled claims arising out of Lincoln's collapse, either with the government or ACC creditors or both,

729

are Sidley & Austin, Jones, Day, Reavis & Pogue, and Kaye, Scholer, Fierman, Hays & Handler. The RTC and Kaye Scholer had been negotiating a settlement, said to be in the area of $23 million, but no agreement had been reached as of the time of the events hereafter recounted, allegedly because the OTS deemed the terms too lenient. Instead, on March 2, 1992, the OTS served the Notice of Charges set out below. One consequence of the OTS's decision to proceed administratively rather than in a court action was that the case would be heard — and factual determinations made — by an administrative law judge (ALJ), employed by the OTS, and not by a federal judge appointed under Article III. ALJs are appointed under Article I of the Constitution and do not have the salary protection and life tenure that Article III judges enjoy. The ALJ's decision in the Kaye Scholer case would have been subject to review by the OTS Director, who has sole authority to "issue the final decision on the disposition of the case," 12 C.F.R. §509.40(c), with only limited appellate review. Akin v. OTS, 950 F.2d 1180 (5th Cir. 1992).

The OTS's charges sought "restitution and reimbursement" from Kaye Scholer in the amount of $275 million, among other relief. On March 8, six days after the charges were filed, still asserting that it did no wrong, Kaye Scholer settled with the OTS for $41 million, of which $25 million was covered by insurance. Kaye Scholer's counsel, Bernard Nussbaum, of New York's Wachtell, Lipton, Rosen & Katz, has stated that the firm was forced to settle because its banks had shut off its line of credit, thereby preventing it from meeting its operating expenses. In other words, it faced dissolution. Nussbaum has also argued that Kaye Scholer could not expect to win before an OTS administrative law judge. Other terms of the settlement prevent two Kaye Scholer partners from practicing before the OTS or participating in the affairs of banks and limit how a third partner, and the firm itself, can thereafter represent banks.

The Kaye Scholer case received much attention in the legal and popular press. See generally: Beck & Orey, They Got What They Deserved, American Lawyer 68 (May 1992); Swanson, Debate Continues on Ethics After Kaye Scholer Accord, 8 Lawyers Manual Prof. Conduct 109 (May 6, 1992); Pitt & Johnson, The Banking Scandal: An Era of New Standards for Professionals?, N.Y. Law Journal 1 (Apr. 23, 1992); the July 1992 issue of the ABA Journal (various articles); and France, Just Deserts: Don't Cry for Kaye Scholer, Legal Times (April 6, 1992).

The facts alleged in the OTS Notice of Charges have never been adjudicated and never will be. Nevertheless, lawyers nationwide have debated whether the OTS was seeking to impose duties on lawyers for banks that are inconsistent with the duties imposed in state ethics codes. Were they? Take note that many of the charges against the firm, though not all, allege *failures* to reveal information harmful to Lincoln. Would the Model Rules of Professional Conduct or the Model Code of Professional Responsibility have required revelation under the circumstances described in the Notice of Charges?

The OTS has emphasized that Kaye Scholer was representing a regulated company before the regulatory agency and had, in fact, "interposed" itself between Lincoln and the regulators, thereby subjecting itself to the same regulations that governed Lincoln. See the Third Claim in the Notice of Charges. Other claims allege misconduct without reliance on an "interposition" theory.

Some of Kaye Scholer's supporters have argued, by contrast, that the dispute between the banking regulators and Lincoln was on the verge of litigation at the time Kaye Scholer represented Lincoln and that, therefore, Kaye Scholer's behavior should be judged according to the standards governing litigators. Among Kaye Scholer's supporters is Professor Geoffrey C. Hazard, Jr., of Yale Law School, whom the firm retained as an ethics expert. He submitted a sworn statement defending Kaye Scholer's conduct on the theory that the firm was acting as litigation counsel. See the Legal Times article, supra; the American Lawyer article, supra, at 75.

Because of the settlement, Kaye Scholer never formally responded to the Notice of Charges. However, it did respond to them publicly. Reprinted below is a document Kaye Scholer released following service and publication of the charges.

Should evaluation of the firm's behavior depend on whether it was acting in a litigation or pre-litigation context? Would doing so change the applicable standards in any event? Of course, no court proceeding was pending against Lincoln while Kaye Scholer represented it. Should that affect whether Kaye Scholer could have chosen to position itself as litigation counsel, even assuming that that status would alter its ethical obligations? Would the firm first have had to alert the regulators to its conception of itself as litigation counsel?

Other issues raised by the Kaye Scholer case are whether Congress empowered the OTS (or its predecessor agency) to impose obligations on a lawyer representing a client before it that may differ from the obligations imposed in the states in which the lawyer is licensed; if the OTS was so empowered, whether it gave adequate notice of the different standards here; and whether Congress can under the Supremacy Clause permit federal agencies to create ethical duties for lawyers that differ from those established in their state codes. Of course, to the extent the duties the OTS sought to impose on Kaye Scholer are no different from those that apply under the law of the jurisdictions in which its lawyers are licensed, these questions might have little consequence. A final issue, appropriate to a course in federal courts or constitutional law, is whether Kaye Scholer had a constitutional right to have the claim against it heard by an Article III federal judge in the first instance. See Fallon, Of Legislative Courts, Administrative Agencies, and Article III, 101 Harv. L. Rev. 915 (1988).

In addition to the Notice of Charges, and receiving as much initial attention, was a document issued ex parte by the Director of OTS and denominated Temporary Order to Cease and Desist. The press and many lawyers called this a "freeze order." The OTS called it an "asset protection order." Pending final resolution of the charges, the order required Kaye Scholer to refrain from transferring its assets without OTS approval and to sequester one-quarter of the earnings of all Kaye Scholer partners (other than recent partners) and an even higher percentage of the earnings of two of the named partners. But the order permitted the firm to continue to pay interest charges on current indebtedness, ordinary and reasonable operating expenses, and capital expenditures up to $50,000 without approval. Separately, the three partners named in the Notice were forbidden to sell or encumber personal property in excess of $5,000. Kaye Scholer initially sought to challenge the Temporary Order in federal court, but then settled with the OTS before the challenge could be heard. The purported refusal of Kaye Scholer's banks to continue its line of credit has been attributed both to the Temporary Order and to the fact that the underlying action sought payment of $275 million.

Excerpts from key regulatory and statutory provisions cited in the Notice of Charges are set out below, followed by the Notice of Charges lightly edited and Kaye Scholer's public response.

KEY STATUTORY AND REGULATORY PROVISIONS

Section 1813(u) of Title 12 of the United States Code defines "institution-affiliated party," which the charges asserted Kaye Scholer had become, as follows:

(u) Institution-affiliated Party

The term "institution-affiliated party" means —
(1) any director, officer, employee, or controlling stockholder (other than a bank holding company) of, or agent for, an insured depository institution; [and]
(4) any independent contractor (including any attorney, appraiser, or accountant) who knowingly or recklessly participates in —
(A) any violation of any law or regulation;
(B) any breach of fiduciary duty; or
(C) any unsafe or unsound practice,
which caused or is likely to cause more than a minimal financial loss to, or a significant adverse effect on, the insured depository institution.

Section 1818(b) of Title 12 of the United States Code gives "the appropriate Federal banking agency" authority to commence cease-and-desist proceedings. Section 1818(b)(6) specifically grants authority to require "an insured depository institution or any institution-affiliated party to take affirmative action to correct or remedy any conditions resulting from any violation or practice," including to

(A) make restitution or provide reimbursement, indemnification, or guarantee against loss if —
(i) such depository institution or such party was unjustly enriched in connection with such violation or practice; or

(ii) the violation or practice involved a reckless disregard for the law or any applicable regulations or prior order of the appropriate Federal banking agency;

(B) restrict the growth of the institution;

(C) dispose of any loan or asset involved;

(D) rescind agreements or contracts; and

(E) employ qualified officers or employees (who may be subject to approval by the appropriate Federal banking agency at the direction of such agency); and

(F) take such other action as the banking agency determines to be appropriate.

Section 513.4 of title 12 of the Code of Federal Regulations provides for discipline of persons practicing before the OTS as follows:

§513.4 Suspension and Debarment.

(a) The Office may censure any person practicing before it or may deny, temporarily or permanently, the privilege of any person to practice before it if such person is found by the Office, after notice of and opportunity for hearing in the matter,

(1) Not to possess the requisite qualifications to represent others,

(2) To be lacking in character or professional integrity,

(3) To have engaged in any dilatory, obstructionist, egregious, contemptuous, contumacious or other unethical or improper professional conduct before the Office, or

(4) To have willfully violated, or willfully aided and abetted the violation of, any provision of the laws administered by the Office or the rules and regulations promulgated thereunder.

12 CFR §563.180(b) (formerly §563.18(b)) prohibits false statements and certain omissions of fact. It figures prominently in the OTS charges.

§563.180 Criminal Referrals and Other Reports or Statements.

. . . (b) *False or misleading statements or omissions.* No savings association or director, officer, agent, employee, affiliated person, or other person participating in the conduct of the affairs of such association nor any person filing or seeking approval of any application shall knowingly:

(1) Make any written or oral statement to the Office or to an agent, representative or employee of the Office that is false or misleading with respect to any material fact or omits to state a material fact concerning any matter within the jurisdiction of the Office; or

(2) Make any such statement or omission to a person or organization auditing a savings association or otherwise preparing or reviewing its financial state-

ments concerning the accounts, assets, management condition, ownership, safety, or soundness, or other affairs of the association.

UNITED STATES OF AMERICA BEFORE THE OFFICE OF THRIFT SUPERVISION DEPARTMENT OF THE TREASURY

In the Matter of

PETER M. FISHBEIN,
KAREN E. KATZMAN, and
LYNN TOBY FISHER,
KAYE, SCHOLER, FIERMAN,
HAYS & HANDLER,

OTS AP-92-19

Former Outside Counsel
of Lincoln Savings
and Loan Association,
Irvine, California,

Respondents.

NOTICE OF CHARGES AND OF HEARING FOR CEASE AND DESIST ORDERS TO DIRECT RESTITUTION AND OTHER APPROPRIATE RELIEF; NOTICE OF INTENTION TO REMOVE AND PROHIBIT FROM PARTICIPATION IN THE CONDUCT OF THE AFFAIRS OF INSURED DEPOSITORY INSTITUTIONS; AND NOTICE OF INTENTION TO DEBAR FROM PRACTICE BEFORE THE OFFICE OF THRIFT SUPERVISION

I. Jurisdiction

1. Until August 9, 1989, the Federal Savings and Loan Insurance Corporation (the "FSLIC") was the regulatory agency with jurisdiction over federally insured, state-chartered savings associations, pursuant to Section 407 of the Na-

tional Housing Act ("NHA"), 12 U.S.C. §1730. The Federal Home Loan Bank Board ("FHLBB") was the operating head of the FSLIC. FSLIC and FHLBB hereinafter are referred to as FHLBB. The Federal Home Loan Bank of San Francisco ("FHLB-SF") was at times relevant hereto the agent and representative of the FHLBB in supervising and examining savings and loan holding companies and savings associations located in California, Arizona and Nevada.

2. As of August 9, 1989, pursuant to the provisions of the Financial Institutions Reform, Recovery and Enforcement Act of 1989 ("FIRREA"), the Office of Thrift Supervision ("OTS") succeeded the FSLIC as the regulatory agency charged with the supervision and regulation of all savings associations and savings and loan holding companies under the Federal Deposit Insurance Act ("FDIA"). . . .

3. Lincoln Savings & Loan Association of Irvine, California ("Lincoln") was a state-chartered savings association organized under the laws of the State of California [and] was a savings association as defined by section 3(b) of the FDIA. . . .

4. American Continental Corporation ("ACC") was a publicly-held Ohio corporation with its principal place of business in Phoenix, Arizona. ACC is a savings and loan holding company that directly or indirectly owned 100 percent of the common stock of Lincoln. . . .

5. Charles H. Keating, Jr. ("Keating") is, and at all relevant times has been, Chairman of ACC's Board of Directors and a principal shareholder of ACC. Keating was President and Chief Executive Officer of ACC from September 1981 to May 1985. Keating is and was a controlling person of ACC and was a controlling person of Lincoln from February 1984 until April 1989 when Lincoln was placed into conservatorship.

II. Respondents

6. Respondent law firm Kaye, Scholer, Fierman, Hays & Handler ("Kaye Scholer") is a New York-based partnership and a large, multi-state law firm. Kaye Scholer represented ACC from and after May 1977 and provided services to Lincoln from its acquisition by ACC in February 1984 until April 1989.

7. Kaye Scholer, acting through its partners, counsel, and associates, served as counsel to ACC and as counsel to and agent for Lincoln during the relevant time period. More than seventy-five (75) partners, counsel, and associates of Kaye Scholer, including the individual Respondents, provided services to ACC/Lincoln, including services with respect to the transactions described in this Notice of Charges. Through its work for ACC and Lincoln, Kaye Scholer gained intimate knowledge of ACC and Lincoln.

8. Kaye Scholer provided legal and other services to Lincoln on numerous matters during the 1984-1989 period. Kaye Scholer lawyers spent substantially more than ten thousand hours in investigating and responding to the matters and con-

cerns identified in the 1986 and 1988 examinations of Lincoln by the FHLBB ("1986 Examination" and "1988 Examination"). Kaye Scholer was paid approximately $13 million by ACC and Lincoln during the period 1985-1989.

9. Respondent Peter M. Fishbein ("Fishbein") was at all relevant times the managing partner of Kaye Scholer with major management responsibilities within the firm. Fishbein served as ACC's and Lincoln's principal outside counsel in all matters relevant hereto. Fishbein was in direct charge of and had supervisory responsibility for Kaye Scholer's performance in each of the matters described in this Notice. Lincoln's responses to the 1986 and 1988 examinations and all other work performed by Kaye Scholer for Lincoln and ACC was done under the supervision and direction of Fishbein.

10. Respondent Karen E. Katzman ("Katzman"), a partner at Kaye Scholer, working under the direction and supervision of Fishbein, had significant and continuing responsibilities for the preparation of Lincoln's response to the 1986 Examination and acted as second-in-command to Fishbein in this work.

11. Respondent Lynn Toby Fisher ("Fisher"), a partner of Kaye Scholer, working under the direction and supervision of Fishbein, and with the assistance of other Respondents and other employees of Kaye Scholer, had principal responsibility for providing ACC and Lincoln with legal advice and representation on securities matters. Fisher also had significant responsibility for the development of factual materials to be submitted in connection with the 1988 Examination.

12. Whenever references are made in this Notice of Charges to Kaye Scholer engaging in any act or having knowledge of any fact, such allegation shall be deemed to include any action taken or known individually by Kaye Scholer or by a partner(s), counsel, attorney(s), associate(s), representative(s), agent(s), or employee(s) of Kaye Scholer, including the individual Respondents, acting with actual or apparent authority.

13. As described more fully below, the Respondents, and each of them, participated in the conduct of the affairs of Lincoln and ACC and were institution-affiliated parties, in that they and each of them:

a. Provided advice to Lincoln and ACC, represented and acted as agent of Lincoln before the FHLBB, and participated in defining the course of conduct by Lincoln and ACC in conducting their business and in responding to the FHLBB's regulation and examination of Lincoln's operations as a federally-insured depository institution;

b. Represented and acted as agent for Lincoln and ACC before the FHLBB and, in connection therewith, omitted material facts from and made misrepresentations in submissions to the FHLBB that are the subject of this Notice of Charges;

c. Acted as securities counsel to ACC, were intimately familiar with its affairs and operations and those of its subsidiaries and affiliates, including Lincoln, and prepared and/or reviewed security disclosure documents that were filed with the FHLBB and other federal regulatory agencies;

736

d. Acted as Lincoln's counsel and agent in providing information and otherwise responding to FHLBB in connection with the examination of Lincoln in the 1986-1989 period.

14. Kaye Scholer and each of the individual Respondents violated and facilitated Lincoln's violations of applicable banking statutes and regulations, as more fully described below.

III. Statement of Facts

A. Background

15. In 1983, Keating decided to expand the business activities of ACC beyond construction and financing of sales of single-family homes and into speculative large-scale real estate acquisition and development and trading of high-risk corporate securities. In 1984, ACC acquired Lincoln and assured that it would continue Lincoln's residential lending focus, maintain Lincoln's required minimum net worth levels for twenty years, and adhere strictly to regulations governing potential abuse of a thrift by a real estate developer. Immediately after obtaining control of Lincoln, ACC began a program that substantially altered Lincoln's lending and investment practices from traditional thrift activities to high-risk investments, particularly the acquisition and development of large parcels of raw land and heavy investment in volatile junk bonds.

[The FHLBB initiated two examinations of Lincoln, the 1986 Examination and the 1988 Examination. In the first of these, Kaye Scholer "demanded on Lincoln's behalf that all requests for information from banking examiners be directed to the law firm." The 1986 Examination identified violations and questionable practices. Kaye Scholer then represented Lincoln in connection with a February 1987 inquiry into forgery and backdating of documents at Lincoln. The 1988 Examination, undertaken in conjunction with California authorities, identified "aggressive, risk-prone" practices at Lincoln, putting "the continued viability of the association in jeopardy." Kaye Scholer was retained to respond to these findings in Lincoln's behalf.]

FIRST CLAIM

Kaye Scholer Knowingly Disregarded Material Facts in Advising Lincoln that its Direct Investments Were Legally Grandfathered

(As to Respondents Kaye Scholer and Fishbein)

22. The FHLBB proposed a rule on May 10, 1984, to place limits on direct investments by insured thrift institutions. Unless expressly approved by the

FHLBB, thrifts which held more than 10 percent of their assets in direct investments were prohibited from making any additional direct investments.

23. By public notice dated December 14, 1984, the FHLBB proposed certain exceptions to the limitation on certain direct investments. That proposal would have grandfathered specified "actual or prospective" direct investments as of December 10, 1984.

24. On January 30, 1985, the FHLBB issued the final direct investment rule, which placed limitations upon direct investments made by thrifts after December 10, 1984. The grandfather clause permitted existing investments and those for which there was a "legal commitment" and further permitted "completing projects pursuant to definitive plans in existence on that date. . . ."

25. On February 1, 1985, immediately after the FHLBB final rule was issued, Lincoln applied to the FHLBB-SF for exemptions for $900.8 million of direct investments, an amount which exceeded 10% of Lincoln's assets. The FHLBB-SF denied the application on the ground that the proposed investments would increase Lincoln's risk of default and thereby expose the federal insurance fund to undue risk.

26. As shown in a May 19, 1985 memorandum from Mark S. Sauter to Keating, Lincoln's strategy with respect to an adverse response to its request for exemption included the alternative course of action of

> taking no action other than to simply operate as if the FHLBB had granted its application by default. Such a strategy would place the onus of administrative or judicial action on the FHLBB. . . .

27. On or about July 1985, Kaye Scholer was retained to advise Lincoln on the legality of Lincoln's direct investments. Kaye Scholer undertook this assignment despite the fact that it had no thrift or other bank regulatory expertise. As part of the assignment, Kaye Scholer lawyers investigated the transactions purportedly affecting the grandfathered direct investments. In doing so, Kaye Scholer interviewed Lincoln employees, reviewed Lincoln documents relating to these direct investments, and otherwise ascertained the facts relevant to the legal status of these investments.

28. By September 10, 1985, Kaye Scholer learned that unanimous consents of the boards of directors of Lincoln and its service corporation purporting to authorize the grandfathered investments had been created after the December 10 grandfather date and misleadingly backdated to appear to have been created before that date ("backdated documents"). Kaye Scholer knew that Lincoln claimed to rely upon these backdated documents as evidence of "definitive plans" that permitted grandfathering of direct investments.

29. On or about September 1985, Kaye Scholer advised Lincoln that certain of its direct investments, in excess of $750 million, were legally grandfathered under the "definitive plans" savings provision of the direct investment rule.

30. The September 1985 legal advice rendered by Kaye Scholer to Lincoln concerning direct investments was embodied in a memorandum provided to Lincoln on or about September 19, 1985 ("the 1985 memorandum").

31. The legal advice in the 1985 memorandum ignored material facts that refuted the factual premise upon which Kaye Scholer's advice was based. In the 1985 memorandum, Kaye Scholer opined that

> Lincoln's plans for investing in service corporations were sufficiently "definitive" because it had taken many concrete steps to invest in these corporations prior to December 10, 1984.

In support of that opinion, Kaye Scholer stated as an example that by December 10, 1984

> Lincoln had definitive plans to invest the full amount authorized [in its service corporation subsidiary, Continental Homes Corporation ("CHC") and] Lincoln's Board of Directors had directed that Lincoln invest the entire $300,000,000 in CHC, subject only to the California Department's approval. . . .

32. When Kaye Scholer opined in September 1985 that Lincoln's direct investments in its service corporations were grandfathered as of December 10, 1984, Kaye Scholer knew that documents purporting to constitute the unanimous consents of Lincoln's directors authorizing such plans at times prior to December 10, 1984, had in fact been created and signed at some time in 1985 and then backdated.

33. At the time Kaye Scholer advised Lincoln concerning its direct investments in September 1985, California law and Lincoln's bylaws imposed certain preconditions before corporate action could be taken. One such condition requires that when the corporation acts by unanimous consent, rather than by vote of the board of directors, the signatures of all such directors are required and the consent is not effective until the date all signatures are obtained. Kaye Scholer knew that the unanimous consents on which Kaye Scholer relied to claim that the direct investments in the service corporations were "definitively planned" were not effective on the date claimed. Kaye Scholer rendered its legal opinion notwithstanding the fact that the unanimous consent documents were signed and backdated and accordingly were not effective means of corporate action on the date claimed.

34. Lincoln relied upon the September 1985 advice of Kaye Scholer concerning the legal status of the purportedly grandfathered direct investments.

35. Respondent Kaye Scholer's and Fishbein's advice in the issuance of the September 1985 opinion, described in paragraphs 22-34 above, violated:

a. Kaye Scholer's professional duty to provide legal advice competently and with due care by recklessly providing legal advice without having the requisite professional knowledge and expertise and by knowingly disregarding the facts that Lincoln had fabricated and backdated the documents purporting to authorize the direct investments claimed to have been definitively planned prior to December 10, 1984; and

b. The prohibition contained in Section 513(a)(4) of the FHLBB Regulations, . . . against willfully aiding and abetting the violation of any laws administered by the FHLBB and regulations promulgated thereunder.

SECOND CLAIM

Kaye Scholer Knowingly Failed to Disclose to the FHLBB Facts Material to the Resignation of Lincoln's Auditor

(As to Respondents Kaye Scholer and Fishbein)

36. In the 1986 Examination Report, the examiners emphasized their concerns about the shift in Lincoln's operations (after its acquisition by Keating) into practices involving higher risks.

37. As early as May 1986, Arthur Andersen & Co. ("Arthur Andersen"), as Lincoln's independent auditor from 1984-1986, had identified Lincoln as having "significant risks." An agenda prepared by members of the Arthur Andersen Phoenix engagement team for an internal meeting held to discuss whether to continue the Lincoln engagement specifically noted the following risks:

A. A small number of highly leverages [*sic*] loans secured by undeveloped land (or land in an early stage of development) make up about $500-$600 million of the loan portfolio. Approximately $120 million of these loans are to Conley Wolfswinkel covering about 5 or 6 different projects. Risk is that a decline in real estate values could result in a sizable loss.

B. Company is an unusual S & L in that it's [*sic*] net interest spread is "0" and it relies on real estate and investment transactions to cover SG&A ($100 million) and profit.

C. Company is somewhat inexperienced at the higher financial levels (CFO, corporate controller).

D. Company is controlled and operated by one dominant CEO.

38. As set forth in a memorandum dated June 30, 1986, George Massaro ("Massaro"), Arthur Andersen's technical partner on savings and loans, had subsequently determined that "the underlying business strategy of ACC involves a significant degree of risk, since, with the exception of deposit gathering, ACC does not follow a traditional savings and loan strategy." In addition, Massaro found that "[t]he elements of risk within ACC are substantially greater than the risk envisioned for insured deposit-taking institutions." These risks arose from the fact that:

Management has taken the posture that they will capitalize on their expertise as a real estate developer, their knowledge of the market, and their skills in speculative equity investments. As a result, they have become *totally* dependent upon the success of their own real estate development projects and those of their borrowers as well as their own ability to realize substantial gains from speculative equity investments or other security transactions. Although such a strategy is not precluded by state regulation it is not one that is consistent with the spirit of the federally insured deposit gathering institution and thus is extremely troubling to the regulators.

[Emphasis in original.]
Massaro further recognized that "many . . . thrift failures are the result of speculative lending to development projects with poor loan underwriting." He concluded:

We must recognize that we have little control in this situation, a downturn in real estate, an upward movement in interest rates, several major loan problems or poor investment decisions could result in major losses. The suggestions above simply serve to better focus our attention and the financial statement user's to the risks inherent in ACC's underlying business strategy. They do not, however, reduce the risk of a business failure and future regulatory involvement in which case the firm will in all likelihood be exposed.

39. On August 6, 1986, Kaye Scholer attorneys interviewed Joseph Kresse ("Kresse"), a senior partner at the accounting firm of Arthur Andersen. Kresse was the national partner who was responsible for reviewing the Lincoln audit. Kresse's statements to Kaye Scholer were based on information received from the Arthur Andersen Phoenix engagement team and Massaro. In the course of that interview, Kaye Scholer learned that Lincoln's financial condition was risky and that Arthur Andersen had serious questions about Lincoln's financial viability and questioned whether ACC's and Lincoln's financial statements adequately reflected the risks inherent in Lincoln's and ACC's business strategy. As shown by an August 27, 1986 memorandum, Kresse told Kaye Scholer that to Arthur Andersen:

Lincoln looks like most of the other S&L's that have failed — it has high growth, unusual investments, very large loans, very high GS&A, negative spread; it takes about $180,000,000 in real estate sales and other non-recurring deals to make up the negative spread, etc. etc. . . . Andersen views Lincoln as a high-risk client.

and:

ACC is a particular risk because it has an $180,000,000 nut instead of zero dollars, after its asset to liability mismatch and GS&A are taken into account.

and:

George Massaro, *the* technical partner on S&Ls (located in Boston) . . . look[ed] at this high risk client [Lincoln]. . . . Massaro said that Andersen should ask Lincoln to show [Andersen] detailed cash flows and analysis of how [Lincoln] plans to make up its negative cash flow so that Andersen can properly sign off on the "going concerns" part of its audit.

(Emphasis in original.)

40. On October 1, 1986, Arthur Andersen resigned as ACC/Lincoln's auditor, effective that same day. In a letter dated October 6, 1986, Fishbein transmitted to Keating, a copy of [the] memorandum of the interview with Kresse advising Keating that the memorandum "gives some insight into what may have motivated Andersen's decision."

41. Notwithstanding its knowledge of the foregoing facts, in an October 9, 1986, letter from Respondent Fishbein to the FHLBB, Kaye Scholer transmitted a Form 8-K stating that Arthur Andersen's resignation "was not the result of any concern by AA [Arthur Andersen] with [ACC/Lincoln's] operations . . . or asset/liability management."

42. In summary, Kaye Scholer knew, prior to the October 9, 1986 transmittal of the Form 8-K stating Arthur Andersen's reasons for resigning, that Arthur Andersen had concerns about Lincoln's risk profile and financial viability. Also prior to October 9, 1986, Kaye Scholer knew and had advised Keating that these concerns showed true motivations for Arthur Andersen's resignation as Lincoln's auditor on October 1, 1986. Nevertheless, Kaye Scholer knowingly omitted to disclose to the FHLBB the numerous statements made by Kresse that contradicted Arthur Andersen's disclaimers of "any concern . . . with [ACC/Lincoln's] operations . . . or asset/liabilities management." Kaye Scholer also knowingly omitted to disclose Massaro's views to the FHLBB.

43. These facts that Kaye Scholer knowingly omitted to disclose to the FHLBB were material to the representations about the reasons for Arthur Andersen's resignation. Kaye Scholer's omissions of these material facts rendered its transmission of the statement in the Form 8-K regarding Arthur Andersen's reasons for its resignation as Lincoln's auditor false and misleading.

44. Respondent Kaye Scholer's and Fishbein's transmission of the Form 8-K to the FHLBB while omitting facts material to the reasons for Arthur Andersen's resignation described in paragraphs 36-43 above, violated:

a. The record keeping and disclosure requirements of section 563.17-1(c) of the FHLBB Regulations;

b. The prohibition against knowingly making false and misleading statements of material facts to the FHLBB and auditors and omitting to disclose material facts concerning any matter within the jurisdiction of the FHLBB in sections 563.18(b)(1) and (b)(2) of the FHLBB Regulations; and

c. The prohibition against engaging in any dilatory, obstructionist, egregious, contemptuous, or unethical or improper professional conduct before the FHLBB in section 513.4(a)(3) of the FHLBB Regulations; and

d. The prohibition, contained in section 513.4(a)(4) of the FHLBB Regulations, against willfully aiding and abetting the violation of any laws administrated by the FHLBB and regulations promulgated thereunder.

THIRD CLAIM

**In Responding to the 1986 and 1988 Examinations
Kaye Scholer Engaged in a Pattern of Omitting
Material Facts from Submissions to the FHLBB
Thereby Rendering Its Representations False and
Misleading and Engaging in Dilatory, Obstructionist,
and Improper Conduct in Its Representation of Lincoln
and ACC Before the Federal Home Loan Bank Board**

(As to Kaye Scholer, Fishbein and Katzman)

45. Kaye Scholer acted as Lincoln's agent and provided advice to Lincoln in connection with the 1986 and 1988 Examinations of Lincoln and in responding to the 1986 and 1988 Examination Reports. Fishbein interposed Kaye Scholer between Lincoln and the FHLBB with respect to all factual matters relating to the 1986 Examination of Lincoln. By a letter dated July 16, 1986 and written on behalf of and as agent for Lincoln and as a Kaye Scholer partner, Fishbein demanded that all FHLBB requests for information made in connection with the 1986 Examination be directed to Respondent Katzman at Kaye Scholer.

46. In acting on behalf of and as agent for Lincoln, Kaye Scholer was obligated to "maintain such accounting and other records as will provide an accurate and complete record of all business transactions," which "records shall at all times be available for such examination . . . , wherever any of said records may be." 12 C.F.R. §563.17-1(c) (1986).

47. In acting on behalf of and as agent for Lincoln, Kaye Scholer was prohibited from knowingly making any statement to the FHLBB that was false or misleading with respect to any material fact or omitting to state any material fact concerning any matter within the jurisdiction of the FHLBB. 12 C.F.R. §563.18(b)(1) (1986).

48. In acting on behalf of and as Lincoln's agent, Kaye Scholer was also prohibited from engaging in any dilatory, obstructionist, egregious, contemptuous, or unethical or improper professional conduct before the FHLBB and from participating in the violation of any laws or regulations administered by the FHLBB. 12 C.F.R. §§513.4(a)(3) and (4) (1986).

49. Kaye Scholer, acting on behalf of and as agent for Lincoln, undertook to respond to the factual concerns and inquiries raised by the FHLBB in connection with the 1986 and 1988 Examinations and Reports issued in those examinations. During the course of its activity on behalf of and as agent for Lincoln, Kaye Scholer interviewed Lincoln employees and others and reviewed docu-

ments relating to the conduct of Lincoln's affairs. Kaye Scholer thereby learned numerous facts relating to Lincoln's regulatory violations. Nevertheless, in the course of making representations to the FHLBB on behalf of and as Lincoln's agent, Kaye Scholer did not advise Lincoln to disclose, and itself omitted to disclose, many material facts, thereby rendering false and misleading many representations that Kaye Scholer made to the FHLBB on behalf of and as agent for Lincoln. Instead, Kaye Scholer participated in, furthered and aided and abetted Lincoln's concealment of those facts from the FHLBB.

[Paragraph 50 incorporates by reference and summarizes the allegations in the Fifth through Tenth Claims. Essentially, these recount instances in which Kaye Scholer allegedly knew damaging information about Lincoln but failed to reveal it even though it was then representing Lincoln before the regulators and presenting them with other information. Claims Five through Nine are set out below. Claim Ten is summarized below.]

51. Kaye Scholer's actions and omissions on behalf of and as agent for Lincoln deprived FHLBB examiners of access to records "provid[ing] a complete and accurate record of all business transactions by" Lincoln in violation of former 12 C.F.R. §563.17-1(c) (1986). Kaye Scholer's omissions and misrepresentations also violated the FHLBB's disclosure requirements set forth at 12 C.F.R. §563.18(b)(1) (1986). Kaye Scholer's actions and omissions also constituted dilatory, obstructionist, and improper professional conduct before the FHLBB and willfully aiding and abetting of laws and regulations administered by the FHLBB in violation of 12 C.F.R. §§513.4(a)(3) and (4) (1986).

FOURTH CLAIM

Kaye Scholer Recklessly Failed to Fulfill Its Fiduciary Duties to Lincoln and Engaged in Unethical and Improper Professional Conduct

(As to All Respondents)

52. Kaye Scholer's actions in the course of its activity on behalf of Lincoln and ACC, described below in the Fifth through Tenth Claims, constituted knowing and reckless breaches of its fiduciary duties to Lincoln, including its duties of care, candor and loyalty. Kaye Scholer failed to advise the board of directors of Lincoln that Keating and others were pursuing conduct not in the best interests of Lincoln, in violation of federal regulations and in violation of their fiduciary duties to Lincoln. Kaye Scholer persisted in representing and acting on behalf of and as agent for Lincoln notwithstanding its conflict of interest in representing both Lincoln and ACC, including the submission of false and misleading information to the FHLBB in connection with the responses to the 1986 and 1988 Examinations. In doing so, Kaye Scholer placed the interests of ACC and Keating ahead of those of Lincoln.

744

53. During the course of Kaye Scholer's representation of ACC and Lincoln, and while preparing Lincoln's responses to the 1986 and 1988 Examinations on behalf of Lincoln, Kaye Scholer knew of: (a) the high-risk nature of Lincoln's real estate development business; (b) Lincoln's pervasive pattern of financial underwriting and appraisal deficiencies and, in particular, that major Lincoln assets had not been properly underwritten or appraised and were overvalued on Lincoln's books and records; (c) improper accounting treatment designed to conceal Lincoln's violation of the direct investment limitations; (d) improper transactions between Lincoln and its affiliates that were manifestly unfair to Lincoln; (e) the massive campaign by Lincoln to create the false impression of compliance with loan underwriting requirements by creating loan file documents long after loans were funded; (f) Lincoln's pressing need to generate substantial profits from repeated, large extraordinary real estate transactions so that it could offset its huge negative spread and show a paper profit; and (g) facts indicating that certain real estate transactions were linked and/or fictitious, and improperly accounted for, so that the resulting profits reported by Lincoln were illusory.

54. Although Kaye Scholer knew that officers and directors of Lincoln and ACC who were participating in the conduct of Lincoln were not fulfilling their fiduciary duties, Kaye Scholer failed to advise such persons that they owed fiduciary duties to Lincoln's depositors and to the deposit insurance fund, and that those duties included the obligation to operate Lincoln safely and soundly and to avoid actions that threatened undue risk of loss to the depositors and the insurance fund.

55. Although Kaye Scholer knew that the officers and directors of Lincoln and ACC were pursuing conduct in violation of federal regulations, Kaye Scholer failed to advise those officers and directors of their statutory and fiduciary responsibilities and failed to notify the board of directors of Lincoln of the officers and directors' unlawful conduct.

56. Kaye Scholer knew that the interests of its client ACC were adverse to Lincoln, which also was its client. Furthermore, Kaye Scholer further knew that due to the conflicts of interest created by its joint representation of Lincoln and ACC, it could not adequately represent the interests of both; and yet it continued such joint representation. Kaye Scholer did not disclose that conflict to or seek to obtain the consent of the board of directors of Lincoln.

57. Kaye Scholer's and the individual Respondents' dual representation of ACC and Lincoln, and their failure to advise Lincoln's officers and directors of their fiduciary duties to the Lincoln's depositors and the insurance fund, and their misrepresentations and omissions of material fact to the FHLBB described in the Fifth through Tenth Claims for Relief described in paragraphs 58-181 below constituted reckless unethical and improper professional conduct, reckless breaches of Kaye Scholer's duty of loyalty and duty to provide competent advice with due care, and demonstrated a lack of the professional character and integrity necessary for an attorney to practice before the OTS.

FIFTH CLAIM

Kaye Scholer Knowingly Failed to Disclose Facts Material to Lincoln's Income and Net Worth

(As to Respondents Kaye Scholer, Fishbein and Katzman)

58. As a result of the 1986 Examination, the examiners determined that as of September 30, 1986, Lincoln's regulatory net worth was substantially less than its required minimum due to adjustments to Lincoln's income that the examiners deemed necessary.

A. Kaye Scholer's June 26, 1987 Representations

59. In the course of the Kaye Scholer investigation conducted for purposes of formulating its response to the examiners about Lincoln's income and net worth, Kaye Scholer learned numerous facts material to the examiners' concerns.

60. Kaye Scholer learned prior to June 1987 that Lincoln had engaged in linked and/or fictitious sales transactions of properties with other entities at overstated values. The fictitious gains realized on those sales were recorded as income and inflated the income reported by Lincoln on its financial statements. For example, Kaye Scholer learned of linked transactions that took place in 1985 between Lincoln and M.D.C. Holdings, Inc. (or its affiliates) relating to properties in Colorado. Kaye Scholer knew prior to June 1987 that Lincoln officials had spoken disparagingly of the transactions as "trading dead horses for dead cows."

61. Notwithstanding its knowledge of the foregoing facts, Kaye Scholer represented in its response to the 1986 Examination that Lincoln had experienced financial "success" and continued to be highly profitable and that Lincoln's reported year-to-year increases in income and net worth up to the time of the submission justified delaying, dispensing with, or minimizing any regulatory action against Lincoln.

62. In summary, Kaye Scholer knew that Lincoln had engaged in fictitious and/or linked transactions and that the FHLBB would view the existence of linked transactions as material to Lincoln's reported income and net worth. Nevertheless, Kaye Scholer knowingly omitted to disclose the linked and fictitious sales transactions in its June 26, 1987, Response to the findings made and adjustments determined by the examiners.

63. These facts, which Kaye Scholer knowingly omitted to disclose to the FHLBB, were material to its representations about Lincoln's success, income and net worth. Kaye Scholer's omissions of these material facts in the June 26,

746

1987, response rendered its representations about Lincoln's profitability and financial viability false and misleading.

B. *Kaye Scholer's September 29, 1987, Representations*

64. Kaye Scholer later learned of other linked transactions, fictitious sales, and contrived real estate transactions that artificially inflated Lincoln's income and net worth. As shown by an internal memorandum dated September 11, 1987 (later summarized in a October 13, 1987 memorandum), in a July 20-24, 1987, review of Lincoln's files, Kaye Scholer had learned that:

> While not a recordkeeping matter, the number of "linked" transactions raises concern. Although the files themselves generally do not indicate linked transactions, it is known in some instances Lincoln or an ACC affiliate purchased a property with all or a substantial portion of the purchase price utilized by the other party for the downpayment in connection with an acquisition from an ACC affiliate. The situation is particularly problematic where there are rights (which may not be reflected in a writing) given the purchaser to trade properties or to reverse the transaction in whole or in part.

65. In summary, Kaye Scholer knew that information indicating linked and other fictitious transactions was material to the FHLBB's view of Lincoln's income and net worth. Kaye Scholer knowingly omitted to disclose the linked, fictitious and contrived transactions in its September 29, 1987, summary of its June 26, 1987, response and instead asserted to the FHLBB that the FHLBB's conclusions regarding Lincoln's net worth were simply wrong:

> [a]s of September 30, 1986 the Association nevertheless . . . had a regulatory net worth of $148 million, or 4.83% of liabilities, which was more than $22 million in excess of the minimum amount required.

66. These facts, which Kaye Scholer knowingly omitted to disclose to the FHLBB, were material to Kaye Scholer's representations about Lincoln's income and net worth. Kaye Scholer's omissions of these material facts in the September 29, 1987, summary rendered its representations about Lincoln's income and net worth false and misleading.

C. *Kaye Scholer's January 17, 1989, Representations*

67. Kaye Scholer subsequently learned of additional linked or fictitious transactions material to Lincoln's income and net worth. As shown by an October 13, 1987, internal memorandum, Kaye Scholer recognized:

"Linked transactions" remain the greatest area of concern. These are transactions such as the recent Crown-Zellerbach deal and the past Crowder Ranch deal. *We know that Charlie [Keating] will probably continue to do these transactions to support ACC's real estate business, but these deals may be a powder keg which could explode if the FHLBB analyzes them carefully.* The number of such transactions appears to have escalated dramatically since the completion of the last exam.

(Emphasis added.)

68. As shown by a subsequent internal Kaye Scholer memorandum dated February 4, 1988, discussing a problem loan to Ernie Garcia for $50 million, Kaye Scholer notified ACC's General Counsel of the apparent linkage between this Ernie Garcia transaction and other transactions, explaining the possibility that the linkage could be uncovered by the regulators:

> Although the file itself does not document how the $10 million of the purchase price of the GOSLP stock was paid, *it is possible that the linkage with the acquisition of the Garcia notes can be determined,* and, as discussed below, giving rise to questions of the soundness of each portion individually. *A further concern is that the discovery of one linked transaction may cause the investigators to seek to uncover other linked transactions.*

(Emphasis added.)

69. The 1988 Examination report stated that "[t]he results depict an association that is managed in an aggressive, risk prone manner that has resulted in a level of problem assets that severely strains capital . . . and that the ability of [Lincoln] to meet its future net worth requirement [was] questionable."

70. Notwithstanding its knowledge of the foregoing facts, in Lincoln's January 17, 1989 response to the 1988 Examination, Kaye Scholer stated that "Lincoln is a well managed, prudent association" and repeated its assertions about Lincoln's financial success, stating, for example, that:

> Lincoln's managerial skill, its sound diversification of investments and its prudent underwriting are all demonstrated by the unqualified success of its investment program. That success cannot fairly be attributable to chance or excessive risktaking. The Association's total return on productive assets since 1984 has averaged in excess of 14.5% per year.

71. In summary, Kaye Scholer knew, prior to the statements it made to the FHLBB regarding Lincoln's income and net worth, that Lincoln had engaged in linked and/or fictitious transactions that resulted in the improper recognition of income. Kaye Scholer knew that the linked and/or fictitious transactions were material to the FHLBB's assessment of Lincoln's reported income and net worth. Nevertheless, Kaye Scholer knowingly omitted to disclose to the FHLBB material facts regarding the linked and/or fictitious transactions.

72. The facts that Kaye Scholer failed to disclose were material to Kaye Scholer's representations about Lincoln's financial success and viability. As a consequence of these omissions of material fact, Kaye Scholer's representations

in the January 17, 1989, response about Lincoln's financial success and viability were false and misleading.

73. Respondent Kaye Scholer's, Fishbein's and Katzman's misrepresentations and omissions of facts material to Lincoln's income and net worth, described in paragraphs 58-72 above, violated [the provisions cited in paragraph 44 (a)-(d)].

SIXTH CLAIM

Kaye Scholer Failed to Disclose Facts Material to Lincoln's Loan and Securities Underwriting Practices and Documentation of Its Loans and Its Securities Transactions

(As to Respondents Kaye Scholer, Fishbein and Katzman)

74. Lincoln's underwriting practices with respect to real estate loans and securities investments were among the matters addressed by the 1986 Examination. The examiners questioned the safety and soundness of Lincoln's real estate lending practices. The examiners also questioned the safety and soundness of Lincoln's substantial investments in equity securities and "junk" bonds, and criticized apparent weaknesses in Lincoln's policies and procedures for underwriting and investing in these securities.

75. Kaye Scholer, in the process of preparing Lincoln's response to the 1986 Examination, conducted meetings with Lincoln officials and employees and reviewed Lincoln's real estate and securities transactions and thereby learned facts material to the examiners' concerns regarding Lincoln's documentation and practices for underwriting loans and securities.

A. Kaye Scholer Knowingly Omitted Facts Material To Lincoln's Loan Underwriting

1. Kaye Scholer Knew Adverse Documents Were Removed from and Apparently Favorable Documents Were Created and Added to Lincoln's Files

76. In preparation for the 1986 Examination, Lincoln undertook to sanitize its underwriting files to conform to FHLBB regulations. As shown by an August 1986 internal memorandum Kaye Scholer knew that:

> [P]rior to the [1986] Board examination, ACC's [*sic*, actually Lincoln's] loan files ran the spectrum from disaster to nonexistent. Before the [FHLBB] examination began, [the accounting firm of Arthur] Andersen sent in a team of five people to assemble the files and get underwriting data.

77. Kaye Scholer also knew how Lincoln sought to mask the deficiencies in its underwriting files. Kaye Scholer knew that Lincoln had duplicated the files of ACC, its parent, which reflected the actual decisions made by ACC (in Phoenix), as to the conduct of Lincoln's business (in Irvine, California). The files were then sent to Lincoln in Irvine for review. Evidence adverse to Lincoln's position was removed from these files. Documents supportive of Lincoln's position were left in those files. Additional documents were created without dates but stated in the present tense, giving the false impression that they had been created contemporaneously with the transaction in question.

78. For example, Kaye Scholer knew no later than July 1, 1986, that in some instances information reflecting adversely or negatively upon the safety and soundness of loans had been removed from Lincoln's files prior to their review by FHLBB examiners. Moreover, as shown by an internal memorandum dated November 6, 1986 memorializing an interview on October 15 and 21, 1986 with Bruce Dickson, Lincoln's President, Kaye Scholer also knew that:

> Dickson dictated memos to [Keating] and [Tim] Westfall after each of these meetings which reflected very negatively on [the borrower]. These memos have since been discarded, precisely because of their negative slant. The memos express concern over perceived marketing and development problems as well as cost overruns.

2. Kaye Scholer Knew of Deficiencies in Lincoln's Loan Files

79. On or about September 1986, Kaye Scholer reviewed files for 27 loans that were originated by Lincoln during the period March 1 through July 31, 1986, for underwriting deficiencies similar to those in other Lincoln loans cited by the examiners in the 1986 Examination. The results of that review are documented in a Kaye Scholer memorandum dated September 29, 1986: (a) 22 of these files lacked sufficient or current financial statements or tax returns for the borrowers or financial analysis of their ability to repay; (b) there was no credit report or verification of credit information for 26 loans; (c) in 20 cases, loan fees or interest reserves were funded from loan proceeds; (d) in 15 loans there was minimal or no borrower equity; (e) in 6 instances, the loans were approved prior to reviewing a current written appraisal report; (f) disbursements were not properly documented in 5 cases; and (g) 6 loan files contained no completed, signed, and/or dated loan application. Kaye Scholer knew that these deficiencies violated FHLBB regulations and guidelines.

80. As a result of other reviews of Lincoln's loan files, Kaye Scholer knew of additional specific instances of underwriting deficiencies. Kaye Scholer knew for example:

   a. No later than July 17, 1986, that the collateral for a Wolfswinkel Marana loan had not been delivered until a full 60 days after the non-recourse loan was funded;

b. No later than October 16, 1986, that: (i) no credit check was done for the "Grand Properties" loans; (ii) no independent analysis of the principal's unaudited financial statement was done and no credit check was done for the "Le Parc" loans; and (iii) on other loans, credit checking was only sometimes done.

c. No later than November 18, 1986, that: (a) "no verifications of financial or credit checks" had been done for the Pima Linda, Key West and Maggio loans; and (b) no verifications of unaudited borrower financial statements were done on the "Arizona Building loan."

81. As shown by another internal memorandum, Kaye Scholer knew no later than November 18, 1986, that a senior Lincoln loan officer held the view that "many of the steps" required for full loan underwriting were "unnecessary" and "a waste of time," and that Lincoln took "underwriting shortcuts."

82. As shown by an internal memorandum dated April 11, 1987, Kaye Scholer knew that the Lincoln loan underwriting deficiencies that were identified in 1986 by the FHLBB examiners and Kaye Scholer's own attorneys continued. In a review of 13 loans originated after October 1, 1986, Kaye Scholer found, as recorded in this internal memorandum, that some files contained: (a) only limited or no analyses of the attributes of the collateral; (b) unexplained negative credit verification material; (c) either no appraisal or no cash flow history for commercial loans; (d) no appraisals in compliance with the FHLBB Regulation R41(c); (e) no loan applications; and (f) acquisition loans incorrectly described as refinancings.

83. Another Kaye Scholer review of Lincoln's loan files, conducted between July 20 and 24, 1987, showed that Lincoln's unsafe and unsound underwriting practices remained uncorrected. Kaye Scholer found, for example, the following deficiencies in loans that originated during the period from Jaunary 1, 1987 to May 30, 1987: (a) Lincoln continued to fail to obtain or document information pertaining to particular projects and borrowers' credit histories, relying instead on generalized information concerning the geographic area in which properties were located; (b) Lincoln still did not explain why loans were made despite borrowers' negative credit histories; and (c) loan applications were still being delivered by borrowers after Lincoln had approved the loans.

3. Kaye Scholer Knew About the Creation of Misleading Underwriting Summaries

84. As shown by an August 27, 1986, internal memorandum, Kaye Scholer knew that Lincoln employees had created loan underwriting summaries designed to give the appearance that loans had been properly underwritten.

85. As shown by an internal Kaye Scholer memorandum dated November 6, 1986, Kaye Scholer knew that the summaries did not reflect what Lincoln actually had done prior to originating the loans. Rather, the information used to prepare these summaries was derived after the origination of the loan from such sources as brochures about the borrowers, correspondence with borrowers, and

conversations with loan officers, without any independent verification of whether the information was used to underwrite the loan. Kaye Scholer also knew that the statements made in the summaries about the financial feasibility of the loan were derived from appraisals and market studies, conversations with loan officers, and supposed "common sense," without any independent verification of whether the information was actually considered by Lincoln in originating the loan. The "repayment analyses" (borrower's ability to repay the loan) were conducted wholly after-the-fact, since they were "extrapolated from the notes, the deeds of trust, and the loan agreements," and were not obtained from financial information provided by the borrowers before the origination of the loans. The borrower's ability to repay was constructed from what the borrower had agreed to repay, and not from the borrower's documented financial condition. No effort was made to verify the accuracy of any of the information.

86. As shown by a February 27, 1987, internal memorandum, Kaye Scholer also knew that some loan summaries were prepared by people who had not worked on the loan origination and therefore could not have known the necessary underwriting information that was missing from the file.

87. As shown by a September 15, 1987, memorandum to Lincoln, Kaye Scholer recognized that:

> [I]n some cases the Loan Summaries which reflected [the] underwriting process and risk analysis were written significantly subsequent to the transaction and there is no other written evidence of underwriting in the file.

4.   Kaye Scholer's Representations to the FHLBB

88. Notwithstanding its knowledge of the foregoing facts, in its June 26, 1987, response on behalf of Lincoln, Kaye Scholer made the following representations to the FHLBB attesting to the adequacy of Lincoln's underwriting practices:

> In making real estate loans, Lincoln has always undertaken very careful and thorough procedures to analyze the collateral and the borrower. What is unusual about Lincoln's underwriting is its particular emphasis on, and the thoroughness of, its underwriting of the collateral. Lincoln is virtually unequaled in the experience, background and talent of its staff.

and:

> The examiners' criticisms of Lincoln's underwriting are unwarranted. In virtually all cases, Lincoln has done a thorough underwriting although, at times, its "paper trail" has been incomplete. Indeed only a small percentage of the over 200 loans reviewed by the examiners were cited for any deficiency....
>
> Lincoln always has analyzed the credit and collateral of its borrowers with great care, examining not only the financial statements of the borrower but also the borrower's reputation and experience in owning and developing projects similar to the proposed project....

752

89. In its June 26, 1987, response, Kaye Scholer also directed the FHLBB's attention to the underwriting summaries in Lincoln's files:

> [I]n some cases, as part of the improved loan documentation, underwriting summaries reflecting the new procedures were compiled by loan officers for prior loans. In addition, underwriting summaries sometimes were supplemented to reflect post-origination information.

90. Kaye Scholer also supplied some of those summaries to the FHLBB as part of the June 26, 1987, response, portraying them as reflecting actual underwriting:

> [t]he Underwriting Summaries state the loan term and summarize some of the aspects of the underwriting taken.

91. Moreover, in its September 29, 1987, summary of its June 26, 1987, response to the 1986 Examination, Kaye Scholer stated:

> [T]he substance of [Lincoln's] underwriting for . . . loans was in fact thorough, even if the files do not always reflect the full extent of the underwriting process, and the number of loans cited by the examiners as having documentation deficiencies is overstated.

And Kaye Scholer stated in its September 29, 1987, response that:

> [I]n the fall of 1985, Lincoln engaged Arthur Andersen to conduct a special audit of Lincoln's loan files. Two thrift experts from Arthur Andersen reported to Lincoln that the loan files were complete, but there was no single document that "told the story" of each loan. Although there was no regulatory requirement for a "loan summary," Lincoln agreed that such a summary would assist anyone reviewing the loan files . . . in understanding the loans. Accordingly, Lincoln undertook to prepare summaries for all loans originated by the Association. The summaries were prepared by a number of Lincoln employees, wherever possible based on their personal knowledge of particular loans. The summaries were not dated because the preparation date was of no significance. The summaries contain the information that the individual preparers thought would be helpful in understanding the transaction including information which postdated the origination date of the loans.

92. In summary, Kaye Scholer knew that there were substantial underwriting deficiencies with respect to Lincoln's real estate lending practices, that Lincoln's files had been sanitized of adverse information, and that underwriting summaries purporting to be reflective of Lincoln's underwriting had been created by persons not involved in the original underwriting and contained only information believed to support the making of the loans. Nevertheless, Kaye Scholer knowingly omitted to disclose Lincoln's underwriting or the deficiencies

in Lincoln's loan files. Kaye Scholer further knowingly omitted to disclose the fact that Lincoln's loan files had been purged of negative or adverse information. Kaye Scholer also knowingly omitted to disclose that the Lincoln loan summaries had been prepared long after the loans were originated and had been drafted in a manner designed to mislead the examiners as to when they were prepared.

93. Kaye Scholer's omissions were material to Kaye Scholer's representations that Lincoln's loans were carefully and professionally underwritten. Kaye Scholer's omissions of these material facts rendered each of its representations concerning the nature and documentation of Lincoln's underwriting practices to the FHLBB false and misleading.

B. *Kaye Scholer Knowingly Omitted Facts Material to Lincoln's Underwriting of Securities Investments*

1. Kaye Scholer Knew of Lincoln's Investment Underwriting Deficiencies

94. Kaye Scholer reviewed Lincoln's underwriting procedures with respect to equity securities and junk bonds in order to respond to the concerns raised by the examiners in the 1986 Examination.

95. As shown by an October 29, 1986, internal memorandum, Kaye Scholer knew that at least 14 of Lincoln's junk bond investment files reflected no internal Lincoln investment analysis. By that date, Kaye Scholer also knew that 41 other investment files rested on purported internal investment analyses that were in "most . . . if not all" cases prepared after the fact, in some cases by outside accountants at Lincoln's request.

96. As shown by an October 29, 1986, internal memorandum, Kaye Scholer recognized these deficiencies and sought to identify junk bond issues that had been diligently underwritten and were profitable to be presented to the examiners as illustrative of Lincoln's junk bond investments. A Kaye Scholer lawyer was directed to:

> Review the junk bond underwriting summaries prepared by [a Kaye Scholer paralegal] and select the 10 or 15 best. Those issues selected should show diligent underwriting, a good yield (positive interest spread), and hopefully a large capital gain realized upon sale of the bonds. We should then speak to [Andre] Niebling for his view as to which of these would show Lincoln's underwriting in its best possible light.

97. As shown by an October 29, 1986, internal memorandum, Kaye Scholer also knew that Lincoln's securities portfolio was not profitable. In that October 29, 1986 memorandum which addressed the quality of Lincoln's underwriting, Kaye Scholer decided they should: "Ask Tom Jones [a Lincoln official] why the present junk bond portfolio is doing so poorly."

98. As shown by a February 19, 1987, internal memorandum, Kaye Scholer knew that the investment summaries in Lincoln's equity and securities files had been edited to exclude information that refleted negatively on the transactions, *i.e.,* Kaye Scholer knew that Lincoln employees "would have tried to edit out things [in investment summaries] that would make it look like bonds should not be purchased."

99. As shown by an April 16, 1987, internal memorandum, Kaye Scholer also knew from Lincoln's own expert, Ostrander, that Lincoln did not have the expertise required to properly underwrite the purchase of junk bonds in secondary market transactions for themselves. As Kaye Scholer recorded in that memorandum, Ostrander recommended:

> Lincoln should either hire or train an analyst who will do actual analysis of financial statements and forecast a company's prospects. Ostrander suggested that a good policy would be that these reports should be in the file within 30 days of purchase for bonds bought from the secondary market, but the report should be done before the purchase of a new issue.

100. As shown by a September 15, 1987, memorandum to Lincoln, Kaye Scholer recognized that Lincoln's underwriting of debt and securities had been in fact "very weak, and there [was] little or no evidence in the files of proper underwriting."

2. Kaye Scholer's Representations to the FHLBB

101. Notwithstanding its knowledge of the foregoing deficiencies, in its June 26, 1987, response to the 1986 Examination, Kaye Scholer stated that there:

> [was] no basis for the . . . conclusion that Lincoln's high yield bond underwriting is inadequate. . . . Lincoln's high yield bond portfolio is characterized by knowledgeable underwriting and constant electronic monitoring of its investments. . . . Lincoln's constant success with high yield bonds is no accident, but rather the direct result of its well-conceived and well executed investment policies.

102. Kaye Scholer further represented to the FHLBB that:

> The exceptional performance of Lincoln's "noninvestment grade" bond portfolio is the result of careful diversification, underwriting, and monitoring.

103. As part of its response to the 1986 Examination, Kaye Scholer portrayed the files for two junk bonds held in Lincoln's portfolio as representative of what it claimed was the exemplary underwriting done by Lincoln personnel. Kaye Scholer also represented that "While Lincoln's investment files do not always have the identical writings contained in the two files described above, a similar process is undertaken for all of Lincoln's investments."

3. Kaye Scholer's Omission of Facts Material to Its Representations

104. In summary, Kaye Scholer knew that: (1) many of Lincoln's junk bond investment files contained little or no evidence of underwriting; (2) the summaries contained in numerous other Lincoln junk bond investment files, which purported to summarize Lincoln's underwriting of these investments, were in fact created well after the transactions had occurred; (3) some summaries had been edited to exclude information that would reflect negatively on the transactions; and (4) Lincoln lacked the expertise to properly underwrite on its own the purchases of junk bonds it had made. Nevertheless, Kaye Scholer knowingly omitted to disclose to the FHLBB the deficiencies in Lincoln's underwriting of the junk bond investments, the deficiencies in and misleading nature of the purported summaries, Lincoln's deletion of negative information from the summaries, and Lincoln's lack of necessary expertise to underwrite the investments.

105. Kaye Scholer's omissions were material to Kaye Scholer's representations that Lincoln's junk bonds were carefully and professionally underwritten and highly profitable. Kaye Scholer's omissions of these material facts rendered each of its representations to the FHLBB that Lincoln's high yield bond portfolio was profitable as a result of careful and professional underwriting false and misleading.

106. Respondent Kaye Scholer's, Fishbein's, and Katzman's participation in the activities in connection with the misrepresentation of Lincoln's underwriting practices and documentation thereof, described in paragraphs 74-105 above, violated [the provisions cited in paragraph 44 (a)-(d)].

SEVENTH CLAIM

Kaye Scholer Knowingly Omitted Facts Material to Lincoln's Direct Investments with Conley D. Wolfswinkel

(As to Respondents Kaye Scholer, Fishbein and Katzman)

107. Beginning in 1985, Lincoln entered into a series of transactions with the Wolfswinkel Group, Inc. ("WGI"), owned by Conley D. Wolfswinkel ("Wolfswinkel"), that related to a raw land real estate development project called "Rancho Vistoso" (the "Rancho Vistoso Transactions"). Lincoln claimed these transactions were acquisition, development and construction loans. As a result of the 1986 Examination, the examiners concluded that the Rancho Vistoso transactions in actuality were joint ventures between Wolfswinkel/WGI and Lincoln, and not loans, and that Lincoln should reclassify the transactions as direct investments.

A. Kaye Scholer Knowingly Omitted Facts Material to the Economic Substance of the Rancho Vistoso Transactions

108. Kaye Scholer had no expertise with regard to thrift regulatory matters. Jones, Day, Reavis & Pogue ("Jones, Day") was Lincoln's regulatory counsel with regard to the issues raised in the 1986 Examination.

109. By July 8, 1986, Jones Day had disclosed to Kaye Scholer by copy of an April 4, 1986, memorandum of one of its partners, Robert Baker ("Baker"), that the Lincoln "loan files contain information which could lead the examiners to reach [the] conclusion" to reclassify "many of the WGI loans" as joint ventures. Jones Day had also disclosed to Kaye Scholer that it was "difficult to assess whether the examiners will put all the pieces together, but they are certainly there."

110. On July 8, 1986, Kaye Scholer lawyers learned from Jones Day that after reviewing Lincoln's files on WGI, Jones Day had major concerns over the appropriate classification of the Rancho Vistoso transactions due to the control and development work performed by ACC on behalf of Wolfswinkel and because the illiquidity of Conley Wolfswinkel's assets could adversely affect his ability to repay Lincoln. Jones Day found that the following specific features of the Rancho Vistoso transactions "may lead the examiners to conclude that Rancho Vistoso is a 50/50 joint venture rather than a loan:"

   (i)   the lack of liquidity of both WGI and Wolfswinkel;

   (ii)   cash flow projections for WGI that projected a "net cash deficit of almost $12 million" for the period December 1, 1985 through May 31, 1987;

   (iii)   that all outstanding Lincoln loans to WGI matured in 1988;

   (iv)   the presence of an "equity kicker" that WGI had granted to Lincoln;

   (v)   that Rancho Vistoso was held out to appraisers and other third parties, and in the ACC annual report, as an ACC project;

   (vi)   that ACC was "managing the development" of Rancho Vistoso, as Lincoln personnel acknowledged; and

   (vii)   that Wolfswinkel "had only guaranteed 50% of the Rancho Vistoso loans (as opposed to his 100% guarantee of other loans)."

111. By July 22, 1986, Kaye Scholer knew facts showing that Lincoln controlled the management of the development of Rancho Vistoso. As an internal Kaye Scholer memorandum of that date states, Kaye Scholer learned in an interview with AMCOR officer Mark Voight ("Voight"):

> When queried with respect to the actual dealings with Wolfswinkle [*sic*] on the Rancho Vistoso property, Mark [Voight] indicated that the Lincoln people do take a "somewhat active" role in the engineering, planning and off and on site development of the property. *I feel very strongly that these raise issues as to whether the Rancho Vistoso deal is, indeed, a pure loan or is rather a joint venture.* For example, Mark

indicated that Lincoln people had participated in obtaining the zoning for the Rancho Vistoso property and contracts with hiring consultants, etc. . . . *Apparently, however, Lincoln runs the project, and keeps Wolfswinkle [sic] advised. When pushed, Mark indicated that if the examiners were to go to Pima County to do a little investigating, it would be no great mystery to determine who was coordinating the project. . . . [N]o one from Lincoln receives any reimbursement* for any services on the Rancho Vistoso project. . . . (Emphasis added.)

112. As shown by an internal July 22, 1986, memorandum, Kaye Scholer knew that a characterization of the Rancho Vistoso transactions as loans was inconsistent with the facts known to it, leading Kaye Scholer to seek to avoid disclosure of facts tending to show that Rancho Vistoso transactions were joint ventures rather than loans:

> [W]e should approach the Wolfswinkel "classification" question from a purely accounting standpoint in that while the facts are not strongly with us we can make an intellectually honest argument if based solely on accounting principles.

113. Another Kaye Scholer memorandum dated August 7, 1986, shows that Kaye Scholer knew at the time it learned of Lincoln's management control of Rancho Vistoso that "the most important factor in addition to joint sharing of profits and losses seems to be control" and that a joint venture exists where a financial institution's management activities during the development period of a project "exceed those of the normal money lender" such as when a lender "exercises substantial control over the development."

114. As shown by Kaye Scholer internal memoranda dated August 12, 1986, and August 25, 1986, the Chief Financial Officer of WGI and WGI's legal counsel reported to Kaye Scholer that ACC/Lincoln "have taken control of Rancho Vistoso;" that Rancho Vistoso operates much like a joint venture with ACC being the managing venturer with many decisions being made by ACC without any involvement by Wolfswinkel, who is often not even informed that the decision had been made; that "control has been an issue all along;" and that WGI's legal counsel is "of the opinion that it would be very difficult to prove *legally* that the relationship is not a joint venture." (Emphasis added.)

115. As also shown by the internal memoranda of August 12 and 25, 1986, Kaye Scholer knew that the parties to the Rancho Vistoso transaction intended to create a joint venture. For example, Kaye Scholer knew, as shown by its internal memoranda, that:

(a) ACC and WGI personnel held out Rancho Vistoso to third parties as ACC's real estate development project;

(b) WGI called Lincoln's financial stake in the project "equity;" and

(c) Although WGI and Lincoln "have tried to structure [the Rancho Vistoso transactions] as a loan," Wolfswinkel and Lincoln considered themselves to be in fact "partners in development."

758

116. As also shown by the August 25, 1986 internal memorandum, Kaye Scholer knew that Lincoln was charging WGI a rate of interest substantially above the market rate. Kaye Scholer knew further that under Generally Accepted Accounting Principles ("GAAP"), Lincoln's profit participation had to be calculated by adding to its share of the net proceeds any interest or fees set higher than the fair market rate. Kaye Scholer accordingly knew that Lincoln's profit participation in Rancho Vistoso (which included the profit on the above market interest rate) was greater than 50 percent.

117. As shown by a September 10, 1986, internal memorandum, Kaye Scholer knew at the time it learned facts about the parties' intent that such facts were material to the determination of whether a project was a joint venture.

118. As also shown by the internal memorandum of September 10, 1986, Kaye Scholer knew that the "joint sharing of profits and losses" was an important "aspect of a joint venture:"

the joint venturers share (according to agreed percentages) in the benefits and losses of the project. This is a primary difference from a loan, in which the lender typically either does not share in appreciation, or shares through a contingent interest participation in upside swings but is generally protected from downswings.

119. As also shown by the internal memorandum of September 10, 1986, Kaye Scholer knew there was a significant similarity between the Rancho Vistoso transaction and other joint land development arrangements between Lincoln and WGI/Wolfswinkel that Lincoln had characterized as "joint ventures:"

[A]s alluded to by Bob Baker of Jones Day, the similarities between the joint venture arrangements and the Wolfswinkel loans may diminish the strength of our argument that the loans should not be reclassified as joint ventures.

120. Notwithstanding its knowledge of the foregoing facts, in its June 26, 1987, response on behalf of Lincoln, Kaye Scholer stated: (1) that there was no justification or support for the examiners' contention that the Rancho Vistoso ADC transactions should be reclassified as a joint venture; (2) that a August 21, 1986 "single consolidated, reorganized loan" to WGI mooted the issue of the classification of the original five Rancho Vistoso transactions, since there was no longer any risk of nonpayment; (3) that "[t]he concerns about liquidity, debt and guarantees, cashflow and working capital loans [to Wolfswinkel] are without merit;" and (4) that "each of the five original Rancho Vistoso loans . . . exhibits the risks and rewards of a loan, not a real estate joint venture."

121. In summary, Kaye Scholer knew, prior to the statements it made to the FHLBB regarding the economic substance and proper classification of the Rancho Vistoso transactions, that there were substantial reasons to treat the Rancho Vistoso transactions as joint ventures. Nevertheless, Kaye Scholer knowingly failed to inform the FHLBB of these facts material to the classification of the Rancho Vistoso transactions.

122. The facts that Kaye Scholer failed to disclose to the FHLBB were material to Kaye Scholer's representations about the appropriate treatment of the Rancho Vistoso transactions as loans or joint ventures. As a consequence of Kaye Scholer's omissions of these material facts, [Kaye Scholer] rendered its representations about the appropriate treatment of the Rancho Vistoso transactions as loans rather than joint ventures false and misleading.

B. Kaye Scholer Omitted Material Facts When It Urged the FHLBB to Rely Upon the Outside Accountants' Opinions

123. In its June 26, 1987, response on behalf of Lincoln, Kaye Scholer stated that the FHLBB was required to defer to the opinions as to the treatment of the Rancho Vistoso transactions of two accounting firms, Arthur Andersen and Arthur Young & Company ("Arthur Young").

124. Kaye Scholer knew by August 1, 1986, however:

(a) that Arthur Andersen and Arthur Young had not investigated or independently verified the facts material to determining whether Lincoln sought to control the development of Rancho Vistoso or whether Lincoln in fact did control the development of Rancho Vistoso; and

(b) that the Arthur Andersen and Arthur Young opinions were prepared based on agreed-upon procedures limited to a review of the *form* of the transaction — that is, the loan documents — rather than on any facts material to the economic substance or classification of the transaction.

125. By August 1, 1986, Kaye Scholer had in its files a May 8, 1986 memorandum prepared by Arthur Andersen that contained Arthur Andersen's "rationale for accounting for [Wolfswinkel] transactions as either loans or real estate investments in accordance with the guidance set forth in the [American Institute of Certified Public Accountants' ("AICPA")] Third Notice [to] Practitioners, our own subject file rider RE 2550 dated August 1985, and Section 517.17 . . . of Title 12, Code of Federal Regulations. . . ." That memorandum reflects that facts showing control of Rancho Vistoso by Lincoln were material in Arthur Andersen's opinion to accounting for the transaction as a loan or joint venture:

> [t]he major distinction of [Wolfswinkel transactions classified by Lincoln as] joint ventures versus [those classified by Lincoln as] loans is that Lincoln and its subsidiaries have full *control of assets* in these joint ventures and have more of the risks of ownership. Conversely, Wolfswinkel has less risk (than he does on his loans from Lincoln) of ownership or *control* of the property. . . .

(Emphasis added.)

126. As shown by an August 27, 1986, internal memorandum, Kaye Scholer knew that it was Arthur Andersen's opinion that facts concerning a putative lender's control over and degree of involvement in the project development may

760

"tip the balance" in classifying the transaction as a joint venture rather than a loan if the issue was close in terms of the accounting treatment.

127. As shown by another August 27, 1986, internal memorandum, Kaye Scholer also knew that facts concerning control of a project's development were material to the Arthur Young opinion:

> AY [Arthur Young] would normally consider the control over a project when classifying an ADC loan, but did not in this case having presumed that AA [Arthur Andersen] had.

128. Kaye Scholer knew as described in paragraphs 110-120 above that Lincoln in fact controlled all aspects of Rancho Vistoso development, including zoning, advertising, and pricing.

129. Kaye Scholer knew that the accountants had not considered the facts demonstrating Lincoln's management control over the development of Rancho Vistoso described in paragraphs 110-120 above, in issuing their opinions.

130. Kaye Scholer also knew no later than August 27, 1986, that Arthur Andersen and Arthur Young had relied on future interest payments by Wolfswinkel to justify their conclusion that Wolfswinkel had sufficient equity "at risk" in the Rancho Vistoso project to warrant characterizing the transaction as a loan rather than a joint venture.

131. Kaye Scholer knew, no later than August 27, 1986, that Wolfswinkel's cash flow was material to the reliance placed by Arthur Andersen and Arthur Young on Wolfswinkel's ability to make good on his personal guarantee.

132. As shown by a Kaye Scholer internal memorandum of November 6, 1986, Kaye Scholer knew that Lincoln used various subterfuges such as sham land "purchases" to funnel cash to Wolfswinkel. As reported in that memorandum, in June of 1986 Wolfswinkel did not:

> have sufficient cash to meet his obligations. It was therefore arranged that Wolfswinkel would obtain $6 million from ACC. The $6 million consisted of a $2.5 million loan on the Ray Road and 48th Street property. In addition, ACC bought three parcels of property, Beaugureau, Cooley, and Pinnacle Peak from Wolfswinkel, for a total of $3.5 million. As part of the sales, Wolfswinkle was given an option to repurchase, for $500,000 a month. The options were to expire on September 13, 1986. Wolfswinkel has since repurchased the properties at the option prices.

133. By August 27, 1986, Kaye Scholer also knew: (a) that WGI/Wolfswinkel had a negative cash flow projected through May 1987 and that, contrary to assumptions made by the two accounting firms, Wolfswinkel was in fact having serious cash flow problems that Lincoln helped to conceal by mechanisms such as interest reserves and by directing cash to Wolfswinkel through additional loans, refinancings and land purchases; and (b) that under the AICPA Notices such projected and actual cash flow shortfalls were material

indicators of Wolfswinkel's inability to repay the loan and thus were among the specific "Characteristics of ADC Arrangements Implying Investments in Real Estate or Joint Ventures" expressly set forth in the AICPA Notices:

> In order for the financial institution to recover its investment in the project, the property must be sold to independent third parties, the borrower must obtain refinancing from another source, or the property must be placed in service and generate sufficient net cash flow to service debt principal and interest. [Third Notice paragraph 8]

134. Nevertheless, as shown by a Kaye Scholer internal memorandum of April 27, 1987 memorializing a meeting of April 24, 1987, Kaye Scholer deliberately omitted facts described in the paragraph above and instead chose in the June 26, 1987, response to

> paste in our argument expressed in the classification letter that it is not Lincoln's cash which carries Wolfswinkel but his own.

135. Notwithstanding its knowledge of the foregoing facts, in its June 26, 1987, response on behalf of Lincoln, Kaye Scholer stated:

> Here, each of the loans sought to be reclassified has been *carefully reviewed* by two of the nation's "Big Eight" accounting firms — Arthur Andersen & Company ("Arthur Andersen") and Arthur Young & Company ("Arthur Young") — and was determined to be properly classified as a loan receivable.... Each of these [Rancho Vistoso] arrangements has been *closely scrutinized* by Arthur Andersen and Arthur Young and determined to be properly classified as a loan receivable.... [E]ach of the Rancho Vistoso transactions ... exhibits the risks and rewards of a loan, not a real estate joint venture, and therefore is properly classified and accounted for as a loan receivable. The analyses of Arthur Andersen and Arthur Young fully support this conclusion.

(Emphasis added.)

136. In summary, Kaye Scholer knew that facts material to the accountants' opinions had been assumed without adequate investigation by the two accounting firms. Kaye Scholer knew that the accounting firms had assumed the facts material to (a) their conclusions under the factors set forth in the AICPA Notices (which the opinions purported to apply) and (b) the economic substance of the transaction. Kaye Scholer knew that the accountants had assumed that Wolfswinkel was not dependent on Lincoln to meet his financial obligations and that Lincoln did not manage the development of the Rancho Vistoso project. Kaye Scholer knew from its own investigation, however, that the facts differed from those assumed by the accounting firms. Thus, Kaye Scholer knew that its statements regarding the "close scrutiny" and "careful review" by Arthur Andersen and Arthur Young of the arrangements between Wolfswinkel and Lincoln were false and misleading. Kaye Scholer knew further that Arthur

Andersen and Arthur Young had not "carefully considered" the facts necessary to apply the applicable accounting criteria. Instead, Kaye Scholer knew they had assumed facts material to their opinions that were known to Kaye Scholer to be incorrect. Nevertheless, Kaye Scholer knowingly failed to inform the FHLBB of material facts regarding the accountants' opinions concerning the classification of the Rancho Vistoso Transactions.

137. The facts that Kaye Scholer failed to disclose were material to Kaye Scholer's representations about the accountants' opinions concerning the classification of the Rancho Vistoso Transactions as loans or joint ventures. Kaye Scholer's omissions of these material facts rendered its representations about the classification of the Rancho Vistoso transactions and the accountants' opinions false and misleading.

138. Respondent Kaye Scholer's, Fishbein's, and Katzman's misrepresentations and omission of facts material to the Rancho Vistoso transactions, described in paragraphs 107-137 above, violated [the provisions cited in paragraph 44 (a)-(d)].

EIGHTH CLAIM

Kaye Scholer Knowingly Misrepresented the Status of Lincoln's Direct Investments and Omitted Material Facts Concerning Those Investments in Oral Presentations and Written Submissions to the FHLBB During the Course of the 1986 Examination

(As to Respondents Kaye Scholer, Fishbein and Katzman)

139. The facts and matters set forth in paragraphs 22 through 34 are incorporated herein by reference and are alleged as if fully set forth herein.

140. During the course of the 1986 Examination, the examiners raised questions about the legality of Lincoln's direct investments.

141. In Lincoln's response to those questions, Kaye Scholer made a series of representations concerning the nature, extent, and basis for grandfathering of the challenged direct investments. In these communications, Kaye Scholer represented that Lincoln's direct investments in its service corporations were protected by the grandfather clause because Lincoln had "definitive plans" to make those investments by December 10, 1985.

142. On March 18, 1986, Kaye Scholer sent a memorandum to Lincoln which was, with Kaye Scholer's knowledge and consent, provided to the FHLBB examiners. The memorandum submitted to the FHLBB stated Kaye Scholer's opinion that as of December 10, 1984, Lincoln had the grandfathered right to make in excess of $750 million in "prospective" direct investments, on the purported ground that all of these "prospective" direct investments were "projects pursuant to defini-

tive plans in existence" on December 10, 1984. The memorandum failed to disclose that documents purporting to constitute the Lincoln Board of Director's authorization of such investments were fraudulent and backdated.

143. During July and August 1986, the examiners requested additional documents relevant to Lincoln's claim that its direct investments were grandfathered. In response to those requests, Kaye Scholer, on September 4, 1986, made a presentation on Lincoln's behalf to the examiners. In that presentation, Kaye Scholer repeated its representation that the direct investments were grandfathered as definitive plans in existence as of December 10, 1984. Kaye Scholer again failed to disclose that documents purporting to constitute the Lincoln Board of Directors' authorization of such investments were fraudulent and backdated.

144. In that September 4, 1986, presentation, Kaye Scholer also transmitted to the examiners the following documents concerning Lincoln's direct investments, knowing that the documents had been created in 1985 and backdated to create the appearance that the Board of Directors had taken action prior to December 10, 1984:

(a) A Lincoln Board of Directors unanimous consent to reduce the investment authority of Continental Homes Corporation ("CHC") from $307 million to $250 million, purportedly dated October 30, 1984;

(b) A Lincoln Board of Directors unanimous consent authorizing Lincoln to return its investment in CHC to $300 million, purportedly dated November 30, 1984;

(c) A Lincoln Board of Directors unanimous consent authorizing Lincoln to invest $100 million in Crescent Hotel Group purportedly dated June 27, 1984;

(d) A Lincoln Board of Directors unanimous consent authorizing Lincoln to invest $100 million in Lincoln Commercial Properties, purportedly dated November 28, 1984;

(e) A Lincoln Board of Directors unanimous consent authorizing Lincoln to invest $150 million in Lincoln Communications Company ("LCC"), purportedly dated September 28, 1984;

(f) A Lincoln Board of Directors unanimous consent authorizing Lincoln to invest $110 million in LCC, purportedly dated October 31, 1984;

(g) A Lincoln Board of Directors unanimous consent authorizing Lincoln to increase its investment in LCC from $103 million to $150 million, purportedly dated November 6, 1984;

(h) A Lincoln Board of Directors unanimous consent authorizing Lincoln to invest $90 million in Lincoln American Financial Investment Company ("LAFICO"), purportedly dated May 23, 1984; and

(i) A Lincoln Board of Directors unanimous consent authorizing Lincoln to invest $225 million in LAFICO, purportedly dated December 8, 1984.

145. In a September 15, 1986, letter to Kaye Scholer, the FHLBB recounted its understanding of and reliance upon the documents transmitted in the September 4, 1986, presentation:

[a]t this meeting, you and other Lincoln representatives presented the documents on which Lincoln is relying to buttress its claim that it has complied with the direct investment regulation, 12 C.F.R. §563.9-8.

The letter went on to note that with respect to Lincoln's service corporations,

[t]he information you provided on September 4 consists in large part of board resolutions and correspondence with the California Department of Savings and Loan. Are we correct in assuming that these are all of the documents on which Lincoln relies in contending that [it had grandfathered investments and definitive plans for its service corporations]? If not, please let us know and provide us with any other documents on which Lincoln relies.

146. By letter dated September 24, 1986, Kaye Scholer, for Lincoln, responded that by transmitting the documents described above, and other similar documents, it had "provided you with documentation concerning Lincoln's definitive plans and legal commitments to invest in service corporations as of December 10, 1984."

147. As shown by a May 13, 1987, internal memorandum, Kaye Scholer had provided the purported unanimous consents of the Lincoln Board of Directors to the examiners at the September 4, 1986 presentation specifically because the examiners found the Board of Directors' minutes and resolutions relating to Lincoln's planned investments in service corporations to be relevant evidence of Lincoln having had definitive plans to invest in service corporations prior to December 10, 1984.

148. As part of its June 26, 1987, response to the 1986 Examination, Kaye Scholer again repeated its assertions that, as a matter of fact, Lincoln's plans for its service corporations constituted "definitive plans" as of December 10, 1984. At the time Kaye Scholer made these assertions it knew that:

(a) Board of Director documents purporting to be unanimous consents had been created in 1985 and backdated to various dates prior to December 10, 1984;

(b) Lincoln's journal vouchers and accounting and computer entries relating to certain direct investments in service corporations had been backdated to November 30, 1984;

(c) Unauthorized signatures had been placed on the unanimous consent documents purporting to authorize Lincoln's direct investment transactions with its service corporations;

(d) Documents in Lincoln's loan files (including loan documents, deeds of trust, and other transactional documents) purporting to show the Lincoln-CHC transaction as occurring on November 30, 1984, had been created in 1985 and backdated;

(e) Board of Director unanimous consent documents purporting to authorize corporate actions relating to the Lincoln investment in CHC were written in the present tense to add purported evidentiary support for Lincoln's contentions that the events critical to the Lincoln-CHC transactions had in fact taken place before December 10, 1984; and

(f) The Board of Director unanimous consent documents misdated November 30, 1984, relating to the Lincoln-CHC transaction recited that certain documents "have been presented" to the Board, notwithstanding that those transactional documents, as described in subparagraph (d), were not created until 1985.

149. In summary, Kaye Scholer knew at the time it made these representations and provided these documents to the FHLBB that: (a) accounting and computer entries had been made on a date later than the date that Kaye Scholer claimed; (b) transactional documents had been created after Lincoln's request for exemption was denied in 1985 and were backdated to 1984; (c) purported unanimous consent documents of the Boards of Directors of Lincoln and its subsidiaries had been created in 1985 and were backdated; and (d) unauthorized signatures had been placed on many of the backdated unanimous consents.

150. Nevertheless, Kaye Scholer omitted to disclose to the FHLBB that the documents had been backdated. Kaye Scholer omitted to disclose to the FHLBB that unauthorized signatures had been placed on certain of these unanimous consents. Kaye Scholer omitted to disclose to the FHLBB that certain of these documents contained misleading factual statements that had been written in the present tense and included in the documents to make the documents appear to confirm Lincoln's position on grandfathered investments. Kaye Scholer omitted to disclose that the transactional documents and journal entries had not been prepared or made on the dates claimed.

151. The facts that Kaye Scholer omitted to disclose were material to Kaye Scholer's representations about Lincoln's definitive plans. Kaye Scholer's omissions rendered its representations that Lincoln had definitive plans to make direct investments prior to December 10, 1984, false and misleading.

152. Respondent Kaye Scholer's, Fishbein's, and Katzman's participation in the activities in connection with the misrepresentations and omission of facts material to Lincoln's direct investments, described in paragraphs 139-151 above, violated [the provisions cited in paragraph 44(a)-(d)].

NINTH CLAIM

Kaye Scholer Knowingly Failed to Disclose Material Facts Concerning Lincoln's Participation in Financing of a Personal Tax Shelter for ACC's Control Persons (Hotel Pontchartrain).

(As to Respondents Kaye Scholer, Fishbein, Katzman and Fisher)

153. On or about December 31, 1984, Lincoln, purchased the Hotel Pontchartrain in Detroit, Michigan ("Pontchartrain"), for $19,500,000 in cash. Lin-

coln made this purchase without securing an appraisal. Lincoln then transferred the Pontchartrain to the Crescent Hotel Group of Michigan ("CHGM"), a Lincoln subsidiary.

154. Following the purchase of the Pontchartrain by Lincoln, Keating and other insiders formed a limited partnership, the Hotel Pontchartrain Limited Partnership ("HPLP"). CHGM was the general partner and Keating and other insiders of ACC were some of the limited partners of HPLP. HPLP was formed as a tax shelter so that the investment tax credits and operating losses would accrue to the personal benefit of its limited partners.

155. On or about March 31, 1985, CHGM sold the Pontchartrain to HPLP for $38,490,000. $38 million of the purchase price was financed by Phoenician Commercial Properties ("PCP"), another subsidiary of Lincoln. Prior written approval of this transaction from the proper regulatory authority was not obtained.

156. The $38 million loan was subsequently refinanced by San Jacinto Savings & Loan ("San Jacinto"). At or about the same time, Lincoln purchased $38 million of San Jacinto's subdebt. The refinancing of the loan by San Jacinto was done in response to concerns raised about affiliated party transactions in the course of the 1986 Examination. ACC, Lincoln's holding company, guaranteed approximately $14 million of the San Jacinto loan.

157. The Hotel Pontchartrain immediately began to experience operating losses and renovation cost overruns. Lincoln, through CHGM, its subsidiary and general partner of HPLP, advanced $10.5 to HPLP to offset the Pontchartrain's negative cash flow.

158. On or about December 2, 1986 (after the 1986 Examination on-site review had been completed) Lincoln, through a third subsidiary, Phoenician Financial Corporation ("PFC"), granted a $20 million line of credit to HPLP without any loan underwriting, financial analysis, or approval by the PFC Board of Directors. The line of credit was unsecured and did not require repayment of interest and principal for five years. The line of credit bore a 10 percent annual rate of interest, which was below prevailing market rates.

159. Lincoln's funding of the Pontchartrain, including the line of credit, was illegal in several respects. Because HPLP was an affiliated person of Lincoln, Lincoln's loans to HPLP were prohibited affiliated transactions in violation of Section 563.43 of the FSLIC Insurance Regulations and Section 584.3 of the FSLIC Holding Company Regulations, formerly 12 C.F.R. §§563.43 and 584.3 (1986). This was also in violation of the FSLIC's conflict of interest policy, as set forth in Section 571.7 (1986) of the FSLIC Insurance Regulations, formerly 12 C.F.R. §571.7 (1986), and was an unsafe and unsound practice.

160. As part of its 1988 review of Lincoln's loan files for underwriting and other deficiencies, Kaye Scholer examined the files relating to the $20 million extension of credit by PFC and learned, as shown by an internal Kaye Scholer memorandum dated February 17, 1988, that the PFC line of credit:

    a.   File lacks virtually all required materials; application, approvals (both as to original making by Phoenician Financial Corporation and transfer to Crescent Landing Corporation), loan to one borrower statement, financial statements and any of the representations (documents true and complete, delinquencies, access) required in connection with a sale of a loan. Also there are no tax returns, credit reports or Underwriting in the file.

b. The loan has serious problems concerning (a) safety and soundness and (b) affiliate transactions. With respect to safety and soundness there is no evidence of the ability of the borrower to repay it. In fact, neither interest nor principal payments are due during its 5 year term. Although the file lacks an Underwriting or any explanation for the loan, it apparently was made because of the weak financial condition of the borrower, in itself raising questions about the likelihood of repayment.

c. Possibly more serious are the affiliate issues presented, both in connection with the original loans and the transfer. Since Lincoln (or ACC) appears to be an affiliate of the general partner, pursuant to the Regulations, Board approval would be required. The situation is worsened by the terms of the loan (10% interest with no payments of principal or interest until the end of the 5 year term) which could be found to be a gift of assets. Board approval would also have been required in connection with the transfer from Phoenician Financial Corporation ("PFC") to Crescent Lending Corporation ("CLC"). Additionally, in view of the low interest rate, risky position and absence of recourse liability against PFC, a substantial discount would be expected, however, instead a premium was paid. ($13,353,316 was paid although $12,122,825 said to be outstanding).

161. Kaye Scholer subsequently participated in the preparation of a March 30, 1988, ACC 1987 Annual Report Form 10-K that was filed with both the SEC and the FHLBB, pursuant to FHLBB regulations that required such a filing with the FHLBB for the purpose of regulatory oversight. The report did not disclose the underwriting deficiencies, the ACC guarantees, the favorable loan terms, or the violations of law associated with the Pontchartrain transactions reflected in the Kaye Scholer memorandum of February 17, 1988.

162. Kaye Scholer also participated in the preparation of registration statements that ACC filed with the SEC on March 30, 1988, April 6, 1988, April 14, 1988, June 3, 1988, and August 23, 1988, in connection with ACC's public offering of its securities. ACC also submitted these materials to the FHLBB pursuant to FHLBB regulations that required their filing with the FHLBB for the purposes of regulatory oversight. Again Kaye Scholer did not disclose in these filings the material underwriting deficiencies, the ACC guarantees, the favorable loan terms, or the violations of law associated with the Pontchartrain reflected in the Kaye Scholer internal memorandum of February 17, 1988.

163. On June 3, 1988 and July 22, 1988, Kaye Scholer participated in the preparation of draft Offering Circulars for the proposed sale of up to

$100,000,000 in the aggregate of subordinated debentures for Lincoln. These Offering Circulars were submitted to the FHLBB, pursuant to FHLBB regulations that required the filing of Offering Circulars for the purposes of regulatory oversight. Kaye Scholer did not disclose in these filings the underwriting deficiencies, the ACC guarantees, the favorable loan terms, or the violations of law associated with the Pontchartrain transactions reflected in the Kaye Scholer internal memorandum of February 17, 1988.

164. On September 6, 1988, a joint examination of ACC as a savings and loan holding company was begun by the FHLBB and the California Department of Savings and Loan ("CDSL"). As part of the joint examination, the CDSL reviewed files concerning the Pontchartrain transactions, and found the $20 million extension of credit from PFC to HPLP to be a "loss, unsafe and unsound, and [a] flagrant conflict of interest."

165. On September 28 and October 4, 1988, the CDSL wrote letters to ACC and Lincoln, detailing its findings as to the viability, safety and soundness, and legality of the PFC-HPLP $20 million line of credit and omissions of material facts in the filings with the SEC and the FHLBB described above. The CDSL correctly informed Lincoln that its filings with the SEC and the FHLBB omitted, *inter alia*, to disclose the following additional material facts necessary for an understanding of the effects of the transactions on Lincoln's financial statements:

(1) The existence of the $35 million dollar San Jacinto first mortgage on the Pontchartrain;

(2) The existence of the approximately $14 million ACC guarantees of a substantial portion of the first mortgage balance with San Jacinto;

(3) The severe operating losses and negative net worth of the HPLP;

(4) The use of unsecured loan proceeds were to cover the large ongoing operating losses and the total amount of the PFC line of credit;

(5) The recommendation by Lincoln officers to place the PFC unsecured line of credit on a non-accrual basis on July 7, 1988, and the approximately $3.0 million loan loss reserve established for it on September 30, 1988;

(6) The commitment by CHGM, Lincoln's subsidiary and the HPLP general partner, to advance funds to meet operating expenses in excess of the $22 million line of credit from PFC;

(7) The extraordinarily liberal terms of the PFC line of credit, including the below market interest rate and the deferral of the payment of interest and principal until its maturity.

166. Respondent Kaye Scholer, on behalf of Lincoln, responded to these deficiencies on October 5 and 13, 1988, by stating, *inter alia*:

(1) The $20 million unsecured loan is not a potential loss to Lincoln. The second and third quarter 1988 operating profit was $160,037 and $238,420 respectively; and

(2) There were no material omissions in the documents filed with the SEC and FHLBB, noting that these filings had been reviewed by Arthur Young and Kaye Scholer.

167. As shown by an October 18, 1988, internal memorandum, Kaye Scholer knew that Lincoln's claims about the operating profits omitted material facts and were false and misleading:

> [T]he month-by-month statement of Operations for the period through the second quarter shows that although an "operating profit" of $60,037 was achieved, this failed to account for $2,192,760 of expenses for interest, property taxes, depreciation, management fees and other expenses. . . .
>
> It seems disingenuous to fail to deduct management fees, real estate taxes and similar items on computing the appropriate profit particularly when the relevant figures are so easily obtainable.

168. Nevertheless, in a letter dated November 4, 1988, Kaye Scholer replied to the CDSL's concerns on Lincoln's behalf, asserting that the concerns identified by the CDSL were beyond its expertise, that the relevant documents contained adequate disclosure, and that Kaye Scholer did "not believe that the ACC documents [filed with the SEC and FHLBB] either intentionally or mistakenly failed to make required disclosures." Significantly, Kaye Scholer in closing also stated in its November 4, 1988, letter that:

> [t]o the extent you are concerned about the viability of the Pontchartrain loan, [Lincoln] responded to these concerns in their October 5 and October 13, 1988 letters. Accordingly, we cannot understand the relevance of your October 13, 1988 letter.

169. Kaye Scholer knowingly omitted to disclose to the SEC and FHLBB facts material to the HPLP transactions memorialized in its internal memorandum of February 17, 1988, and described in the CDSL letters of September 4 and October 4, 1988. Moreover, Kaye Scholer knowingly omitted to disclose to CDSL in the course of the joint examination the material facts memorialized in its internal memorandum of October 18, 1988, that contradicted Lincoln's claims of the HPLP's financial viability upon which Kaye Scholer had asked the CDSL to rely.

170. The facts Kaye Scholer omitted to disclose were material to Kaye Scholer's representations to the SEC and FHLBB regarding the Pontchartrain and to the CDSL during the joint examination about the viability of the HPLP loan. Kaye Scholer's omissions of these material facts rendered its representations about the HPLP transactions in the filings with the SEC and FHLBB and to the CDSL false and misleading.

171. Respondent Kaye Scholer's, Fishbein's, Katzman's and Fisher's participation in the activities in connection with the misrepresentations and omission of facts material to the HPLP transactions, described in paragraphs 153-170 above, violated [the provisions cited in paragraph 44(a)-(d)].

770

TENTH CLAIM

Kaye Scholer Participated in Obtaining a Loan on Favorable Terms for the Benefit of One of Its Partners in Violation of Lincoln's Procedures and Applicable Law

(As to Respondents Kaye Scholer and Fisher)

[The Tenth Claim asserts that Fisher, a Kaye Scholer partner, obtained a loan from Lincoln and that the loan was "not in compliance with Lincoln's applicable loan policies and procedures, not in the normal course of business in the savings and loan industry, not in compliance with applicable federal regulations, and not in a safe and sound manner."]

V. Injury

182. As a consequence of Respondents' reckless breach of its fiduciary duty of competence and due care, Lincoln made direct investments that resulted in substantial losses.

183. As a consequence of the Respondents' failure to inform the Board of Directors of Lincoln of its fiduciary duties to the depositors and to the federal insurance fund in light of the material facts of which Respondents were aware, the Board of Directors was deprived of the opportunity to take appropriate action with full knowledge of its fiduciary duties concerning the transactions described in this Notice of Charges.

184. As a consequence of the Respondents' knowing misrepresentations and omissions of material facts in communications to the FHLBB, the FHLBB was deprived of the opportunity to exercise its official regulatory judgment and discretion with full knowledge of all material facts concerning the transactions and other matters described in this Notice.

185. As a consequence, Lincoln, ACC, and the federal insurance fund have suffered actual losses from the transactions described in this Notice of at least $275 million.

VI. Prayer for Relief

186. In light of the charges set forth in the foregoing Notice of Charges, the OTS seeks the following remedies with respect to the Respondents:

a. The issuance of a final cease-and-desist order pursuant to Section 8(b) of the FDIA, 12 U.S.C. §1818(b), which order shall include affirmative corrective action provisions requiring the Respondents, *inter alia*: (i) to refrain from the participation in the violations described in the Notice of Charges;

and (ii) to make restitution and reimbursement for losses to Lincoln with respect to all expenses and other losses or damage paid or incurred in conjunction with the activities described above, including without limitation the costs of this proceeding and the underlying investigation; which liability shall be the joint and several liability of Respondents and each of them;

b. the issuance of a final order of removal and prohibition, which would provide that Respondents shall not: (1) participate in any manner in the conduct of the affairs of any institution or agency specified in Section 8(e)(7)(A) of the FDIA (hereinafter referred to as "Paragraph (7)(A)"); (2) solicit, procure, transfer, attempt to transfer, vote, or attempt to vote any proxy, consent or authorization with respect to any voting rights in any Paragraph (7)(A) Institution; or (3) vote for a director or act as an institution-affiliated party; and

c. the issuance of a final order to debar Respondents from practicing before OTS pursuant to 12 C.F.R. Part 513 (1990). . . .

OFFICE OF THRIFT SUPERVISION

Mar. 1 , 1992   BY: s/_____

TIMOTHY RYAN, DIRECTOR

KAYE, SCHOLER'S RESPONSE TO OTS'S NOTICE OF CHARGES

The Notice of Charges by the Office of Thrift Supervision (OTS) against Kaye, Scholer (KS) consists of ten claims purporting in essence to allege violation by KS of provisions of the Code of Federal Regulations applying to communications between thrift institutions and their regulators. While we address each of the specific counts below — and none of them have factual or legal merit — there are certain concepts underlying the OTS's position that are wholly at war with generally accepted professional standards and ethical obligations for lawyers representing a client.

1. KS is *not* alleged to have been involved in the underlying transactions or practices complained of at the time they were done, accounted for or reported. With respect to virtually all of the matters at issue, KS was retained as *litigation counsel* by Lincoln Savings and Loan (Lincoln) only *after* Bank Board examiners had identified and criticized specific transactions or practices previously engaged in by Lincoln, and only *after* an adversary relationship had developed between Lincoln and the Bank Board. The firm's role was to assist Lincoln's Board of Directors in preparing Lincoln's answer to the Examiner's Report and to prepare for litigation in the event the answer was not credited by the Bank Board.

Significantly, the Bank Board had retained its own litigation counsel to prepare a lawsuit against Lincoln.

2. Thus, the KS role here was the traditional one of counsel representing a client in a matter before a regulatory agency that has become adversarial and involves anticipated litigation. In that role, KS assisted Lincoln's Board in preparing written reports of more than 1000 pages responding to the examiner's criticisms of well over 20 separate transactions and virtually all of Lincoln's business operations. The OTS does not seriously contend that any of the material in this report was false. Rather, the OTS's criticism of KS is for advancing arguments on its client's behalf which it believed were supported by the facts and law, without going further and disclosing weaknesses in its client's position, or contrary arguments which could be made by the OTS.

3. Completely refuting this OTS contention, Professor Geoffrey C. Hazard, Jr., of the Yale Law School, the nation's foremost authority on legal ethics, is of the opinion that Kaye Scholer was not required to disclose to the Bank Board client confidences or to provide to the Bank Board possible adverse characterizations of Lincoln's conduct. On the contrary, it is Professor Hazard's opinion that:

> The disclosures and representations that the OTS alleges should have been made to the Bank Board by Kaye Scholer in fact would have violated the standards of ethical conduct and professional responsibility generally recognized as applicable to Kaye Scholer in its role as litigation counsel.

It is further Professor Hazard's opinion that: "Kaye Scholer did not violate existing standards of ethical conduct and professional responsibility, and acted in accordance with its duties under the law."

4. A large part of KS's actions criticized by the OTS involve the firm's reliance on financial statements certified by Arthur Andersen (AA) and Arthur Young (AY) — highly reputable big 8 accounting firms — or other statements filed by them with government regulators. The OTS's unprecedented position is that lawyers do not have the right to rely on the accuracy of accountants' work, but were required to second guess the accountants on issues within the accountants' expertise.

5. The OTS does not contend that the alleged omissions by KS were the proximate cause of any loss or damage to Lincoln. Instead, the OTS is trying to hold KS liable for substantial damages on the ground that the traditional requirement of proximate cause does not apply.

6. After reviewing literally tens of thousands of documents generated by KS's attorneys during the course of its representation of Lincoln, including extensive notes of interviews and internal memoranda, and deposing under oath more than twenty KS present and former attorneys, the OTS has managed to come up with only a handful of alleged omissions out of submissions totalling more than 1,000 pages dealing with Lincoln's business practices. And these alleged

omissions, as can be seen from the refutation of the OTS's specific charges which follows, either did not take place or were clearly immaterial.

I. Claim 1 questions advice given to Lincoln by KS that Lincoln's prior actions in establishing service corporations and obtaining approvals by the California Department of Savings and Loan to fund them at specified levels "grandfathered" those direct investments under the applicable Bank Board regulation.

- The OTS does not contest that KS's interpretation of the applicable grandfathering regulations was reasonable. Rather, OTS's complaint is that KS — although it had been told by Lincoln's directors that they had held meetings to approve applying to the California Savings and Loan Department for permission to make certain investments in its service corporations — should have advised the Lincoln Board that the documentation of the directors' actions was incorrect because written consents were prepared after the meetings had already occurred.
- But the key issue under the grandfathering regulation was whether Lincoln had definitive plans to invest in its service corporations, and it was clear to KS that the directors knew of and approved the applications being filed.
- Obviously, if the Lincoln Board had in fact approved the applications, as KS was advised by the directors themselves, whether such action was correctly documented could have no bearing on the grandfathering issue.

II. Claim 2 concerns the reasons why AA resigned as auditors for Lincoln and its parent, ACC, in October 1986.

- As required by law, ACC filed a Form 8-K with the SEC expressing those reasons; and AA filed a statement, approved by its senior management, explicitly stating that those reasons were correct.
- KS is accused of having failed to bring to the attention of the regulators an earlier statement made by an AA technical partner concerning Lincoln which did not contradict AA's explanation for its resignation and did not contain any information concerning Lincoln that was not known to the Bank Board.
- It appears that the OTS doesn't believe the reasons given by AA for its resignation, and is suggesting, without a shred of evidence, that we knew that AA was lying in a formal statement, approved by its senior management and its partners responsible for the ACC account, and filed with the SEC. We didn't, and we had no reason to doubt the accuracy of AA's stated reasons for resigning as told to the SEC.

III. Claim 3 is a catchall, repeating allegations in other claims and concluding that KS misled the Bank Board by omitting to state various facts.

- The answers to these other claims completely refute this catchall allegation.
- In fact, as the Bank Board knew at the time, KS was retained by Lincoln to represent it in presenting Lincoln's answers to the criticisms contained in the Examination Report. KS was obligated under the Rules of Professional Responsibility to defend its client and present the client's arguments and positions as persuasively as possible so long as they had a reasonable basis. What the OTS really is complaining about is that KS failed to volunteer negative information about Lincoln or to set forth the potential weaknesses of Lincoln's position to the Bank Board. Not only is this *not* the role of counsel in such a position, but it would have violated KS's professional obligations to its client to have done so.

IV. The **fourth** claim repeats allegations of other claims and charges KS with breaching fiduciary duties to Lincoln and not disclosing to Lincoln's board a conflict of interest because it represented both ACC and Lincoln, ACC's wholly owned subsidiary.

- At no time did we believe that the positions that we took on behalf of Lincoln, with the full knowledge of the Lincoln Board of Directors, were other than in Lincoln's best interests.
- Neither we, nor the bar in general, perceived any conflict of interest in representing a parent and its wholly-owned subsidiary in defending the subsidiary's conduct before a regulatory agency.

V. The **fifth** claim relates to Lincoln's income and net worth.

- The Lincoln directors' response to the examiners' criticisms stated that Lincoln was in compliance with its regulatory net worth requirement. This was based on Lincoln's 1986 financial statements certified unequivocally by AY.
- The OTS alleges that we knew that Lincoln had on occasion engaged in simultaneous transactions with the same party (or related parties) and should have brought that fact to the attention of the FHLBB because those transactions were material to assessing Lincoln's income and net worth.
- It is undisputed that when we learned of these transactions, we contacted ACC's general counsel and were assured that AY knew the full details of all these transactions, carefully scrutinized them and had determined that they were properly accounted for. AY's contemporaneous workpapers make clear that they in fact knew all the facts known to KS regarding those transactions.
- Clearly, the KS lawyers involved in this matter believed that AY had performed a complete and competent audit, and knew all the pertinent

facts, when it certified ACC's 1986 financial statements. There simply was no reason for KS to assume that AY's certification was unwarranted.

VI. The **sixth** claim charges misrepresentations and omissions in connection with portions of Lincoln's response to the Examination Report dealing with loan and investment underwriting.

- There are two aspects of this underwriting issue: substantive underwriting and documentation of that underwriting. At all times it was acknowledged that Lincoln's documentation of its underwriting was deficient, although it did improve over time. But the point that the Lincoln officials repeatedly made to us, and that we repeated to the regulators, was that in virtually all cases *substantive* underwriting had in fact been done.
- To support its claim that KS knew that substantive underwriting was not done, OTS points to a few snippets from a couple of interview memos by KS associates in which they discussed a very small number of loans as to which there was very substantial, albeit not perfect, underwriting; and it totally ignores the dozens of interviews reflected in KS memoranda covering about 100 loans that support the conclusion that Lincoln in fact did extensive loan underwriting. The KS lawyers who conducted the interviews of the Linicoln loan officers had good reason to and did believe those people.
- With respect to documentation, the OTS alleges that we failed to disclose that Lincoln removed certain documents from its loan files which contained negative information; and that certain underwriting summaries were prepared after the transactions had closed.

    (i) As for the removal of documents claim, once again the OTS is attempting to generalize from a few snippets — one specific loan mentioned in one interview memorandum, and a handwritten note by an associate which indicates that certain documents that did not belong in the loan files were removed.

    (ii) As for the fact that the underwriting summaries were prepared after the loans and investments were made, we learned that after the fact, but so did the regulators, because it was acknowledged to the regulators by ACC's president and others *before* Lincoln responded to the Examination Report.

VII. The **seventh** claim has to do with the treatment of certain transactions as loans rather than as joint ventures.

- On this one both AA and AY opined that Lincoln was correct in treating them as loans.
- The regulators took the contrary position, claiming that the arrangements were joint ventures.

776

- OTS asserts that KS knew that the AA and AY opinions failed to consider the issue of control, and that we had no right to rely on those opinions.
- The fact of the matter is that our lawyers had several discussions with the accountants and were advised that the issue of control was irrelevant to the proper accounting treatment of the transactions.
- We also know from the regulators' internal documents that they were fully aware of the fact that Lincoln exercised control over the project and that they nevertheless themselves treated the issue as an accounting matter where control was not relevant. The only difference was that their accountants disagreed with Lincoln's accountants after applying the same criteria. The short of the matter is that KS had no reason to question the validity of four separate opinions by AA and AY, which were rendered in between two unqualified audit opinions by those two firms, stating that Lincoln's loan accounting for these transactions was proper.

VIII. The **eighth** claim concerns statements to the regulators concerning the grandfathering of the same direct investments covered in Claim 1.

- The real dispute between Lincoln and the regulators involved a question of law. We contended that the applicable regulations, as a matter of their plain meaning as well as their legislative history, covered definitive plans to invest in service corporations. The regulators, on the other hand, maintained that the regulations only protected definitive plans to invest in actual real estate projects.
- We felt so strongly that we were correct in our interpretation that we urged the regulators at the time of the examination to join us in seeking a declaratory judgment by a court to resolve this question of law. But the regulators steadfastly refused to litigate the question. One of the regulators even acknowledged that the question was a fair ground for litigation.
- No matter how a court would come out in deciding the legal issue, it is inconceivable that it would have the slightest doubt that we acted in complete good faith in concluding both that the definitive plans provision applied and that such plans existed as of the grandfathering date.
- The OTS's allegations in this claim focus again on the dating of certain consents. But in addition to the fact that these consents were immaterial to the argument KS was making to the regulators, the dating of the consents after the date on which, KS was informed, directors' meetings had taken place was also immaterial.

IX. The **ninth** claim relates to Lincoln's loans to the Hotel Ponchartrain Limited Partnership.

- According to the OTS, KS was responsible for material omissions from ACC's SEC filings and from certain correspondence with the California regulators concerning whether a $20MM loan to the Ponchartrain limited partnership was an affiliated transaction and a safe and sound loan.

- The fact that the $20MM loan had been made to a related party was disclosed in ACC's proxy statement and Form 10K annual report. The regulators knew who the parties were to the transaction and therefore had all the disclosure they needed to raise the affiliated transaction question — and they ultimately did.
- As for the safety and soundness of the loan, the examiners began their second examination of Lincoln shortly thereafter, at which time they had complete access to the relevant loan file.

X. The **tenth** claim is based on a loan from Lincoln to a KS attorney for the purchase of a home at a competitive interest rate and completely secured by a mortgage on the property and a pledge of securities.

- The OTS does not dispute that the loan was at a competitive interest rate and adequately secured, but criticizes Lincoln's internal record-keeping because the loan application was "incomplete" and the appraisal of the property was performed without a physical inspection.
- The OTS does not suggest that Lincoln lost a dime on this loan or that there is any prospect that it will not be paid back in strict conformity with its terms, just as every interest payment has been made. We are therefore at a total loss to understand the basis for bringing this claim.

In conclusion, it is apparent from this Notice that the OTS is intent on making a statement to the bar on what it perceives to be the proper role of a lawyer for an insured depository institution: to be a public watchdog with primary responsibility to the regulators rather than the client. Whatever the merits of that view as a policy matter, one thing is clear. It is patently unfair to attempt to impose that view retroactively on a single firm that was operating under professional standards previously thought to be universally accepted — standards that not only permitted but mandated that KS vigorously represent the interests of its client in accordance with a lawyer's pre-eminent duty of loyalty to his or her *client*.